D0207658

A Pragmatist Philosophy of Life in

Ortega y Gasset

A PRAGMATIST

Ortega

The first volume in a series of comprehensive studies on the thought of Ortega y Gasset.

PHILOSOPHY OF LIFE IN

y Gasset

John T. Graham

University of Missouri Press   Columbia and London

Copyright © 1994 by
The Curators of the University of Missouri
University of Missouri Press, Columbia, Missouri 65201
Printed and bound in the United States of America
All rights reserved

5   4   3   2   1   98   97   96   95   94

Library of Congress Cataloging-in-Publication Data

Graham, John T. (John Thomas), 1928–
    A pragmatist philosophy of life in Ortega y Gasset / John T.
Graham.
        p.   cm.
    Includes bibliographical references (p.   ) and index.
    ISBN 0–8262–0938–6 (alk. paper)
        1. Ortega y Gasset, José, 1883–1955.   1. Title.
B4568.074G64   1994
196'.1—dc20   94–6736
                                                CIP

♾™ This paper meets the requirements of the
American National Standard for Permanence of Paper
for Printed Library Materials, Z39.48, 1984.

Designer: Kristie Lee
Typesetter: Connell-Zeko Type & Graphics
Printer and binder: Thomson-Shore, Inc.
Typefaces: Galliard, Eras Medium, Pepita

Contents

WHY A HISTORICAL APPROACH
TO SYNTHESIS?

preface is the last thing one writes, to *justify* a book, and there have been so many books on José Ortega y Gasset already. More than twenty years ago Ciriaco Morón Arroyo asked in the preface to his critical synthesis of Ortega's philosophy: "Another book on Ortega?"[1] He had spent more than two years in scholarly labor to elucidate a "Heideggerian" existentialism in Ortega, but he had to leave ill-explained what he recognized as the "radical historicism" in his last ("idealist") stage of thought. To date, no one has devoted enough time, care, and documentation to the "radicalism" of either Ortega's beginning or ending. Now to deal in depth with origins and conclusions is a historical imperative, as much as with continuity and changes in between, even if they be in philosophy. Many of the stubborn problems can be answered only within a historical *time*-frame of origins and development, and only by historical methods.

This critical synthesis is the work of an intellectual historian, one who has culled Ortega's archives and examined his private library to find scattered and fragmentary answers to a definition—or at least a description—of his supremely varied and puzzling philosophy as a whole: a "philosophy of life," as he insisted on calling it at the end. It comprised a long-hidden beginning in a pragmatist metaphysics inspired by William James, and with a general method from a realist phenomenology imitating Edmund Husserl, which served both his proto-existentialism (prior to Martin Heidegger's) and his realist historicism, which I situate somewhere between Wilhelm Dilthey and Benedetto Croce.

Perhaps the sheer quantity of "missing" and implicative evidence required

---

1. Ciriaco Morón Arroyo, *El sistema de Ortega y Gasset,* 7.

to put Ortega's philosophy together into a coherent synthesis—especially data on his origins and his end—constitutes a task of search and discovery more suitable for a historian than for a philosopher. By attempting a fresh analysis of beginning and end, within a synthesis of the philosophy of life as a whole, this study is *not* like any other. It has consumed a decade of effort, largely in *historical* analysis and comparison of parts, from undetected basic sources in pragmatism ("radical positivism"), even to neglected final consequences in what is in fact a "realist," pragmatist historicism within his philosophy of life.

The title "A *Pragmatist* Philosophy of Life" itself needs explaining, for, if Ortega named the general type, I have imposed the qualifying adjective as a species to make it unique—since he postponed till too late any explicit acknowledgment of his original basic debt to James's pragmatism. Oriented to life and to history, his basic pragmatism underlay and pointed to all his later developments. With a phenomenological method, "philosophy of life" sufficed to cover the *duality* of existentialism and historicism, into which his philosophy (as *unitary*) resolved and extended. Life is (largely) history as present, and history is life as past. The component of history so dominated his ongoing later thought (or "second voyage") that one is tempted to add "History" to the title, but "philosophy of history" would complicate too much the unitary duality of his philosophy of life. He went decisively over to "history" in order to go "beyond philosophy" into the "human sciences," in order to "complete" his philosophy of life from broad interdisciplinary studies,[2] which are better known than his philosophy.

Do the persistent problems of beginning and end justify a *historian* undertaking a study of Ortega as a *philosopher* who was immersed in fully half a dozen philosophies? Do not traditional disciplinary boundaries forbid it, despite many inter- or cross-disciplinary ventures in our time? Where Dilthey, Croce, and Ortega all regarded "history of philosophy" as a truly necessary "propaedeutic" (introduction) to philosophy itself, none of them expected historians to "do" philosophy the way they thought that they as philosophers could "do" history. Of course, I make no pretense to "doing" philosophy. It is *ultra vires*—beyond my capacity—as well as outside my field. But for a long time now, intellectual historians have taken past philosophy, like science and culture, as legitimate concerns: human thought as historical phenomena viewed from a historical perspective. And this holds

---

2. See my "Pragmatism and Philosophy of History in Ortega y Gasset." On intentional interdisciplinary and historical dimensions of Ortega's thought, see my "Historiology and Interdisciplinarity." Here and elsewhere a large part of the studies on Ortega are not on philosophy but on his historical, political, social, cultural (literature, art), linguistic, and educational writings. Most of these attempt some relation to his philosophy, however.

true for *a* philosopher and his philosophy, done "genetically" and even by careful analysis of texts.

That most extreme of historicists, Croce, once seemed to think that it would be prudent and safe to entrust the history of philosophy to historians, who have the patience, an exacting discipline, and impartiality, instead of to philosophers with their "passion" of commitment to "schools." But he shortly rejected historical "objectivity" as "absurd" and insisted that "whoever would judge the philosophers" must himself *be* a "philosopher who by virtue of his thought *is* a historian."[3] As it happened, I had already done this study before I encountered Croce's ban. Unable to philosophize or "judge" authentically, this poor historian can only submit humbly to the critics and beg pardon for lacking proper garb and expertise. Since my study was not at first planned to be about Ortega's philosophy, however, but about his historical thought, it is an unpremeditated extravagation, offered in hopes it may be useful.

No effort is made here to "judge" the worth or validity of Ortega's philosophy qua philosophy, however much the historicism and historical ideas may appeal to a historian. Similarly, in presenting his case as he stated it vis-à-vis other philosophers—such as Nietzsche, Bergson, Husserl, Scheler, Unamuno, Comte, Croce, Heidegger, James, and Dilthey—I do not attempt to decide his merits, for that assessment also properly belongs first to philosophers. One cannot even be confident of having described Ortega's own philosophy always correctly, as a philosopher would have done it, although much care was taken. A historian can attempt to *do* only intellectual history with Ortega, not philosophy per se. It is hoped, however, that philosophers may find this new historical overview of Ortega's philosophy, so basic for grasping his thought on history and the human sciences, also helpful for possible reassessment of his philosophy.

For a personal disclaimer, as a historian I have never been an Orteguista ("Orteguist") in the sense of disciple or imitator of his philosophy. Although I had been superficially interested in some of his non-philosophical works, until about eleven years ago I did not try to get "inside" his "way of thinking" or his processes of thought, basic assumptions, and methods, as he tried to get "inside" Goethe and Kant and Dilthey. Although he has proved very stimulating as a thinker, he is also a very hard challenge to the historian's craft and has required much study and preparation. One's methods, gained by learning, practice, and instinct, as dictated by the difficulty of intellectual history and by Ortega as subject matter, were taxed to the limit and in

3. Benedetto Croce, *Philosophy, Poetry, History,* trans. C. Sprigge (London: Oxford University Press, 1966), 121–30 and (to clarify) 8, 30, and 512; idem, *History: Its Theory and Practice* (1916), trans. D. Ainslie (New York: Russell, 1960), 160–62. See Angelo de Gennaro, *The Philosophy of Benedetto Croce: An Introduction* (New York: Greenwood, 1968), 44–46.

application took much time and effort. Anything less fails. As Ortega once said of quick, easy critics, many "literary cowboys" have galloped through and shredded their lassos in vain. A few weeks or months are too little to rope Ortega's synthesis or system.

After starting with a legitimate historical topic—the idea of "historical crisis" in Ortega's *Man and Crisis* as the concluding chapter in a history of crisis thought[4]—I found that this book just "growed like Topsy." As in history itself, "one thing led to another," and another, and another. That chapter became ever more complex, until it had finally *dragged* me, sorely against my will and instincts, into his philosophy, first existentialism and then historicism, etc., as logically supporting (as well as prior to) his thought on "crisis," history, and the "human sciences." That chain of implicative research thus has forced me into two more book manuscripts in a decade, but, logically, "the last shall be first." Thus I got involved with Ortega's philosophy via history—ending with his philosophy instead of beginning with it, as would have been proper for philosophers.

This study has required more than a decade of dogged, patient, documentary research into the many sides of Ortega's life and thought, published and archival, and into many kinds of related literature. Before ever an editor's pencil, how humbling it is to look back at some five hundred earlier efforts and on all of my own revised versions of text, title, and structure (see Contents), which eventually produced, I felt, a "fit" that "hangs together" and "works" in pragmatic fashion, after so much "trial and error." Possibly no other historian nor any philosopher (except Julián Marías) would have undertaken such an almost endless quest. In that sense, Croce's first instinct was right, but I ask to leave "judgment" of the result to philosophers *and* historians.

My approach as a whole is historical, for historians also analyze texts, if in a way differing from that of many philosophers: by empirical and inductive, not abstract and deductive, method; as genetically developing, as logically "systematic" in topics; and, finally, as open-ended and tentative instead of closed and conclusive. The pragmatic research strategy and the piecemeal historical procedure that I use—of sheer necessity—seems to be one way of getting hold of Ortega as a whole. Alone, the analytical methods of philoso-

---

4. Ernest Breisach, *Introduction to Modern Existentialism* (New York: Grove Press, 1970), 3, 11: "The mood of crisis has come to be an unwanted but permanent guest. . . . Wherever we turn, someone hurls the word crisis at us." For Ortega on crisis, see *Obras Completas,* 4:398, 8:280, and *Man and Crisis,* trans. Mildred Adams (New York: Norton, 1958). Two chapters from my book manuscript, "A History of Crisis Thought"—in which Ortega will also have a chapter on his theory and model—have appeared in the *Proceedings of the Consortium on Revolutionary Europe.* See for example, "Repeatable Paradigms? General Crisis Theory for the 17th and 18th Centuries" (1989).

phy have not sufficed, probably because he left us no compact, manageable body of systematic philosophy to assess. His thought is full of lacunae and hard problems, almost as if designed for application of historical methods. Actually, Ortega understood "historical reasoning" very well. Such procedures do not, of course, assure that this study of his philosophy is any "truer" or more "scientific" than others, but I have tried to follow a research strategy that, as H. S. Hughes said, has long been practiced in historiography, and particularly by the intellectual historians trying to "relive" and "re-create" the past—including past thought—from primary sources of various kinds, besides philosophical treatises.[5]

Because this pluralistic yet holistic interpretation of Ortega's philosophy reflects not only my own judgment but the opinions of the critics over the past seventy years, perhaps informed readers will want to begin with the bibliographical essay at the end, even before the introduction. For the sake of more casual readers, the many footnotes, which contain much supporting data and extraneous information, do not contain the longer and heavier commentaries of the bibliographical type. These have been placed in a section of supplemental endnotes on the general topical background of the chapters and their more complex problems, which critical specialists will want to examine separately. Readers may be helped to follow my argument and Ortega's "open" and developing philosophy not only by the compressed "structure" of a topical and chronological kind in the Contents but by the many additional subtitles that are included in the text only, so as not to clutter the clean lines of the inductive "model" in the Contents.

5. H. S. Hughes, "Vico and Contemporary Social Theory," in *Giambattista Vico: An International Symposium,* ed. G. Tagliacozzo and H. V. White (Baltimore: Johns Hopkins University Press, 1969), 320; also see Paul K. Conkin and Roland N. Stromberg, *Heritage and Challenge. The History and Theory of History* (Arlington Heights, Ill.: Forum, 1989), 212–14. In his classic *Consciousness and Society, 1890–1930* (New York: Vintage Books, 1958), Hughes did not examine Ortega, who was too late for the "generation of the 1890s" but might have fitted into his ("half"-) "generation of 1905" (18, 336)—ideas that Hughes could soon have found in *Man and Crisis* instead of in Marc Bloch. He would have found him puzzling for rejecting "consciousness" as basic, an idea first in William James to which Hughes did not advert. However, what he did say of James (and of Mach, Vaihinger, Bergson, and Dilthey in relation to James) would have given him a great advantage—as it did me—in properly understanding Ortega, whom he later rightly placed with the existentialists and phenomenologists (if wrongly seen as sharing their *idealist* view of "ultimate reality") and with Pareto's and Croce's elitism (*Contemporary Europe: A History* [Englewood Cliffs, N.J.: Prentice-Hall, 1961], 180). One of the better post-centennial studies of Ortega's social thought is by Ignacio Sánchez Cámara, *La teoría de la minoría selecta en el pensamiento de Ortega y Gasset* (Madrid: Editorial Tecnos, 1986), who makes usually overlooked comparisons with Comte, Pareto, and Mosca.

Acknowledgments

ermission to cite and quote from unpublished documents in the archive of José Ortega and from his published works was graciously granted by Señora Soledad Ortega, President of the Fundación Ortega y Gasset in Madrid, Spain.

I wish to express my special thanks to those who have generously helped me by one or more of many favors and services during the course of this long research project: Professors Julián Ruíz, Antón Donoso, and Jorge Gracias and Sister María Teresa Arias (Mercedarians), for timely advice and encouragement, for assistance with bibliography or sources, and for kindly hospitality; Dr. Henry A. Mitchell, for partial funding of short trips to Argentina and to Spain for a paper and research on Ortega y Gasset; Professor Hans Uffelmann, for advice on pragmatism and phenomenology; my dearest wife, Alsy Izurieta Graham, for patient personal support and frequent help with a recalcitrant computer that was not "the apple of my eye" and a very capricious and *im*perfect word processor, which did their utmost to prolong this project.

A Pragmatist Philosophy of Life in

Ortega y Gasset

Introduction

ORTEGA AGAIN

As Philosopher of "Our Time"

ame is so fickle and fleeting. How many today in the United States know who or what José Ortega y Gasset (1883–1955) was? A few who were in graduate studies at the time of his death may remember that he was then Spain's greatest philosopher, was one of the hundred most "famous" names in the United States, that he inaugurated the Goethe Festival in Aspen in 1949, was reported in the *New York Times, Time,* and the *Atlantic,* and was nominated for a Nobel Prize—by philosopher Alfred Stern, among others. In the United States as in much of the Western world, however, he was less known to philosophers than to professors in other fields and to students, to journalists, pundits, notables, and the educated public, who were fascinated with his ideas *beyond* philosophy. North Americans first encountered his provocative, quasi-ironic view of "modernist" art in *The Dehumanization of Art* (1925) in 1930. In 1940, Rex Smith of *Newsweek* wrote to him: "A large sector of the intelligent people in this country are devoted followers of yours since *The Revolt of the Masses*" (R 20). This work, translated in 1932, dealt with "mass man," overspecialization, and the "United States of Europe."[1] None then realized that perhaps we liked

---

1. Donald B. Robinson, *100 Most Important People in the World Today* (New York: Pocket Books, 1952), 337–40; Franz Niedermayer, *José Ortega y Gasset,* 86; Alfred Stern, *The Search for Meaning: Philosophical Vistas,* 256, claimed to be one of many who proposed Ortega for the Nobel Prize in literature. Rex Smith to Ortega, May 8, 1940, "(R 20)" in the text refers to microfilm Reel 20 of the Ortega y Gasset archive at the Library of Congress; this parenthetic method will be used henceforth to give locations in that archive; for a subject index of the reels, see *Hispanic Focus,* ed. Everette E. Larson (Washington: Library of Congress, 1982). Smith, a former Associated Press bureau chief in Madrid from 1931 to 1935, knew Ortega in his *tertulia,* or discussion circle, and in the Cortes; he wanted him to come reside in New York City; and he mentioned Edward Weeks of the *Atlantic Monthly,* which published Ortega's "The Unity of Europe" in April 1940, pp. 432–42. Like *The New Yorker*

him in part for the "pragmatic" attitudes and values that he had derived tacitly from William James. He seemed to be what a later generation would call "so relevant"—so up to "the level of the times" with his variegated "themes," if not with his "advanced" but unidentifiable philosophy in *The Modern Theme*. But, if readers did not fathom his philosophy, could they truly understand his other striking ideas? He *was* a philosopher.

As a rational philosophy of life, the very badly misnamed *Modern Theme* (1923), literally "the theme of our time" that was intentionally "post-modern," puzzled more than persuaded critics and philosophers with a pot-pourri of "metahistory," generations theory, subdued pragmatism, and proto-existentialism. Several of those ideas, however, with others from *Revolt of the Masses, History as a System* (1936), and *Man and Crisis* (1958), intrigued some premier North American historians, such as Carl Becker, Crane Brinton, and Jacques Barzun, who sensed in Ortega's "philosophy of history" a pragmatist flavor.[2] In the stricter sense, however, his philosophy won neither adherents nor much interest.

After Mortimer Adler asked his advice on the Great Books, he placed not Ortega but Santayana with James and Dewey among notable contemporary philosophers. Oddly, his *Man and People* (1957), which he had edited especially for the United States with very insistent pragmatism, did not attract sociologists. In 1949 and 1950, by contrast, R. M. Hutchins invited Ortega to take part in the launching of the Aspen Institute, so impressed was he with *The Mission of the University* (1930), which contained parallels to his own educational reforms at the University of Chicago, but he was unaware of any debt his guest may have owed Dewey. Echoes of that encounter with a Spanish educator who sought to *open* the mind of "mass man" and the "specialists" continued on through Alan Bloom's rare academic best-seller, *The Closing of the American Mind* (1987).[3] In person and by his works that

---

(June 1, 1946, p. 94), *Time* (whose Henry Luce was a "fan" of Ortega) reviewed his *Concord and Liberty* (June 10, 1946, p. 102) and reported on the opening of his Institute of Humanities in Madrid in 1948 (January 17, 1949, pp. 44–46). There were more than twenty reviews and notices in the leading U.S. magazines and newspapers (including the *New York Times*) between 1944 and 1949, when he made the trip to address the Goethe Festival in Aspen.

2. Crane Brinton, review of *Man and Crisis*, in *America* 100 (November 1958): 218; Jacques Barzun, *A Stroll with William James*, 300 (on Ortega and James).

3. Correspondence (R 24, 33, 73) reveals Ortega's role in planning the Aspen Institute for Humanistic Studies for more than a year afterward and inquiries related to the Great Books program; also see James S. Allen, *The Romance of Commerce and Culture* (Chicago: University of Chicago Press, 1983), 207–57. Prior to Bloom's book, his friend Saul Bellow wrote the prologue for a new edition of *Revolt of the Masses* (Notre Dame: University of Notre Dame Press, 1985). In *The Closing of the American Mind* (New York: Simon and Schuster, 1987), it is true that Bloom did not bother to cite Ortega, but his preface (19–20) stated a plainly Ortegan "perspective" on "generations" in cultural "crises"; in fact, when

were translated in the United States from the 1930s through the 1950s, Ortega then addressed the mood and interest of many Americans—except for his philosophy, the unappreciated source of his other ideas.

A bold and lucid but "unsystematic" thinker, Ortega aspired to reform "radically" the long philosophical tradition not only of modern times but of 2,500 years past. He tried to go back beyond Parmenides and "being" to start afresh from "life"—to "examine" first his own life (as Plato advised) and then that of others—via Heraclitus's neglected mode of "becoming," as did James with "stream of consciousness." Yet he was also timid, cautious, and reticent about making his views and "system" clear by way of well-organized treatises for the critical minds of his profession, to whom he responded with thirty years of "silence." He preferred the privacy of classroom lectures and dispersion into countless essays in newspapers and journals for the broad, literate public. Before such uncritical audiences he called for a new way to "do" philosophy, by standing Descartes on his feet instead of on his head: a new principle of "vital reason" ("I live and so I think") was the basis for "authentic" philosophizing, versus the "mummified" professional philosophy that was taught and repeated on occasion instead of thought out and lived out constantly (12:194, 301).⁴ By "historical reason" he meant to incorporate the long philosophical tradition and the social, historical past into his "system" as necessary dimensions but to cease "doing" philosophy the old way. Few critics were aware of his Nietzschean and Jamesian temerity. Fellow philosophers mostly ceased trying to figure out what Ortega meant, went on with philosophical business as usual, and gradually forgot him.

---

he discusses "uncivilized" students (341) and teachers with excessive "specialization" (59, 338–40) trying to satisfy the needs of human life with a failed "physico-mathematical reason," he sounds as if he is paraphrasing *Revolt of the Masses* and *History as a System* (182–85, 199). Similarly, Benjamin Barber's review in *Harper's Magazine* (January 1988), without mentioning Ortega, recast Bloom's arguments in terms of "barbarians," "mass men," and (yes) "Revolt of the Masses" (61–65). Mortimer Adler, however, lamenting "the state of higher learning in America" in *Newsweek* (August 21, 1978, p. 15), had attributed the phrase "The Barbarism of Specialization" to Ortega's *Revolt of the Masses* and had praised his *Mission of the University*. It is clear, of course, that neither Hutchins nor Adler knew about Ortega's anti-"scholastic" historicism. See Fred Matthews, "The Attack on 'Historicism,'" *American Historical Review* 95 (April 1990): 429–47.

4. Henceforth, references to Ortega's *Obras Completas*, including volume and page(s), will be incorporated in both text and notes thus: (12:194, 301). Citations from other members of his family will always carry the first name, if not the full surname. Ortega was seldom cited, however, in older American and British histories of philosophy—not at all by Will Durant nor Bertrand Russell, both of whom (after tributes to Bergson, James, and Dewey) ignored existentialists and historicists. Maybe Ortega's secret kinship with pragmatism would have been detected by Philip A. Schilpp, editor of so many "living" philosophers (including Santayana in 1940, and Dewey, Whitehead, and Russell in 1951), who had contracted Julián Marías to write up Ortega in 1955, then his subject died (*The Philosophy of Gabriel Marcel* [La Salle, Ill.: Open Court Press, 1984], 553 [Marías]).

Not surprisingly, today Ortega is almost forgotten in the United States, except (ironically) by the specialists, although he was an attractive stylist and a provocative thinker whose ideas are still useful in approaching North America's various unresolved problems and crises. Neglect is true even of Spain and the Hispanic world. In 1980, Guillermo Morón, reissuing a work from more than twenty years earlier, regretted that Ortega now interested only specialists and "heirs," but he also predicted that Ortega would undergo a revival—if only as a Spanish *literary* classic. Yet Morón admitted that when he had written his doctoral dissertation on Ortega in 1958, he had regarded him as both a "good philosopher" and a "good writer." "I have, to my own disadvantage and cultural loss, forgotten" him, because he was too difficult to grasp as a whole. The same regret about the current "ostracism" of Ortega by the Spanish cultural world was echoed by Rabade Romeo in 1983 and by Cerezo Galán in 1984.[5]

In the United States, Ortega has never had any followers or disciples in philosophy per se, because he was even harder to understand there. Nevertheless, his relevance may be seen by a strange coincidence. The National Book Award in 1989 went to Professor Robert Nozick of Harvard, whose *Examined Life* has a surprising resemblance to Ortega's philosophy of life. "I want to think about living and what is important in life, to clarify my thinking—and also my life." From that opening statement, Nozick set forth an explicit "philosophy of life," a personalist creed developed through related popular "themes": not just living but dying; creating, loving, begetting; even politicking and historizing. But life or living, he admitted, "is not the kind of topic whose investigation philosophers find especially reward-

---

5. In North American bookstores one can still find some of Ortega's works, like *Revolt of the Masses, History as a System,* and *What Is Philosophy?* He was cited in a former "best seller," Daniel J. Levinson's *The Seasons of a Man's Life* (New York: Knopf, 1978)—basic to Gail Sheehey's *Passages*—for his concept of generations (28–29, 214, 323). In George Seldes, ed., *Great Thoughts* (New York: Ballantine, 1985), his *Revolt of the Masses* made up one column of quotations (315–16). Strangely, both Ortega and Dilthey were omitted by Frank N. Magill, ed., from *World Philosophy: Essay-Reviews of 225 Major Works,* 5 vols. (Englewood Cliffs, N.J.: Salem, 1982), although James, Dewey, and many lesser writers were included. Walter Kaufmann's *Existentialism from Dostoevsky to Sartre* (New York: Meridian, 1975), 152–57, included "Ortega: Man Has No Nature"—a theme for which he is also cited in books on historicism. John Butt, "Ortega y Gasset," in *Makers of Modern Culture,* ed. J. Wintle (New York: Facts on File, 1981), 391–92, claimed that Ortega was of no current interest or influence in the United States. Apparently Butt's view was not extreme, because the *Social Science Citation Index* for 1983, 1984, and 1985 showed only four, one, and two citations: from *Man and Crisis, Revolt of the Masses,* and *History as a System,* which were his three most popular and enduring works in the United States. Guillermo Morón, *Historia política de José Ortega y Gasset* (Caracas: Ateneo, 1980), preface; Sergio Rabade Romeo, *Ortega y Gasset: Filósofo, hombre, conocimiento, razón,* 7; Pedro Cerezo Galán, *La voluntad de aventura: Aproximación al pensamiento de Ortega y Gasset,* 12.

ing." "Unsystematic," it lacks that definite "finishing line," never gets to any "general and complete theory" that can "cover it all" but that might make "life overintellectualized."[6] It is a philosophizing from life, with which ordinary literate people may feel comfortable. Apparently Nozick was unaware of any kinship to Ortega (or even to William James) in subject and style, but an affinity might seem natural in both cases.

If the world (learned and popular) now knows (and cares) much less about Ortega than when he lived, it is largely because the overall synthesis (*The Dawn of Historical Reason*) that he often promised he finally could not deliver. Nor has anyone else been able to bring it together coherently—even to the present. My own study of his philosophy as a whole is only the first volume of a critical overview of his thought in several dimensions, which may later include his theories of history, sociology, politics, aesthetics, and education. It is high time for a major effort at synthesis, because we can no longer see the forest (Ortega) for the trees of specialization (studies of his varied aspects). There is still no sustained analysis with a simplifying synthesis, not even of his whole philosophy, which this volume attempts with the aid of his archive and the rich and diverse body of past criticism.

A CENTENNIAL COMES AND GOES

In and around 1983, academics in Spain, Europe, and the Americas marked the centennial of Ortega y Gasset as the most celebrated of modern Spanish philosophers with conferences, symposia, colloquia, and the predictable outpouring of scholarly books and articles in learned journals. Because it was more than a half-century since he had begun to attract critical attention internationally, we might have expected an overall synthesis or at least a general assessment of how his philosophy has come to be identified and evaluated around the world. However, in twelve extremely varied volumes, Ortega had become too much for anyone to master on short notice, and the basic bibliographical task for expositors and critics was too vast to encompass.

The very large undertaking of listing, augmenting, and indexing the great mass of studies on Ortega (since a first attempt by Udo Rukser in 1971) was at last accomplished in 1986 by Professors Antón Donoso and Harold Raley, both noted Ortega scholars.[7] Their *Bibliography* will be invaluable for grate-

---

6. Robert Nozick, *The Examined Life: Philosophical Meditations* (New York: Simon and Schuster, 1989), 11–12, 298.

7. Antón Donoso and Harold C. Raley, *José Ortega y Gasset: A Bibliography of Secondary Sources*. Their up-to-date alphabetical author listing and subject index are indispensable, and it is the general bibliographical source most often cited in this study. Udo Rukser's *Bibliografía de Ortega* (Madrid: Revista de Occidente, 1971), a chronological listing of both

ful researchers everywhere. It can be a data base for *comparative* critical surveys of how scholars have interpreted Ortega over the past fifty years on all sides of his thought. They turned up more than four thousand publications from twoscore nations and two thousand writers in diverse fields and in more than a dozen languages.

Numbers of publications on Ortega by each scholar range up to seventy for Julián Marías, and fifteen or twenty or more for Raley and Donoso and for Iriarte, Gaos, Ferrater Mora, Garagorri, González Caminero, Rodríguez Huéscar, Abellán, Granell, Jesús Herrero, and Orringer. Five to ten or more articles are not uncommon among such as Alluntis, Aranguren, Araya Goubert, Benítez, Cano, Ciusa, Csejtei, Curtius, Díaz Arrieta, Díez del Corral, Durán, Fernández, Fraile, García Astrada, García Morente, Giusso, Guy, Laín Entralgo, Maravall, Vicente Marrero, Martínez Gómez, Mataix, McClintock, Morón Arroyo, Muñoz Alonso, Oromí, Pellicani, Recasens Siches, Roig Gironella, Francisco Romero, Rukser, Salmerón, Sarmiento, Silver, Torre, Vela, and Zambrano. Single studies abound.

Clearly, to judge by numbers alone, Ortega has become an "academic industry." Of course, not everything that has been published has much merit as scholarship—some is very light and shallow—nor contributes to our right understanding of Ortega's philosophy or his thought as a whole. But there is substance enough in Ortega to attract a wide variety of tastes and interests, both scholarly and popular. His thought and themes have inspired more than eighty Ph.D. dissertations, no few of them in the United States. At least two hundred different topics, themes, and aspects related to him have drawn six or more writings, and there are more than nine hundred total items related to him that different writers have covered.

Even if we allow for duplication of indexing, the philosophy alone has been the subject of about five hundred studies, around one hundred each on Ortega as a philosopher and on his doctrine, more or less undifferentiated by school or type, and sixty-five on him and "Spanish philosophy." On his "system," there have been sixteen studies indexed and many more on its parts: more than fifty on his "perspectivism," twenty on phenomenology, seventeen on vitalism, fourteen on "ratiovitalism," sixty on "vital reason," thirty-five on existentialism, thirty-five on "historical reason," and eight on historicism, even two that (in a cursory way) dealt with pragmatism. These figures show that his philosophy was not only extremely variegated but that more than half of the critics could not make up their minds about just what he was in philosophy. And clearly there was little agreement among those who had opinions. Criticism was a labyrinth with no exit.

Ortega's works and other authors by *nations,* is still a useful supplement for its arrangement and for Ortega's own publications.

The overflowing cornucopia of secondary literature that Donoso and Raley have presented us is cause for worry over what Ortega called academic "overspecialization" that may lead to a "crisis of superabundance" (5:503) that can muddy a thinker's clear identity, kill public interest, and greatly diminish his influence. Excess of criticism reflects both the difficulty of the subject, which made critics reassess him repeatedly, and the very wide choice of perspectives, themes, and interests that his thought offered. What we need now is not just a new perspective so much as a simplifying synthesis of the whole that measures past criticism against his extraordinary complexity of thought.

Ortega himself provided us with a "superabundance," and he did not help us with any works of synthesis. He continued spinning out a profusion of works of all types and varieties, including philosophy, but never did he succeed in summing up his "system." In his lifetime, his works came to six volumes that comprised more than 260 distinct works, if one breaks up his anthologies and journals. Even after promising "books" instead of newspaper articles, he averaged 32 items each for volumes 4, 5, and 6 of his *Obras Completas*. His posthumous volumes 7, 8, 9, and 12, of historical and philosophical works, averaged only 14 each, but his earlier pieces on politics were 150 in volume 10 and 58 in volume 11. As a whole, his production constituted more than 500 separate works. Few besides Voltaire surpassed that.

Because of the mass and complexity of both Ortega's works and those of his critics, the centennial year(s) could not have been expected to yield the long overdue syntheses reassessing either his very problematic philosophy or his total thought. There were some fine studies in depth and some of relative breadth. On the one hand, Ortega was simply too diverse to assign to any one school of thought—or even to philosophy alone. On the other, his lifetime output has been too much and too dispersed to take in without excessive time and effort.

Not only is the bibliographical challenge of past critical opinion so formidable, but all of Ortega's own "works" are not yet available. Now we must add to the "Complete Works" what his daughter Soledad announced (half in jest to the symposium at the Library of Congress in 1982) as the future "Completer Works."[8] The great bulk of archival papers and correspondence (little used yet) will be edited some time in the future, but the first of the new series could well be volume 12 (1983), which reproduces some course materials that Ortega maybe never dreamed of publishing. Since it took almost forty years to bring out the first set (1946–1983), we may not see much

8. The addresses and papers given at the Library of Congress on September 30 and October 1, 1982, were published not in English in the United States but in Spanish in Buenos Aires: *Sur*, no. 352 (January–June 1983).

of the next one for years. Hence, a full and authoritative synthetic study of a truly "complete" Ortega must still wait. Much about the personality of Ortega and about his changing relations with a great many people in Spain, and especially in Germany and the Americas, has still to be revealed by careful analysis of the voluminous correspondence.

So the centennial observance passed with multiplication of special perspectives on Ortega that did not make him any more accepted and accessible even to the academic world. But a long-needed critical, general synthesis was not yet possible. Julián Marías's tireless efforts from *Circumstance and Vocation* (1960) to *Trayectorias* (1983) did not culminate in synthesis, although at last he moved from "vital reason" toward "historical reason."[9] Meanwhile, the rest of us must strive to move toward synthesis with the published materials at hand, including the critics (at least the generalizers who sought synthesis after the 1940s) and the unpublished archives—where possible.

CRITICS AND DEFENDERS IN PRESENT PERSPECTIVE

In the bibliographical essay the reader will find a brief history of Ortega criticism, grouped by nations and regions, since the 1920s. More than sixty-five years ago in Argentina some of the first critics of Ortega's philosophy suspected that a basic pragmatism underlay his effort to keep up to "the level of the times" with a vitalist (even historical) "theme of our time." Then he apparently shifted abruptly in 1924 from "vital reason" to "historical reason" (really historicism), which *seemed* so idiosyncratic that it confused all the critics, until (by the later 1930s) they were able to recognize the existentialism in his varied themes. Not until about fifty years ago, after he had published *History as a System* in Spanish in 1941, were there critics bold enough to call him both an existentialist and a historicist. Because he refused to respond to the attacks and because his disciples denied one or both attributions then and ever since, critics could never afterward reach consensus about Ortega, as they added still other names to define his thought, such as philosophy of life or phenomenology, past 1983.

Why has Ortega been such a long and difficult problem for interpretation? A part of it was surely his own fault: his secretiveness, his diffuseness, and his dilatoriness. More yet was owing to the great difficulty of the task, or "trajectory," he set for himself of a new kind of philosophy, or new "way of thinking," that could bridge the gulf between the old realism and idealism,

---

9. Julián Marías, *Ortega y Gasset: Circunstancia y vocación* (Madrid: Revista de Occidente, 1960), trans. F. M. López Morillas (1970); idem, *Ortega: Las Trayectorias.* Ortega's most prolific and loyal disciple has attempted synthesis, but always within an invariable reduction of his master's philosophy as "vital reason."

and between life and history and "science." Much, too, was due to the passions of a few critics (like Iriarte and Marrero) who stung him to silence in his final years (when he might otherwise have clarified the issues) or to the myopia of a few well-meaning defenders (like Marías and Vela) who refused to see what was before their eyes. Even without all of that past misunderstanding, he has left us fertile soil for continuing controversy, which this investigation may kindle again, despite my irenic and inclusive intentions.

This study did not set out to be (or even to include) an examination of the critics, for it would have been impossible to understand Ortega's philosophy by arranging and blending such a diverse and often mutually contradictory mass. This critique has come as an afterthought, to see when, where, and how my own complex view of him may have been anticipated by earlier critics. A historian examining philosophy needs all such reassurances that he has not been a presumptuous fool.

An initial encounter with the wilderness of criticism was very disillusioning, without any evident, structured, dominant interpretation leading out of it. Ferrater Mora impressed me in the matter of verisimilitude by his concessions about several general types of philosophy in Ortega, but he could not help me much with the obvious historicism. So I rashly decided to tackle Ortega afresh, from published primary sources. This course seemed easier than to make either sense or patchwork cover out of the tangle of critical opinions. Hence, I put off further consideration of the critics for insights into Ortega's overall philosophy, until I had formulated my own view of his "system" the hard way: part by part toward elusive whole.

Thereafter, in a search for support and "justification," I still found no general interpretation that coincided precisely with my own, but I met with enough similar views on greater or lesser parts of the whole both to humble and to encourage me. And my respect for Ferrater Mora increased, as I realized that his conception of the general structure and relationship of Ortega's thought was sound and could be stretched to "fit" more or less with my own schema of interpretation. Thus encouraged, I again revised the chapters so as to encompass, in text and notes, as many critics as possible who were relevant to each successive level or stage of Ortega's philosophy.

My first task with the vast critical literature is to try to accommodate "generalists" in this introduction, which thereby anticipates the bibliographical essay that provides an orienting survey of Ortega criticism around the Western world. A summary of viewpoints, it helps define Ortega's philosophy as a whole and in parts, and it is a "first" critical effort to survey such a wide, varied mass of criticism as an ongoing, interacting enterprise from a variety of nations, regions, and languages.

In coping with all the criticism, I have had to be rather selective; no one could obtain and absorb so very many studies. But one may not just balance critic and defender so as to promote one's own solutions. So often I found that I agreed with neither or agreed with both. A growth of acuity and breadth has been evident on both sides in the decades since Ortega's death, and also a limited convergence of opinion, on which I have sought to capitalize. Of course, the critics have helped me change my mind on very many points, even though my general conception of the structure of Ortega's "system" and most of the supporting data resulted from my own research and reflection.

Not all of those critics have been praised whom this investigation ought to have acknowledged. Some studies could not be obtained; others surpassed my linguistic limits. One can only regret omitting scholars and views that one *ought* to have recognized but failed to mention. Bibliographies, citation indexes, and data bases, which now answer Ortega's dream of new research aids in "Mission of the Librarian" (1961), are still not enough to protect the researcher from myopic errors of one's own "self and circumstance." Many specialized studies are cited in the notes, and some in the bibliographical essay, but only a few generalists can be assessed ensemble here.

FROM CRITICAL ANALYSIS TO HISTORICAL SYNTHESIS

From a limited number of generalizing critical analyses of Ortega's philosophy by Hispanic and non-Hispanic scholars since 1955, we can easily confirm his extraordinary *diversity*. No agreement, however, has emerged on how to put it all together as a unity, or "system." Moreover, opinion has split on whether it was idealism or realism essentially, and on whether it was unitary as a unique "Spanish philosophy" simply of "vital reason" (ratiovitalism) or dual as a European (or Western) philosophy by its varieties of existentialism and historicism, perhaps unified in a basic yet comprehensive philosophy of life, with methods from phenomenology and from history, and a flavor of pragmatism. International criticism shows no recent signs of advancing further toward a single or comprehensive definition of Ortega's thinking, unless it be as "philosophy of life"—with renewed emphasis on the phenomenological and the *historical*.

With a historical approach, perhaps one can discover an authentic synthesis in Ortega, a "covering" structure sufficient for all the known "stages" and levels of his philosophy, that can serve as a firm basis for interpreting the very large remainder of his thought. It would have to be a broad kind of philosophy more capacious than ratiovitalist existentialism or a realist variation of phenomenology from Husserl, whom Ortega claimed to have outgrown (gone "beyond") very early. "Philosophy of life" (with "history") can truly integrate Ortega's many-sided philosophy, but another factor—as basic and nearly as pervasive as life and history—is also required: *pragmatism*. The realist metaphysical foundation of all of his complex philosophy was pragmatism. Several earlier critics glimpsed it, but they neither placed it precisely nor demonstrated it. Here I add pragmatism to the vital and historical core and unity of Ortega's thought, even define it as a *"pragmatist philosophy of life"* that still needed history to complete it. Among the critics, as noted in the bibliographical essay, life and history in his philosophy—dual yet united—are old, recent, and current interests. Overlooked as root and linkage, pragmatism binds it all together.

What does *this study* try to accomplish? No new stage, nor "label" for a type of philosophy in Ortega, is proposed here that was not previously discerned by one philosopher-critic or by many. No one before now, however, has *integrated all* of them in a "system" of philosophy with an ordered structure of temporal growth, nor *demonstrated* all of them from the published sources, and *confirmed* them from the archives, nor shown how far all those types were such—least of all, pragmatism.

In addition, I try to flesh out or complete, by added data from the primary sources and the critics, the main existing interpretations of what Ortega's philosophy was between his pragmatist beginnings and his final holistic philosophy of life: neo-Kantianism, phenomenology, and existentialism and historicism. It is remarkable that he had six philosophies, successively or in combination, that the critics have identified. Properly to distinguish, locate, and integrate all of that variety within his *unified* philosophy of life and to relate it to philosophies of his time raises many problems. The solutions proposed here make it part of other movements but also unique: one and various, a "radical unitary duality" (8:43).

The diversity in Ortega's one body of thought is very rich. Each chapter topic here has already been the subject of one or many books on Ortega, with two exceptions: (1) pragmatism, which (from chapter 4 and portions of others, and from encyclopedia essays very probably Ortega's) could well constitute a book by itself; and (2) historicism, which (from chapter 7 and a book still to come) could easily become an extensive treatise. Even his philosophy of life, too fragmented and ill-defined to elicit more than a chapter in a book previously, was the subject of a whole (collective) volume in 1990. In my synthesis, it now constitutes a comprehensive cover to redefine his philosophy as a whole, including elements of his "theory of life."

By all its particulars, my investigation is thus virtually several "books" in one, so it is unavoidably a bit "fat" or long—like this introduction. As a *synthesis,* however, it would be short on credibility and thin in data and insights, if it did not look into all major aspects of his philosophy and take into account analytic and synthetic judgments of two generations of critics.

May readers be indulgent with these fat chapters as concise "books." Subtitles in every chapter round out the spare schematic chronological "structure" of the Contents, and they are meant to help the reader follow the complexity of developing thought and interpretation more easily.

In the comprehensive synthesis attempted in this study, I do not seek to "refute" the varied general definitions previously made of Ortega's philosophy; I try to incorporate them into the complex, overall structure of his philosophy of life. Earlier attempts began too late, halted too soon, or claimed too much with aspects or parts they selected; mainly they left out too much. However, they have been generally right about what they have examined closely, so they are kept and honored herein.

Julián Marías proved more right than we had thought of late: Ortega was *not just* an existentialist, a historicist, a philosopher of life, or a phenomenologist. But he was *all* of them—and more—in unique ways, and this fact Marías did not see. Ironically, long ago he *could* have arrived at a comprehensive synthesis not so unlike the one presented here. Already in his *History of Philosophy* he had discerned in Dilthey just such a combination of philosophy of life with historicism,[10] yet he refused to see a similar mixture in Ortega. Like other generalizers, of course, he overlooked the initial and pervasive pragmatism.

The very mass and contrast in a half-century of ongoing publication and critical evaluation of Ortega's thought forbid any final or conclusive interpretation as yet—perhaps ever. Ortega's philosophy is a Gordian knot that no one has yet cut through by merely logical analysis, but maybe we can loosen it more by a historical approach. We are able to compare all those variant viewpoints and add them together chronologically as successive but overlapping aspects, levels, and stages of his philosophy—an "open" philosophy, in Ferrater Mora's words, or a philosophy in "evolutive" development, as Orringer maintained.[11]

Like his "perspectivism," this study has developed a number of successive (ever wider) "viewpoints" on the reality that was Ortega, adding one to another, so as to get a fuller view of the philosophical whole, but without ever encompassing all of that unfinished project. This inductive and empirical approach is broadly similar to his phenomenological epistemology of "opening the eyes," "looking," and "seeing" what is really there, instead of trying to force on him any abstract ("utopian") schema, gotten from outside him like a ready-made Carlylean "philosophy of clothes" to "cover the

10. Ironically, "circumstances" that Marías considered in *Circumstance and Vocation—Lebensphilosophie*, pragmatism, and Bergson (78–85), only to *reject* them (e.g., 381)—are crucial to my own study. On Dilthey, see idem, *Historia de Filosofía*, 6th ed. (Madrid: Revista de Occidente, 1956), 353.

11. José Ferrater Mora, *Ortega y Gasset: An Outline of His Philosophy*, 9–10, 26. Nelson R. Orringer, *Ortega y sus fuentes germánicas*, 351.

appearances." It is possible now to have Ortega himself, from publications or archives, acknowledge that he saw himself as pragmatist, phenomenologist, existentialist, historicist, and philosopher of life—in some respects.

What has been lacking till now for the unification of that "plurality" of elements into *one* philosophy of life—one that is not "eclectic" but integrated, realist in basic perception but idealist in concepts (both together)— was Ortega's always overlooked formula of 1934: "a radical unitary duality" (8:43), a neglected "key."[12] That principle meant not just life as "self and circumstance" at its "radical" (pragmatist) basis but a higher development, by phenomenological and historical methods, as existentialism and historicism within a philosophy of life.

Of course, to obtain a philosophical unity out of such a variety of parts requires much research and exemplification. It takes many hundreds of loci cited from Ortega's *Obras Completas* and from his archives to demonstrate the "system" that he claimed was in his head and in his thought as a whole. All the parenthetical citations will let readers satisfy themselves about the evidence from Ortega himself on which this generalizing interpretation has been painstakingly erected.

This historical study is not offered with a naive illusion that it is the "totality" or the "last word" on Ortega. Too many previously have claimed to have found "the key" to his enigmatic "system,"[13] and too many partial views and perspectives have been promoted as revealing the hitherto undiscovered "secret" of his mental processes and philosophical coherence. No one will ever have the last word on Ortega, because he was so very diverse, so "many-sided." There will always be other themes, facets, nuances, problems, relationships, and newer interpretations to expose to public view—including my own projected study of his thought "beyond philosophy," on history and the "human sciences." With studies of Ortega proliferating to the present, however, there is all the more need for periodic attempts to bring some synthesizing unity into that diversity—some balance, relationship, and struc-

12. The unitary-dual formula was cited by John Graham in 1987 in "Pragmatism and Philosophy of History," 1332; and idem, "On Qualitative Modelling: Ortega y Gasset" (Paper presented at the Social Science History conference, Chicago, 1985).

13. For "keys" to Ortega, see, besides Marías, Ferrater Mora, and Morón Arroyo, the following: Jorge Mañach, "Dualidad y síntesis en Ortega," *Papeles de Son Armadans* (Palma de Mallorca) 5:13 (1957): 13–32; Santiago Ramírez, "Ortega y el nucleo de su filosofía: El tema del hombre," *Punta Europa* (Madrid), no. 40 (1959): 41–87; Casanovas Sánchez, *Ortega, dos filosofías* (Madrid: Studium, 1960); Paulino Garagorri, "Ortega y Zubiri en un sistema abierto," *Cuadernos Hispanoamericanos*, no. 66 (1966): 5–12; Guillermo Araya Goubert, *Claves filológicas para la comprensión de Ortega* (Madrid: Gredos, 1971); Abelardo Herrero Alonso, "Claves estilísticas de filosofar en Ortega," *Conversaciones sobre Ortega*, ed. Ana E. Velázquez Fernández et al. (Aller, Spain: I.N.B. Príncipe de Asturias, 1983), 153–65. Like Garagorri and Ferrater Mora, Marías too (*Trayectorias*, 493) saw Ortega's as the "open system" it was.

ture to it all—so as to interest not just specialists and philosophers but general, educated readers again in what is still vital, living, in him.

LIMITATIONS AND OBSTACLES

So many, and such seemingly contradictory, opinions compete about Ortega's philosophy. The dominant Western view of him as one of the existentialists may have sufficed for his crisis thinking, yet with what could we cover the later historical remainder of his thought? Silver proposed phenomenology for his overall system, but even in Merleau-Ponty that had been only minimally concerned with history. Historicism has been rejected by most philosophers instinctively—both as a philosophy and in Ortega. If he is not generally regarded as "a philosopher's philosopher," however, might not the "old aficionado of history" (4:158) have been "a historian's philosopher"—some kind of "philosopher of history" after all? But historians are ill-made to explicate historicism as ontological or metaphysical.

Obviously one volume cannot cover everything related to Ortega's philosophy. On one side, the studies (books, articles, and addresses) on Ortega since 1955 are enormous in number, and, on the other, his twelve volumes and the more than eighty reels in his archive, make it impossible to cite every opinion, essay, or set of class notes—useful to support this interpretation or maybe to contradict it. This book is only a relative whole, even for his philosophy, let alone his thought "beyond" it as interdisciplinary studies in culture and the human sciences.

Short of a lifetime—a luxury granted only to Julián Marías—one cannot do a truly *conclusive* study of Ortega's philosophy, in part because not all the sources are available yet. As persistent "digging" into them goes ever deeper and wider, the excavated material piles up and branches out with no certain terminus in sight, until one looks like Burckhardt's "capricorn beetle." For that reason, when one thinks he has at last a coherent grasp of *most* of Ortega's ever-elusive "whole" as a "philosophy of life," he must present the structure, with supporting evidence and argument.

At this point of surfeit, I feel less pain than gratitude that—with the lecture "course" materials put out in 1984 or into volume 12 (1983)—published writings of Ortega remained relatively "complete" after the centennial years, excepting the *Cartas de un joven español* (1991), the youthful correspondence edited by his daughter, Soledad Ortega. However, her promise of "Completer Works" from the archive tells us the task of interpretation (and hence of revision) will long continue.

Some of the "open" microfilm reels in Ortega's archive at the Library of Congress are utilized in this book, and others that were closed (but were perused with the consent of Señora Soledad) will be cited briefly for general content and import, where permitted. The archive especially helps us to grasp a *second* stage in Ortega's study of Nietzsche's mad vitalism, Heidegger's sad existentialism, and Dilthey's lifeless philosophy of life. His notes on them illuminate his growing hostility to the former two and his mild critical reaction to the third. Isolated archival data were essential to show that he was briefly a conscious idealist during his youth and that he later recognized that indeed he had a type of "historicism," but the archive was not needed to demonstrate that he knew he was an existentialist and had a philosophy of life. By names and books, archival notes let one establish how early James's pragmatism, Husserl's phenomenology, and Bergson's vitalism were known to him, or how one related to another. Many pages of his notes and correspondence, however, are too dim to decipher from microfilm. If some materials that I *ought* to have used in this study are illegible, at least the very many I was able to read have not contradicted my integration of the *published* Ortega but sustain, supplement, and embellish it.

My general interpretation, as roughed out about 1982–1983, has not changed basically, despite all the archival materials subsequently used to verify and polish it. Instead, my original study was much enriched and expanded in details and variations; in numerous cases I could confirm what I otherwise could only surmise or suspect. Similar support derived from the vast critical literature, from the many insights and data.

No exhaustive bibliography will be added to the very many citations in the footnotes and supplemental endnotes of this study. Only major synthetic interpretations in Spanish and English, which are frequently cited, will be included. The vast number of items in Donoso and Raley make a comprehensive bibliography unfeasible and superfluous for such a large work as this. Virtually everything that anyone has found to be significant by and about Ortega's philosophy is used, however—and much besides that is peripheral—all needed to support and to clarify this complex interpretation of his very problematical philosophy of life.

PROBLEMS CONFRONTING A SYNTHETIC INTERPRETATION

Ortega's philosophy has remained a problem, even an enigma, almost half a century after his death. As Philip Silver remarked in 1978, despite all our attempts to pin down and to define his philosophy, it "continues to elude us."[14] Much of it no doubt eludes me too, with my new or different emphases. At least, one

14. Philip W. Silver, *Ortega y Gasset as Phenomenologist: The Genesis of Meditations on Quixote*, 1.

hopes it now seems more complete in parts and more coherent as a whole, as a pragmatist "philosophy of life." Exercising "the imperative of all history" while expounding Ortega, I have tried "to complete" the *tendency* of his thought into our mental world, much as he tried to do with Dilthey (6:174). Overall, I have sought to show that—in Ortega—pragmatism actually could (as has recently been argued) undergo a logical development into most of the leading philosophies of the twentieth century.

More than a long generation after his death, what is more problematical about Ortega than a generally acceptable definition of his philosophy? After so many efforts by philosophers to define him, how can an intellectual historian hope to do it? There is no sense in simply repeating well-worn labels and formulas, unless one can demonstrate them convincingly and solidly out of the sources and then integrate that plurality into one "system": pragmatism, phenomenology, existentialism, and historicism within a comprehensive whole as a "philosophy of life" that is still "authentically" Ortega.

Major obstacles, apart from those of an "outsider," face every researcher here: (1) objective problems of sources (organization, mass, accessibility) and (2) more subjective problems of established translations (Norton's series) and of more or less authoritative interpretations (like Marías's). There are also, of course, problems of "proof" by the researcher himself, which finally reduce to persuasion by evidence and argument—here mostly for my two related theses: that, in fact, Ortega was a pragmatist and that he was coherent as a whole in his philosophy.

The arrangement of the *Obras Completas* sometimes hinders more than helps the researcher. Because Ortega, long lacking a national journal of philosophy, was so chaotic in his mode and order of production, so much of which was dispersed in newspapers, some of the twelve volumes are arranged neither very logically by topic nor chronologically. Even volume 6 does not present a clear line of break (1932) between the first and second stages (or so-called voyages) in his thought, and the indexed contents (mostly unnumbered documents) of the eighty-some reels in the archive are often extremely diverse. Some titles chosen by Ortega are a poor gauge of content, so one must read everything. Of course, the multitude of his interests and the accidents of his life prohibit anyone from putting everything from before and after 1932 into uniform, tightly integrated volumes, by field and period. Although they are very helpful, book indexes have many mistakes of location (usually by only a page or two), and inevitably editors have limited or omitted references to some important topics. Extensive or intensive research into Ortega will require anyone to make corrections, additions, and even supplementary indexes—built on and into the extant ones.

Through all areas of investigation of Ortega, but nowhere more than in respect to his philosophy, one may occasionally be misled by the English translations. At times not only specific words and phrases—as essential as "radical" and "radicalism" and "radical empiricism," which are *crucial* for grasping what he was about—are altered from their authentic meaning in Spanish. Whole books or chapters may (by variant title) be given a pallid or wrong meaning. The classic instance was the British decision to call what was literally a post-modern "theme of our time" by the very misleading name *Modern Theme*. However, Ortega himself warned us that translating is a "utopian" task, but we have to do it—and to double-check for verisimilitude. All translations here—from Ortega's works and archive and from the critics—are my own. Where his essays have appeared in English, I have consulted and often closely paralleled such renditions if they were sufficiently accurate. Rarely, however, are their versions precisely the same as mine, even where no error occurs. *De gustibus non disputandum est*—tastes vary.

Most of the errors of the translators stem from inevitable lack of familiarity with the whole. Ortega himself was emphatic about the need to get a grasp of the whole—of European and Western history, or of the life and works of an artist or of a thinker. Holism is no less necessary for dealing effectively with Ortega himself, with his ever-recurring but variable themes and his incomplete "complete works." Because essential things are missing, the effort is difficult and the result tentative, as on his pragmatism and on his coherence as a whole. Neither can stand solely on objective evidence or on subjective judgment or argument, but both are required for a solution.

Because Ortega was omnivorous in his reading, ecumenical in his interests and efforts, and encyclopedic by intent (and by production in part), he cannot be neatly categorized. His thought cannot be represented simply as another academic philosophy with precise limits of metaphysics, epistemology, ontology, ethics, and logic. Such sharp bounds do not exist even in his philosophy, much less in his thought as a whole. He keeps spilling out and running over—and into much that is not strictly philosophy, that is "beyond philosophy." But his work in the human sciences was consistent with his philosophy, and the two areas were coherent in themselves and together. Evidence and argument, of course, have still to be presented—for philosophy (in this volume), and for the human sciences (in another).

It may help to predispose readers to accept pragmatism in Ortega if they learn of the main evidence here at the beginning. So many of Ortega's basic concepts (even his notion of "concept" itself) were from James that in 1916 he confided to a class that his "system of vital reason" had been crudely anticipated by "so-called 'pragmatism'" and by German *Weltanschauung* theory, or Dilthey's historical "worldviews" (12:392). Not until near the end of his life, however, in what he called an "autobiographical" account by "historical reason," did he again directly confess his early debt to James and to *Pragmatism* (1907).[15] The subtitle of that book was about a new "way of thinking" (a phrase Ortega used often and prominently), and where the last part of the book referred to a "living reason," it evidently inspired his own later *razón vital*.

We find a basic Jamesian metaphysics of "the given" already in 1910 in his "Adam in Paradise," before he formalized it as "absolute positivism" in 1916. James's Heraclitean idea of fluid time and reality became, with Ortega's "metahistory" (1923), a new ontology of "becoming." Later, in 1928, pragmatism as a "radical empiricism" gave Ortega half the four elements of his method of historiology, which was also inspired by Dilthey's "basic discipline" for history and the social sciences.

Initially Ortega was a tacit, teasing borrower from James, but his secret debt was quickly buried (by 1913) within elements taken from Husserl. Thereafter he assigned what were essentially the same pragmatic concepts to Kant, Dilthey, and Comte in turn. Quietly pragmatism entered his phenomenology, existentialism, and historicism, and finally his covering philosophy of life—five relatable movements in the philosophy of his time to which he responded creatively and successively, after a false start in Kantianism. Because he had so many masters, he finally was a disciple of none. He was the maker of a very complex "system" of his own that had close affinities with all of them, especially with James first and with Dilthey last.

One hopes that the evidence and reasoning that follow in this study will indeed persuade readers to see that Ortega truly had "a pragmatist philosophy of life"—a very complex and comprehensive "system" or "way of thinking" that imparted unity or cohesion to all of his interdisciplinary and multidisciplinary ventures.

Ortega *is* still interesting and instructive. He is still a philosopher for "our time" because he participated creatively and critically in so many philosophical developments that are still ongoing. And he foresaw or encouraged so many things "beyond philosophy" that we have either already experienced or still anticipate.

15. Ortega, "Medio siglo de filosofía," 5–6, 15–16.

Chapter 1

FROM PROBLEMS TO SOLUTIONS

Ortega's Open "System"

ccording to Ortega, "everything is problematical" in philosophy. "A philosophical system can be understood only in its totality."[1] "The history of philosophy," however, "is an integrating part of the system of philosophy" (R 76). We ourselves have to use a historical approach as well as textual analysis in order to integrate *his* "system" of philosophy, which has always been very problematical, in parts and as a whole.

What this introduction attempts is a succinct overview of the complex and comprehensive historical study that follows. It seeks to identify the main problems that have always confronted critics and to find in Ortega himself the answers and solutions to them, either in his words or in his life by its stages and potentialities. We shall put to the test his claim in 1932: "My vocation was thought, zeal for clarity on things" (6:356). I also try to show how his philosophy was a "systematic" unity of life and history: a "radical unitary duality" (or plurality).

Because Ortega was so diverse (in parts, areas, and modes of thinking) and so dispersed, with his "works" still coming out, it has been virtually impossible to define him (or to understand him) as a whole. Silver has made a fruitful approach to his method (as phenomenological), and, like Ferrater Mora and Orringer, he has rightly seen in Ortega an always *developing* philosophy. Moreover, as has been said of Dilthey, so it is with Ortega: "By

---

1. Ortega, *¿Qué es conocimiento?* 26, 93, three lecture courses (1929–1931). The passages from R 76 are not datable. However, in 1913 he stated: "In fact, there is no *first* problem, no problem in itself. To each stage in the progressive series of solutions, the previous solution is a problem." The history of philosophy "is the history of what was once a vital problem but is not so for us now" (12:496). That is largely so with Ortega's philosophy, but each "stage" that solved *his* problem became a problem for critics.

its very nature [his] thought cannot be presented in serial fashion" alone, because it not only "evolved but also revolved" through his hermeneutical procedure. Even so, his thought must be viewed historically and in the ongoing context of life, era, and world. As Marías pointed out, interpreting Ortega's thought demands both the "text" and the "context" of his life and historical circumstance. We look in vain for one or several substantial works sufficient to define him analytically.[2] Instead, like Marías (but more radically), we ought to track him through the whole "trajectory" of "self and circumstance," from beginning to end—not just in his vocation of philosopher in the narrower traditional sense but as a wider-ranging thinker who dared to speculate about problems relevant to the arts and literature and to the human sciences. Both interdisciplinary and synthetic by interest and effort, his thought has exceeded the grasp of everyone who has tried to see him whole and integrated, even in philosophy alone. His philosophy itself was many things and intentionally led into projects that went "beyond philosophy" but still reflected it.

Working on Ortega is like attempting to put together a vast jigsaw puzzle, with the pieces all scattered and without a sure and agreed-upon picture of the whole: a "mosaic philosophy" like that of William James.[3] Since some portions have now been integrated more or less, however, the whole may be almost within our reach. But let us not be tempted to force it to support arbitrary schemas instead of trying to fit together the chaos of parts by patient labor. By heeding closely the historical details of his life, thought, and circumstance (with help from his own theory of life and private revelations), we can identify and understand Ortega partly "from within," from himself. If we search diligently, we can find in the history of his life and thought answers for most of the problems that his diversity, secrets, delays, and lacunae have presented. We can glimpse the unity under his diversity, especially for his philosophy. If we then compare him with contemporaries and predecessors as part of his "circumstance," we can identify him in part from "without."

ORTEGA "FROM WITHIN"

"A system of secrets," Ortega warned us, "cannot be discovered . . . from outside" (R 64), but only from an effort to live "inside." He admitted that his own work was "very complex, very full of secrets, allusions and elisions,

2. Philip Silver, *Phenomenology and Art,* 9; idem, *Ortega as Phenomenologist,* 4; Orringer, *Fuentes germánicas,* 349–51; Michael Ermarth, *Wilhelm Dilthey: The Critique of Historical Reason* (Chicago: University of Chicago Press, 1978), 10; Marías, *Trayectorias,* 35, 37.

3. James, *The Writings of William James,* ed. John J. McDermott, 195, 199 ("mosaic").

very interwoven with a whole vital trajectory . . ." (6:349). In 1961, Marrero alleged that Ortega had concealed his sources, but, boasting that he had discovered them all, he denied that any "secrets" remained.[4] By appearances, however, Ortega still had some big secrets: James, Schlegel, and Croce, even Comte and Tocqueville—sources that Marrero never suspected.

Merely to attempt a critical exposition and "construction" (like that by Morón Arroyo) of what Ortega called "the thought . . . of such a man" (8:17) is not truly to get at his thought from inside. Several have already tried to show us Ortega "from within," but here we essay only a schematic relationship of his life and thought according to his own "theory of life," which he occasionally applied to his personal experience. This project concerns his generations theory and a contrasting theory of *intellectual* life, but it does not pretend to be an intellectual biography, although it provides some biographical details.

Where did Ortega get his idea for "Goethe from Within"? In *A Pluralistic Universe* (1909), James recommended approaching a thinker not from "outside" by "putting together dead fragments" but from "inside": from the center of a man's "philosophic vision," so as to understand his ideas as "things in the making" and his life as *élan vital,* by a "living sympathy." This "way of knowing" from life, instead of from rationalist "intellectualism," shows us how "what is manifold [can] be one," as life is "continuously changing," whereas our conceptualizations "cut out and fix, and exclude." But "the real concrete sensible flux of life experiences compenetrate each other," and none can be excluded. What Ortega attempted in "Goethe from Within" (1932), and with Kant even earlier, was very like James's advice.[5]

Knowing Ortega "from within" is a fine ideal—Ortega's own—but it is for us still an unattainable desideratum. He wanted "biography" to enter into "the life," "calling," or "vocation" of the subject, which for us will be only his philosophy as a kind of "history of ideas." "A life viewed thus, from its intimate side, has no form. Nothing seen from inside has one" (4:400–402). For Ortega himself, however, we must supply the *external* "aspect." "Unfinished, indeterminate," life "does not tolerate being contemplated from without" as a mere "object." Nevertheless, we may have to do so to a greater extent than we would wish, because his life was so "secret." He wanted life *not* to be as subjective as "psychological biography" but to include both "I and my world" as "the true within." If psychobiography is really not possible here, neither can we bring in much of his world. Our approach has to be a compromise, not an Ortegan "bio-graphy," except

---

4. Vicente Marrero, *Ortega, filósofo "mondain,"* 120, 242.

5. James, *A Pluralistic Universe* (1909, 1977), 113–16, 118. See Ortega, 4:48, on Kant "from within." Where more than one edition of a work by James is cited, the later version is usually the most recent critical edition from Harvard University Press.

where we are able to discern thought and life in contact. That kind of visible "compenetration" is as yet very limited for us. We simply lack enough "auto-biographical" details from him to fulfill such a project in "historical reason." Regardless of our limits, however, let us strive in that direction, for he anticipated the "genetic" injunction that we cannot very well understand disembodied thought historically (8:17, 21).[6]

If an analytical, topical approach by conceptual schema is not sufficient to cope with Ortega, neither is a purely genetic-chronological approach by history or biography. We need both. His ideas and themes changed too much for the former way, but they also displayed a degree of recurring (if developing) permanence. There are a limited number of major themes in his system, but one can rarely assign a precise beginning or end for them. And the whole system is unfinished at the end, like an "open" system that is meant to be "continued." Perhaps the whole is not attainable by any method or combination of approaches, because it was in fact still *intentional,* as befitted such a phenomenologist. Part of his thought (vitalist, historical, and linguistic) was not completed, and the histories of his life and thought were not finally perfectly integrated with each other.

Judicious interpretation of Ortega is, therefore, rather like balancing on a tightrope; one must not tilt too much in any direction. His philosophy was a delicate balance between realism and idealism, subjectivism and objectivism, ontology and epistemology, one school and another. Marías erred not so much in denying that Ortega's philosophy *was* any one of these types (phenomenology, existentialism, historicism, or philosophy of life) but in not seeing that he participated in *all* of them. But such comprehensiveness meant that he was indeed "unique."

Despite all critical opinion, Ortega must be our first and final source for what his thought was: in relation to his predecessors and contemporaries and in relation also to himself and his own life and circumstances. Always he strove to be at "the level of the times" (as he put it), and he took pride in going "beyond" others (3:185, 187), even beyond himself, over the years. For him, thinking was a lifelong project of constant growth and adjustment. Unlike Hegel or Comte, he saw his own and every philosophy as time-bound, never absolute, and never finished so long as life did not end (6:417–18). Ever striving to innovate, as late as 1951 he wrote of the need for a new

6. Among those who have sought to grasp Ortega's thought from "within" are: Marías, *Trayectorias,* 36; Morón Arroyo, *Sistema,* 4; Manuel Durán, "Pidiendo un Ortega desde dentro," in *Ortega Hoy,* ed. Durán (Xalapa: Veracruz University Press, 1985), 35–40; Juan D. García Bacca, "Pidiendo un Ortega y Gasset desde dentro," *Entregas de la Licorne* 4:8 (1956): 69–77. All, of course, imitated Ortega on Goethe. See Silver, *Ortega as Phenomenologist,* 13, 156: Ortega did not expound his doctrines at length, but sometimes he did so historically and genetically.

"point of departure" and a "new road" in philosophy (R 33). Rarely was he "finished" with any theme or idea, so it was inevitable that when he died his work was still "incomplete," even by its very name. For that reason, it is called here a "philosophy of life," because he was still trying to complete it out of history (with a historical linguistics and sociology). Although he once criticized both "philosophy" and "history" as "ridiculous names" for the realities and sciences that they signify (6:361–62), he finally admitted that "Life" was a poor name for a philosophy, whatever the latter were.

"WHAT IS PHILOSOPHY?"

Around 1930, Ortega proposed a very Jamesian "theme," as against any "perennial philosophy": "The Meaning of Philosophy: 'Philosophy is perpetual overcoming,' surpassing, going beyond" (R 54). "What Is Philosophy?" was the name of a course Ortega taught in 1930, which is now a book, his most openly pragmatist one. His answer to that question was the work of a lifetime, in part because of his aim of ever "overcoming," which he explained as "conservation" (7:404), or *keeping* somehow (instead of discarding) his whole philosophical past, while developing that heritage into something new. "Philosophy," he said, "is the story that never ends" (12:183)—as in James.[7]

At that time Ortega defined philosophy as a "hypertechnical question" about what "philosophizing" is. It involves "what 'our life' is"—"day by day." Hence, "doing philosophy" is "a form of living," a "type of life," but also is "de-living" in order to make the "universe" (and life) knowable. It is "first of all . . . a theory of life" (7:297–98, 287, 428–30). In another 1930 course he argued that "we need a new philosophy or system of concepts," because traditional ones were inadequate for a "new reality" such as *life* and "all [that] is in it."[8] Real, "authentic" philosophy, "a philosophy that *be*" such, he said in 1944, is active, growing, a part of living and doing—is wrestling with life's "radical problems," not merely *teaching* a "system" previously worked out, which is thereby a lifeless "mummy" (12:150, 205, 210). Life is self *and* world.

In 1947 in his "Leibniz," Ortega observed, "Philosophy is a system of radical interpretative (therefore intellectual) attitudes that man adopts in view of the gigantic event that for him is finding himself living" (8:266). Already in 1929 he averred: "*Cogito quia vivo*" (4:58). Thought is a function

---

7. Craig R. Eisendrath, *The Unifying Moment: The Psychological Philosophy of William James and Alfred North Whitehead* (Cambridge: Harvard University Press, 1971), xiii: "Such a scheme is developed by Whitehead," but James "ran out of time."

8. Ortega, *¿Qué es conocimiento?* 113.

of life. The event of living involves not only oneself but "a whole world of other events" in which for him other things exist. Hence, if philosophy is a "system of radical opinions" about both self and world as events, then time, place, and *history* are necessarily part of it.

Already in 1930 (even in 1923), Ortega had brought history into his definition of philosophy (7:284–85; 3:198). Later, in a historical approach to "origins," he found the reason for "doing philosophy" authentically in historic losses of faith, or beliefs, during crises of doubt[9] wherein our *quehaceres,* acts, or doings, follow our ideas or "theories" (8:265–66). Philosophy supplants a lost "faith." So it was for the ancient Greeks, and for him personally too. Philosophy is comprised of both *ideoma* and *draoma;* the former is the "system" of conscious, explicit concepts and principles set "apart from time and place," but the latter is "a 'system' of vital actions" and "beliefs" that are "essentially latent"—and *historical* or changing (8:258–59). So philosophy at bottom was a *belief* that at top was *ideas*—a distinction from James that he developed in an interesting way.

HOW ORTEGA SAW AND NAMED HIS OWN PHILOSOPHY

A very proud intellectual, Ortega reluctantly admitted the "enormous limitations" that his "supremely questionable figure" cut in philosophy (12:273). His style was unorthodox, his method was not very obvious, and he did not write solid tomes. Unlike Kant, Hegel, Marx, and Comte, and most contemporaries, he made no "utopian" pretense of excogitating an abstract universal or "definitive" philosophy (6:418). Instead, he philosophized for and from "life," for his personal "destiny," for his concrete circumstance (or "situation") of time and place, and in response to "shipwreck," or crisis (6:350–51). His "system" was therefore vitalist, ever developing, ultimately, consciously historicist.

It may be surprising that Ortega used different names for successive stages and different levels of his developing system. Until later years he had not settled on "philosophy of life" as sufficiently general and comprehensive, but even then what it included and excluded was not clear. "I am not going to say," he wrote in 1947, "what I am, of course, but . . . what I am not, namely a materialist and an idealist" (8:256n). Over the years he had described his philosophy in turn as "absolute [radical] positivism," "perspectivism," "vital reason" or "ratiovitalism," and "historical reason"—all before choosing "philosophy of life." Only the last of these terms is still recognized as once a

---

9. On philosophy's origin in crises of doubt, see Ortega, *The Idea of Principle in Leibniz,* trans. Mildred Adams (New York: Norton, 1971), 273, 295–96, 354–55.

general type (or current) in European and Western philosophy; the others were peculiar to Ortega, to his idiosyncrasies of nomenclature. Much confusion has arisen from this pluralism of types and proliferation of names, but also from the *duality* in them, which doubles the confusion. In 1932, Ortega regretted that his disciples had not been able to "think together" the dual elements of his philosophy, of "vital" and "reason" (4:404n). Some twenty years later he found that neither Marías nor Curtius—favored confidants with opposite perspectives—could do so with both vital reason and historical reason (R 2—1938–1949; R 33—1952). We are still trying to think them together, to unify his duality and plurality into a kind of "system" that coherently reflects his thought in reality.

The variety of names and types of philosophy in Ortega can be reconciled by seeing that each was *in* a growing whole, a covering "philosophy of life." But even those parts that were not dual in name were dual to some degree, including the life-whole. In a subtle way, his radical positivism was at once epistemological and ontological. It assumed that one's self "sees" phenomena that were "self-posited" or "given," the *presence* of the "things" comprising "self and circumstance" in the "intuited" life-reality. While perspectivism may sound more epistemological, and philosophy of life more ontological, both reflected that basic metaphysical duality. Formally dual, but alternately reversing the emphasis from methodical reason to substantial life, were vital reason and ratiovitalism. In contrast, historical reason seems mainly epistemological, because "historical" modifies reason, but it also implies life. Life is historical, and history is about life (5:401). Philosophy of life, finally, comprised both historical reason and vital reason, so it was dual from bottom to top.

Except for calling his metaphysics "absolute positivism" and his chief method "perspectivism" (both in 1916), Ortega did not assign a specific name to his philosophy publicly, nor substantively, until 1923, when he proclaimed it "vital reason." The term "ratiovitalism," which he later claimed to have used for "many years" thereafter (6:196n; R 37—1929), may have been private and implied, but it did not appear in print until 1932 (4:404n). From 1923 and 1924 he alternately denoted his philosophy formally by his dominant general methods of vital reason and historical reason. In *Modern Theme* he gave "vital reason" the dimensions "vital, historical, and perspectivist," and in "Atlantises" (1924) he first spoke of a "historical reason" (3:201, 314). He did not imply that the whole might be called "philosophy of life" until he promoted Dilthey as his revered exemplar in 1934 (8:46; 6:205). Dilthey was the only other philosopher, moreover, who had used the terms "philosophy of life" and "historical reason" to describe his own thinking.

What kind of *general* philosophy, or variations therein, did all Ortega's idiosyncratic terms signify? Then (1934) he meant to let German critics know that what he himself had called "philosophy of vital reason" was equivalent (in his "Idea of Life" as "radical reality") to Dilthey's "philosophy of life" on one side and to Heidegger's "philosophy of existence" on the other, except that it was *more* than (or more rational and vital than) "existential thinking" (8:45–47). He also stated then very explicitly that Husserl's "phenomenology was not for us a philosophy: it was . . . good luck" as a method, or a "prodigious instrument" (8:42). That same year he equated his "radical positivism" with "radical empiricism" (6:202, 210), as if they were Dilthey's, but the former was of his own coinage and the latter was James's quasi synonym for pragmatism. The term "perspectivism" had been his near equivalent for phenomenology, but in a *realist* mode that combined James and Husserl. "Vital reason" was his earlier form of existentialism, and "historical reason" was a vital and "rational" historicism akin to Dilthey's.

That year (1934), the midpoint of his philosophical career, was the acme of his efforts to adopt a distinctive name for his whole effort, a "philosophy of life" as related to a general Western philosophy. Later he praised Husserl and Heidegger as better, or luckier, than he in "denominative" talent for naming the new developments in philosophy. Still, he considered and rejected as *insufficient* for his total philosophy such general names as phenomenology, existentialism, historicism, and even philosophy of life; he likewise did not use pragmatism as a name for his metaphysics. Although he finally reduced that "radical positivism" to Husserl's "radicalism" and quit mentioning "perspectivism" and "ratiovitalism," he never discarded the name "vital reason." In later years, however, he referred to "historical reason" almost exclusively—as then constituting his philosophy (at least his major effort in it) after the mid-1930s (5:534). He did not directly and *publicly* call it "historicism," but that is what it was. At Geneva in 1951, although he still preferred "philosophy of life" to either historicism or existentialism for his *total* position vis-à-vis Merleau-Ponty, he deferred amicably to the latter's defense of "being" over "life" as more precise.[10] Because of those later developments, I have in this study assigned the name "philosophy of life" to the whole.

From the foregoing relationships of one type of philosophy with another, and of ontology with epistemology, it is clear that Ortega's total "philosophy of life" grew into a complex, interdependent, and comprehensive body of thought. "Radical positivism" (or "radical empiricism") was his basic pragmatic metaphysics throughout. It was also at the basis of (and was expressed by) his "general phenomenology," which was in turn his basic realist method for both perspectivism and vital reason and even, to a more limited degree, for historical reason. Hence, his phenomenology as *method* was also visible in

10. Ortega, "Troisième entretien privé," 289.

all phases of his thought, as Silver says, although more diluted and dependent in the last stage of historical reason, which was a more or less Diltheyan kind of historicism. He certainly believed that parts of his thought were truly existentialism and historicism and phenomenology. They were all included *in* his own philosophy of life—more than in Dilthey's (see 6:175, 185, 208 n. 1).

DEFINING ORTEGA HISTORICALLY BY STRUCTURE, LIFE, AND STYLE

The nature of Ortega's thought is a many-sided problem. Historical research can aid critical analysis in defining and interrelating the "stages" of his philosophy. He himself stressed a genetic, historical, and circumstantial approach to all philosophy, his own included. Examination of his life from a circumstantial angle certainly helps understanding, but he also recommended a genetic-structural approach to thinkers such as Descartes, Kant, and Dilthey. Applied to him, this last approach utilizes his life theory, including his generations theory, for he clearly believed that it was reflected in his thought too.[11] What he was and did and thought apart from philosophizing also had a great effect on his philosophy, which grew and changed through a series of stages and levels. His diversity is, of course, much more evident than any unity ("system") in his thought, but it is the latter that we now seek—first for his philosophy. How can one hope to find therein a meaningful and coherent structure that others have sought in vain? If it was not in his style, was it in his life?

With an amazingly diverse and prolific output of "themes" for a half-century, Ortega represents a formidable obstacle to all efforts to "reduce" his thought to any tidy order, although he always claimed to have a "system." Trying to systematize him, however, is like trying to render poetry by prose. Regarded by some as the greatest essayist in the history of philosophy, he has to be read in the original or else most of the *charm* that captivated many for a whole generation gets lost. Still, we do need a systematic framework for Ortega or most of the *content* and *coherence* in his ideas also gets lost. Either way, tampering with his work is a bad compromise, but maybe pragmatic usefulness will excuse the inevitable necessity of first carving it up before trying to serve it up whole. After all, his work comprised parts.

11. Apart from studies of Ortega's idea of generations as studied systematically by Marías in *Generations: A Historical Method,* there apparently are no extensive studies published on Ortega's general theory of life, although perhaps some dissertations, several of which have "life" as a topic, might serve. Also see Daniel J. Levinson, *The Seasons of a Man's Life* (New York: Knopf, 1978), 214, 289, 323, for Ortega's contributions to crises and "stages of life." For a short inquiry, see Domingo Marrero, "El constructivismo orteguiano y las categorías de la vida," *La Torre* 4:15–16 (July–September 1956): 15–16, 34–36.

One would like to have a self-explanatory Ortega, but he did not ever become that candid and comprehensive. At times he was very revealing of one side or another of his thought but never of the structure of the whole, except for the enigmatic formula "radical unitary duality" (8:43). Several times, on the contrary, he confessed that he had *concealed* under his style the "dialectical musculature" or "architecture" of his thought (3:270; 8:292 n. 1). Even when he promised to do so by "brief formulas" (12:152–53, 195), he backed out of candid exposition, since it was too "difficult to transmit to others."

Therefore, the only way to grasp Ortega as a whole, to get beyond savoring superficial impressions of his notable popular essays, is to ignore his reluctance and instead to follow James and "break up" the "original chaos" in any "given reality," not excluding his or Ortega's thought.[12] We have to cut his work apart and put it back together again, "remodeled" in a way more historical, systematic, and structured. His innumerable themes, essays, articles, and prefaces were often special perspectives on life that contained little distillations, or concentrations, of his basic philosophy of life, which become very tedious with repetition. They entice but they are never enough to satisfy our appetite, for they raise as many questions as they answer. But that was Ortega's way. He would never sum up his whole philosophy in any one or several works, and he was so reticent on some essential relationships and dependencies. We can get at the whole only by patiently analyzing and chronologically relating a great mass of material over many years. His diversity was as staggering as his secrecy was irritating.

The Diversity of Ortega in Life and Thought

Clearly Ortega was a wide-ranging thinker, a veritable "polymath," who is hard to "pin down" and categorize succinctly. For he did not believe that his "mission" or "vocation" in life was to be just a "specialist" in philosophy, a narrow academic "profession." Except for its "utopian" implications, he agreed with Scipio's motto: "I am a man and nothing human is foreign to me" (3:226–27). He regarded philosophy itself as a *quehacer,* something to "do," particularly to "make" one's own self, or being, so that life itself is "the repertory of our *doings*" (6:350–51). In the preface for the German edition of *Modern Theme* he said that he was a *polypragmosyne,* by which he meant a "doer" who was many things at once: teacher, writer, journalist, editor, political theorist and activist, conversationalist in *tertulias,* and aficionado of bullfighting (8:16). But all of his various avocations were "secondary forms of intellection" that "derived" from his radical "vocation" of

12. James, *The Philosophy of William James,* ed. Horace M. Kallen, 69.

philosophy, of thinking (6:352–53). In such breadth, he was intentionally very unlike the German *Gelehrte* (Cohen and Heidegger, for example) in narrow specialization, "profundity," and formal style (8:57).

Refusing to wear the professional "uniform" and "grotesque masks" of formal style and format (12:274–76), he feigned not to care whether critics took him for a philosopher, a poet, or a "duckbilled platypus" (4:150). Sometimes, in mock humility, he disarmingly called himself Mr. "Commonplace" (*Perogrullo*), or "Everyman" (5:316; 8:497). An aficionado of bullfighting (mainly for its art and history), he later described himself as "a little Spanish gentleman with the face of an old torero" (9:651). When venturing thus outside the traditional bounds of philosophy (as a critic of art), he confessed he was just such an "incorrigible," rash amateur (8:559–60). Even in his two chief philosophical preoccupations of life and history, however, he saw himself as an aficionado (4:158; 8:405). "The *afición*," he explained, "is an authentic, intimate, spontaneous motive that has the character of a desire or appetite toward a thing" (5:175). Such a motivation, he believed, distinguished all "authentic" philosophy from the merely professional type—regardless of style.

Most analysts have granted that Ortega's style set him apart as a gifted writer, lecturer, and teacher, but there agreement ends. Many have not been able to detect any "system" in him, and indeed a few captious critics denied that he was properly a philosopher at all—perhaps a "poet" or a "mystic"?[13] For thirty years he kept silent in the face of Spanish "pseudo-intellectuals" who saw him as only a litterateur instead of a philosopher because of his style of writing in metaphors and for newspapers (2:387–88).

Style or Substance?

In the 1920s, Ortega historized Aristotle's theory of tropes (3:373–75). He decided that *metaphor* (for which he was so often criticized) was a proper way of speaking about a new situation, about a newly perceived reality, that

13. Ventura Cumillas, ¿*Es Don José Ortega y Gasset un filósofo propiamente dicho?* (Buenos Aires, 1940); Angel Rosenblat, "Ortega y Gasset, filósofo o poeta?" *Revista Nacional de Cultura* (Chile) 19:123 (July–August 1957): 23–32. Two hostile critics, former admirers, J. I. Jiménez-Grullón, *A Margen de Ortega y Gasset* (Havana: Puentes Grandes, 1957), and Patricio Canto, *El Caso de Ortega y Gasset* (Buenos Aires: Leviatán, 1958), both denied that there was any "system" in Ortega's "disorderly" thought; as "historicism," it was a soulless, imperialist, and class-inspired "mysticism" of a relativist skeptic. J. B. Trend, who studied under Ortega in the 1920s, felt obliged to ask (on inviting him to Britain): "What is his system," when one saw in him traces of Plato, Descartes, Hegel, Nietzsche, the neo-Kantians, Scheler, Weber, Simmel, etc.? ("Boceto de Memoria," *Sur*, no. 24 [July–August 1956]: 204–5).

thus required a new mode of expression that could not yet be reduced to formal concept and exposition. Citing Schlegel, he regarded irony as characteristic of modern literature and art since the eighteenth century (3:382), and he felt that rationalism had ironized life (3:177). Just as irony fit the negative, incipient stage of a crisis, so metaphor suited Ortega's later, positive efforts to emerge therefrom with a new solution.

When Ortega died, many recalled him more for his stimulating presence, questions, suggestions, dialogue, and metaphors than for any formal doctrines or system of philosophy. Certainly he had "style" and was both proud of it and apologetic. To write for newspapers, instead of expounding his ideas in "compact" books that were "technically well articulated" (6:355–56; 8:54), may have been appropriate, given Spain's public disinterest—*in partibus infidelium* (1:311). But at times he might well have criticized himself as much as his era for having lost "the great style of thought," for requiring "pages and pages to hide our dialectical poverty" (3:432). Some of his lectures were in truth rambling and superficial. Until after the 1930s, his "books," he granted, were hardly books; they were mere collections of newspaper articles—or of classroom lectures—that had been addressed to Spaniards, not to "humanity" or to everybody (8:20). As such, they were "lighter" than customary philosophical treatises, and they were colloquial, because he did not edit "self" and "circumstance" out of them before publication. They had to be understood in terms of both author and audience. With an "altruistic" concern for the other's "point of view" and "reality," he sought to preserve "dialogue" even in his books (8:17–18).[14]

In a colloquium in 1951 he spoke on "philosophical style" as a new theme. He commended Aristotle's and Brentano's style but, paradoxically, not Plato's, whose dialogues were mainly literary, even "baroque" (9:638–39; compare 8:218). Since he had felt that "realism" was "my style" (R 43), and that this matched his new "objective realism" in philosophy (R 78), he was closer to Aristotle and Brentano than to the idealism of Plato or of Husserl. However, literary and philosophical styles had two different purposes. Thus, Heidegger had a "marvelous" style to *expound* philosophy but a heavy, opaque style for literature (9:634), to *persuade* a public that wanted clarity. For clarity, Ortega much preferred Husserl, if not Dilthey. Of course, his own dialogue was literary (3:270; 8:292–93), but since he professed clarity as a "courtesy" that the philosopher owes his public (7:288), he sought formal clarity too (6:352). Unlike the romantics and neo-romantics, "We demand that one speak with simplicity, clarity, and exactness, in words as fresh and disinfected

14. For Ortega on dialogue, see 3:255–57, which includes his notion of Socratic dialogue as "dialectic," and his proposal for a society (or *tertulia*) in Madrid to be called "Dialogue," in which philosophizing would be "sportive" in conduct and rules.

as a surgeon's instruments." Those were the three "divinities" he worshiped (7:437). Nevertheless, it pained him that critics could not see the philosophy in and under his literary metaphors (8:292n). His problem of style and substance was thus opposite to Heidegger's. Many regarded him as primarily a stylist, one whose supremely varied "themes" had no unity or systematic consistency, but others have liked both his style and his thought.[15] In fact, however, the lucid realism of his style matched an ontological realism in his "system" of philosophy, although the way he put forth his philosophy was not formally systematic but *thematic*.

THEMES IN ORTEGA

In 1932, Ortega's faithful collaborating editor and disciple, Fernando Vela, gave vent to his frustration over the apparent lack of coherence and order in his master's philosophy-in-essays—always just one theme after another, sometimes resumed but sometimes not. "Ortega, who has been the greatest raiser of themes," he lamented, "is also the one who has killed the most of them. He has drawn them out, has held them aloft dazzling," made us dizzy by his juggling, and then dropped them with: "it will be continued" (4:384). One day, before their *tertulia* convened, he demanded that Ortega write down for him the "key to the enigma." Naturally, his master refused, and instead launched into "a new theme, a theme on themes: the biography of themes."

> They live in us like we ourselves live in the world, as, like us in our circumstance, terrible things happen to them. Some are fortunate; others, hapless. Themes, like men, have their destiny. They have their childhood, their acme or flowering, their decline. They begin by being a mental game, "a happening"; later they become a fervor, when not an obsession. Still later they drain out and are left bloodless, stiff, and act in us only mechanically. (4:384)

The latter were "encysted themes," "decrepit or dead," that could ruin a writer who clung to them. In contrast was "the happy theme," whose acme comes when we have "time for it." Alas, Ortega never had time enough to finish any theme in a conclusive and systematic sense. Sometimes, he sighed,

---

15. On Ortega's style, see Manuel Durán-Gil, "Spanish and Catalan Literature," in *World Literature Since 1945*, ed. Ivav Ivask (New York: F. Ungar, 1973), 620: "clarity and elegance" and "almost baroque brilliance," but "his metaphors made his most difficult philosophical concepts accessible to the nonspecialist." Jan H. Walgrave, *La Filosofía de Ortega y Gasset*, 11, 15; Teresa Rodríguez de Lecea, "Ortega: Evolución de un pensador frente a su circunstancia," *Razón y Fe* (Madrid) 207 (May 1983): 487–94. For opposite views, see n. 13 above.

a writer's "most authentic themes" were virtually "left unborn"—such as his "new linguistics" at the end—or got "misplaced."

After exemplifying several species of themes, he abruptly concluded: "Et cetera, et cetera, et cetera." "As you see, the theme is not finishable. The same can be said of architecture, sculpture, theater. And cinematography. Note that this theory is not independent and apart from my other work. It is the general theory of my philosophy: perspectivism. But it is not 'point of view' in the idealist sense, but the opposite: it is that the seen, reality, is *also* point of view." These last words, he warned, would provoke a new theme. "Be content with continuations and enlargements . . ." (4:390).

And so Ortega's "themes" usually leave us *dis*content. Nevertheless, if he had a *system* it was made up especially of what he called his two greater "themes": "vital reason" and "historical reason"(12:193, 195), which were also the two "voyages," or stages, in his philosophy.

"SYSTEM" IN ORTEGA'S PHILOSOPHY

Defending his own "loose" philosophy, James criticized other philosophers for their "absolutism" with regard to intellect—an "intellectualism" that saw reality in terms of fully integrated "systems" of absolute truths. He protested that "no philosophy can be more than an hypothesis." "Life lies open, [but] . . . the philosophy that their intellects desiderate must wear the form of a closed system." Ortega's philosophy too was "loose," as befitted life, but he did not despise "system," so long as it remained "open"—just as several saw his, including Marías, Walgrave, Ferrater Mora, Morón Arroyo, and Díez del Corral.[16]

Like Croce's, Ortega's philosophy was an ongoing series of "attempts at a system" that never quite got there in a *formal* way. As he said of Dilthey, he too was one of those "thinkers who think without rushing to arrive at formulas" (9:290). But something else he said of Dilthey seemed to apply to himself: "Philosophical thinking is system and in a system every concept includes all the others." One cannot, of course, say everything at once (6:170). He could well have agreed with Croce that "I shall go on philosophizing, even if . . . I one day give up 'philosophy'" in the traditional systematic sense. Already in 1956, one of Ortega's admirers, Díez del Corral, pointed out how "problematical" was his master's philosophy in regard to "system," because Ortega had begun by rejecting "those coherent and closed systems" of comprehensive treatises, since he had found his prede-

16. James, *Essays in Philosophy* (Cambridge: Harvard University Press, 1978), 93; Marías, *Trayectorias,* 493–95. Recently repeating the view that Ortega's was an "open system" was Rodríguez de Lecea, "Evolución de un pensador," 487.

cessor, the Krausist Salmerón, imprisoned by a system and the neo-Kantian systematism suffocating. If Ortega had a system, it was open-ended and never finished, and so Díez del Corral refused to try to put a name to it.[17]

Despite his efforts at clarity, Ortega's philosophy was not clearly one thing instead of another. Largely on the basis of his most widely read work, the so-called *Modern Theme* (1923), a number of critics outside of Spain eventually decided that he was indeed a philosopher, one whose vitalism was an existentialism that fitted between Unamuno and Heidegger. At first a very few (in Argentina and the United States) had also detected some traces of (affinities with) James's pragmatism in that same work. With or without his insights in the "Preface for Germans" (1934), others also have found phenomenology in it, even a philosophy of life. Still others discovered historicism in his *History as a System* (1936). So his philosophy in general has thus been defined as at least a half-dozen things, with no consensus yet. Some scholars therefore continue to ignore his ever-disputed philosophy and concentrate on his historical, social, political, aesthetic, or educational theories, as if he were simply an ad hoc "thinker" or an eclectic essayist, which he was not.

Actually, his philosophy informed all of his variegated thought, and it was a vitalist (life) "system" that at bottom reflected a Jamesian "radical empiricism." As a whole, it was a general, synthetic "philosophy of life," but it was originally and always *pragmatist* at its metaphysical basis, and, while developing, that *prima philosophia* came to support and penetrate other "ways of thinking": phenomenology, existentialism, historicism, and philosophy of life. Pragmatism also entered into his thought "beyond" philosophy in his ventures into history, the "humanities," and the "human sciences."

Could one thinker "do" all those philosophies without becoming grossly *eclectic* at best or very confused and chaotic at worst? Well, Heidegger (with whom Ortega has been compared most often) has been seen not only as an existentialist but also as both a historicist and a phenomenologist, and recently even as a sort of pragmatist. And critics who have seen as many (or more) aspects to Ortega include Marrero, Ferrater Mora, Morón Arroyo, McClintock, and Holmes. An early Argentine critic regarded him as a "mirror" of all that was current in the 1920s. During times of rapid change and development in philosophy, as in the early twentieth century, it is not so unusual for thinkers to espouse several successive positions and yet remain consistent. One was Scheler. None, perhaps, has gone through so many

17. Benedetto Croce, *The Autobiography of B. Croce*, trans. R. G. Collingwood (1927; reprint, Freeport, N.Y.: Books for Libraries Press, 1970), 107, 109; Luis Díez del Corral, *De Historia y Política* (Madrid: Instituto Estudios Políticos, 1956), 22–23. Luciano Pellicani, *Introduzione a Ortega y Gasset*, noted that he was not a systematic *thinker* but always strove for a systematic *structure;* his philosophy was "one of the most complex, suggestive and stimulating" (11).

stages or contrasting phases as did Ortega, and kept a sense of direction and identity. Throughout he was consistent, for he had a "system," even if it was in his mind and never expounded in print. In 1948, at sixty-five, Ortega put his finger to his forehead and told Granell: "I have the system here."[18] Since he never set it forth clearly, as many have denied it as have struggled to illustrate that putative system. His coherence of system *can* be demonstrated, not just affirmed.

"System" as Integrated Life Philosophy

As has been said of William James, "scattered throughout" Ortega's work is "a system *in posse*," a potentiality that was never finished: "no conclusion." As his first editor noted, James had intended to give a "systematic statement" to his formally unsystematic philosophy in *Some Problems of Philosophy*, but "he died before the book was half done."[19] In like manner, Ortega meant to do the same in his *Dawn of Historical Reason*, which not only was left unfinished at his death but disappeared.

In 1908 in response to Maeztu's accusation that he strove for "excessive precision" with words and too much "synthetic systematization" of ideas (1:111–12, 439–40), Ortega agreed that he had shown too much "systematic rigor" in exposition—which no one else has ever thought to protest. It was his "mental habit," he said, to see everything "systematically," and he took for certain Hegel's affirmation that the "truth can exist only under the shape of a system." Moreover, Spain had since 1898 needed such precise and disciplined thinking. "Systematization" meant to him mainly overall consistency and relation. "It is not honest to keep storage boxes in the soul, without communication between them; the hundred problems that make up our vision of the world have to live in conscious unity. It turns out, naturally, that one has no system ready; but one must try to form one. System is a thinker's integrity. My political conviction has to be in synthetic harmony with my physics and my theory of art" (1:114). It seems, therefore, that from the beginning system was his *intention*, despite his always unsystematic appearance.

Clearly Ortega did not as yet possess an actual *system* of philosophy by 1915 (12:392). He had only a potential or putative one, whose relationships with *life* in every area had to be worked out gradually, although his "system" flowed logically from that "root," or dual first principle: life as "self and

18. Mark Okrent, *Heidegger's Pragmatism* (Ithaca: Cornell University Press, 1988); Homero M. Guglielmini, "Algo más sobre Ortega y Gasset," 30–31, 33; Manuel Granell, *Ortega y su filosofía*, 144.

19. The last words of James's last essay (1910) said of his philosophy: "There is no conclusion. . . . Farewell!" (quoted by Gay W. Allen, *William James: A Biography* [New York: Viking, 1967], 496). Kallen, "Preface," *Philosophy of James*, v.

circumstance." By the mid-1930s he wrote "History as a System" and at the same time gave a course he entitled "Theses for a System of Philosophy" (12:131–36). The latter began with a metaphysics (*prima philosophia*) of "radical reality" (life) and a philosophical search for "radical certainty" about that same reality, from things "given" or learned by "experience of life." The variety in life can be organized by philosophy (vital reason) and the human sciences into a "system that is permanent and is constitutive of 'directions of spirit or consciousness'" in worldviews of types religious, philosophical, scientific, and cultural. Any one of these may be paramount at a given "historical conjuncture": they are a "dialectical series of systems of beliefs" whose views of radical reality ranged historically from realism to idealism. In very abbreviated form, that was his own system, which this study will examine extensively in terms of parts and whole. It was a system of development—about life as he perceived it both immediately and historically—and a system for integrating philosophy *and* history with the human sciences. Formally Ortega never worked out a systematization of his philosophy, but what he said in 1939 about one concept could apply to his thought as a whole: "though appearing to be fortuitous and disjointed, [all my effort] is from a terrible systematism . . ." (8:428). In 1949, adverting to his lectures on Toynbee and history, he again asserted that whatever he was saying therein was "rigorously systematic," even what was seemingly adventitious (9:215).

By "system" Ortega certainly did not mean a few volumes comprising a compact body of doctrines, principles, and methods on truth or reality, all tightly articulated with logical rigor and clarity. In the 1930s he defined "a system [as] always a simple, general idea, to which are subordinated hierarchically, in different degrees of decreasing generality, other ideas that are or are not in accord with the concrete phenomena of the real world" (R 75). For him that basic idea was "life." All of his philosophy was subordinate to it.

What Ortega said about his interest in "system" in 1934 is very revealing about his sources and his intent. His generational group derived their "will to system" initially not from Husserl, whose phenomenology was (in itself) "incapable" of system (8:41–42). Inspiration came, first, from the neo-Kantians Cohen and Natorp, who had rigorously systematized Kant; second, from the German Romantics (Hegel, Schelling, and Fichte), who thought that "philosophy, whatever else it may be, is, one way or other, system as such"; and third (apparently), from the *schöpferische Synthese* of Dilthey and his generation (which included James), which gave priority to the whole over the parts (8:27–37 passim) and to unity over plurality (or duality). As a relativist, Ortega found Cohen's "spirit of system" too simplistic and absolute (R 75), so he derived his "will to system" mainly from the Romantics, but his *idea* of system came from Dilthey and James—"connection" and putting life as a whole before the parts.

He could long see his system in his mind's eye, although he could not express it systematically (or schematically) in words, except for the enigmatic formula (1934), "a radical unitary duality" (8:43). In that context, his philosophical *unity* could have come only from phenomenology or from philosophy of life, both "translatable" there as "vital reason." Which overall "system" was it by then? Was it the prominent phenomenology that Silver has stressed but that Ortega then rejected (at least as "philosophy," *un*systematic and idealist)—or was it an unobtrusive Diltheyan philosophy of life (implying history too) that is so easy to overlook (8:46)? Or was it, in a complex and doubly dual sense, both of them together, as method and as substance— the method being made systematic by the historical life substance that was "system in itself"?

Critics on Ortega's System: "Keys" and "Stages"

Besides Silver, critics who claimed to have discovered the "key," "nucleus," "marrow," or "secret" to Ortega's presumed system were: Domingo Marrero (1951), Gaos (1957), Gaete (1962), Morón Arroyo (1968), Araya Goubert (1971), López Quintas (1972), Alvarez González (1980), Rabade Romeo (1983), Ríu (1984), and Cerezo Galán (1984). Most have found, like Granell (1960) and Ferrater Mora (1956), that the "key" or "central nucleus" in Ortega's philosophy was *life* as "radical reality." But is one key enough to open such an enigma? Closely related to Ferrater's key is the one that is stressed in this study: his philosophy was, Ortega himself claimed, a "radical unitary duality" (8:48). This formula (1934) is a clue not only to the dualist metaphysical basis but to the very structure of his philosophy. Ríu, however, saw another "key"—even to that basic life reality—at least for his later thought: "historical becoming."[20]

Several more inventive critics have divided Ortega's overall philosophy (system or not) into successive "stages," or phases, that he called "themes" or "voyages." Beginning with Nicol and Gaos, these analysts included Ferrater Mora, Morón Arroyo, and Cerezo Galán. Ferrater's schema has been the most often cited and imitated, even by Morón and Cerezo, who subsequently sought to correct it or to refine stages. In 1957, Gaos merely formalized the dualism that critics had already found: there were "two Ortegas" represented in the earlier "ratiovitalist biologism" of *Modern Theme* and in the later "ratiohistoricist biographism" of *History as a System,* that is, in "two successive stages of progressive philosophical deepening." Then Ferrater

20. On "keys" to Ortega, see introduction, n. 13; and Granell, *Ortega,* 135–36. Federico Ríu, *Vida e historia en Ortega y Gasset: Pensamiento filosófico,* 150. Cf. "metaphysics of becoming" in Ortega's philosophy, as seen by Ferrater Mora (*Outline,* 48).

subtracted one and added two to Gaos to obtain *three* stages: objectivism, perspectivism, and ratiovitalism, with historicism subordinated to the third. In 1968, Morón resurrected biologism from Gaos and refined Ferrater's types from a general nomenclature of *four* precise stages: culturalist neo-Kantianism (1907–1914); phenomenological perspectivism (1914–1920); biologism and psychologism (1920–1927); and existentialism (1928–1955). If Morón did little with Ortega's "inclination" toward historicism, Cerezo quite ignored it in 1984 in a schema of four stages that were meant to be still more precise: neo-Kantian idealism (to 1911); phenomenology (as method) (1911–1914/17); sociologism (1917–1930); and, finally, Heideggerian existentialism (like Morón). Cerezo found a "key" in each stage—phenomenology in the second, for example, and sociological anthropology in the third—but the latter is only a level or layer.[21]

What have we gained by multiplying and refining stages since Gaos and Ferrater? We now have a greater discrimination of both personal nuances and European categories; his biologism, psychologism, and sociologism are dubious, but neo-Kantianism, phenomenology, existentialism, and historicism are obvious. And Ferrater's objectivism is no more incomplete than neo-Kantianism for Ortega's beginnings. But do we need so many stages, when Ortega himself spoke of only two "voyages" or of two main "themes"? Are some of the reputed stages only nuances, *levels,* or aspects of his thought (like biologism, psychologism, sociologism, and anthropology) that need to be put into a more limited place and role? Are his basic metaphysics of life and his phenomenological method really stages of his philosophy or only layers or levels within it?

Ortega himself offers us additional clues to the structure, order, and coherence of his thought that are still helpful.

Clues to Coherence and Consistency

Like many other critics, J. B. Trend saw contradictions in Ortega's philosophy.[22] Although there are certainly conflicts and non sequiturs in everyone's thinking, here we shall look primarily for elements of consistency and coherence. These unifying aspects are as characteristic of Ortega as any real or apparent contradictions or inconsistencies.

21. José Gaos, *Sobre Ortega y Gasset y otros trabajos,* 89–90, 99–100; Ferrater Mora, *Outline,* 12–13, and chaps. 2, 3, 4. Also see Granell, *Ortega,* 135–36. Morón Arroyo, *Sistema,* 10, 77–81 (chap. 2), 305, 58 (on "levels"). On "layers": Walgrave, *Filosofía de Ortega,* 38. Cerezo Galán, *Voluntad de aventura,* 15 n. 1, 16n, 182–84. Also see the review by Calvo Martínez, "Ortega, España y el pensamiento europeo," *Revista de Occidente,* no. 48–49 (May 1985): 219–21.

22. Trend, "Boceto de Memoria," 204–5.

In tracing philosophical synthesis in history, Ortega made an observation in the 1940s that is extraordinarily pertinent to help us grasp the successive sources and dependencies of his own philosophy, especially for its early stages, where he claimed always to be going "beyond": Kant, James, and Husserl.

> In each philosophy all the other [previous] ones exist as ingredients, as unavoidable steps in the dialectical series. Their presence will be more or less acknowledged and, perhaps, an entire older system will appear in the newer one only as a stump or rudiment. . . . But the reverse is also true, if we take an older one, we see shining through it, like seeds, like faint outlines, not yet embodied, many later ideas. . . . Since the problems of philosophy are radical ones, there is no problem that is not already in all philosophies. (9:360)

Now continuity between and overlapping of distinct philosophies were very true of Ortega's own total philosophy. In 1915, he had acknowledged he had borrowed from predecessors, he used this related organic metaphor: "contrary to the biological order, in ideological generation recently born ideas carry their mothers in their wombs" (12:388). "Maternal" sources that "shine" (rather dimly) through his own more advanced and complex philosophy are James's pragmatism and Husserl's phenomenology.

Equally autobiographical was Ortega's remark that "each new philosophy begins by denouncing the error of its predecessor," by discovering its "fracture," and thus becomes "another philosophy" (9:353). This "dialectical" process resembled his resort to Husserl to remedy the formal philosophical crudity of James's pragmatism and the "error" or inadequacy of his idea of truth, then his use of James in turn to discover "the hole" in Husserl's idealist notion of consciousness (8:54; 1:256). But he also borrowed James's insight into the nature of Kant's "Copernican revolution" and of Dilthey's *Idealismus-Realismus*. Accordingly, his own philosophy was more properly the reverse: realism-idealism, or a basic perceptual realism of concrete "things" capped by a conceptual idealism of abstract general terms. These maneuvers and distinctions ensured Ortega's originality and his "independence" of any one "master."

In part, these relationships are witness to the historical succession and development of ideas in the minds of a series of thinkers. In Ortega himself (as he saw in Hegel and Dilthey too), it is very difficult (or impossible) to separate history from philosophy, or vice versa. "Philosophy begins then," for Dilthey, "very simply, by being its own history, 'indispensable propaedeutic for systematic philosophy'" (6:202, 208). The "first task" of philosophy is to bring—by such introduction—"the subject to full and concrete consciousness of his place historically," by a reconstruction of "the stages," or successive positions, man has adopted during his collective mental (spiritual) life. Such a preliminary task meant that philosophy must begin as *history* of philosophy, dealing with the temporal succession of worldviews throughout the whole of human history—as well as individual stages of thought.

Before studying Dilthey, Ortega had formulated how one should write the history of philosophy as a "history of ideas"—not as merely an evolutionary "cinematic" continuity of ideas and systems but also with marked crises of discontinuity (6:299). It must be genetically integrated with the thinker and his time and generation and be set within the historical "totality" of human life (4:48–51; 6:179). What he said of Kant and Dilthey applied equally to himself: "the whole human past" was a "historical collective" heritage and "mental subsoil" from which he derived his ideas "empirically" and began to "do" philosophy (6:175, 207). With that example and his help, we can do such an operation on Ortega's sources too.

ORIGINS, SOURCES, AND TYPES

Ortega's philosophizing had its radical roots in a historic sense of crisis— of loss of personal and social "faith." Hence, he felt deep empathy with Socrates and Nicholas of Cusa as crisis-ridden purveyors of *docta ignorantia* (2:347; 7:508–9)—of "learned ignorance" and questioning as proper responses (set in stylistic "tropes" of irony and metaphor) to a crisis of doubt in one's traditional "beliefs." With Descartes and James, he found philosophy a "vital necessity" and of "vital urgency" in historic crises of belief (8:262), which was the experience then in Europe (6:353–54). Spain's political crisis of 1898, when the pragmatic Yankees were victorious, was a critical personal experience that turned him to philosophy: first as a Nietzschean devoted to life, then as a secret Jamesian pragmatist.

In some undated autobiographical notes captioned "History of my ideas" (R 36), Ortega claimed that his two most basic ideas were not from specific philosophical sources but were as fortuitous as "Newton's apples." Thus, his "idea of life" first came to him from "the constant impression of presentness" in his own experience of living—it was "a native and original intuition." And his notion of "circumstance" was owing first to another Spaniard having said to him: "Everything is a question of circumstances." Thus were life and country his starting point, but other more *philosophical* sources were obviously important for the definition and development of those key ideas.

Ortega's inspirations, and the sources from which he drew, were more international than Spanish, and more recent than ancient, medieval, or "modern." In public and in private he identified most with European leaders of early twentieth-century thought. "These two men whose heirs we are were Dilthey and Husserl. Neither of them were in a hurry and they resisted going to a system—Dilthey till his death and Husserl till his last years and only in a certain way [in] *Meditations*" (R 40). He praised their "veracity" but claimed that his generation had "to go on to *system*," as veracity demanded. System aside, he was heir to many more.

As Silver has observed, Ortega did not often expound his philosophy systematically at length, but sometimes he explained it historically and genetically, that is, by its place and sequence relative to his life and generation and to other philosophies.[23] Thus, in his remarkable "Preface for Germans" (1934) he meant to clarify "the meaning of [his own] ideas . . . by sketching the profile of the *man* who *says* them . . ." (8:25). Using its revelations, we can analyze his philosophy in *Modern Theme* (1923) against the background of his own life and studies. We can thus present it more exactly and completely—and in a manner less diffuse than in Julián Marías's picture in *Circumstance and Vocation* (1960). And with the aid of so many critics, we can then define more confidently than previously the sources, elements, and stages that together made up his presumed but elusive "system."

In the "Preface for Germans," Ortega identified more of his individual sources than in any other work, but there they were limited to German philosophers. He named Nietzsche, Cohen, Husserl, and Dilthey, and he implied Heidegger. After he cited Brentano, he also strongly implied James (8:30–31), but he in no way alluded to other non-Germans, such as Vico and Croce, or Hume and Russell, or Comte, Renan, and Bergson. However, by 1923 they were all present in his work to some degree, although his new "philosophy of vital reason" (8:47) in *Modern Theme* was more than all of them together, for (since he did not parrot nor lump them eclectically) it was unique to, consistent with, his own mind.

In a few pages of the "Preface for Germans" (8:31, 37, 41–42), Ortega also alluded to most of the major types of philosophy that he had absorbed to constitute his complicated philosophy of 1923—romantic idealism, neo-Kantianism, phenomenology, existentialism, and "philosophy of life"—even a "radical . . . empiricism." Bifurcated, this last element (the first, logically and chronologically) of his philosophy was all but "elided" for "secret" motives. It was a new vital *realism* from James that he elsewhere called a "radical positivism" (6:190, 210); here he applied it to realist, empirical phenomenology, not idealist as in Husserl but like Brentano's or James's. And it was James's opposition to "intellectualism" that he directly repeated now. That kind of realist phenomenology he related to the manifest, "given" or "self-posited" nature of life as self and circumstance, wherein his philosophy had begun— with James, before the *Meditations on Quixote* (8:31–32, 48, 53, 273 n. 2).

In the "Preface for Germans," Ortega was very reticent about his pragma-

23. Silver, *Ortega as Phenomenologist*, 13.

tist origins and his later historicist development. However, he gave many hints of the *complexity* of his maturing philosophy. As he had warned in a "prologue" for his works in 1932, his thought was indeed "very complex, very full of secrets, allusions and elisions, very interwoven with a whole vital trajectory . . ." (6:349). In short, his philosophy in general, his "system," was a *historical* development parallel to his life by themes, aspects, levels, and stages. For the most part, that development was not open but "secret"— something we have to discover, dig out, and describe, part by part.

STRUCTURE OF LEVELS AND STAGES (OR "VOYAGES")

Obviously, Ortega's system, scattered through the extremely varied corpus of his thought, was so loose and complex that it has defeated both the casual reader and the serious student. They need what Ortega himself (echoing James) called a sketch-map that simplifies (without forcing) the "authentic," synthetic structure (or "anatomy") of his ever-developing philosophy. My historicized schema (see Contents) is such a flexible, fluid, mobile structure that sums up Ortega's system of philosophy in two main levels (metaphysics and method) and two big stages—or "voyages" or "themes," as he put it. For the reader's sake, the following description of that schematic structure is meant both to epitomize and to justify, to answer briefly and ahead of time some of the problems posed or implied in the detailed analysis and exposition of the later chapters. As a metaphysics, his pragmatist "new realism" came first, from 1909 till 1916 and on through the 1920s and 1930s in refinements and restatements. It was so recondite, however, that it was the last part to be clearly detected. His chief method, a realist phenomenology, was the next to emerge. To move from phenomenology into existentialism, in a cloak of "vital reason," was much longer coming to maturity—from 1916 to 1923 and beyond into the 1930s. Historical reason, as historicism, was more than thirty years beyond 1924 in developing fully, although the often-promised *Dawn of Historical Reason* as its summation was never to appear. Nevertheless, to Ortega's mind, the whole "system" had coalesced within a "philosophy of life" of personal, social, and historical dimensions from around 1933 onward, but that system—which waited for *Dawn, Man and People,* and a "new linguistics"— was likewise never finished. Through it all, pragmatism remained his basic metaphysics and a "philosophy of life" was the focus of his overall "system."

Pragmatic "Radical Empiricism" as Basic Metaphysics

The chief discovery of this study is Ortega's Jamesian pragmatism. Perhaps it would be better to say re-discovery, but at least this is the first effort at *demonstrating* that connection. James was Ortega's first master, after he deserted Nietzsche as not properly a philosopher, before he had taken up Husserl in 1912 and before he felt he had fathomed Kant in the 1920s. His critical grasp of both Kant and Husserl, in fact, depended in part on James, from whom (by 1909) he took his basic metaphysics of "radical empiricism." Strangely, he never admitted James's influence—never even mentioned his name—in anything published in his lifetime. There is no easy identification of his precise debts nor simple explanation for his long, persistent silence.

Although James had expressed a similar sardonic view of Teutonic pedantry and Ortega had a special liking for the Greek word *pragma,* such parallels do not prove that the latter was a pragmatist. That claim must still be demonstrated, with regard to his basic, *radical* "way of thinking" (a phrase prominent in the subtitle of James's *Pragmatism*), in which "radical empiricism" was also touted. That book, he admitted around 1950, had a basic influence on his philosophy.[24]

Why did not Ortega acknowledge at the beginning that he had adapted James's "radical empiricism" for his own new "way of thinking"? Already in 1908 he had proposed (in jest) to be a "pragmatist," but he was not prepared to confess any debt until almost the end of his life. To fathom the motives for his secrecy, we can only hypothesize—circumstantially and even sympathetically. After the bitter crisis of 1898, "pragmatism" had a bad name in Spain. Would Spaniards have accepted for the honored chair of metaphysics at their Central University in 1910 a young professor who admitted taking his principles of reality (if not of truth) from the grossly "pragmatic" Yankee victors? If he wished to serve his country as a philosopher, he could not do so and agree openly with James on metaphysical realism.

Renan's examination of German philosophy after 1870 was a sound precedent for studying the foreign foe. Once persuaded and committed, young Ortega could not turn back, but he had to conceal his American source. His solution to the dilemma was to derive similar ontological and epistemological principles from other more acceptable sources in Europe: first, after Nietzsche, Bergson for "life"; next, a "radical empiricism" from Mach and Ziehen (12:489–91); then a philosophical "radicalism" and some basic concepts and methods from Husserl (whom James obviously influenced) that lent *form* to James. Later he wrung a "radical positivism" or "radical empiricism" even from Kant and Comte, but chiefly from Dilthey (6:193n, 202n, 210), whose kinship he was proud to acknowledge. Not until Jacques Barzun in the 1980s did anyone see that Ortega had been attributing James's ideas to

---

24. James, *Writings,* 488–89, on German philosophy, its methods and style. Ortega, "Medio siglo," 5–6.

Dilthey.[25] If Dilthey was closer to where Ortega ended his philosophizing, however, James was certainly closer to where he had begun—in a *new,* very sparing, basic metaphysics. For more than a quarter of a century (1910 to 1936) at the Central University in Madrid, Ortega held the chair of metaphysics, taught courses on it, but never in his lifetime published a book about it. Indeed, with Comte, Dilthey, and James, he regarded the *traditional* metaphysics as having become something "impossible," an outdated "'absolutism' of the intellect," or "intellectualism" (6:206). Actually, he developed a pragmatic and vitalist metaphysics, and a "metahistory" too, but they have been even less well understood than his philosophy as a whole.

Although so basic for defining his general "philosophy of life," Ortega's metaphysics has been its least-known part, one that previously has been viewed from only one angle, or level: his brief formula of 1913–1914 that one's reality is "life" as "self and circumstance" (for example, 6:349). That was his basic "pocketbook metaphysics"—his constant vade mecum (3:432). In fact, for the most part, that formula had rested first on James's "radical empiricism," which became Ortega's "absolute [later, radical] positivism" after 1916. James's "viewpoint" on (or "seeing" of) *things* that are "given" was the basis of his metaphysics from first to last. When he gave a course on the "metaphysics of vital reason" (12:13) in 1933, it was still pragmatist at its base. If *life* "given" as "self and circumstance" was his ontology, however, what then was this "method," or epistemology, of vital reason? Clearly it was more than just pragmatism; it was phenomenology and was also an existentialism. The further Ortega developed his vitalism and historicism beyond his Jamesian metaphysics, the more obscured became his "radical" roots and the more secure his "secret." Eventually, James was so forgotten among European philosophers that Ortega (in "Leibniz" manuscript of 1947, later *The Idea of Principle in Leibniz,* trans. 1971) could safely emphasize a "radicalism" of his own "roots" (chapter 29) as his formal, *explicit* basis—as if it were of his own devising. Undoubtedly he had personal and native predispositions toward such a realist "way of thinking," but those ideas were already in the public domain.

By the 1940s, Ortega surely had no need to continue to conceal his initial and basic debt to James. He was a philosopher of international repute, quite original in his own right, and 1898 was long past. Since the 1920s concealment had become a habit, however, no longer a necessity but a *game* of "catch me if you can." Not until after his trip to the United States in 1949 did he finally decide to acknowledge his debt. Unfortunately, the chronic illness of his final years prevented him from making a public disclosure, which came only in the 1980s.

25. Barzun, *Stroll with James,* 300.

All his life, Ortega confided, he had maintained, as a "psycho-physical apparatus" of defense, "a very strong system of inhibitions and restraints" (4:306). Always timid and often secretive about his philosophy, he ruefully admitted—in regard to his "existentialism" in 1932—that not even those closest to him had "a remote idea of what I have thought and written" (4:404). Both earlier and later, however, he had granted that he had *concealed* the structure ("musculature") of his thought (3:270; 8:292–93) under style, and that was true also of his metaphysics and his methods. He was so "cagey" about sources and so dilatory in publishing works in his lifetime that, when his metaphysics at last came out posthumously (1966), little attention was given to its affinities or to its type, but by 1933 it was already much *more* than James's pragmatism or radical empiricism.

Once it is recognized, Ortega's "pragmatism" gives us a new realist and practical perspective on his thought as a whole, on his philosophy and on his contributions to history and other "human sciences." Besides giving him a basic metaphysics, it was a natural link with phenomenology as a still newer "way of thinking," but without Husserl's idealism. Pragmatism related also to existentialism for Ortega, as it did for Unamuno and for Heidegger. Much more than Dewey, he went on to develop James's emphasis on time and place (8:44) into a new sort of vital historicism. Pragmatism proved very fertile and malleable in his hands, even if he never admitted its inspiration publicly. Husserl was too convenient and, sans idealism, so compatible.

Phenomenology as Method

From 1912 through the 1920s, Husserl's phenomenology was so useful to Ortega's purposes that he could scarcely praise him enough. His stress on "description" was a natural entry into vitalist existentialism and historicism, if it were done in the realist mode. Eventually, however, all this adaptation muddied the clarity of his own composite "way of thinking" to the extent that his logic and originality were being questioned by critics and students alike. Was he just an imitator of Husserl and Heidegger?[26] As he tried yet again to explain his own "way of thinking" after 1940 in "Leibniz," he noted defensively:

> . . . It does not matter whether or not a philosophy makes evident the method by which it operates. Plato, Descartes, Locke, Kant, Hegel, Comte, Husserl dedicate a part of their philosophy to expound their method, . . .

26. On Ortega's reputed indebtedness to Heidegger, see Nemesio González Caminero, "Ortega y el primer Heidegger," *Gregorianum* 56 (1975): 98; J. Saínz Mazpule, "De Ortega a Heidegger," *Haz* (Madrid), February 18, March 25, September 15, 1941; Juan Saiz Barberá, "De Decartes a Heidegger," *Revista de Filosofía* (1941).

but this does not mean that those who do not do so are less "methodical" than those [who do], that they do not also have their method. On studying their dogmas we easily discover in what this [method] consists. But . . . , on the other hand it is a bad sign when, looking at a philosophy against the light, we cannot see clearly, as in filigree, what is its "way of thinking." (8:70–71)

Is it a "bad sign" that his expositors and critics have not fully identified his own basic "way of thinking" through all these years? That was largely his own fault: he was secretive and had a synthetic intent for a new, extremely complex system.

Given his propensity to define (name) a philosophy by its "way of thinking," method, or epistemology as often as by its ontology, or notion of reality, it may seem surprising that Ortega *insisted* that his own "philosophy"—even in its earlier stage of development from 1913 till 1923—was not simply "phenomenology." We may still ask whether, in trying to systematize phenomenological *method* after 1925 (8:273), he should not have admitted that his philosophy as a whole might be called phenomenology, because its Husserlian content in both concepts and method was substantial.

Except in method, Ortega's philosophy was never a "system" of phenomenology at its "radical" base nor as a whole. It is easy to confirm from his earliest writings on phenomenology (1913) that the very useful "instrument" mentioned in 1934 in both the "Preface for Germans" (8:42) and in "Dilthey" (6:208 n. 1) was already phenomenological "scientific method" (1:256). Contrary to Silver, phenomenology had become his "system" not as *philosophy*—not as idealist ontology—but as *method*.[27] What Silver has called Ortega's "existential phenomenology" was actually more of a "phenomenological existentialism," as in Heidegger. Subordinated in that way, phenomenological method was always a large and important *part* of his general life philosophy as "system"—but a part dependent on the vital and historical whole. From the mid-1920s history supplemented and finally outweighed phenomenology as Ortega's method, or epistemology, even as life (vitalism) defined his ontology.

From Existentialism to Historicism: Twins of Life and History

"Vital reason" was Ortega's preferred name for the first stage ("voyage") of his life philosophy up to 1923 (8:47)—and beyond. As a translation of James's "living reason," it included both pragmatism (or "radical empiricism") as a concise metaphysics and phenomenology as method. However, by 1923 his vital reason was also explicitly "historical," because "*Life* is . . .

27. Silver, *Phenomenology and Art*, 7; idem, *Ortega as Phenomenologist*, ix. Actually, Silver stresses "method" (9–10) in the first work and *philosophy* or "system" in the later study (xi).

history" (3:198). Already by 1924 he began to appeal to "historical reason." In short, his phenomenological vitalism or existentialism began to "turn" historicist. Existentialism and historicism became "twin" concepts, like "knowing and being."

Did Ortega *define* his mature philosophy by its ontology (its idea of life, existence, or "being" as radical reality) or by his method (phenomenological-historical) of getting there? Despite his insistence to the contrary (8:42, 273), method might seem enough to describe his philosophy, were we to take at face value the "decisive" insight he offered in 1947 in *Leibniz* about method as "way of thinking" or way of "knowing"—equating them as he had done in 1925:

> A new idea of Thinking is the discovery of a way of thinking radically different from those known till then, although it retains this or that *part* in common with them. It is equivalent, therefore, to the discovery of a new "faculty" in man, and it is to understand by "thinking" a reality distinct from the one known till then. According to this, a philosophy is different from another not so much nor primarily by *what* it says to us of Being, but by its very *saying* it, by its "intellectual language"; that is, by its way of thinking. (8:70–71)

This "way of thinking" must match the "idea of Being." To understand a "philosophical system," we must begin by finding out what they mean by "thinking," which shows us "'what game they are playing' in that philosophy." The "idea of Being" for Ortega himself, however, was *life* becoming, life as *history,* which the larger context shows. So his own "way of thinking" (or method) had to fit historical life. That was *his* "game": a "philosophy of life"—largely as "history."

To introduce the text above, in a chapter called "Thinking and Being, or the Gemini," Ortega stated, "Philosophy is a certain idea of Being. A philosophy that innovates brings forth a certain new idea of Being" (8:70). Hence, a philosophy may be defined by either of these "twins"—by its idea of being (ontology), or by its method, or "way of thinking"—or, rather, by the two *together.* A "weak and colorless" word, *method* as "way of thinking" is not always strictly equated with epistemology (or "theory of knowledge") in Ortega's thought, but in this context they seem to be the same. "Knowing and being," or epistemology and ontology, had been more or less equated with one another by him ever since 1913, in reference especially to Kant's thought (12:496). Since he stressed his difference from both Heidegger and Husserl over the primary reality that is perceived—life or being or consciousness—rather than way of *thinking,* we cannot conclude that, for Ortega, the former is of little or no importance compared to the latter. Again he reiterated his long disagreement with Husserl about ontology by recalling his proposal in 1925 to "systematize" the phenomenological method, which he had used to establish his own difference. The relationship of thinking and being is one not of exclusion but of priority, for a philosopher "discovers his new idea of being thanks to having previously discovered a new idea of thinking, that is, an intellectual method previously unknown" (12:70). Not an interchangeable identity, interdependency and interpenetration of thinking (knowing) and being gives the proper meaning of the passage (quoted above) about distinguishing one philosophy from another through its "intellectual language," or way of saying.

Even earlier in *The Origin of Philosophy* (1946), as against all previous notions, Ortega had described knowledge as "an 'interpretation' of the thing itself [that is, of reality or an aspect thereof] by subjecting it to a translation, as . . . from one language to another, so to speak, from the language of being, which is mute, to the fluent language of knowing" (9:372–73). On one side, reality is an "epistemological concept"; on the other, an "ontological concept." The implication of all of this is that Ortega did *not* define philosophies by method (way of thinking, or knowing) alone—that is, by epistemology only—but by concept of being, too. As he put it in *What Is Philosophy?* (1930): " . . . every theory of knowledge, against its will, has been an ontology—that is, a doctrine about what being is, for its part, and what, for its part, thinking is (finally and at the end, a particular thing or being), and therefore a comparison between the two. Hence, it turns out that sometimes thinking was discovered as a result of being—and this was realism—and at other times, on the contrary, it was shown that the structure of being derived from thought itself—and this was idealism." But, since Kant, it has been necessary to show "the structural identity of both terms" (7:325). In Dilthey and in Scheler this notion was expressed as "Idealism-Realism," and, like them and James, Ortega sought a similar dual compromise.

In Ortega's case, his original "discovery" (*aletheia,* or "intuition") of life-being came first (1909–1910), with James's new "realism." His formal perception of life as *dual* (as "self *and* circumstance") seems, however, to have coincided with his absorption of the phenomenological method from Husserl after 1912. His *concept* of intuition had also come to him less from Bergson (as James's "second") than from Husserl, whose "fracture" was the ontological idealism in his idea of "consciousness of . . ." (8:273–75 n. 2). Then, through this "hole" (with James's aid) Ortega's own initial ontological *realism* had poured into his later phenomenological method (8:53–54). His basic realist ontology of life was clearly *prior* to his use of phenomenological method in his "independent" philosophizing. Apart from vital reason (as ontological *and* epistemological), philosophy of life (as formally more ontological) therefore seems a more proper (if belated) designation for his philosophy than is phenomenology. Of course, the latter (as a *realist* "method") had "known" and clarified life-reality, but "ontological" priority seems clear.

In fact, first "vital reason" and then "historical reason" were more often used by Ortega to describe his unitary-dual philosophy than any other words, perhaps because they are doubly "twin" terms. "Reason" in either case denotes a general method in epistemology, varying only in techniques, which in the first are mainly phenomenological but in the second, historical. In regard to the reality of life, "vital" and "historical" are virtually exchangeable—except that the one is more *basically* ontological than the other. Yet both adjectives are subordinate to "reason" as *method*. Still, the term he favored between 1924 and 1933 was "ratiovitalism" (4:404n; 6:196n), wherein the knowing and being relationship was reversed to ontology. Then in 1934 he turned to "philosophy of life"—an ontological name that could include a methodological "game" of phenomenology and history.

In order to make method alone enough for defining Ortega's philosophy, we would have to disregard the substance of his critique of phenomenology in the years from 1913 to 1916, 1934, and 1939, and again in 1947, to say nothing of his critique of Kant in the 1920s. The rest of his *Leibniz* offered little further clarification of the problem of how to define his philosophy—whether by its method or by its ontology—except to note that, whereas Husserl had insisted ever since 1910 that philosophy is a "strict science" (or method), Ortega now said that "philosophy has no interest in being considered *a* science" (8:82–83), and he did not even agree that it is a "rigorous *science*" (7:145). Contrary to Kant, Husserl, and positivism, "The method of Philosophy is at bottom the opposite of the method of Physics" (8:84). By that time (1947) his own "new[er] way of Thinking"—which distinguished his philosophy from all others better than "the idea of Life" he shared with Dilthey, James, Bergson, and Nietzsche—was "historical reason," which was doubly epistemological, unless life *is* history.

In short and in sum, let us interpret the problematic text in *Leibniz* about developing "a systematic phenomenological thinking" after 1925 as meaning that phenomenological method was to be made systematic by containing it within a broader and newer whole, by integrating it as part of a larger ontological and methodological system of vital reason and historical reason, the dual-featured "twins" of his philosophy of life. Thus, from several angles, Silver's unitary thesis that Ortega's philosophy *is* phenomenology, even if he meant only an all-embracing realist method-as-philosophy, seems to contravene Ortega's intention.

Why should we now identify Ortega as a whole with a *unitary* "philosophy of life"? In 1934, referring to his rejection by 1913 of the "philosophy of culture and of consciousness" (Cohen and Husserl), he praised "philosophy of life" in Dilthey and he called his own basic idea of *life* in "self and circumstance" a "radical unitary duality" (8:43)—to which we add a duality of existentialism and historicism. In 1951 he still preferred the name "philosophy of life," which included historical reason.

Again we find Ortega going "beyond"—now beyond merely phenomenological method, which was to be *given* a "dimension of *systematic thinking*" within vital reason and historical reason by his adapting it to them as "synthetic or intuitive thinking" built upon that ontological phenomenon (life) "that is system in itself" (8:273–74). But "history *is* a system," too, for Ortega regarded life as both history and system. But that was a problem for his "second voyage"—beyond the position he defined in 1934.

Historical Reason as the "Second Voyage"

How strange it is that Ortega announced with his selected works (*Obras,* 1932) that he was ready to set out on a "second voyage" (6:256)—the first having started about "1911" (really in 1910)—which involved a change in both the form and the substance of his now fast-growing philosophy. Virtually everyone agrees that the "second voyage" (stage) of his philosophy was historical reason, but he had first introduced it in 1924. (Perhaps he regarded that overlapping interval of eight years merely as preparation.) He wanted to produce "books" after 1932 that were "systematic" works, but *The Modern Theme* (1923) was itself a book, was systematic in his sense, and was also oriented to history. Of course, the new books would contrast to the timely essays in newspapers or the lectures that had till then constituted the style and most of the output of his developing philosophy, so that he could address the limited capacity of Hispanic readers and audiences. The first of his new "books," however, was only the chapter called "History as a System" (1936), where he again referred to a "second voyage" (6:29) but did not "systematize" history in any customary sense. Probably he meant that history (or "historical reason") would help to impart more system to his philosophy of life (and vice versa) and—largely by means of a "metahistory" or "historiology" (6:30n, 44n)—also to the *human* sciences. This was implicit historicism (6:41), but it was also pragmatism as anti-"intellectualism" (6:30, 32) at his metaphysical (or metahistorical) basis.

His renewed "will to system" pushed him into promising then (6:38n) more than he could ever finish, so that he had to reannounce his projects periodically for the rest of his life: systematic books setting forth his newer *historical* thought in philosophy and sociology. "On Living Reason" was initially the title of the first, but he soon changed it to "The Dawn of Historical Reason." The second was to be "Man and People." Because of illness and the tragic interruption and exile from Spain in 1936 through World War II, his admitted "rhythm of starts and stops" (8:57) stopped too abruptly. Although he resumed his efforts in the 1940s, he was never to bring those two great projects to conclusion, so as to "systematize" formally his philosophy and thought in general.

In his final philosophical work, the historical *Leibniz* (1947), where Ortega first hinted what his new "systematic" way of thinking (or method) comprised, he referred to history and to history of philosophy (8:85, 90). He connected *methodos,* the "safe way" out of the "doubt" and "loss of faith" when crisis periodically engenders philosophy anew, with the "historical condition" of all philosophy, explicitly in the context of "historical reason" (8:268). Now historical reason was a new method, but it was also a new ontology of human life viewed historically. Of course, "historicity" modifies *life* as becoming but does not really substitute for it. Ortega's historical reason was not contained in his phenomenology, not even as method; rather, his earlier and less extensive method was included in his later, more "pregnant" one. As Silver saw, there does seem to be a "mother-daughter" relationship, but with "genetic phenomenology" inside historical reason.

In the end, Ortega could not—even as he said of Dilthey—finish his "system," perhaps because he lacked the favorable time and circumstance. Almost completed, *Man and People* soon came out posthumously, as did several other substantial works. But "The Dawn of Historical Reason" seemed to have vanished without a trace. Perhaps the numerous levels and stages in his very complex philosophy were too much for an old man finally to integrate and to unify within more or less systematic and connected treatises. Even so, they would not have been like the denser tomes of the German *Gelehrte,* whose turgidity he disliked as much as did James. Had he succeeded with *Dawn,* his philosophy would have addressed not primarily Spain but the West, if not "humanity" (as "Adam") (8:20). Thereby he would have moved from a personalist and "Spanish philosophy" to one that was general Western (if not "universal")—balancing *An Interpretation of Universal History* (1948–1949).

THE WHOLE: A "PHILOSOPHY OF LIFE"—WITH HISTORY

In view of the proliferation of names that Ortega and his critics have assigned to his philosophy as a whole, I have opted for a "safe way" out of the "crisis" of nomenclature by defining his philosophy both ways at once— by ontology combined with epistemology, or method. He had a philosophy of life resting on a basic ontological "radical empiricism" of Jamesian inspiration and including a realist phenomenological method, a vital reason that was in fact proto-existentialism, and a historical reason that was historicism—two stages that were both ontological and epistemological in varying degree. Such a "radical unitary duality" on *two levels* (metaphysical and systemic) may satisfy most critical views and still be faithful to the evidence and to Ortega's intent. This solution is a logical *and* historical way to unify (or "think together") the dual (or pluralist) terms of his complex, ever-growing philosophy.

Over the years Ortega rejected as inadequate to describe his philosophy as a whole such current terms as phenomenology, existentialism, and historicism. After "vital reason" and "historical reason," his own choices of newer names—notably, "biognosis," or "bi-ology" (literally, study of [human] life), or "General Theory of Life" from 1940 into the 1950s—were not felicitous enough to supplant (even for him) the phrase "philosophy of life" as a general descriptive *type*. He had favored it first in 1934 and still preferred it in 1951, although he admitted it was weak nomenclature. Actually, he was stuck with it; there was, in fact, no better definition for the whole, for it alone was capable of containing all the parts, including the mature historicism of 1936 to 1955.

Finally, Ortega's life philosophy was like a Chinese puzzle to which he once adverted. There were boxes inside boxes, but this was opposite to his "mother-in-daughter" metaphor. Each level and stage was the product of an expanding methodology, or "way of thinking," but throughout all kept the same ontological basis and integument: the primary and ultimate reality of human life, a basic unitary-dual ontological principle (self and circumstance) that he first "intuited" spontaneously but thereafter supported first from Nietzsche, James, and Bergson, and later confirmed in Dilthey, if not in Husserl. That first little box grew and grew, until it enclosed all the other later boxes, including the expansive historicism of historical reason. His "philosophy of history" was ultimately a philosophy of life, and vice versa—a "one-two," as he put it—but history was subordinate to life.

All of the layers and stages in his thought constitute an ascending and broadening "dialectical series" of Ortega's own "ways of thinking" within his one philosophy of life, which comprised "duality" or "plurality" and "development" (Orringer) within unity. In the "Preface for Germans" (8:44) he said that "the rest of my production," after the *Meditations on Quixote* (1914), hinged on that "intuition" of life, and he repeated this basic orientation over and over again in every kind of context. We can see in almost all of Ortega's more substantial writings, from *Meditations on Quixote* onward, that a unitary-dual intuition of life as self and circumstance was the core idea, the metaphysics, on which his philosophy always turned and grew.

His "philosophy of life" therefore amounts to a "unity in variety"—an ancient paradox that Ortega found restated in Guizot and in Cousin as well as in James. He himself employed such terms as "twin," "dual," "two-in-one," "bi-lobar," and "radical unitary duality" to describe this unified complexity that was his philosophy. The two sides of his mature philosophy of life gradually became vital reason and historical reason, which amounted to *phenomenological* existentialism and realist historicism. These two main branches of Ortega's philosophy were reducible—through their dual, combined forms of "vital" and "historical" with "reason"—to the basic ontological and epistemological elements united in them, even as they were unified in an overall philosophy of life, as two successive stages and coordinates. All of this may seem peculiar, but it reflects Ortega's intention and his perception of what his philosophy was in fact. Thus one tries to "think together" his dualities into a presumed philosophical unity or "system."

As synthesis, Ortega's philosophy of life encompassed all of the phases of his philosophizing, both before and after 1934, in a very complex, seemingly unsystematic "system." For decades he had stretched this vitalist system to cover all the parts of his philosophy and all of his special, idiosyncratic names for those general movements of Western thought. Philosophy of life was a higher "radical unitary duality"—truly a *covering* philosophy.

Because he never finished his intended synthesis formally, Ortega's "system" remains an apparent duality: a philosophy of life *and* history. In fact, the historicism of historical reason pointed "beyond philosophy" to a new critical "philosophy of history," that in a general sense and in specific ways was also "pragmatic"[28]—a big problem that is reserved for a later volume. His philosophy in its most comprehensive sense was a philosophy of life that continued in his historical "way of thinking" by means of historical reason. The latter was meant to complete the former as a theory of life that he wanted to derive from history and sociology in a *general* way to supplement personal introspection into his own life via vital reason.

THEORY OF LIFE: GENETIC STRUCTURE

Now named and linked in chronological relationship, the whole and the parts of Ortega's philosophy of life have not yet been placed in a general theory of life that relates to his own personal life and thought. We should do this before we try to place them within the general philosophical tradition, in the following chapters. No intellectual biography is intended here but only a brief schema of relationships that does not confuse thought with life, or vice versa. Ortega agreed: *living is not philosophizing,* but every philosophy is "from life."

We can be confident that Ortega's "philosophy of life" is intimately con-

28. See Hans Meyerhoff, ed., *The Philosophy of History in Our Time,* 57–64 ("History as a System") and 44 (pragmatism).

nected with his own life, but he warned in 1932 that "every life is secret and hieroglyphic" (6:344–45; 8:406), and he offered no "sure method" or "key" for his own. In his frank revelations, "Preface for Germans" (1934; unpublished till 1970), he reminded us that "ultimately, strictly, and truly what we usually call 'ideas,' 'thought,' does not exist; it is an abstraction, a mere approximation. The reality is the idea, the thought, of such a man" (8:17). His own ideas need to be understood against the background of his entire life and "concrete existence." All his "circumstances," despite two substantial studies by Marías and by Gray, will not be known until the archives and correspondence are exhausted,[29] but we must do what we can with what is available meanwhile. He left numerous hints to help us link his thought to his life.

Ages, Stages, Crises, Generations

As Ortega developed his philosophy over the long span of fifty-one years from 1904, when he received his Ph.D., on a theme of historical life, until his death in 1955, there are many indications that he was developing a "theory of life" covering "stages" of a vital regularity of which he had become aware. At the 1949 Goethe Festival in Aspen he adverted to a kind of "model" of "the knowing of our life." "What are called the ages of man—childhood, youth, maturity, and old age—more than differences in the condition of our bodies signify different stages in the experience of life," which he proposed for a group project (9:573). Earlier in that year at his own Institute of Humanities in Madrid he had spoken of regular "aspects" in "the experience of life," one of which was a "vital chronology" that included a certain limited number of "forms" and key "ages" that were "repeated" (with variation) in individuals, in collectives, and in "the process of world history" (9:27–28). That regularity at times corresponds more or less to his theory of generations, at other times to certain of his ideas on mental maturation, or to more recent notions of "ages of life" and "life crises." More than once he himself cited coincidences among dates, years of age, and new departures in his thinking (see 8:57), or that of other philosophers. Later and in a more general way, Romano Guardini argued for a loose connection between "the stages of life and philosophy." Thus Ortega modified Freud's psychological influence (not on sex but on critical ages) with insights from James and Dilthey. For him, the successive "ages of man" (childhood, youth, maturity, and old age) signified "different stages in the experience of life," with appropriate *crises* and stages

29. There are, of course, such "biographies" (translated) as Niedermayer's short *Ortega*, and Marías, *Circumstance and Vocation*, as well as Rockwell Gray's much fuller work, *The Imperative of Modernity: An Intellectual Biography of José Ortega y Gasset*. As a kind of memoir-biography, Miguel Ortega's *Ortega y Gasset, mi padre* is very useful for intimate details.

of thought (9:573).[30] Not always is there a precise coincidence between different stages of Ortega's thinking and the phases of his life. However, his theories of generational change, life crises, and years of relative maturity help to strengthen a historical and genetic interpretation of his philosophy over a merely critical analysis of content. We would be foolish, in fact, to disregard some connections made by Ortega himself, for he stressed often that we think in response to life's needs and crises.

It is clear that Ortega's theory of generations and his theory of life are not identical, at least in regard to the life-ages of intellectuals. According to his schema of half-generations, every fifteen years or so a notable change of activity and of social circumstance accompanies an individual's growing older with his age group. Perhaps the generational sequence of imitative learning (1–15, 15–30), assertion of independence and sharing of power (30–45), full exercise of "power" and influence (45–60), and status of mere "survivor" thereafter may be relatable to mental development and to life crises in general, as well as to careers in politics and letters.[31] For intellectuals, however, he assigned a somewhat different (earlier and later) sequence: the ages of 26, 50–51, and after 70 for mental "independence," ripe maturity, and loss of "power," with awareness of senility and approaching death. Although there is no *quantitative* agreement at any point, there are two ways to calculate possible coincidences of his special theory of intellectuals' life-ages with half-generational periods: from his birth and from the center of his generation. Sometimes, apparently, these coincidences fit marked changes and notable publications in his philosophical career.

Evidences of a theory of intellectual life are scattered widely through Ortega's writings. His idea of the *general* significance of the twenty-sixth year, seemingly from James, was first related by him to the life of Descartes; his idea of the fiftieth to fifty-first year apparently came from Aristotle, if not from Croce.[32] He seems to have experienced close personal "parallels" with

30. Romano Guardini, "The Stages of Life and Philosophy," *Philosophy Today* 1 (June 1957): 75–79. Also see Adrian van Kaam, "Existential Crisis and Human Development," *Humanitas* 10 (May 1974): 109–26, on positive and negative phases of life in change, crisis, death, and "rebirth." Apparently there has been no extensive study yet published on Ortega's general theory of life, but see Marías, *Generations;* Levinson, *Seasons;* and Domingo Marrero, "Constructivismo."

31. A primary source for Ortega's theory of generational conflict and succession in fifteen-year units was perhaps Renan (who used it differently); this feature was not yet in *Modern Theme,* chap. 1 (his basic theory—3:145–50), but was a later refinement in chaps. 3, 4, and 5 of *Man and Crisis* (5:48–66) and was applied in "Preface for Germans" (8:30–32) and 9:517–18.

32. Marías, *Circumstance and Vocation,* 321–22 (on the twenty-sixth year). In *Trayectorias* (395), Marías quotes Ortega stating that Aristotle "says that the mind grows until fifty years of age. I have spent several years waiting for the evidence of my decline and harbinger

Dilthey that extended to both the twenty-sixth and fiftieth years, and perhaps to seventy and beyond. Thus, around 1860, or "from his twenty-sixth year Dilthey possessed the essential intuition of what was going to be, of what ought to be, his doctrine": namely, the "idea of life" (7:60). Moreover, "Dilthey was fifty years old when—in 1883—he published the first volume of his *Einleitung* . . . ," where he introduced not only his "philosophy of life" but his promise of a "Critique of Historical Reason" connected to the "human sciences" as a second intended volume. "His life lasted thirty years more, but the second volume never appeared" (7:59).

Could Ortega help wondering at certain "coincidences"? As he noted (R 40), he was born in the same year the *Introduction* appeared; he too was twenty-six when he had his basic intuitions on life and on history in 1909–1910 (Dilthey died in 1911). He too was fifty when he published his study of Dilthey in 1933–1934 and launched his "second voyage" from a "philosophy of life" parallel to Dilthey's out onto the sea of "historical reason." Finally, more than twenty years were not enough to bring out his books on sociology and historical reason, which were meant to be like volumes 2 and 3 to *Modern Theme* (1923) and its "vital reason"—both volumes being reoriented on the human sciences. Instead, the parallels for the seventieth year and afterward were the almost completed *Man and People* and the unrevised lectures, "Interpretation of Universal History." They were not equivalent to the "shift" that Ortega observed in Dilthey's thought (and in Kant's and Plato's) at old age, however, for he continued to pursue life, historicity, and crisis to the end. Maybe his shift was a "linguistic turn," so often forecast.

If we try to correlate such life theory for intellectuals to generations theory, the significant years of Ortega's life from his birth in 1883 forward by fifteen-year intervals make the so-called adolescent identity crisis and the beginning of his youthful Nietzschean revolt coincide with the very unsettling national crisis of 1898, the Spanish-American War. This crisis became a badge of identification for the so-called generation of 1898 and at the same time a precipitator of young Ortega's crisis thinking. His youthful era of passionate reactions and imitative thinking had ended before his "twenty-sixth" year, the year of his intellectual independence, "around 1911"—or more accurately in 1909–1910 with "Adam in Paradise." This crucial point of departure, then, came well before the biologically (or generationally) mature

---

of my idiocy, but, with great surprise, I see that it is *all to the contrary.*" Hence, he interpreted fifty (to fifty-one) as being the height of mature powers for synthesis (5:46; 8:41), which also parallels Croce, *Autobiography,* 19: fifty is an "ideal pause" to look back and ahead. For his debt to James (on twenty-six), see my chap. 3, on his books; also see the persistent use of twenty-six in his *Obras Completas,* 6:198 and 7:60 (Dilthey), 8:32, 34, 42 (Ortega's own generation), 9:574 (Heine), 9:518 (Vives); also "Medio siglo," 12, 13, for similarities in Liebmann and Cohen.

age of thirty, when, in 1913, he wrote *Meditations on Quixote,* a Spanish philosophy of life that he afterward viewed as his entry into a professional reputation and influence. After 1913, the next pivotal generational date was 1928, when, notable and influential at forty-five, he published "Historiology" as a new "basic discipline" of vital and historical reason and as the beginning of a new historicist ontology. Long before his sixtieth year in 1943, however, owing to the extraneous "accident" of Spain's civil war, he had already lost position, power, and repute at home, and had fled into exile abroad. Struggling to hold off the decline of his vital and mental vigor and to recover fame and influence, he strove on till his death in 1955 to make up the lost years. As it turned out, the expected decline after sixty did not occur; the era was the most productive of his life—in major (if unfinished) works.

The merely generational schema above clearly does not fit everything, especially not the two chief denouements ("voyages" or stages) in Ortega's thought, which began at age twenty-six in 1909–1910 and age fifty to fifty-one in 1933–1934. We can match his key age-dates with his generational sequence only if we start from his own generation's "central" year: "1911." Ortega himself thus manipulated this scheme and the dates, to make his twenty-sixth year seem to correspond more closely to his generation's center. Then it was that his "generation of 1911," declaring their intellectual independence of neo-Kantian and Husserlian idealism, "launched their ship to sea" and into "the unknown," sailing toward "an imaginary coast" (8:41–42). Philosophizing was thus like a bold voyage of discovery.

As we have seen, Ortega's twenty-sixth year was 1909, when he was preparing new ("pragmatic") ideas for "Adam in Paradise" that were evident in his philosophy ever after, in 1913 as in 1953. But he himself stressed that it was "around 1911"—if not in 1912 (8:47, compare 42)—that he "discovered" his basic *dual* principle. Presumably, he meant the dual *formulation* of life as reality, for he already had conceived of "self" and "circumstance" separately. The later date did not imply that the precocious Ortega was a "late bloomer" in his generation, for life's two elements had been stated in "Adam" in 1910.

In other ways, 1911 was very significant for Ortega's key historical outlook, if not for life ontology. At a conference on mathematics in 1911 (or 1912?), he expressed his first intimations of a great crisis and inversion in general European thought and culture. "But when I came to those years of life [circa twenty-six] when the intellectual by deepest vocation receives his first [basic] illuminations—years which . . . are not just any but can normally be determined with exactitude—I had the vision that human history was going, once again, to turn on itself 180 degrees, to execute one of those great radical tacks or turnabouts that are characteristic of it; that the modern age, having exhausted the sources of its inspiration and the validity of its principles, was finding itself in agony . . ." (12:246–47). In *Man and Crisis* he states he had then predicted that another great reversal, like the one in 1600, was imminent. About to succeed the great regnant ideas of "*continuity, evolutionism, and infinity* in mathematics, physics, biology, and history" was a "tendency to *discontinuity* and finiteness" in all of them (5:57). As he recalled elsewhere, the *unitary* views of Newton, Darwin, and Marx, were about to be supplanted by the *pluralist* outlook of Planck, Einstein, and Spengler (3:303–4 and n)—and James. Although Ortega did not simply abandon the old "modern" ideas, the new "great Ideas" played a decisive role in his thinking thereafter. Nevertheless, he had "discovered" the "great Idea of life," his most decisive "belief," *before* 1911.

Did Ortega's fiftieth year also relate to the generational schema? "Around fifty" is the "stage" when life, or "experience of life," becomes "transparent" in its "aspects," general "order," "rhythm," and "totality" (9:26–27). For his own "generation," 1911 was the "central" year in a "zone of dates," whose boundaries were approximately seven years to either side, 1904 (his Ph.D. dissertation) and 1918, when no clearly dramatic changes occurred in his thinking. Fifteen years forward from the latter date, however, gives the key year of 1933, when (at fifty, ripe intellectual maturity) he united vital reason to historical reason in the "Galileo" lectures on the theme of "historical crisis" as both a personal and a generational experience. Preparatory to his "second voyage" of historical reason, he had summed up his past philosophy with the introduction of his selected works (*Obras,* 1932). In the next year (1933–1934), he *should* have brought out "The Dawn of Historical Reason" and *Man and People,* or so he confided to Curtius.[33] At that time the former could only have been a part called "History as a System," which he had to put off until 1936, while the sociology still needed much work. So instead, out came "W. Dilthey and the Idea of Life" (if not yet "Preface for Germans"), in which he hinted that his own thought too had been a synthetic "philosophy of life." Then the dreaded crisis intervened in fact, in both Spain and Europe—and for Ortega personally. It was to be fifteen years (1948–1949), before he was ready for another major part of "Dawn" ("Universal History") and then for "Man and People"—at his Institute of Humanities.

Anomalies of Life and Theory

However we structure them, it is obvious that (in any strictly *quantitative* sense) schematic fifteen-year periods are not exact tools for interpreting

33. Ortega, "Epistolario entre Ortega y Curtius," *Revista de Occidente,* no. 6–7 (June 1963): 340 (December 3, 1937).

Ortega's thought as a developing whole, with clear denouements that begin or end distinct stages. Here and there life and thought do "fit," but rather loosely. If there is anything truly normal about mental development in a life-and-generational model, then clearly we must make ample allowance for disruptive external crises. In the distinctive schema of first and second *mental* maturations and senility, the idea that twenty-six is the normal age of intellectual maturity and independence may fit Descartes, Dilthey, Einstein, and Ortega too. However, the twenty-sixth and the fiftieth year do not fit regular generational sequences, or meet them only approximately or by manipulation. If indeed intellectuals have a life cycle, it seems to be somewhat different from that of other people—if theirs in turn normally obeys a fifteen-year periodicity.

In sum, there *are* indeed some rough coincidences between Ortega's biological (or genetic) and mental schemata of general development and the crises and scholarly productions of his own lifetime. Those limited approximations are important for our understanding him, because he himself called attention to such correlations between life and creativity, particularly for the years 1898, 1910 to 1913, and 1932 to 1934. The first provoked his lifelong commitment to "saving" Spain. By the second interval he had both discovered and united the dual principles of his basic outlook on reality: "life" as "self and circumstance," which became both vitalistic and historical. By the third date he had set out on his "second voyage" toward systematizing his "philosophy of life" by means of historical reason. Ortega himself lent an emphasis and an authenticity to these points of coincidence. Other chronological points, however, excepting his launching of historiology (1928), are not so clearly pivotal.

Life and thought, obviously, cannot be neatly boxed into half-generational sequences of fifteen years. Sooner or later, the crises of the outer world upset any natural rhythm that our individual lives *might* otherwise follow. And if the world does not frustrate us, problems of health or personal relations from self and outer circumstance are enough by themselves to do so. What is often considered a major line of demarcation in Ortega's philosophy, *Modern Theme* (1923), reflects neither the stated regularities of life and generation in his theories nor chance events of history. Nor does it fit any natural "life crisis," except maybe the onset of middle age, to which he adverted but never as a fruitful crisis.[34] Possibly already from around forty years of age (as in fact he announced his intention in 1925) he then meant vital reason (now historized) to become his program for full intellectual maturity and synthesis, as "synthetic" and "systematic thinking" 8:273). He had not then discovered

34. See Ortega, 5:70 (*Man and Crisis* [New York: Norton, 1958], 86), where he says that in eras of historical and social crisis (like his own era), at "about forty years of age," one's generation becomes "annulled," because one cannot live any longer on the former political and cultural "fictions" but seeks to live "in truth."

the magic of "fifty." For a decade yet, at any rate, he was not ready for the stage of *overall* mastery and *synthesis* of his philosophy of life, which (by 1933–1934) he had decided to pursue mainly with historical reasoning.

Synthesis, Ortega later claimed, was not for passionate, shallow youth but for *ripe* maturity in the early fifties. For him there were no genuine young prodigies in philosophy, except perhaps Schelling, whose exception proved the rule (8:269). Only in the sense of a long-term project (12:392), as both Marías and Silver have perceived it,[35] could he feel intellectually mature enough even by 1916 to claim a "system" of philosophy (compare 1:311, 318). As fully developed, his "system" was still the "unknown shore" toward which he was always sailing and swimming, or where he has "shipwrecked" like a "Robinson" (Crusoe). Not until 1923 did he make land (with a first, tentative synthesis) and publicly name that first stage of his philosophy "vital reason." But not until 1932–1934 did he feel mature enough to put his earlier works behind him, to begin a "second voyage" by a compass (new method) of "historical reason," and to rename the "systematic" whole a "philosophy of life" (6:205, 356). But another great crisis of self and world—the second in his life—long delayed that "voyage."

The crisis of 1898 was apparently the only crisis in which Ortega's thought and bio-psychological nature coincided more or less fully with an external event. Outbreak of the Great War in 1914 was pure "coincidence" unrelated to *Meditations on Quixote,* for only later did the slaughter convince him that a historical crisis he had foreseen in 1911–1912 was now becoming both general and actual. When he published his selected works in 1932, he had intended to accomplish his "second voyage" in his now *generalized* "philosophy of life," via a new "theme" and method ("historical reason"), that was to culminate, following "Schema of Crisis" (1933), in *Dawn of Historical Reason* by 1934. Grimly confirming this continuing and deepening crisis in Western civilization, however, civil war in Spain in 1936 and World War II in Europe in 1939 more or less fit his fears and analyses in *Invertebrate Spain* (1921) and *The Revolt of the Masses* (1929). But vital and historical reason had no effect on the outcome, and history seemed anything but "systematic" when he wrote "History as a System" (1935–1936). Moreover, anticipated vital and mental patterns for his own life and career were wholly upset by external circumstances and by exile and the collapse of his health. Severe illness recurred periodically thereafter.

By 1933, Ortega's deepest and longest personal crisis was beginning. More than an "upper-middle-age crisis," it was at first in response to his keenly felt need to leave politics and to get on with his "mission" as a thinker dedicated to life, to complete a historical "synthesis" of his thought, undisturbed by

---

35. Marías, *Trayectorias,* 35; Silver, *Ortega as Phenomenologist,* ix.

the disappointments of the new Spanish Republic he had helped create in 1930. This crisis, however, proved more difficult to resolve: stoically "withdrawing" into "solitude" did not allow him to contemplate and to philosophize "authentically" again. Then, "faced with the difficulties of life today" (1933), the sated "lover" and reluctant *político* even contemplated returning to Christianity, at "my fifty years" of age[36]—a decision he avoided, however. He was forced to admit that he had embraced "the spirit of the time" too eagerly and too actively, without an adequate understanding of Spain's present possibilities and impossibilities—intractable problems that new editions of his *Invertebrate Spain* could not resolve.

Personally, Ortega wanted no truck with the "mass-man" activists of either right or left, as his *Revolt of the Masses* made clear. The fascist founder of the Falange, José Antonio, publicly reproached him in 1935 for refusing to lead it.[37] Thereafter, leftists and Communists so harassed and threatened him (4:306) that (now seriously ill) he escaped in 1936 into what became a prolonged exile of a decade's duration and his long "silence." In Paris in 1937 he almost died before an operation. As World War II began he went to Argentina, feeling like a "drowning man" (8:394–95, 401–3), still sickly and hounded by leftist refugees fleeing Franco's Spain. In 1939 he ruefully described his life since 1935 as having become "an uninterrupted series of private and public misfortunes" (R 32).

His new circumstances, though partly foreseen, brought the greatest crisis of his personal life, not at all foreseen, which corresponded with the deepest crisis of modern Western civilization.[38] In 1949 he would look back on the previous "fifteen years" as a great crisis for him and for all intellectuals: it was a long time of "silence" for those charged with clarifying the causes and effects of human destiny (9:73). Then a "political avalanche" had buried philosophy, had left it "without social power or presence," even without notable production (R 36). That was certainly true in his own case.

When he had withdrawn into private life again after 1933, Ortega was disgusted with politics and eager to start writing his intended books of synthesis. However, he was too exhausted. By strenuous effort he was able to complete "History as a System" in time for a British publication related to "philosophy of history" in 1936 (R 20). His worsening health had forced him to cancel a trip to the United States to give the Gifford Lectures at Harvard

---

36. Ortega, *History as a System* (New York: Norton, 1961), 207–9. These passages of 1936 are not in the *Obras Completas*.

37. José Antonio Primo de Rivera, "Homenaje y reproche a don José Ortega y Gasset," *Haz*, no. 12 (December 5, 1935).

38. See Niedermayer, *Ortega*, 67–69, on Ortega's embarrassments and his illness and flight into exile.

on the social theme of man and people in 1935, but he planned to go to the Netherlands and then on to the United States (Harvard, Princeton, and elsewhere) in 1936 to give a series of public lectures on four new themes (R 6; R 20), historical reason, historical crisis, sociology of man and masses, and a new linguistics (philology). Several years late, Ortega was ready at last to launch his "second voyage."

Then the Spanish Republic (and his health) had collapsed, and political terror and looming civil war had sent him fleeing. The rest of his troubled life as exile and outcast was not enough for him to complete any of his four new themes—except for *Man and Crisis* (1941), an ironic mockery of his experience. Wretched in exile (5:375), despite fitful work on philosophy, history, and sociology, he could seldom make rapid progress on his great projects. Revolution, war, and sickness had disrupted and delayed the biological and mental rhythm of his life cycle. That fifteen years (forty-five to sixty) of his full maturity, which should normally have brought him the fruits of honor, power, and *synthesis*, had met disaster and "ended" a decade prematurely. He was never able to make up that lost time.

After 1943 as a "survivor" in Portugal and (after 1946) barely tolerated in Madrid by Franco, Ortega began to bring out his complete works through 1941 (six volumes) while pressing to finish (at his new Institute of Humanities) manuscripts begun in the 1930s and 1940s. However, he was often incapacitated for months by illness and began to experience symptoms of the so-called old-age crisis. In March 1952, he felt that life was losing its savor, had become too pressured and busy (R 33). He realized that his life's work was ending, not completed yet and thus publicly unknown—in fact, it was partly still secret. Successful postwar trips to and lectures in the United States, Germany, Switzerland, and France, when he debated Heidegger and Merleau-Ponty, had helped restore his fame and optimism by midcentury but had not made his philosophy any better understood or liked—as existentialism *and* historicism in one "life" unity.

In 1955, at seventy-two years of age, the old "mariner" succumbed to stomach cancer and died in passage but closer to his anticipated second (synthetic) "coast." He had *Man and People* almost in hand—for W. W. Norton in the United States—but his *Dawn of Historical Reason* vanished mysteriously, as did his "New Philology." Accordingly, little was known of Ortega's "second voyage" except *History as a System* and *Man and Crisis* in 1941—too little to reveal the full dimensions of his mature "system" of philosophy. Despite a massive outpouring of commemoratives around the Western world in 1955–1956 for Ortega y Gasset the person, the thinker still had to be discovered as a whole.

Obviously, Ortega's hints about the connections of his life and thought according to the formal schema of his theory of life and generations, with its "epicycle" for intellectuals, are of some use for illuminating his philosophy. However, objective theories could not account for unforeseen chance and crisis, both personal and circumstantial. His very background, crises and all, both helped him develop and hindered his finishing his unusual and extremely variegated system of philosophy.[39]

39. We have seen how Marías and Ferrater Mora both described Ortega's philosophy as unfinished and "open." Walgrave, *Filosofía de Ortega*, 315: "He did not succeed in constructing a complete philosophy, without deficiencies"—a philosophy "sketched" only in "outline." There was, however, a metaphysics, of which Walgrave was unaware, and there was more to the historical "second stage" than anyone has demonstrated.

Chapter 2

BACKGROUND

Life, History, Philosophy
(1883–1914+)

A *living being,*" said William James, "must always contain within itself the history, not merely of its own existence, but of all its ancestors."[1] How one views love, religion, politics, and society (and philosophy, too) depends—argued Ortega in the original English and American version of "History as a System" (1936)—on his *past,* on what he has been in life ever since childhood, and on the history of his society and nation. Present "possibilities" (such as Christianity, liberalism, maybe becoming Hermione's lover at the sated age of fifty) *contained* his whole past. But, he noted further on, man is compelled "always to advance on himself." He is ontologically "irreversible"; "he cannot go back to being what he has been," because "time does not recur."[2]

Allowing for development and change (and with certain things excepted), Ortega nevertheless was at the end—in a very general way—pretty much what he had been at the beginning, in his youth. An acute experience of life and crisis, an intense interest in European culture and science, a historicist general "philosophy of life," an "aristocratic" liberalism in politics, and perhaps even an unorthodox, very undogmatic "Christianity," remained in him from beginning to end. And all his adult life he was a Spanish *galante* with women. In such ways, while working out his "theory of life" and "program of life," he stayed true to himself, to his own intellectual and social history and destiny. Throughout, he remained broadly consistent.

1. James, *The Will to Believe and Other Essays in Popular Philosophy* (1897; London: Longmans, 1931), 231 ("Great Men and Their Environment").
2. Ortega, 6:36–37; cf. *History as a System,* 207–9. Here the original version differs from the later Spanish; it is apparent from the former that Ortega himself was the reluctant Lindoro of the latter. Cf. 9:519 and 12:236 on the complexity of heritage.

ROOTS OF LIFE: YOUTH, LEARNING, CRISES, FAITHS

Ortega himself called "the reconstruction of origins" a "historiological operation" (9:411), something we are obliged to try with him. Late in life, at Geneva in 1951 at the age of sixty-eight, he described himself as "a little Spanish gentleman with the face of an old torero" (9:651). In fact, he later remarked there that he had been a bullfighter in his youth—a rather dubious claim. Although he was fascinated by the history of the sport, he had no stomach for the brutal spectacle itself. Hella Weyl, who may have been his Hermione in the 1930s, then recalled a middle-aged "Don Juan of the Spirit," whose eyes at least still flashed in his olive-hued "Castilian peasant's face" with "an Andalusian *torero*'s haughty grace." Always he was more exciting for his ideas than for physical presence, even in the 1920s, when (with Pío Baroja as his boon companion) he often caroused with women in a roadster, when he was "researching" his "Studies on Love," Don Juan, and "the interesting man."[3]

Lack of an intellectual biography that fully utilizes his works both published and archival to illuminate the background, origins, and early development of his main features of mind and character obliges us to scrape together here whatever "vital facts" seem relevant, from whatever sources. His brother Eduardo's recollections of José's precocious childhood and youth are most helpful, despite their brevity, and so are some of José's (Pepe's) own early writings (*mocedades*) that reveal more about him than he perhaps intended.

Eduardo recalled several incidents that helped mold José's character and give him permanent direction in life. His first significant recollection was of José's prodigious memory. At only five years of age he memorized in less than two days and then recited verbatim the whole first chapter of *Don Quixote,* in order to persuade his father to buy him a cordovan cask. That feat presaged the boy's voracious appetite for reading, a habit (especially during summer vacations) that became so intense that it brought him to a precocious "crisis of . . . intellectual development" in 1895 at twelve years of age—a "crisis so deep" that he was in bed with "nervous fevers" for several days.[4] It seems that he had buried himself in Balzac's *Human Comedy* so completely that he finally could not distinguish fiction from reality. As he came out of

3. Ortega remarks in "Troisième entretien privé," 298: a torero in his youth. But see remarks by his son, Miguel Ortega, *Mi padre,* 182–83: his *afición,* at least, began as a youth. Helene (Hella) Weyl, "José Ortega y Gasset," *Toronto Quarterly* 6 (1937–1938): 461, 474; on Hermione, see *History as a System* (1941, 1961), 207. That personal involvement was replaced by Lindoro (6:36), but their correspondence was not (on her side) always intellectual. Miguel Ortega, *Mi padre,* 70–71. See n. 5 below.

4. Eduardo Ortega y Gasset, "Mi Hermano José: Recuerdos de Infancia y Mocedad," *Cuadernos Americanos* 87 (May–June 1956): 174–211.

that pre-adolescent "identity crisis," José observed: "I have acquired an experience as if I had lived, not one, but several lives. I am already an old man weighed down with experience" and ideas, which he now feared losing. To Eduardo he revealed: "I have found in these days the principle or motto that is going to be my guide. . . . 'Let us be in our lives like archers who have a target.' One has to choose an end in life, . . . to go straight forward progressing even through shortcuts without wasting time in doubt and disorientation." That symbol of the archer and the arrow he did indeed make his motto, often repeated; it was an emblem on his later publications. Life itself became the target of this archer, and it was clearly not something he learned first from philosophy. However, life presented him with deviations and detours. Experienced both directly and vicariously (through art and literature), life became his obsessive interest, his *idée fixe*, from the onset of puberty until his death.

José's well-known jest that he "was born on a rotary press" refers to the fact that his Cuban-born father, José Ortega Munilla, was a journalist, director of Madrid's *El Imparcial*, a newspaper belonging to his wife's family, the Gassets. Well-connected with personalities in politics, literature, and art, Ortega senior passed on to his sons a lively interest in these fields.[5] From an early age they were exposed in the family dining room to free and open discussions with people of note on all manner of subjects. This stimulating "banquet" environment promoted in young José both mental agility and verbal eloquence, and an immediate orientation toward art and literature. There he first encountered that *fin de siècle* attitude of elitist snobs and poseurs that "Life is Art." "His vitalism," claimed Eduardo, "was a doctrine that arose in him with his love of art" and literature. Some of his first essays (of literary criticism and in praise of life) appeared as articles in *El Imparcial*, an advantage that naturally turned him from the first toward a journalistic style and medium. The family milieu thus played a major part in the shaping of his mind and character, his broad literary and humanistic tastes, and his lifelong preference for liberalism.

Jesuit Education

Both José and Eduardo Ortega y Gasset provided direct or indirect accounts of their formal schooling under the Jesuits from 1891 to 1898, first at

5. Niedermayer, *Ortega*, 14, 15-18, on his education. Also see Fernando Salmerón, *Las mocedades de Ortega y Gasset*. Occasionally useful on the early years is Miguel Ortega's *Mi padre*, by the oldest son (a physician); it is filled with intimate, vital details that are not encumbered by direct relation to his ideas and philosophy—so valuable to us because José kept his family life and most of his private experiences out of his writings. Also useful is Raúl Roa, "Dichos y hechos de Ortega y Gasset," *Cuadernos Americanos* 85 (January–February 1956): 122.

Miraflores del Palo near Málaga and then (for the latter) briefly at the Jesuit university in Bilbao in the North. In "A.M.D.G.," a book review written by José in 1910 of a poignant "documentary" novel about Jesuit secondary education in Spain, there seems to be much retrospective personal meaning. Like the author, Ortega himself had had just such experiences. He too had been one of their prize pupils—an "emperor." "On reading the book," he recalled, "my lost childhood has come back to me with a dangerous rush . . ." (1:523).[6] One might be hard put to identify young Ortega as simply another bright Bertuco, but he definitely did not belong to the other two types of students drawn nationwide from the well-to-do families: neither the earthy, bull-like "Pantagruels" nor the colorless "inert mean" of the middle (1:533–35). More than a little autobiographical were those of Bertuco's type, as Ortega described them. They were of "tremulous spirit, prematurely sensitized, with incredible energy of imagination," those "centrifugal souls, always ready to fly from collective human action, like the arrow from the hand of the archer." As "the only ones who can draw the gross masses after them toward higher forms of existence," these are the elite poets, thinkers, political leaders, and inventors, in short, the "salt of the earth." Instead of developing suitably this promising rank of talent, the Spanish Jesuits rendered it useless for the world by their narrow, hostile, suspicious attitude toward the rest of humanity, by their distortion or suppression of the classics of ancient and modern thought and science ("Democritus, Plato, Descartes, Galileo, Spinoza, Kant, Darwin, etc."), by their rigid and outdated ethics, and by minimal "art" or culture.

Bertuco's socially alienated, boxed-in feeling was evidently similar to young Ortega's visceral reaction in 1898, when no teachers nor books nor largeness of spirit were at hand to inspire a gifted youth during the deep personal and national crisis that year. Unlike Bertuco, young Ortega did not long to retire uselessly into himself, renouncing "all social labor" as he grew older. Rebounding, he escaped from the Jesuits, like other great minds and spirits who had benefited from their classicism and discipline but had gone on to outgrow their views and influence—Descartes, Galileo, Voltaire, and so many others. His severest censure of his Jesuit masters, as he looked back, was not for pride, greed, or the often alleged "Jesuitism," or Machiavellian pursuit of power and partisan ends (5:156). Instead he blamed them for purposeful "ignorance," or "intellectual incapacity" (1:535). But that was the very same failing that, with the rare exception such as Unamuno, he found

6. There seems to be little written specially on Ortega and the Jesuits, except for Eduardo Ortega's essay and Joaquín Iriarte, *Ortega y Gasset: Su persona y su doctrina*, 29–30; also see Marías, *Circumstance and Vocation*, 98–100 (on "A.M.D.G."). In a letter of 1905, Ortega boasted that he had been an "Emperor and little Greek" (*emperador y gréculo*) at his Jesuit school (*Cartas de un joven español*, 637.)

also in the Spanish state universities among lay professors. These disillusioning experiences guaranteed that when irrepressible young Ortega grew up he would become an educational reformer of note—and not just for his famous *Mission of the University*.

Eduardo's account of their Jesuit educators squares well with José's hints about the deficiency of their intellectual vigor and pedagogy—except that Eduardo was even more hostile. At Málaga they had an "excellent teacher of talent and culture," Father Gonzálo Coloma, brother of a noted novelist, who provided both boys with special tutoring and let them read books denied to other students. Learned and eloquent, he taught a very popular class in world history. Unfortunately his superiors, recalled Eduardo, felt that learning ought not be pleasurable nor a teacher eloquent, so they transferred him. His dull replacement was Father Barba, a mathematician, whom the students renamed Barbáro (Barbarian) when he mistook the Parthenon for a Greek ship.

If José's lifelong fascination with history began under Father Coloma, another Jesuit fostered his interest in history and linguistics—Julio Cejador (1864–1927), a noted philologist. Cejador was teaching him Greek during "the sad date of 1898," and his simplicity and dialogue were a refreshing contrast to the usual "rules, exceptions, etc." of the Jesuit method (1:66–67). Taking his ideas and style to heart, José studied the humanities under Cejador at Bilbao for a semester before going on to the University of Madrid. When Cejador was expelled from the order and gave up the habit, Ortega continued to call him "friend and master" as late as 1907, even as he tried to convert him to a neo-Kantian "philosophy of culture" with historical and linguistic dimensions.[7] Besides classical studies and a *Dictionary of Quixote*, Cejador produced a "New Method" that was etymological and "historical-comparative." Many years later, Ortega made etymology a basic tool of "historical reason."

In 1911, Ortega and Cejador differed over the interpretation of Joaquín Costa's program of Europeanization, which both supported as a response to 1898. The younger man saw a contradiction between "reconstitution" (as reactionary) and Europeanization (as progressive), a conflict that he attributed to the national narrowness of Costa's romantic "historicism." Gently he

---

7. At the beginning of Reel 32 (also in Ortega, *Cartas,* 71–77, 188–90) are three letters from Ortega (at Marburg) to Cejador, one of which is dated June 26, 1907. His "pragmatic of evaluation" already posited that "man, the human, is not something that is, but something that should be." A later letter based the *casticismo* (of Spanish culture) in a "philosophy of culture," and then he turned to linguistics and comparative history; finally he would explain "genetic psychology" by "space and time." He urged Cejador to turn to philosophy, study Kant, and create a philosophy of classicism. Debts to James, Nietzsche, and Cohen by 1907 are evident there.

criticized Cejador for lacking "intellectual altruism," that is, for a tendency to master things too quickly in muscular fashion and from his own limited viewpoint, instead of entering thoroughly into and informing himself on "things" and men in their "original complexity" (1:165). Many years later, he recalled with pride that Nicolai Hartmann had praised him (Ortega) in 1906 for his "intellectual altruism," which he then interpreted as meaning that he spoke openly with others and entered into their "point of view" (8:17–18). Since he never referred to Cejador again after 1911, possibly that mild reproof was too much for the former Jesuit's pride.

To Ortega's credit, he did not continue to pursue the Jesuits in the petty, vengeful spirit of a Voltaire or Quinet, who clamored publicly for the suppression of the order and its schools. Once free of them, he rarely mentioned them collectively, but he remained resentful and critical.[8] As one critic observed, despite everything he had gotten a good, solid grounding in basic skills and in the classics. Even without their help, he was able to fend for himself with "the moderns." Incidentally, he later found one Jesuit contemporary whom he admired, the noted French philosopher-scientist, Pierre Teilhard de Chardin, whose idea of "planetary man" he adopted into his own thought (9:568). Teilhard was an ill-tolerated rebel and misfit within the order, scarcely less than Cejador.

Adolescent Crisis of "Self and Circumstance," 1898

Did young Ortega lose his Catholic faith because of his bad experiences with the Jesuits, or because of much reading in Renan and Nietzsche? His later critic, the Jesuit Iriarte, concluded that something happened in his relations with Jesuit officials in 1898 at Bilbao (perhaps involving Cejador) that deeply angered him and even drove him out of the Church.[9] Later he considered for a "theme" this laconic Latin axiom: Homo homini lupis,

8. In a letter of 1905, Ortega blamed the Jesuits, "ignorant and conceited" barbarians, for having made him "timid and pedantic" (*Cartas*, 329, 657). In a speech to the Cortes after 1930, he distinguished his attitude from anticlericalism, Protestantism, and even "laicism"; he agreed to prohibit Jesuit teaching simply because they were "very bad educators, . . . inept instructors" (*Discursos Inéditos* [Madrid, 1967], 160–61).

9. Iriarte, *Ortega* 30; he also alleges the pagan influence of young Pepe's reading in Renan, Nietzsche, and Goethe (202–5). In 1906–1907, Ortega explained himself to his pious sweetheart (later wife), Rosa Spottorno, whose "faith" he promised always to respect: he distinguished *religion* from Catholicism, the Catholic church and clergy (especially the Spanish), which he blamed for doing "horrible damage" to Spain, citing the Inquisition and the Galileo affair (*Cartas*, 476, 553, 561). He scorned the "monstrous pride" of the clergy, who "blacken life" with imagined "sin" (436–37). Nevertheless, he somewhat paradoxically aspired to turn Spain into a "Christian Greece" (716), and he admired Spain's later Middle Ages. Evidently his deep love and respect for Rosa made him restrain his anticlericalism then and later.

femina feminae lupior, clericus clerico lupissimus ("clergyman to clergyman most like a wolf" [R 54]). In that era, however, many, if not most, educated young Spaniards automatically adopted a skeptical, indifferent, or hostile outlook on matters religious. Indeed, around the turn of the century, most Western and European intellectuals—Catholic, Protestant, Orthodox, and Jewish—became at least "agnostic" when not openly atheistic. Yet a number of them, both older and younger (Dilthey, Weber, Freud, Durkheim, James, Jaspers, Heidegger, and Sartre), manifested keen intellectual interest in religious phenomena, not mere indifference or hostility as in earlier generations.

A profoundly Frenchified youth like Ortega could hardly have escaped that alienated but interested atmosphere of the *fin de siècle*. Even under Jesuit tutelage, he had soon put aside pious works like those of Menéndez y Pelayo and Donoso Cortés, with their traditionalist, fideistic Catholicism, and had taken up Renan, even his critically agnostic *Life of Jesus*. "Renan's books accompany me since childhood," he remarked in 1909; "on many occasions they have served me as a spiritual breviary, and more than once they calmed certain metaphysical griefs that go with boyish hearts sensitized by solitude" (1:443). Yet at the "decisive" age of twenty-six he had concluded that Renan had been less than fully truthful and committed in questions of religion. "Ah, M. Renan, have you . . . discovered the historical figure, divinely human, of Jesus of Nazareth?" (1:449). Or had the "master of smirks" simply repeated what he had learned from such German works as Strauss' *Leben Jesu*? For himself, however unorthodox his views about Christianity, Ortega continued to respect it as a great historical force, and, as he matured, he (like William James) came to regard Jesus as a consummate model for the resolution of human life in crisis (5:110), if not precisely *his* model. But all of these "second thoughts" were indeed more from the head than from the heart. After life itself, philosophy became for him a "religion" or surrogate "faith" to fill the void that he experienced after his personal crisis, which paralleled the nation's in 1898.[10]

Even while the precocious student was chafing to be free to explore new horizons of intellect and art, fifteen-year-old José Ortega experienced acutely Spain's defeat and loss of empire to the United States in 1898. That painful crisis forced a rethinking and reorientation in the intellectual, literary, and political life that is associated with Spain's "generation of 1898"—Unamuno, Azorín, and Pío Baroja, whom José admired, studied, and imitated (9:491–

10. See John Delvin, *Spanish Anticlericalism: A Study in Modern Alienation* (New York: Fordham University Press, 1966), 141–48, on Ortega. Ortega, *Man and Crisis,* trans. Mildred Adams (New York: Norton, 1958), 142, 136. By 1905 young Ortega had resolved to live by "general ideas"—not necessarily religious—even those of Nietzsche that were "applicable to life" (*Cartas,* 643). They clearly included the vague aspiration to a "philosophy of life," "becoming" over "being," and emphasis on "solitude" as conducive to creation.

94), although he was too young by several years to participate directly in it. Nevertheless, that humiliating defeat also sparked as deep an identity crisis for him personally as it did for his nation collectively. He identified with Spain.[11]

Defending Unamuno as one of the few heroes of 1898, Ortega recalled in 1914 how profoundly that crisis had moved him: "1898. Enough." That reminiscence confirms on so many points what has been said above about that period of his youth.

> Ah, . . . it suffices for me to enter into my own heart and boyhood, . . . enthusiastic and patriotic. It is that age, when entering life, every pure and energetic soul searches around for higher principles, ideals to inflame oneself and to serve. Those are shaped in strong disciplines that incite one to live. But in our milieu we heard only outdated, cringing, stupid, and pompous voices. We went looking for teachers and found none: the universities, with rare exceptions, taught us nothing. Books that were representative of the era failed to stir our beings with their stupid rhetoric. For several years, . . . every sensitive youth found himself like a Robinson [Crusoe] in the midst of spiritual Spain—obliged to erect from his own grief a creed for shelter. . . . (10:267)

His dramatic picture of the impact of 1898 on him personally, although hyperbolic, rings with sincerity. It seems evident enough that his loss of religious faith combined with the shock of Spain's national crisis became—or provoked—in young José what psychohistorians call an adolescent identity crisis. For several years after 1898 he posed as a Nietzschean "superman" rebelling against the recent past and dreaming of starting "history over" again. His creed was Barrès's "cult of the self."

In the years following 1898, in alienation from the older generation and from the Church, young Ortega did not live without enthusiastic and passionate "beliefs" that he substituted for his losses and disappointments. Later he would tell his students that " . . . every age of life takes a special form that requires appropriate virtues" and passions. Several such that are suited to tender youth who are oriented outwardly to life and world include laughter, friendship, love, and "enthusiasm" that is akin to faith. For himself, he avowed that such a faith had moved him deeply ever since childhood—a love of Spain, a fervent patriotism. At thirty-three he had half lamented, half

---

11. On Ortega's youth (mostly after 1898), see Salmerón, *Mocedades de Ortega*. On the crisis of 1898 as part of Ortega's "circumstance," see Marías's *Circumstance and Vocation*, 46–48, for a non-personalized account; also, António Millán Puelles, review of *Ortega y el 98*, by G. Fernández de la Mora, in *Nuestro Tiempo* (Pamplona) 14 (June 1961): 808–16. As portions of previous notes imply, Soledad Ortega's edition of her father's youthful letters, *Cartas de un joven español,* is very informative on dreams, disappointments, and ambitions between 1891 and 1908, especially from 1905 to 1907.

boasted that "my boyhood was not mine, but my race's. My whole youth, like Moses' bush, burned beside the path that Spain travels as history."[12]

Among his youthful enthusiasms were some that he quickly learned to moderate and to subordinate to this nationalism and to other higher aims. From Renan and later from his German masters, he imbibed an almost religious devotion to Culture, which he soon recognized as virtual idolatry (*beatería*) (1:466). The same imbalance was also true initially of his youthful ideals of "Europe" and "science" (7:304–5). But these were more sober beliefs, which he added to another equally intellectual and practical: philosophy. But Nietzsche first, and then James, Bacon, Vico, and Scheler, all taught him to beware of "idols," which he later detected in all "utopian" thinking, especially in traditional rationalism. As soon as he had left his native faith, however, he had fallen first into just such other "religions," starting with Nietzsche's radical postures.[13]

The Young Nietzschean

Later Ortega frankly and openly acknowledged his youthful Nietzschean rebellion from 1898 until around 1903. In 1905 and again in 1908, he recalled to Maeztu how much he had "absorbed" (*mamado*) from Nietzsche as he had passed, sweating "horribly," through that "torrid zone"—inflamed over a page of that "tyrant," "sophist," and "ingenious fabricator of indecencies" that flatter and puff up the unwary reader into an adamantine history-maker, "beyond good and evil" (1:441). His debt to Nietzsche was even more forcibly stated a month later in "The Superman," where he described his naive enthusiasm as "all burning sand and fiery wind, . . . and unbearable heat." Yet he was not now ungrateful, for, without that haughty pride, he felt he would have drowned in the "cultural shipwreck" and universal "coarseness" that was Spain after 1898. He had been intoxicated by Barrès's Nietzschean dictum: "You are called to start history over"—admittedly a ridicu-

12. Ortega, "Elogio de las virtudes de la mocedad," *Revista de Occidente*, no. 15–16 (August–September 1982): 65–71.

13. See R. G. Collingwood, *The Idea of History* (New York: Oxford University Press, Galaxy Books, 1956), 68–69, on Vico taking Bacon's "idols" as "conceits." Nietzsche's *Twilight of Idols* (1888) declared "new war" on "inflated" idols that were never so called. On his boast of "idol smashing" already in 1905, see *Cartas*, 613. After Bacon, Vico, and Nietzsche, a decisive influence on Ortega's idea of *beatería* as "utopian" was probably James's *Pluralistic Universe*, 51 (as pt. 2 of *Essays in Radical Empiricism*), where there is a reference to the "beatific vision" of perfect and absolute wholes, of the "intellectualist" or rationalistic type. James regarded things cultural as ideal, as utopias (*Writings*, 92). See Ortega, 5:306, on "beatería de la Cultura." In an essay of 1911 (later called "Die Idole der Selbsterkenntnis"), Scheler also touched on this theme (Silver, *Ortega as Phenomenologist*, 57).

lous idea but culturally useful and necessary then for young Spaniards who wanted to shed the "morbid heritage" of the recent past (1:91–93). Years later, he still recalled how a "whole generation has burned with heat radiated by Nietzsche's slogan: 'transmutation of values'" (1:318). But "today [1908] we are just any two men for whom the moral world does exist," after all (1:441)— at twenty-five years of age.[14]

Around his twentieth year, young Ortega had begun to desert Nietzsche and Barrès. By 1905 he had decisively repudiated the "solipsist [*yoista*] ideal," and with it "*immoralism, amoralism,* or *Nietzscheanism,*" as well as "skepticism"; it was the "disease" of his generation. Meanwhile he turned to Bergson and devoured Renan and French literature again (8:24). His first published work, however, was "Glosses," in *Vida Nueva* (New life) in 1902, and it was still openly Nietzschean in style and content. He offered aphorisms on what it is to be a critic, with no pretense of "impartiality." Although he cited French critics, it was clearly Nietzsche who was still inspiring him by three central ideas that he carried over into his later philosophy: life, perspective, and history, along with the cliché of "strong man," or hero, eyes ablaze and eager to lead the stupid herd of his fellow citizens (1:13–18). Before he had finished with Nietzsche, around 1903, Ortega had not only launched himself as critic but, for his future career and for new "faith," was studying philosophy from a historical perspective. Within two years he had focused on "human life" and the "problems of living," for which the mythic literary image of Don Quixote provided inspiration.[15]

LIBRARY AND HISTORY OF PHILOSOPHY

To "do" philosophy, Ortega found that he needed books (an adequate library) and a historical approach as much as solitary reflection on basic problems, as his Diary of 1915–1916 well demonstrated (R 36). Since he was always keen on the practical value and applications of his ideas, his library needed to cover a broader spectrum than was at first available to him. In 1908 he lamented that no public library in Madrid (nor scarcely a private one) contained the works of such German masters as Kant, Fichte, and Harnack (1:108). Very early, then, he began to accumulate his own books in the fields of his interest. By 1910 he could boast of "the ocean of my library," wherein

14. For Nietzsche and Ortega during his youth, see Salmerón, *Mocedades de Ortega;* and Gonzalo Sobrejano, *Nietzsche en España* (Madrid: Gredos, 1967), 527–65. Ramiro de Maeztu said that their "Nietzscheanism" was a reaction to defeat by the United States in 1898, to national weakness (*Autobiografía* [Madrid: Editorial Nacional, 1962], 115). Evidently Ortega confused Barrès here with the French revolutionist Barère. Cf. Ortega, *Cartas,* 616, 639.

15. Ortega, *Cartas,* 137–43, 148, 636.

he never felt "shipwrecked" or lost (1:155). He continued collecting until (by the 1930s) his library filled his house "from basement to attic" and had no more room for shelving.[16] When he had to go into exile after 1936, he sorely missed his own books, and he bemoaned the dearth of adequate libraries in Argentina (5:375).

His holdings on various leading philosophers past and present (some of whom are cited in this study, such as Plato, Aristotle, Descartes, Leibniz, Kant, Schlegel, Hegel, Comte, Dilthey, Scheler, James, and Russell) are basic evidence of his sources (which Orringer especially has utilized) and of his scholarly habits. Over the years he acquired sets of complete works, specific essays and treatises, autobiographies, biographies, and histories, including histories of philosophy, that his approach by analysis combined with history of philosophy demanded, if he were to stay up to the vital "level of the times."[17] In 1934 he claimed that he had taken the whole intellectual past as the "mental subsoil" for his "collective heritage," from which he did his own current "work of knowledge" (6:207).

In his later years Ortega regarded philosophy as a "human thing"—not as something substantially, universally, and perennially human in Heidegger's sense but as something that "happens" (like other historical "events") to some people. Already for young Ortega as for Dilthey, the *history* of philosophy had become a necessary "propaedeutic" or entrée for doing philosophy, because the European and classical "whole" of two and a half millennia gave meaning to the contemporary national or personal part. Not until he had produced a historico-sociological interpretation of his native "circumstance" in *Invertebrate Spain* (1921), however, did he emphasize to his public that a general *historical* sense and dimension had always been essential for his philosophizing. That same year, for Spanish students and serious dilettantes, he promoted a translation of Karl Vorländer's *History of Philosophy*. "When I was beginning my training in philosophy, this history, then recently published, I always kept close by. Customarily the novice feels urgent appetites, sudden eagerness to possess quickly the ideas of a great thinker, to whom, here or there, he has seen an allusion. . . . How grateful he is to find a work

---

16. Weyl, "Ortega," 473.

17. Miguel Ortega, *Mi padre*, 63–66, on Ortega's study habits and bookcases (with editions of Descartes, Hegel, and Goethe). He worked in "great disarray" on the dining-room table but always knew where everything was located. Compare with the information on his library in my chapter 4—in regard to the books of James. In its final contents, his library is well supplied with the works (individual or complete) of most of the major philosophers of the Western tradition, especially in German and French editions: for example, three sets of Plato, at least one set for Aristotle, Descartes, and Hegel, and numerous individual works for Leibniz and Kant, including (in German) both the *Critique of Pure Reason* and the *Critique of Practical Reason*—the former so heavily marked up that it demonstrates the depth of his effort.

that is simple, clear, concise, and reliable to offer him a schema of the system in question!" (6:292).[18] One could not learn philosophy, he noted, without studying current problems and past systems in parallel. "In no other science does the history of its development acquire the value of unavoidable instrument for new . . . investigation." In fact, the philosophical past "perdures" and acts in present philosophy. "Every contemporary thinker, if he looks through his own doctrine, sees swarming the whole philosophical past" (6:296)—which at first appearance looked like a babble of competing errors instead of dialectical progress and continuity through partial truths.

Let not the historic diversity and clash of philosophical opinion turn you into skeptics, Ortega warned the beginners. What he feared was not the skepticism of the learned few but that of the many "specialists" of the dominant "social mass," the good "engineers, doctors, and politicians"—the current "common intellectuals" with their proud "aggressive ignorance" of everything outside their narrow "specialism." These potential "barbarians" were precisely the "mass men" whom he attacked almost a decade later in *Revolt of the Masses*. They scorned diversity in philosophy as "unscientific." Both these "mass men" and their "scientism" had their roots in the "defective heritage" of the nineteenth century, beginning with parallel "subversions" of the Third Estate against absolute monarchy and of the bourgeoisie against the nobility, and going on to the romantic rebellion against rationalism and finally to the positivist and scientistic rebellion of "specialists" against romanticism. There had then followed an "eclipse" of philosophy for half a century while only "pseudo-philosophy" survived (6:296–98).

Out of that historic gap in philosophy, however, several things intellectually worthy had emerged. Current philosophy had to take cognizance of these interim developments: the maturing of history as a science (especially among the Germans), as wedded to the biological idea of evolutive *continuity*, and applying even to philosophy. The history of anything and everything, he noted, consists primarily in establishing "these lines or series of evolution." But this advantage that tends toward unity becomes a vice, if we overlook differences and *discontinuity*. By 1911 the twentieth century seemed to be moving again into an epoch of discontinuity in science and philosophy

18. Apart from Salmerón's study of Ortega's ideas on history (not history of philosophy per se), no one seems to have examined specifically his early historical conceptions and judgments on the philosophical past. He later encouraged Marías to undertake his *History of Philosophy*. Karl Vorländer, *Historia de la filosofía*, 6th ed., 2 vols., trans. J. V. Vigueira, prologue by Ortega (Madrid: Beltran, 1921). Ortega probably used the second German edition (Leipzig: Durr'sche, 1908) as a postgraduate in Germany; it had sections entitled "Philosophy of Life" and "Philosophy of History" but its "vitalism" was naturalistic (biological), as in 2:488; also it had basic information on individual philosophers such as Dilthey, on philosophy of history (472, 482, 487) but nothing at all on James and little on Bergson or Croce.

(6:298–300). Still, the present and the future of philosophy were rooted deeply in the past, especially the unphilosophical last half of the nineteenth century. European positivism and materialism had been the weak background and basis from which he had been obliged to begin, for Spain had offered him next to nothing from which to begin philosophizing.

In his old age after 1950, Ortega began another history of contemporary philosophy, which was explicitly a narrative of historical reason and intentionally autobiographical. If he had completed it, it might have made at least this chapter unneeded. Unfortunately that self-revealing fragment lay unpublished until 1980 and therefore without effect on current interpretations of the sources of his thought. After a nod to the ancient Greek "way of thinking" since Parmenides' *aletheia* and the emergence from it of the particular sciences, Ortega swept through modern philosophy after Descartes, when the effort was made to turn that generalizing mode of thinking into "*a science*," which had left the discipline "cross-eyed," until Kant turned it (and metaphysics) into a Newtonian imitation of mathematical physics, whose proper conclusion, despite Hegel and the idealist romantic reaction, was materialistic positivism. Comte himself excepted, positivism was as good as "no philosophy."[19] Then began a hiatus in "authentic" philosophy that he projected forward through his youth until 1910 or after.

Unfinished though it is, his "paradigm" of philosophy's "historical reality" reveals many details essential for an understanding of his own philosophical background, origins, and earliest development, but it requires many other insights from him to fill in the gaps and to complete the story. At least it persuades one that the historical approach to his "systematic" mind and thought is a proper one, so we imitate and follow him.

The Past Half-Century in European Philosophy

Already in 1913, barely at the philosophically "mature" age of thirty, Ortega dismissed the previous hundred years as the time of "least weight" in European philosophy for centuries. The further he developed, the broader and more critical became his attitude toward the past,[20] although eventually

19. On Comte and positivism, see Ortega, "Medio siglo," 5–8, 11–12, 16.

20. Informative on Ortega's philosophical background and early development are Marías, *Circumstance and Vocation;* Morón Arroyo, *Sistema;* Orringer, *Fuentes germánicas;* Silver, *Ortega as Phenomenologist;* and Julio Bayon, *Razón Vital y dialéctica en Ortega* (Madrid: Revista de Occidente, 1972). Also see Hernán Larraín Acuña, *La Génesis del pensamiento de Ortega* (Buenos Aires: General Fabril, 1962); Franz Niedermayer, "Ortega y Gassets Erstling (Meditaciones)," *Hochland* 5 (1961): 479–82; E. Holz, "Ortega y Gasset, Meditation über Don Quijote. Triumph des Augenblicks. Glanz und Dauer," *Bucherei und Bildung* 13 (1961): 551–52; and Udo Rukser, "Gründzuge von Ortegas Philosophie," *Zeitschrift für philosophische Forschung* 19 (1965): 668–88.

he became much more tolerant than in "Nothing Modern and Very Twentieth Century" (1916), which was his defiant manifesto for younger generations shaking off the yoke of ideas and values from the immediate past (2:22–24). Ideas of "progress" and "modernity" in the elders were only their arrogant attempt to dictate the future as well as to condemn the past. Not only their democratic and parliamentary politics but also their positivism in philosophy now had to be overcome, surpassed. "Other ways of thinking, moving in the same path as positivism, keeping and reinforcing whatever it had in respect to strict purposes, have supplanted it" (2:23): pragmatism, phenomenology, and life-philosophy.

Of the second half of the nineteenth century, especially its last quarter, he later remarked (1929): "Those were the times of positivism, that is, of no-philosophy" (4:51). Philosophy had then suffered a kind of senile forgetfulness, if not an identity crisis, up to the end of the century. An "anti-philosophical age" (8:286) had then sacrificed its authentic purpose and historic character to modern material science. Between the 1840s and the 1870s, two generations had ignored philosophy in order to make revolutions and to build railroads and industry through the era of Napoleon III, Disraeli, and Bismarck; they represented "a gap, a rupture, in the historical continuity of philosophical questioning" (8:221). "Philosophy having been exhausted by materialism and positivism, which rather than two philosophies are two manners of philosophical ignorance, the European mind lost the scholarly tradition of this science" (6:306) and had had to go "back to school" to relearn the classic systems of philosophy (7:29). In 1939 as World War II was beginning, in his view largely because Europe had no integrating and inspirational common "faith" anymore, he observed that after Kant and the Enlightenment, which was the "last integral system of opinions in force," only partial faiths survived for groups and individuals, such as German romantic idealism in the earlier nineteenth century, the scientistic positivism of France and England around 1870, and thereafter Marxism. The absence of a common conviction, to give "system" to the human mind and existence, had become a "radical illness" for Europe (6:364).

Positivism as Worldview and Philosophy

The positivism that had prevailed in Europe in the last half of the nineteenth century was, according to Ortega, both "more and less" than a philosophy, properly speaking (8:31). Like Kolakowski more recently, he recognized that positivism was a very broad phenomenon that extended back through European thought well beyond its so-called founder, Auguste Comte, to roots in the Enlightenment and in English empiricism. There was an authentic (true) and inauthentic (false) positivism in the philosophical sense, the first of which was an empirical epistemology that he had adopted and that he deemed always valid, whereas the second was a science-aping epistemology (method) that had now run its course. Eventually he shifted Comte to the first category, and he typified the second by Littré. Ortega's notion of what is properly positivism is almost the opposite of William Simon's distinction, for he did not construe it strictly as scientism in methodology, history, and history of science, nor did he limit it to the equally narrow ideological (even religious) Comtism of the little coteries of British and French true-believers,[21] some of whom he may have met in Paris. In its most important aspect, positivism was a broad "governing philosophy" (9:359) that had gained the status of a dominant "worldview," "a mental attitude to which man comes historically, the result of a chain of intellectual experiences forged during two centuries," deriving especially from English and French sources since 1760 (8:31). Among the intellectual "faiths" of the nineteenth century, positivism was the last *nearly* general such mentality (6:365). Out of the positivist background, partly by reaction and partly by more acute development of its basic insights, there had come later in the century those great innovators who, because of the failings of positivism, had had to give rebirth to philosophy.

For Ortega, materialism, positivism, and "biologism" were "exceedingly bad philosophy" (R 77), a "tragicomic illusion" that aped the natural sciences and took mechanistic physics as the model science—indeed, as the *only* "science" (3:347). Yet physics dealt only with "intermediate" questions, not the ultimate ones proper to philosophy. "Materialism consisted simply in the divinization of matter. As the physicist manipulates matter but does not know what it is, he . . . therefore divinizes it. More cautiously, positivism renounces the attempt. . . . Convinced that physics can resolve only penultimate questions, it declares impossible those that are ultimate" (3:347). Positivism thus ended in agnosticism, abandoning the supreme problems as mere "myths."

As a philosophy, positivism "of the old stamp" (3:303) was indeed narrow, but Ortega regarded it as historically necessary and unavoidable after 1870. For, "had the men of 1880 not been positivists, we ourselves would have had to be so" (4:507)—evidently, to sweep away now useless debris of the past before beginning afresh. In its anti-metaphysical stance, it denied essence, being, nature, and natural rights, ultimately reducing to a doctrine of immediate sense perception, which greatly diminished the bounds of reality in

21. On nineteenth-century positivism, see Leszek Kolakowski, *The Alienation of Reason: A History of Positivist Thought,* trans. N. Guttermann (Garden City, N.Y.: Doubleday, 1968), v, 70; William N. Simon, *European Positivism in the Nineteenth Century* (Ithaca: Cornell University Press, 1963), 245–47. Ortega was closer to the first view: positivism as a broad and broadly penetrating movement.

man's world, leaving only evident "pure facts." "The European positivist of 1880 was [thus] a tightrope walker" over "the void of the world" (4:507). He sought to fill that void with rather illogical causal relations and frequencies expressed as scientific "laws" that let him make "predictions" and machines (4:508). The error in positivism, he repeatedly pointed out, was to admit *only* the sensual as real, as "fact."

Positivism, finally, was the philosophy of the middle-class man, of the bourgeois, who was "the dominant type of man" in the second half of the nineteenth century. The worldview of "positivist man," or the "positivist generation" of the 1880s, rejected metaphysical "being" but retained the greatest faith in "facts," and (thanks to science) in "laws"; this was now no longer possible (6:508).

Materialism and Marxism

The most famous of the critics of the positivistic bourgeoisie was Karl Marx, a materialist and a "positivist" *malgré lui* in his philosophy, since Marxism was not at its core very different from positivism.[22] Both were scientistic and materialistic. Modeled on material science and deterministic, they were thus a "peddler's view" of reality and of history in the end. If positivists were agnostic on ultimate questions about matter, he maintained that "Marx and Engels never had a clear idea of what they wanted to say by their presumed 'materialism,' which in the strict sense was only 'economism' . . ." (5:495).

The prevalence of merely economic aims, of a "religious materialism," had corrupted contemporary Spaniards, had deprived them of ideals and ethics for the future, and had undermined even the economy and the current democracy (1:119). Only science, and philosophy in a more scientific *and* idealist mode, could serve as an "instrument" to supply what Spain was lacking.

In 1924, Ortega remarked that the second half of the nineteenth century had "lived under the double sign" of Darwin and Marx, both of whom conceived a one-dimensional evolution that supposed "struggle for existence, conflict, and triumph of the better adapted" (3:302). Not only in Marx

22. On materialism in 1911, Ortega cited Lange's *History of Materialism* (1:493); in 1909 he had rejected the materialism of Haedsel as outdated and erroneous (10:97). For a Marxist study of Ortega, see Bayon, *Razón Vital*. More specifically on Marxism, see Jesús Herrero, "Ortega e suas correccoes ao Marxismo," *Brotéria*, no. 107 (June 1978): 43–61. Ortega's later *Revolt of the Masses* attracted attention in what was Soviet Russia and the eastern European countries: Zdenek Kourin, "Ortega y orteguismo: Un tema actual de la crítica soviética," *Cuadernos Hispanoamericanos*, no. 403–5 (January–March 1984): 467–84.

and Darwin, he found, but in the "positivist" Taine, conflict theory seemed a consequence of a more basic and radical philosophical pessimism (6:81). Ortega saw that these three materialistic movements—all of which espoused the idea of historical progress—were paradoxically pessimistic at their root. Growing out of modern idealism since the Renaissance, this pessimism had climaxed in the second half of the nineteenth century (2:527; 5:599).

Darwinism and "Biologism"

Contrary to Nicol and to Morón Arroyo, I see little evidence for a genuinely "biological stage" in Ortega's philosophy, but there was one in his pedagogical theory, and it corresponded to the more childish, biological phase of one's life cycle. Although Darwinian biology provided him a basic "perspective for evolutionism," or the changes and historical development of life, Ortega was never entirely comfortable with it. Comparing the mechanistic philosophy of the seventeenth and eighteenth centuries with "our evolutionism" in 1908—"all of us are *developmentalists*" and accept "the developmental hypothesis" (stated in English)—he detected a sane turning-back to the concept of "end" (as in Aristotelian "biologism"), wherein (since Kant) ideas were to serve as ends (1:115). Although young Ortega sensed a chasm between Kant's proud view of man as creator and Darwin's theory of his humble animal origins as a product of environment's physical forces, he felt that the very existence of Darwin (and of biology as science) demonstrated that Kant was equally right (1:161). If he could not disregard the biological side of life and of "vital phenomena," neither could he agree with a merely materialistic concept of man and life—which is "our last hope"—as bound to "physical necessity" that obliterated freedom, originality, and heroism (1:400). In fact, several times in his earlier lectures he had explicitly denounced such "biologism" (R 77).[23]

The dangers of social and political applications of Darwin's ideas in the form that we call "social Darwinism" became obvious to Ortega during World War I, in German attitudes about European dominance, notably in the propaganda of Max Scheler (2:197–200). By that time he was aware of a "new biology," especially Uexküll's (3:304n), that regarded the living organism not as a result of parts and functions adapting to the milieu but as a functional *whole* acting on its environment and that viewed life as a "composite of material and spiritual organs" directed toward the external world (2:149). This kind of biology also suited his emerging historical and cultural perceptions: for example, the ideas that "non-organized life created organization," and, accordingly, that it was primitive man (and the historically

23. See supplemental note 23, chap. 2.

recurring spirit of primitivism) that had created culture and civilization (2:280–82; 3:324). "Darwinian biology begins precisely where life, in the strict sense, ends."

In his *Meditations on Quixote* (1914), Ortega rejected the notion that life (or, to live) is simply adaptation, as a false Darwinian definition (1:400). Despite his discontent with Darwinism, however, Ortega was unable to break decisively from it until revisionists of the physical and biological sciences had provided him the means. In 1912, recognizing that radical changes were already afoot in physics (3:303n), he was thereafter able to formulate Einstein's worldview as going beyond the "evolutionary spirit" of the preceding century, with its emphasis on unity, continuity, and common features. This new outlook stressed plurality, difference, and discontinuity—not just in biology but now also in history and all things human (3:303, 308–9; 6:299). He had translations of both Uexküll and Spengler published in Spain by the early 1920s (3:304n), but he was too open and critical to remain a Spenglerian, and he did not then go through a "biological stage" of thought as he perhaps once seemed to imply (8:54) and as Nicol and Morón Arroyo have thought. To call philosophy of "Life" *literally* "bi-ology" (in contradiction to material "zo-ology") was the closest he came to it (9:650).

CONTEMPORARY SPANISH BACKGROUND

Men do not philosophize in a vacuum, even when they withdraw into an ivory tower. For Ortega, man lives and man philosophizes in a definite time and place, not in "uchronic" or "utopian" circumstances. Thus a modern Spaniard does not philosophize in precisely the same fashion, or for the same motives, as an ancient Greek or a seventeenth-century Frenchman or a twentieth-century German. As he emphasized more than once, his circumstance was not "Humanity" (4:116; 8:20), nor eternity, but contemporary Europe in the broader sphere and Spain since 1898 in the narrower—his own country being his immediate context, problem, and inspiration.

The Spanish Heritage

Ortega strongly admonished both the Germans (1934) and the French (1937) that he had till then been preeminently *Spanish* as a philosopher—in the sense that he had labored especially for his own nation and had addressed himself chiefly to Spanish problems in a journalistic and Socratic manner that Spaniards could understand. We may easily forget that the author of such international essays as *Revolt of the Masses* and *Dehumanization of Art* had aimed the overwhelming bulk of his periodical pieces at his own land.

Indeed, his repeated rooting of authentic philosophy in the crisis experience and situation strongly suggests that Spain's crisis of 1898 was also his own personal crisis, which drove him to philosophize to seek to "save" his native "circumstance," as in *Meditations on Quixote* (1914).

Young Ortega judged his homeland as being virtually without culture or philosophy of its own, but he nevertheless regarded himself as very "Mediterranean," a "Southerner," "Celtiberian," and "Spaniard to the brim" (9:510) in temperament, thought, and culture. Maturing as a philosopher from 1911 onward, he soon presented himself as preeminently a *Spanish* philosopher, yet he felt he had received virtually nothing to build on by way of a genuinely Spanish tradition in philosophy. The "traditionalism" that he had learned as a boy from Menéndez y Pelayo did not seem to him to merit the name philosophy, and it had derived from French Romantic sources. Under the Jesuits he apparently had encountered also some of the old scholasticism going back to Suárez and beyond, in a revived form as neo-Thomism, but little firsthand acquaintance with modern philosophy.

Spanish Realism

Sánchez Blanco has shown how Ortega *could* have related to Spanish traditions in philosophy of "life and history" that were realist (without being materialist), and in fact he did so quite consciously, but not to any great extent in philosophy. In regard to realism, vitalism, and historical orientation, he was at least compatible with predecessors and contemporaries. If he wanted to exert an influence, he needed to stress continuity with his nation's past and present in that way: "Spanish art, say Alcántara and Cossio, is realist. Spanish thought, says Menéndez y Pelayo, is realist. Spanish poetry, . . . says Menéndez Pidal, more than any other sticks to historical reality. Spanish political thinkers, according to [Joaquín] Costa, were realists" (1:186). "What am I," among such famous compatriots, "going to do except draw the line and add it up?" We should not let "imagination" come between us and touching and seeing *things* clearly in their natural state. Obviously, that confession of realism, from a 1911 essay on aesthetics in which he cited his "Adam in Paradise," was meant to affirm a philosophical realism too. His rejection of the old rationalism had been anticipated by Unamuno and Pérez Galdós, but his "Robinsonism" of withdrawal into solitude led him not to mysticism, nor to materialistic "biologism," nor to utopian "intellectualism," but to a realist philosophy of "life and history," for which Spain also had precedents—even in the traditionalism of Balmes, Donoso Cortés, and Menéndez y Pelayo.[24]

---

24. Sánchez Blanco, "Continuidad," 606–8, pointed out that both Unamuno and Pérez

Traditionalism

"When I was a boy, imbued with faith, I used to read the books of Menéndez Pelayo" (1:341). Ortega's later criticism of that author extended to more than his alleged distinction of "Germanic mists" (8:24) from "Latin clarity." Menéndez was also the defender and promoter of "traditionalism," a kind of fideistic "philosophy" whose roots were in Louis XVIII's France with Maistre and Bonald and whose Spanish representatives were Balmes and Donoso Cortés.[25] The two French traditionalists he mentioned only as archreactionaries and as collectivists before the socialists (4:125), and he seemed to have known as little of the other two. "What idea, what emotion, what living molecule of my soul do I owe to this man"—Balmes—to enrich "the inner life"? (1:143). He disagreed with the extremism of "the excellent Donoso Cortés" on the relation of thought and truth, but he maintained what Donoso would have readily admitted: that political interest or utility is the father of lies as often as not (1:186). Many years later, in *Revolt of the Masses,* he repeated Donoso's views on the totalitarian dangers of the modern state.[26]

As a philosophy, traditionalism was something Ortega never seriously entertained. He denied that he was "conservative or traditionalist by temperament." "I am a man who truly loves the past. Traditionalists, on the other hand, do not love it; they want it to be not past but present" (2:43). That kind of "contemporary traditionalism" was "a philosophical and political theory." The truly traditional is a historical reality, is a "real mechanism" that functions in certain eras (3:212, 228–30). Later he opposed "traditional" to "modern" in one of the earliest of "modernization" theories applicable to historical societies and values. As related to such a "model," his own values were neither those of a Spanish traditionalist "idolater" of the past nor those of a European rationalistic and "utopian" modernizer, but something in between (or "beyond") those two extremes. "Our extreme race, our extreme climate, our extremist souls"—he said of Spaniards other than himself— "are not called to leave the record of a form of reasonable and continuous life in history." Oddly, this view, which he attributed to Menéndez y Pelayo in 1906, was in fact pure Donoso, who likewise had aspired to rational but non-rationalistic alternatives for his times. Such too had been Ortega's intent since at least 1916: "nothing 'modern'" (2:22–24), but very contemporary.

Galdós had rejected the old rationalism, and (much earlier) so had Donoso Cortés. For Ortega's (unindexed) metaphor "Robinson," see 1:229–30; 2:79, 85, 86; 3:145; 8:82n, 225; 9:497. For his "Robinsonism," see idem, *¿Qué es conocimiento?* 30; also Marías, *Circumstance and Vocation,* 61.

25. See supplemental note 25, chap. 2.

26. See supplemental note 26, chap. 2.

How otherwise avoid both traditionalist and modernist extremisms in Spain? Besides defending traditionalism, Menéndez y Pelayo had also been a promoter of scholasticism, which he had tried to unite with the Scottish "common sense" philosophy that Ortega was to call the most worthless of philosophies (8:285). In later years Ortega recalled that one of the most "comical things in the hapless intellectual life of Spain" in the nineteenth century had been Menéndez's attempt to match those two incongruent philosophies (8:249).

Thomist Scholasticism and "Christian Philosophy"

In fact, Ortega regarded Thomist (or neo-Thomist) scholasticism as a bad joke, or as a tragicomedy (8:217) of incongruences in philosophy, for either the thirteenth or the twentieth century. Although he later studied it in greater depth from around 1927, essentially he never changed his mind: it was an anachronism and had not been an *authentic* philosophy, not even with Saint Thomas (8:214–16). For Ortega, the term "scholasticism" came to signify also a *type* of merely revived and received philosophy. The Medieval and the contemporary were just two of many varieties—and not the weakest— of a generic scholasticism that now included such secular versions as neo-Kantianism (8:214n, 219n) and contemporary Marxism.

That Aristotle, who had not believed in God, should have been turned into "the official philosopher of Catholicism" in medieval and modern times struck Ortega as "one of the strangest and most confused facts of world history" (8:166–67). The Church had clung to Thomism as "an inveterate habit," not understanding what Aquinas had been or what he had done historically by elevating independent reason (5:130). His first public reference to Saint Thomas in 1902 was contemptuous of his Aristotelian definition of man: a "gray bird" of typifying generalization that compared ill with the "perspective" of life in the actual individual (1:14). Otherwise, during his formative years as a philosopher, Ortega ignored scholasticism as unworthy of comment. Not until it caught attention again in the 1920s as French "Thomism" claiming to be philosophy did he reassert: "The life of man and the course of history are things more serious and more tragic than all of that" (3:566).

Unamuno and Spanish "Existentialism"

Disagreeing with Unamuno's romanticism, Ortega nevertheless had learned from him some of the negative, "tragic" side of a way of thinking about life that was later called existentialism. Over the years from 1906 to 1912, Unamuno carried on an intimate correspondence (R 5), now mostly published, that undoubtedly was meant for the spiritual and intellectual guidance of young Ortega, even as it made him more aware of their essential and permanent differences as well as their agreement on liberalism and individualism. "Unamuno's spirit is too turbulent and drags along in its dizzy current some things of gold and many others useless and unhealthy," he remarked in 1908. He had responded to Unamuno's idea of life as "desperation" in 1907 by observing that such life as "a metaphysical existential problem" was both true and false. Little of what Unamuno said was specifically philosophical, although there were "existential" elements with respect to Christianity and mysticism. Ortega adopted some of his elder's ideas and terminology, in *¡Adentro!* (1900), which he later turned into his own idea of individual "withdrawal" (as *ensimismamiento;* see 2:459)—an existential "turning inward."

Already in 1907, Ortega raised the issue of idealism or realism and criticized Unamuno's understanding of *Don Quixote*.[27] Unamuno frankly disliked science and things German. The positions that the younger man then took successively in public against Unamuno in favor of Europeanization and science are well known. When they briefly resumed an exchange in 1919, some of Unamuno's views on history were too present-minded for the taste of the other, but he was pleased that Ortega admitted that "you read me and above all reread me."

After Unamuno's death in 1936, Ortega honored him as "a giant in his virtues and vices," essentially a "poet" who spurned "all doctrine." More than Heidegger, he had spent his life in a *meditatio mortis*—fascinated with death (6:261–62). Ortega rejected such morbidity in existentialism.

Krausism and External Influences

The specifically national, Spanish background in philosophy of which Ortega was aware had included very little intermixture with Germany, with whom contact had been broken off since the Counter-Reformation (8:21). By the 1860s and 1870s, however, some Spaniards had responded to a peculiar brand of German thought called Krausismo, although their Krause had no clear comprehension of any of the great German philosophers—Kant, Hegel, or the Romantics. Still alive in his youth and surviving weakly past 1900, the Krausist movement probably helped arouse his interest in German thought.[28] The Spanish Krausistas were, he said, "excellent people, but wretched musicians" (8:21). Prior to his time, in the 1870s, they had tried to subject Spanish minds and hearts to a "Germanic discipline," only to be thwarted by the fanatic nationalistic jealousy of Spanish Catholicism toward everything for-

27. See supplemental note 27, chap. 2.
28. On Krausism, see Marías, *Circumstance and Vocation,* 107–13, 175–82.

eign or non-religious (1:212). If Ortega's few references do not make clear whether Krausism had direct influence on his own philosophical formation, perhaps it added to his resentment of the Jesuit restrictions on exploring German thought for himself—first Nietzsche, then Hegel and the Romantics, finally Kant.

Customarily, he noted, Spaniards took their philosophy from outside, but with about as much discrimination as they bought things in a store (1:167). In Juan Valera he encountered a kind of Spanish positivism of no great depth or authenticity that aided, if it did not inspire, his interest in Renan and Taine. Besides liberalism and Europeanization, he drew from Joaquín Costa his first exposure to German romantic historicism (1:166–67), which he eventually developed in a more contemporary form related to historical reason and to an etymological method that probably owed something initially to Cejador. Altogether, he judged, the era in Spain since 1874 was philosophically a mishmash, leaving a crisis of mental poverty and "shipwreck" for his generation's heritage. Spanish youth felt they were drowning and so had grasped at such straws as the then-fashionable international Nietzscheanism.

CONTEMPORARY INTERNATIONAL INFLUENCES

Of other nations' foreign philosophical influences on his country, Ortega remarked that when he was twenty (in 1903) "Spain was enormously influenced by ideas and forms from France. Add to this a slight influence of certain things English. From Germany little more than nothing" (8:21)—notably, Krausism and Nietzsche. Looking back from the 1950s, he recalled that in reality Germany had been the "visceral center" of Western philosophy since the nineteenth century, France its "epicenter," and England "virtually nothing." However, "there were things begun or brought to perfection outside Germany—American pragmatism as an example of the first; [British] mathematical logic of the second," although their "decisive effect," "historical force," and "full reality" came only when they were "integrated into German thought."[29]

Ortega explained what had been "the structure or anatomy of 'philosophical' reality between 1900 and 1915"—the span of a half-generation when he had become a philosopher. It was an "interregnum" between a declining neo-Kantianism and the rising Husserlian phenomenology. Then, during Dilthey's long "latency," he recalled a "layer" of "great solitary facts of thought whose real and precise historical role" he meant to treat after giving some background information on positivism (like the one above). Those "solitary facts" were Sigmund Freud, Bertrand Russell, Henri Bergson, and

29. Ortega, "Medio siglo," 5–6, 15–16.

William James, and their works, respectively: *The Interpretation of Dreams* (1900), *The Principles of Mathematics* (1903), *Creative Evolution* (1907), and *Pragmatism* (1907).

About Ortega himself, the connection with Germany (after he went there for postgraduate studies in 1905) has been the more renowned and better documented, the French has been studied but incompletely, and the English and American hardly noticed at all. Britain's impact was indeed scant and late (except for Russell's logical positivism) while, of his two primary sources, France came first (with positivism), then Germany (with heavy idealist emphasis), then North America, then France again, but German influence was always paramount, if not most basic.

There were some other sources about which Ortega was very quiet. Most important was James's pragmatism, but also important was Croce's historicism. What effect they had on Ortega was unknown in his lifetime, however, and has yet to be demonstrated here.

France and Positivism

If the Latin, Mediterranean side of Ortega's mind had received very little philosophical nourishment from his native Spain, he admitted having received "much, much from the French," an influence to which scholars generally have given short shrift compared to the German orientation that he acknowledged so emphatically in the "Preface for Germans."[30] The great impact on Spain of "ideas and forms from France" he had always regarded as beneficial for the period from 1700 to 1900 (1:207; 8:21–22). He himself had plunged so deeply into the sea of French culture that he felt his feet touch bottom—a thorough immersing that convinced him, however, that "Spain could no longer nourish herself from France" (8:24). He himself later returned to France, however, again and again.

Influenced perhaps by the examples of Valera and Costa (1:159), as a youth Ortega had devoured Gallic sources, especially "positivists" such as Renan and Taine, and in his maturity during the 1920s and early 1930s he returned to feast again, this time with the master of positivism, Comte, and his master, Saint-Simon, as well as Maistre and the traditionalists, Guizot and the "doctrinaire liberals," and finally Tocqueville in the 1940s. His "Prologue to the French" strongly implies that the positivist strains of thought had been of greater consequence in his development (4:126, 137) than all others, including Ballanche and Cousin (4:122–24). Naturally his emphasis

---

30. For the French influence on Ortega's Spain, see Marías, *Circumstance and Vocation*, 174–75 and 183–87 on Ortega himself, especially for Chateaubriand, Barrès, and Renan. French scholars on Ortega have not investigated all the probable connections.

was on matters political (European and French) and social, rather than philosophical as such, so that even Descartes, whom he studied in depth in later years, was related ahead to a "demagogic" political rationalism that had ended finally in revolution—a view that repeated Comte and Maistre, even Donoso Cortés (4:134–35). Definitely, there *was* a positivist side to Ortega.

To overlook the influence of the quasi positivists, Renan and Taine, is to ignore a substantial part of Ortega's youthful formation, although he was to outgrow them in a few years. Nevertheless, their influence was more literary and historical than philosophical. Taine's "milieu" served to confirm his idea of "circumstance," if indeed it did not have a *suggestive* effect. To inspire his youthful pride and hope of national recovery and progress, he found "Renan—always Renan!" (1:92).

It was not so much positivism as the sway of Germanic influence ("Germanismo") over Latin culture that he observed transforming France intellectually by the early twentieth century. "Nowadays [1911] philosophy is not a kind of rhetoric, as in the idyllic times of Cousin and Renan, but reflection on the complex methodology of the sciences: only M. Bergson keeps up the wisdom of the old order by expounding a *demi-mondaine* philosophy before a numerous audience" (1:207). From Renan and Taine, Ortega had evidently drawn the conclusion that German thought (Kant and Hegel) and English thought had since the eighteenth century been in ascendancy over a declining French culture, which still retained artistic and literary vitality. He deemed the cultural influence of French classicism a thing of the past, however, largely of the seventeenth century, with its language, absolutism, Catholicism, and geometric conceptions (1:548–49). After the Enlightenment, he deemed French romanticism and neo-romanticism as basically conservative and as ending in *fin de siècle* "decadence" (1:550–51), which even Bergson had not been able to overcome. Probably the "decadents" had influence on Ortega's pessimism about progress, the corruption of politics, the banality of the bourgeoisie, and the crisis of modern civilization and culture, even as exemplary *beatería* of culture. Except for "M. Homais" from Flaubert, however, the effect was more diffuse than specific.[31]

Bergson: Vitalism and Intuition

It was to Henri Bergson, great "solitary" genius, the most renowned vitalist in Europe, and to his *Creative Evolution* that Ortega surely owed at least secondary inspiration for his basic idea of life as fundamental but "fluid" reality. His earliest public reference to Bergson was in 1910, as merely one of

31. There are some striking parallels between Ortega and the "decadents" on history, modernity, and culture as "religion" and "faith." See Eric C. Hansen, *Disaffection and Decadence* (Washington, D.C.: University Press of America, 1982).

the "great thinkers" (1:395). But he had cited him, along with James, Russell, Dilthey, Husserl, and Trendelenburg, in some notes of 1908–1909 (R 76). In 1916, when he adverted to Bergson's "*je profonde*" in *El Espectador* (2:84), he had talked with him when the latter vacationed in Spain. Bergson was impressed with Spanish "intellectual independence" (R 77). Although he found in Bergson one of the key "solitary" thinkers who had influenced him in his youth, Ortega was by that time rather critical of the French philosopher.[32]

He had given a critique of Bergson as a neo-romantic philosopher in some lectures in 1912–1913, in which he had identified "Bergsonism" with a so-called philosophy of life or vitalism that dealt with the problems of "knowing and living" (R 76). For Bergson, "to know is to live problems, not to think them." But Ortega had little sympathy with those who shout "Life" against science and philosophy. Nevertheless, he found some value and meaning in that vitalism. It "coincides with epochs of crisis" as a "natural expression" of "doctrinal deficiency" and uncertainty. "In one of those epochs we find ourselves. . . ." For himself, Ortega saw in "life" a "new theory" promising growth and maturity in science, morality, and art, but Bergson had not really gotten down to life-reality.

Ortega was suspicious of Bergson's work as too literary, as full of "gratuitous affirmations and rotund negations," written for dilettantes and for public applause. From a "scientific point of view," most of it was valueless. "Only his first book, *Time and Free Will* (*Essai sur les données immediates de la conscience*, 1889) had made a positive contribution to philosophy, and its ideas were simply repeated attractively but tiresomely—in *Creative Evolution* (1907), which he later designated for its influence on him. They were a "bit naive" who deemed Bergson one of the greatest philosophers of all time. "Not a single motif has Bergson brought to philosophy for the first time" (R 76). Later he saw in him an "intellectualism," despite contrary claims (R 50).[33]

Much later Ortega reevaluated Bergson as a "thinker of genius," a "mar-

32. Ortega, "Medio siglo," 14–15. On Bergson, Marías seemed to deny any dependence, despite noting some patent similarities: *Circumstance and Vocation*, 79 (life philosophy), cf. 83 ("viewpoint") and 84 (knowing an object by circling around it or getting inside it). Bergson's *Creative Evolution* (1907) expressed the idea that *life* is the "unique reality." This book, *L'Evolution créatrice* (Paris: Alcan) in the 1911 edition, is still in Ortega's library, and is well marked up, although the marginal notations are mostly illegible, having been cut off in part, so that we are deprived of his valuable opinions from that time. Also see Alain Guy, "Ortega y Bergson," *Revista de Filosofía* 7 (1984): 7–9; Juana Sánchez-Venegas, "Orígen común y desarrolo divergente en Bergson y en Ortega," *Pensamiento* 41 (1985): 57–67.

33. Compare with James, *Pluralistic Universe* (1977), chap. 6, on Bergson's "intellectualism"; Ortega was probably echoing James's critical reference to Bergson's "kinetoscopic camera" shots of life, when he criticized Bergson's "cinematic" view of reality, which he found also in Einstein (2:242n).

velous thinker" (5:451; 9:292), whom we must acknowledge as "right today on so many points" (6:32–33 n. 1). However, he never came to agree with Bergson's *kind* of vitalism. This he firmly rejected in 1924 as too intuitive, a "transrational" form of irrationalism (3:272) that rejected reason, analysis, and "conceptual thinking" to make "living," or life, itself a "way of knowing." More than once he compared Bergson to Plotinus as starting with philosophy but as ending with something else—with a mysticism that was of no use to a rational, philosophical mind (5:451, 453; 7:338, 431). Bergson's later work, *Two Sources of Morality and Religion* (1932), seemed to him essentially a "sociological" treatise, but nevertheless acute thinking (7:81, 213).

Clearly, what he found compatible in Bergson was not the general system but only some specific concepts and striking phrases, notably the idea of *l'être en se faisant,* which was similar to his own "man makes himself" (*hacerse*), except that the latter had the added "radical difference" of meaning not just passively "becoming" but actively, purposefully *making* oneself (6:32–33 n. 1) in and out of history. Once he praised Bergson for the notion that one's place in his generation is a "modifiable fatality" (7:494). In *What Is Philosophy?* (1930), Ortega rather generously saw Bergson's "admirable" appeal to "common sense" against the "reason of physics" as equivalent to "what I have formerly called 'vital reason,' a reason according to which no few objects are rational that to the old *raison,* or conceptual reason or pure reason, are in effect irrational" (7:327). Years later he credited Bergson with being almost the only one, besides himself, who did not regard primitive man as simply illogical in his thought processes (7:464). Although not by *historical* insight, Bergson anticipated here the viewpoint of Ortega's historical reason, for example, by implying "sequential" thinking (R 37).

All of this adds up to no very extensive or fundamental dependence by Ortega on the ideas or "system" of Bergson, despite notable coincidences in regard to ratiovitalism, vital reason and historical reason. These areas of agreement were marginal compared to basic differences between Bergson's supra-rational and intuitive processes of knowing and Ortega's ratiovitalism, which he characterized as another (newer) form of reason, but not that of "antihistorical" rationalism (3:159, 277). Of course, he did not reject the role of intuition in human knowledge; he simply did not think that a philosophy could be built up out of it alone, and he found Bergson's idea "confused" (R 50). In contrast, perhaps Husserl's doctrine of intuition might have opened up a new epoch in philosophy (1:335). His own discovery (*aletheia*) of human life (or self and circumstance) as the basic reality was intuitive, and his own philosophy was developed rationally from that original intuition (6:349). Moreover, the first step in Ortega's historiological method was intuitive (4:530). On balance, it seems likely that he derived from Bergson's *élan vital* some initial clues and encouragement for his own vitalism in 1913, and, from that very unhistorical philosopher, some intimations compatible with his reflections on fluid time, becoming, and historicity in human reality as apt concerns of philosophy (R 36).

Comtism and Social Science

Only in the positivism of Auguste Comte and in the accompanying Realism and Impressionism in art and letters, did young Ortega see a valiant but unsuccessful attempt to return to the "substantial" (1:552). Of course, his vitalism of 1913 owed something to Bergson, but he chose Germany, with its scientific culture, over France after 1905 and for the next fifteen years or so. Not until he had outgrown German "culturalism" during World War I and realized that not only postwar Germany but all Europe was as sick with crisis as Spain itself, did he turn to seek inspiration again from the French past—afresh from Comte. Then he concluded that his own basic philosophical doctrine of "radical positivism" had been anticipated by Comte, who had discerned "the substantial," historical basis of life-reality, at least in part. Comte was a primary source of his idea of "historical crisis" and of his interdisciplinary efforts, but also of his elitism and perhaps of his politics too. Belatedly he concluded that Comte had had a great but very misunderstood ("unknown") philosophy (8:277–78), that he was perhaps the only real philosopher between 1830 and 1860.[34]

French influence was not as great on Ortega's philosophy as it was on his ideas about history and the social sciences. That was certainly the case with Tocqueville as well as with Comte. Not until the 1940s did Ortega study Tocqueville closely, with results for his methods ("pragmatism") and his view of America (this will be discussed in another volume). Briefly, he found his sociology too much influenced by abstract rationalistic concepts and insufficiently historical.

Germany and Idealism

Before 1914, Ortega sought to exchange Spain's dependence on decadent Paris for "an introduction to the essential life" of Germany. He was not interested in the average German's Protestantism, poverty of intuition, liter-

34. Curiously—since Ortega urged study of Comte by Marías, who found both "life" and "milieu" present in Comte as "correlatives" (in *Cours de philosophie positive*, 3:295–96)—the disciple did not see much Comtian influence on his master (*Circumstance and Vocation*, 183–85, 353–58). Ortega's interest in Comte has been overlooked even by French scholars; see Ortega, "Medio siglo," 11–12. Virtually all of Comte's works are in Ortega's library, and the last two volumes of the *Cours de philosophie positive* (two sets of 6 volumes; Paris, 1864 and 1908) are well marked up.

ary and artistic insensitivity, nor political obtuseness, nor even German culture in an uncritical way, but in German *science* instead (1:208–10)—and especially German philosophy.

The story of Ortega and Germany has been told often enough by Ortega himself, by his biographer Niedermayer, and by Orringer's and other scholars' accounts,[35] so it need not be repeated with full factual and chronological information. What he expected to gain from German philosophy, and what he actually derived from it in his "thirty years of Germanism" (8:25), are our chief concern. That is too big a question, however, to take as background, and so requires separate treatment of the philosophers and schools that he mentioned or implied in the remarkably self-revealing "Preface for Germans" (1934) for *Modern Theme*. Not just Nietzsche's iconoclasm but all German *idealism,* in general and particular, was therein rejected (8:40–41). He mentioned Kant's idealism, Cohen's neo-Kantianism, Husserl's transcendental phenomenology, Hegel's romantic historicism, Heidegger's existentialism, and even Dilthey's "philosophy of life." Their main influences on Ortega's emerging philosophy actually came in that order. Of course, idealism aside, they all had much influence on him. Here we can merely identify the general German impact on his philosophical formation as detailed mainly in the "Preface" and, except for Nietzsche, leave the others till later.

Nietzsche: "Pragmatism," Historicism, and Vitalism

Although he twice cited Nietzsche in his autobiographical "Preface for Germans" (1934), Ortega left no hint there that he owed any part of his intellectual formation to him. He dismissed his pre-pragmatic equation of will with truth and of life with fiction (8:38). In Nietzsche, however, were the roots for his mature historical definition of man in "History as a System" and of his effort to "historicize" everything (including pragmatism and phenomenology in philosophy). Also in his earlier critique of Nietzsche first became visible his native inclination to a "philosophy of life," or vitalism—before he had made serious study of pragmatism or phenomenology. Clearly Nietzsche had first confirmed both of those ingrained characteristics that

35. For the German influences on Ortega, see P. Bruno Ibeas, "La filosofía de Ortega y Gasset." Best to date on his library of personally "annotated" German books is Orringer's *Fuentes germánicas,* on Cohen, Natorp, and Simmel, and lesser neglected or overlooked parallels and sources; idem, *Nuevas fuentes germánicas de ¿Qué es Filosofía? de Ortega* (Madrid: Consejo Superior de Investigaciones Científicas, Instituto de Filosofía Luis Vives, 1984), treats Scheler, Heidegger, Hartmann, Husserl, and Dilthey. General treatments are Marías, *Circumstance and Vocation,* 187–205, on Ortega's "German experience" and "Germanism"; Miguel Ortega, *Mi padre,* 46 and (later) 121–23; and Robert McClintock, *Man and His Circumstances: Ortega as Educator,* 39–58. Major studies of Ortega and Husserl and Heidegger are covered later.

identify Ortega's thought, although he was certainly not the first nor the only source.[36]

The very first lesson he had drawn publicly in reassessing Nietzsche in 1907 was to see "the only plausible interpretation" of "Superman" as the progressive improvement, or surpassing, of man (1:74). With the support of Simmel's study, he then expanded on this new moral and historical view of man as superman. He saw Nietzsche's main effort as having been a new philosophical view of man, as necessarily historical, and as involving a new morality, too (1:92–93). "The definition of man, the true and unique problem of ethics, is the motor of historical variations." In contrast to the generally extensive and quantitative definition of humanity in terms of the common and the social (in socialism, for example), Nietzsche had opted for an intensive and qualitative definition that settled on outstanding individuals as being or creating the norms of value and culture, not as isolated from, but as inspiring, the masses at every stage of history. Gifted individuals represented objectified, ever-advancing stages, or degrees, in "the type Man," or Humanity, and in the living ideal of free human organization. "This ideal is Superman" (1:94). This idea of life is progressive, historical. "For Nietzsche to live is *to live more,* or to put it another way, life is the name we give to a series of progressive qualities, to the instinct of growth, of perduring, of capitalization of forces, or power. The principle of life, the will of life, is 'Will to Power'" (1:94).

Ortega insisted in 1934 that he "did not reach the idea of life as the fundamental reality, as the pure event of man's struggle with his circumstances, by way of positive intimations from anyone. I was directed to it by the very problems that confronted philosophy" (8:47). He found a contradiction in the idea of life, or vitalism, in Nietzsche, who sometimes thought life was an "instrument of knowing," or intellectual experience, and sometimes that knowledge was "an instrument of life." Nietzsche was a mere "impressionist in metaphysics" (R 39).

Although he finally concluded that Nietzsche's idea of life was worth little intellectually (R 39),[37] Ortega kept on quoting Nietzsche's burning words or

36. See supplemental note 36, chap. 2.

37. On Reel 39 (Ortega archive, Library of Congress), some parts of which are dated 1923 but others seem much earlier, Ortega criticized Nietzsche's "hostility to everything received" as "false, wicked, perverse." Like "all of us," he was "a devaluer" of things traditionally seen as good: "Baudelaire and his Black Venus." He also found the "feminism" of ideas like "eternal return" contradicted by the grossly masculine style of this "German madman" whose emotionalism offered "nothing concrete" for use. In his library Ortega had three sets of Nietzsche's *Werke,* one of 11 volumes, at least ten other individual works of his, and about twenty studies on Nietzsche—some marked up, some not—but few from his own formative period predating 1920: only *Human, too Human!* and *Will to Power* in German and French.

phrases—many times not for substance but only for effect, for the "sparks" that fly from his iconoclastic blasts (8:307). Ortega especially liked to repeat him on "life." In 1916, when he began to develop his perspectivist philosophy of life, he cited Nietzsche's *Genealogies* on "perspectivist seeing" and "knowing" (R 54). Later he denied that his own "perspectivism" and ratiovitalism had anything in common with "will to power," but he hailed Nietzsche as a prophet of genius who had first intuited the immanent values of life that later generations had to rediscover in their own common sensibility (3:192). "Notwithstanding his pathetic gesturing, Nietzsche manages to seduce us when he invites us to dance in honor of life and of every instance of life" (2:89).

That "supreme seer" had found one of the most fruitful vitalistic ideas that Ortega inherited: "the distinction between ascendant life and descendent life, between life achieved and life wasted" (3:190). The first of these signified to Ortega optimism and openness to one's destiny; the latter, the very opposite. He liked to repeat Nietzsche's "That is life? Good, come again" (3:179; 8:249), not necessarily for any cyclic or regenerative implications but for its optimism. His phrase "living more" (4:477) caught the essence of mankind's life lived historically in successively new and different forms, and implied a historicist definition of man.

Although Ortega incurred debts for vitalism and historicism, he soon came to reject as false to the core Nietzsche's scintillating imperative, "Live dangerously" (1:351). It was a product of *fin de siècle* security and pretension, or playacting, like his and Burckhardt's "strong man," or superman, of the Renaissance (5:76, 303; 8:307). " . . . Despite his genius, Nietzsche did not realize that the very substance of our life is danger, and that, therefore, it becomes rather affected and overdone to propose as something new, added, and original that we seek and hoard up danger" (7:91). Twenty years later, however, he came to see "Renaissance man" (like Machiavelli's Cesare Borgia) as an exemplification of acute historical crisis, when life is indeed more dangerous than usual.

Although he never acknowledged the debt, it is probable that Ortega was initially tempted by Nietzsche to reject the whole rationalistic tradition of the past 500 years, to strike boldly out on his own. He noted in the 1920s that Nietzsche was hostile to everything received or traditional, as if it were "false, wicked, perverse." Yet "this anti-traditionalism is characteristic of us all" (R 39). Eventually, in *Origin of Philosophy* and in *Leibniz*, he tried to reexamine critically the whole philosophical tradition of the past 2,500 years, especially its pre-Socratic origins and Cartesian rebirth with respect to crisis. He regarded *The Tragic Philosophy of the Greeks* as a "splendid essay," but he maintained that Nietzsche "did not know how to see things clearly in their fundamental structure," and "as the last romantic, he did not know how to be truthful either" (8:307; compare 7:487).

Among the literary and philosophical themes that he dreamed about on summer vacations, Ortega contemplated one entitled "Quixote and Nietzsche." The parallels were obvious. "Don Quixote is a madman: but [seen from within] his madness has a transcendent content." Similarly, Nietzsche: "Genius and heroism are madness" (R 43). Citing an oral tradition, Ortega related that Nietzsche had roused from madness to observe: "The Spaniards. The Spaniards: Those men wanted to be too much" (2:557; 8:58). Of his style and thought, he noted in 1923, Nietzsche "is a mad German. He has no delicacy, no finesse, nor is he very intelligent." His philosophizing was "musical"—an "expression of the emotions." The famous "will to power" finally reduces to "I want to 'be on top'" (R 39).

In his final, mature assessment of Nietzsche in the 1940s, Ortega was most unflattering. If Nietzsche was a prophetic genius, he was a flawed genius for philosophy, since he walked "a tightrope with ideas." "Nietzsche never came to know either what tragedy was or what philosophy was. He entered into both subjects like a maniac . . ." (8:307), without opening his eyes to see what reality was. If Nietzsche to some degree anticipated the "I" (or self) for Ortega, Dilthey and Husserl were his predecessors in "seeing" circumstance. Perhaps it is too much to affirm that the egotism of Ortega's youthful Nietzscheanism, or Barrès' Nietzschean *culte de moi,* was a source of the *yo* half of his basic equation of reality, *yo y circunstancia.* Nevertheless, in the year (1914) he enunciated it, he also cited Nietzsche in *Yo y Mi Yo* as having come up with a distinction between saying and doing, thinking and being, that "is exactly the same as between *thing and I*" (6:253; compare 3:335).

Ortega might have been more grateful and generous as a critic. Clearly he owed part of his foundation to Nietzsche, but he was also indebted to other German philosophers. He went to Germany seeking a "system," only part of which was the "I"—much transformed. In 1907 he acknowledged that "My German education has consisted precisely in overcoming my unconscious *self,* my uncultivated *self,*" by a *new* "personal self."[38]

"Rebirth": Neo-Kantianism, Dilthey, Husserl

After 1870 scientistic materialism and positivism had come to dominate to such an extent, claimed Ortega, that no genuine philosophy any longer existed in Europe (8:30). Soon Nietzsche had stimulated a new generation, but he was hardly a philosopher. Hence, the only recourse was to go "back to school" to learn again the classical systems of philosophy (8:221). The resulting neo-Kantianism, neo-Hegelianism, and neo-Fichteanism were, to his judgment, largely anachronistic and "inauthentic" philosophy, like all "neo" movements (3:253; 6:306; 8:28)—they were old clothes on new bodies. In

38. Ortega, *Cartas,* 556, 616, 635.

contrast to Kant and his strict followers, however, Rickert at least had oriented himself on "historical science" instead of physics or biology. After 1900 the neo-Kantians, Husserl, and Dilthey had corrected, filled, and widened the narrow vision and shrunken world of positivist man (4:508–10), restoring value, being, and essence in a veritable rebirth of philosophy. In the long run, the radical cause of such "great historical changes" was, in Ortega's judgment, "a simple mutation in man's mental apparatus that makes it gather in reflections previously unnoticed" (4:520). It accompanied a great shift in the dominant "worldview." Until after his *Meditations on Quixote* (1914), Ortega's reciprocal "give and take" relation to Germans was all "take."[39] Eagerly, enthusiastically, he had gone to Germany as a "pure Celtiberian flame," a fierce young "hawk" ravenous for something "meaty" in philosophy, culture, and science to seize, swallow whole, and carry back home to digest (8:20, 24–26). "Spain needed Germany," which also satisfied his own keen appetite for learning. Having found Spain intellectually barren, and now French culture virtually played out, he went to Germany with the belief that Spain could benefit from cross-fertilization with a different national culture. The fruit of that miscegenation in his own thought can be seen in his later reflections on Kantianism as a typical German "philosophy of the self" contrasted to a naturally Spanish philosophy of worldly "circumstance." In 1934 he boasted that, almost alone in the past fifteen years, he had brought to Spain and South America an enthusiasm for German ideas (7:22, 25–26). Two years earlier, he had acknowledged that he was "enormously indebted to German philosophy," and he felt he had repaid the debt by promoting the "treasure" of German thought widely among Hispanics (4:404n).

Although "shocked" at the violence and the barbaric changes brought about by Hitler's domination in 1934 and 1935, Ortega still admitted that his youthful years in Germany had been "a decisive stage" of "permanent importance" in his formation as thinker (5:184–85). Nevertheless, having seen firsthand "the rebellion of the masses" and the triumph of the "mass man" in Nazi Germany, he refused to publish his new "Preface for Germans," disowned Heidegger, and turned his back on Germany until after its defeat and ruin, when he returned (in 1949 and 1951) to repay the debt he owed for his intellectual formation. Now he encouraged Germans to rise from the ashes and to begin again, not in Heidegger's spirit of pessimism but with a

39. On the German content of Ortega's thought, see Max Rychner, "Ortega deutsch," *Arachne* (1957): 144–53; Aurelio Fuentes y Rojo, "Ortega y Gasset and der deutsche Geist," *Göttinger Universitätzeitung,* no. 21 (1949): 8–10; Alain Guy, "Ortega y Gasset et la pensée germanique," *Ibero-romania* 2:3 (197?): 197–215; Carlos Talamas, "Ortega y el pensamiento alemán," *Alcala,* no. 79–80 (1955): 4–5; Marías, *Circumstance and Vocation,* 187–205; and McClintock, *Ortega as Educator,* 39–58.

Mediterranean optimism. To offset an exaggerated "culturalism" and idealism, Germans too needed cross-fertilizing—from Spain's Latin realism.

Britain and Empiricism

In contrast to the French "prologue," his "Epilogue for the English," written for the 1937 translation of *Revolt of the Masses,* focused on the approach of World War II, promoted European union, praised British liberalism, individualism, and the Commonwealth of Nations, and criticized pacifism and mere internationalism. He said not a word about British philosophy. When he had discussed Mill's and Spencer's individualism and liberalism for France (4:126–28), he encouraged England's resistance to "totalitarianism," since that stalwart nation was still Europe's best hope (4:137). In philosophy, then, Britain hardly influenced young Ortega—except for Bertrand Russell and Alfred North Whitehead, and perhaps David Hume—because he studied Locke and Bacon only later.

There is no evidence of deep or immediate familiarity in Ortega's references prior to 1914 to past British philosophers (Bacon, Locke, Hume, Bentham, and Mill) whose empiricism and utilitarianism he deemed more vice than virtue, even in things economic and political (1:315, 549; 2:197–98; 3:341–42). Accordingly, we can rule them out as having had any important influence on the *Meditations on Quixote* (1914), or on its basic epistemology and ontology that he later called "radical empiricism," or "radical positivism." Having learned his Newton through Marburg and Kant, he regarded British philosophy as a "frigid moral climate," until well after he had clearly grasped the basically "empirical" character of his own residual positivism.

Except for Mill (12:466–67) and Darwin, it seems that Ortega first took British thought—Locke's empiricism and Hume's skepticism—in the company of Kant and through Husserl (12:417, 450–51, 458–60). For him, their epistemology was more intellectualist than Dilthey's or Brentano's positivistic empiricism (6:186–87). In their influence on continental "positivism" from the eighteenth-century French materialists through Comte (7:64), he saw their thought as essentially "not a philosophy, but a series of very acute objections to all philosophy" (8:220 and n). "Few things seem less like philosophy than the books of [John] Stuart Mill"; they seemed a "renunciation" of philosophy. Not until the 1940s do we find him reading Locke directly (compare 12:459; 5:538–40). Similarly, he did not read Bacon carefully until late in life (9:539)—and liked him (R 39). Clearly, Ortega came to his own basic empiricism, or neo-positivism, not mainly through British thinkers; it was William James who fitted his instinctive "Mediterranean" reaction to German idealism. British thinkers interested him more as he expanded his study of empiricism through the 1920s in connection with James. Hume's shift from philosophical empiricism to history intrigued him, especially as relatable to historiology and modeling.[40]

It is hard to know just what in Russell's *Principles of Mathematics* (1903), with its mathematical logic, then most appealed to Ortega philosophically. He saw it as "representative of the more normal currents of triumphant mathematics," and he quoted Russell (p. 158): "Quantity in fact, though philosophers appear still to regard it as very essential to mathematics, does not occur in pure mathematics, and does not occur in many cases at present amenable to mathematical treatment" (R 76). In this instance, Ortega used that argument against Cohen's quantification of "existence."

In 1909, Ortega cited Russell (with Whitehead and Poincaré) on logic and intuition (R 76), and later Russell's "logical positivism" surely interested him.[41] However, he *reacted* to Russell and Whitehead as continuing the old physics-dominated philosophy of positivism. Their philosophy represented an "extramural physics," a sort of "metaphysics" in the literal sense of a physics "beyond physics" (7:317). Nevertheless, Russell initially helped legitimize James for Ortega, who eventually took from Russell ideas on quantification, constants, and variables.

North America and Pragmatism

When he was young, Ortega mentioned the United States in regard to philosophy only on rare occasions to express his contempt for its brash pragmatism, which had attracted some attention in Spain after 1898. As suggested previously, his negative attitude seemed intended to divert attention from his own secretly pragmatist principles in metaphysics. But it is significant that he almost always coupled criticism of the formal crudity of pragmatism with praise of one or another of its naive insights into truth or reality. His camouflage was so effective that no one, including the few Argentine critics of his *Modern Theme,* suspected the depth or extent of James's influence on him. That was revealed only after 1980—from an unfinished essay.[42]

40. See supplemental note 40, chap. 2.

41. Ortega, "Medio siglo," 14. Russell's *Principles of Mathematics* (1903) is not now in Ortega's library, not even in translation, but he had eleven of his books, several without any date of publication but others all from the 1920s through the 1940s in Spanish or French translations. If not on "mathematical logic," he differed with the "linguistic positivism" of the early twentieth century, its rejecting any "true" sense of words, for he insisted on an "authentic" *original* sense (or meaning) related to a life situation in *history* (9:637). J. B. Trend, "Boceto de Memorias," *Sur,* no. 24 (July–August 1956): 199. Ortega was thus well aware of Russell, but he did not find himself in the copy of Russell's *Outline of Philosophy* (1927) that he bought.

42. See supplemental note 42, chap. 2.

After a trip to Aspen in 1949, Ortega began an account of the past half-century of philosophy, told in "autobiographical" terms of "historical reason." Among the few new things that were begun outside Germany in philosophy was "American pragmatism," but it had not had full effect and *vis historica* until Germans had "integrated" it into their own philosophy. He acknowledged that James's *Pragmatism* (1907) and individual works by Freud, Bergson, and Russell had been formative influences for him.[43]

Breaking off abruptly, he left us to wonder precisely what James had contributed to his own formation. It is probably significant that in other works both Russell and Bergson were in part advocates of James. Bergson later wrote an enthusiastic preface for a 1911 French edition of *Pragmatisme* that Ortega read, and Russell had announced in 1910 that pragmatism was "a genuinely new philosophy" embodying "the prevailing temper of the age." Like Russell, Ortega preferred James's "radical empiricism" to his "pragmatism." In fact, careful study and comparison will show that his own "radical positivism" was essentially James's "radical empiricism" as a "new way of thinking" metaphysically. This proposition will have to be demonstrated in later chapters, of course, but James thus helped him in the most basic way to get started as a philosopher. He could relate some of James's views backward to moderate or reinforce Nietzsche[44] and Bergson on "life" and forward to Husserl and Dilthey to counter their transcendental idealism with the "new realism."

43. Ortega, "Medio siglo," 5–6, 14, 15–16. Any consideration of Freud and Ortega is put off for another volume, but a copy of *Die Traumdeutung* (3d ed.; Leipzig: Deutige, 1911) was in Ortega's library and was well marked up. James's *Pragmatism* (1907) was another matter; see my chap. 4.

44. Bertrand Russell, *Philosophical Essays* (New York: Longmans, Green, 1910), 87, 118, 120 (Bergson as "ally"), 127; idem, *Philosophy* (New York: Norton, 1927), chaps. 20, 26, 32. His ideas of "neutral monism," duality of mind and matter, and reality as "pluralism" of "events" were much indebted to James and are very like Ortega's; Russell agreed with James on empiricism, pluralism, compresence, working hypothesis, and consciousness as "not an entity." Before he died, James read Halévy's *Nietzsche* and bought two of Nietzsche's books, according to Gay W. Allen, *William James: A Biography* (New York: Viking, 1967), 483, who shows that Nietzsche and he were very comparable on life and will. Jacques Barzun, *Darwin, Marx, and Wagner,* 2d ed. (New York: Doubleday, 1958), 305, described Nietzsche as a pragmatist and a Freudian ahead of his time.

Chapter 3

BEGINNINGS

General, National, and Personal
(1904–1916)

L ooking back on the history of philosophy from the dark hiatus of 1943, Ortega reflected that philosophical "production" had suffered "displacement" in about 1840 by literature, politics, and the sciences, but about 1910 had begun a "return" that World War I had cut off, and had resumed after 1920 (R 36). It is noteworthy that he began his own authentic philosophizing in 1909–1910 and 1913–1914 and that his chief work came out in 1923. Prior to 1910 he had made an embarrassing but instructive faux pas with his Ph.D. thesis (1904) before going to Germany for postgraduate study, for depth and enrichment (1905 to 1911).[1]

Out of a varied background that was more international than national and as historical as it was contemporary, young Ortega had begun to try to philosophize around 1902–1903. In his first published essay, a Nietzschean-French mélange on literary criticism in 1902, he had stressed "life," "perspective," and "individuality" (1:14), all of which principles later became cornerstones of his philosophy. Evidently it was not Unamuno's but Maeztu's urging that persuaded him to go for a degree in philosophy instead of literature or law.[2] What started as a mere career soon turned into a lifelong "vocation" or "destiny." His first formal effort (in his thesis) was shallow and read like an essay in history, but it was indicative of the path he was to follow stubbornly for a half-century of hard endeavor in philosophy. It took

---

1. Ortega said he went there in 1905 seeking a "system"; by 1907 he realized that his "German education" had resulted in a deepening of the conscious "self" (*Cartas*, 635, 639, 556).

2. On Maeztu's influence here, see Iriarte, *Ortega*, 32; Ricardo López Landiera, *Ramiro de Maeztu* (Boston: Twayne, 1978), 26; and Marías, *Circumstance and Vocation*, 124, 128–31.

him about a decade, after 1904 and after savoring German thought,[3] to find his own new "way of thinking"—one that was unitary-dual, that was authentically and forever his own, yet was heavily indebted to diverse Spanish, French, German, American, and British sources.

Not until 1916, with his essay "Nothing Modern and Very Twentieth Century," did Ortega publicly identify his philosophy as a new "absolute positivism" opposed to the old positivism (2:23, 66). Even then, privately in his classroom, he called it a "system of vital reason" (12:392, 399). As a new Hispanic light in Argentina, at age thirty-three, he then ended his novitiate in philosophy, and he exuded confidence and maturity. No one yet, however, knew just what he was, or where he stood, in relation to existing schools and new trends in philosophy in 1916–1917.[4] Even his post-modern *Modern Theme* (1923) did not clearly "place" his "vital reason."

THESIS IN "PHILOSOPHY": SOCIAL LIFE AND HISTORY (1904)

Despite Nietzsche's seductive but absurd pretensions of beginning again, history was a "perspective" that restrained Ortega's youthful "utopian" bent and passions in life and thought. After a happy first exposure under Coloma, he had continued to follow history as a major interest, despite or even because of Nietzsche,[5] until his education culminated in December 1904 with a Ph.D. in philosophy at the Central University in Madrid, where he later spent his teaching career.

The topic of Ortega's thesis was historical: "The Terrors of the Year 1000: Critique of a Legend." Why such a non-philosophical title? Evidently the subject intrigued him because it was, in a fashion, on a new beginning of history and of thought (of Europe's culture and civilization, at least), after a long night of barbarism terminating in an illusory apocalypse. Moreover, the

3. The fullest and most revealing source for Ortega's earliest (contemporary) views on German culture and education is Soledad Ortega's edition of Ortega's letters (*Cartas*, 1991), including his earliest schemes for reform of education.

4. Kessel Schwartz, "José Ortega y Gasset and Argentina," *Anales de la Literatura Española Contemporanea* 8 (1983): 59, 78, said that there were 260 articles by Ortega in the Argentine press, 210 in Spain, and 110 in Germany by 1970, as compared to approximately 400, 500, and 225 critical responses. So Argentina was "as important" as "any other element in the development of his original philosophy."

5. For Ortega's indebtedness to Nietzsche, see especially Gonzalo Sobrejano, *Nietzsche en España* (Madrid: Gredos, 1967); and chap. 2, n. 14, and supplemental note 36. The influence in Ortega of Nietzsche's reflections in "The Use and Abuse of History," from his *Thoughts out of Season*, will be evident to anyone who makes the comparison, especially with secs. 6 through 10.

supposed sense of deep crisis prevailing in 1000 had a closer parallel in Spain and in his own spirit since fateful 1898.

Faculty examiners categorized Ortega's work as "excellent," but, as philosophy, it was a strange specimen. Although it was cited in an early biographical article on him, Ortega himself, after he had the meager text (fifty-eight pages) printed by *El Liberal* in 1909, never adverted to it afterward and did not publish it with either his selected or his complete works. A hostile clerical critic, the Jesuit Iriarte, denied in the early 1940s that the thesis had "any philosophical content." In 1959, Fernando Salmerón, who analyzed only the introductory *Notas* (abstract), confirmed that it was "in reality a historical investigation."[6] It was indeed historical—poor history at that—but it was not solely, purely history. To judge from it, we might think that Ortega, like Dilthey, *began* as a "historian" and was already a "historicist" of sorts in philosophy (compare 6:171–72; 8:46; 1:166–67); but maybe he was something else besides. The contents of Ortega's thesis as a whole could, in fact, justify rating it as historicist and pre-existential: its theme was supposed historical life and crisis, with an effort at social psychology. His summary of Frankish history relatable to the legend was subordinate to his main *intent,* which was to devise a kind of "social logarithm" of life and mind at that time. His "reconstruction" of a basic "reality" that was supposed to be a vanished *type* of human "life,"[7] in sentimental and intellectual conditions, anticipated his later metahistory or historiology. However, it turned out to be a poor sort of psychosocial history, in which he mingled narrative "stories" from the chronicles with sketchy reflections on emerging medieval social and cultural institutions.

Moreover, Ortega's critique of the historians (Taine and Michelet) who had mistaken legend for "historical fact" seems to foreshadow his much later critical philosophy of history. He traced the origins of the myth to a "historical climate" of apocalyptic millenarianism in the sixteenth and seventeenth centuries, which was mainly reinvented by nineteenth-century historians.[8]

For its emphasis on a collective psychological *life experience*—mythical though it was—his thesis as a whole evinced a personal kind of basic, still inchoate "vitalism" that certainly owed something to Nietzsche, if not also to Bergson. Under Husserl's influence, he would soon reject "psychologism" in philosophy (12:420, 465), as he later did in history too (5:27). But a

6. The thesis was cited in *Enciclopedia Universal Ilustrada* (1919), s.v. "José Ortega y Gasset." The copy quoted below, graciously sent to me by Señora Soledad Ortega, had several earlier pages missing. Manuel Durán, "Ortega antes de Ortega: La tesis doctoral" (paper presented at State University of New York, Albany, April 1982); Iriarte, *Ortega,* 32, 39; Salmerón, *Mocedades de Ortega,* 173–74, 175.

7. Ortega, *Los Terrores del Año 1000* (Madrid: El Liberal, 1909), i, 4, 35.

8. Ibid., 57.

psychological interest was a lifelong motivation for the vitalism and historicism in his developing philosophy. Thus his "arrow" followed its course, or "trajectory," true to the original intention and intuitions of the "archer." His thesis was more like a prospectus of his life and thought than a worthy philosophical performance, however.

In the context of philosophy, therefore, Ortega had good reasons simply to forget about his doctoral thesis. Surely he soon realized that it was premature, that it had failed because of the very same flaw that he later criticized in Scheler and Jaspers: "lack of [philosophical] technique" (4:511; 12:91). Still another and weightier reason to forsake "The Terrors," however, could have been his belated discovery that it was very deficient even in its primary *historical* dimension. It was "much ado about nothing"—not worth the time and effort.

Unfortunately, Ortega had selected a theme for his thesis that was already passé among well-informed historians. He did not realize that French and German historians had already quite demolished the legend as pure invention and myth. In his thesis, Ortega assumed that there were at least some valid social and historical "facts" in the legend with regard to France, despite the errors of earlier historians affirming the universality of the "terrors" in Europe. (His mistake, let us admit, has been repeated too often in both basic history texts and advanced treatises up the present.)[9] To discover that he had labored hard over *nothing*—a phantasmagoria of "utopia" and "uchronia"—must have caused him painful embarrassment, when he later found out his mistake—as he very probably did. Perhaps from this experience derived his lifelong battle against utopianism.

Other historical embarrassments awaited Ortega because of the sources and "authorities" on whom he had relied. The "scientific" repute of the "positivist" historian Hippolyte Taine, renowned for his critical principles of "time, race, and milieu," was demolished soon afterward by the historian Alphonse Aulard. With "melancholic" reflections, Ortega painfully reported that famed academic spat in 1908. Although Taine had been historical meat for him and his contemporaries, Ortega now acknowledged that he had been fundamentally flawed—a mere literary historian and rhetorician (1:86–88) who lacked precision, patience, and scientific "integrity." Nevertheless, at twenty-five he now admitted the debt of mental stimulus that he had owed Taine at

9. Debunkers included, for example, George L. Burr, "The Year 1000 and the Antecedents of the Crusades," *American Historical Review* 6:3 (April 1901): 432–35, which surveyed earlier discrediting by French, German, and Italian historians. That exploded myth continues to evoke studies. See Henri Focillon, *The Year 1000*, trans. F. W. Weck (New York: Ungar, 1969); and Richard Erdoes, *A.D. 1000: Living on the Brink of the Apocalypse* (New York: Harper and Row, 1988), the latter concocted merely to fit our *fin de siècle* mood.

"around" the age of twenty-one—when, incidentally, he had written his thesis on the millennial "terrors."[10]

Another French authority whom Ortega had cited was Ernest Renan, quasi positivist and quasi historian, who had also posed as a philosopher.[11] Disillusionment came swiftly there too, for in the same article on Taine, Ortega noted that Renan's works in history—like *History of the Origins of Christianity*—were all "ruins" now (1:86–87). Two years later he observed that, although Renan "views everything under the species of the historical, . . . for him the historical is the divine . . . , his philosophy of history is, in reality, a theology" (1:134).

An "aficionado of history" since boyhood, Ortega—now forced to repudiate Taine and Renan—did not despise all historians thenceforth. Instead, he became ever more devoted to "scientific" history over the years, viewing it as a necessary test and "dimension" of sound philosophical thinking about human realities. Small wonder that when he went to Germany for postgraduate studies to "relearn" philosophy from the ground up, he was also looking for more reliable historians. These he found (from 1910) in Ranke's peers and in his successors of the Prussian historical school, especially Theodor Mommsen (d. 1903), the great historian of the Roman Empire (1:135). To a degree, Mommsen restored his shaken confidence in historians. From him Ortega derived the first generalization, or principle, of a sociopolitical kind that he applied ever afterward in his own thought: "incorporation," or integration—first for Spain, then for Europe, and finally for the West.

Although Salmerón noticed how he had slacked off from philosophizing about history in the years immediately after his thesis,[12] Ortega persisted through his German reeducation and afterward in trying to define "the historical," to assess the place of history in the total structure of reality and human knowledge, and to schematize human types and life experience historically (see 1:155–57). Thus, his youthful inclinations were not lost, nor abandoned, but the Kantianism to which he was being subjected in his postgraduate studies at Marburg was basically inimical to his original vitalist and historical interests in philosophy, especially the historical, but he man-

10. On Taine, see Salmerón, *Mocedades de Ortega,* 174, 178. There are no good studies of Ortega and Taine.

11. On Renan, see chap. 2 in António Rodríguez Huéscar, *Perspectiva y verdad: El problema de la verdad en Ortega,* which speaks of an objectivist realism there that carried over into "Adam in Paradise."

12. Salmerón, *Mocedades de Ortega,* 175–77. Also, for young Ortega's views on history, see his *Cartas,* 652 and passim (indexed); in 1905 his heroes of "holy History" were still Taine and Renan, but with "Ranke, Raumer, and Treitschke" added (655). Clearly he was already a historicist by 1906, in his emphasis on Bergson's "idea of becoming," that is, "things are not; they become" (711).

aged to combine the two in 1910 when he wrote about New Testament life and history, vis-à-vis Peter and Paul on Jesus (1:156–59).

COHEN, NATORP, AND NEO-KANTIANISM AT MARBURG

After 1900, Ortega recalled, there was "properly speaking no philosophy" in Europe, only stale neo-Kantianism—still regarded as a "terror" in Germany and abroad because of its reputed difficulty. Like James previously, he soon learned a bemused contempt for the formal rigidity and abstractions of German philosophers, whose arid systems seemed so far removed from the problems of life as he experienced them. Before long he felt almost "suffocated" by the "systematic narrowness of neo-Kantianism." He wrote to Unamuno, who had no use for mathematics and science in philosophy: "I believe with Cohen that philosophy as science is a function of physics; and therefore there will be no new philosophy—as science—while there is no new physics." Thus Descartes after Renaissance science and Kant after Newton. Was mathematical physics already undergoing a revolutionary change that required "a new philosophy"?[13] He had not yet heard of Planck and Einstein.

Going "back to school" for postgraduate work to study Kant under Hermann Cohen and Paul Natorp at Marburg in 1908 and again in 1911, Ortega had worn "callouses" on his head pondering the *Critique of Pure Reason* (8:26). Natorp he found wanting in personality, and that, despite his "great acuteness" as a critic, prevented him from being a "great original thinker," but Ortega had great respect for Cohen. Those were the years (1908–1909) of his "received" neo-Kantianism. For a while he passed as an "idealist," with a "philosophy of culture." An example of that imitative period was "Descartes and the Transcendental Method," a paper he gave in October 1908. Marías has judged that it was definitely a *Kantian* study—maybe "Ortega's only Kantian piece of writing." However, more than a year later he also gave in Madrid a lecture that was still neo-Kantian in spirit: "On the Meaning of Philosophy" (December 15, 1909). "I do not need someone someday to point out to me with irony those winged words in Kant's immortal book, the book to which I owe all the content (much or little) of my soul: the philosopher is, before all else, a professor of the 'ideal'" (R 76). With a "religiosity" of attitude, he went on to say that into all our actions we carry an ideal as a guide to systematization. "That is, in all our acts we shall live, we shall realize the ideal and thus, although this seem a game of words, we shall idealize

---

13. Ortega to Unamuno, January 27, 1907, in "Epistolario entre Unamuno y Ortega," *Revista de Occidente,* no. 19 (October 1964): 11–12.

reality. If life be not this, if living be not thus living the ideal, life is a crime. . . ." And philosophy—"No, philosophy is not a trivial thing, not a textbook"; it is "the central science of humanity, the prime basis of cultural pedagogy." Such words certainly lend support to the critics who regarded Ortega (at least at the beginning) as an idealist in philosophy. "Reality is not what one sees, hears, touches—but what one thinks." He was at least a *scientistic* idealist, for he identified his philosophy in June 1907 as that of "Plato, Galileo, Descartes, Newton, and Kant."[14] However, soon he was attempting to blend that idealism with a new realism. Even then, his search for an *objectivism* in culture that could serve a specifically Spanish national purpose had distinguished him from the subjectivism and universalism of his Marburg mentors.

A preponderant influence on Ortega from Kant and from Cohen seems evident through 1909, but then he began to go "beyond" them. By 1912–1913, in schematic notes for some "lectures on current philosophy," he apparently regarded neo-Kantianism as already a thing of the past. Science had "overcome" nineteenth-century Hegelianism and positivism by what he called "the 'turning to Kant.'" "Cohen-Kant as master of philosophy.—Reconstruction of Kantianism— . . . Thirty years of neo-Kantianism. In 1901 begins its system—which already is not neo-Kantianism" (R 76). Here he seems to have anticipated Natorp's later judgment on Cohen.[15]

Since 1908, Ortega had been stressing "space and time" as "principles" and "concepts" related to "life": "the real or existential." "Existence = being temporal spatial," and the latter three terms were all *concepts*, not facts or "things." But he felt that Kant himself had given us the example of "overcoming" even his own earlier positions as merely "relative" (R 76). And here Ortega also adverted to Bergsonism as an insufficient "philosophy of life."

14. For Ortega's early opinions on Kant, see his *Cartas*, those to Rosa Spottorno in 1906–1907: "Philosophy is a substitute for love" and "This old Kant is a road I have to run to get to you, but it is work and weariness" (453). However, that "hurdle" should be of "historical value" to Spain, for it will divide philosophy there into two epochs. Kant was his "Galileo" of philosophy (481, 560). See Ortega, "Medio siglo," 12–13 (neo-Kantians). He offered a troubled acknowledgment of his own "idealism" in 1907: "Man has to be an idealist, and, under pain of not being a man, he has to idealize life," although life is "not ideal but real," and "an ideal life . . . is a false life" (*Cartas*, 557–58). He also said, "Reality does not exist; man makes it" (557). Compare Ortega with James, *Some Problems of Philosophy* (1911; Cambridge: Harvard University Press, 1979), 10, a "text-book approach" and a generalizing, "intellectualized attitude toward life." James, *The Letters of William James* (New York: Atlantic Monthly Press, 1920), 1:263–64. On Ortega and Kant or the neo-Kantians, see Marías, *Circumstance and Vocation*, 323; Luis Díez del Corral, "Saber y personalidad en Ortega," *La Torre* 4 (July–December 1956): 52–54; Orringer, *Fuentes germánicas*, 77–83; Morón Arroyo, *Sistema*, 90–97; and McClintock, *Ortega as Educator*, 56–57.

15. These excerpts are from the third lecture (R 76). On Natorp's critique of Cohen, see *Encyclopedia of Philosophy* (1967), s.v. "Natorp."

Between 1909 and 1912 he was clearly moving rapidly "beyond" Cohen's Kant and into a new kind of philosophy of "existential," "vitalist aspiration" that fixed upon "the concrete" as the real. In fact, in his correspondence with Unamuno, he had expressed a concern in 1907 with overcoming the traditional dichotomy of idealism and realism. His emerging distinction between the concrete (real) and the conceptual (ideal) was crucial to his new position, which nevertheless included some influence and carryover from neo-Kantianism. New names cropped up in fragments of his notes by 1908–1909—James, Husserl, Dilthey, and Russell—along with a new interest in phenomenology (R 76).[16]

Not ungrateful to Cohen, Ortega dedicated the *Meditations on Quixote* (1914) to him, and he still praised the Marburg school in "Meditation on the Escorial" (1915). "To it I owe half, at least, of my hopes, and nearly all of my discipline." "One of the greatest philosophers now living," Cohen had had the insight to discern a type of commonplace philosophy of "will, decision" in Sancho Panza (2:559). Nevertheless, Marburg and the Escorial were contrary types, an opposition that he soon discerned in his own Spanish and Mediterranean predispositions and Cohen's Germanic spirit. It is not surprising that when he again adverted to Marburg in 1918, he declared that "neo-Kantianism is not the current science, much less that of the future" (3:25–26). He hinted, moreover, that the Kantian "practical reason" was only an "empty formalism."

Later (1929) Ortega was more brutally direct: in reacting to the crudities of positivism, neo-Kantianism was one of those "little provincial philosophies" pretending to be "philosophies of culture" rather than "philosophies of the real." The former were "arbitrary syntheses conventional in structure, sordid utopias that confused bright, supple reality with the wretched schemas of so-called idealism" (3:253). All considered, his summary description of Cohen and Marburg in "Preface for Germans" (1934) was no more flattering. Neo-Kantianism, especially Cohen's powerful intellect, had done philosophy a real service by awakening it and raising it to the level of contemporary life, after the bleak positivist interlude (8:27), but neo-Kantianism was not a genuine philosophy. And Cohen and his colleague Natorp did not so much teach philosophy as teach themselves, their peeves, passions, and idiosyncrasies (8:34–35). One had to *know* philosophy before ever going there.

Not surprisingly, Ortega had much the same objection to his Marburg masters as to his old Jesuit teachers of neo-Thomist scholasticism, that is,

---

16. Up through July 1907, Ortega's *Cartas* made reference not to James, Bergson, Freud, or Russell—the four formative influences that he admitted after 1950—but only to a "practicism" (702, 719), although he had nothing by C. S. Peirce. Besides Kant and neo-Kantians, he mentioned German philosophers such as Hegel, Simmel, and Vorländer, but only Renan from France and Croce from Italy, all for his study of Hegel (280).

their deep hostility to and prejudice against (and distortion of) thinkers from outside their systems (compare 1:534). In this case, from Plato to Hegel, all had to pass through the neo-Kantian wringer or be rejected. In addition to their failure to *teach* philosophy, the neo-Kantians had avoided opening students' minds to questions that did not interest them or fit their system. A third fault, which he then charitably passed over, was apparently what he called a lack of "truthfulness" in their philosophy (8:28, 36), because they followed aims other than the longing for certainty. It is clear that he included the Marburg group—"quasi-romantic idealists" (8:39)—among the "post-Kantian" idealists and rejected them for their "insufficient scrupulousness" and their "excessive zeal to be right" (8:40), for example, their present-minded will to make all philosophers from Plato forward say what Kant said, and to make Kant think what they themselves thought (7:385, n. 2). But one could still learn much from their time-bound and ahistorical critiques of both Kant and Plato (4:51–54; 6:385n).

Cohen's narrow, overzealous righteousness was also reflected in the devotion to German and European culture in which Ortega's generation at Marburg was indoctrinated with a veritable "theological attitude" that he likened to a surrogate religion: the cult of "culturalism." "There is but one God, Culture, and Hermann Cohen is his prophet" (9:560). He could as well have substituted "Kant" for "culture." Hence, it was appropriate that Ortega should finally call neo-Kantianism a "scholasticism" of "minor scale" (8:220–21) that was content with interpreting another's philosophy—and not very well at that. It represented not so much continuity with Kant as a mere "reception," or resumption, after materialism and positivism.

Such criticism, even veiled by good humor, makes it hard to determine just what Ortega had learned at Marburg to influence his own philosophy later. As an old man himself, he would remember "the great Cohen" for his handsome Semitic head and nose and his white mane. From that passionate and fierce "Isaiah," who evoked enthusiasm in his students, he gained valuable examples of a pedagogic style with electric energy and a "pure rhetoric" of verbal exactness and appropriateness—and a "will to system" (8:27, 34) but not a philosophy "from life."[17]

Something from Cohen's "philosophy of culture" survived in Ortega's

17. On the Marburg experience, see "Marburg as 'Level,'" in Marías, *Circumstance and Vocation*, 193–204; also António Galego Morell, "Ortega en Marburg," *Cuadernos Hispanoamericanos*, no. 403–5 (January–March 1984): 441–44. Around 1951 in "Medio siglo" (13) Ortega said in retrospect that Cohen had not been treated justly: he had raised the level of philosophy "at one stroke" by his key work of 1871, had obliged philosophers—himself included—to "turn to Kant" and to treat philosophy again as a "difficult" and "very complicated" thing. Also see Ortega, 8:273 n. 2 ("Leibniz"), where he said that he started his investigation of "Being" in 1902 from what he got from Cohen's books—only to abandon it.

abiding interest in culture and its theory. A few critics defined his thought by that perspective. In fact, in his "Adam in Paradise" (1910) he began with what was *formally* a philosophical aesthetics, if not truly a "philosophy of culture."

Kantian Heritage: History, Ethics, Culture

Ortega admitted deriving from Cohen the idea of "unity of thinking," a fruitful concept he later pursued in Kant till he felt he had reduced both epistemology and ontology to unity (4:56–57), as a "unity of knowing and being," which he called Kant's "Copernican revolution."[18] He also retained a Kantian commitment to conceptual, "schematic" thinking and theorizing— a paradoxical idealist "positivism." For a while only, he showed a devotion to mathematical and physical science as *the* model of knowledge. It is not clear, however, that this residue came more from his teachers than from his studying Kant directly then and for many years afterward. Beyond that, the debt was mainly negative, a deep conviction that he had to abandon all idealism, even Kantianism, or go "beyond" it by preserving features of it in his new realism-idealism. At Marburg, Ortega encountered ideas and attitudes that made for philosophical contrast or continuity with Kant, some of which he had almost immediately rejected, others he retained for a while and discarded, and still others that he worked and modified for most of his life. Some fruitful interactions between his historist and vitalist predispositions and his reception of Kantian doctrine were evident by 1907 and 1908. On his side the usefulness of history in philosophy and the paramountcy of life clashed with the absolute and timeless "intellectualism" (James's word) in Kantianism. Naturally, Kantian epistemology was his abiding problem and interest, but Kant's ethics did not attract nor persuade him.

Influenced partly by Nietzsche, Hegel, and Cejador, Ortega inclined toward a "historical-comparative method" (1:66, 114) and toward a historical, developmental view of human "nature," thought, and culture[19] that collided head-on, it *seems*, with Kant's ethics and absolute, abstract view of reality. Initially he tried to reconcile his original interests with neo-Kantianism by supplanting Kant's ethical implications of "radical evil" in man with Kant's commitment to indefinite progress, so that "superman" could mean the rejection of any "historical type of insurpassable goodness and perfection."

18. See supplemental note 18, chap. 3.

19. On Ortega as a philosopher of culture, see Karl J. Weintraub, *Visions of Culture: Voltaire, Guizot, Burckhardt, Lamprecht, Huizinga, Ortega y Gasset*, 247–82; August Buck, "José Ortega y Gasset als Kulturkritiker," *Universitas* (Stuttgart) 8 (1963): 1031–41; Charles Cascalès, *L'Humanisme d'Ortega y Gasset*; K. M. Dolgov, "Filosofía Kultury i estetika Khoje Ortegui-i-Gasseta," *Osovremennoi burzhauaznoi estetike* (Moscow) 1972, no. 3:3–60; K. Kuipers, "Ortega y Gasset als cultuur-en-geschildfilosoof," *De Gids* (1957): 197–201.

Also, "true" classicism in culture should no longer be limited to the ancients (1:66), who should not be regarded as definitive, for we must accept modern (or German) and future "classicisms" as well. Kant's (and Fichte's) idea of truth as infinite task or problem should be consistent with Hegel's evolutionary historical idea of it as a process never finished (1:74, 83, 97, 114). Nevertheless, Ortega's actual development of historicism had to wait for more than ten years, until he had mastered and absorbed Kant, whose general outlook on reality, truth, and culture was in fact the opposite of the concrete and the historical. As he remarked more than once, Kantianism was "utopian" and "uchronic," that is, absolute, or outside space and time (3:185, 238, 279; 7:191).

Apparently the first thing that Ortega's original and spontaneous historical vitalism had obliged him to question in Kant, or the *Critique of Practical Reason,* was his ethics and the "categorical imperative."[20] After Ortega's adolescent, Nietzschean aversion to scholastic ethics as merely a "heap of rules" (1:534), he had sympathized with Kant but would not accept his implication of "radical evil" in man (1:74) that seemed to carry over from the theological background (4:44). Through 1914, however, he interpreted Kant's ethics optimistically, seeing the categorical imperative as a "formula of morality" or "criterion and schema of all duty" that was equivalent to the Gospel's "golden rule"—treat others not as things (6:250).

By 1916 and 1917 (perhaps through James's influence), he had rejected Kant's ethics as too like that of the Greeks: absolute, general, and ideal. It was an ethics hiding behind "a hideous legal mask." "No, duty is not abstract and generic. Each of us bears our inalienable and exclusive self" (2:38). "I can fully will only what bursts in on me as the longing of my whole individual person." Having forgotten that individual happiness is a dimension of culture, Kant and later figures of the nineteenth century had presented us a sad "moral climate of below freezing" (2:89). Kant had committed a major "error of perspective": "an interpretation of ethics that formally obliges man to be discontent with himself" (2:142). Against Kant's "metaphysical morality," Ortega argued that "ethics cannot invent, rationally construct the good; it has to limit itself to discovering it . . ." (2:285). If he did not become a situational relativist in ethics, it was owing not to Kant or to Cohen but to Scheler.[21]

20. Deliberately excluded here is any consideration of Ortega's ethics as a minor topic. See José Luis Aranguren, *La Etica de Ortega* (Madrid: Taurus, 1958), only 62 pages; and Morón Arroyo, *Sistema,* 395–416.

21. In "The Moral Philosopher and the Moral Life" (1891), which also appeared in *The Will to Believe* (1897), James refused the moral a priori and an "ethical philosophy made up in advance," but he rejected skepticism as much as a "clean-shaven" and "stable system" by a "closet philosopher"; he called for a "test" and "trial" by a pragmatic approach that

"My generation," confessed Ortega in 1949, "was educated in . . . [a] theological attitude toward culture," notably by Cohen at Marburg (9:560). That reverent outlook on culture is not hard to find in the younger Ortega (1:83, 458–59), even in his idea of a "new" (continuous and contemporary) classicism, wherein he had first contrasted complementary northern and southern, Germanic and Latin, types (1:201, 341–43, 469), which he would later apply to philosophy. "God, in a word, is culture," he wrote in 1910 (1:135). "Modern culture," he observed thirty years later, "is like all cultures, a faith: [in this case] faith in reason" (5:449). But this was not the same thing as his youthful faith in culture, which he later realized was an "idolatry" of culture.[22] The scientific side of German culture "enthralled" him even more, so that for many years he found himself "almost drowned" in it (8:20). During those years he was preaching to Spain science as "equal" to Europeanization: "Europe = science" (1:99, 102). Here too he later saw Kant, as a worshiper of Newtonianism, as having initiated a century of scientism and of minimal philosophy, to which Comte and positivism fell heir—as did Ortega, of course (8:74, 88).

It was not just a Hispanic trait nor individual perversity that made Ortega do his early philosophizing in the form of literary, artistic, or scientific essays and addresses. It was the influence of the neo-Kantian emphasis on science and culture. Accordingly, he put his first statement of a general philosophy of life in an essay on painting and aesthetics, "Adam in Paradise" (1910), in which both Morón Arroyo and Orringer have seen clear evidences of Cohen's ideas and influence.[23] His first expression of a "national philosophy" was in a work of literary criticism, *The Meditations on Quixote* (1914).

"over the whole course of history" could "never be final" (*Essays on Faith and Morals* [Cleveland: World, 1962], 184–213). Alfred Stern, "¿Ortega, existencialista o esencialista?" *La Torre* 4 (July–December 1956): 395–96, attributes to Scheler's influence an absolutism or "extreme objectivism" in Ortega's ethics and values in the early 1920s.

22. See Buck, "Ortega als Kulturkritiker," 1031–41; Patrick Dust, "Ortega entre el naufragio y la cultura," *Aporia* 6 (1983–1984): 125–54; Jorge Uscatescu, "Ortega y la idea de la cultura," *Cuadernos Hispanoamericanos,* no. 403–5 (January–March 1984): 149–65; and Egon Schwartz, "Ortega y Gasset and German Culture," *Monatshefte* 49 (February 1957): 87–91.

23. Ortega's *Obras* (Madrid: Espasa-Calpe, 1932) did not include "Adam," so his secret beginning was buried and secure. See Orringer, "Adán en el paraíso: On Cohen in Ortega's Early Esthetics," *Hispanic Review* 47 (1979): 469–85; and idem, *Fuentes germánicas,* 49–74. Teresa Rodríguez de Lecea, "Ortega: Evolución de un pensador frente a su circunstancia," *Razón y Fe* (Madrid) 207 (May 1983): 487–94, incorporated Orringer's view of "Adam in Paradise," and also included the influence on Ortega's metaphysics from Natorp's psychology that de-emphasized consciousness and added the world to self (490–91). That may be a paradoxical idealist carryover into his basic realism, but there were others more properly realist, Renan (as Marías stressed) and James, just as early or earlier. With Ortega, one source was rarely decisive and sufficient, especially for making the crucial shift from neo-Kantian idealism to vitalist realism.

The beginning of a critical attitude toward the abstract idealistic schema of culture in Germany was evident in those *Meditations*. There he insisted that the primary reality, from which all culture was (and is) "born one day," is the immediate circumstance of individual life (1:320–21). For neo-Kantianism and other philosophies at that time, however, "man's *reality* was culture" (8:43). Culture's proper function, countered Ortega, is to give "security" to the "circumstance" of the basically insecure life of the individual (1:322, 354–56). Rather than the source of things, culture (or civilization) is only secondary, a "fiction," a "mirror" of past or living reality (1:385, 387). By 1920 he could see culture and civilization as secondary and tertiary activities of the human spirit, which were but mechanical "precipitates" or the "overflowing" of the primary activity of life itself, of its psychic "powers and innate appetites" (2:278).

All the while he was at Marburg, *life* remained for Ortega the basic reality, always acknowledged as the first perceived from 1904 onward. History became mainly a needed nuance, a necessary perspective on his informal philosophy of life during the next twenty years as he reoriented and developed his "vitalism" both in continuity with and rebellion against the recent philosophical past in Europe.

Limits of the German Heritage

During his final years of postgraduate study in Germany, at Marburg, Leipzig, and Berlin (8:20–21), Ortega took for his basic vitalist philosophy more inspiration from Husserl's and Scheler's phenomenology than from neo-Kantianism, but even more from James's pragmatism. This claim contradicts the accepted critical opinions, but there is good evidence to support it, both circumstantial and coming from Ortega himself.

In his reflections on a half-century of philosophizing, Ortega told us briefly what was "our case" between 1900 and 1915. Then neo-Kantianism was still clinging to power and influence, and the phenomenology of Husserl (after the *Logical Investigations,* 1900–1901) was going to take almost another fifteen years to get established, after his *Ideas* (1913) and Scheler's *Formalism* (1913). In that "interregnum," when he was first beginning to philosophize, young Ortega had filled the "vacuum" with other "profiles— erratic, magnificent, or only curious": Bergson, Russell, James, and Freud.[24] Now we know that he regarded Freud as "curious" and Bergson as "erratic," so who was "magnificent"? Since he made little identifiable use of Russell, it must have been James, from whom he drew basically and extensively beginning around 1908. It was, then, mainly the "magnificent" James who in-

24. Ortega, "Medio siglo," 5–6, 15–16.

spired the basic philosophy of Ortega's "Adam in Paradise" (1910), just as Cohen inspired its aesthetics.

With Husserl's methods and Scheler's example, he eventually developed an incipient pragmatist, "existential" vitalism into something that approximated the historicism of Dilthey, whom he later honored as having reacted most fruitfully to the positivism and materialism of the previous century. But Ortega rejected the idealism of Husserl as surely as Kant's, and the residue of idealism in Dilthey himself as well. The new realism in which he employed phenomenology as an "instrument," however, was compatible with his Spanish values and it was neo-positivist in character. "Absolute positivism" he called it at first, to mask his debt to James's "radical empiricism."

Although Ortega meant to tell Germans in his 1934 preface how much he owed them as he explained himself solely in relation to their own thinkers, he felt he had become a Spanish philosopher to the roots of his being (8:24).[25] The German orientation of the preface has misled critics into assuming that the *only* major influences on him were German. His style of writing and his own philosophy (8:20–21) until 1923 were, however, only partly in response to German philosophy. His "dialogue" shifted between his native Spanish "circumstance" and his adopted German milieu. What he said about "positivism" and a "radical . . . empiricism" related to a realist phenomenology (8:31, 53) that was basic to his philosophy pointed beyond Brentano, Dilthey, and Husserl to James.

His decision to accept his "Spanish destiny whole and without reserve" in 1913 was only indirectly the outcome of his studies in Germany (8:55). If Ortega had felt "obliged then and for many years afterward" to adopt a style of writing philosophy "exclusively and *ad hoc*" for Spaniards and for Latin Americans (8:18, 21), to become a popular, national thinker, his model was obviously no one in the stiffly formalized German professorate; it was James or Bergson. At first he had tried, like the Germans, to address himself to "humanity," to "Adam," but in vain.

It had been the German professors' privilege, in a stable and well-ordered society, to be concerned with abstract general questions in philosophy instead of with concrete problems of their nation, and it was possible for German university students to feel that their national character and way of life was still to be realized. As a young Spanish philosopher, Ortega had had to devote himself "obsessively" to national problems, for, after 1898, all Spain was problematical, its destiny an enigma, and its character already lived out and perhaps not to be revived (8:56–58). The expense and the contrast of Wilhelm II's Germany were painful for a young Spaniard after 1898.

25. Following Orringer, Rabade Romeo was "forced" to conclude that almost all roots of Ortega's thought were in German philosophy (*Ortega filósofo,* 49).

If he were going to philosophize for the "salvation" of his circumstances, he had to analyze his Spain as a whole and to address Spaniards as they were: in all their diversity and as "infidels" too long disinterested in deep philosophical problems to take them in an abstract and systematic German form. Instead, only in popular, journalistic essays and lectures, mainly on the Spaniard in his landscape and among his own people (8:54), would Ortega philosophize until he was nearly fifty years of age. The most notable exception was his first effort, "Adam in Paradise," in regard to both audience and sources. Nevertheless, it was from German philosophers—if not from Natorp, then from Simmel, Scheler, and Mach—that he seems first to have learned of William James.[26] James's pragmatism was the new, non-Germanic source of his initial *general* philosophy for mankind, for "Adam."

BEGINNING "IN GENERAL": "ADAM IN PARADISE" (1910)

The origin of Ortega's "philosophy of life" is a troubling problem, if we assume that his "authentic" philosophizing began only with the *Meditations on Quixote* (1914), which he wrote (8:43) when he was thirty years old. In "Preface for Germans" he designated "the twenty-sixth year" as the normal one for young intellectuals (including his "generation of 1911") to reach mental maturity and to think independently (8:34, 42). For him personally, however, the crucial twenty-sixth year was not 1913, nor "about 1911," but 1909–1910. Then he was writing his "Adam in Paradise," which introduced his principle of life as the basic reality. Metaphysically, ontologically, *life* was first, and that idea had come from his personal, native experience before it came from Nietzsche, Bergson, or James.

Ortega's own twenty-sixth year and "Adam in Paradise" really marked the

---

26. Natorp's concern with psychology made his knowledge of James at least possible, and his denial of consciousness and his treatment of life and the "natural attitude," which Orringer affirms (*Nuevas fuentes germánicas de ¿Qué es Filosofía? de Ortega* [Madrid: Consejo Superior de Investigaciones Científicas, Instituto de Filosofía Luis Vives, 1984], 12, 22), were more compatible with James than with Cohen. Natorp also came closer to Husserl's *Ideen;* two of his students, Hartmann and Ortega, soon went over to phenomenology. Likewise, Scheler's "'natural' vision" and his critique of pragmatism (Orringer, *Nuevas fuentes,* 35, 53, 59) were later than Ortega's, so Scheler was not a likely *source* for his realism in "Adam" or later but was confirmatory at most. See *Encyclopedia of Philosophy* (1967), s.v. "Neo-Kantianism" (by L. E. Loemker). Vorländer, who had nothing on James, identified realism with Mach and Avenarius but not with Brentano (*Geschichte der Philosophie* [Leipzig: Durr'sche, 1908], 475–76, 483). Ortega cited Vaihinger in 1916 (2:19n), so perhaps it was from the latter's *Philosophy of "As If"* (1911) that he learned, if belatedly, something of James. Simmel joined themes borrowed from pragmatism with a Kantian theory of knowledge, according to Raymond Aron, *La Philosophie Critique de l'Histoire,* 2d ed. (Paris: J. Vrin, 1950), 159.

beginning of his independent philosophical thinking, more than anything in 1911 or in 1913–1914, such as *Meditations,* to which Marías, Morón Arroyo, and Silver devoted most attention. He first expressed his basic philosophical positions in "Adam" and other essays equally unphilosophical in form and title. In the 1930s did he single out *Meditations* as his basic study in philosophy just because it was the one early work that anticipated Heidegger's existentialism? Actually, before that, he had written several short "philosophical" pieces: reflections on Renan (1909); aesthetics, "Adam in Paradise" (1910); and literary criticism, "Ideas on Pío Baroja" (1910). All of them took life as basic.[27]

From Neo-Kantianism to Pragmatism in "Adam"

The most developed, philosophically, among Ortega's long-neglected *mocedades* (youthful works) was "Adam in Paradise" (May–August 1910), whose conception and opening fell within his twenty-sixth year. Its significance for his philosophy has not gone wholly unnoticed, because Marías both linked it with Ortega's mental maturity in the "twenty-sixth year" and saw an "Adamism" in it.[28] No one, however, has given it full credit by discerning James's basic influence there, for Marías thereafter deferred to the *Meditations on Quixote* as his "terra firma," or real beginning in philosophy. On the contrary, "Adam" fitted Ortega's "theory of life" about the twenty-sixth year as crucial for intellectual "independence" much better than *Meditations* did, and, as Marías saw, it also first contained the basic *doctrine* of life. Granted, "Adam" gave no clear evidence yet of the method of realist phenomenology that he used thereafter. Following Marías, Morón Arroyo reexamined "Adam," called it "the overture" of Ortega's system, and found therein the influence of both Husserl and Cohen. Nevertheless, he too affirmed much greater significance for the *Meditations on Quixote,* which manifested more clearly a "natural affinity for phenomenology." Later Silver sifted "Adam" for evidence of Husserl's phenomenology, but, finding none, he followed Morón

27. Morón Arroyo, *Sistema,* makes *Meditations on Quixote* pivotal (77) between the first and second stages of Ortega's system; and Silver, *Ortega as Phenomenologist,* felt that everything he wrote afterward had its "key" therein (157). Although Ortega did not include "Adam" in the *Obras* (1932), he himself in 1932 (4:403n), 1934 (8:43), and even later (8:273n) emphasized *Meditations on Quixote* as basic and original, and therefore scholars have followed his lead.

28. On "Adam," see Marías, *Circumstance and Vocation,* 326–28; Morón Arroyo, *Sistema,* 93–94; and Silver, *Ortega as Phenomenologist,* 2, 21, 55. Also see Rodríguez Huéscar, *Perspectiva y verdad,* 47–59, 262–84; Frederick C. Copleston, "Ortega y Gasset and Philosophical Relativism," 173, on I *and* world in "Adam"; Ernest W. Ranly, *Scheler's Phenomenology of Community* (The Hague: Nijhoff, 1967), 9:28–29, who points out that in psychology Scheler stressed "I" related to world.

in citing only Cohen's influence on the aesthetics, which Orringer then detailed.[29]

Examination shows how right was Marías about "Adam" having the nucleus of Ortega's doctrines on life (even with "self and circumstance" adumbrated). There was little clear evidence of Husserl's influence yet, and more of Cohen's, but most of all it was James's. Certainly Cohen's doctrines were a major source for Ortega's aesthetics, and even for a residue of idealist philosophy, which had been more assumed than studied, before Morón and Orringer. However, "Adam" was more notable for *realist* ideas that were new, that were Ortega's declaration of "independence" from Cohen's idealism and subjectivism. No one has recognized James as a probable source for that "new realism." Pragmatism, or radical empiricism, covered the more prominent features of philosophy in "Adam" better than did Husserl's phenomenology. Evidence to support this view can be found in "Preface for Germans," where basic principles of realism that he used then (8:47–53) against Husserl's "intellectualism" and idealist "consciousness" included "coexistence," which was not in *Meditations* but was in "Adam" (1:487). Other concepts, such as the factual "given" or life as "self and circumstance," were common to both essays, but were in James and in "Adam" before they appeared in Husserl in 1913. In *The Meaning of Truth* (1909), James referred to "world" or "circumstance" three times.[30]

29. Morón Arroyo, *Sistema*, 208; Silver, *Ortega as Phenomenologist*, 26–30; Orringer, *Fuentes germánicas*, 49–74, and "Adán in el paraíso." Although Silver found there no phenomenology, Juan Saiz Barberá, *Ortega ante la crítica: El idealismo en "El Espectador"* (Madrid: Iberoamericanos, 1950), traced Husserl's phenomenology in Ortega back to "Adam" (21–44). See Rodríguez de Lecea, "Evolución de un pensador," 490–91; and María González-Gardón, "Presencia de algunos temas neo-Kantianas en el jóven Ortega," *Cuadernos Salamantinos de Filosofía* 6 (1979): 359–77.

30. From Iriarte in the 1940s until Morón Arroyo and Orringer, Ortega's initial debt to (and early imitation of) Kant and Cohen's neo-Kantian idealism had been more taken for granted than carefully investigated; for example, see the general studies by Julio Bayon (*Razón Vital y dialéctica en Ortega* [Madrid: Revista de Occidente, 1972]), Cascalès, Gaete, Guy, Alfonso López Quintas (*El Pensamiento Filósofico de Ortega y d'Ors* [Madrid: Guadarrama, 1972]), and Vicente Marrero. Also see Saiz Barberá, *Ortega ante la crítica*, and "El perspectivismo: Fundamento y orígen de esta teoría orteguiana; su sentido idealista," *Revista de Espiritualidad* (Madrid), no. 9 (1950): 74–87; González-Gardón, "Presencia"; José Luis Molinuevo, *El Idealismo de Ortega* (Madrid: Narcea, 1984); and Antonio Rodríguez Huéscar, "Crítica y susperación del idealismo en Ortega," *Revista de Bachillerato* (Madrid) 22 (1982): 126–33, who cites his "metaphysical innovation." The evidence for James's influence on Ortega's "Adam" is multiple and cumulative; however, we cannot rule out Husserl's in the emphasis on "things" as basic. See Herbert Spiegelberg, *The Phenomenological Movement: An Historical Introduction*, 2:656: "Ever since Husserl's phenomenological manifesto, 'Philosophy as a Rigorous Science', . . . 'to the things themselves' has been the leitmotif," which was a goal "closely related to that of William James." James, *The Meaning of Truth*, 91.

The title "Adam in Paradise" may well have been intended (as Marías suggested) as a metaphor for "life" as "self and circumstance," just as was the metaphor of *Dii consentes* or the Gemini, but the unity with duality was from neither Husserl nor Cohen; it was from James. However, the fictitious Dr. Vulpius, a German philosopher of culture, whom Ortega pretended to have asked for a preface to "justify" his strange title "Adam in Paradise," may have been not himself but Cohen.[31] Yet it is not the aesthetics of the essay that concerns us here but its paradoxical philosophy, which aimed to reconcile a basic realism of "things" with a conceptual idealism, as did James.

If Ortega was silent about Cohen in "Adam in Paradise," he was equally so about James. By a very peculiar coincidence (for Ortega would not have known it then), James too in 1910 referred to Adam. In an essay not then available, James adverted to "the primordial Adamic surprise of Life" and to an "old Adamic secret" of supreme "simplicity," that is, "being is knowing" (and knowing is being)—a Kantian "idealistic vision" capable of bringing unity ("monism") to "pluralistic" reality.[32] Either Ortega soon afterward discovered this insight in James, or he "re-discovered" it in Kant, for within a few years (by 1916) he too had enunciated that principle. Other influences from James, however, were clearly evident in "Adam in Paradise."

Like Renan after 1871, young Ortega after 1898 studied the philosophy of the victorious nation—in his case, the United States and James's pragmatism or "radical empiricism." Where and when did he come upon James? Possibly Ortega first read about him in Husserl, but neither Cohen nor even Natorp was a likely source. Another of his revered teachers in Germany (at Berlin) was Georg Simmel (2:93n), who influenced him toward sociology and philosophy of history. In an anonymous article entitled "Pragmatismo" in 1922, which Ortega may well have written, German pragmatists were identified as Simmel, Ostwald, Mach, Avenarius, and Vaihinger.[33] Elsewhere Ortega com-

31. Marías, *Circumstance and Vocation*, 251–52, 327; cf. Ortega 1:477. Compare *Personas, Obras, Cosas* (1916) with "Adam in Paradise," which reappeared there with the other *mocedades;* the first and last terms are equivalent to "self and circumstance." Although Mestanza was clearly Ortega himself reacting to Comte, Vulpius sounds more like Cohen to me, as it did to Silver, in contrast to Marías's opinion.

32. Ortega, "Medio siglo," 19; James, *Memories and Studies* (1911; reprint New York: Greenwood, 1968), 386n, 397. Ortega apparently read this memoir later, when it may have reinforced his lifelong Adamism, but he obviously knew nothing of it in 1909–1910. If the metaphor was not original with him, a possible source was Leibniz, who wrote to Arnauld (1686) about a "possible Adam whose posterity is of a certain sort, and an infinity of other possible Adams." This was said to be very important in regard to "the self as an individual" in Leibniz's philosophy. See Benson Mates, "Adam's Concept," *The Philosophy of Leibniz* (New York: Oxford University Press, 1968), 138–39.

33. *Enciclopedia Universal Ilustrada* (1922), s.v. "Pragmatismo." Since Vaihinger's work (Ortega, 2:19n) did not come out until 1911, Simmel was probably Ortega's first German source on pragmatism.

mented on all of them except Ostwald. Wherever he first heard of James—in Spain after 1898 or in Germany after 1905—he read the German translation of *The Will to Believe* almost certainly by 1908. His chief mentor in unitary-dual principles of realism was James; in the idealist critique of culture, it was Cohen.

Thus, pragmatism first appeared in Ortega's philosophy under the cover of Cohen's idealist "philosophy of culture" in "Adam in Paradise," and it appeared next under the forms and terms of Husserl's idealist phenomenology in *Meditations on Quixote*. In both cases, however, he kept the forms but discarded the idealist content for the "new realism" of James's pragmatism. Even in forsaking Germanic idealism, he not only kept some idealist trappings for a while—and the concept as idealist always—but he sometimes fell back too close to the old classical realism.

By 1908–1909 Ortega's new realism, which Marías has called "objectivism" in deference to Ferrater Mora, involved a compromise with idealism, one that preserved the "unity of life" in the "two faces" ("nature and spirit") of "the vital," in realism *and* idealism (1:485–86) or in the objective and the subjective. This was certainly a more moderate reaction to Cohen's idealism than was Ortega's essay on Renan (1909), where he denounced the subjectivism of the self as a leprous "error," a judgment that would seem to him in 1916 very extreme (1:445n, 447n). Even there, however, he sought a "compromise" between the "dualism" of "nature and culture": a "centaur" that needed a "third" world with a "unity" beyond the "variety" (1:451, 455)—a compromise that recalls James.[34] Even earlier, in 1908, he had agreed with Maeztu that in any important matter both "men and ideas" figured, that "the intellectualism (?), the idealism that I defend" allowed for both (1:439), although in current Spanish politics (and generally in history), ideas must lead, even if they do not "go alone" (1:441). By this reference to intellectualism, he implied a knowledge of James, which he soon turned against Maeztu by feigning to *pretend* to accept pragmatism (its conceptualist instrumentalism) for the sake of mere argument (1:119). He accepted it in fact.

Apparently pragmatist realism and objectivism were rapidly eroding his idealist subjectivism in 1908–1909, but he did not simply discard idealism, even in "Adam." Looking back on it from 1916, he saw its "idealist" notion of "functions" constituting "organs" as "blasphemously" ingenuous, and the "Kantian" idea of "relations" as thing, life, or being was also extreme (1:478n, 482n). For reality both the real and the ideal were required, as

34. James had used the metaphor of the "winged horse" (Pegasus) to make a point about the imaginary (but nevertheless "posited" or "given") *thing* in reality. Cited by James Edie, "William James and Phenomenology," 507. Ortega used the "centaur" not only in "Renan" but on other occasions for purposes like those of James (Marías, *Circumstance and Vocations*, 324).

"coetaneous." Not until around 1916 did he attain a suitable *balance* between subject self and objective world (1:419–20). In "Adam" he had been within reach of life as self and circumstance, so that he felt relatively "tranquil" about his *mocedades,* despite any "tactical errors." James's pragmatism had provided Ortega with inspiration for his unitary-dual formula, but at first he had overreacted, going back to his native realism against the Germanic self ("I") of idealism. Pragmatism did not actually require him to reject subjective self for objective circumstance. They belonged together.

"Adamism" in Ortega and "Adam" as His Philosophy

"Adam" became a fixation in Ortega's thought, to which he adverted time and again, so often that Marías has dubbed it "Adamism." Just how important "Adam" was to his philosophical foundations and to the start of his *first* "voyage," which was vitalist, may be judged by an enigmatic reference he made to Max Scheler as, after Husserl, the "first man of genius, Adam of the new Paradise" (4:510). Not exactly of his "generation" but intellectually close kin, Scheler died in 1928 as Ortega was preparing for his second "voyage," which was historicist. At that time, what did "paradise" mean—pragmatism, phenomenology, or philosophy of life? Probably he meant phenomenology, for in both vitalism and historicism he had preceded (and exceeded) Scheler, and evidently also in pragmatism. The latter's noted *Formalism in Ethics* (1913), which predated Ortega's *Meditations* and which he cited in 1923 (6:329n, 330n) as the most "formidable book yet in the twentieth century," was notable chiefly for its phenomenological description of essences. Although Scheler had ended with a promise of an "Essay on a Philosophy of Life,"[35] Ortega finally concluded that he had not come to a proper "idea of life," or philosophy of life. Accordingly, Scheler as Adam was a phenomenologist, for Husserl's type of phenomenology was not very evident in Ortega's "Adam," whereas a realist ontology of life as self and world was there. In 1928 he was hinting that his own incipient vitalism had still needed the phenomenological method, and that Scheler had beaten him to the challenge. That such was his meaning is clear, for not until 1913 did he develop a "realist" variation of phenomenology for *Meditations on Quixote:* a mixture of Husserl and James.

What Marías called Ortega's Adamism was to be evident in many later references to "Adam" or "paradise" as he developed his basic metaphysics over the years (7:269).[36] These odd metaphoric references, like those to the

35. See supplemental note 35, chap. 3.
36. "Adam" and "paradise" are unindexed themes; see Ortega, 11:185, 209–10, for a related one for theologians, a new theme on man as forever unadapted and unadaptable in the world but obliged to "transform" it.

Gemini (7:417; 12:35, 388), served to link his efforts together in continuity, but the Adam-paradise metaphor also denoted the insufficiency of his first notable effort at philosophizing in 1910. After all, life was not a paradise, nor the self an Adam, or first man, so the terms were "utopian" and "uchronic." Everyone is a definite person, living in a *resistant* and hostile world-circumstance (12:84). "Adam could not be a philosopher," at least not in paradise (8:268, 273). Ortega continued to employ the basic metaphysical principles of "Adam in Paradise," but the "anyone" subject and the "nowhere" or "eternal" setting had to give way to the real dimensions of concrete person, time, and place. As he remarked in 1936, he had soon come to exclude *uchronisms* and *utopisms* from the basis of his philosophy of life as "radical reality" (6:22), so *Meditations on Quixote* was the logical sequel to "Adam in Paradise."

"Adam in Paradise" was a complex, rather comprehensive, but still indirect statement of his incipient philosophy, in the guise of an aesthetics of art. Of course, he disavowed any *intention* of expounding philosophy—"a picture cannot be a trampoline that suddenly bounces us up to a philosophy" (1:491)—but he did try, nevertheless, and in many more ways than previously. How surprising to find so many elements of his later philosophy (as described in 1934) already detectable there at the end of his twenty-sixth year. The very title showed an interest far transcending Zuloaga's painting of that name. "Who is Adam? Anyone and no one in particular: life." "Where is Paradise? . . . It doesn't matter: it is the ubiquitous scene for the immense tragedy of living, where man struggles, renews his strength, and returns to the contest" (1:480, 492). Shortly before, however, he had put paradise in "Mesopotamia" (1:480), and that was where (with Victor Hugo) he would put "Humanity" (Adam) in "Preface for Germans" (8:19–20), in contrast to Cervantes' Don Quixote, who belonged to a more specific place (country) and time. And so "Adam," therefore, was a first, tentative expression of his *general* philosophy of life—for "mankind," or "anyone"—in contrast to his later *Spanish* vitalist philosophy in *Meditations on Quixote*, itself a philosophical aesthetics of literature to all appearances, instead of a customary systematic treatise in philosophy. Truly, Ortega *began* with "secrets" (6:345). Aesthetics was a cover for philosophy wherein James was his prime source and prime secret.

James's Influences in "Adam": Metaphors and Concepts

In *The Will to Believe* (1897), which was probably the first of James's works that Ortega read, was a passage inspired by Tennyson that certainly evokes his later pelagic metaphors, in such a graphically prophetic way that we may justifiably regard it as a source for his attitude toward philosophy of life, first and always—in "Adam" (1910) as in "Preface for Germans" (1934).

> Philosophies, whether expressed in sonnets or systems, must all wear this form. The Thinker starts from some experience of the practical world and asks its meaning. He launches himself upon the speculative sea, and makes a voyage long or short. . . . [But] the utmost result they can issue in is some new practical maxim or resolve, or the denial of some old one with which he is sooner or later washed ashore on the terra firma of concrete life again.
>
> Whatever thought takes this voyage is a philosophy.[37]

James was the unnamed captain, then, under whom Ortega now began his first speculative "voyage": to vital reason as a philosophy of life. That dependence was first evident in "Adam in Paradise."

If we disregard the open aesthetics of "Adam in Paradise," wherein Morón Arroyo and Orringer discovered Cohen's influence, and look for its covert "metaphysics" (ontology), what new concepts can we find that were "pragmatist"? Were the ideas of "life" that Ortega put forward there still idealist, now realist, or somehow new as *both*—a Jamesian "new realism" in basic experience but also a residue of Kantian idealism in "concepts"? Was his realism James's pragmatism or (better) "radical empiricism"?[38] In his "metaphysics of vital reason" (1933), where he took a position of "radicalism" on "life" as "coexistence" of "self and circumstance," Ortega mentioned that "Adam" had been expelled from Paradise into a world that resists the self (12:83–84). This world-circumstance was not only physical but sociotemporal. That metaphysics was not purely neo-Kantian idealist nor pragmatist-realist; it was both together. But James was the primary source of what was new in "Adam."

In "Adam" we encounter Ortega's earliest intuitions and statements of new principles and concepts: "life" as basic reality; life as "self" and "world" ("circumstance"); "point of view" ("perspective") on life; and several corollaries that related to "presence," holism, unity and duality, realism and idealism, and orientation to "becoming" and to history. We also sense, therefore, a will to go "beyond" both traditional realism and idealism. Here were beginnings of ideas and methods that he worked on for the rest of his life.

Life as Basic Reality

Who besides Royce and Ortega ever looked to James for a "philosophy of life"? Almost lost in his stress on pragmatism and radical empiricism were a number of appeals (especially to youth) to turn their attention to life as the object of philosophical reflection. "The return to life can't come about by

37. James, *The Will to Believe and Other Essays in Popular Philosophy* (Cambridge: Harvard University Press, 1979), 112 ("Reflection and Theism").

38. See *Encyclopedia of Philosophy* (1967), s.v. "New Realism," wherein James and Russell are representative, with roots identified in Brentano and Meinong. Against the idealist doctrine that the mind creates the perceived object, new realism had as its primary tenet that what is perceived exists independently of perceiving and knowing.

talking." It would take action and example. "Or I must point, point to the mere *that* of life, and you by inner sympathy must fill out the *what* for yourself."[39]

Young Ortega took up James's challenge, and he found in him (among other sources) the root idea of life as the basic reality. There he could have found almost the form of his own later "Cartesianism of life" ("I live and so I think") in James's Kantianism of life ("I 'breathe' instead of Kant's 'I think'"). More likely he found there separately (in loose association) the elements of his unitary-dual principle of self and circumstance. In opposition to Kantianism and consciousness, James argued that "pure experience" was duality and that "not subject, not object, but object plus subject is the minimum that can actually be."[40] Ortega came around to that view in his *mocedades*.

Life as Self and World of "Things"

Ordinarily one would assume that the sources of Ortega's idea of self (I) were Germanic and those of circumstance (world) were Latin (if not simply Spanish). Who would think that there was also a Yankee-American root for both of them? In *The Meaning of Truth* (1909), James referred to a "world with circumstances," the "circumstance" of truth and reality, and a "*fundamentum* of circumstance surrounding object and ideas."[41]

Apart from James, Ortega's "Renan" seems to show that the roots of *yo y circunstancia*, or "self and circumstance," were more directly French than German.[42] In French intellectuals such as Renan, the "individual self," or "subjectivity," was linked inseparably with objective "things" (*cosas*) or "world." And, he noted, in the Spaniards Cervantes and Velázquez the self is submerged in a national "world" (1:446–47). In "Baroja" he developed the point that "living" (or reality) and "feeling oneself living" are two different things (1:82). Further, he contended that living is most basically *action:* "Action is the whole life of our consciousness when it is busy transforming [external] reality"; it is "being outside oneself." This is just the opposite of reflection (or consciousness) in "contemplative life," which "de-realizes" things by turning them into ideas, or concepts (1:90–91). Nevertheless, he rejected the "extreme activism" of the overt, thoughtless "men of action,"

39. Josiah Royce, *William James and Other Essays on the Philosophy of Life;* James, *Pluralistic Universe* (1977), 131.

40. James *Writings*, 183, 170 (from "Does Consciousness Exist?" [1904]).

41. Concern with world, worldview (*Weltanschauung*), and history—as related to his radical empiricism and pluralism was evident in James's *Will to Believe and Other Essays in Popular Philosophy* (London: Longmans, 1931), vii, 129, 244, where (231–32) he referred to world as our "environment" and "situation." For more evidence (later) on self and "circumstance," see supplemental note 42, chap. 3.

42. See supplemental note 42, chap. 3.

whom the dyspeptic Baroja praised (1:92). Such remarks of 1908–1909 show that Ortega had in substance a basic principle of life as dual reality in "self" and "world"—all, that is, except the unified formula, which came only with *Meditations on Quixote*.

By 1910, before he had ever studied Husserl's phenomenology seriously, Ortega had rejected the idealist notion (if not yet the phrase) that "consciousness of" life is most basic. A contrary realism, moreover, is already there: life is *at bottom* the self's action and reaction to the external world of things. Here we can see the root of his idea of the "executive I" of the 1920s and 1930s. Beginning with the *Meditations* in 1914, however, he would always give more effort to analyzing worldly *circumstance* than *self,* whether active or contemplative. From almost the beginning, then, he was closer to objective realism in James than to subjective idealism in Cohen.[43]

"Presence" of "Things"

In "Adam," the ontological foundation—a self-presenting "thing" (1:479)—emerges not first but much later, after all the various epistemological theses of "seeing," "viewpoint," and touching, even after "thinking" and "historical point of view" and "historical concept" (1:474–75). This focus on "things," which was similar to Husserl's Jamesian motto "Back to the things," was clearly not from neo-Kantianism, which never looked "at things—[either] present [or] past." Yet what counted first to Ortega was the perception of a "thing"—life as the basic reality. It is "percatarse de una cosa" (1:479), as he stated again in "Dilthey and the Idea of Life" in 1934 (6:206–7). But "awareness" (*percatarse*)—or merely taking account of a "thing"—is *not* the same as "knowing it" (*conocerla*). Hence, our first contact with primary reality is not epistemological alone but is still half in the ontological frame of reference: "something that presents itself before us" (*ante nosotros se presenta algo*). Here was the very essence of Ortega's later "radical positivism."

Where did he come by this notion of "presence," when it was not yet in Husserl, when he did not yet know Dilthey, to whom he later attributed it? Evidently it was from James, because his "instrumentalism" was also appar-

---

43. See Ortega, *¿Qué es conocimiento?* 13–19 (his analysis of "the subject of life, or who am I?"), 122–38 ("Life as Execution"). But self (*yo*) as "executive" dates from 1914 (6:250–52). To exemplify the evident relatability of Ortega's "self and circumstance" to James's idea of self and world, see Eugene Fontinell, *Self, God, and Immortality: A Jamesian Investigation* (Philadelphia: Temple University Press, 1986), chap. 2, which begins with a quotation from Ortega's *Some Lessons in Metaphysics,* trans. M. Adams (New York: Norton, 1969), on self "coexisting" with circumstance, or world. Since there was no other reference to Ortega, Fontinell clearly saw the remarkable similarity of conceptions. On realism that is as relatable to Ortega as to James, see E. B. McGilvary, *Toward a Perspective Realism* (La Salle, Ill.: Open Court, 1956), 1, where philosophy is a perspective on one's world—subjective, partial, and never finished.

ent (1:488). In several ways Ortega could adjust James to his own Kantian heritage. He found it logically possible to combine the former's realism of things with the latter's idealism of concepts and a priori judgments, for James had "pointed" the way.[44]

With such an outlook on "thing" as reality as early as 1909–1910, Ortega clearly was *not* yet taking up phenomenology in Husserl's idealistic sense of "consciousness of" consciousness as basic, not even here at the very beginning of his independent philosophizing. Besides, the appropriate work, Husserl's *Ideen,* with its "presence" of "thing" or "given," came out in 1913.[45]

For Ortega, "thing" then included "life." Already he saw life as *multiple* or many-sided. Not only man and animals but the very stones "live: are life" (1:479). But only with man (Adam) does that mute "existing" fully become "living," mean "feeling oneself living"—or awareness of life—and thus become an "endless problem" for us (1:480). "Man is the problem of life" (1:481). And what a problem it was, for Ortega himself and for all who have tried to interpret him.

Life as Fluid: "Biologism" or "Scientism"?

Since Nicol and Gaos some (like Morón Arroyo) have assumed from the ambiguity of later statements by Ortega that his early theory of life was simply biological, or "biologism." According to his admission in 1934, "in those years" (around 1913 to 1915) he had written a "series of essays" that extended "the biological ideas of von Uexkull into philosophy" (8:54) in reaction to the "utopian" notion of the "ubiquity" of man—which had been precisely the viewpoint of his own "Adam." But in that earliest context he immediately and explicitly gave to "life" a *supra*-biological significance that it never lost in his thought thereafter.

"Contrary to all of this [biology and physics], I oppose a concept of life more general, but more methodical." "The life of a thing is its being. And what is the being of a thing?" (1:481). The being of anything, he explained, is

44. James, *Writings,* 75; Ortega, 1:487–88. On the "pragmatic function" of Ortega's "theory of conceptual perception," see Eugenio Frutos, "El 'Ortega' de Julián Marías" (review of *Circunstancia*), *Revista de Filosofía* 19 (1960): 503, where he disagreed with Marías. On James and Kant, see John E. Smith, *Purpose and Thought: The Meaning of Pragmatism* (New Haven: Yale University Press, 1978), 123: "Despite the many differences between Kant and James, the . . . parallel is striking." John Wild, *The Radical Empiricism of William James,* 4, found that (paradoxically) "James is thoroughly Kantian" (49–57) in some respects. For example, full knowledge requires conceptual as well as sensory elements—precisely Ortega's position—with the sensory perceptual as an "existential" a priori (again in historiology).

45. In Husserl's *Ideen* (1913), possibly the prominent use of "given" served to make Ortega more aware of that synonym and to use it thereafter in his metaphysics. See supplemental note 54, chap. 3.

the part (and place and function) it occupies within a greater whole, or "system," which itself was (we learn later) life as self and world-circumstance. Here and now he rejected the traditional metaphysical concept of "substance" for "the category of relation." So much, then, he accepted from "modern idealism." "Everything is a mixture: its life, its being, is the aggregate of relations, of mutual influences, in which are found all the others" (1:482). Now a "thing" is "a piece of the universe" (1:474). To "exist," a stone needs the rest of the world. The "vitality of each thing" is constituted by "that inexhaustible being"—the whole. "Every concrete thing is constituted by an infinite sum of relations" (1:483). And life is not just matter but spirit, and both are essentially an "aggregate of relations." Natural science settles on some one or other of these relations, to generalize it via abstraction into a "law," or "general relation." Is that James or Husserl?

Now Ortega knew well that modern philosophy had followed science in search of "the general," had even of late claimed to be "a science" (Husserl). At this incipient stage, however, he regarded his own philosophy not as "a science" but—like the arts—centered on *individual* life as the basic reality. "Life is individual"; the vital is "the concrete, the incomparable, the unique" (1:482). Hence, his own method (like art's) would be a "method of individuation and concretation"—at least for the first, the vitalistic stage of his thinking. Life is, at once, "something concrete, unique, individual." Further, life is, then, the opposite of "nature" meaning stable and permanent; instead, life is absolutely fugitive (*pasajero*) (1:483).

Life of the "spirit" was "successive" in the fluidity of time and "living together" (*convivencia*) (1:489). As fluidity, "life is change of substances" (1:491). Eventually logic made him restate these propositions as "life is history." With Rickert, Windelband, and Dilthey, Ortega at "twenty-six" had taken a historical view of reality (12:247), had thus already distinguished the vital (with the historical and the aesthetical) from the natural sciences in object and in method (1:483). In his incipient philosophy, he preferred "biography" to "biology" as the proper approach to man (1:484).

Holism and Generality

Explicit in the principle of subordination of part to whole was the "totality" of relationship (1:484) that he later acknowledged having learned from the generation of Dilthey and Brentano (8:31–32)—and James. Of that inexhaustible whole in every life, he believed that we can possess "at least" (or "at most") its "form." This form, which was general and abstract, was a side of his philosophy only incompletely and imperfectly developed at the end of his life. That "general theory of life," as he called it later, remained a problem, project, and dream for the future: the search for "system" that is already adumbrated in "Adam." System itself he defined here as a whole of parts, interrelated and interdependent (1:481)—a "system of relations," as in sociology (1:476). " . . . Every element of a system needs all the others" (1:481).

Unity and Duality

Already, too, we see stated clearly the combined *duality* and *unity* of life, which is definitely an augury of his much later description of his "philosophy of life" as a "radical unitary duality" (8:43). " . . . The individual, as thing or as person, is the result of the total remainder of the world: is the totality of relations" (1:484). Thus, the human person (or self) exists in fact inseparable from the world of things. "Science," however, analytically "breaks the unity of life into two worlds," nature and spirit. Art (and philosophy) then have to reunite (*fundir*) "those two faces of the vital," for nothing that we see exists as either matter or spirit alone (1:485). The "problem of life" resolves into a "coexistence" of things in space (1:487)—hence, of person and things—and not just coexistence but co-living: "*Coexistir es convivir*." Here again, therefore, without his pronouncing it explicitly until his *Meditations on Quixote*, Ortega leaves us in "Adam" almost touching his basic formula of "self and circumstance." Above this coexistence of self and world in "Adam," Ortega posits a *unity,* or "synthesis," through a "unitative instrument" that is "light" in art (1:488) but is "dialogue" or "narration" in the novel. Above both, of course, in philosophy is the unity of life—which goes unsaid. This "unified life-world" was also to be found in James.[46]

Realism and Idealism

Already in "Adam" we can see Ortega striving for a type of philosophy that might avoid the errors of both classical realism and modern idealism, yet preserve in combination some of the advantages of each.[47] His notion of life and being as an "aggregate of relations" (1:482) even then justifiably can be called "relativity" instead of "relativism," and that doctrine clearly pointed forward to his later perspectivism (1:475, 477). "Realism" and "idealism" he regarded as "ingenuous words"—our "weasel words"—that are capable of quite different (even contradictory) meanings in various times and fields. In his historically and conceptually more precise rendering of these supposedly mutually exclusive terms, "realism [becomes] more exactly idealism," and "Idealism would more truly have to be called realism" (1:485–86). The realism of things must be *related* (referred) to the whole, which can be perceived only through an "idealistic" operation of the mind, to apprehend the "gen-

46. Edie, "James and Phenomenology," 508.
47. Silver, *Ortega as Phenomenologist*, 26, cites Manuel García Morente, *Ensayos* (Madrid, 1945), 206, on Ortega's intent already in 1906 to "breach idealism."

eral," the stable, the "absolute." And as ideal, concepts must be related constantly to the "chaos" of real things in order to obtain "a principle of orientation to dominate them."

So soon, then, under James's influence, young Ortega tried to approximate Dilthey's *Idealismus-Realismus*. He wanted to merge realism and idealism into one by making the basic *concrete* reality of things truly (fully) knowable only through ideal *concepts*. On his ladder of "knowing and being," realism was the bottom rung and idealism the top, however.

"Point of View" or "Perspectivism"

By 1910, Ortega's newborn philosophy had assumed a doctrine of "viewpoint" akin to James's but also from James—so early—an anticipation of Einstein's still unformulated "general theory of relativity."[48] This universal "system" of relationships he attributed not just to things, life, and values but described in a way appropriate to physics. "The astronomer needs to determine exactly the place the globe occupies at every instant within the enormous supposition of starry space. . . . The example could be extended indefinitely" (1:475). His own Einsteinian "perspectivism" in *Modern Theme* (1923) was as much an outgrowth of this early concept of "viewpoint" as was the "relativism" of this and succeeding years (in 1913 and 1915), which led him eventually back into his original historicism.

The Historical

The search for general unifying concepts of idealist provenance was present but muted in the mainly concrete and realist "Adam." References to "the form of life" (1:484), to "the concept of life" as fluidity (1:491), are pale anticipations of a "general theory of life" in *historical* terms[49] that Ortega sought during his last twenty years. Nevertheless, in saying that "matter is an idea" (1:485), and that El Greco's paintings reduce, distill, "dis-articulate" the essence of an actual individual "model" so as "to articulate its aesthetical form," he opposed naive naturalism (1:487). This was in fact an artistic expression of *generalizing* the individual, concrete, changing thing (or life), to "realize" it in Cézanne's sense, which for Ortega was to *idealize* it. "To paint something into a picture is to endow it with conditions of eternal life" (1:491).

Now this generalizing aim was patently akin to what he later called "metahistory," to formalizations—called "schemas" and "models"—of "historiol-

48. See Rodríguez Huéscar, *Perspectiva y verdad,* 47–59. James, *The Meaning of Truth,* 79. For other Jamesian terms besides "point of view" that Ortega used later, see 58–59 ("consistency") and 49 ("dramatic temperament" of life).

49. Ortega, *Sobre la razón histórica,* 132, affirmed his "vision" of a great historical crisis and turn of direction at "precisely" his twenty-sixth year (1909–1910).

ogy" from the 1920s onward. At this point (in "Adam") Ortega was first anticipating the highest development of his philosophy of life—the *side* of vitalism and historicism that sought to "transcend" from concrete, changing individual things to the *general,* which in different ways was the object of both natural science and of that traditional philosophy from which modern philosophy since the seventeenth century had initially drawn its aspiration to regularities and laws—even before Newton or Kant.

In the still unembarrassed profusion of names (words) that Ortega then used untechnically—in equating thing, life, being, existence, and person (man), and individual (1:484, 492)—we discover here at his beginning the solution to many of the problems of comparing his later philosophy to others of a similar kind. But what was this, his "proto-philosophy"?

The Roots of Philosophy in "Adam"

What *philosophy,* finally, was contained in "Adam"? A systematic aesthetics, he admitted, was like trying to "square the circle," since it concentrated on concrete and individual things that always change, whereas philosophy has dealt with the absolute and the general (1:492). Hence his tongue-in-cheek pretense that he was not yet attempting philosophy here. Still, that particularistic bias was the beginning, the foundation of support for the first floor of his proto-philosophy, which was a "perspectivist" ratiovitalism that most disciples and many critics have fixed on exclusively. No critic has discerned its concealed pragmatist footings in "radical positivism," and few have grappled with the later, higher "systematic" structure of the second floor, the historicism. Fewer still have beheld the roof, overarching but largely hidden from public view: the philosophy of life that gave unity to the duality, and that was concerned with a *"general* theory of life." In "Adam" a careful observer can discover inchoate elements of all those different levels, although the historical part was still more implied and promised than developed. It is as though the novice architect were trying to rough in a drawing of the whole structure, but had not yet figured out the precise relationship and fit of all the parts, which therefore do not always appear in a proper logical order.

Obviously, young Ortega could not then see where all the parts and principles of his fledgling philosophy would lead. Over the years they would carry him through a succession of more or less distinct philosophies, which he endeavored to keep integrated into one. Chief among those related philosophies were, in order: James's "radical empiricism," Husserl's phenomenology, Heidegger's existentialism, and Dilthey's historicism and "philosophy of life." The problems of Ortega's relationship to them have evidently to do with *nuance* and *development,* more than radical difference in philosophy. He sought to provide a unity to that plurality.

From "Adam" to *Don Quixote*

When one has searched out, through long investigation of its constituent parts in mutual relationship, what Ortega's philosophy became as a whole, then to reread "Adam in Paradise" brings surprising discovery. It does not look like just another of his several early efforts to establish an aesthetics of art and literature. Anticipating the *Meditations on Quixote,* it was the first, partly disguised statement of his incipient unitary but dual philosophy of life expressed in Jamesian terms. Only the explicit formulation of "self and circumstance" (his hallmark) and a phenomenological method were lacking to "Adam." As his first metaphysics, from James, it was a first aesthetics mainly of Cohen's type, but pre-phenomenological as a whole. Some of James's ideas, however, appeared in his later aesthetics: hypothesis, plurality of forms, and "cash value."[50]

In a lecture that he published from a metaphysics course in 1934, Ortega was tacitly explaining what he, as a fledgling philosopher, had undertaken in "Adam in Paradise" in 1909:

> [We] have to behave as if there were no [metaphysics] and decide to do it as the first man who began it. Everyone, if he truly wants to live, must behave like a first man, is obliged to be the eternal Adam, to revive in himself the essential and permanent springs and themes of life. Only on the road of trying this rebeginning and simplification of life does one find that he is not and cannot be a first man but is instead numbered so far down the very long chain of men and generations that succeeded him [Adam]. (5:178)

Then one discovers that he is a successor, an heir, a "historical being," who has to learn the metaphysics that others have done already, from the first even to the very last one. In short, to avoid "utopia," one has to follow the historical road and to compare traditional metaphysics with one's own efforts (5:179).

As a whole, "Adam" was actually an earlier and clearer—but much shorter—revelation of the structure and fundamental ideas or principles of his philosophy than one can find in *Meditations on Quixote* itself, for good reason. "Adam" was a universalist first statement of his philosophy, a metaphysical breviary (in literary guise) of his general philosophy, whereas *Meditations* is a later, particular national variation on it. In fact, he almost predicted the latter in "Adam," where several times he implied that something of that type and title soon would be forthcoming. For example, by its fixation on things individual, unique, and concrete (not just any stone but "the stone of Gua-

---

50. Cf. Ortega, "Aesthetics on a Streetcar," *Obras Completas,* 2:35, 39. On "cash value," where Ortega's essay ended, see James, *Writings* (ed. McDermott), 207, 311. Aesthetics, James held, dealt with "an ideal world, a Utopia" (92).

darrama" [1:482–83; compare 8:16]), even a unique and concrete "world," *Quixote* was a necessary next step: his *native* part of the world "totality." "*Don Quixote*," he said then, "leaves in us, as a divine font, a sudden and spontaneous revelation that lets us see effortlessly, at only a glance, the broadest ordering of everything: we might say that immediately, without having studied, we have been raised to a higher intuition of the human" (1:484). Cervantes' work was the firstborn of modern novels, wonderfully combining dialogue and narration (1:489).

After "Adam" essayed man in general, *Meditations on Quixote* suited perfectly Ortega's next purpose of philosophizing via aesthetics: "Not this historical man, nor that other: [but] man, the problem of man as inhabitant of the planet. To reduce this problem to a national type, for example, is to reduce it to the proportions of an anecdote." That anecdote, as it turned out, comprised the many "themes" of *Meditations*. "Historical man" would have to wait much longer—until after his *Espectador*, with its impressionistic perspectives of the daily world in its "perpetual change of substances," the world in movement and flight. This, too, "Adam" had forecast naively (1:492).

It is strange that Ortega should so soon have intentionally "forgotten" the basic "universalizing" purpose of "Adam," to confound it with the national viewpoint of his yet unborn *Meditations on Quixote*. Only a year later (July 1911), with reference to Worringer, he wrote: "According to what I have heard, what I wrote then [in "Adam"] was not clear, and this pains me, because it was concerned with an essay of Spanish aesthetics ... as a theoretical justification of our artistic peculiarity." Thereby he sacrificed the whole of his "Adam" for merely one of its intentional, future variants—on Cervantes. But when he proposed that "someday" he might attempt "the scientific (i.e., philosophical) history of Spain" (1:190), could he also have foreseen his *Invertebrate Spain*, or "historical reason" and "historiology"? Vaguely, at best.

Thanks to "Adam," we can now understand better the nature and purpose of that nationally oriented work of philosophical literary criticism, *Meditations on Quixote*, another cultural work that served a hidden but serious philosophical purpose. As aesthetics it represented his "graduation" from Cohen's concepts into a phenomenological aesthetics reflecting Husserl's ideas. All the while, however, with James's help, he was rejecting both mentors' philosophical principle of *consciousness*.[51]

Ortega later decided to acknowledge *Meditations* as the *formal* origins of

---

51. For Ortega's works in phenomenological aesthetics, see Silver, *Phenomenology and Art*. David K. Herzberger, "Ortega y Gasset and the 'Critics of Consciousness,'" Herzberger did not realize that Ortega's idea of consciousness (with specific object)—which made Ortega a forerunner of the Geneva school of critics—was a rejection of Husserl's influence (even early on.)

his basic doctrines and style of philosophy. "Adam in Paradise," however, remains the real (but only hinted) beginning of his independent philosophizing in 1909–1910, at the conclusion of his "twenty-sixth year." Although he did not explicitly mention "Adam" in his revealing "Preface for Germans," three references clearly bring it to mind: (1) identifying himself with Guadarrama granite; (2) equating Mesopotamia with "Humanity"; and (3) acknowledging "Mesopotamia" universalized as the "ultimate" terminus of his "perspective" or "circumstance," as Spain was always its "primary" or proximate boundary (8:16, 19, 54). There "humanity" and the general or world-circumstance appeared as his *final* interest; in "Adam," they were his first—a kind of forecast in miniature of his maturest philosophical development.

If the *Meditations on Quixote* rates more than "Adam in Paradise" in his mature recollections, it is not just because Ortega introduced there his formula "self and circumstance" and a phenomenological method. It was also his "first book" (8:43, 440) of philosophy and therefore more impressive and more available to German readers in 1934. Out of print from 1916 until 1946, "Adam" was part of his *mocedades,* or youthful works. Universalist and general, however, it was not one whose "subjectivism" and individualism he rejected in 1916 (1:419–20). Except for his dual formula and phenomenology, its principles anticipated what his mature philosophy had become by 1934, as well as his study of Cervantes' classic.

NATIONAL BEGINNING: *MEDITATIONS ON QUIXOTE (1914)*

By his own account—everybody agreeing—Ortega *formally* launched his philosophy, as an independent thinker, in 1914 with the *Meditations on Quixote,* which he wrote during the preceding year when he was thirty years of age. As he was approaching fifty in 1932, he wrote in the prologue to his selected works (*Obras*) that the basic principle of "self and circumstance" (formally enunciated first in the *Meditations*) "condenses into least volume my philosophical thought," and "my work is a case of executing that very doctrine." Deliberately, "my work is, by essence and by presentation, circumstantial" (4:349).

Deferring to several detailed studies of the fundamental *Meditations on Quixote,*[52] we need here only summarize its importance in the development

52. For reviews and commentaries on *Meditations on Quixote* that are not primarily literary, see relevant pages in the general treatments of his thought (already cited above) by Marías, Morón Arroyo, Silver, Orringer, and Rodríguez Huéscar. Jean-Paul Borel's *Raison et vie chez Ortega y Gasset* was typical of studies that began with "self and circumstance" in the *Quixote* and traced it as a basic theme through the later works. Also see Angel Benito y

of his philosophy as Ortega himself saw it. With "the idea of life," which he later denied getting from Dilthey, Kierkegaard, or any other individual source, but which stands out clearly in *Meditations,* he was launching what he viewed (by 1934) as a "philosophy of life" akin to Dilthey's (8:46). Years later (1947), he still affirmed that in his *Meditations* "the intuition of the phenomenon 'human life' is the basis of all my thought" (8:273). That was his "discovery" (*aletheia*) of life (in "coexisting" self and world), which was like James's idea of "uncovering" reality.[53]

There he represented "life" by the "dual" principle of basic reality, "self and circumstance" (*yo y circunstancia*), which he had conceived by 1910 and worked together by 1913, very probably with the help of both James and Husserl, and maybe Scheler too.[54] Or, as he explained it twenty years later to the Germans, "that radical reality that is life itself does not consist in [Kant's or Husserl's] 'consciousness' . . . , but in a radical unitary duality . . . that is *one-two*" (8:43). His "basic discovery" thus was twofold, or "double": "personal life is the radical reality and that life is circumstance" (8:44). The word "existence" is not enough in itself to cover this duality; neither is "being." The reality of life is "my *coexistence* with things," not statically being but dynamically "happening" (8:51–52). This initial *unitary dualism* in Ortega's basic thought, or ontology, developed over the years into a conscious "philosophy of life" in two dimensions, one existential (the vitalist self) and the other historicist (circumstantial with regard to time and place).

Despite his earlier references to Cervantes' perennial popularity even with scholars (10:82, 139–40) including Unamuno and Cejador, it is unclear what "circumstances" induced Ortega to offer his initial *philosophical* program in a literary form with national "salvation" themes (1:322–23; 8:56) about *Don Quixote*. He had accused Unamuno of a "terrible historical injustice" in 1907 for having presented Cervantes, "the only Spanish philosopher," as a litterateur. His great novel was at once a "Spanish melody" set within the "universal harmony" of European culture and potentially a "universal song" reflecting a national crisis for Spaniards, "for whom life is not a technical problem, but a metaphysical-existential problem." Like a "superman" overcoming his superiority and "ironizing" his circumstances, Cervantes had arrived "theoretically at Man" in *Don Quixote*. Beyond realism or idealism,

Durán, "Ideario filosófico de Ortega y Gasset en las 'Meditaciones del Quijote,'" *Cuadernos de Estudios Manchegos* (1950–1951): 29–52; Franz Niedermayer, "Ortega y Gassets Erstling (Meditaciones)," *Hochland* 5 (1961): 479–820. Also see two papers in *José Ortega y Gasset,* ed. Nora Marval-McNair (New York: Greenwood, 1987): Anthony J. Cascardi, "Between Philosophy and Literature: Ortega's *Meditations on Quixote*," 15–20; and Ronald J. Jones, "José Ortega y Gasset and Arthur Koestler: Meditations on the Two-Faced Forest," 151–56.

53. James, *Essays in Philosophy,* 160.

54. See supplemental note 54, chap. 3.

Cervantes "places life in front as an absolute problem and looks at every manifestation of life under the form of ultimate value [and] end," from a variety of perspectives.[55] Certainly Ortega carried forward those insights into his own *Meditations on Quixote,* whose themes of life and crisis, or of life *in* crisis, were leading, motivating interests. Perhaps because Cervantes knew so much about life (8:419) in an earlier age of national crisis, his work may have seemed the most convenient vehicle for stating the basic dual principle of Ortega's new "philosophy of life": of "self and circumstance" after 1898. An "epic of the forever and essentially defeated" type (8:21), the novel's protagonist represented an "extremist" (or crisis) figure, which might serve as a prototype for Spaniards in general (6:126).

The *Meditations* seems to have reflected Ortega's continuing "anguish" over Spain's long decadence, especially acute since the great crisis of 1898. Hence, his decision now to accept "Spanish destiny," however painful. Possibly conversations with Cohen (2:559) had influenced Ortega to cast his incipient philosophy in this loose, literary form. Specific inspiration for *Meditations on Quixote,* whatever it was, came suddenly at twilight one spring day near the Escorial in 1913 (1:363).

As befitted his still limited capacity and his precarious situation *in partibus infidelium* (an uninterested Spanish public), the young professor of philosophy offered a new "way of thinking" on philosophical themes about Spanish "circumstances" and the "shipwreck" of life that were really intended as a patriotic labor of love to "save" Spain from rancor and self-contempt (1:311–13). His "philosophical intentions" were not to display erudition but merely to offer for the reader's consideration some "new ways of looking at things" (1:318–19). Circling Cervantes' book—as if it were Jericho—in tightening hermeneutic circuits, he hoped to penetrate through its "Quixotism" to the very pith and basis of Spain's "ethnic consciousness" and there discover and save its "primary substance," shake off the dead hand of tradition, and find, finally, a "new way of living," a "new sensibility" to reawaken Spain to cultural creativity (1:361–62). Reading Spain's history in reverse, he sought the fullness of its "essential experience" as concentrated in Cervantes, whose style also complemented his "philosophy," ethics, and politics. Cervantes' marvelous realism, which embraced the will and the ideal as well as material things (1:382–84, 388), was compatible with Ortega's own position. The "chief question" Ortega asked of the *Don Quixote* in "anguished cries" was: "My God, what is Spain?" What is "this spiritual promontory of Europe. . . ?"

55. See Ortega's letter (February 17, 1907), "Epistolario entre Unamuno y Ortega," *Revista de Occidente,* no. 19 (October 1964): 14, promising to reconstruct systematically the main idea (madness) of Unamuno's *Quijote.* The intent of "salvation" perhaps reflects James's *Meaning of Truth,* wherein pluralistic pragmatism sees the world's "salvation" as depending on our efforts and actions (123).

What is its destiny, its "mission in history?" (1:360; 8:58). Such was his "patriotic" purpose in launching this new *national* philosophy.

Starting formally as very clearly a *Spanish* philosopher by choice of format, themes, and style, Ortega nevertheless also sketched out a kind of ingenuous prospectus comprising or anticipating his various philosophical themes and principles over the next twenty years and more. In 1934, in the "Preface for Germans," whose purpose was in part "to establish the dates of my writings, especially those that define political realities [such as the crisis of 1898] and collective states of spirit" [for example, of his own "generation of 1911"] (8:57), he described the *Meditations* as "my spontaneous reaction to what I had received in Germany," which was, essentially, neo-Kantianism and idealism—thus including also phenomenology. "The rest of my output, which was to be a ceaseless battle against [idealist] utopianism, is, then, already formulated in this my first book." But his opposition to such "intellectualism" (8:43–44, 47, 53) was really more from James than from Germany.

In *Meditations* was a variation on "one and many" with a homely metaphor about "the forest and the trees" that James had used in *Pragmatism,* which also contributed other basic ideas to Ortega's purpose, including a "living" (like "vital") reason. "With having recognized in the forest its fugitive nature, always absent, always hidden—an aggregate of possibilities—, we do not have the whole idea of the forest. If the deep and latent is to exist for us, it will have to present itself to us, and on presenting itself to us it has to be in such a form as does not lose its quality of depth and latency." Here are, in short, James's ideas of "compresence," "percept," and "concept"—even if mediated now through Husserl. Besides that part of reality open to our senses as "pure impressions," there is "a transworld constituted by structures" that is "no less real" (1:330–32). If he thus retained here something Kantian in the "transcendental" character of the concept, his distinction between "thinkers" and "feelers" differed little from James's appeal to "tough-minded" empiricists over "tender-minded" rationalists and their "intellectualism".[56]

Thus, where Ortega preferred "impression" to "percept" (1:353), the meaning was still James's (1:349–54). The primary, immediate "impression" of the "fluid" and floating world of "things" was sufficient perhaps for "feelers," but "thinkers" required greater "depth" of a secondary order in the "concept," which was an "organ," "instrument," or "apparatus" for grasping things by their "schematic content." Concepts comprised the "relations," "reflections," and "connections" between things—in short, their limits (which James had called their "fringes"). One might say that for Ortega "the

---

56. James, *Pragmatism,* 138, 24. See his metaphor of the squirrel and the tree trunk in *The Meaning of Truth,* 84. Idem, *Writings,* 356. The adjectives are from *Pragmatism* (1907).

concept" was tantamount here to James's "pragmatic method." But, for him as for James, a concept, one which gives "fullness" to knowledge, is ideal and "hypothetical" rather than real and so cannot "substitute" for the thing. "Reason cannot, does not have to aspire to supplant life" (1:353). In short, it must be a "vital reason" (as he would soon put it) or a "living reason" (as James put it).

Here in the *Meditations* we find already outlined the idea of a "vital" reason arising out of his initial "intuition" of life (in self and circumstance) as reality; this idea was not formally enunciated in the press for another decade. It was not the purpose of Kantian or Hegelian conceptual reason "to dispossess intuition, the impression of reality." Reason must not, cannot, supplant life (1:353), as lazy minds want. "As if reason were not a vital and spontaneous function of such kind as seeing or touching!" The world was "too vast and too rich" to be contained in merely "schematic" conceptual reason. "But on dethroning [this] reason, let us be careful of what we put in its place. Everything is not thought, but without thought we possess nothing fully" (1:354).

Even so early, it is clear that he did *not* replace reason in human life with the will or passions of material life in a so-called biologism, in the sense of an irrational vitalism, despite any later equivocation (1:54). On the contrary, he always emphasized man's freedom to choose and his rational capacity to mold or modify his "landscape," or "circumstance," instead of determinism (1:322; 2:296–98; compare 8:54–55).

As Ortega would recall in 1934, in the *Meditations on Quixote* there were already anticipations of what the Germans later called "existentialism" (8:45). In his view, words like "restlessness," "darkness," "obscurity," "worry," "problematical," "insecurity," and culture as "*aletheia*" or "discovery" and as "security"—all represented his spontaneous, "first reaction" to his experience of life as reality. For this new philosophy he had come to prefer the name "vital reason" by 1916, or "ratiovitalism" after 1924 (4:404), or by 1933 even "philosophy of life" (4:404; 8:45).

Besides anticipating "vital reason" in the *Meditations,* Ortega also found places for other concepts to be developed further for Spain and later universalized for "humanity," such as frontier culture, the indocility of the masses, and the unconscious hold of history upon them (1:324, 355). Indeed, the *Meditations* is a rich "repertory" of ideas and themes, including his determination "to treat the past as a mode of life" (1:325) in the perspectives of time and space (1:349). There is even the use of an etymological technique (derived from Cejador) that he later made a method of "historical reason." It is important to emphasize that Ortega himself regarded the *Meditations on Quixote* as having unwittingly paralleled Dilthey's "philosophy of life" (8:46), besides having more or less anticipated Heidegger's existentialism; the work has also recently been seen (by Philip Silver) as expressing mainly a "mundane" phenomenology overall. Philosophically it was all of those things and more. Of course, "around" 1911, when he first formed the half-conscious "generic position" and "decision" that neo-Kantianism was "forced and untrue" (6:350; 8:35), he had no name for his complex philosophical insights and knew not where they would lead him. In rejecting neo-Kantian "Culture" and idealism, he and his generation did not at once find a single "clear and positive idea" (like Dilthey's "Idea of Life") to put in their place (8:41–42), but, with the help of phenomenology as a "prodigious instrument" (method), he admitted, they set sail for an "imaginary coast"—its generic name unknown.

PERSONAL BEGINNING: LAUNCHING AND SETTING SAIL

Life, Ortega reminded his audience in his 1930 lectures entitled "What Is Philosophy?," is very personal. It is the life of "each and everyone" (*cada cual*), and accordingly the philosophy of life that he was launching in 1910 was also—besides general and then national—from first to last necessarily a very *personal* philosophy. He had been like a "Robinson Crusoe" trying to escape his desert isle *in partibus infidelium,* to "navigate" upon the "high sea" of philosophy, and to make landfall on a new continent (7:288, 335, 405–6). "To sea! To sea!" (12:182).

Ortega's "ship" was built of largely secondhand materials—all fastened to a newly designed double keel, "self and circumstance." It too had yet to get a name—for he had painted over *Pragmatism,* which had marked his metaphysics in "Adam." He had repaired, modified, and outfitted his bark with many other elements past and present, not least of which were much tamer versions of Nietzsche's "unphilosophic" visions of life and history and a more rational version of Bergson's "intuition." Taking Husserl's phenomenology for "instrumental" method and rudder, he adjusted Nietzsche and Bergson to James's basic hull and added (as compass) Dilthey's historical worldview (*Weltanschauung*), all by 1916, when he at last christened his basic metaphysics "absolute positivism"—or "radicalism"—and his general philosophy a "system of vital reason."

ORTEGA'S BEARINGS: EARLY LECTURES

Among the unpublished papers in the archive is "Course of 1912–1913," which included four lectures on contemporary philosophy. Those talks were as autobiographical as they were analytic. In explaining the historic break from positivism by its current "belated but more subtle" representatives, devotees of science such as Mach and Ziehen and Herbart, he was also explaining his own relation to Nietzsche, Bergson, James, and Dilthey—if not yet to Husserl. "The continuity of historical evolution requires that every new sensibility be born of the preceding one as a negation of it." "It always happens so: for the disciple to come someday to produce new affirmative doctrines, to come to be a master himself, he has to traverse an intermediate stage in which he is going to disengage himself from his master, in that he is his negation" (R 76). These negative "bridges" are "epochs of crisis, of pain and discontent," and Europe was now in that situation. He detected "great crises" already in modern thought, manifested in the "deep crisis" in philosophy and also in history. Bergson's vitalism, or "philosophy of life," for example, "coincides with epochs of crisis" and is a "natural expression" of them. In his polemic against positivism, he refused to reduce being and truth to either mere "facts" or to "existential characters."

There were, however, some "existential" and historicist implications in Ortega's reflections about historical "science" in crisis. History assumed that the world was a "network" of "space and time." It involved the "real or existential." "Existence = being temporal-spatial." "Being, on the other hand," is "a concept . . ." (R 76). The crisis in history and the problem of "historical reality" were tasks for what Ortega even now called "integral historiological thinking" to give "structure" to the "historical substance" of "human acts."

Thus, Ortega was already "on course" toward his future "terra incognita" of existentialism and historicism within a "philosophy of life." First, however, he had to work out a basic pragmatist metaphysics as a starting point for general philosophy and a "general phenomenology" as a basic method. It is a remarkable characteristic of pragmatism that various of its principles or positions were capable of being developed in phenomenology, existentialism, historicism, and philosophy of life. In fact, they were thus elaborated through a number of philosophers but no one brought all of these things into harmony, except Ortega.[57] That was to be his "vital task," his unique "project" or "program" of life, in short, his "destiny." Now it was beginning.

Toward a Metaphysics

For a professor of metaphysics, Ortega was a long time at developing this basic discipline to maturity, beyond "Adam" and *Quixote,* beyond his mysterious "absolute positivism" (1916), into a full-fledged "metaphysics of vital reason"—that is, into one of existentialism, in 1933. Beforehand he had to

57. For one of numerous instances of projecting James (or pragmatism) into later philosophies, see Wild, *Radical Empiricism,* vii. Also see n. 4, my chap. 4.

absorb critically the heritage of traditional metaphysics over the past 2,500 years. As he reflected in 1950:

> Certainly metaphysics was born, there in Greece, in the first third of the fifth century, as the investigation of the being of things, but understanding by their being what they are, let us say, on their own account and not merely what they *are for* us. It is the being of things in itself and by itself. That science, which a Cartesian, at the end of the seventeenth century, called ontology, exerts itself boldly and strenuously and grows feeble after twenty-five centuries in finding that *being* of things. But [what] . . . is sought has not yet been found sufficiently. (7:128)

He suspected "that they do not have it"—that "being" is still "problematical"—because philosophers cannot "show" to us what should be "obvious and very well known." "This [likelihood] brought me many years ago to the daring opinion that the being of things, insofar as it belongs to them apart from man, is only hypothesis, as are all scientific ideas." "With that," he acknowledged, "we turn all philosophy topsy-turvy, a devilish task . . ." (7:128–29).

If Aristotle's answer to the question of being—that it is "substance"—was the best in the past, for antiquity, the Middle Ages, and modern times, it no longer satisfied our Western minds, so "we have to seek another" elsewhere. Actually, this context (from 1950) was concerned with *life* as "authentic or radical phenomenon" and with "things as *pragmata*" and "pragmatic fields" (7:127–29). Thus, in pragmatism and phenomenology, he had sought his own answer to the metaphysical problem of being.

Ortega had approached the problems of metaphysics from a historical point of view. Considering its origins, he observed in "What Is Philosophy?" (1930) that in reality it had not been a "meta-physics" in the sense of "after" or "beyond" physics but had instead been an "ante-physics." Like philosophy itself, its root had been in "primary life," born out of life itself, before physics existed (7:317). As he explained to a class in 1934, "doing metaphysics in the fullest and most real manner begins by being a feeling that all doing is impossible, . . . that life is unlivable" (5:176). Thus, like all philosophizing, "authentic" metaphysics, as distinguished from merely studying it or teaching it, is rooted in a sense of crisis, in a feeling that "our whole life is in itself negative, illusory, absurd, and senseless." That, at least, is what it was in the first metaphysicians, but, since then, regardless of feeling lost, one is "a historical being," born with a *heritage* of metaphysical thought that one perforce must take into account. "Inevitably, we do metaphysics from a determinate place in the history of philosophy and, in general, of human history" (5:178).

A syllabus for a metaphysics course whose date is uncertain reveals how Ortega apparently had normally approached the subject. First he had stated general metaphysical problems for the "present situation." Then he surveyed historically the "great classical systems" from Greek antiquity and from modern rationalism and materialism since Descartes. Next he took "the modern systems [that were] negative toward metaphysics": British empiricism, positivism, neo-Kantianism, pragmatism, and phenomenology. Only after that introduction did he get around to discussing epistemology and ontology analytically (in themselves), and finally pursue the problem of reality in relation to physics, psychology, and the "historical sciences." He ended with "theory of values" (R 57). He was already giving courses structured in this way from 1915 to 1918 (R 77).

Of all the metaphysicians of history Ortega praised Leibniz most—not for his precise ideas of reality, however, but for his brevity and clarity. Like Ortega, he had been a factotum and a philosopher, one who had created a "whole new metaphysics." His *Monadology* was "a pocketbook metaphysics," and, averred Ortega, every metaphysics should be such a *vade mecum* (3:432). His own was such—essentially, "self and circumstance"—but it rested on a pragmatist basis of "things" borrowed from William James, a basis that he tried to keep just as brief and as clear.

In fact, the evidence indicates that Ortega developed his metaphysics mainly out of almost contemporary sources that were very paradoxical: from James's pragmatism, with methods and insights borrowed from Husserl's phenomenology and from Cohen's neo-Kantianism. These were what he called "anti-metaphysical" philosophies. The result to which he aspired was a "whole new metaphysics" for his time, parallel to what Leibniz had done.

Notes for a number of Ortega's early classes survive in his archive. One in print, on problems of psychology, was for semesters in 1915–1916 and is most revealing of his fundaments, as he reached for a "system" via phenomenology. So is another one, still unpublished, from Argentina, for 1916–1917. In them we can see elements developing in his private, personal philosophic thought that were not made public till years later. At the beginning of his course on psychology he affirmed a general "crisis" of the European mind and sciences—in this case a crisis of "transformation" that promised "an incalculable broadening and renewal of human thinking" (12:343–45).[58] One side of this was "relativity" in physics—before Einstein put forth his general theory. By the seventh lecture (1916), he had arrived at his "system": "what I call the system of vital reason." This was clearly related to "the phenomenological or purely descriptive sciences," as in logic, mathematics, and ontol-

58. For an analysis of that course (in Ortega, *Obras* [1932], vol. 12), see Julio Bayon, "Problema y verdad," *Cuadernos Hispanoamericanos,* no. 403–5 (January–March 1984): 93–104, which ends as "Verdad e Historia."

ogy, but also to "*Weltanschauung* or worldview, and in a form still poorer and more absurd in the so-called 'pragmatism'" (12:392). Shortly, in the same context, he announced the "alpha and omega of my logical and methodological convictions: *absolute positivism against partial positivism*" (12:399). This was a first name for his Jamesian metaphysics of "radical empiricism," but in the "form" of a Husserlian phenomenology, for example, in the fifteenth and last lecture (12:445–47).

Less than a year later Ortega was a guest lecturer at the University of Buenos Aires in Argentina. There he developed a number of topics that carried his thought further forward. Themes on crisis, history, utilitarian thinking, positivism, radicalism, consciousness, and subjectivism were continuations or anticipations. "Philosophy so oriented will thus extend its domains incalculably," he predicted, and he promised his youthful audience that he would someday bring out these ideas officially, in published form.

> We live in an hour of profound crisis in the depth of human consciousness. I refer not to the fact of the war. . . . Wars neither create nor destroy anything spiritual[;] they simply accelerate or bring the expansion of the intimate changes that were found before them. Before the war, human thought and emotion had changed their center of gravity. All the sciences were experiencing a radical transformation. (R 77)

He urged Argentine youth to be faithful to the new currents and thus be true also to themselves and to their country.

Among those themes the most significant for us—and perhaps for some of his audience with long memories—were those relating to thinking as a utilitarian, anti-positivist radicalism and his observations on history. The former were a new epistemology that tacitly combined pragmatism and phenomenology; the latter reaffirmed the historicism in his thought, which (apart from his remarks) had then seemed in suspension—in Husserl's "brackets."

He explained that he fought against positivism, "because it is not positivist." It does not "humbly heed . . . phenomena as they offer themselves, the facts as they are manifest." Refusing Mach's ultra-positivism and "biologism," he found "in the primary and universal phenomenon of consciousness . . . the object before me and myself before the object, radically distinct from each other but mutually dependent." "I am not alone in the world! Objects are neither more nor less real than I!" For himself, "I aspire to a super-positivism—one that does not give form to the body . . . of phenomena with preconceived dogmatisms."[59] Then he summed up his position with a

---

59. Marías, *Circumstance and Vocation*, 278; Silver, *Ortega as Phenomenologist*, 153, 157, on this so-called super-positivism of 1916. Few critics have ever noticed Ortega's "absolute positivism," and none have seen what it truly was: a basic pragmatism. Marías therein conceded to Ortega (271, 278) that it was the "basic thesis" of "the reigning philosophy of

unitary-dual metaphor of the *Dii consentes,* or Castor and Pollux, who were "born and died together" (R 77): self and circumstance.

Because of all of the discord in traditional doctrines of knowing and being, he invoked history to find a way out of this "plurality" and "chaos" of learned opinion. "History's task consists precisely in seeking behind the variations and differences" in human views "their essential identity over the long run. History is an exercise in comprehension. . . ." Referring to Heraclitus's "river of life," he observed that "History is the organic reconstruction of the variations of a subject" that keeps throughout "its own radical identity." "Such is the science of history" (R 77). Such was the historicism in Ortega's fledgling philosophy at that point, in 1916. At the same time he also anticipated his "historical reason": "This reason, in the concrete sense we have just given the word, is history, the protagonist of universal history, . . . to investigate the formation and progression of those enduring historical forces that . . . go falling upon every people and sowing a new science, a more perfect morality, a new style of art. . . ." And this new historical rationality related to time and place. In 1924 he would call it "historical reason."

In view of this early course, it was perhaps to be expected that Ortega's pragmatism and historicism would be recognized first in Argentina in the 1920s, ahead of "metropolitan" Spain and Europe in the 1940s–1950s. During the next fifteen years he continued to use Argentina as a testing ground for his ideas. Philosophy had begun, he pointed out, in the Ionian "colonies" of Greece—so why not re-begin in the erstwhile colonies of Europe? Over the decades he published more writings there than in Spain, and there he evoked almost as many critical responses. When Ferrater Mora, at the end of the 1950s, defined the first "stage" of Ortega's philosophy as an "objectivism" of sorts, he was not so wrong, given Ortega's strong opposition to "subjectivism" in Argentina in 1916–1917.[60]

ORTEGA'S TEACHING, DIALOGUE, JOURNALISM

How were Ortega's early lectures in philosophy regarded by those who heard them? Perhaps the first recorded impression was that of María de Maetzu, who as a student attended an opening lecture in Madrid in 1908, when he was still expounding neo-Kantianism. She was fascinated by his enthusiasm and by his "clear, precise, and elegant" delivery. "It seems that we are witnessing, not the teaching of a magisterial class, but the progress of

---

life" at that very time but he then rather illogically denied that a philosophy of life (as *Lebensphilosophie*) could be assigned to him (78–80, 381–83).

60. Ferrater Mora, "Objectivism," *Outline,* 15–24.

a dramatic theory whose protagonist is the very life of the philosopher." Another witness was Victoria Ocampo of Buenos Aires, who heard Ortega there in 1916, when he was thirty-three years of age. Holding forth spontaneously in private conversation or developing a theme "out of the air," he embodied a "prestige," an *élan vital,* and a "frank enthusiasm" that were as fascinating to her as were his "radiant" eyes and his polished phrases. Coriolano Alberini, later dean of the Faculty of Philosophy and Literature at the University of Buenos Aires, recalled Ortega's lectures there in 1916, when as yet he offered no mature system but a philosophy still "in the making." "For one [not semi-learned] who knows how to understand him, he is always a philosopher," even though he is usually *applying* his concepts to specific problems. He repeated the view that he was a "specialist on our time" and on the "values in force." No one surpassed his "acute perception" of contemporary philosophy. "No one, not even Bergson, whose magic is notorious, excels Ortega in philosophical dialogue," or in "intimate colloquy." And back at the University of Madrid in 1923, another student experienced how "exceptional" he was in "oral exposition, either in augmenting a text or in dialogue with students" on a "theme," spontaneously but clearly—surely a "natural gift," one bestowed in "superlative degree." Students responded so positively because it was not only in writing but in teaching that Ortega carried on "a kind of hidden dialogue" with the reader or auditor—to "caress" or to shock, for "language is essentially dialogue and is more effective in this form than in any other."[61]

Off the lecture dais and apart from discussion with peers in questions of philosophy, Ortega also made his mark from 1909 or before in a *tertulia,* a kind of discussion club for learned gentlemen of all professions. Having started his own group in the noisy café Granja el Henar, he moved it (after 1923) into the quiet offices of his *Revista de Occidente.* Like the review itself, the *tertulia* took up all manner of personages and problems of Spain, Europe, and America—Einstein, Spengler, Joyce, Picasso—anything in literature, art, science, the social sciences, history, or politics. In the 1920s, Walter Starkie described Ortega as its "center and master," a chubby Socrates with "magnificent leonine head," who cited philosophers and historians while coordinating the variety of theories and viewpoints into a coherent vision *sub luce aeternitatis.* He was "the most European mentality" in Spain also for

61. María de Maeztu, *Antología—Siglo XX* (Buenos Aires, 1943), quoted in Marías, *Circumstance and Vocation,* 230–31; Victoria Ocampo, "Mi deuda con Ortega," *Sur,* no. 24 (July–August 1956): 209–11; Coriolano Alberini, quoted (at length) in Iriarte, *Ortega,* 258–59; Alfonso García Valdecasas, "José Ortega y Gasset: Primeros recuerdos," *Revista de Occidente,* no. 26 (June–July 1983): 69.

Hella Weyl, who witnessed him still holding forth in the 1930s: flashing eyes, torrential words, and gesticulating hands.[62]

Before his famed *Revista de Occidente,* Ortega's most notable project in *haute* journalism was *El Espectador,* a review of philosophy and literature that he launched for the whole Hispanic world in 1916. Among the initial reactions was one that looked for whatever *philosophy* there was in the "absolute positivism" he announced that first year. "But this philosophy is not a system" but only a "method," not a new one either, and not Comte's. "We have here a professor of metaphysics. . . ." More than a decade later, another opinion of his production in that review was similar: "Thinker and litterateur always; never philosopher." Like a drone among the flowers, he was ever gathering nectar but never making honey. It was still impossible to define a system in this "independent rationalism."[63]

Even when Ortega published his theme of themes, the so-called *Modern Theme* of 1923, no one saw that his *philosophy* (or "system") of "perspectivism" and "vital reason" was a historizing existentialism—five years before Heidegger—that rested on a realist metaphysics (or method) that was basically pragmatism, misnamed "super-positivism," or "absolute positivism." Already in Argentina, however, a few critics even then could detect pragmatist connections, as did some critics a decade later in the United States.

62. Ortega, 2:255 (on his society called Dialogue); also 8:17–18 and 9:765; Walter Starkie, *Spanish Raggle Taggle* (New York, 1935), quoted in Iriarte, *Ortega,* 114–15; Helene (Hella) Weyl, "José Ortega y Gasset," *Toronto Quarterly* 6 (1937–1938): 461.
63. Q. Saldana and V. Cano quoted in Iriarte, *Ortega,* 245, 253.

Chapter 4

METAPHYSICS

"Radicalism" as Pragmatism
(1909+)

ccording to William James in *Some Problems of Philosophy* (1911), "philosophy means metaphysics," and the problems of the latter are largely the problems of life. Ortega agreed that "all the problems of metaphysics have their roots in the study of life, of vital reason." Moreover, "one can say of philosophy as metaphysics, fundamental science or *prima philosophia*, at once and at least, that it is something one does" (12:137). When his metaphysics was finally published (posthumously) as "doing" (*hacer*) a "metaphysics according to vital reason" (12:13, 24–26), a number of critics had already recognized a "metaphysics of life" in him,[1] but none saw that his metaphysics was pragmatist: Jamesian "radical empiricism," which he first called "absolute positivism," then "radical positivism," and finally simply "radicalism."

Most basically Ortega's philosophy was about "life" as "self and world," or "I and circumstance." But what else might this unitary-dualistic formula have meant? For many years it has been repeated uncritically by followers and sympathetic critics as uniquely and quintessentially his logos. But was it self-explanatory, or was it only a verbal mask covering a yet more "radical" knowing of a more basic and "radical" reality? Have we been merely skipping along the literary surface of his metaphysics without plumbing its depths and its relationships? Unlike Morón Arroyo, I do not regard Husserl's idealist phenomenology as *the* source of Ortega's original metaphysics of "absolute

---

1. William James, *Some Problems of Philosophy* (1911; Cambridge: Harvard University Press, 1979), 19–20, 24; Ortega, *¿Que es conocimiento?* 158 (from 1931). For example, J. A. Maravall noted that Ortega's "reform of philosophy" was a "metaphysics of life," and he "did metaphysics" in his course in 1933 ("Testimonio de Ortega," *La Torre* 4 [July–December 1956]: 72–73).

positivism"; at bottom, that metaphysics was mainly a version of James's realist "radical empiricism." Such a pragmatist metaphysics, formulated in phenomenological terms, supported his well-known formula: "self and circumstance." Yet it was paradoxical, his merging of these kindred types of philosophy (positivism, pragmatism, and phenomenology), all of which he had designated "anti-metaphysical" in an early course (R 57). Exploiting such unlikely sources, he was trying to *do* a new kind of metaphysics, very different from the traditional: metaphysics from "the point of view of vital reason" (R 75). Consequently, many critics did not recognize his metaphysics as such, much less as pragmatism, or radical empiricism.[2]

Nowadays, perhaps "pragmatism . . . is back," or at least has been reexamined in relation to other later philosophies of this century, so it is now recognized as "formidably diffuse."[3] That is true of James's metaphysics, too, for those who have detected a metaphysics in James, such as Sidney Hook and John McDermott, are not all agreed that it was his radical empiricism. Outside his metaphysics, pragmatism was also very "diffuse" in Ortega, because it affected his whole philosophy, beginning with "Adam in Paradise" (1910), as we have seen, and including *Modern Theme* (1923), *What Is Philosophy?* (1930), *History as a System* (1936), *An Interpretation of Universal History* (1948–1949), and *Man and People* (1950). Those extensions of pragmatism will be shown in each chapter (especially the last) of this study.

After Unamuno, Ortega was the first notable Spanish thinker to absorb in part the "practical" and "useful" philosophy of the Yankees—into his metaphysics, as well as his phenomenology, existentialism, historicism, and philosophy of life. What makes him so unusual is the fact that scholars have long been relating James's ideas or influence to these general movements in twentieth-century philosophy.[4] He proceeded where James had "pointed."

2. See supplemental note 2, chap. 4.

3. See supplemental note 3, chap. 4.

4. On Unamuno and James, see Pelayo H. Fernández, *Miguel de Unamuno y William James: Un paralelo pragmático* (Salamanca: CIADA, 1961); and Luis Farré, *Unamuno, William James, y Kierkegaard y otros ensayos* (Buenos Aires: Aurora, 1967). Unamuno sometimes used James's "will to believe" as a motto; Angel del Río, *Estudios Sobre Literatura Española* (Madrid: Gredos, 1972), 40. See Migotti's review, in supplemental note 3, chap. 4. On the relatability of James's philosophy to later movements, such as historicist existentialism, see John Macquarrie, *Existentialism* (Philadelphia: Westminster Press, 1972): "There are indeed existentialists who come close to a kind of pragmatism"—notably Unamuno and (more so) Ortega—for a focus on life more inward than outward in orientation (16; thanks to Antón Donoso). Ortega's "vitalistic bias" and instrumentalism brought him closer; his sense of crisis also put him with the existentialists. See Gerald E. Meyers, *William James: His Life and Thought* (New Haven: Yale University Press, 1986), for his view on freedom and determination, as related to becoming. For other movements, see the following scholars or the appropriate works as cited in other chapters of this study: (historicism) Jacques Barzun; (phenomenology) James Edie; (philosophy of life) Otto

ESTABLISHING ORTEGA'S "PRAGMATISM"

How can one demonstrate such unaccustomed claims about Ortega as a pragmatist fundamentally and throughout? Only a few Argentinian critics ever suspected any *direct* relationship or dependence between Ortega and James, but they dropped their inquiry in the 1920s after he had demonstrated some differences from popular "pragmatism."[5] Several (including Heidegger, Brinton, and Silver) have recognized that positivism of some kind was in Ortega's philosophy. However, no one as yet has noticed that his "radical positivism" was his basic metaphysics, and connected it to James's pragmatism as "radical empiricism,"[6] or extended this to all the levels and stages of his thought. In truth, the connections were easy to miss, unless one happened to be studying James and Ortega at the same time—a fortuitous conjuncture in my own case in 1984. But even marked similarity in a few ideas is not enough to establish any truly significant dependence, unless other links and resemblances become evident. As I investigated more fully, I discovered numerous connections, similarities, and basic identities, so that definite influence and dependence seem much more plausible than mere "coincidence" for Ortega and James. And the dependence extends from Ortega's idea of philosophy to his metaphysics and "beyond" to his work in history and the other human (social) sciences.

This complex thesis on pragmatism is very difficult to demonstrate adequately. One has to alternate the historical and the analytic: first, the direct evidences of various kinds (even critics' insights) from the formative through the maturing years; next, parallels (or identities) from texts of all levels and stages in regard to ideas, terms, and attitudes about philosophy, metaphysics, and the structure of reality and thought; then the later evidences of pragmatism in regard to history and sociology. In this way we can follow Ortega in his encounters with pragmatism from beginning to end and anticipate his varied applications of pragmatism to newer kinds of philosophy and even within the social sciences. It is a complicated procedure.

"Proof" of Ortega's basic pragmatism is, of course, in part necessarily subjective. Although I show it first historically (by sequential evidence) and then analytically (by comparison of positions and doctrines), the reader must finally be convinced personally by the evidence and persuaded by the demonstration. In nonspecific ways, Ortega at times admitted basic parallels with

---

Böllnow. On James's anticipating analytic philosophy, see Morton White, *The Age of Analysis: Twentieth-Century Philosophers* (Boston: Houghton Mifflin, 1944); he found James like Russell in "deflating" the pretentious obscurity of Continental philosophy (237), but unlike him in having a "philosophy of life" (190).

5. See supplemental note 5, chap. 4.
6. See supplemental note 6, chap. 4.

pragmatism and, at the end, an early and seminal influence from James. Where coincidences of doctrine and terminology relate to the books he had or used, we may reasonably assume that specific influences and borrowing were very probable. Between their basic metaphysics, crucial points of resemblance and of identity can be shown textually and chronologically. Of course, this demonstration selects only such aspects of James as were "congenial" with Ortega's own interests, problems, and native development, chiefly his "radical positivism," which owed so much to James's "radical empiricism."

Why did not Ortega admit James's basic influence at once and openly? As noted earlier, after 1898, for a young Spanish philosopher aspiring to a national chair of metaphysics, having professed publicly a close affiliation with James would probably have been fatal to his reputation and his career. It was easier for him at first to admit a limited kinship with German "empirical" thinkers such as Mach, Ziehen, and Avenarius, to insist on the basic differences of his own position, and, later on, to acknowledge Husserl and Dilthey and Comte for anticipations and "parallels" that he probably first found in James. Accordingly, we should view skeptically any of his intimations that "self and circumstance," his initial "intuition" (and "verification") of a unitary-dual principle in metaphysics, was entirely his own "independent" discovery (8:43–45). *Separately* those elements were first in James, later they were *united* in Husserl, but not so prominently in either case as they became in Ortega after 1910. But can one affirm such specific dependence even while affirming Ortega's overall originality in philosophy? Yes.

James in Ortega's Thought

Probably the most guarded of all of Ortega's "secrets" (6:349) was his initial dependence on William James. Like Dilthey, Bergson, Husserl, and Russell then, later British and American thinkers, such as Whitehead and (after Dewey) Barzun, have regarded James as original and "seminal," one for whom the often pejorative name "pragmatist" is inadequate. He was a "genius" who "gave to philosophy . . . a perspective and a context wholly novel in implication." After numerous hints for many years, Ortega barely admitted his early debt to James's "solitary" genius only near the end of his life, after 1950, in an explicitly "autobiographical" account, "A Half-Century of Philosophy," which lay unfinished and unpublished until 1980 and has not yet been well utilized.[7]

7. McDermott, "Preface," *Writings of James*, xi. Edie, *Invitation to Phenomenology*, 111, said James's "thought has more fundamental meaning for the evolution of 20th-century philosophy than even his most partisan followers have yet claimed for it." Bertrand Russell, *Philosophical Essays* (New York: Simon and Schuster, 1967), 87, 118; idem, *Unpopular*

In a retrospective analysis, Ortega explained by "historical reason" the "structure or anatomy of 'philosophical' reality between 1900 and 1915" (when he began to philosophize) as an "interregnum" between declining neo-Kantianism and the rising Husserlian idealist phenomenology. Then, during Dilthey's long "latency," there existed a "layer" of "great solitary facts of thought whose real and precise historical role" he meant to explain next: Sigmund Freud, Bertrand Russell, Henri Bergson, and William James— the last for *Pragmatism* (1907).[8] Russell was an advocate of James in part; Bergson, at times, was almost a like-minded "twin." After a long introduction on positivism, Ortega stopped in mid sentence before defining his specific dependence on James, but clearly an early connection was real and basic, and probably he would have linked pragmatism (taken as "radical empiricism") to his own "radical positivism."

Let us try to fill in the story Ortega left unfinished.

James in Ortega's Library

If Ortega were influenced by James's ideas in ways either basic or extensive, he had to know his chief works. Otherwise, we could dismiss his remarks as ill-informed, prejudiced, second-hand opinions out of histories, encyclopedias, and dictionaries of philosophy. In fact, he owned four works by James: *The Principles of Psychology,* two volumes (1890) translated into Spanish by Sorro in 1909; *The Will to Believe and Other Essays in Popular Philosophy* (1897), in the German translation by Paulsen in 1899; *A Pluralistic Universe* (1909), in French as *Philosophie de l'Expérience,* translated by Le Brun in 1910; and *Pragmatism: A New Name for Some Old Ways of Thinking* (1907), as *Le Pragmatisme,* again by Le Brun (with Bergson's very laudatory introduction, 1911) in 1929. These dates suggest that pragmatism interested Ortega most from around the time he became a philosopher until about 1930, which years fit well enough with my hypothesis and other evidence. The list is assuredly incomplete, for he probably read most of James. Ortega had indirectly cited *The Will to Believe* in 1908 (to Maeztu) and in 1916 (on James); *Pragmatism* in 1910 (on Baroja); and, in 1914 and 1915, *The Principles of Psychology* (lectures on psychology). And in 1930 he implied the posthumous

Essays (New York: Simon and Schuster, 1950, 1969), 167, calls James "a great man" and "a natural aristocrat." Craig R. Eisendrath, *The Unifying Moment: The Psychological Philosophy of William James and Alfred North Whitehead* (Cambridge: Harvard University Press, 1971), x, observed that Whitehead thought James's work was part of a "decisive turn in Western thought. . . ." Ortega, "Medio siglo," 6, 15. Oddly, this essential source, which was published in *Revista de Occidente* in 1980, was not included in *Obras Completas,* vol. 12 (1983), nor do I recall anyone citing it in the 1980s.

8. Ortega, "Medio siglo," 14–15; pragmatism, he said, was one of the few things "begun" in philosophy outside Germany.

Collected Essays and Reviews (1920) by reference to Peirce and "practicalism" in a course entitled "What Is Philosophy?" He also made both direct and implied reference (unpublished) to *The Varieties of Religious Experience* (R 56; R 61). Almost certainly he knew *The Meaning of Truth* (1909) and *Essays in Radical Empiricism* (1912), for the ideas therein are so like his own.[9]

Knowing that Ortega had several of James's books and that he probably used still others, we can more confidently look for evidence of likely influence, dependence, and borrowing. Only the *Principles* is "marked up" in the margins and by underlining, where in "The Stream of Thought" the self (*yo*) synthetically *unites* thoughts of things and their relationships (298–99); and, under "Instinct," the mind's instinctual plasticity for imitative learning for the first twenty-five years prior to metaphysical, psychological, or religious maturity (403).[10] These markings seem relevant to Ortega's basic metaphysics for union of self and things (world, or circumstance) and to his "theory of life," wherein the *twenty-sixth* year is normal for intellectual

9. My original knowledge of the contents of Ortega's library in regard to William James was courtesy of Señora Soledad Ortega. *Will to Believe* was a good introduction for Ortega to James's popular style of philosophying and to most of his key concepts and pragmatist terminology, including "radical empiricism," "pluralism," "working hypothesis," "concept," and even pelagic metaphors. See Ortega, 1:119; 4:87; 12:388, 417; perhaps the reference to Peirce's pragmatism as practicalism (7:310) relates to James's *Collected Essays,* but the reference to Peirce's practicalism may have come from certain "essays in philosophy" included in *The Will to Believe* (Cambridge: Harvard University Press, 1979), 131, 134. There is no work by Peirce in the library, so not he but James was Ortega's source. Ortega's identical quotations of Chesterton from 1914 to 1915 (1:413; 9:487) are from the first page of *Pragmatism,* surely from the 1911 French edition (with Bergson's preface), because Bergson's name is in both contexts. Regrettably the 1911 edition, which Ortega almost certainly read (and probably marked up in his distinctive way), is not in his library at the Fundación Ortega y Gasset. This is a great loss. Likewise, the only older version of *Varieties of Religious Experience* (1902)—*Las Variedades de las experiencias religiosas,* trans. S. F. Yuaes (Barcelona: Peninsule, 1926)—is cataloged but missing. Since the formative influences that Ortega acknowledged were much earlier, one should not expect to find much in the 1929 edition of *Le Pragmatisme,* but he marked both "instrument" and "instrumental" (68) in it, and he underlined the statement that pragmatism is "concrete thought" and "efficacious action" (61). That these volumes are now missing is not strange; the marvel is that so many have been preserved—approximately 15,000 with his "archer" stamp (red) in them, and many with his black, blue, and red marginal marks or underlining, sometimes with significant marginal comments—and the Fundación has added about that number since 1955. Of those four books by Freud, Russell, Bergson, and James, only Freud's and Bergson's are still in the library. They contained numerous marks and comments, but the latter were regrettably chopped off when the original paperback came back from the binder—the sad fate of too many of his annotated books.

10. My thanks to Professor Julián Ruiz, University of Seville, for arranging to have examined in Madrid Ortega's copies of James's books—which did not include the 1911 edition of *Le Pragmatisme* (already missing in 1985)—and to have photocopied for me those marked pages in James's other books.

independence. He was that age when he wrote "Adam in Paradise," which forecast a Jamesian philosophy of "life" stated in terms of "self" and "world."

An additional connection between Ortega and pragmatism may be surmised from several books by John Dewey that he owned. The first to leave a clear mark in his thought was *Democracy and Education,* from which he seems to have taken the idea of "trial and error" as the "pragmatic method" in 1916 (2:21) The former phrase (in English) he repeated in 1943 in a rerun of his "What Is Philosophy?" course (1930) wherein pragmatic elements were prominent (R 36), including "doing philosophy" (7:428), a term he repeated (R 78; R 80). Here we shall not attempt to pursue his debt to Dewey and "doing." Others have approached Ortega and pragmatism from that secondary angle, where the most direct influence—partly reactive—was probably in educational theory.[11]

Pragmatism Criticized but Accepted

If we were to take at face value Ortega's initial public scorn for pragmatism, it would be foolish or pointless to investigate his early thinking on knowledge, truth, and reality for possible fruitful relationships. Moreover, in *nothing* he published during his lifetime did he ever even mention James. Referring to pragmatism for the first time in reply to Maeztu in 1908, he dismissed it as a "sect" whose doctrines were a "shame for the scientific seriousness of the 20th century," and whose only deep or respectable ideas (on will) had already been anticipated by Fichte (1:119). Nevertheless, with obvious reference to James's *Will to Believe,* even then he accepted some of its ideas on science and ethics: he agreed "for a moment" to "become a pragmatist" by admitting that the will creates its object via conceptualization as an "instrument." In fact, he had soon quietly accepted a version of that idea, and he became a "pragmatist" for good.

In Ortega's archive is part of a manuscript of 1908–1909 with a bibliography citing James, along with Russell, Bergson, Husserl, and Dilthey (R 76). Evidently his familiarity with James began no later than that date, and from

11. Señora Soledad Ortega also provided a list of John Dewey's books that her father owned. A careful search through all of James's works did not turn up the phrase "trial and error," which evidently first appeared in Dewey's *Democracy and Education* (1916), a book in Ortega's library. The same expression also appeared thrice but much later in George Herbert Mead, *The Philosophy of the Act,* ed. C. W. Morris (Chicago: University of Chicago Press, 1938), 368–69. Ortega used the term again in 1939 (5:358), relative to technology and "instruments" as a "biological law," and also in 1943 in another version of his "What Is Philosophy?" lecture course on the second page along with "tropism" (R 36). As before, he used the English, "trial and error." This rough method was implicit in his "Historiology" (1928). On scholars recently or currently working on Ortega and Dewey, there is an unpublished paper by Antón Donoso, "Ortega's Critique of Pragmatism" (1987).

so early in his development he had associated James with the main European thinkers to whom he thereafter related pragmatism.

Having turned with Maeztu first to Nietzsche, Ortega now probed James against him. Other Spaniards of the "generation of 1898" who had reacted to Yankee pragmatism were Azorín, Baroja, and Unamuno.[12] Only the last was able to grasp pragmatism philosophically, but (having first *learned* James from Germans) Ortega approached him not through Unamuno but against Maeztu and the others, whose understanding he deemed erroneous and so he set out to refute or correct.

It was also in 1908 that Ortega reviewed—in fact panned—*El Político* by Azorín, who proclaimed the "bankruptcy" of democracy on the authority of socialist H. G. Wells and of "pragmatism." Briefly paraphrasing Azorín, he stated: "it is characteristic of pragmatism not to prejudge any dogma. All philosophies are true according to that new-old theory, when they serve to tune the heart of the individual. Action determines contemplation and distinguishes its solutions." Hence, decided Ortega, "pragmatism is *not* the enemy of democracy; far more is it the enemy of discretion" (10:53). This first encounter with a *political* pragmatism was not his last, and he did not wholly reject it.

In 1910, Ortega began a "Meditation" on novelist Pío Baroja, who had attacked Spain's "national pragmatism" (9:483–84). "Around 1910 . . . a crisis occurred in the soul of the nation." A "generation of Spaniards . . . doubted the reality of Spain," but doubt soon "turned into the denial of so-called 'national pragmatism'" (9:484). Ortega regarded this name as unsuitable for summing up that general disposition. "Why call that pragmatism? This fashionable word signifies the acceptance of an idea as true in view of its efficacy to augment or sustain life. Well, an old pragmatism would mean an assortment of non-efficacious ideas, therefore a pragmatism that does not exist." Baroja had thus given a "frivolous name to a very tragic reality" (9:490) that was the object of his "modernist" rebellion. But Ortega could soon have agreed that true ideas serve life. What "works" *may* prove true, by "trial and error."

His distaste for the term "pragmatism," at least as it was currently misused, did not deter Ortega too from using it in *El Espectador* in 1916 to describe more or less what Baroja had meant: politics as "utilitarian thinking." "For half a century, in and out of Spain," he noted, "politics—that is, subjection of theory to utility—has invaded our spirit completely. The extreme expression of it can be found in that pragmatic philosophy that dis-

12. See n. 4 above. Fernández found that Unamuno possessed James's *Will to Believe, Varieties of Religious Experience,* and *Pragmatism.* I found no reference to James or to pragmatism in the correspondence between Ortega and Unamuno, and Maeztu's works show no depth of interest at all in pragmatism.

covers the essence of truth, of the theoretical par excellence, in the *practical,* in the useful. In such fashion, thought is left reduced to the operation of finding good means for the ends without worrying about the latter" (2:15). For the past century Europe had been overly "concerned with collecting instruments: it has been a culture of means"—until world war had caught the nations unprepared for "ultimate questions" of ends, with a "culture of endings." Hence, such devotion to the useful might finally prove *not* useful. But, if it were generally bad and false for philosophy, it was often sensible "to think in utilitarian ways" in politics. "Situated in its range of secondary mental activity, politics or thinking of the useful is a salutary force from which we cannot prescind." But a politics "of lies" must not rule our consciences and our whole mental life, in education, literature, and history. "It is necessary, therefore, again to affirm . . . the rights of truth"—a question of reality (2:16), which was to be found only in "individual perspectives" on life *and* by "trial and error" methods. Hoping to catch for his new generation a glimpse of a "better epoch" for the future, Ortega promised to seek it out like an "arrow from the bow" (2:20–21).

Despite his unfavorable comments on pragmatism from 1908 to 1916, Ortega had derived basic inspiration and some key ideas from James during those very years. Not the least of these was his "perspectivism," or epistemology of "point of view." The announced purpose of *Espectador* was to "observe," or "see," life and the multifaceted world of things in flux, from the *true* perception of reality—through varying individual "perspectives" or "points of view" (2:18–20). Ortega's philosophical *intent,* then, still related as much to James's "viewpoint" and "stream of consciousness" as to Husserl's phenomenology.

James's *A Pluralistic Universe* (1909) had ended with a plea to youth to "gather philosophic conclusions . . . from the *particulars of life*" in imitation of Bergson—something Ortega (as "Spectator") now tried to do: "seeing life as it flows before one." Similarities just as marked (but a bit more specific) and equally basic to him and James were "pluralism" and "radical empiricism," ideas he first expressed between 1911 and 1916.[13]

Privately, in lectures on psychology in 1915–1916, Ortega cited mainly Husserl, but he also mentioned James (12:417)—in the context of plurality, relativity, and belief. Therein he first called his new rational approach to life by the name "vital reason." At the same time, he had again adverted to "so-called 'pragmatism'" as having—along with the historical idea of *Weltanschauung*—somehow anticipated "vital reason" and as being one of the "purely descrip-

13. William James, *Pluralistic Universe* (1977), 149. Ortega, 12:190–92, "radical empiricism"; 2:35 (1916), "plurality" with "hypothesis"; his reference in 1912 to pluralism, continuity and discontinuity (3:303) was almost certainly inspired by James's *Pluralistic Universe*, 146–47.

tive . . . phenomenological sciences," but in a "poorer and more absurd form" (12:392).

That brief, isolated reference to pragmatism is of capital importance for understanding Ortega's philosophy at that stage of development—in two senses. First, pragmatism had *anticipated* his own idea of vital reason, and, second, pragmatism was *compatible* with phenomenology, which was his current fixation. However, since pragmatism was so "poor" and "absurd" in *form,* he preferred to *express* his philosophy of vital reason in the form and terminology of Husserl's phenomenology. That did not deter him from using what was actually James's critique of idealist "consciousness" against Husserl even there (12:393, 407).

It was then too that he approved explicitly of James's larger view that "truth is the sense of evidence—belief, . . . the emotional reaction of the whole man" (12:417). Here he linked pragmatism to the "emotional" side of vital reason, which had resembled Unamuno's proto-existentialism and had anticipated Heidegger and Sartre since 1914 (4:403–4; 8:45).

The link Ortega saw between pragmatism and phenomenology in 1916 revealed them—along with historical "worldview" (Dilthey?)—as basic components of his "system" of philosophy of vital reason. Like Husserl's phenomenology, James's pragmatism both repelled him as a system and attracted him by its useful ideas. In 1916 he first cloaked the latter in a "formula" of "*absolute positivism,*" which he called "the alpha and omega of my logical and methodological convictions" (2:399). Theories and systems are true, if they fit our "direct vision of . . . the phenomena themselves"— before Husserl, a pragmatist maxim.

One additional bit of information ties Ortega irrefutably to James, for having had a major basic interest in pragmatism up through 1916 at least. A letter to Ortega from one of his graduate students, Fernando Vela, in that very year mentioned that he was preparing for his doctoral examinations by studying psychology in Wundt, Ziehen, and James. "But what *sensation* is for James, I still do not know . . ." (R 5). Now a master does not thus assign sources that are of little or no importance to himself.

Although perhaps he had never mentioned James outside the classroom, it becomes abundantly clear that Ortega was familiar with his pragmatism early enough to account for much—though obviously not everything—that then made up his basic philosophy. As noted above, by 1916 his philosophy was compounded of elements from James's pragmatism, Dilthey's historicism, and Husserl's phenomenology. Such a composite he reaffirmed in *Modern Theme* (1923) as the "vital, historical, and perspectivist" dimensions of his philosophy of vital reason (3:201). Critics could not assess his philosophy as a whole until he summed it up in *Modern Theme,* which a few took for pragmatist.

Ortega and Critics of His Pragmatism

Scarcely any of the numerous parallels between James and Ortega were detected by critics in the latter's lifetime, but general similarities were noticed both in Argentina and in the United States. In his public responses to critics who suspected him of pragmatism in the 1920s—for *Modern Theme*—he usually supported it in part but criticized it in general. His lectures "What Is Philosophy?" (1930), with several references to pragmatic themes, represented his final public answer to critics and was the acme of his public concern with pragmatism. His commitment to a paradoxical pragmatist metaphysics was lifelong, however. Already before 1923 it had influenced his development toward phenomenology, existentialism, historicism, and philosophy of life, all of them "beyond" mere pragmatism.

Accordingly, it must have surprised Ortega greatly when Argentinian critics accused him of being a pragmatist in his *Modern Theme* (1923). There was nothing *obviously* pragmatist about it, unless it was his "Doctrine of Point of View." Otherwise, any specifically Jamesian elements were scattered and diluted, if not disguised.[14] And new ideas were prominent, as in his "meta-historical" introduction about the role of generations in the history of thought and culture. A critic well informed on James might have noticed a general flavor of pragmatism in his proposition that *the* "theme of our time," in a crisis of European culture (3:186–88), called for a more precise "instrument" of thinking that would go "beyond" the extremes of the old rationalism and relativism (3:156). But the new philosophy that was proposed—at once "vital, historical, and perspectivist"—was obviously much more than James. If very alert, the critic might have noticed subtitles that embodied a dualist view (3:169, 174). But rationalism was not called "intellectualism" here, and the alternative of a very "rigorous positivism" (3:164) was not offered as a Jamesian metaphysics of "the given." "Relativity" (3:234), to supplant relativism, invoked Einstein instead of James.

In short, a critic who detected pragmatism in Ortega's new book had to be either very sharp or predisposed to suspicion. After 1916, *El Espectador* had won a good reception and following for Ortega in Argentina, especially among intellectuals of the younger generation. Perhaps someone had remembered therein his initial concessions to pragmatism (2:15, 21). Maybe he was suspected of having written a fine article on pragmatism in 1922 in

14. In *Modern Theme*, one can find isolated instances of Jamesian "instrumentalism" (cf. Ortega, 3:156, 187, 241) and vitalist functionalism, and "point of view" as "perspectivism" (3:178, 197, 234–35), but Ortega's longtime opposition to "intellectualism" here became pallid as mere "antirationalism" or "anti-utopianism" (237–38). His criticism then of relativism (3:207–9) was not exclusively James's, nor were the hopes for a "new time," or "new passages," in philosophy (3:146, 156)

Espasa-Calpe's *Enciclopedia Universal Ilustrada*. At any rate, he was accused too openly of pragmatism to ignore it.[15]

The anonymous review in *Inicial*, he answered, had failed to comprehend adequately the "theme" of his book and to evince a "positive" attitude. In an open letter in April 1924, therefore, he tried to set the issue straight. His philosophy, he insisted, was not pragmatism, and, from James's own outlook, that was technically true.[16] "Moreover, such a crime cannot even be committed in philosophy because, on intending it, one has ceased to be a philosopher. Pragmatism has never been a philosophy of philosophers, but at the most, a philosophy for those incapable of having one" (8:272–73).

That disingenuous disavowal of pragmatism was very like Ortega's later claim that for his generation phenomenology was not a "system" or "philosophy" but only a useful *method*, or "instrument" (8:42). He denied only that his *philosophy* was pragmatism, and, in a strict sense, that was true enough about his overall "system." Any "pragmatism" that appeared in him then seemed limited to a vague "method" of "viewpoint," or "perspective." As later with phenomenology, he was less than candid about his debts and affinities. He remained silent about having been *influenced* by any of James's ideas. If he were correct technically, he nevertheless misled his critics.

What Ortega denied and admitted in 1924 in response to *Inicial* was at least the most thoughtful of his public comments on pragmatism till then. Up to a point, he did not refuse a certain validity to the pragmatic thesis, but he felt that he had corrected its flaws and gone beyond it in *The Modern Theme*. "No, I have never thought that truth is a simple process of adaptation to practical ends." I have always believed quite the contrary. His intent was "to harmonize the trånscendent, ultra-biological character of truth with the immanent, biological character of thought."

> Truth is transvital—so says Socrates' and Plato's rationalism. Thought is a vital process—so says relativism—, of which pragmatism is only a discolored manifestation. And the case is that both affirmations are true. For that

15. See supplemental note 15 chap. 4.

16. James, "Preface," *Pragmatism*, 6: " . . . there is no logical connection between pragmatism, as I understand it, and a doctrine which I have recently set forth as 'radical empiricism.'" Thus he distinguished his pragmatism (as practical method relative to truth) from his "world-view" (or metaphysics) of radical empiricism, which Ortega especially took up. In an interview in 1907, James insisted that radical empiricism, which "sounds idealistic," has "nothing to do with pragmatism" and should not be "confounded with" it (*Writings*, 449), although at other times he connected them as interdependent (*The Meaning of Truth*, 6). What he predicted in *Pragmatism* (1907) pretty well described Ortega's own reaction to it over the years: "First, . . . a new theory is attacked as absurd; then it is admitted to be true but obvious and insignificant, finally it is seen to be so important that its adversaries claim they themselves discovered it" (*The Moral Philosophy of William James*, ed. J. K. Roth [New York: Crowell, 1967], 292).

reason it is impossible to shut oneself into one of them and to deny the other, as do rationalism and relativism. (8:373)

He cautioned that we must not "confuse thought with truth"; as an "organic function of the individual," the former could be true or false in its development, but "truth is indifferent to all vital co-living." His critic had missed the refinements that distinguished truth from thought, at the *historical* level.

Although Ortega was not a grossly popular pragmatist, was not his "two-horned" approach to relativism and rationalism, after all, rather Jamesian at bottom?[17] Then what else was he intimating by his dual distinction between thinking and truth (or reality)? He was trying to synthesize ("harmonize") neo-Kantian idealism and empirical realism, in a unity of knowing and being. Even this daring synthesis was not very different from James's intent.[18]

Although Ortega regarded his difference from James as real and crucial, actually it appears to be more a matter of *degree,* and not nearly so great as the following diatribe on truth seems to say. After all, pragmatic "truth" was only one of his many doctrines that interested Ortega, but he judged that it contained the most critical error: an "absurd" identity of truth and subject that made pragmatism a "vulgar skepticism."

> Pragmatism is an example of audacity without equal. Without stopping for an instant to reflect on the most elementary ideas that intervene in the problem of knowledge, it has wanted to build a philosophy. The result has been a grotesque confusion. Instead of speaking of truth, it should have been speaking of conviction, of certitude, that is, in effect, of subjective facts. In the formation of our convictions practical factors clearly intervene. . . . The "acquisition" of truths . . . is a historical process, a biological phenomenon. (8:376)

Against the popular notion of pragmatism—not against James—Ortega argued, "Truth cannot be relative to the condition of a subject, be it individual or the species. Something is true for me, when I believe it true in itself, and not vice versa."

Perhaps echoing Scheler's refutation of pragmatism, Ortega was "protest-

17. In "Dialogue," from *Meaning of Truth,* James spoke of the "horns of a dilemma" concerning truth and reality and said that one had to take it by both horns (*Writings,* 444); also see his *Psychology: A Briefer Course* (1892; Cambridge: Harvard University Press, 1984), 371.

18. Andrew J. Rick, "Epistemology in W. James' 'Principles of Psychology,'" *Tulane Studies in Philosophy* 22 (1973):79–115, sees James's work as "revolutionary," in its dualism of empiricist and rationalist emphases. Conkin, *Puritans and Pragmatists,* 310, observed that in radical empiricism, as "a new and revolutionary view of reality," James was torn between "pure experience" and "conceptual thought," although he was usually a "realist." His pluralism had "a key metaphysical import" (319).

ing too much," for he did not go so far in fact.[19] He took "leave" of pragmatism *too* "quietly"—maybe a little ashamed of ingratitude. Obviously, he felt that something was right philosophically with pragmatism. If not pragmatist "Truth," at least he accepted James's ideas on "truths" and "beliefs." But pragmatism was no longer up to the level of the times. "To be busy with it implies being far removed from the big new problems. Philosophy has traveled far from 1880 till today. It is not too much to say that in that interval it has been reborn, and that today, as adult, it sees before itself vast, shimmering horizons" (8:376). It is ironic that even in his hopes for the philosophical future, he echoed James.

In epistemology and ontology his metaphysical foundation had been— and still was—James's radical empiricism, if not all of "pragmatism." While it is true that his own *philosophy* had already become much more complex, nuanced, and subtle, James's influence was still there waiting to be discovered by anyone who looked closely and comparatively at some of the key ideas. To Ortega's embarrassment, despite all his denials and distinctions, his "secret" was detected. Argentinian critics stubbornly repeated their suspicion in 1924 and again in 1925—precisely on his close resemblance to James in pragmatism and finally even in "radical empiricism."

Responding to his April 27 rebuttal, Homero Guglielmini admired the skill with which he had there treated the basic problems of philosophy in attempting a synthesis of Platonic idealism and of relativistic realism. He had written an "intimate diary" of his era: on the one side an "impossible Platonism" and on the other "a mischievous little devil of relativism that seeped through every crack in his philosophical armor," like an "ironic grimace." Such was the "essential contradiction" that Guglielmini saw in Ortega's philosophy, and did not believe that he had indeed succeeded in surmounting subjectivism and "a certain echo of pragmatism." "His theory of perspectivism is and always will be a subjectivist way of confronting problems." In his search for a solution Ortega had eagerly tried to adjust to his "doctrine

---

19. Like Ortega, Scheler spent some time and effort investigating American pragmatism, which he accused of "grave errors" with regard to history and ethics and of turning "all philosophy into a bog." See Scheler's *Formalism in Ethics and Non-Formal Ethics of Value,* trans. M. S. Frings and R. L. Funk (Evanston, Ill.: Northwestern University Press, 1973), xiii, 398, 431–32, 518, 582n. Also see John H. Nota, *Max Scheler: The Man and His Work,* trans. T. Plantinga (Chicago: Franciscan Herald Press, 1983), 157, on Scheler's "exquisite refutation of pragmatism"; like Ortega, he thought the pragmatists right on *practical* but wrong on conceptual knowledge and its a priori character. Ortega, however, came to see James as merely not clear nor developed enough on the latter. Where Scheler's position was *Idealismus-Realismus,* Ortega's was "realism-idealism." The fact that Ortega accepted "Martha" along with "Mary"—action and reflection—was noted by Carl J. Burckhardt, who said he "denied any [sharp] limits between thinking and working; thought should be action" ("Encuentro con Ortega," *Sur,* no. 24 [July–August 1956]: 181).

of point of view" the ideas of Spengler in history and of Einstein in mathematics and physics. But, "more than a systematic philosopher," he was a mirror and his perspectivism was an interpretation of his era's thinking. In his fight against utopian systems of "culturalism," cut off from life, "is he not translating a position, in a certain way, loftily pragmatic?" An "immediate subordination of the idea to the practical ends of our life" was, after all, the "primitive and rudimentary orientation of the pragmatism of '80."[20]

Summing up, Guglielmini noted that Ortega's "pragmatism gravitates around the formulas" set up in *Modern Theme* that concerned truth and culture in a subjective setting. Promising a "definitive" study after he could examine all the works still to come, Guglielmini was not heard from again, perhaps because in 1924 Ortega turned abruptly to a new "horizon": to "historical reason," only hinted in 1923, for a new opening to objectivism.

How right was the Argentinian critic in identifying the pragmatism in Ortega? Actually his critical judgment did not rest on a very direct or complete knowledge of either James's pragmatism or of Ortega's works to date. As he granted, there was much more to be said on the subject. Apparently he had no suspicion that Ortega depended on James's radical empiricism for the "rigorous positivism" in *Modern Theme* or the "strict" positivism of his public letter (3:166; 8:375). Yet these phrases summarized Ortega's attempted compromise between realism and idealism—a "synthesis" that comprised three "elementary distinctions," without which (as James too had said) "all of philosophy's cats will be gray": the things thought, the ideas thought, and the act of thinking, with their epistemological and ontological "relations" and "connections" (8:374).[21] While this was not pragmatism as "vulgar skepticism," it *was* James's radical empiricism—spliced with Kant. And, feasible or not, Ortega's "synthesis" was genuinely an *effort* to go "beyond" general pragmatism—even as James himself had "pointed" the way.

A muted return to that dispute over pragmatism came six months later (October 1924) in Ortega's essay "Neither Vitalism nor Rationalism," where he clarified some points misunderstood about *Modern Theme*. Distinguishing three kinds of vitalism, he linked "the beatific pragmatism" with "the empiro-criticism of Avenarius or Mach" in the *basic* vitalist theory of knowledge, as mere "biological process" (3:272). Now that was hardly fair to James, whose "radical empiricism" as theory of knowledge was by no means such a

---

20. Guglielmini, "Algo más sobre Ortega."

21. Curiously, the very phrase about "gray cats" (which Ortega used more than once over the years) was also in James, who got it from a dictionary of aphorisms, although it was originally (whether or not James realized it) from Cervantes' *Don Quixote*. Compare with Wild for James's similar expression about "things thought" and "not of thinking" (*Radical Empiricism*, 233–34).

simplistic *beatería* of scientism, but was closer to Ortega's second (Bergsonian) type of vitalism that confronted "rational method" with theory as "intuition." "For me," however, objected Ortega, " . . . reason and theory are synonyms," thus distinct from Bergson "and others similar in form" (3:273). In fact, his third variety, the vitalism of *Modern Theme,* which accepted *rational* method related to life but not the old rationalistic theory that contradicted life, was at base indebted to James's conceptualism and anti-"intellectualism."

If the newer distinctions by Ortega were valid, how deep did they go? He had separated from the basic "biological vitalism" of a material-scientific type another (fourth) kind (much more like James's), which he denoted as a "pure 'biologism'" (simply "study of life," literally) that was "a rigorous empiricism." This biologism was "limited to studying vital phenomena in the unpolished particularity that they manifest, without supposing behind them any specific vital entity . . ." (3:271). Neither this primary nor the material meanings of vitalism, he argued, "can be applied to a philosophy" in a "strict sense," but "I see in pure 'biologism'—not in its impoverished and insufficient form . . . —the direction of the most fruitful future." Clearly, any "fruitful" *philosophical* application for this "rigorous empiricism" would be as a raw metaphysical basis for the third type of vitalism that he called "vital reason."

In short, expounding ratiovitalism in 1924, Ortega implied that pragmatism was a "biologist" vitalism that was indeed *basic* to his own philosophy—past, current, and future. But he felt he had clearly gone "beyond" that "rigorous empiricism." Thus did James's radical empiricism still reside within his larger philosophy as its epistemological and ontological point of departure, which now he also called a "rigorous positivism."

A more direct admission of pragmatism than that, no one was going to get out of Ortega. Since first encountering American pragmatism, he had diluted it within—or assimilated it to—much wider fields of European philosophy: empiricism, positivism, and phenomenology. Among all of those affinities, however, James's "radical empiricism" was still the most singly important fundament of his philosophy. Now, however, Ortega was preparing to bury that pragmatist connection ever more deeply under his new historical point of departure. The higher "historical reason" of "Atlantises" (1924) owed much more to Dilthey than to James. Apparently Ortega's grudging concession about pragmatism in the article on vitalism and rationalism had been too minute or too subtle for his critics. Misled by his reference to Mach, they now turned away from their well-founded suspicion that he was somehow a pragmatist. Reviewing the perspectivism of *Modern Theme* in *Nosotros* in 1925, Alberto Rouges briefly compared his realist empiricism to James's "radical empiricism," but he saw Ortega basically adhering to Ernst Mach's "radical phenomenism."[22] Having thus led critics off the track, Ortega could henceforth safely apply the qualifier "radical" to his own metaphysics.

A last echo of the debate with the Argentinians over pragmatism came in 1930. His public lecture course, "What Is Philosophy?" was the most directly concerned with pragmatism (alongside phenomenology, existentialism, and even historicism) of all his works. Several parts of the lectures were printed as letters in *La Nación* (Buenos Aires), wherein he saw Yankee pragmatism offering a "congenial cynicism" in its view of *truth*. However, he now granted that, besides ingenuous boldness, "there is something profoundly true, if centrifugal, in pragmatism." This time he rejected as mere *beatería* any "preconceived disdain" for its genuine insight into that *half* of the truth represented by its "practicalism" (*practicismo*), or the "active life" of "Martha," as a necessary part of the "perennial duality" in human life (4:97). And he noted, too, that Einstein had said to Planck that the truth or superiority of any theory in physical science is ultimately determined *practically* by "the world of our perceptions." Then Ortega concluded that neither the reality nor the knowledge of physical science is absolute, but is limited—a rather Jamesian position (4:101–2). In fact, like the very title and content of his lectures, his argument was at times very reminiscent of James's "popular" essays in philosophy, notably those in the 1920 collection on "practicalism" as the basic principle of pragmatism that James had attributed to Peirce. Since 1923 Ortega had probably written (at least edited) anonymous articles for Espasa-Calpe on James, Peirce, and Schiller.[23]

If Rouges and Guglielmini read the letters, they did not take the bait. Because Ortega had had the last word in the debate, he had won the game. His secret safe, he impishly teased Argentinians again in 1939 on *pragma*, "pragmatism," and encyclopedias (6:350–59), for a new venture of Espasa-Calpe in Buenos Aires. After 1930 he could enjoy an "ironic grimace."

In the United States, where their basic pragmatism might have been detected more readily, *Modern Theme* was not published until 1933 and *What Is*

---

22. Rouges, "Perspectivismo," 340, 344, 348, 346 (as opposed to Kant). The suspicions of Rouges apparently went back to 1916, to Ortega's conferences in Argentina. See *José Ortega y Gasset: Dos conferencias* (Tucumán: Universidad de Tucumán, 1916). My thanks to Roberto Arias for data on Rouges and Guglielmini, neither of whom ever again published on Ortega.

23. James, *Collected Essays and Reviews* (New York: Russell, 1920), 410. For Peirce's realism and "social philosophy" as contrasted to James's "nominalism" and individualism, see Susan Haack, "Pragmatism and Ontology: Peirce and James," *Revue Internationale de Philosophie* 31 (1977): 377, 393–99. See supplemental note 15, chap. 4, for the encyclopedia essay on James, which differs in emphasis but not in essentials from "Pragmatism"; for shorter ones on Peirce, Schiller, and other pragmatists, all probably by Ortega, see corresponding volumes.

Philosophy? not until 1960. That was a decade and a generation too late for reviewers to pounce on them, but in the 1930s there were two who sensed a vague similarity. R. A. Scott-James of the *Christian Science Monitor* feared that Ortega's laudable effort to bring philosophy down from airy heights and into contact with human life "may expose him to the charge which is constantly brought against William James and the Humanists—that they are not philosophic." Irwin Edman of Columbia University saw similarities with Schiller's "New Humanism." Since that movement was already passé, however, he concentrated on other features of that "provocative" essay that were of more current interest. No other reviewer then came close to recognizing the pragmatist connection of *Modern Theme,* including Henry Hazlitt in *The Nation* and H. M. Kallen, who had edited *The Philosophy of William James* in 1925. Apparently misled by "perspectivism," Kallen compared Ortega's relativistic and functionalist view on life and reason not to James but to Nietzsche. Fifty years later, however, Barzun saw that his "point of view" was properly James's "perspectivism." In the interval, in 1957, James Conway in *Thought* described Ortega's philosophy of "a-thing-to-be-done" as a "pragmatic *faciendum*—"a pragmatistic 'vital reason,'" and in 1967, Neil McInnes compared Ortega's vital reason in *Modern Theme* to what Dewey and the pragmatists "would call . . . practical reason."[24]

From his bouts with the critics, it looks as if Ortega used the crass popular perception of pragmatism—with James's more incautious utterances—as a convenient "decoy" to distract them, while he continued developing several of James's crucial, seminal insights as basic to his own "systematic" philosophy that grew far "beyond" the sparse metaphysics of radical empiricism from which he had started. Dewey did much the same thing, but Ortega gave that basis a much greater extension. Where Dewey freely admitted his debt to James as his master, however, Ortega was more like Bertrand Russell, whom Barzun later chided for having written publicly against pragmatism while learning it and teaching it to students.[25] Never acknowledging James openly, Ortega nevertheless remained at basis more Jamesian than Kantian, Husserlian, or Heideggerian.

24. R. A. Scott-James, review in *Christian Science Monitor,* April 22, 1933, p. 10; Irwin Edman, review in *New York Herald Tribune Books,* February 19, 1933, p. 3; Henry Hazlitt, review in *Nation* 136 (February 1933): 209; Horace M. Kallen, review in *Annals of the American Academy of Political and Social Sciences* 167 (May 1933): 245; Barzun, *Stroll with James,* 300; James I. Conway, "Ortega y Gasset's 'Vital Reason,'" *Thought* 32 (December 1957):595, 601—a review of Marías's *Reason and Life,* trans. K. S. Reid (New Haven: Yale University Press, 1956); *Encyclopedia of Philosophy* (1967), s.v. "Spanish Philosophy" (by Neil McInnes).

25. Barzun, *Stroll with James,* 299; Elizabeth R. Eames, *Bertrand Russell's Dialogue with His Contemporaries* (Carbondale: Southern Illinois University Press, 1989), 170.

MAJOR AND MINOR PARALLELS WITH JAMES

When we turn from the history of Ortega's encounters with pragmatism and critics and approach the problem analytically by texts and ideas, we find that broad but remarkable similarities between James and Ortega begin with their attitudes and concepts toward philosophy (or philosophizing) and metaphysics. Along with Bergson, James stated an opposition to the old rationalism and "intellectualism" that Ortega echoed for the rest of his life. Likewise, James's emphasis on the functional nature of thought relative to the problems and "crises" of life, which both experienced in different ways,[26] was repeated in Ortega's rooting of reason in vital needs and experience—in practical ("pragmatic") *usefulness*—even to provide a rational "faith" for life in lieu of an inherited one.

As the basis for knowing reality, James's metaphysics of "radical empiricism" was grounded in "fact" and "thing" and in "experience of life" and "viewpoint" or "perspective" thereon, with basic relations and "connections" included. All of that is scarcely different from Ortega's "radical positivism" in any significant respect. The near-coincidence both verbally and conceptually of "radical empiricism" and "radical positivism" extends to the type of Heraclitean and Bergsonian ontology of "things" *becoming*. Tied to this concrete, "perceptual" basis of philosophizing were higher "conceptual" operations of the intellect. This duality was the same in Ortega as in James.[27] Similarities of this kind continue even into higher forms of generalizing by concepts, hypothesis, and verification in Ortega's metahistorical historiology.

Continuity with James is also true of Ortega's "dualism" (or "pluralism") balanced by "unity" (8:43, 330; 9:379, 389–91), in their positions respecting reality and truth—or ontology and epistemology. Similarly James's epistemological "knowing things together," is very like Ortega's "thinking [things] together" and "unity of knowing and being" (12:491; 8:70–71). These aspects are structurally basic.[28]

---

26. See James, *Writings*, 170 (*functional* nature of consciousness) and 6–7 on his own crisis at the age of twenty-eight.

27. See James, *Will to Believe* (1979), 5–6, where radical empiricism is closely linked to "pluralism," "point of view," and fact and *givenness*"; compare with Ortega in "Adam in Paradise," as discussed in my chap. 3. James, *The Principles of Psychology*, 2 vols. (1890; reprint, New York: Dover, 1950), 1:233, in "The Stream of Thought" related Heraclitus's "river of life" to a "*continuous* stream" (240); compare with Ortega, 6:33n, 36, "History as a System." For James on "intellectualism," see *Writings*, 519, and supplemental note 37, chap. 4; on "duality," 183, 252–54. Compare with Ortega's "Meditations on Quixote," the concept in regard to the forest and the trees, in my chap. 3, and on dualism in Ortega, see my chap. 8 (on James).

28. In James, see *Memories and Studies* (1911; reprint, New York: Greenwood, 1968), 385–86 n. 1 ("being is knowing" and vice versa); idem, *Writings*, 151–53, 252.

Semantic likenesses (even *identities*) between them hold for peculiarities of terminology in cases major and minor. Besides "pluralism" and "intellectualism" mentioned above, even James's expression "consciousness of consciousness"—denied of Kantian rationalistic idealism—also reappears in Ortega's rejecting of Husserlian phenomenology. Moreover, Ortega's emphasis on new "ways of thinking" (2:23; 8:91, 155, 240), reiterated throughout his career, was topically prominent as the subtitle of *Pragmatism* in 1907. Even James's emphasis on the word "beyond" has an exact counterpart in Ortega's often repeated *mas allá* (7:120, 313, 421), which meant to "overcome" or surpass but to keep by incorporating. "Presence," "compresence," and "concatenation" are additional Jamesian terms that carried over directly (in "What Is Philosophy?") into his philosophical diction, as did "primal stuff" and "copies."[29] Nor are these the only instances. (See chap. 3, on "Adam," for others.)

Some of the similarities between James and Ortega *may* be coincidence, and probably several of them are (such as "Adam," "Cartesianism of life," and "gray cats"), for both minds were working on similar problems from similar principles, and both searched widely for inspiration, often in the same sources. James himself borrowed freely (from Dilthey and Brentano) and was borrowed from (by Husserl and Bergson). But not all, nor even most, of the similarities are coincidences—especially not for views on philosophy.[30] The parallels between "radical empiricism" and "radical positivism" represented the most basic part of their philosophies, and here they were almost identical. Even through his "middle" stage of philosophizing (vital reason as

29. Locations in James (as in Ortega) for these and other expressions are extremely various and repetitive, and most are given below (as "beyond": James, *Writings*, 213). For specific expressions, as they appear in the text, see the appropriate notes below. One example of semantic identity, which is not repeated elsewhere in this study, is the word "zigzag," which both James and Ortega used—see *Pluralistic Universe* (1909), 394, and *Essays in Radical Empiricism* (1947), 162; cf. Ortega 1:450; 2:734; 10:223; 8:500n; 9:320n—and which both preferred to Hegel's strictly triadic form of dialectic. For "compresence" in Ortega, see 7:118–20, 332; and 6:43 (history as a "chain" [*cadena*] of human experiences); cf. James, *Essays in Radical Empiricism*, 106–7.

30. On "gray cats," see n. 21 above. A good example of multiple sources (or coincidence) of ideas, terms, and metaphors occurs with Herder. Many of Ortega's maritime metaphors, *aurora* (dawn), Castor and Pollux (the Gemini), and human nature as historical appear in Herder's *Social and Political Culture*, trans. F. M. Barnard (Cambridge: Harvard University Press, 1969), 65, 71–72, 83–84. Herder's, *Reflections on the Philosophy of History of Mankind*, ed. Frank E. Manuel (Chicago: University of Chicago Press, 1968), refers to time, place, and circumstance, including history as a "concatenation of circumstances" (196, 213, 265–66). A similar point is made in my chap. 8 about Friedrich Schlegel and Ortega. Did James also read (and borrow) from Herder and Schlegel? Is it a likely "coincidence" that the Chesterton quotation on the first page of James's *Pragmatism* should have reappeared exactly in Ortega (9:487; 1:413–14)—both times (1914, 1915) in connection with Bergson?

"perspectivism"), Ortega resembled not only Husserl and Heidegger in phenomenology and existentialism but James, too, in ideas and *intent*. Only in his final stage of "historical reason" did Ortega clearly, unequivocally, go *far* "beyond" his Jamesian heritage and become fully independent as a thinker. But in his historicism, too, one can discern a Jamesian root in his insistence on the *temporal* and *spatial* correlatives of reality (6:350; 7:285). Like Dilthey, James had at least investigated the history of thought in philosophy. It was not typical of new peoples like the Americans, observed Ortega, to be very much concerned with history (4:203, 240–41).

The similarities and identities of expression become altogether too many and in some cases too exact to suppose mere "coincidence" between James's ideas and those of Ortega. Clearly, among other things, young Ortega was a Jamesian, and he never ceased to be such at bottom. Let us not stop here prematurely, however, but add a specific demonstration. The many resemblances can be grouped and reduced to (1) philosophy in nature and purpose; (2) "radical empiricism" as metaphysics; and (3) unity and plurality as chief structural principles. Each of the three general likenesses has several subordinate elements.

On Philosophy and Philosophizing

When he talked about philosophizing, William James often sounded like the José Ortega we have come to know and to like. Besides *Pragmatism* (1907) and *A Pluralistic Universe* (1909), young Ortega probably found encouragement in *Essays in Radical Empiricism* (1912), wherein James explained his philosophy not just to other philosophers but to youth and to the educated general public. "Fortunately our age seems to be growing philosophical again," mused James.[31] His deliberately "popular" lectures, like Bergson's applause from "the broad public" (R 76), were noteworthy anticipations of Ortega's later style.

One suspects that young Ortega took to head and heart such lines as the following on a new realism, except that he came to it through Kantian idealism. "Believing in philosophy myself most devoutly, and believing also that a kind of new dawn is breaking upon us," James had an acute sense of unrest and of change, with attendant borrowing and innovation, by the first decade of the twentieth century. "What the younger generation 'seeks' is more of the temperament of life in its philosophy, even though it were at some cost of logical rigor and of formal purity."[32] James felt that the new

---

31. James, *Pluralistic Universe* (1977), 7; idem, *Writings*, 317, 362–63.
32. James, *Writings*, 359, 363 ("new dawn"), 380, cf. 387, 390 (positivism).

Weltanschauung would be a "natural realism," like "pragmatism," or "radical empiricism," which was the culmination of years of thinking in opposition to idealistic rationalism.

By no later than 1910–1911 (7:288; 6:19), as he began to philosophize, Ortega too sensed a turning point (a "crisis") in philosophy away from both idealism and materialism, toward "pluralism," realism, and the concrete individuality of human *life* and "historical empiricism" (3:303–4; 5:57). For him, as for James, individual "point of view" was inseparable from a philosopher's grasp of reality and truth.[33] His vital reason was for him a philosophy of "everyone," so also a philosophy of "viewpoint" (or "perspective"). It was something (*un quehacer*) for anyone or everyone (*cada cual*) to "do" in life (4:366–67; 7:405, 415), by using concepts as "instruments"—a viewpoint so pragmatic that it recalls Dewey. And, like James, he expected his kind of philosophy to become a general worldview, a new "revelation" or "dawn" (5:45, 375) of vital and historical reason, as opposed to both positivism and "intellectualism" (6:30) or Cartesian and Kantian idealism.

Seeking "postmodern" solutions, Ortega in 1916 observed: "Other ways of thinking, moving in the same trajectory as positivism, keeping and strengthening whatever it has of strict purposes, have supplanted it" (2:23)—meaning pragmatism, phenomenology, and his "absolute positivism," of course. Not the old rationalism, the last was not vitalist *ir*rationalism, as he stressed in 1924 (3:276–78), but a *rational* vitalism.

Can one help recalling the later Ortega also in these words of James? "I know that you, ladies and gentlemen, have a philosophy, each and all of you, and that . . . it determines the perspective in your several worlds." "Philosophy is at once the most sublime and the most trivial of human pursuits . . . . No one of us can get along without the . . . light it sends over the world's perspectives." Even earlier James had asked: "What is the task which philosophers set themselves to perform; and why do they philosophize at all? . . . They desire to attain a conception of the frame of things which shall on the whole be more rational than the somewhat chaotic view which everyone by nature carries about with him under his hat."[34]

How James's exhortations on "popular philosophy" must have reverberated in Ortega's spirit, as he went on to develop his own version of "Everyone his own Philosopher" in his popular "What Is Philosophy?" lectures

33. As in Ortega's *History as a System*, so also in *What Is Philosophy?* trans. Mildred Adams (New York: Norton, 1960), one finds lines that are not in the Spanish text that is presumed to be the "original"; here on pages 30–31 is a reference to philosophy between 1900 and 1910 that is not in the other (7:288), but the dates impress one as authentic, fitting what Ortega said elsewhere. James, *Writings*, 195, 379–81, 304, 362.

34. James, *Will to Believe* (1979), 57; idem, *Writings*, 317, 362, compare with Ortega's *What Is Philosophy?*

(1930). That philosophy of *life* (and history), addressed to "everyone," especially to a new "generation" of youth, was (in part) the most openly concerned with pragmatism of all his works. Therein he directly adverted to pragmatism, to Peirce, and to several ideas, such as "multiverse" and "compresence" (7:297, 310, 320, 332), that were patently James's. Besides he offered a "radical" positivism of "immediate presence" as a metaphysics of life, the "radical reality" (7:351–52). To philosophize was to start from one's life and to work toward the world.

Then and always their popular styles of philosophizing were similar: chatty "dialogue" in exposition, both for lectures and for writing. What James acknowledged as the "artlessness of my essays in point of technical form"[35] was repeated by Ortega about his use of informal dialogue, even in his books (7:17–18, 20). In his lecturing, he often rambled and once had to excuse a rude "burst of philosophic gas" (9:83, 184). In their intellectual and popularizing temperaments they were often alike.

According to James, subjective temperament, however much despised, has always helped make the kinds of philosophers we find throughout history. Most of us have *mixed* temperaments, but everyone still "*sees* things" in "his own peculiar way," so obviously "beliefs" count. In general, however, philosophers divide into "tender-minded" rationalists, who hold to idealism, monism, wholes, principles, and absolute universals, and "tough-minded" empiricists, who hold to realism, pluralism, parts, life experience, and concrete individual "facts." To range himself on the latter side, against the old rationalism as an "intellectualism," was only an *apparent* "irrationalism," for he also deemed conceptual thinking essential.[36]

We also find an empirical and realist position, over and over again, in Ortega's perspectivism and later, balanced with emphasis on conceptualization. Looking back from the 1930s, he too stressed the role of temperament (his "altruism") in the shaping of his own philosophy, in balancing off the solipsist "Robinson" Crusoe in all of us (6:346; 8:18). Already in 1914, moreover, he had contrasted "feelers" and "thinkers" but had put himself more with the conceptualizers (1:349–51), without forsaking realism for idealist "intellectualism."

Not "Intellectualism" but Open, Social Philosophy

Throughout his career, Ortega repeatedly used James's term "intellectualism" to describe the old idealist rationalism. In 1934 he claimed: "Against

35. James, *Will to Believe* (1979), 7, incidentally adjacent to the term "overcome" (in quotes), which Ortega often used in its Spanish equivalent.

36. James, *Writings*, 356, 374; idem, *Will to Believe* (1979), 7, 65; idem, *Pluralistic Universe* (1977), 144; cf. Ortega 1:349 ("thinkers" or "feelers" in "Meditations on Quixote").

intellectualism, as the root of idealism, I have argued constantly" (7:44). On the problem of knowing (epistemology), or "what is the seeking or apprehending of truth, or the being of things," he called for greater "radicalism" against the "'intellectualist' error" that "dealing with things" in our lives is simply an "intellectual relation." Against Descartes, he argued, "I think because I exist, because life poses hard problems for me." For Ortega as for James, the life of the mind is not self-sufficient; it is for "intellectualists." For traditional rationalists dwelling in a supernal world of universal absolutes and immutable relations, the concept was a "self-sufficing revelation" independent in origin from "perceptual particulars," in contrast to empirical absolutists for whom the *only* significance of concepts was tied to particulars, so as to give control of one's world. James related function and value of concept to "perceptual" experience of reality, but he also recognized a certain reality and utility in the concepts themselves, always with *full* value found only in application to perceptual reality again. Ortega could agree with James here too, but not with his "pragmatic Rule" that "particular consequences" are the only criterion of a greater relative autonomy in concepts. Nevertheless, James granted a less than "exclusively practical use" of concepts in life higher than the infantile or the primitive.[37]

As much borrowed as new, James's pragmatism was all rather eclectic in appearance. He himself once called it a "mosaic philosophy" that was held together not by formal, systematic exposition but by the continuity of his own life, experience, and thought. His "philosophy of pure experience" was harmonious with "radical pluralism," freedom, morality, and religion. Supporting "unity and duality" together, but with primary emphasis on the "pluralism" of the concrete facts of life experience, his philosophy—for all its looseness—had a certain unity and coherence. It also hoped to be "a *social* philosophy, a philosophy of 'co,' in which conjunctions do the work."[38]

As a whole, Ortega's philosophy was similar. It too *looked* loose and eclectic, but—upward from its basic metaphysics of "radical positivism"—it held. together as a "radical unitary duality" (or plurality) in a complex "philosophy of life," which he developed in accord with his own life experience, far beyond pragmatism. Like James's, his own philosophy included "co's" to help bind it together. "Coexistence" and "co-living," or "living-with," which he had stated by 1913 or before (1:256n) as *convivencia*, were always central

37. See supplemental note 37, chap. 4.

38. James, *Pragmatism* (1975), 79–82 (quotation on p. 81); idem, *Manuscript Essays and Notes* (Cambridge: Harvard University Press, 1988), 66, 68, 71–72, 84, 95 (on "co" and "co-ness"); idem, "The Knowing of Things Together," in *Essays in Philosophy* (Cambridge: Harvard University Press, 1978), 71–89; also *Writings*, 195–97, 206, 212, 305–6 on his social philosophy of "co's," which included Ortega's "coexist."

principles, for which he developed a *social* dimension in *Man and People* at the end.

Finally, each was a relativist, and did not regard his own philosophy as permanent. Each generation and era would see the great perennial problems differently. Like James, Ortega saw his philosophy as not "final" nor closed (6:410, 418), and he aspired to change the "existing realities," in philosophy and in the organization of life and politics in Spain, Europe, and the West during the general crisis of this century. Both often aspired to something "beyond" what was past or current. That "beyond" (*mas allá*) was virtually their common motto.[39] In those ways, Ortega's philosophizing had very "pragmatic" aims.

Why Philosophize?—Useful for Life in Crisis and Danger

Although he philosophized with an assumption that "if it works, it's true," James was not just a "commonsense" thinker who eschewed conceptual and abstract thinking. He acknowledged that concepts were essential for the richness of rational living and for the effectiveness of practical ("pragmatic") results of our knowing, for control over the natural and human world. In fact, "we must translate experience from a more concrete or pure into a more intellectualized form, filling it with more abounding conceptual distinctions . . . ." Why? Not because "theoretic life is absolute" (as rationalists claimed), but because (as the naturalists maintain) "the environment kills as well as sustains us." So elements with "a practical bearing on life are analyzed out of the continuum" and "fixed."[40]

Now that Heraclitean rationalization of reasoning by James was essentially what Ortega repeatedly used but he mixed it in a Nietzschean metaphor (7:91n): life *is* "dangerous," so we must "swim" in the perilous river of life, or we sink and drown in its terrors and crises (9:416–17). Life is ever "problematic": hence, our "natatory" efforts in conceptual solutions. We philosophize because life is dangerous and crisis-ridden. But for both James and Ortega, after this almost instinctive functional reaction, we must apply our acquired mental techniques to *serve* life, by "doing" useful things.

39. Relating to James's view that philosophy is not permanent, not perennial, see *Writings*, 810; idem, *Essays in Philosophy* (1978), where he says, "No philosophy can be more than an hypothesis," because "Life lies open" (93); similarly *Will to Believe* (London: Longmans, Green, 1931) on the first page of the preface. Ortega observed, "Not only is there no *philosophia perennis*, but philosophy itself is not forever" (8:269). James, *Writings*, said: "The beyond must, of course, always in our philosophy be itself of an experiential nature," so experience of life can "grow at its edges" (213, 353); idem, *Essays in Radical Empiricism* (1947), 88–89 ("the beyond").

40. James, *Writings*, 216; idem, *Pluralistic Universe* (1909), 118, 121 (on origin of philosophy in crisis).

Ortega too had turned to philosophy in response to personal crises of life, which James described as a kind of "counter-conversion" crisis in *The Varieties of Religious Experience* (1902), and philosophy also became for him (for a while) a "faith," "revelation," and virtual "religion" (R 56). "Belief" also became for Ortega an absorbing interest—not so much as formal religion as all manifestations of conviction, including philosophy. More than the mere "ideas" of "intellectualism," *beliefs* were the center of life and action, and they constituted effective "worldviews" (5:383–84).

Metaphysics: "Radical Empiricism" as "Radical Positivism"

According to one expositor, "radical empiricism is the name given by James to his entire philosophical endeavor" and "position." Apparently it was his metaphysics at least.[41] An earlier term, it was mentioned in *Will to Believe* as equivalent to what he later called "pragmatism" and was also mentioned in *Pragmatism* (1907), before the *Essays in Radical Empiricism* (1912). Since he continued to use both names more or less interchangeably in virtually every work he wrote, it appears that they were two distinct *aspects* of his general life-oriented philosophy as a whole. Pragmatism, he acknowledged, was more restricted to *method,* as an "instrument" (precisely as Ortega later defined Husserl's phenomenology), but one for testing the truth of ideas by their practical results. In contrast, radical empiricism seems to have been his *basic* philosophy in ontology and epistemology. It was this "metaphysical" foundation of James's thinking (more than the "method") that had mainly attracted young Ortega. He borrowed it, or emulated it, from his own positivist and idealist backgrounds in philosophy and with a varied emphasis and terminology.

Although Ortega spoke primarily of a "radical positivism" instead of a "radical empiricism," that was not an *essential* difference. James himself once called pragmatism a "more radical" form of empiricism that was distinct from the older British empiricism. His kind "harmonized" with traditional philosophy as a whole and with positivism, too, yet it was as distinct from previous "positivistic empiricism" as from the old rationalism and empiricism. Hence, when Ortega selected a name for that philosophical point of departure, it came to him legitimately from James and naturally from his

41. Edie, *Invitation to Phenomenology,* 118, cf. 122. See James, *Writings,* 134, 136, 195, on "radical empiricism" as his new worldview and as his metaphysics (experienced "things," the "stuff" of philosophy and its generalized conclusion). It was anti-rationalist. McDermott, *Writings of James,* comments on "radical empiricism" as the name of James's "entire philosophical endeavor" (134).

own positivist background.[42] He thus *adapted* James's metaphysics, and instead of changing its substance, he changed chiefly its name.

As Croce had recommended, he also made radical empiricism more "systematic." Later relating it to Comte's positivism, he often expressed the basic "given" as "the posited," but that variation was in James too. In addition, Comte's *General View of Positivism* had as a subtitle *System of Thought and Life;* its first chapter took "a systematic view of human life" as "the object of philosophy" and the means of progress.[43]

Metaphysically, what was radical empiricism? As with pragmatism, James defined it differently on several occasions. In *Will to Believe* (1897) he first gave the essence of it. "He who takes for his hypothesis the notion that it [pluralism] is the permanent form of the world is what I call a radical empiricist." He went on to explain that whatever "*your* point of view," there is always "mere fact and *givenness.*" This plurality of "given" fact and individual viewpoints was at the heart of James's radical empiricism, as it was later of Husserl's *Ideen* (1913) and of Ortega's "absolute positivism" in 1916. James had expressed this insight rhapsodically. "There is no possible point of view from which the world can appear an absolutely single fact." An overflowing reality in "*real*" possibilities, determinations, beginnings, ends, evils, crises, catastrophes, and escapes—"a real God, and a real moral life" in "common sense" and "in empiricism" cannot be "'overcome' . . . in monistic form." In *The Meaning of Truth* (1909) he defined "radical empiricism" in terms of "*experience*" with "relations," both "conjunctive and disjunctive," holding "*things*" together. Therefore, "the directly apprehended universe needs . . . no extraneous trans-empirical support, but possesses in its own right a concatenated or continuous structure."[44]

<hr />

42. James, *Meaning of Truth* (1975), nevertheless denied that pragmatism was "only a re-editing of positivism" (100); in his *Principles of Psychology* (1950), 1:vi, he calls his work "strictly positivistic" in "point of view," suitable for a "new kind of metaphysics." For Ortega on radical empiricism and one version or another of "radical positivism," see 2:66; 3:166, 303; 6:164, 210, 271, 323; 8:213; 12:399. James foresaw that someone might later come up with "the right word," "some unifying and conciliating formula" better than "radical empiricism" (*Essays in Radical Empiricism* [1947], 156).

43. Croce, *Philosophy, Poetry, History,* trans. C. Sprigge (London: Oxford University Press), 45 ("The Logic of Philosophy"), attributed pragmatists' failure at "systematization and demonstration" to their hostility to "the idealist tradition of Kant and Hegel"; idem, *The Autobiography of B. Croce,* trans. R. G. Collingwood (1927; reprint, Freeport, N.Y.: Books for Libraries Press, 1970), 99, where he calls his own philosophy "a new positivism" or "a new Kantianism." For another such view—that Comte's positivism somehow contained (or anticipated) pragmatism—see Raymond Aron, *Main Currents in Sociological Thought* (New York: Basic Books, 1965), 1:108–9. Auguste Comte, *A General View of Positivism,* trans. J. H. Bridges (Stanford: Stanford University Press, 1953).

44. James, *Will to Believe* (1931), vi–vii (on radical empiricism as pluralism and givenness) and cf. 280 (no "single proposition"); positivism somehow contained (or anticipated)

Such "radically empiricist" ontological and epistemological attitudes from James reappeared in Ortega as he *developed* his metaphysical "first philosophy" from "Adam in Paradise" forward, but more analytically, systematically, and subordinated and "transcended" in a larger, more definite philosophy of life. Metaphysics was a "method" of "intellectual radicalism" that was "distinct from every other science," that was the "authentic . . . *prima philosophia*" (R 77) that all other sciences presuppose. For all his efforts with "form," however, Ortega could not express "radical positivism" in significantly clearer or different terms: James had put it in a "nutshell." But what constituted almost the last phase of James's philosophy[45] was only Ortega's first phase. As he developed his metaphysics (and metahistory), he put greater emphasis on the "transcendent" or "supra-historical" character of concepts—not an idealist "transcendentalism" but somewhat "beyond" James's realism.

For the first time (and repeatedly) in an address called "Sensation, Construction, and Intuition" (1913), he used James's expression "radical empiricism." However, he misdirected it—with more extreme meaning and content—to Mach and Ziehen. The original text, which was unpublished until 1983, has been too loosely translated, giving "extreme," "root," and "fundamental" for *radical*. This term, as well as *radicalíssimo* and *radicalismo*, came to assume a special significance for Ortega by the 1930s and 1940s. Those words are better kept as "radical," "most radical," and "radicalism," but etymologically "root" is also from *radix*. There he was already probing, in "radical" fashion, to the "roots" of the problem of "knowing and being" (12:488–90). His search for roots may sound like Husserl's "foundationalism," but such a radicalism was also implicit in James.[46]

---

pragmatism; also cf. Ortega, 8:48 (1934); 12:493, 499 (1913). The fact that these ideas on "the given" (self-presenting, or concrete, unique "thing"—1:479, 482) were already in Ortega ("Adam," 1910), shows that he got them initially from James, not from Husserl's *Ideen* (1913). Silver, too, recognized "the given" in Ortega but felt that he balked at accepting Husserl's idealist reversal of it in *Ideen* (*Phenomenology and Art*, 58–59, 88). James, *Will to Believe* (1931), 280—no viewpoint on the world as a single fact; (1979), 104, 106—life as overflowing with possibilities; God and morals; James, *Writings*, 136, 217–19, 221, 240 ("system" as "connections"), 314.

45. Wild, *Radical Empiricism*, chap. 4, "The Last Phase."

46. Spiegelberg, *Phenomenological Movement*, 1:67–68, on James's unfortunate dependence on Mach. Edie, *Invitation to Phenomenology*, 117–18, says that although James on occasion sounded much like Mach, "unlike Mach, James did not erect his radical empiricism into a metaphysics or go to the extreme" of materialism, but cf. 122 "necessarily a metaphysics"). Whereas Silver translated the positions of Mach and Ziehen as "extreme empiricism" in *Phenomenology and Art* (1975), in his *Ortega as Phenomenologist* (1978) he more accurately said "radical empiricism" (79). John T. Blackmore, *Ernst Mach* (Berkeley and Los Angeles: University of California Press, 1972), claims that James and Mach influenced each other (55, 176–77, 202), both were "neutral monists," as far from materialism as

The "absolute positivism" that Ortega advanced as his own "radical" solution to that problem of knowing and being in 1916 (2:66; 12:399)—and reaffirmed in 1930 (7:352) as "radical"—was very like James's "radical empiricism," which was not "extreme" but was one of "roots." Later still he would also misdirect this same idea to Dilthey as both "radical empiricism" and "radical positivism" (6:202n, 210). Finally, in the 1940s, he called it simply "philosophical radicalism" (7:271, 280), which thus echoed Husserl too.[47] As Ortega described or elaborated it, however, as "super-positivism" in 1917 (R 77) or as "strict," "rigorous," "authentic," or "radical" positivism in later years (3:166; 6:210–11; 8:375), his metaphysics at bottom was Jamesian "radical empiricism" from first to last. Once he linked "pragmatism" with such an expression (8:376).

What this metaphysical "radicalism" always involved was the directly perceived, "given," or self-posited "thing," which included self and world together. These basic elements were repeated over and over by Ortega from 1908 until 1950, surely with help from Husserl for actual formulation. They are evident in "Adam in Paradise," *Meditations on Quixote,* several early phenomenological essays from 1912 to 1916, *Modern Theme, What Is Philosophy?, Some Lessons in Metaphysics, Leibniz,* and in many lesser works. Moreover, like "presence," "compresence," "representation," and other terms, the "given," or the "positive," is mentioned repeatedly in unpublished sources, usually related to "positivism" of one kind or another (R 40, 46, 76, 77).[48]

At a higher level, however, knowing required concepts, so that a basic realism of things perceived was combined with a conceptual idealism. Something similar was in James, but Ortega gathered added force from Kant and Husserl for his own version of "realism-idealism," so to speak, that matched his "self and circumstance" as corollary. In his metaphysics of 1933 he still spoke, like James, of "testing" the realist thesis as "hypothesis" on the reality of things, but he also referred to the idealist thesis on ideas; since he found

---

from idealism (126–27). James Edie, *James and Phenomenology,* x–xi; Spiegelberg, *Phenomenological Movement,* 1:76, on Husserl's "philosophical radicalism" as an "urge to go down to the sources."

47. See Spiegelberg, *Phenomenological Movement* 1:32, 94, on Husserl's "philosophical radicalism," which (as in Ortega) meant going to the "roots," beginnings, of knowledge, which initially were "things," or "phenomena." Husserl, however, pushed this "foundation" on to transcendental subjective consciousness, which Ortega rejected.

48. James, *Will to Believe* (1931), vii ("givenness"). Rodríguez Huéscar, who earlier (1966) saw his metaphysics as "perspective" (epistemology) or "realism-idealism," has found a "new metaphysics" of "radical reality" and related "presence" and "compresence" to it (*La innovación metafísica de Ortega: Crítica y superación del idealismo* [Madrid: Gómez, 1982], pt. 2 and pp. 23, 144–75, 134, 155), but he never connected it with James and pragmatism. On the contrary, he saw Ortega "overcoming" not only idealism but also "intellectualism-pragmatism" (27). For "the given" ("posited"), also see Ortega, 8:48 or 52 ("self posited"); and 7:351–52 ("presence" and "positive"), related to a "radical" absolute positivism.

neither adequate in isolation, he affirmed a "coexistence" in life of both immanent realism and transcendent idealism (12:120–28). Both were in "centaur" Ortega—together.

Meanwhile Ortega had extended his search for life-reality beyond metaphysics even into a metahistory that was meant to be pragmatically "useful" for life and for the human sciences. Even there James inspired him. "Life is always a place and a date," Ortega wrote: " . . . life is of itself, historical" (12:76).

Some Pragmatic "Principles"

In his "Leibniz" (1947), Ortega stated that we cannot fail to recognize that "since philosophy is exploration toward authentic principles, it is essential or unavoidable that the philosopher wear himself out trying to dig out those latent, pragmatic 'principles' that act within his own secret depths and impose on him—as 'evident'—arbitrary assumptions on which he does not reflect, or which, if he reflects on them, he solemnizes with the pompous title of principles" (8:261). Proclaiming such principles was not only the business of philosophy, he maintained, but its very "alpha and omega." To do so is to philosophize authentically—to "do" philosophy—as distinguished from merely taking one's philosophy "ready-made." We are at once reminded of his claim in 1916 that "absolute positivism" was the "alpha and omega" of his "logical and methodological convictions" (12:399). If Ortega "did" his philosophy in the primary, original principles that supported (or extended) his basic "self and circumstance," however, he was actually *reliving* (redoing) what James had already done, for the most part, even though it fitted his own experience and intuitions. At least he showed a notable degree of originality of expression, and in systematic integration and consistent application he surpassed James.

At bottom, most of Ortega's principles were pragmatic, or quasi-pragmatist. They followed fairly closely what James had identified in "The Problems of Metaphysics" in 1911; he put off defining metaphysics except through the problems by which we can "get at" it. These were the problems of life and thought, truth and thought, things and reality, "unity and diversity" (or "the one and the many"), "percept and concept," continuity and discontinuity (or the continuum and the infinite), space and time, freedom and determination, and mind and body. "Is thought for the sake of life? or is life for the sake of thought?" Of course, Ortega opted for the first of these alternatives, which he turned into "vital reason." He took seriously James's advice that "philosophers may be into as close contact as realistic novelists with the facts of life." Moreover, he came to agree with James that "the problem of Being," the "so-called ontological problem," was the greatest, most difficult of these problems. Yet he did not pursue it as James posited it: "what" it is, and "how there comes to be anything at all." Instead, Ortega mainly investigated what (or where) and how the concept of Being itself ever came to be, in history.[49]

Let us now examine and compare some of the main pragmatic principles that Ortega seems to have derived from James.

Utility of Conceptual Knowledge

Conceptual knowledge represents "a *theoretic* conquest over the [chaotic] order in which nature originally comes." James thus acknowledged the great "practical utility" of concepts to guide, inform, and give values. They clarify our "percepts" and open the way to further truths of a different, "conceptual order," which may be "rationalized" into a "*system*" showing the distribution and "*connections*" of things and relations. "The conceptual order into which we *translate* our experience seems not only a means of practical adaptation [to perceived, fluid reality], but the *revelation* of a deeper level of reality in things." But, contrary to rationalists, these "deeper features of reality are found [verifiable] only in perceptual [concrete] experience." "Here alone do we acquaint ourselves with *continuity,* or the immersion of one thing in another, here alone with self, . . . with activity in its various modes, with time, with cause, with change, with novelty, with tendency, and with freedom"—things that have appeared "unreal or absurd" to the traditional conceptual thinking.[50] Those words and ideas of James that are italicized in this paragraph proved to have "cash value" for Ortega, notably for his idea of "system" and his notion of *historical* reasoning, as in "History as a System."

The relation of immediate life experience (or "percept") to concept was that of part to whole, and James saw the perceptual part as prior in the order of reality, but not exclusive in a monist way. "Empiricism proceeds from parts to wholes, treating the parts as fundamental both in order of being and the order of our knowledge. In human experience the parts are percepts built out into wholes by our conceptual additions." Being singular, percepts "change incessantly," bring "concrete novelty into our experience," whereas rationalism is a "closed system" that excludes novelty. In the radically "empiricist view," reality is continually "created" in time, so that concepts provide only a "sketch-map" to give us our bearings but can never "fitly supersede" perception. Reality "overflows, exceeds, and alters" the "ring fence" of concepts. Yet, "Concepts are . . . as real as percepts, for we cannot live a

---

49. James, "The Problems of Metaphysics," in *Some Problems of Philosophy,* 21–25. Also see 19, 21–30 passim.

50. See these words in James, *Writings,* 240, 243. See Allison H. Johnson, *Whitehead's Theory of Reality* (Boston: Beacon, 1952), 146, on "connectedness" and "concepts" in James.

moment without taking account of them. But the 'eternal' kind of being which they enjoy is inferior to the temporal kind, because it is so static and schematic and lacks so many characters which temporal reality possesses." While they "interpenetrate" in practice, contrary to rationalism, it is the "concrete percept" that is "primordial" and the "concept-stuff" that is "secondary" in nature and origin.[51] Such was the epistemology of James's radical "realism." All of this, too, is very consistent with Ortega's thinking, first as "absolute positivism," later in historiology.

Not developing *systematically* his distinction of our knowledge of experienced reality into two interacting levels, primary (perceptual) and secondary (conceptual), James still anticipated to a remarkable degree the essentials of Ortega's later systematic "way of thinking" on two levels. As intimated in *History as a System* (6:44n), Ortega went "beyond" the usual abstract, static concepts of Eleatic philosophy into a new kind of fluid Heraclitean conceptualization. Generalizing "schemas" and "models" were intended to move and "change" with history so as to "fit" ("work" better with) the flux of concrete events, or individual happenings, to lend them form or structure. Although his metahistory or historiology was inspired from other sources, James nevertheless provided him a rational epistemological and ontological foundation.

James's very expressions ("skeleton" and "map") for describing such empirical concepts have close equivalents in some of Ortega's metaphors for the model (11:161; 3:239). When Ortega said of his "concept" or "schema" of "historical crisis" that if it "fits" it is true (5:69), he was echoing James's pragmatic notion of "true" concepts: "Any idea that helps us to deal, whether practically or intellectually, with either the reality or its belongings, . . . that *fits* in fact, and adapts our life to the reality's whole setting, will . . . be true of that reality."[52]

Life as Self "Being-with" the World in "Time and Space"

"Radical empiricism . . . is fair to both the unity and the disconnection" of self and things. The relation between the self and the world of experienced things was one of those "conjunctive relations" of which James treated. "Change," "doing," "happening" were "synonymous with the sense of 'life,'" starting with "our own subjective life" immediately involved in the world, which was the original sense of "being." Here one can detect the roots for several of Ortega's key ideas on life, some of which he enunciated

51. The ideas mentioned here as constituting James's metaphysics are not all in his *Essays in Radical Empiricism* but are widely scattered in his essays; see *Writings,* 195, 214–15, 235, 237, 239–43, 252, 253–54.

52. James, *Philosophy,* 85–87; idem, *Writings,* 253.

soon after the *Essays in Radical Empiricism* appeared, but some much later. James rejected rationalists' *addition* of "transexperiential agents" such as substances and the hermetic self to give unity to their "world-picture." He refused to separate self and world, which were bound together by a variety of conjunctive relations starting from merely "to be with," and going on to include such terms as time and space, like and unlike, continuity and discontinuity, or disjunction. Possibly it was from this conjunctive relation of "being-with" that Ortega derived his ideas of "self and circumstance" in 1913 and *convivencia* ("living-with") as a Spanish equivalent (1:322, 256n). In "realist" phenomenology, experience of continuity in the self and with the world also went with awareness of *change* in the "spatial and temporal determinations," and likewise of discontinuities in personal and historical crises (1:256–57, 270–73). Thus Ortega turned the phenomenon of life implicitly toward history—all consistent with what James implied by his emphasis on "time and space."[53]

"Consciousness of" Consciousness Not Basic

In attacking the neo-Kantian doctrine of "consciousness," James implicitly rejected that idealist concept in Husserl's phenomenology, too—in a way that probably set young Ortega on the path to "independent" thinking (8:34, 42–43, 54), precisely about the problem of "consciousness of," already in 1913 (1:255–57). To James (in 1904) it should be "discarded":

> To consciousness as such nothing can happen, for, timeless itself, it is only a witness of happenings in time, in which it plays no part. It is, in a word, but the logical correlative of "content" in an Experience of which the peculiarity is that *fact comes to light* in it, that *awareness of content* takes place. Consciousness as such is entirely impersonal—"self" and its activities belong to the content. . . . [54]

Clearly, James did *not* accept "consciousness of consciousness" as an "'epistemological' necessity," because it was not factual—"we had no direct evidence of its being there." So, contrary to "almost everyone," he denied any "immediate consciousness of consciousness itself." In his *Essays in Radical Empiricism* he refused to accord consciousness the status of metaphysical reality, as "aboriginal stuff" or quality of being.

"Consciousness of" was seized by Ortega after 1912 for his own initial

53. James, *Pluralistic Universe* (1947), 161; idem, *Writings*, 196–98; idem, *Will to Believe* (1979), 61. J. E. Smith, *Purpose and Thought*, comments on the tendency of pragmatists "to give priority to time and change over the fixed and immutable"; they did not "deny the reality of the past" (120).
54. James, "Does Consciousness Exist?" (1904), *Writings*, 169–72, 183, substituted for fictitious "consciousness" the "stream of thinking" about the *concrete* "stuff" that is reality; and see "consciousness of consciousness itself" (170).

insight into the basic "error," "breach," or "hole" that he found in Husserl's idealist phenomenology in 1913 (1:255–56; 2:63; 8:274n, 296): that "'consciousness' be capable of reflecting on itself" (8:47, 50, 54). "Vital reason, then, does not start from any idea [consciousness] and therefore is not idealism" (5:541). Obviously it was first James who had found the "hole" and dismissed consciousness as "a nonentity" with no place among first principles. It was an "external relation," "content," a function, *not* a primary reality. And so it was for Ortega, who later called for a "quarantining" of the idea.[55] He was addressing this very problem of "content of consciousness" in 1915–1916, when he first identified his realist solution as an "*absolute positivism*" that judged the truth of ideas and theories by how they fitted our "direct vision of the objects, of the phenomena themselves" (12:398–99). In short, such was the reality of "life" as "self and circumstance": "things" *given*.

Pragmatism as "Method" (or "Instrument") and "Theory"

Beyond his basic epistemology of "seeing" or perceiving things, Ortega took pragmatism as a "method" or "instrument" suited to many aspects of human and worldly reality and truth (4:357). If it were workable and useful, however, it was only "probable" and "relativistic" with regard to truth,[56] so how far could he utilize its rather limited method? Here the question resembles his problem with Husserl's phenomenology—how far did he accept James's "pragmatism" as philosophy and how far as *method*? But the relationship is reversed; he made less use of James's method than of his "philosophy," especially as "radical empiricism," of which pragmatic method was an aspect.

According to James, his handy "pragmatic rule" signified that the truth and meaning of a concept, whether simple or complex, are judged *functionally*, by concrete or particular *consequences*—the difference it makes, if it is true. In practice his "rule" meant chiefly "test," or "verification." Now "pragmatic method," he tells us, is "nothing new," since it had been used by Aristotle, Locke, Berkeley, and Hume in fragmentary ways. It represented in James himself a "radical" empiricist attitude that abandoned the "inveterate habits" of philosophers who depend on abstraction, "verbal solutions," "a priori reasons," "fixed principles, closed systems, and pretended absolutes and origins." Instead, it means relying on *facts*, or concreteness, and action. It was openness and naturalness against "dogma, artificiality, and the pretense of finality in truth." As "method only," pragmatism should effect an

55. Ortega, 8:51; oddly, the phrase is also translated by Silver (*Phenomenology and Art*, 66) as "discard," precisely as James put it; Ortega was still treating of the problem of "consciousness of" in 1933 in *Some Lessons in Metaphysics* (1969), 49, 60, 139, 143, 145, 157. On "consciousness" in Ortega, see Osvaldo Lira, *Ortega en su espíritu*, vol. I.

56. James, *Some Problems of Philosophy*, 111–16 (against intellectualism and for probabilism and relativity); idem, *Will to Believe* (1979), 62 (concepts as "instruments").

"enormous change in . . . the 'temperament' of philosophy." Science and metaphysics would "work . . . hand in hand"—for example, by the "working hypothesis" and "trial and error," both of which terms Ortega stated in 1916 in the original English. It would mean testing in practice, in the stream of experience, the meaning of power-endowed words like "God," "principle," "matter," and "reason." Pragmatic method is, therefore, less "a solution" than "a program for more work," a search for "ways in which existing realities can be *changed*."[57]

Besides "method" in a particular sense, James also defined pragmatism as "a certain *theory of truth*." As a means to wider knowledge beyond the flow of concrete experience, James saw concepts as "thin extracts from perception"— but they were "insufficient representatives thereof" that must not be taken in rationalistic ("intellectualist") fashion to afford "a deeper quality of truth." These concepts themselves were "theories" with some practical utility for trying to extend our knowledge of self and of world. "*Theories thus become instruments*," observed James, "*not [absolute] answers to enigmas in which we can rest*." They invite us to "move forward" to "make nature over again by their aid." "Pragmatism [thus] unstiffens all our theories, limbers them up and sets each one at work." Again he insisted that this was nothing new, that pragmatism "harmonizes" with much of philosophical tradition, like utilitarianism and positivism.[58]

With the "instrumental" side of pragmatism, Ortega obviously agreed, for he regarded phenomenology itself as a "prodigious instrument" (8:42). Like John Dewey, he went on to develop his own "instrumentalism," first in "perspectivism" as both pragmatic and phenomenological method, and later in other ways. Apparently from Dewey he took "trial and error" as a "pragmatic" method in 1916—more than twenty years before George Mead employed that term.[59] This homely procedure implied much that later went into historiology. Thus James had pointed out or intimated part of the method

57. James, *Writings*, 238 ("pragmatic rule"), 311 (verification), 377–79 (method and consequences); idem, *Will to Believe* (1979), 79 ("working hypothesis"). This phrase also appears in several other works, for example, first on p. 13 (a subheading set in bold-face type) in James, *Psychology: A Briefer Course* (1892), which was the one-volume version in Ortega's library. For Ortega's use of both terms, see 2:21, 164n; also see n. 11 (this chapter) on "trial and error." James, *Writings*, 374, 381–85. Victor Lowe, *Understanding Whitehead* (Baltimore: Johns Hopkins University Press, 1962), 341: "The proper general method, both [James and Whitehead] believe, is that of the 'working hypothesis'"—with the need to test and elucidate. James, *Writings*, 311–12, 363–64, 374, 379.

58. James, *Writings*, 380.

59. Edie, *Invitation to Phenomenology*, 110–11 (James's "instrumentalism" or "functionalism"). See Ortega's references to "instrument" in ¿*Qué es Conocimiento?* 90 (with "work"); also in *Modern Theme* (3:156, 187, 241) and *History as a System*, trans. Helene Weyl (New York: Norton, 1941, 1961), 176, 222 n. 17. Refer also to my n. 11 and supplemental note 37, chap. 4. Dewey, *Democracy and Education*, 169–81; Mead, *The Philosophy of the Act*, 368–69.

that Ortega was to use in his own philosophy. Taking pragmatism not only as a useful instrument, he would also seek to reconcile and to unify the "utility" with the "theory" in it.

For a truly effective method, of course, Ortega had to go "beyond" James. Finding pragmatism insufficient here, he added Husserl's phenomenology. Through the stage of vital reason, phenomenology clearly outweighed pragmatism in his developing philosophy. But, after 1925, he had to go beyond phenomenology too for the final stage of historical reason, wherein elements of the pragmatic method were more evident than phenomenological aspects.

With almost the whole program of James's pragmatic method—as far as it went—Ortega could agree, except that he refused simply to abandon the concern with a priori, reason, and historic origins. Taking these elements in a non-idealist way, he both utilized James and went "beyond" him in a complex methodology for historical reason in "historiology" in 1928 (4:530–32). There, "working hypothesis" and "verification" by inductive "testing" are very evident, and perhaps a Jamesian a priori.

The Pragmatic Theory of Truth and Reality

Besides an old-new method, pragmatism for James was "a genetic theory" of truth. Ortega had some problems with the practicality and relativity of James's theory of truth, but not with its developmental character. He could assent to his basic definition of pragmatism in *The Meaning of Truth* (1909) that truth means the agreement of "our ideas" with reality and that "truth should have practical consequences." What he rejected was the *adequacy* (or universality) of the crasser version of the pragmatic "test"—"what 'works' best"—as a criterion of truth.[60] For truth was often more than, even *other* than, practical utility or workability. Otherwise, he could accept the notions that (for humankind) truths (contingent and plural) were more appropriate than Truth (one and absolute), that truths are often "useful" and "practicable" but not so in every case. "Always, publicly or privately, philosophy implied 'primacy of practical reason.' It was, is, and always will be (so long as it exists) the *science of doing something*" (compare 7:404–5, 430; 12:25–26).

Like James, he could see human truth and error as something that "becomes," "is made," "happens" in the course of time or history (6:409), as "event" and as "process" of verification or validation. What he objected to strenuously was the popular notion of pragmatism, to which James's careless utterances gave credence and standing: that truth itself is *merely* expedient,

---

60. Although James himself attributed the notion of "works" to Schiller (*Writings* [ed. McDermott], 442), he had already used it in *Will to Believe* (1931), xi; idem, *Writings*, 390, 430 ("cash value"), 441; he rejected the merely materialistic meaning of "works" by including also the mental (*Meaning of Truth*, 100).

utilitarian, variable. Certainly he agreed that truths "*should* have practical consequences" and that both knower and object (self and circumstance) were experienced in "one continuous scheme," in a subjective relation to objective reality.[61]

On the ontological side, Ortega was in more complete agreement, not only on "life" but on the word that James had preferred over the traditional "substance": "consistency." He likewise preferred "consistency" even to phenomenological "essence" (4:510; 5:531).[62]

Less absolute in rejecting "rationalism" and idealism, Ortega sought to salvage more of that tradition from Plato, Descartes, Leibniz, and Kant. His own "radical positivism" developed so as to "harmonize" or accommodate both realism and idealism, both a posteriori induction and a priori intuition. In this way, starting from James's radical empiricism and even using "pragmatic method," he went "beyond" James, as he thereby later went beyond Husserl, Scheler, and Dilthey. He "borrowed," it is true, but he was, throughout, following his own "arrow" to his own "destiny." From personal yearning and by the tendency of his time and generation, James's invitation to a philosophy of life experience based on a radical empiricism as a pluralist unity and using a pragmatic method—as a practical, functional "living reason"—was going to greatly attract and influence young Ortega.

"If it is true that James's radically empirical philosophy and particularly his notions of 'pure experience' and a 'pluralistic universe' leave many questions unanswered and even unformulated," observes John McDermott, "it is also true that his thought wedges us into areas on which genuine problems exist."[63] It is clear that Ortega took up the challenge to respond to James's unresolved problems and unasked questions.

"Unity and Duality" ("Plurality")

Next to radical empiricism, James's handling of the ancient and perennial philosophical paradox of "the one and the many" seems to have exerted the greatest influence on Ortega. This idea of "radical pluralism" gave him the metaphysical *structure* of his philosophy from beginning to end. Convenient roots for his uniquely phrased resolution—"a radical unitary duality"—were already in James, who had returned to that puzzle time and again, but always gave the same "Hegelian" answer: reality is both many (dual or "plural") and

---

61. James *Writings*, 439, truth itself as "mutable" or (442) expedient. James observed: "Truth *happens* to an idea. It *becomes* true, is *made* true by *events*. Its reality is in fact an event, a process . . ." (312); this is very like Ortega's historical view of truth. On verification and validation of "hypothesis," which were incorporated into "historiology," see Ortega, 9:530, 534. See James, *Writings*, 430–34; idem, *Meaning of Truth*, 38, 73, 75, 89.

62. James, *Meaning of Truth*, 58–59. Also see Ortega, 5:136; 6:199n; 8:49.

63. McDermott, "Introduction," *Writings of James*, xliv.

one at the same time. His essentially Heraclitean way of thinking about "being" as actually *becoming* inspired him to try to cut through this ages-old Gordian knot and thus bring the one and the many together. For him, concrete "radical" plurality (of parts) retained continuity and contact with "the whole."[64] One strongly suspects that Ortega also found that way, through reading James.

For an answer to the paradox of "unity and diversity" James started from a commonsense pluralism of distinct parts against rationalistic monism, whether idealistic or materialistic, but he strove to preserve "the whole" as end result. "The full nature . . . of reality [is] . . . given only in the perpetual flux." Hegel's notion that dialectic resolves contradictions in a higher unity James saw borne out empirically, since life finds "ways of satisfying opposites at once." "Our 'multiverse' still makes a 'universe,'" a "manyness in oneness." Radical empiricism posited a "pluralism in its ontology": "concatenated union of things" in the reality of living experience.[65] The whole is approached from the concrete plurality of things.

On an ontological level, James reduced plurality to the old duality of mind ("spirit") and matter, and to the duality of knowing and being, truth and reality. He believed that radical empiricism brought a certain harmony to these traditional polarities. By "harmony," he meant that he went "beyond" the antagonism of monism and dualism and brought them into fruitful relationship. A critical attitude that James expressed in *Essays in Radical Empiricism* (1912) related directly to the problems that Ortega had been facing at Marburg with the neo-Kantians Cohen and Natorp. "If neo-Kantism has expelled earlier forms of dualism," mused James, "we shall have expelled all forms if we are able to expell neo-Kantism in its turn."[66]

64. James, *Writings,* 258, 299 (the "many-in-one" character of reality), 359; idem, *Essays in Radical Empiricism,* 89 ("pluralism and unity"). Another way James put it was: "not subject, not object, but object plus subject is the minimum that can actually be"—in "pure experience" (*Writings,* 170). Also see James, *Memories and Studies,* 375, where he calls his philosophy "sometimes monistic, sometimes pluralistic"; James confessed himself "churned" by the Kantian "idealistic vision" of ultimate unity (410), a unity of pluralism and vice versa. In *Pluralistic Universe* (1909, 1977), James noted that Bergson's "Heraclitan 'devenir réel'" said much the same as he (397), and that radical empiricism explains "wholes by parts" and vice versa (9). Ortega first encountered "pluralism" (like "radical empiricism") in James's *Will to Believe,* probably in 1908. James, *Pluralistic Universe* (1977), 45 (on the "whole" and environment), cf. Ortega's "circumstance"; idem, *Writings,* 258, 259.

65. James, *Writings,* 134, 258, 299, 362; idem, *Will to Believe* (1931), vii, 175, 280 (pluralism); idem, *Pluralistic Universe* (1977), 146; *Writings,* 195 (whole and parts); *Will to Believe* (1979), 56, 58–59 ("unity and diversity" obtained theoretically by concepts of *simplification* and *clarity*).

66. James, *Writings,* 184–87 (on neo-Kantian and other forms of "inveterate dualism"), 214, 170 (on "expelling" Kantianism). Wild, *Radical Empiricism,* says that James tried to overcome the traditional dualism of life and world; it was both *subjective* and *objective:* the self thinking and the thing thought (361–62).

James has been called a great light and relief to students of philosophy in those years who were "breaking their heads" over Kant's famous *Critique of Pure Reason*. One who apparently found him very refreshing in a stale field was young Ortega, who then was wearing "calluses on my head," pondering Kant (8:26).[67]

Unity as Continuity and "Concatenation" in Diversity

The problem of "practical dualism" was not so readily resolved by James as was "consciousness of" itself. " . . . Dualism of matter and thought, this heterogeneity of the two stuffs posited as an absolute, has always presented difficulties for me." Representations, or concepts, he decided, were not just "little copies" of sense "percepts." Experience itself "has no such inner duplicity" of consciousness and content, which are simply mental "additions." He did not claim that he had "a final resolution," but he suggested that to suppress consciousness as entity or "stuff" would result in the abolition of this "ontological dualism" for a "vague monism" of "pure experiences" of the "primary reality," that is, phenomena or facts. At most, it was a very "rudimentary monism" that was "absolutely opposed to the so-called bilateral monism of scientific positivism" or Spinozism. Experience is a "double composition" comprising both matter and consciousness, neither of which exists as "ordinarily understood." He distinguished them not ontologically, but in the "*functional* order only."[68]

Contrary to rationalism, which separated unity from variety in things, James affirmed "conjunctive relations" between concrete things as "concatenated union," or loose "hanging together" as a whole, within a kind of ontological unity. But because many concrete relationships seemed "so external," "a philosophy of pure experience must [also] tend to pluralism in its ontology." Hence, once again reality is both "one and many" in radical empiricism.[69]

Beyond his "radical positivist" metaphysics, Ortega took this Jamesian unitary-pluralist ontology on into a metahistory. In historical "becoming," as in *History as a System*, concrete phenomena are men, individual human lives and events, within an overall "concatenated" unity, order, or system of world history. "History is a system—the system of human experiences that form an inexorable and unique chain" (6:43).

67. The relationship of Ortega to Kant needs study, a problem undertaken for an appendix here but omitted for the sake of space.

68. James, *Writings*, 170–72, and 172–79 (on dualism, concepts not copies; suppression of consciousness).

69. James, *Essays in Radical Empiricism*, 107–8 ("concatenation"), 134 ("philosophy of pure experience"); idem, *Writings*, 136 ("concatenated or continuous structure"); idem, *Pluralistic Universe* (1977), 147; *Writings*, 196–98, 221, 240, 314.

On "Nature" as "Continuity" and "Compenetration"

How like Ortega's later famous "denial" of human "nature" is the following observation by James about such static "absolutes": "There is no other *nature*, no other whatness than this absence of break and this sense of continuity in that most intimate of all conjunctive relations, the passing of one experience into another when they belong to the same self."[70] "Practically to experience one's personal continuum in this living way" is so similar to what Ortega later meant by claiming that *history* is man's only "nature," or that he has no nature but only a history (6:41). In James (as in Ortega later) reality—man as well as world—participated in this Heraclitean *becoming*, instead of mirroring rationalistic absolutes of being and substance. Ortega differed from James mainly over how far *truth*, like reality, is "mutable" or "useful."

In discussing the "thing" and its relations, James described the world of living experience as "fluent," flowing, a "flux" or *stream*, until it is broken into discrete parts by the analytical, reflective intellect. "The great [original] continua of time, space, and the self envelop everything, betwixt them, and flow together without interfering." They "compenetrate."[71] Now this conception of human self and world of things—thus initially compounded in one experiencing and experienced reality as human life—is very like what Ortega began to call "self and circumstance" (*yo y circunstancia*) in 1913 and later justified as the "radical unitary duality" comprising our "life" reality. He had distinguished those elements since 1910, but he had not brought them intimately together until after James's *Essays in Radical Empiricism* appeared posthumously in 1912.

A Unity of Truth and Reality (Knowing and Being)

Another side of "inveterate dualism" tending to "a sort of" unity of the whole that we find in James earlier we see in Ortega as "unity of thinking" ("knowing and being") or the "Gemini" of "like-minded" twins (8:70; 12:64, 388). "If 'knowing' and 'being' are the two fundamental problems, for us to define metaphysics as radical knowing" alone is insufficient (12:27; compare 9:373). Through Cohen, he had first come to a theory of "unity of knowing and being" in Kant—which he took to be his fundamental doctrine, or "Copernican revolution." James had said almost the same thing: "Being is knowing" and vice versa, in "thought (life)," and he stressed that there is "no breach in humanistic epistemology. Whether knowledge be taken as ideally perfected, or only as true enough to pass muster for practice, it is hung on one continuous scheme" connected to reality. James's idea of the

70. James, *Writings*, 198–99.
71. Ibid., 214–15.

consonance (or unity) of truth and reality was very similar. As in *Pragmatism,* he said in *The Meaning of Truth* (1909) that truth "agree[d] . . . with reality." For pragmatists, "True ideas are those we can assimilate, validate, corroborate, and verify." But they are not static, or stagnant. "Truth *happens* to an idea. It *becomes* true, is *made* true by *events.* Its reality is in fact an event, a process."[72]

Although he agreed about the historical development, testing, and "mutability" of truth and error, as perceived (knowable) by human beings, Ortega balked at James's merely "expedient" definition of truth and right (4:97). In one way or another, he always upheld truth and right as absolutes per se, even though they were thus unattainable by human effort or experience. Still, he too was committed to the *utility* and *practicability* of truths and rights relative to life. Although he would have found repugnant James's remark that the truth of an idea or a belief depends upon its "cash value in experiential terms," he accepted "plurality" and even "cash value" for female beauty (2:39). A limited relativism he granted, but not *absolute* relativism—in everything—which James did not intend either, despite often loose and equivocal statements. Distinctions between "subject" and "object," "thought" and "thing," each thinker admitted only as practical, or *functional,* not as *ontological* separation into a "classical dualism."

The fuller dimensions and implications of James's pragmatic doctrine of unity of truth and reality come out in his contrasting of "percept" and "concept," where he refused fully to separate them—as primary and secondary—from each other and from basic experienced reality. Here the *parallels* between James's and Ortega's "ways of thinking" become ever clearer, ever more extensive. Two levels of knowing are united in *one* level of reality, in our experience of life and world.

"Percept" and "Concept"—Two Levels of Knowing One Reality

In *Some Problems of Philosophy* (1911) James distinguished primary or immediate perception of experience from secondary mediated knowing in concep-

72. James, *Memories and Studies,* 383, 385 n. 1: on "a 'twin' question of *sameness and difference*" related to "subject-object knowing itself as a seamless unit," and to the proposition that "knowing is being" and being is knowing as bound to "thought (life)," or "*both* in the same thing"—which James acknowledged as a Kantian "idealistic vision" of unity and simplicity that balanced his pluralism. Also see James, *Writings,* 151–53, 252. Ortega, 12:492–93, 496 (1913): "this perfect mutuality between being and knowing." Also see the introduction ("System and Unity") to "Some Lessons in Metaphysics," 12:27 (1933). James, *Memories and Studies,* 385–86 n. 1, commented on Benjamin Blood, who by "mystic" means had reached the same conclusions that he himself had developed rationally—a coincidence that he regarded as "ludicrous and astounding at once" in its simplicity. James, *Writings,* 311–12, 439–46; idem, *Pluralistic Universe* (1977), 9 (on Kant's "unity of perception"), cf. Ortega, 12:496 (1913) on Kant's "unity of apperception" and Cohen's "unity of thinking."

tual thinking. Here too he denied any rigid dualism. Percept and concept "interpenetrate" as two levels of knowledge of a common, experienced reality. In this fashion (no less than Ortega later) he fitted knowing, or truth, to reality, or being—as all of one continuous, fluid stream or continuum from object to subject, from thing perceived to knowing self. "'Things' are known to us by our senses" as "presentations," and these perceptions are distinct from "representations" or concepts, but the latter "flow out of" the former "and into them again." They "interpenetrate and melt together, impregnate and fertilize each other." So "interlaced" and "mingled" are sensation and thought. "Feeling must have been originally self-sufficing; and thought [compare Ortega, 1:349–51] appears as a super-added function. . . ." However, both were indispensable for "complete knowledge of fact."[73] Concept relates to perception as a "transcendence" in knowledge, pointing to something higher than the particular and concrete, but not as transcendental idealism.

"The intellectual life of man consists almost wholly in substituting a conceptual order for the perceptual order in which his experience originally comes." James displayed none of that contempt of modern rationalists—so proud of their "godlike" universals and absolutes—for humble sense perception. "The world of common-sense 'things'; the world of material tasks to be done; the mathematical world of pure forms; the world of ethical propositions; the worlds of logic, music, etc., all abstracted and generalized from long-forgotten perceptual instances, . . . return and merge themselves again in the particulars of our present and future perception."[74]

We can find very similar views in Ortega (see 6:185), who often characterized the rationalist, "intellectualist" attitude as "utopian" and "uchronic" *beatería*, like "idols" of the abstract and universal venerated by the opponents of pragmatism (4:97). "Pure contemplation does not exist," not in the "strict sense," because theory always leads to the "manipulation of things," excepting such "transcendent realities" as "God, universe, and the meaning of life." "The error of pragmatism is not rooted in considering ideas as instruments, but in wanting to reduce things with which man must deal to the perceptible and experimentable, to what is at hand and present" (4:357). Compared to other animals, man has the advantage of a longer *memory*—a history—and therefore the ability to use the past and the *imagination* to create for the future.

73. James, *Writings,* 214, 236–43, 252–55. Also see James, *Pluralistic Universe* (1947), on percept and concept—like a revolving lantern (232–36); cf. Ortega, 1:248, especially instances of "the given" or self-"presented" in his radical positivism, and for "transcendence": 2:493–95; 3:166, 168; 6:45–48. Cf. 5:534 and James on "transcendence," from *Essays in Radical Empiricism,* excerpted in *James: The Essential Writings,* ed. B. Wilshire (Albany: SUNY Press, 1984), 218–21.

74. James, *Writings,* 234–35, 239–40; idem, *Philosophy,* 77.

A SUMMARY VIEW OF ORTEGA'S BASIC PRAGMATISM

My effort to persuade skeptical critics that there was indeed significant influence, dependence, and borrowing from James in Ortega's early philosophy (in his basic metaphysics), has required a long demonstration. We have seen his references (clear or equivocal) to pragmatism from 1908 onward, the several insights of critics, and the many coincidences in ideas. To confirm his real involvement with pragmatism was his own very belated acknowledgment (circa 1950) of James's influence on his half-generation in formation. That confession, and all texts and parallels, may not be enough, but when one includes the books in his library, and other evidences from his teaching, his own editing (or writing) for encyclopedias,[75] and his archives, they indicate more than probable influences. Indeed, Ortega was a pragmatist at basis, but he went on into much else besides, "beyond" the pragmatism of "absolute positivism." Where James *ended,* Ortega *began.* If James had "pointed" to phenomenology, Ortega pursued it eagerly, and likewise a historicism and an "existential" philosophy of life.

The "principle" of "my whole philosophy," said Ortega as he criticized but half-accepted pragmatism in "What Is Philosophy?" (1930), is: "living comes first and then philosophizing" (7:417). Essentially, philosophizing is "theoretic life," a "type of life," "theory of life" (7:344, 429–31). Pragmatism, however, at least Peirce's *practicism,* proposed "supplanting all theory" with mere "practical utility." Ortega granted that this was partly true for life and for the special sciences, even as Comte had foreseen, but he recognized that an unnamed kind of pragmatism accepted theory (7:297, 310). That was true for James but to a greater degree for himself. For him philosophy was, finally, both "Mary" and "Martha" (7:328), contemplation and action, or theory and praxis, idealism and realism—or, by implication, Kant and James. It was also life and history.

Ortega's interest in pragmatism extended to Dewey, and later to Peirce and Quine, to educational theory and even to connections between pragmatism and politics. Oddly, if in *Revolt of the Masses* (1929) he paradoxically viewed "Yankees" almost as quintessential "mass-men," at the same time he took the Union as the model (more or less) for European union. He both scorned and admired the United States. Not until his visit in 1949 did he pretty well overcome his childhood aversion and develop a warm liking for the United States and its ways and institutions. Thereafter he concluded that Tocqueville's "pragmatism" was too pessimistic, was unrealistic about U.S. citizens. He did not just relate American character to James's pragmatism, but if both were crude, they were very instructive. Apart from Ortega's

75. See supplemental note 15, chap. 4.

insistence on the inadequacy of any exclusively pragmatic test of *truth* and his greater respect for Kant and idealism, his later, mature thought was to develop consistently with its foundation in James, so that he was a more faithful "disciple" than was John Dewey. Of course, he was a secret "continuator," and, using James against himself, he found "holes" in him. Keeping much more abreast of the times than did Dewey in things new philosophically (from phenomenology through existentialism and historicism), he went "beyond" pragmatism.[76]

In archival notes that seem to be from the 1930s, Ortega mentioned a "*great* suspicion" he had come to in regard to "thinking": "that far from thinking making being, reality is what by its consistency and structure has been creating the consistency and structure of our intellect. This would be the true overcoming [*superación*] of pragmatism because this idea would absorb it within itself" (R 64).[77] If the first proposition were idealist, the second was realist and seems to be compatible enough with pragmatism. If the latter also implied his realist historicism, however, in the final development of his philosophy after 1930, he "overcame" pragmatism by absorbing it "within" history. He did much the same with phenomenology.

76. See n. 23 above. On Peirce, see Ortega, 7:310; on Quine, 5:524n, and R 2. Alfred North Whitehead, *Dialogues of . . . Whitehead*, recorded by L. Price (Boston: Little, Brown, 1954), 338: "In carrying on the philosophy of William James, I think he [Dewey] enormously narrowed it"—in regard to "complexity and possibility in human experience." Whitehead called James "one of the great philosophic minds in history." In contrast to Dewey, Ortega *expanded* James's ideas in several directions and into new philosophies. He did not mention Dewey in his writings, but his library included *Democracy and Education* (1916). See James, *Essays in Radical Empiricism,* 48 (on "the hole" through which "fictions" pour into one's philosophy), 88–89 (on "the beyond); and idem, *Writings,* 213. Thus Ortega apparently found both ideas in James.

77. This statement is undatable; R 64 contains papers of very different dates, from 1911 into the 1930s.

Chapter 5

METHOD

"Perspectivism" as Phenomenology (1912+)

erspectivism" was the name Ortega favored to cover the epistemological development of his philosophy of life from approximately 1912 through *The Modern Theme* in 1923. His perspectivism was phenomenology.[1] Since it was related earlier to "point of view" in James, who was as unconsciously "phenomenological" as Husserl was consciously "pragmatist," he logically connected his new perspectivism openly with Husserl's phenomenology. Thus were James and Husserl "like-minded twins" of his youthful firmament, as were James and Bergson. However, it was a *realist* ("anti-idealist") interpretation (8:53) that he gave to the great movement of phenomenology in European philosophy, to which he eagerly gravitated as the then-dominant force. The realism of an "empirical sort" so evident in his own "general phenomenology" reflected not only James but apparently also Husserl's original "neutral" or "naturalist" position.[2]

Like James, Ortega might have preferred to say "thing" but he now described even "life" as "phenomenon," as essentially "perspectivist" (3:169, 201). While he defined perspectivism and phenomenology alike as *method* (7:286; 8:42, 273), as "theory of knowledge," their ontological implications also related to *life*. The "phenomenal" is our "representation of authentic reality." "It is the 'perspective' in which reality presents itself," and, as such, it is *"grounded* in reality itself" (8:333). "Phenomenon" itself might be a "ridiculous" word, a heritage from Leibniz through "pedantic" Kant, but

---

1. Rabade Romeo, *Ortega filósofo,* says that Ortega's "radical perspectivism" is "difficult to see except as a form of phenomenism" (67). Armando Savignano, *Filosofia de Ortega,* observes that Hartmann, Heimsoeth, and Ortega (circa 1911) all took up phenomenology "more as a method than as system" (436). See Spiegelberg, *Phenomenological Movement,* 2:658, 684–85, on Husserl's *method* of seeing "modes of appearing" (givenness), also described by him in terms of "aspect" or "perspective."

2. See supplemental note 2, chap. 5.

philosophers were stuck with it (12:279). The radically basic thing, the "fundamental phenomenon" for him, was *life:* "the phenomenon of phenomena" (12:392).

In the 1920s, Ortega openly boasted about his promotion of phenomenology in Spain and Latin America, even telling Husserl that he was the leader of a "phenomenological school" in Spain. He praised phenomenology as "the gigantic innovation" and "the greatest influence" in philosophy between 1900 and the 1930s (4:508; 7:161; 8:47). Doctoral dissertations by Zubiri and Gaos, which he supervised, dealt with phenomenological questions. Given such prominence, what role did phenomenology play in his own developing philosophy as a whole? In 1990 in the *Analecta Husserliana,* Anna-Teresa Tymieniecka, Harold Raley, and Nel Rodríguez Rial assigned to Ortega a "phenomenology of life," even a phenomenological "philosophy of life." Did phenomenology then absorb, even constitute, his "system" of philosophy? Or was it only a major part—his principal *method* (or epistemology) for a philosophy of life in those years?[3]

Properly defining the complex character, place, and role of phenomenology in Ortega's thought is very difficult and fraught with traps. The problem is a veritable "can of worms" that, once it was opened in the 1970s by Philip Silver, who demonstrated that Ortega was (in a new realist way) a phenomenologist, may not be ignored—nor easily closed again by a simple, clear, and generally satisfactory resolution.[4] One can only try (and hope) to persuade that he was a phenomenologist *in part.* Yet he was indeed a phenomenologist, and in even more (and different) ways than Silver proposed in his fecund thesis.

TRANSITION: FROM JAMES TO HUSSERL

Even before his *Meditations on Quixote* (1914), Ortega had made an easy and natural transition from James's "radical empiricism" to phenomenology.[5] We have seen that his point of departure in philosophy was not imme-

3. See supplemental note 3, chap. 5.

4. L. Brenneman and S. O. Yarian, *The Seeing Eye: Hermeneutical Phenomenology in the Study of Religion* (University Park: Pennsylvania State University Press, 1982), 1:4, 7, 26–27, on "ambivalence" in phenomenology, which "crosses boundaries," because its definition and its "limits are vague." Ortega's type (like Dilthey's) was "hermeneutical" and in response to crisis, and his epistemology co-opted the "seeing eye," notably (with Spengler) "the historian's eye," aspiring to the "transhistorical." The difficulty of being definitive on phenomenology in general (much less Ortega's) is exemplified by Spiegelberg, *Phenomenological Movement,* 2:655, who observes that no "coherent system [was] shared by all phenomenologists"—"idealistic, realistic and neutralistic."

5. The article "Fenomenología" in *Enciclopedia Universal Ilustrada* (1924) was originally

diately phenomenology, however, but something "more radical": his pragmatic metaphysics was a so-called absolute positivism, which he nevertheless
later denoted as merely "radicalism" in imitation of Husserl, who, he nevertheless maintained, had failed to get to the "roots" (5:451; 8:270, 274–75,
280). If he had first discovered in James his unitary-dual principle of life
reality, he found it formally restated as a *unity* in the "presence" of "self *and*
world" in Husserl's *Ideas* (1913). Therein was no philosophy as "system"[6] but
the method and concepts—a "fine structure of meaty tissues"—for developing his metaphysics into a full-fledged philosophy, for building up "the
architecture of a system" (12:392; 8:42). In his course "Psychological Investigations" (1915–1916) he acknowledged "Husserl—to whom we owe so much
in all these matters" (for example, doubt, probability, and "modulations of
belief") and James as well, also for "belief" (12:417, 434).

Despite his own idealism, Husserl had admired James and borrowed from
him freely, as various critics have affirmed. Noting that "Husserl seldom
cites his living precursors" (12:451), Ortega certainly detected in him key
ideas from James, such as the initial "presence" of "things" and "viewpoint." Surely he also saw that (except for using it as a "methodic instrument") not only Dilthey but James "possessed in principle what in 1901 was
going to [be] exploited in the philosophical world with the name of 'phenomenology'" (6:208n).[7] Thus, he experienced no need to abandon the
"realist" ontology and the epistemology of "perspective" that he had adopted
earlier from James. Before 1916 he had added Husserl's phenomenology as a
refined and neutral "method" (or "instrument") that he found more effective than the vague and crude pragmatic method (12:392). To take up Husserl

---

written a good two decades earlier, given its reference to Husserl's "recent" propaedeutic
(*Prolegomena*, 1901) to logic, seen from "the empirical point of view" and separated from
its "historical vagueness." The article was perhaps by Ortega himself, since it fits in time
and viewpoint. As we have seen (R 76), he was apparently studying Husserl together with
James by 1908. Also see the anonymous article "Husserl" in the same encyclopedia (1925),
which related him to Brentano and saw his phenomenology as a "neutral discipline." It
also stated that Scheler "is today an independent thinker."

6. See supplemental note 6, chap. 5.

7. Spiegelberg, *Phenomenological Movement*, 1:111–15, 128–31, 161, 649, shows Husserl's
admiration for James, which most works cited in my supplemental note 2, chap. 5, affirm,
notably Edie ("James and Phenomenology," 487). In Edie, ed., *Patterns of the Life World*
(Evanston, Ill.: Northwestern University Press, 1970), contributor Enzio Paci states "As
long as the *epoché* is maintained, there could be no harm in viewing phenomenology as a
critical, non-naive pragmatism fully aware of its implications" ("The *Lebenswelt* as Ground
and as *Leib* in Husserl," 123). Also see Joseph J. Kockelman, *Edmund Husserl's Phenomenological Psychology* (Pittsburgh: Duquesne University Press, 1967), 73–77. What Ortega
said of phenomenology and Dilthey (6:208n) applied equally (or more) to James, as can be
determined from the reference to "intellectualism" on the previous page, if not by his
reference to "pure historical empiricism" (207).

was like slipping a smooth glove over a rough hand—to disguise it. Now he could cite Husserl instead of James on such things as "belief" and "*whole and part*" (12:468).

Clearly Ortega owed much to Edmund Husserl, and even called him "my master" years later (12:179), but from the first he had distinguished the latter's type of phenomenology as "particular" and "transcendental" in contrast to his own realist and "general phenomenology" (1:253–54; 5:542; 8:53). Several times from 1913 to 1916, under James's influence, he examined Husserl so as to correct "the description of the phenomenon 'consciousness of . . . ,'" which was "the [idealist] basis of his doctrine" (1:256; 2:62–64; 8:273n). Although he acknowledged Husserl's influence on twentieth-century idealism and philosophical investigations being dominant into the 1930s (12:285), he himself rejected this "ultra-pure" idealism as too extreme (12:106, 178). He preferred James's moderate new realism.

Having investigated Husserl "seriously" only after 1912 (8:47) while continuing to study Kant, Ortega used these two Germanic sources to enrich and modify his basically pragmatic and realist ontology with a more "transcendent" epistemology. By 1915–1916 he was ready to attempt a *synthesis* of all these diverse elements—realist *and* idealist—into what he was already calling a "system of vital reason" (12:392), a comprehensive synthesis that by intent resembled Dilthey's *Idealismus-Realismus*. Did "vital reason" thereafter remain only a loose and eclectic potpourri of disparate sources and influences—phenomenological, Kantian, and pragmatist? If he truly effected synthesis in a "system"—mentally—what part did phenomenology play in it?

ORTEGA'S PHENOMENOLOGY: PHILOSOPHY OR METHOD?

One of the most challenging, innovative, and informative interpretations of Ortega's philosophy has surely been that of Philip Silver, who (against Spiegelberg) has defined it as a "mundane" (realist) phenomenology—hence, not as Husserl's "transcendental" type in a strict sense, but one at least partly of his own devising. By thus affirming that Ortega was a realist, Silver rejected Morón Arroyo's view that he was instead an "ultra-idealist." With support from others,[8] Silver has thus opened up, by his combined analytical and historical approach, a new way to understand Ortega more fully. However, he has based his view of the later Ortega too much on an interpretation of two key texts ("Preface for Germans" [1934] and *The Idea of Principle in Leibniz* [1947]) that can be well construed very differently, so that on "being" and on historical reason he seems off the mark because of

8. See supplemental note 8, chap. 5.

misdirection and exaggeration. These criticisms of Silver's thesis are not meant to deny its very great utility within narrower limits, for he has certainly given us a clearer understanding of Ortega's earlier thinking, from 1913 to 1923, and he has identified an important strand in his thought even to the end. But was he right to think that a quasi-Husserlian phenomenology was truly Ortega's *philosophy*—was it (in itself) his "system"? Or was Spiegelberg right: did Ortega (even as he claimed) see phenomenology as mainly a useful method, since he never defined a philosophy by method alone? Or was Ortega's a "transcendental" ("naturalist" yet idealist?) kind of phenomenology, very Husserlian from beginning to end, as Nel Rodríguez Rial maintained in 1990?[9] Either way, phenomenology was indeed his chief "new" method, or epistemology.

According to Ortega himself in 1934, Husserlian "phenomenology was never a [general] philosophy" for him, but it served him well as a new "instrument," or method (8:42)—first to describe life as reality and later to redefine "Being." His distinction echoed Croce but also sounded like Heidegger in *Being and Time* (1927), where he had stated that phenomenology's "essential character does not exist in being *actual* as a philosophical school" but only as a "*possibility.*" Heidegger too had come to Husserl around 1911, but through Brentano instead of James—even as Ortega seemed to say in his own case (8:31). The *Logical Investigations* and the *Ideen* of Husserl had given Heidegger a "procedure," but his interest was less in method than in "Being." In contrast, Ortega used phenomenology as a method to show that Being was actually Life, but to do so he had to supply phenomenology the "system" it lacked and of which it was "incapable" (8:42, 273). If Heidegger could reduce phenomenology to system and being to life, then, according to Morón Arroyo, Ortega's claim was doubtful.[10] Right or wrong, however, that was his view of Husserl's phenomenology, and he had sought to go "beyond" it, to get outside it in part.

Far from comprising the *essence* of his ongoing philosophy, or defining it as a whole, Husserl's phenomenology was for Ortega and his generation a

9. See supplemental note 9, chap. 5.

10. Croce distinguished between "philosophy as methodology" and "philosophy as metaphysics" (*History: Its Theory and Practice* [1916], trans. D. Ainslie [New York: Russell, 1960], 152–54). Martin Heidegger, *Being and Time*, trans. John Macquarrie and E. Robinson (London and New York: Harper, 1962), 62–63, 76–77, 78–79. Also see Heidegger *On Being and Time*, trans. Joan Stambaugh (New York: Harper, 1972), for "My Way to Phenomenology" (1963). Stern defined Heidegger's existentialism as "phenomenological description and interpretation of human existence," *Sartre: His Philosophy and Existential Psychoanalysis* (New York: Delarte, 1967). For a distinction (contemporary to Heidegger and Ortega) between "method" and "philosophy" in phenomenology, see Marvin Farber, *Phenomenology as Method and as a Philosophical Discipline* (Buffalo: Buffalo University Press, 1928). Morón Arroyo, *Sistema*, 211–18.

very useful thing but extraneous—a "stroke of good luck," as he put it (8:42). With some of its "instrumental" concepts (for example "bracketing" and "description" [1:252]), he clearly used phenomenology as a "science" to develop his own philosophy of life as "perspectivism," or "vital reason" on its epistemological side. But he also meant (from 1925) to use "phenomenological method" *systematically* to reform (restate) the basic ontological problem of "Being" (8:273).

In his first stage of philosophizing, Ortega very obviously utilized phenomenological method, but *life* was still the radical reality, not Husserl's idealist "consciousness" (8:47–49; 1:256). Thus, his metaphysics remained a variation of James's realist "radical empiricism," whose terminology of "presence" and "given" Husserl had also adopted. But Husserl's phenomenology brought with it "the methodic instrument" that "let some of my generation immediately situate the problem [of the "given"] beyond Dilthey" (6:208n), who (like James) had already had phenomenology "in principle" but not in name. After 1924 this method also served his second (historical) stage of thought, but meanwhile he added "metahistory" (3:149). So it was from life and history that he proposed to make merely "*synthetic*" ("intuitive") phenomenological "method" also "systematic," now to investigate "being"—by starting from life, which is "system *of itself*" (3:273), yet also from history "as a system."[11]

"The novel thing about [Husserl's] phenomenology," Ortega had said in 1913, was that it made "a scientific method" out of its treatment of "the lived, the immediate and visible as such" (1:256). And this is precisely how he then used phenomenology: as a *method* more revealing of basic reality and truth than was traditional induction or deduction (1:250–51; 12:498). Insofar as his "general phenomenology" of 1913 originated with Husserl, therefore, it did so in technique, in instrumental concepts, notably "intuition," "description," and "intentionality" (1:251–53; 12:407), and "reduction" and "suspension" at times.

Ortega took Husserl's (and James's?) idea of intentionality as of capital importance for himself (12:460).[12] With it, "we leave traditionally modern doctrines; with this we intend to overcome modernity" (R 77) in philosophy and psychology. At that point he adverted to the "little book" of 1916 that he called "Nothing Modern and Very Twentieth Century." Thereby he deserted modern principles and mere "facts" in still influential positivism. With "faith" in the future, he proclaimed that "the radical duty of every free

---

11. Spiegelberg, *Phenomenological Movement,* observed: "Phenomenology . . . has served as a tool for extremely divergent enterprises" (2:653).

12. Spiegelberg said: "Husserl's conception of intention shows . . . unmistakable traces of William James' inspiration" (ibid., 1:111).

man is to free his spirit from the past by making it, in effect, be a past and not a ghostly survival" that oppresses both present and future.

Between December 1914 and March 1916, Ortega kept a diary in which he explored various concepts and problems involving phenomenology, in regard to which he "reread" both Husserl and Scheler on such topics as relation, self-deception, intuition, value, essence, and being. From the latter he gained "little harvest," and he found the *Ideen* deficient on "noematic nucleus" and in "radical error" on another idea. To his class he said: "But where the science of phenomenology ends, the problem does not. We have to ask ourselves what corresponds in the purely metaphysical plane to the ultimate concepts of science. This will give a knowledge that will be like an applied metaphysics . . ." (R 36).

Intentionality and phenomenological method and terminology did not of themselves comprise Ortega's general *philosophy*, and his method was not purely Husserl's, whose "phenomenological reduction" (of basic reality to idealist "consciousness") he always rejected (1:255–56; 12:181; 8:48, 275n).[13] He also used a pragmatic method of "trial and error" (2:21) from 1916, as with "working hypothesis" (2:164n), and later as "testing" with "historical reason" in a "new methodology" (12:313) of historiology (4:530), which was phenomenological only in part—by its use of "intuition" and "description."

Accordingly, Ortega's *philosophy as a whole* cannot be sufficiently covered by a "system" of phenomenology, whatever the variety, and not as exclusive method, even for the period from 1913 to 1923. However, like his "positivist" version of James's "radical empiricism," a realist variation upon Husserl's phenomenology is surely contained *in* Ortega's philosophy—as a very important epistemological ingredient in the larger, more complex whole.[14] After James's metaphysical ideas about the "radical" life reality, Husserl's "methods" and "instrumental" concepts helped him *develop* those basics into a unitary-dual philosophy of life and of history. Insights from James limited his use of Husserl, even as Husserlian precision "informed" his Jamesian metaphysics. Dependence, thus bifurcated, diminished.

Both Silver and Rodríguez Rial have disallowed Ortega's "*intentions*" by making him appear to deny what he had explicitly claimed with respect to phenomenology. Silver has also represented him as already mature in philos-

13. Spiegelberg found, by his reckoning—by the first four out of seven methodological characteristics of observing or describing "instincts," "relationships," "appearances," particular phenomena, and general essences—that Ortega was a phenomenologist in method; where he was not was by the "suspension" (*epoché*) of existence and by rejecting the "phenomenological reduction" to consciousness (ibid., 2:658–60).

14. Silver, *Ortega as Phenomenologist*, 58–59 (cf. 88), thinks that Ortega would not go along with Husserl's "transcendental turn" from "things" or "facts" into idealism in the *Ideas* (1913). On the original realist possibility in Husserl, also see my notes on Edie and Farber in supplemental note 2, chap. 5, and also see n. 41 below.

ophy, with his "mundane" phenomenology, by 1914 in the *Meditations on Quixote*. He argued that Ortega developed this firm basis first into an "existential phenomenology" (vital reason), and then into a "phenomenology of origins" (historical reason). Rodríguez Rial now views Ortega's "transcendental" phenomenology as developing along much the same pattern. From too limited a perspective on Ortega's origins, both scholars (in apparently opposite ways) thus have mainly extrapolated the two stages of his philosophy as phenomenology. Silver has assumed that phenomenology *is* existential vital reason and then historical reason—until the end of the book, when the latter identity became problematic even in his own eyes.[15] Here I grant to Silver and to Rodríguez Rial that phenomenology was *in* both stages of Ortega's philosophy, but it proved insufficient for his overall "covering" philosophy.

The foregoing observations are not meant to deny any claims that by 1914 Ortega's philosophy was phenomenological; rather, I question that it was even then *merely* phenomenology or that it was so soon a "mature" philosophy. That after the period from 1913 to 1923 his very loose "system" of thought remained phenomenological *to some degree* is not disputed, just any idea that phenomenology is enough to encompass either the metaphysical origins or the later development in either of its two stages. Phenomenology was, for Ortega, never more than a very major but subordinate part of the larger whole that was—"intentionally"—a philosophy of life.[16] And that philosophy of life was more than a "phenomenology of life" or a phenomenological philosophy of life, just as his historicism was something more than Husserl's or Merleau-Ponty's "phenomenology of origins" or "genetic phenomenology."

As for the basic *Meditations on Quixote*, Ortega tells us more than once that it was more akin to what came to be called "existentialism" than to phenomenology (4:403n; 8:43, compare 45–46). That makes very problematic Silver's identification of the *Meditations* as essentially "mundane" phenomenology, even if he were to see this as *already* an "existential phenomenology." With residues from still other youthful interests, his philosophy then seems to have comprised elements of both pragmatism and phenomenology that were loosely synthesized and extended into a phenomenological vitalism or proto-*existentialism* that within a decade had become Ortega's overall philosophy in all but name.

For the period from 1912 to 1916, Silver presented his thesis about Ortega's phenomenology very well, but he overlooked too many sources and parallels

15. Silver, *Ortega as Phenomenologist*, ix–x, 114, 160.

16. Silver clearly recognized that *life* was Ortega's "systematic principle" and basic reality, of course: see *Ortega as Phenomenologist*, 28–29, 84. Rodríguez Rial, "Ortega—Phenomenologist," 107–34; also see supplemental note 3, chap. 5.

and so defined his philosophy too narrowly. The influences from Kant and the neo-Kantians along with Brentano and phenomenologists Husserl and Scheler are not enough. For example, if Ortega's realism justified not pursuing a suggestion that the *Meditations* might be "an 'existentialist' version of certain of Kant's ideas," he also ignored influence from Unamuno's contemporary proto-existentialism. Nietzsche had first turned Ortega toward a philosophy of life and history, but he was barely mentioned. And if Silver was vaguely aware of a "super" (or "radical") positivism, he did not suspect its nature or its relation to James's pragmatism, nor did Rodríguez Rial, who noted that Ortega was an "omnivorous reader" but considered no sources other than Husserl.[17]

For Ortega's later production, Silver and Rodríguez Rial cast nets both too wide and too loose. If not for vital reason then for later historical reason, they claimed too much influence from Husserlian phenomenology, compared, for instance, to the complex relation of Dilthey to Ortega. True, something like historical reason may have been *implied* in Ortega's phenomenology in *Meditations on Quixote* or in lectures or articles before 1920.[18] But that is not to concede that mere phenomenology covered (or contained) even vital reason as it continued developing, much less historical reason.

In *Phenomenology and Art* (1975), Silver put Ortega's earlier perspectivist works together uncritically with other much later ones that were informed by historical reason. His *Ortega as Phenomenologist* (1978) did not clear up the unavoidable problems of continuity and relationship of phenomenology and historical reason from the mid-1920s. Given Spiegelberg's very broad definition of the scope of the "phenomenological movement" from Brentano, through Husserl, to Heidegger, and finally to Merleau-Ponty, Silver's and Rodríguez Rial's contentions would be very plausible, *if* there were not (as Spiegelberg emphasized) major differences in Ortega. In fact, only limited coincidences with phenomenology can be found in his philosophy's second stage that have yet to be studied carefully.[19]

In his development Ortega was obviously ahead of, and maybe consistent

---

17. Silver, *Phenomenology and Art,* 11; idem, *Ortega as Phenomenologist,* 153; Rodríguez Rial, "Ortega—Phenomenologist," 107–10.

18. Silver, *Ortega as Phenomenologist,* x.

19. Herbert Spiegelberg, "Spain: Ortega's Past and Its Significance," *Phenomenological Movement,* 2:611–19. On Ortega's historical thought and phenomenology, see especially John H. Nota, *Phenomenology and History,* trans. L. Grooten (Chicago: Loyola University Press, 1967); and cf. idem, *Max Scheler: The Man and His Work,* trans. T. Plantinga (Chicago: Franciscan Herald Press, 1983). Also see José R. San Miguel Hevia, "Fenomenología y ciencia de la historia: Lectura libre del 'Prólogo' a Brehier," *Conversaciones sobre Ortega* (Aller, Spain: I.N.B., 1983), 407–21; and Oliver W. Holmes, "La fenomenología y la historia en Ortega," in *Ortega Hoy,* ed. Manuel Durán (Xalapa: Veracruz University Press, 1985), 225–36.

with, other European phenomenologists who dealt with existentialism and "phenomenology of origins" in later years. However, he differed by becoming distinctively, authentically an existentialist *and* a historicist. His conception and intention went beyond Husserl's phenomenology, Heidegger's existentialism, and Merleau-Ponty's almost ahistorical "structuralism." Given his diverse roots, Ortega's vital reason cannot be "reduced" to simply "transcendental" or "existential phenomenology," nor his historical reason just to Husserl's "genetic phenomenology." He was different; he was *more*—or "beyond"—those positions.

Ortega adjusted phenomenology to the rest of his thought, to its "living" and historical kernel, as much as the reverse. Thus, after 1925 he even sought to render phenomenology itself "systematic" via life and history, as a method for "restating" the problem of "being." If phenomenology were *most* of the *methodological* side of his philosophy of vital reason, however, did it also serve so much for historical reason?[20] Ortega did not think so. In method, historical reason was more complex.

Several sources relevant to his later historicism were prior to his study of Husserl and distinct from phenomenology—even where they were relatable to it. When he wanted to take up *historical* phenomenology (10:60) several years before he began to study Husserl seriously in 1912, he had already been predisposed toward vitalism and historicism by Nietzsche, Renan, James, and Bergson. There were also later influences of Comte's historical positivism and of Dilthey's variations on both vitalism and historicism. Despite undoubted similarities between Ortega's historical reason of 1924 and "phenomenology of origins" *later* in Husserl and later still in Merleau-Ponty, he therefore could rightly deny that his second stage ("voyage") of thought was covered sufficiently by *any* type of phenomenology. In 1941, when he became aware of Husserl's final extension of his undeveloped "genetic phenomenology" in a historical study entitled "The Crisis of the European Sciences and Transcendental Phenomenology" (1935), he refused to believe that it had been his own doing to thus "leap" suddenly to the level of "historical reason" (5:541–42, n. 2).

---

20. Compare with Farber, *Aims of Phenomenology*, who observes that no "single method" can be used exclusively for all problems in philosophy; hence, phenomenological method "must be used in cooperation with other kinds of method. The extravagant claim that it was the only genuinely philosophical method led to a strong reaction" (14–15); moreover, the method was too subjective and idealist (by bracketing out the natural) on life and history, as it was for Ortega. But in his chapter "Phenomenology as a Method" (43–62), Farber included other elements than "general seeing" and "description" of "essences," such as "reduction" and (re-)"constitution," to make phenomenology not a metaphysics ("suspended") but a "first science" for all the "special sciences" and disciplines. This was also the aim of Ortega's metahistorical historiology—a probable connection with Husserl that has gone undetected.

As a *whole* and in its final stage, Ortega's *philosophy* seems unlikely to have been phenomenology, although it certainly contained some major elements thereof. For the first stage, for vital reason, however, phenomenology was *very* important—for method and concepts, as Silver maintains, and for a "new epistemological paradigm," as Rodríguez Rial holds. Maybe it is a mistake, then, to try to separate very strictly Ortega's metaphysical concepts from his phenomenological methods. Much from both of these aspects of phenomenology was undoubtedly incorporated into Ortega's mature philosophy. Nevertheless, *he* insisted on distinguishing phenomenology as "philosophy" from its "methods"—in order to uphold his own independence. That distinction was valid as *intent,* for in fact his philosophy *and* his method were more than Husserl's phenomenology, more too than his own "general" phenomenology in metaphysics and psychology.

"GENERAL PHENOMENOLOGY" IN METAPHYSICS AND PSYCHOLOGY

After James, Husserl undoubtedly contributed most to Ortega's basic metaphysics, to reinforce "presence" and "given," for the epistemological concept of *intuition* from the *Ideen* (1913), and to "describe" so many "essences" of his worldly "circumstance." He could even apply the idea of intuition (after the fact) to account for his earlier perception of the "phenomenon" of life itself as primary reality. Because it was separable from "transcendental" phenomenology, Husserl's idea of intuition now became the subjective side of his self-positing (or "objective") principle of life as "self and circumstance" by 1913–1914. By then, in psychological studies James's "radical empiricism" (misassigned to Mach and Ziehen) was the source of Ortega's "correction" of Husserl's idealism and "consciousness of."[21] Instead of Husserl's "pure phenomenology," then, Ortega opted for a "general phenomenology," as he put it (1:254). This is what Silver has called "mundane phenomenology," but it could just as well be named "empirical" phenomenology. Its new realism Ortega took more from James than from Brentano, although (as a "natural mode") it too derived in part from Husserl (1:253). Realism nevertheless made a "real," a major, difference.

Ortega's early phenomenological essays (1913–1916), which Silver published, greatly illuminate his "Preface" and *Leibniz*—and show how long he had held those later positions. They also reveal that he was well acquainted with

21. Husserl, *Ideen,* on "presence and "given"; see supplemental note 8, chap. 5. See Rodríguez Rial, "Ortega—Phenomenologist," 109–10, on "intuition." Also see Silver's *Phenomenology and Art,* wherein the repeated translation (82, 84, 85, 87) of "radical empiricism" (Mach and Ziehen) is given as "extreme empiricism," but not so altered in meaning in *Ortega as Phenomenologist,* 79; cf. Ortega, 12:489–91.

Husserl's basic concepts, terminology, and methods. They do not clearly support the thesis that he then adopted or used merely a quasi-Husserlian "mundane" phenomenology either for his basic metaphysics or for his overall "philosophy." His "general phenomenology" was something more modest—not yet a "system," even as *method*, and it derived from others besides Husserl: from Hume, Hegel, and James.

Of the term "phenomenology," he said: "When I use it, it means (by full intent) something distinct from Husserl, and it nevertheless coincides materially with one side of Husserl's phenomenology—*neomatic* phenomenology" (R 36)—that is, where it dealt not with ontology but with epistemology, or the mind. Where he "suspends Reality," "I suppress 'consciousness of. . . .'" "The 'phenomenon' in Husserl arises when by 'reduction' he turns Reality into 'consciousness of' . . .": "transcendental ego."

As Silver points out, long before "1912," when (Ortega later admitted) he began "serious study" of Husserl (8:47), he was interested in phenomenology.[22] Probably it was even before 1907 (Silver's estimate) that he first became aware of phenomenology. In some early (undated) notes, he mentioned "doing phenomenology by surprise" (R 76). Although exact years are impossible for us to establish, already in 1908–1909 he cited Husserl, along with James, Russell, Bergson, Dilthey, and Mach, among others, in regard to both psychologism and "concepts" (R 76, ms 5). Also in 1908 he remarked: "For a long time now I have been meditating on the problems of historical phenomenology" (10:60)—twenty years before Husserl did more than state a "program" (5:542n). Then whose "phenomenology"? As historical, was it Hegel's? Already he admired Hume's great "phenomenological talent" in psychology (R 76). We cannot surely identify source or type for his pristine phenomenology, but he did not mention Husserl again until his *Ideas* (1913) for a "pure phenomenology" (1:244, 251). Hence, his early basic interests in life and history, as well as in metaphysics and psychology—all predating 1912—cannot simply be annexed to a Husserlian phenomenology, remade sui generis as either "mundane" or "transcendental" version.

So, what was Ortega's "general phenomenology" before 1913 and until 1916, or whence was it? Clearly he had other sources of inspiration besides Husserl. Lesser works of that period show that after 1912 he knew Husserl's phenomenology very well, in its concepts, terminology, and methods, but they also confirm that he had not just adopted it for his own "general" phenomenology. For that reason, Silver thought that Husserl's teacher, Franz Brentano, had inspired the "worldly" streak in Ortega's phenomenology.

Ortega's "Essay on Aesthetics" (1914) seemed to Silver to manifest "a Brentanian critique of Husserl's transcendental-phenomenological reduc-

---

22. Silver, *Ortega as Phenomenologist*, 2.

tions" that compares well with Sartre's much later work of 1936–1937.[23] Thus, Ortega was seeking to "naturalize" a variety of "Husserlian phenomenology" in Spain with the aid of Brentano's earlier "empirical" phenomenology. But was this source then likely or even possible? A more likely source was William James, if not Max Scheler, whom he was then reading in regard to "Idealism-Realism." He noted that Scheler did not contain "a special phenomenology of facts (at least of the perceived)" (R 64), but he continued to "reread" him on "inner perception" and "observation in itself" (R 36).

According to the later "Preface for Germans," Ortega linked himself mentally with the "generation" of Brentano and Dilthey, that of 1836 (which implicitly included James), as superior philosophically to any before Husserl's. Yet, no more than Husserl, he noted, did Brentano have "what is called a philosophy" (8:30–31, 42). Only Dilthey then possessed an "authentic philosophy" and "system"—even if unknown at the time. The influence of Anglo-French positivism had imposed a basic, radical mental disposition of empiricism on Brentano and Dilthey. Subsequently, phenomenology was born out of Brentano through Husserl. Hence, Brentano's and "especially Dilthey's" positivistic and phenomenological way of being empiricists "continues today to be the future of philosophy." (He could have said the same of James.) Ortega saw this new type of empiricism as both anti-Kantian (or anti-idealist) and anti-positivist (meaning oriented merely to fact-thing).

That proto-phenomenology sought to "construct the world" on the basis of the psyche, or on psychology taken as "fundamental science" (8:32). In one sense, Ortega followed Husserl in rejecting their "psychologism" (4:282), but he insisted that the thought of his own generation was actually closer to those "radical tendencies" of the generation of Brentano and Dilthey than to later generations of the neo-Kantians and of Husserl. One must therefore conclude that it was more in the sense of Brentano, Dilthey, and James that Ortega had first taken up phenomenology in a limited and "empirical" way.

Since Ortega had not yet read much of Dilthey, was his "phenomenology" before 1913 and until 1916 in fact Brentano's? In the "Preface for Germans" (1934) he did not say that he had known anything about Brentano's works and ideas during that period. "Today," he said, we know "that the swan of phenomenology" hatched from the "chicken's egg" that was Brentano's admirable *Psychology from the Empirical Point of View* (8:31). He recalled that when he had asked Cohen about Brentano in 1911, however, he had gotten no useful response (3:433). In lectures on psychology in 1915 he referred twice to Brentano's *Empirical Psychology*, but only for its non-synthetic view of judgment related to values (12:402, 408). Since he did not mention him in the early phenomenological essays (1913–1916), perhaps he then knew no more

23. Ibid., 42–44.

about Brentano than about Dilthey (8:30–31). There are no other references before 1923, when he said that he had just put out a Spanish edition of Brentano's *On the Origin of Moral Knowledge* (1889), related to values (6:322n). In his preface to Brentano's *Psychology* in 1926, Ortega seemed to have learned of its part in the historical origins of phenomenology from the German second edition of 1925. Only then did he note that among the younger disciples decisively influenced by him was Husserl (6:340). Such a belated realization was implied in his remark to Albert Einstein (at Toledo in 1923) about Brentano having been unknown to both of them until after his death in 1917 (3:433). As with Dilthey, Ortega evidently knew about Brentano but did not grasp his general doctrine or his important ideas until years later.

If the "general phenomenology" of Ortega from 1913 to 1916 was not Brentano's, or purely Husserl's, then was it partly Jamesian, compounded with positivism and Kantianism? Given his acknowledgment of philosophical immaturity in those years (1:311; 8:41), and his later insistence that Husserl's phenomenology did not become his philosophy (8:42), his "worldly" phenomenology could not have been solely of his own devising. Like Brentano and Dilthey and James, he came from a background of positivism (more French than English); so if we add to his Kantianism a Jamesian "radical empiricism" as "absolute positivism," his early phenomenology makes more sense, for he saw it in 1915 as compatible with pragmatism (12:392).

His essays on aesthetics (1914, 1916) did not manifest any greater orthodoxy in phenomenological concepts but revealed again his basic realism and rejection of pure idealism (6:253; 2:35, 37). In fact, the whole corpus of those earlier works has the appearance not of purity in his general phenomenology but of compromise, and of admixture with other elements—notably with pragmatism. For example, his "Aesthetics on a Streetcar" impishly concluded with a relativist Jamesian "cash value" (2:39). If his key idea of "life experience" (*vivencia*) may have come from Husserl, it could as well have come from James first. A strong Kantian imprint also is evident, however, in the idea of style as "schema" and as "de-realization." Moreover, his combination of the *real* with hypothetical "ideal-type" models looks like a Weberian compromise anticipating "metahistory." Yet both schema and "hypothesis" were very compatible with James.

As early as 1913, residues of realist positivism and scientism in Ortega were in conflict with the idealism of Kant and of Galileo (1:84–86, 88, 255–56). He sought a compromise by means of Husserl's phenomenology, especially through use of the "principle of intuition," which was too new in 1913 for him to see "its limits and its constitution." But perhaps with it, he hoped, "a new epoch in philosophy has begun." Using Husserl's concepts and techniques (for example, 1:252–53), he now rejected the "extremes" of empiricism in positivistic science (1:246) and of idealism in Kantianism for something partaking of both idealism and realism. Both Dilthey and Scheler sought that combination as *Idealismus-Realismus*. In 1913, Ortega called the result his own "general phenomenology" of "pure description," one differing from Husserl's "particular phenomenology of human consciousness" (1:253–54). Not so extreme as Mach's positivism, James's "radical empiricism" (which he disguised as "absolute positivism" in 1916) was—more than the others—what made the essential link with and difference from Husserl in phenomenology.

If it was not Brentano, finally, who inspired a *realist* "general phenomenology" in Ortega, unless James? Since it was so late (1912) that he studied Husserl "seriously," it is very unlikely that he had first learned of James through him years before. On the other hand, he might not have recognized any "phenomenology" in James except *through* Husserl after 1912. Does this process of elimination then leave Hegel as the most likely source of Ortega's early interest in trying to "historize" phenomenology? Perhaps, but his realist emphasis on time and place could as well have come initially from James, whom Husserl had tried to get to read his works and to recognize that phenomenology was affiliated to pragmatism.[24] James died in 1910 without doing so, but Ortega certainly saw and admitted it (12:392). Thus, his "general phenomenology" was Husserl's type as "corrected" by James's pragmatism, or vice versa: a synthesis of the two.

PHENOMENOLOGY AND PROBLEMS OF CONSCIOUSNESS AND PRESENCE

When Ortega expounded Husserl to Spain after 1913 (for example, 8:273), it was critically and it reflected James in several ways. In some notes from that time captioned "Phenomenology—Husserl," he held that it made empirical psychology possible, that it fixed "the description and phenomenological nature" of "mental objects" that were related to theory of knowledge (R 76). In the idea of consciousness, however, he cited several "mistakes" and problems, such as whether the contents of the consciousness were "immanent or transcendent" in terms of "being," realist or idealist in terms of interpretation. In fact, "consciousness of" was his crucial problem with Husserl, and his solution seems to have come straight out of James.[25]

In his university course on psychology in 1915–1916 phenomenology and Husserl's name and terminology are prominent, but we also find reference

24. Spiegelberg, *Phenomenological Movement*, 1:111–14. Edie, *Invitation to Phenomenology*, 116: James never read Husserl.

25. For James's denial of "consciousness of consciousness" as applicable to Husserl, see Edie, "James and Phenomenology," 499, 509–19 ("James' Non-Egological Theory of Consciousness"), as "existential phenomenology" (509, 515), and as related to "*the central active self*" (513) and to Sartre and existentialism (cf. Ortega's "executive self," n. 29, 30 below).

to James there (12:417) and to pragmatism as having anticipated "the system of vital reason" (12:392) and as being compatible with phenomenology. Moreover, just as he recalled in 1934 (8:54), in the lesser works of the period 1913 to 1916 he had already discovered a basic "error" in Husserl's phenomenology (1:256; 12:407): the primacy of "consciousness of" *consciousness*—as James had put it. But primary perception is not consciousness, which relates object to subject (12:377–79). Ortega had begun with an idea (clearly not yet Husserl's, but very possibly James's) that philosophy is born of crisis, of a "desperate situation," and he concluded that series with the open assertion of his philosophical *independence* by means of "absolute positivism" (2:66; 12:399), which was in reality much closer to James's "radical empiricism" than to Husserl's phenomenology.[26]

The problems of *immediate* fact, "given," or "presence," in contrast to mediated "consciousness," frequently crop up in Ortega's notes and lectures between 1913 and 1916 (as in R 76). He manifested therein the conflicts between the realism of James's pragmatism and the idealism of Husserl's phenomenology. "If man is consciousness, Cartesian man is the consciousness of consciousness. In effect, the problem of consciousness is the first that philosophy has to resolve and on whose solution the rest depends." For Ortega as for James, "consciousness does not exist"—unless in its "content." There has to be a "presence" of both object and subject for consciousness to exist. But "the self" cannot be that content or object, although it is truly a part, or "element," of consciousness. "Certainly, from the phenomenological point of view," he conceded, "the immediate is what we find immediately," without reflection, as our "radical point of departure." "What that *datum* is, is something more elemental than thinking: when I open my eyes I find something placed absolutely. . . . The 'things are' serves us a prototype of spontaneity. This is Being as Existence—being that is" (R 76). In such contexts, Ortega pushed beyond pragmatism and phenomenology, to the borders of existentialism—not just in terminology but in the principle that "existence [of self and things] is prior to essence"—more or less as in James, for whom perception is prior to conception. Moreover, the idea of "presence," or "compresence," noted above is most certainly from James, and was stated by Ortega in "What Is Philosophy?" in a clearly pragmatist context.

In those years from 1914 to 1916, while he was working hard to reconcile his different sources of realist and idealist viewpoints, Ortega kept a diary to record his progress. On "Day 27" (in September 1915), he was mulling over the problems of essence, form, and intuition. Rereading Husserl's *Ideen* and

26. Also see Ortega, 7:351, on a "radical" type of "absolute positivism," which demands "the presence of the object itself," or "the 'positive'" (1930); and 8:296, on the "huge error" that phenomenology had committed in its "point of departure" by its "description of the phenomenon 'consciousness of'. . . ."

Logische Untersuchungen (on "noematic nucleus"), he noted that he had found a "radical error" and a "serious mistake" in each of them. "But what is an 'essence' concretely?" Later he noted: "But where the science of phenomenology ends, the problem does not. We have to ask ourselves what corresponds in the purely metaphysical plane to the ultimate concepts of science. This will give a knowledge that will be like an applied metaphysics"—as for psychology (R 36).

Precisely as he claimed in 1934, Ortega had after 1913 rejected as an error Husserl's idea that "consciousness of" is basic reality (8:54; 1:256). Now that was precisely what James had rejected in neo-Kantianism. For Ortega, human life (*Erlebnis, vivencia*) is the "primary and all-encompassing reality," and it was a "boundless field" for phenomenological investigation (1:256–57). More than either Husserl or Scheler, Ortega gave to the "phenomenon" of human life its coordinates of time and space—and this by 1915 (1:252, 255). He was also more "radical" than Husserl with his "first principle": before they are real or unreal, objects are immediate to consciousness, but consciousness itself, or "consciousness *of*" consciousness, is not primary, is not the point of departure for reality.[27]

In such ways Ortega used the "rigorous" phenomenological technique on Husserl himself. Already in 1912, as he studied phenomenology carefully, "it seemed to me that it had committed the same carelessness in the microscopic order that the old idealism had created in the macroscopic" (8:47–48). This recollection from the "Preface for Germans" (1934) was followed immediately by what ("*put by itself,* the 'positive,' or 'given'") was—in light of his early phenomenology—clearly his "absolute" positivism applied to the problem of "primary" reality. Thus, he had used Husserl's "instrument" against its author to defend his own intuition of basic reality as *life* rather than mere consciousness,[28]—a new moderately realist view.

In 1930, again on the problem of "self-consciousness" that "idealism and phenomenology do not clarify," he stressed that the "radicalism" of his own "system" rejected consciousness as the last three centuries of idealism had taken it. "Phenomenology says that it attends radically to the given and the

27. On Ortega's realist and objective idea of "life" as basic, and his rejection of "consciousness" as basic, and as idealist and subjective in both Husserl and Dilthey, see Tuttle, "Ortega's Vitalism."

28. On the problem of "consciousness" in Ortega with regard to Husserl, see Silver, *Ortega as Phenomenologist,* 9–12, 77, 83, 85; he did not, of course, trace it to James, although he recognized (85) that Ortega had seen that "man's primary relation to the world was really 'pragmatic,'" and that "things" perceived are *pragmata,* and also Heidegger's basing of ontology on "this same Greek notion of *pragma*" (86). On this "pragmatic" quality and on phenomenology and consciousness, see Rodríguez Rial, "Ortega—Phenomenologist," 112, 116–17; and Lester E. Embree, ed., *Life World and Consciousness* (essays for Aron Gurwitsch) (Evanston, Ill.: Northwestern University Press, 1972).

present as such." But in fact it introduces as "intermediate" between self and object a "presence before me." "I confess that I have never found it." So this requires a "radical restatement of the theme 'perception' and therefore of the theme 'consciousness'" (R 78). Ortega moved to integrate consciousness, or the things that are its objects, into "my life," which is "the primordial and absolute reality"—one with "executive, not objective being."

Apparently from the same course "What Is Knowledge?" in a "new theme" called "Life as Execution," he stated: "Phenomenology leaves out of consideration the executive character of the act." In phenomenology, by an "inner contradiction in idealism," the meaning of "consciousness of" is "being outside of something" in regard to the act. He found that, as idealism, phenomenology did not "clarify" the problem of the "universal and executive presence" of things relative to "consciousness." On the distinction between "objective being and *executive being*," "our theme is strictly the inverse of that of phenomenology, and of its method, therefore."[29] Was this new "executive" realism inspired belatedly, but chiefly, by James?

Ortega's "executive I" was finally very different from Husserl's Cartesian "I" of the "pure consciousness," which was "*reduced*" to mere passive contemplation of both self and outer reality but lacked both "belief" and "action."[30] Thus *vivencia*, or "life experience," is reached only by the "manipulation" of Husserl's "phenomenological reduction," which "instead of *finding* reality fabricates it" and "suspends" the true reality of life (8:48–50). In 1940, Ortega averred that "Husserl's famous 'phenomenological reduction' is clearly and plainly impossible" (12:181, 185). He insisted that "a reality that consists in being immediate to itself—and this is *consciousness*—does not exist." The term should be eliminated from "basic philosophy," or metaphysics. He admitted that his proposal was "scandalous" and "unheard of," but he resolved to stand by it.

Husserl's phenomenology had made a big "intellectualist," idealist error: it had committed the "crime" of making reality "vanish by turning it into consciousness." "Consciousness, then, is a concept contradictory in itself" and the very "term 'consciousness' ought to be quarantined" (8:51).

> What must be done is to uproot from the word "*Erleben*" (*vivencia*) all residue of intellectualistic, "idealist" meaning, of mental immanence or consciousness, and leave it its awesome original sense, according to which

29. Ortega, *¿Qué es conocimiento?* 14, 18–19, 51, 58–59.

30. "Executivity" is covered by Silver, *Ortega as Phenomenologist*, 85, 97–110; more extensively by Cerezo Galán in *Voluntad de aventura*, which is based partly on the lectures in Ortega's *¿Qué es conocimiento?* See Rodríguez Rial, "Ortega—Phenomenologist," 111–12, for a critical remark on Cerezo and executivity. That James was a source for Ortega's idea seems likely: cf. Edie on "*the central active* self" in James's *Principles of Psychology* (1:298–301), in "James and Phenomenology," 513.

something happens absolutely to man; that is, being—and not only thinking he is—, existing outside thought, in metaphysical exile from himself, handed over to the essentially foreign world of the Universe. Man is not a *res cogitans*, but a *res dramatica*. He does not exist because he thinks, but, on the contrary, he thinks because he exists. (8:52)

In 1940, against the "intellectualist" and idealist "false Cartesianism" of *Cogito, ergo sum* (or "I exist because I think"), he proposed this inverse "Cartesianism of life": "I think because I exist," or live (12:194). "The *cogitatio*, or the *consciousness*, is therefore entirely other than what Descartes supposed. It is, in an essential way, *transcendence;* it is, precisely, *presence* of reality" (12:186).[31] Radical reality was life, self and circumstance, mutually "positing," "presenting" themselves "absolutely," an idea originally from James.

"ABSOLUTE POSITIVISM" AND PHENOMENOLOGY

By "the Idea of Life as radical reality" Ortega was able to "avoid the prison that the concept of 'consciousness' had been" and to substitute for it "simple coexistence of 'subject' and 'object'" as self and circumstance (8:53), as *Dii consentes*. That unitary-dual "symbol" for a realist phenomenology (which he got out of James before Husserl) first appeared in his psychology lectures of 1915–1916 (12:388), wherein he admitted owing much to Husserl (12:399, 434, 444) and stated that "the alpha and omega of my logical and methodological convictions" was "absolute positivism over relative positivism" (2:66). And what did this mean? "All deduction, theories, and systems are true if what they say derives from direct observation of objects themselves, of the self-same phenomena." But this "positivism" of immediate facts, or objects, was from both James and Husserl.[32]

Undoubtedly Ortega's "absolute positivism" reflected not only (primarily) James's concept of "radical empiricism" but also Husserl's methods. By rigorous "revision" of idealism, the latter had provided a "technique of exactitude" for defining consciousness and its content (8:47). So often,

31. On Descartes and Ortega, few consider the latter's (mostly posthumous) revelation of his "Cartesianism of life," which Nietzsche probably first suggested to him—"*vivo ergo cogito*" in *The Use and Abuse of History,* trans. Adrian Collins (Indianapolis: Bobbs-Merrill, 1957), 69. Also see McClintock, *Ortega as Educator,* 414–15, 432; and Jean Vuilleumier, "Ortega y Gasset, el anticartesiano," *Journal de Geneva* (October 1955); Juan Saiz Barberá, "De Descartes a Heidegger," *Revista de Filosofía* (1941); Marías, *Circumstance and Vocation,* 323. See Edie, "James and Phenomenology," 523, on the "dramatic" in James's concept of life.

32. For Husserl's contribution to the idea of life as "radicality," see Francisco X. Martins Prata, "O nivel de radicalidade da filosofia de José Ortega y Gasset," *Filosofia* (Lisbon) 8 (October–December 1961): 245–82.

observed Ortega, "the great advances in knowledge" come not from "great new intuitions" but from observing "little differences." Such contraction and concentration of attention, of course, then characterized generic "neo-positivism," including Husserl's. Ortega credited his "integral positivism," idealist though it were, with helping Dilthey "overcome" the old empiricism (R 40).

Although his "Preface for Germans" and early essays in phenomenology illuminate each other, a fuller coordination of Ortega's metaphysics involves also his essays on Kant from the 1920s.[33] Together they show that, even with phenomenology, his "theory of knowledge" remained essentially James's, though called "radical positivism." Into it he combined James with Husserl and Kant for a unified ontology and epistemology. Moreover, James gave him insights to cope with the others.

Ortega's "Preface" of 1934 used some epistemological terms that were not so evident in his early phenomenological essays—except in regard to Mach's scientific so-called radical empiricism. These words, "*given*" and "immediate," appeared in early lectures.[34] "Certainly, from the phenomenological point of view, the immediate is what we find immediately," without reflection and not as a "fact of consciousness," as our "radical point of departure" (R 76). "*Things* are given me in the plural [and] spontaneously," and they are "real being." The terms "given" and "*self-posited*" had become more prominent in his Kantian critiques of 1924 and 1929. In seeking a firm and primary reality on which to base everything else, a philosopher decides that "to think is the subject positing something." But he seeks an objective case that will "consist in something that he does not posit, but, on the contrary, comes *imposed* on him, in something, therefore, *posited by itself,* the 'positive,' or 'given'" (8:48). For Husserl this positive, given, primary reality was (ultimately) "pure consciousness." For Ortega, as for James, it was ("radically") the "thing," as "phenomenon."

What Ortega regarded as "primary" was not consciousness, then, but something simple, "unreflective," and irreducible beyond the immediate reality of our contact "with things themselves, with the world." Thus, reality is not idealist reflection but is "activity," happening, and *vivencia,* or life experience (8:49, 52). Thus, "the positive and the given" are "self-posited," imposed on us. What *truly* is there, or radical reality," needs no further "intellectual step," or "reduction"; it is "life in its uncoercible and insuperable spontaneity."

His concern with the "pre-philosophical," self-posited, and imposed had led Ortega to his discovery of "life as the radical reality" (8:53). Such was

33. For lack of space I have omitted an appendix on Kant and Ortega.
34. For example, see Silver, *Phenomenology and Art,* 84, 86 ("positing"), 90 (Cohen's "unity of thinking").

ontology in Ortega's metaphysics: clearly more Jamesian than Husserlian. Now, except by hindsight in *method* and concepts (like "intuition"), this discovery owed to phenomenology little that was not previously in pragmatism. Phenomenology was thus not identical with his basic metaphysics in 1914—nor in the 1920s, 1930s, or 1940s. Then what was Ortega's phenomenology? Most basically, his phenomenology was "seeing" as "perspectivism"—an *addition* to the epistemological side of his Jamesian metaphysics, but also rooted in James.[35]

"PERSPECTIVISM" AS PHENOMENOLOGICAL METHOD FOR "VITAL REASON"

Following his discovery of life as basic reality around 1909–1910 by a unified metaphysical operation of Jamesian "radical empiricism" that was both epistemological ("given"; "presence") and ontological (self and things), there came the first stage of development in Ortega's life philosophy as vital reason. Phenomenological "perspective" was its most prominent *method*. By 1916, the same year that he named his new metaphysics "absolute positivism," he had substantialized "perspective," or "viewpoint," as "perspectivism." Perspectives were a way of "seeing" his world "circumstance" from about 1913–1914 in the *Meditations on Quixote* through *The Modern Theme* of 1923 and beyond. Until the 1930s he was content—"for better or worse"—to let this method be called "perspectivism," a name deriving from the Germans (7:286), from Leibniz (R 36), Nietzsche, and Vaihinger (2:19n) and maybe from Scheler,[36] although Ortega's meaning for it was "point of view" as in James and Husserl. This perspectivism was closely aligned, therefore, to phenomenology. Indeed, by its more notable features, perspectivism *was* Ortega's "general phenomenology," not idealist but a moderately realist type that at bottom thus reflected James as much as Husserl.

When he later denied ever having been truly a Husserlian phenomenologist in philosophy, he meant not only in overall "system" but also in ontological origin and basis: *life* (in self and circumstance) as reality that was more "radical" than Husserl's "consciousness." However, when he defined his philosophy by its epistemology, its methods, and its "way of thinking" about that life reality, then (until after 1923) his philosophy could have been qualified as a realist phenomenology as well as perspectivism. Obviously he was then very concerned with both Jamesian "viewpoints" and Husserlian

35. For a potent passage from Husserl's *Ideas* (1913) that Silver thought had a "catalyzing" effect on Ortega, see his *Ortega as Phenomenologist*, 91–92, for such (actually Jamesian) expressions as "thing," "percept," "aspect," and "appearing" (cf. "seeing"), and 93, on Ortega's "perspectivism," as in *Meditations on Quixote* (118–19).

36. See supplemental note 36, chap. 5.

"description of essences," as he himself had characterized phenomenology in 1913 (1:253, 258) and (in Scheler's work) again in 1928 (9:339–40). Husserl's influence was also apparent in his references not only to "seeing" but to "phenomenological reduction" (*epoché*), "consciousness" (of), and "bracketing," among others.[37] Therefore, as a name for this methodological *level* of his thinking, what Silver calls "mundane phenomenology" is not inappropriate.

"POINT OF VIEW," "ASPECT," AND "PERSPECTIVE"

With evident overlapping earlier and later, perspectivism was a method of the earlier stage of development of Ortega's philosophy of "vital reason."[38] Introduced inconspicuously from 1908 (1:111, 440), James's "point of view" and "aspects" were incorporated into the basic "Adam in Paradise" (1:475, 486). In 1911 his "Books of Walking and Seeing" already manifested a simple epistemology of "seeing" (1:17–19). By 1914 viewpoint and seeing became "perspective" in *Meditations on Quixote* (1:321, 343). Even before that, distinguishing his own more basic and realistic "general phenomenology" from Husserl's, he had separated the whole (as a synthetic act of consciousness) from the primary perception of the "surface properties" of things—the "points of view" that were to be synthesized. "Viewpoint," or "perspective," therefore reflected both James's pragmatism and Husserl's phenomenology. He confirmed that "from 1913" forward he had expounded "perspectivism" in his university courses, which were then largely on phenomenology.

Ortega also recalled (3:200n) that his "doctrine of perspectivism" had first been publicly "formulated" in 1916 in a "limited" way by his *El Espectador.* In "Truth and Perspective" (2:18n), which introduced "Confessions of 'The Spectator,'" he had begun by reference to "pragmatist philosophy" related

---

37. Not every critic would agree that Husserl always overlooked life as basic, or that phenomenology itself (if not in Husserl, then at least in Ortega himself) could not get down to the "roots" in life as reality. See Holmes, *Human Reality,* 46: "Clearly Husserl's idea of *Lebenswelt* was the kind of notion Ortega discussed in his own philosophy of 'human life.'" On the other hand, Marías argued that one cannot "grasp and understand . . . life itself as fundamental reality," as in Ortega's philosophy of vital reason, unless "one go beyond phenomenology, beyond all 'description' and *consciousness* thinking" ("Metaphysics as a Science of Fundamental Reality," in *Spanish Philosophy: An Anthology,* ed. A. R. Caponigri [Notre Dame: University of Notre Dame Press, 1967], 368). But see Tymieniecka, "Phenomenology of Life," 3; and Rodríguez Rial, "Ortega—Phenomenologist," 115–16. In the collection of phenomenological essays in Silver's *Phenomenology and Art,* Ortega entitled one (1913) "What Is Phenomenology?" (101). He stressed its "scientific methods" (110) and concepts, meaning "intuition" (93, 104), bracketing (105, 108), description (106)— all appropriated for his own "general phenomenology" (107), which immediately rejected "consciousness of" (107, 110–11).

38. See supplemental note 38, chap. 5.

to Spanish life and politics and had ended by appropriating the pragmatic method of "trial and error" (2:21). The "Spectator's" purpose was to observe "life as it flows before one" and to speculate on it (2:18). One did not arrive at the truth in theories and schemas except through "the individual point of view," which avoided both skepticism and the old rationalism. "Reality, then, presents itself in individual perspectives," visual, intellectual, and evaluative (2:19). All of this was strikingly like James but was largely duplicated in Husserl.

From pragmatic "viewpoints" and by phenomenological "description," Ortega had a way to get at "essences" on a conceptual level. His reduction of phenomenology to "pure description" and "viewing" is a source of perspectivism, which thus largely reflected Husserl's methods.[39] As "seeing," phenomenology was an "instrument" of vital reason, just as Ortega later claimed in the "Preface for Germans" (8:42, 47). It would be an error, however, to regard his perspectivism as simply a variation of phenomenology, for, in discussing existentialism later, Ortega said that he had found a "viewpoint of life" in several forms of vitalism (12:192)—one of which (unidentified) was certainly James's, but not Husserl's.

"Perspectivism" was, then, "in force" from 1916 through at least 1923, when it concerned life, or "the *vital human phenomenon*" (3:169) in *Modern Theme,* where he also adverted to it as "Doctrine of Point of View" (3:200n). Contrasted to absolutist and "utopian" philosophies, his vital reason had a "*vital, historical, and perspectivist dimension*" (3:201). Finding a "perspectivism" in Einstein's theory of relativity (3:234), he made "the particular perspective that reality offers when seen from our point of view" an essential part of the whole, of "the order and form that reality assumes for the one who contemplates it." Thus it "acquires an objective value" and is not just individually subjective and "provincial." "Against the Kantian thesis, time and space turn out to be forms of the real" (3:236–37). Introducing his selected works (1932), he again affirmed that "the world is . . . a horizon whose center is the individual. This is the basic perspective of life" (6:347).

A New Text: James, Husserl, and "Consciousness Of"

A potential "clincher" for the preceding arguments is an undated page of his unedited notes that Ortega titled "Vital Reason, *Realdialektic,* and Phenomenology." The very caption links him not just to Husserl but to Dilthey—if not to James. Therein he explicitly identified the first term with the third *initially,* but he also viewed vital reason as being somehow different because of the second. Insofar as it was realist, his phenomenology was indebted to

39. Silver, *Phenomenology and Art,* 106 (1913); Ortega, 4:509.

James before Dilthey, despite the German term for a "realist dialectic." The heart of the argument follows: "Vital reason is 'immediately' Husserlian *seeing*. But the latter arrives at the 'fiction' of the transcendental ego. What has happened? What difference *results* ('later' as compared to 'immediately') [or] turns out between the two [ways of] seeing? The 'thing' that is seen in H[usserl?]., therefore the being (absolute being of *Erlebnis*)[,] is obtained previously [by] a fiction—that of which the 'seeing it' is 'conscious of . . .' and not that *from which* this is consciousness. In vital reason being (absolute) is from the outset *given*—because that H. lives—exists . . ." (R 39). Here Ortega again rejected the "*consciousness* of" for the "*presence* of being." The "conflict" that he affirmed between these two terms (or ideas) was then reducible to the difference between Husserl and James, or between idealism and realism.[40] In fact, "presence" was first not in Husserl but in James, who had repeatedly denied that "consciousness" is primary, or is the immediately "given."

If we were to forget whose terms Ortega was really talking about, then the unique text above might seem to validate Silver's contention that his *philosophy* was indeed a "mundane" Husserlian phenomenology—even from its metaphysical origins. Better stated, it was so in part and by second hand, *after* a primary Jamesian realism of radical empiricism.

Ortega clearly stated above that his vital reason had taken its *departure* from Husserl's initial "natural" mode of "seeing," prior to the idealist "reduction" in *Ideen*. The "perspectivism" in "vital reason" was rooted first in the realist (Jamesian) mode or variation in Husserl's early epistemology.[41] When he rejected Husserl's idealist "consciousness" as not sufficiently basic (or radical), he opted instead for James's realist "presence," in the sense that *life* is the "given" ground, or source, of "being" and of consciousness. So, *ontologically*, vital reason was always something distinct from Husserl's idealism, which contradicted realist epistemology by means of an a priori "consciousness of."

Phenomenological "Perspective" in Later Thought

The influence and impression of Husserl's phenomenology on Ortega was permanent, even though he had "abandoned" it in its stricter and fuller sense already in 1913, as he claimed. Thereafter he "reduced" it to *method*,

---

40. R 39. The interpolations into the text seem necessary for proper sense, but it is conceivable that the "H" could have stood for *hombre* instead of "Husserl," although Ortega did not capitalize it elsewhere.

41. On the "naturalist" mode in Husserl, see Silver, *Ortega as Phenomenologist*, 60–62; Husserl, *Ideas*, chap. 1, for "suspension" of the "natural standpoint." Also see supplemental notes 3, 6, chap. 5; and Silver, *Ortega as Phenomenologist*, 2.

chiefly as perspectivism. This "perspectivism," he said in 1930, was a "method" he had initiated to "bring together" in philosophy the "temporal" and "eternal" aspects of reality from nineteenth-century positivism and historicism (7:285–86), or realism and idealism (3:201).

As idealist "pure consciousness," phenomenology in *Modern Theme* seems tacitly consigned to the rationalism of "pure reason" as "utopian" and "uchronic." Years later, he called Husserl "an extreme rationalist, the last great rationalist," who had tried to recover Descartes's "point of departure" and had thus "looped the loop of rationalism" (5:517). Now his kind of perspective had to be "supplanted by a vital reason that is localized and acquires mobility and the power of transformation" (3:201). But in vocabulary Husserl's phenomenology survived in Ortega's philosophy of life, as "transcendent," if not transcendental: "Human life—or the ensemble of phenomena that integrates the organic individual—has a transcendent dimension in which . . . it emerges from itself and participates in something that is not itself, that is beyond it" (3:169). This other thing was culture, which comprised "vital functions" such as thought, will, aesthetic sense, and religion—with a *historical* dimension and conceptual form.

In his "reduction" of the complex phenomenon of life to "pure facts," one can see much more clearly in *Modern Theme* (1923) than in "Concept of Sensation" (1913) Ortega's reliance on James's radical "empiricism," which (in deference to Husserl) he now called "the most rigorous positivism" (3:166). Thus he made his own formerly "absolute" positivism of 1916 parallel to Husserl's "rigorous" science in attention to detail. "Suddenly the world solidified and began to ooze sense from . . . all things," when he had started from the experienced life-world (4:509). James had done the same, and his "things" were "facts."

Perspectivist phenomenology became less evident in Ortega's later works. It cropped up again in 1925 as "points of view" and "aspects" in "Some Drops of Phenomenology" in *The Dehumanization of Art* (3:360–62). Commenting on Heidegger in 1932 (4:403–4, n), Ortega traced his own existentialist ideas back to 1914, to his *Meditations on Quixote*, where he had enunciated a doctrine of perspective (1:321). But "today I prefer to this term [perspectivism] others more dynamic and less intellectual," obviously "vital reason," as in *Modern Theme*. In effect, it seems, he was thus annexing perspectivism to his own later existentialism as well. He meant that, as perspectivism, this phenomenology was in vital reason, which in turn became Ortega's existentialism. Now if perspectivism is phenomenology as method, then existential vital reason is phenomenological in precisely the same way—but with a progressive complexity.

"Perspective" remained a distinct (but seldom prominent) term and method subordinated to historical reason in his later philosophy of life (8:333; 9:371–

73, 339). In *The Origin of Philosophy* (1946), which was preeminently a work of historical reason, the second chapter ("Aspects and Entirety") was patently perspectivist (9:369–73). "Knowledge . . . is perspective," not the thing itself, nor a copy, nor a construction, but an interpretation that "translated" it from the language of being to the language of knowing (9:372). Here perspective sounds more like James than like Husserl, however.

In *Origin* we can see the basic connection of perspectivism with both pragmatism and phenomenology more clearly, although now Goethe had to substitute for James. "This [looking at the surfaces of things from a variable focus] is at times a compelling phenomenon of paradigmatic value . . ." (9:368). "For me this unpremeditated experience has been unforgettable— what Goethe called a 'protophenomenon'—and to it I owe, literally, a whole dimension of my doctrine: that *the thing is man's master . . .*" (9:368). From one aspect, therefore, this *looking at the thing* was ontological, where the object was human life; from another it was methodological, or epistemological. As he wrote the following year (1947) against Heidegger, such a philosophy of seeing (or looking) was not only Husserl's but Dilthey's (8:298)—and, of course, it was James's.

As late as 1954, with reference to Scheler again, Ortega connected "human space" with "living perspective" (9:339). Thus, phenomenological perspectivism was always part of his thought—through his existentialism, even historicism. Already by 1934, however, he had gone "beyond" phenomenology as his vitalism became self-consciously existentialism.

PHENOMENOLOGY, VITALISM, EXISTENTIALISM: LATER TEXTS

In a variant form of the sixth lecture of his 1930 course "What Is Philosophy?" Ortega dealt with problems of phenomenology and existentialism. "Our theme, then, is strictly opposite to that of phenomenology and therefore [of] its method. On describing an act, phenomenology eliminates, reduces its executive character. We ourselves are concerned exclusively with this latter" (R 78). At that time he was proposing an "executive," "objective" *realism* of a new kind. Of course, life (vitalism) remained the basic, radical reality for him, what "exists radically 'for me.'" "My existing is, then, to exist in coexistence and *for* it." Since idealist phenomenology did not clarify the problems of "self-consciousness," he stressed the "radicalism" inspiring his own "system"—from James, of course.

In 1941, looking back on Husserl's phenomenology as a thing of the past, Ortega observed: "Phenomenology has forty years of life that has not passed in vain, and it would indeed be fitting" to show (as Croce did with Hegel) "'what is living and what is dead' in it." For himself, "unquestionably" he had "for some time now" put phenomenology "behind" him. "However, let me counsel students of philosophy to study phenomenological method deeply as incomparably the most fecund, efficacious, and rigorous in this discipline." These lines, in a variant draft of his "Points on Thought," were part of "a radical critique of phenomenology's point of departure—the 'phenomenon [of] consciousness'" that built upon a then unpublished study ("Preface" for *Modern Theme*) written years ago "for Germany" (R 80).

Taking a later and more *historical* perspective on Ortega, I have naturally understood the "Preface for Germans" (1934) somewhat differently from Silver and from Rodríguez Rial. With a more complex view of his "mature" philosophy, I see it as including phenomenology but as going "beyond" it too. I accept Ortega's claim then and later that neither phenomenology nor existentialism adequately covered or defined his philosophy as a whole; nor did historicism, much less the ever basic pragmatism.

Actually, Ortega did not say in 1934 precisely *what* his "philosophy" was in 1923 besides "vital reason." However, he hinted strongly about Dilthey's "philosophy of life" as a "first-class, authentic philosophy," in which "the fundamental tendencies nourishing us today realized their fullest and purest possibilities" (8:30–31, 46). By 1934 he was projecting James onto Dilthey: in the basic "radical empiricism," which appeared (unidentified) here too (8:48–49, 51–52, 55). Beyond James, however, Dilthey also represented a more highly developed and often compatible vitalism and *historicism*. If he admired Dilthey more, Ortega praised Husserl for the rigor and beauty he had brought to idealism. The "Preface for Germans," however, was not a confession—direct or oblique—that phenomenology of any kind had ever fully constituted his own general philosophy.

In that "Preface" of 1934, Ortega revealed only part of his sources and intellectual odyssey up through *The Modern Theme* (1923). He saw himself as a "resistant" (reserved), independent, and "mature man who has already seen the underside of things" (8:21–22). Evidently, the "underside" was "life experience," or "facts" (as self and circumstance) that he had discovered as basic reality by an "intuition" Husserl helped him formulate. By use of Husserl's "marvelous instrument" of phenomenology he had defined this basic reality metaphysically as (Jamesian) "absolute positivism" in 1916. But the *upper* side of his later mature philosophy was not phenomenology per se but "vital reason" that was closer to the newer existentialism and to Dilthey's older philosophy of life, of which he had been unaware in 1923 (8:31, 32, 46). His later historicism went unmentioned in 1934.

Also in that preface, Ortega pointed out that apart from truth, there are three things that a philosopher is driven to seek: *reality, problem,* and *system*—apparently in that order chronologically (8:36–37). His initial discovery (*aletheia*) of "reality" before 1913 was not Husserl's "consciousness" but "life" as "self and circumstance." This discovery had then "launched" him on a "voyage," onto a sea of "problems," his "destination unknown," as he abandoned the philosophy of "the 'Modern age'" (Husserl's idealism included) for a shore "never . . . reached before" (8:41). One of those problems was that of "being." That shore, as a new "system" of philosophy, for a long while lay out of reach if not out of view. By 1934 it was not phenomenology but a kind of rational vitalism that he saw as akin to existentialism, but more positive and historical.

To sum up, from 1913 forward Ortega was sure of his own originality, but he did not yet know quite what he was creating philosophically upon his new (basically pragmatic) metaphysics of life-reality. Evidently, beginning in the *Meditations* and lasting through the perspectivist period into the middle 1930s, he was solving "problems" of life by phenomenological method, and by *historical* "addition" to it after 1924. These were problems about what Silver calls repeatable "life-themes," which he worked into his growing body of philosophy as "truthful" implications of his basic unitary-dual principle of reality. Finally, by 1934, he had reached the ripe maturity of fifty-one years of age, which, so Aristotle told him (8:41, 269), was the time to begin Plato's "second voyage" to consolidate and to "systematize" in books (7:315). For that historical "second look" (7:285), he had *added* "metahistory" and "historical reason" to the methods of phenomenology utilized in his "vital reason." To systematize was no easy task, however. Such had been Ortega's constant "will," or intent, since before 1913–1914, but for twenty more years he had found it beyond his powers. The first notable fruit of his renewed effort at systematization was "Historiology" (1928), which was indeed partly phenomenological. Next came "History as a System" (1936), where "vital and historical reason" was then openly more historicist than phenomenological.

To make of Ortega an "existential phenomenologist" in the mainstream of the "phenomenological movement" Silver needed to restrict himself to *method,* to fit the "Preface for Germans."[42] Most of the ten relevant pages there were actually about how Ortega had formerly used Husserl against himself, to find the "careless" errors, the "hole" in his thought, the "crime" of making reality disappear (8:48, 50, 54). Moreover, if "system could not be the work of youth," he said, neither could it result from phenomenology, which is "incapable of systematic form or shape" (8:42, 273). The "Preface" does not, therefore, support Silver's notion that he held then or ever a *systematic* phenomenology for his general philosophy; quite the contrary. But Silver's view is sustained neither by the *Leibniz* text, nor by its context, nor when it is compared to the "Preface."

42. Silver, *Ortega as Phenomenologist,* 60, 88, 90.

PHENOMENOLOGY, VITALISM, AND HISTORICISM IN *LEIBNIZ*

The autobiographical data of the "Preface" do help illuminate a not very clear reference to phenomenology in *The Idea of Principle in Leibniz* around 1947. Silver's thesis defining Ortega as essentially an "existential phenomenologist" rests on part of the chapter "The Level of Our Radicalism"—a very complex and difficult passage that Silver translated and interpreted more freely than as follows (Ortega's italics).

> In 1925 I stated my theme . . . saying literally: first, that the traditional problem of Being has to be renewed [*renovar*] from its roots; second, this has to be done by the phenomenological method so far and only insofar as this means a *synthetic* or *intuitive thinking* and not merely the conceptual-abstract type like traditional logical thinking; third, but it is necessary to integrate the phenomenological method by adapting to it a dimension of *systematic thinking*, which, as we know, it does not possess; fourth, and finally, in order for a systematic phenomenological thinking to be possible, it is necessary to start from a phenomenon that is system *in itself.* This systematic phenomenon is human life and one has to start from the intuition and analysis of it.(2) In this way I abandoned phenomenology at the very moment I received it. (8:273)

Concentrating on phenomenology, Silver (and O'Connor) analyzed the passage apart from either its immediate or its extended context and without close attention to key terms that Ortega stressed. "Radicalism" itself implied, if not Comte (8:277), then James as much as Husserl, and the text implies that Ortega "adapted" *vitalism* ("vital reason") to phenomenological method, thus "integrating" the latter into something larger. Before Heidegger, moreover, he had set out to develop a new ontology with a new method of "systematic thinking"—that is, by an altered phenomenological method (8:273) that was to be made systematic by study of "life" as an object already "systematic."

Critique of an Interpretation

Now what Silver italicized for emphasis in that passage, "systematic *phenomenological* thought," is better rendered active—as "thinking"—which befits "method" more than does passive "thought," which implies "system," or *philosophy*. Moreover, it is not the phrase that Ortega himself stressed ("*systematic thinking*"), which obviously was not initially "phenomenological." Next, it is equally clear that neither the first phrase nor the second is exchangeable with "phenomenology" as a *philosophy*, to which he referred last of all (as "abandoned"). The phrases can be attributed only to the "phenomenological method" that he mentioned twice. As Ortega's addendum to phenomenological method, "systematic thinking" was a "dimension" that had to be "adapted to" it, since he explicitly denied that this method was systematic in itself. Now the context makes it obvious that the "systematic" part of the resulting compound came from an extraneous source, a "phenomenon that is system *in itself*"—namely, "human life"—that is, from vitalism. Finally, contrary to Silver, the intervening footnote (2) did not cancel out Ortega's plain reassertion that he had "abandoned phenomenology"—meaning "system" ("philosophy")—already in 1913. There (in note 2) he had again affirmed that he had rejected Husserl's "consciousness of" for "life" as "self and circumstance"—which was his basic, pragmatist metaphysics of "radicalism" (or "radical positivism") in a "nutshell."

So the systematic addition to Ortega's method had come from *outside* phenomenology, from his ratiovitalism, which was then (1925) still his philosophy-as-a-whole, with its "*vital, historical, perspectivist dimension*" (3:201), or methods at once from life, history, and phenomenology. To assert, with Silver, that "a systematic phenomenological thought" is "the philosophical method" of "vital or historical reason" *is* surely admissible,[43] *if* one has altered the "phenomenological method" to make this (perspectivist) aspect *systematic* by incorporating it into the greater vital and historical whole.

Thus limited and encompassed, "existential phenomenology" can indeed be said to be the chief *method* of Ortega's vital reason as late as 1925. For "historical reason,"[44] however, he was very soon working out a new "systematic" method that was "metahistorical" and (in part) phenomenological: "historiology." In later years the accustomed phenomenological method was not therefore dominant in his "way of thinking" but was coordinated with, and subordinate to, a historical method in his total "system" of vitalism—which was thus only partly phenomenology.

Alternative Interpretations

A first impression that one could just as well gather from the *Leibniz* text (above) is an apparent contradiction: Ortega had abandoned *phenomenology*

43. Ibid., 8, 50–51, 70–71, 96 (cf. x). For the basic importance to Silver of the *Leibniz* text ("from which our study set out"), see 8, 71, 96; and idem, *Phenomenology and Art*, 10. Also see O'Connor, "Ortega's Reformulation," 53–63.

44. O'Connor, "Ortega's Reformulation," 55. Compare with Paul Ricoeur, "The 'Existential' Turn of 'Transcendental' Phenomenology," *Husserl: An Analysis of His Phenomenology* (Evanston, Ill.: Northwestern University Press, 1967), 204, on the later Husserl's return to perception and 'thing'—an "empirical" shift in accent over to "existential phenomenology." Clearly Ortega preceded Husserl in this "existential turn," just as in the *historical* turn. Ricoeur notes that Husserl's phenomenology "becomes a method" (203), and consciousness is directed to the "outside," as "world-for-my-life," for the "living ego"—as in Ortega, incidentally.

by 1913, but twelve years later he proposed to give to phenomenological *method* a new "dimension" of "systematic thinking" that it had always lacked. Was he then returning to phenomenology, or did he in fact never "abandon" it? Since the first alternative seems too foolish in view of all his phenomenological terminology after 1913, Silver chose the second, although that seems to make Ortega contradict himself. A third, commonsense possibility is that Ortega, like Heidegger and others, simply distinguished phenomenology as a *philosophy* (or "system," in Silver's sense) from its *method,* which might be used systematically when combined with something else, in a philosophy that thus utilized phenomenology but was itself something distinctly different. Was this the case?

Footnote (2) actually identified what Ortega's philosophy was in fact: since the *Meditations on Quixote* (1914), "the basis of all my thought is the intuition of the phenomenon 'human life'" (8:273n)—that is, a philosophy of life—which became a philosophy of vital reason and (eventually) historical reason, or of existentialism and historicism—including (let us admit) a *systematic* "phenomenological method," which would be very hard to identify, except as part of historiology, to which he had adverted (8:272) just before the disputed passage.

One's second impression, from the larger context preceding and following the *Leibniz* text, is that Ortega's philosophy of life was not merely a "phenomenological" existentialism of Heidegger's type, but was, here too, something more "radical"—which he had been discussing just before digressing about Husserl's phenomenology. The footnote, moreover, repeated what he had already said in 1916 and in 1934: Husserl was not "radical" enough in his perception of primary reality, which was neither "consciousness" nor "consciousness of" (both of which were secondary, or hypothetical) but "experience of life" (*vivencia; Erlebnis*). And life is the twofold "*coexistence of the self and the thing,*" or "I and circumstance": "man is being to things and things being to man; this is to live humanly" (8:274n). It was not Dilthey who influenced Ortega here, for he "had no idea of these things and believed ardently in 'consciousness.'"

In short, neither Heidegger nor Husserl, nor even Dilthey, was up to "the level of our radicalism" (in chapter 29 of *Leibniz*). Not one of them really began their philosophies with intuition of human life as the radical, ontological reality. On the other hand, that was the hallmark of Ortega's philosophy of life—more basically than even Dilthey's. After Nietzsche, it was *James* who, still unacknowledged, had helped Ortega there.

Did that passage in *Leibniz* mark only what O'Connor has called an "existential turn" in phenomenology in 1925, or was it a vitalist and a historical turn in Ortega's "phenomenological method" too? In the "Preface for Germans" (1934) as later in *Leibniz* (1947), Ortega rejected both phenomenology and mere existentialism for his "system." Instead, his was a philosophy of *life,* as a more basic, "radical" and primary reality than either Husserl's consciousness or Heidegger's "inflated" concept of Being, *Dasein,* or *Existenz* (8:272–77). The "radical reality" was life, that "phenomenon that is system *in itself,*" from which, by "intuition and analysis," he had started and continued to build. It is clear, however, that in developing his philosophy of life, Ortega already had used Husserl's phenomenological *methods* more or less "systematically": to "intuit" life as radical reality and to "view" and "describe" life from different "perspectives"—increasingly, after 1925, historical. Apart from preferring "life" to "being," it is clear that he had anticipated and had many existentialist terms and concepts in common with Heidegger. But in "History as a System" in 1936 he had historized "being" into "becoming" (6:33n, 34, 39–41) and was now (1947) much more "historicist" than either Heidegger or Husserl. Besides, in 1928 he turned his metahistory into a historiology, a complex new method for a new historical ontology, half of it phenomenological and half pragmatist (4:530), which historized "being" itself.

O'Connor saw the intent of Ortega's words of 1925 in *Leibniz* about "restating the problem of Being" as pointing toward "What Is Philosophy?" as an existential and vitalistic metaphysics.[45] That is true, but in fact his metaphysics of 1930 was still pragmatist at bottom and already historical. Besides, for restating being, that was not his first attempt, which was "metahistorical" in *Modern Theme* and—as Ortega in fact said in *Leibniz* (8:272) explicitly—in his essay "Historiology" (1928). There he had begun to historize Being (or human life-reality) "systematically" with a special mode of historical reason. Then, and at a higher level, his one philosophy of life had become dual, or "bi-lobar"—that is, metaphysical *and* metahistorical at once, before 1930.

Still another perspective on Ortega's odd "two in one" philosophy was implied on the same page of *Leibniz,* where he referred to his "Annex to Kant" as his second effort to restate the problem of Being with a "radicalism" that Heidegger had never attempted. Heidegger had merely "inflated" the concept of Being instead of reducing it to the bold question: "what is something?"—much less had he really *historized* either Being or truth (8:272–73, 279 n. 2) in *Being and Time.* Now what Ortega had done with Kant in the 1920s—and what he was doing with Heidegger in the 1940s—was to take both an analytical and a historical approach to his thought, which no doubt his now "systematic" phenomenological method facilitated. The result, however, was to make Kant's "Copernican revolution" a unifying of epistemol-

---

45. O'Connor, "Ortega's Reformulation," 53. Silver, in *Ortega as Phenomenologist* (71), took note of "Historiology" but drew no inferences thereon; he also concluded that phenomenology underlay his "philosophy of history" in *History as a System.*

ogy and ontology that was more or less equivalent to James's "radical empiricism." Indeed, the "Annex" was ultimately Kant with a Jamesian twist (4:55–57), which he expressed much more directly and clearly in 1930 (7:325) as a "unity of knowing and being"—a phrase that Ortega used boldly in his *Leibniz* (8:70).

Intuition, Synthesis, System

Sensing a general crisis broader than what Husserl had found in the natural sciences, extending even to *principles* and to reason itself, Ortega believed it called for a deeper "philosophical radicalism" than what Husserl could claim. Only such a radicalism could get "under the very foundations" of things, get to the bottom of the problem of Being itself (8:280–82). "Philosophy is formally radicalism because it is the effort to discover the roots [Latin: *radices*] of everything else" that is not manifest—including the concept of Being.

To dig so deeply required an "intuitive," "synthetic," *and* "systematic" way of thinking (8:273). Those key terms, as Ortega used them, notably the first two (given as equivalents), were not transparent in meaning, but all related somehow to altering the method of "phenomenological thinking." Carefully defined, they can help show us what he meant by "systematic" use of a phenomenological method in relation to life and history.

Having taken Husserl's "new principle of intuition" as a method for grasping basic life-reality and essences already in 1913 (1:251), Ortega by 1930 had still not defined intuition beyond "that mental state in which an object is present to us" (7:353–55). Such "intuitive" evidence was "the basis of the philosophy most characteristic of our time"—phenomenology. In 1947 in *Leibniz* he would praise Husserl for having provided the first "controllable clarification" of what intuition means. He interpreted it here as partaking of both vision and imagination. Partly Euclidean and partly Kantian (8:134–36), intuition also somehow combines both observed external reality and an internal mental operation. Thus is it "synthetic."

What else intuition may have meant to Ortega is not clear, but he found Bergson and Husserl only enough to get started. Apparently he utilized their ideas of "intuition" so as to combine James's naive "percept" with an *un*contrived concept. In 1928 he thus made intuition the a priori first step for knowing human reality in a scientific method of "historiology" (4:530).

For "synthetic" thinking, if Husserl did not provide him a usable method, at least his conception was open to development. Although synthetic thinking had always existed in philosophy, Ortega observed in 1946 that no one before Kant had so named it and considered how it was distinct (9:35in). Kant, however, had seen synthesis only negatively—as neither analysis nor implication. Fichte, Schelling, and Hegel had regarded it as evident but had not known its source or rules. "Husserl, who hardly mentions synthetic thinking, is the one [nevertheless] who had clarified its nature most." Even yet, Ortega felt, we have only begun to grasp it. He hoped to *develop* it.

Equating synthetic with "dialectical" thinking, Ortega developed a "dialectical series" of alternately "backward" and "forward" searching in the history of philosophy. Trying to improve on Hegel, he related this dialectic to historical reason and to historiology (9:362, 368). This historical orientation of synthesis was very evident as he explored the "historical origin" of philosophy itself in the 1940s.

In Ortega's dialectic, one thing (or idea) connects with another in both forward and backward progression (9:350–51). If contradiction is involved in this process, so is continuity. Each philosophy in the historical series has thus been partial error and partial truth. However, each successive system has also represented a "path, road, method" that could develop only so far, so that its successor had not only to continue but to try a different way and direction (9:359). Thus, the methods of historical reason presumably contain and succeed to the phenomenological methods of vital reason, not by a simple displacement but by addition, correction, and continuation. Here Ortega thought that he was providing something else that was not in Hegel's dialectic nor in Husserl's phenomenology—an *immanent* process that was a *historical* method. By "progressive complication or synthesis," the historical dialectic thus leads logically and historically to "historical reason" as a new and comprehensive system (9:365–66 n. 2).

But "system," Ortega held, was not in phenomenology itself, nor in its intuitive and synthetic thinking (8:42, 273).[46] It could come only from life and history. But how could "life" be "system in itself"? In 1916, he had remarked that theories and "systems" were true if they come "from direct observation of the objects" or "phenomena themselves" (2:66). However, "systematization" was not a primary coincidence of knowing and being, as assumed by the scientific "radical empiricism" of Mach and Ziehen; instead, it was secondary, separated from subject and object in themselves and supposing connection—relationship. Actually he got this idea not from Husserl or Mach but from James. Such "system" came not directly from life but from reflective operations on it that took the form of concepts. As "models" or "hypotheses," such concepts he derived (from the 1920s onward) as meta-

46. Silver, *Ortega as Phenomenologist*, 49–51, seemed to reject Ortega's claims (as "inconsistency") that neither phenomenology nor its method was a system. Hence, he seemed to imply, if Ortega were a "mundane" (or "existential") phenomenologist, then his *philosophy* is phenomenology and *is systematic*. I do not dispute Silver's view of Husserl, only his disallowing of Ortega's very explicit *intentions*—whether right or wrong in themselves. And Ortega's idea of "system" was more complex than Silver realized.

historical "constants" from historiology, which was intended to make not only history but philosophy and the "human sciences" *systematic,* as he projected in 1936 in "History as a System" (6:30n, 44 and n.). "History is the systematic science of the radical reality that is my life." His "Theory of Life" was, finally, historical and comparative and used historiological models, such as crisis, generations, and life stages.

It is time to conclude with Ortega's problem of "systematic phenomenological thinking" or "method" of 1925. In the "Preface for Germans" (1934) he stated that his own generational group had derived their "will to system" from the neo-Kantians and from the idea of Hegel and the German Romantics that "philosophy, whatever else it may be, is, one way or another, system as such" (8:27, 37, 41). Implicitly against Husserl's claim of "rigorous science," he then also attributed to the Romantics the first "clear" perception that "philosophy as problem, as intention, and as mode of the mind is something that has scarcely anything to do with the sciences: in short, it is not *a* science."[47] Now then, if phenomenology is a "science," can it be truly a philosophy? Or is it essentially an instrument, a technique, a method? For his own purposes, Ortega clearly settled for the latter definition: it was a "prodigious instrument" (as he had said already in 1913) for "the description of essences"—even historical ones. Phenomenology may serve history and vice versa.

His own generation, Ortega wrote in 1934, did not "entrust itself fully to phenomenology after 1911." "Phenomenology, by its very consistency, is incapable of arriving at a systematic form or shape." "Therefore, phenomenology was not for us a philosophy. . . ." But, if phenomenology in itself was not a "system," maybe it could be turned into a systematic *method* ("instrument") for constructing a system of life and history in philosophy (8:273). Contemporary life and history of life, in turn, could provide elements of system for phenomenological method. Did the later phenomenology of Husserl after 1934 seem to Ortega at last a "system" of "philosophy" (5:536–38), by its new concern with "crisis" and with history? But, first, let us examine Scheler as a possible influence on the new historical thinking of Ortega, if not of Husserl too, even in phenomenology.

ORTEGA AND SCHELER'S PHENOMENOLOGY

In *developing* phenomenology, Ortega perhaps depended less on Husserl than on Max Scheler, most of whose books he had gotten, for Scheler too

---

47. As late as 1921, Ortega still called philosophy a "science"—a "true science" with clarity and order as aims, after which he mentioned Husserl (6:292, 294, 295).

was "more than" a phenomenologist, had studied pragmatism, and turned later to history and sociology. Scheler strove for a "meta-anthropology" while Ortega was developing a "metahistory" and even a proto-existentialism. One suspects, however, that Ortega praised him so highly not because he had borrowed so much from him but because he was so pleased to find someone else using common sources in a way similar to himself.[48]

A text that Silver did not utilize might, as examined by Orringer, considerably strengthen his contention that Ortega's philosophy was a "system" of phenomenology that extended into vital reason and historical reason.[49] In an obituary where he commemorated Scheler as a "Drunkard of Essences" in 1928, Ortega asserted (contrary to positivism) that "the eternal concern of philosophy—the grasping of essences—was attained, finally, in phenomenology in the simplest way," by a "new optics" (4:510). From a later text we learn that this new epistemology was merely opening one's eyes and "seeing" how things actually are (8:298). That was the way of Husserl's phenomenology (but it was James's way, too). Fascinated by its possibilities, "the thinker *par excellence* of our era," Scheler, "forgot" the larger truths of "metaphysics, theory of knowledge, and logic" in order to concentrate on problems close at hand: "human types, sentiments, historical valuations." Such immediate problems Ortega too had undertaken during his perspectivist phase by "describing" the concrete essences of his world-circumstance. Now Ortega was preparing to go "beyond" Scheler to provide phenomenology with "system," even while continuing to define human types (like mass-man). What he found still missing in Scheler was precisely what he had found lacking in 1913 and 1925 in Husserl (compare 8:42–43, 273), "architecture, order, system," which he was now ready to "add," to "complete" Scheler's phenomenology (4:511). And history was sooner compatible with phenomenology in Scheler than in Husserl, but Ortega preceded both of them in that development and maybe anticipated Scheler's "philosophical anthropology"

48. See supplemental note 48, chap. 5.

49. Spiegelberg, *Phenomenological Movement,* 1:239, 241, 248; Nota, *Max Scheler,* 88, 143 (Heidegger and meta-anthropology). Silver gave emphasis to Scheler's influence on Ortega's phenomenology (*Ortega as Phenomenologist,* 20, 57, 64, 153). See p. 60, for example, on Ortega's rejection of Husserl's transcendental *idealism.* Nelson R. Orringer (*Nuevas fuentes germánicas de ¿Qué es Filosofía? de Ortega* [Madrid: Consejo Superior de Investigaciones Científicas, Instituto de Filosofía Luis Vives, 1984], 13) saw Scheler's influence in Ortega's writings from 1920 to 1927 in both metaphysics and "philosophical anthropology," before the latter read Heidegger. For my reservations and doubts, see the immediately following notes and the next chapter. Also on Ortega and Scheler, Manuel Durán, "Dos filósofos de la simpatía y el amor: Ortega y Max Scheler," *La Torre* 4 (July–December 1956): 103–18; Martha S. Mateo, "Los valores in Max Scheler y Ortega," *Humanitas* 9 (1961): 157–70; and Antonio Pintor-Ramos, "Max Scheler en el pensamiento hispánico," *Revista de Occidente,* no. 137 (August 1974): 40–61.

too.[50] But was phenomenology here "system" as fully "philosophy," or was it again only "method" ("optics"), or epistemology, that he meant to systematize?

Although the context is ambiguous, Ortega also seems to say that he intends to impart order and system to areas neglected by Scheler's type of phenomenology, areas such as metaphysics, epistemology, and logic, because the "era for discovering essences" had closed with Scheler's death. Soon, from 1929 to 1933, he would expand his inchoate Jamesian "radical positivism" into a formal "metaphysics of vital reason." In 1923 he had introduced a "metahistory" in *Modern Theme,* and in 1928 with "historiology" he produced an alternative to Scheler's merely "philosophical anthropology" (4:467–69). In the 1940s he would develop a new version of historical dialectic. Accordingly, if it was in historical thinking that he went so beyond Scheler, was "History as a System" historical phenomenology or at least phenomenological historicism? In short, was his philosophy in its historical stage indeed phenomenology of "genetic" type? If so, it went far beyond what either Scheler or Husserl attained.

As a whole, the relationship with Scheler seems not to have been mere dependency and imitation on Ortega's part but one of amicable mutuality, with perhaps reciprocal influence. Ortega praised Dilthey, Husserl, and Scheler not because he had taken over ideas or systems from them uncritically but because he found in them parallels to his own development, so that they justified what he was doing and bolstered his self-confidence. Thus he clearly preceded his "great friend" Scheler (5:297) in historical (if not also sociological) development, and perhaps he influenced *him* therein.[51] Although he regarded Scheler as "a formidable thinker and a mind of the highest purity," by the mid-1940s he stressed "the unquestionable inadequacy of his philosophical knowledge and technique," even in his "insight" into *person,* one of "the few ideas" from Scheler that he admitted still following (12:212).

Clearly, for Ortega's earlier period, much more study of his relationship to Scheler is needed, to sort out priority in some remarkable parallels, like "philosophical anthropology."

50. Ortega (12:319) did not regard "philosophical anthropology" as central to Scheler's philosophy, and he himself had considered it (2:451–53; 4:467) in 1924–1925, two years earlier than Scheler seemingly enunciated it in *Philosophical Perspectives* (9–10, 68–69). Ortega had praised the anticipation of a "historical perspective" in Scheler's "phenomenology of war" a decade earlier (2:194–95). In chap. 6 (110–32) of *Invitation to Phenomenology,* Edie attributed "philosophical anthropology" to James originally, as central to James (115), where perhaps Ortega and Scheler got their common idea.

51. On Scheler, see supplemental note 48, chap. 5.

THE LATER HUSSERL ON CRISIS
IN SCIENCE AND PHILOSOPHY

One of the more enlightening, yet finally perplexing, of Ortega's commentaries on phenomenology—in "Points on Thought" (1941)—shows that he had consciously subordinated it to his philosophy of life in a larger sense. Nevertheless, the essay ends with a further reflection that shows him vexed by Husserl's later convergence with his own existentialist and historicist way of thinking. The context is "The Historical Character of Knowledge." In an "annex" he subjects phenomenology to a critique shaped by vital reason and historical reason (5:540–42); finally, however, comes a long footnote examining Husserl's later departure into crisis thinking that corresponds—illegitimately, thinks Ortega—more or less to historical reason.

Philosophy must *justify* itself. " . . . Phenomenology has in common with all previous philosophies the character of 'ingenuous or unjustified philosophy'" (5:536). Answers appear to be "forced," or doubtful, as to *why* anyone philosophizes at all. "Every human occupation has to be justified," however, not only to others but "to the one who is so occupied"—openly or implied—and philosophy especially, because it tacitly insults all "brutes" who are not philosophers. "And the justification that I demand will exist only when the ideas that constitute the system of philosophy itself are derived from it, as from a principle" (5:537–38). Stated as a "thesis," this meant that a philosophy's justification is its first principle. "All that induces a man to philosophize forms a part doctrinally of the philosophical theory itself." To illustrate what he meant, he took Locke and Husserl for examples.

In Husserl, Ortega found no conscious preliminary fundament from which first principles, or a philosophy of phenomenology itself, properly derived. Although Husserl never paused to reflect on his original, pre-doctrinal motives, Ortega insisted here that "Man does philosophy in virtue of certain needs or advantages [that are] pre-theoretical or non-theoretical, that is, vital. These are not vague but precise and they condition very *determinatively the intellectual exercise* called 'reason.'"[52] If it was Locke's unconscious principle that knowledge was a "vital function" of conduct, then Husserl's notion that reason is a function of "humanity" (equivalent to "men who live and have lived") should have implied both vital and historical reason. Instead, "phenomenology, which aspires to be the maximum of reason, is not formally a function of life but is an independent activity: knowing for the sake of knowing." Even as late as Husserl's *Formal and Transcendental Logic* (1929), "hu-

---

52. Spiegelberg, *Phenomenological Movement*, 1:73–74, disagreed with Ortega over Husserl's lack of serious (vital) motivation for philosophy, although Husserl was nearly forty before beginning phenomenology.

manity, life, and the functional character of reason nowhere appear and cannot appear. Their character as vital function remains extrinsic and informal" (5:540).

The "radical reflections" of Husserl were therefore not "radical" enough to get to the very "roots" of knowledge, which are pre-theoretical and vital. Apart from their name, his "pure life experiences" really had nothing to do with life. "The attitude of phenomenology is [therefore] strictly opposite to the attitude I call 'vital reason.'" Instead of life as the basic (absolute) reality in our world, Husserl's idealism made him settle on "consciousness"—ultimately consciousness *of* consciousness. Now to start philosophizing from that circular basis, which locks "the self" into itself, is "the opposite of what we call *living,* which is to be outside oneself entrusted ontologically to the *other* . . . [as] world or circumstance" (5:540–41).

By not being sufficiently radical, by not getting to the vital roots, phenomenology had failed to "justify itself" (5:541). "Consciousness of" is not primary to our life but is a secondary idea that "we discover or invent. Vital reason, therefore, does not start from any idea and therefore is not idealism." After measuring Husserl's phenomenology against vital reason, he compared it with historical reason, but in this case too found that it was not "radical" enough (5:541–42 nn. 1, 2).[53]

As an offshoot of "general phenomenology" that was meant to deal with pre-theoretical "living" reality, Husserl's "genetic phenomenology," claimed Ortega, was never developed in his lifetime beyond the statement of its programmatic intent in *Formal and Transcendental Logic* (1929). Although he expected some attempted investigations posthumously, he was already convinced of "the essential limitation of genetic phenomenology before the great problem of the 'genesis of reason.'"

At the last moment Ortega had encountered Husserl's final paper and article, "The Crisis of the European Sciences and Transcendental Phenomenology" (1935–1936), but it too failed to persuade him to withdraw his view that Husserl had only *one* "intellectual style." Detecting in the article too much of Fink, Husserl's disciple and editor, he refused to believe what he now saw there with a certain satisfaction and pleasure: that phenomenology should suddenly "leap" to the level of his own historical reason, for logically it simply was not in that phenomenology (5:542n). Moreover, he noted, he had developed this idea for "History as a System" before it had appeared in Husserl's "Crisis." In fact, he had announced historical reason, as an adjunct of vital reason, more than a decade before that, and his concern with crisis in the sciences went back almost a generation's time to 1915 and before (12:343–45).[54]

---

53. See Silver, *Ortega as Phenomenologist,* x; supplemental note 8, chap. 5, on historical reason and genetic phenomenology.

54. Silver, *Ortega as Phenomenologist,* 154: "*The Modern Theme* itself has been consistently

Less questionable was Ortega's point that Husserl had been *initially* unaware of the crisis circumstances from which modern philosophy had first emerged and into which it was now entering again. In contrast, he himself had been acutely aware of the personal, national, and European circumstances of crisis in which he had begun to philosophize. But it was just such a crisis of common "faith" that Husserl had finally described in 1929 (5:517; compare 518–20), although Ortega regarded the causes as much more "radical" and "historical" than he did even then. In his "Crisis," Husserl had stated that "the actual situation in the European sciences calls for radical reflections," for our world had become "problematical" (12:313, 316), which Ortega regarded as similar to his own view that philosophy begins in the crisis sense of disorientation, when one feels lost and hence has to try something "radical" in order to survive and live. So, where Husserl finally ended, Ortega had begun.

Ortega found the "Crisis" too late to be a convincingly consistent and "systematic" conclusion for Husserl. Whatever coincidence there may have been between their historical "turns" (or "second voyages"), Ortega's was years earlier, much more complicated, and continued to develop far longer than Husserl's. In *Leibniz* (1947), we have seen, he still held that "systematic thinking" in a historical mode simply was neither legitimately nor logically *in* idealist Husserlian phenomenology.

As his own "historical reason" was distinct from Hegel's "dialectical reason," so, he believed, it differed in kind from Husserl's "genetic phenomenology": as a realistic reason *in* history contrasted to an idealistic reason imposed *on* history. With it, he investigated how philosophy began in *Origin of Philosophy* (1946) and, in *Leibniz,* even the origin of principles. But was Ortega right about Husserl's "Crisis"? Or did his historicism in fact *anticipate* Husserl's development of genetic phenomenology?[55]

PHENOMENOLOGY AND HISTORY: PROBLEM AND FUNCTION

If the *possibility* of two different "styles" or "paths" (idealist and realist; analytical and historical) were already in Husserl's thinking between 1901 and 1913, as some contend (and Ortega too noted his "natural" mode [8:274n]),

misread," for "it is the rough equivalent of Husserl's *Crisis,* Part III A." In fact, he had anticipated it in 1914.

55. Silver pointed out that "Ortega had been a practitioner of 'genetic' phenomenology, even in his first book, whereas Husserl's first essays in the historical method date only from the last years of his life *after* his discovery of the life world" (*Ortega as Phenomenologist,* 64–65, and see 156); also, Ortega did indeed anticipate the turn toward historicity in Husserl's later work (84)—his "phenomenology of origins." Cf. Rodríguez Rial, "Ortega— Phenomenologist," 124–27.

then it might seem that Ortega had after 1912 simply turned Husserl inside out by seizing upon the neglected path for his own *mundane* "general phenomenology." The latter way, moreover, was also compatible with his perennial interest in history, with his "Mediterranean" inclinations to realism, and with his prior Jamesian "radical empiricism", which stressed time and place. Already in 1908, when he first mentioned both James and Husserl, he had referred to having long "pondered problems of historical phenomenology" in a context of themes that connected forward (through Maeztu) to James's pragmatism and to some "main problems of historical methodology" (10:60; compare 1:439, 119–20). That link suggests that James's emphasis on time and place was a more likely first source of his realist "*historical* phenomenology" than were Hegel, Husserl, or Scheler. But surely he found those four sources (and Nietzsche too) somewhat compatible therein from the beginning. Although Ortega stated "historical reason" five years before Husserl set out "genetic phenomenology," the one did not have to contradict the other.

If Ortega had let the historical side of his vitalism await any substantial "systematic" development for so many years, then Husserl could legitimately have waited even longer to put into practice the realist and historical alternative in his earlier phenomenology. As he was to James initially, Husserl may finally have been indebted not only to Scheler but also to Ortega himself.

Although he was ailing and seemed rather senile in 1934, Husserl was entranced by the visit, the talks, and perhaps the works that the "wonderful" Ortega left him then. In German editions of *Modern Theme* (1930) there were references to the "*most radical crisis*" of modern Western history, whose "symptoms" were in culture, art, and science (3:186, 193–94) and of *The Revolt of the Masses* (1931), to a "very grave and dangerous crisis" even for the physical and chemical sciences (4:198–99). This crisis threatened not only an outer indifference or hostility from the States of mass-men but, notwithstanding Einstein, excessive specialization in the sciences themselves (4:216–17). "Physics is entering into the deepest crisis of its history" and required new "systematic" generalization (4:219–20). Such remarks, from such an admitted phenomenologist, maybe encouraged the aged Husserl to publish his "Crisis of the European Sciences."[56]

Neither Husserl nor Scheler could develop a new historical (and sociological) way of thinking fully or coherently, of course, but Ortega went much further, both earlier and later, than did they. He learned little directly from Husserl about historical method from so-called genetic phenomenology,[57] but perhaps he helped Husserl "leap" to the level of historical reason.

56. See supplemental note 56, chap. 5.
57. See supplemental note 57, chap. 5.

Since Ortega's mature philosophy was not simply a "system" of phenomenology, he did not try to conceal his debt to Husserl in specifics. His clarity of style he prized above Heidegger's touted "profundity" (9:632, 638). He especially admired Husserl's clarification of "intuition" (8:134) and several other instrumental concepts, which he deemed still in need of further analysis and development—notably his "admirable analysis" of abstraction (8:164 and n., 228). In 1954 he still praised "the great philosopher" for his analysis of time as interpenetration of past, present, and future (9:705), an idea he himself did much to develop as basic to his own historicism.[58]

PRAGMATISM AND PHENOMENOLOGY

Ortega's debt to Husserl, finally, is comparable to what he owed James. Quite early he had found a basic error, or "hole," in the thinking of each philosopher—about "consciousness" and "truth" respectively—but in neither case did he just "abandon" them. He appropriated the ideas, methods, and terminology that were useful to him. In Husserl's case, he admitted specific debts; in James's case, he finally lacked time and strength in the 1950s. Although his basic argument against Husserl—that "consciousness of consciousness" cannot be basic—surely came from James, it was thanks to Husserl that he admitted in 1916 that pragmatism was compatible with phenomenology, which in turn helped him see the insufficiency of pragmatist methods and theories of truth and life. By the 1930s he had gone well "beyond" both thinkers. He had played each against the other to come to a "middle" position different from both: by that time to a definite "philosophy of life"—one yet plural—existential and historicist, wherein he felt independent.

Most of all, Ortega was indebted to Husserl for his basic phenomenological *method*. He added it to pragmatist method for a combined new methodology for historical reason in historiology, in order to *develop* his realist general philosophy of life. His philosophy (or "system") as a whole became a philosophy of life, which clearly was *not* just phenomenology but went "beyond" it to include both existentialism and historicism. First, however, his "existential phenomenology" had become a "phenomenological existentialism"—even a phenomenological historicism in part.

58. See supplemental note 58, chap. 5.

Chapter 6

STAGE I

"Vital Reason" as Existentialism (1914–1923+)

irst among the existentialists after Unamuno was Ortega, well before Heidegger and Sartre, who were phenomenologists too.[1] He was, that is, an existentialist in all but name, a name he never liked, but he was somewhat untypical and something more besides. His "vital reason" was a "happy" (not "gloomy") existentialism, and he stressed that his optimistic emphasis on "life" and "reason" had made him different. Undoubtedly he also went "beyond" that movement into a distinctive historicism of "historical reason" and also into "philosophy of life." He both assailed existentialism and grudgingly admitted kinship. Hence, properly defining his existentialism has been as great a problem as assigning it a rightful place within his total philosophy.[2]

1. Several studies emphasize Ortega's priority (after Unamuno) over Heidegger and Sartre in developing what was a personal variation on an existentialism *sans nom*. The role of phenomenology (as a method) in existentialism was acknowledged by both Heidegger and Sartre. See Robert C. Solomon, ed., *Phenomenology and Existentialism* (Washington, D.C.: University Press of America, 1979), xi–xii, on a "common-law marriage of association" that commentators have seen between these two closely related movements. Ortega would fit such overall characterization of phenomenological existentialism, except for his aversion to "sensationalism" and to the idealist roots in Descartes and "consciousness," while he combined Husserl's (and James's) emphasis on knowledge and belief with Heidegger's and Sartre's emphasis on practice and action.

2. Not until 1940 did a critic publicly identify Ortega as an existentialist, an identity repeated till his death: Julio E. Moreno, *Filosofía de la existencia* (Quito: Romero, 1940); J. Saínz Mazpule, "De Ortega a Heidegger," *Haz* (Madrid), February 18, March 25, September 15, 1941; Juan Saiz Barberá, "De Descartes a Heidegger," *Revista de Filosofía* (1941); S. Alonso Fueyo, *Existencialismo y existencialistas* (Valencia: Guerri, 1949); Agustín Basave Fernández del Valle, *Miguel de Unamuno y José Ortega y Gasset* (Mexico City: Jus, 1950); Niso Cuisa, "José Ortega y Gasset e la filosofía dell'esistenza," *Giornale di Metafísica* 9 (May–June 1954): 251–57; T. M. McTigue, "Spain's Christian Existentialism: Unamuno, Ortega y Gasset, Buero Vallejo, Sastre" (Ph.D. diss., Louisiana State University, 1969).

Of themselves, neither *Meditations on Quixote* (1914) nor *Modern Theme* stood out as obviously proto-existentialist, and no subsequent work, such as his 1930 lectures, published as *What Is Philosophy?* (1960), struck critics as being clearly or purely existentialist.[3] He was always "more" and different, having a special type within a philosophical context broader than the existentialism of his contemporaries.

Since the 1940s when he was first publicly identified and then harshly attacked in Spain as an existentialist, various professional philosophers have viewed him sympathetically as an existentialist with very distinctive traits but still belonging to the European group of that name. Notable among scholars before or soon after 1955 who approved of vital reason as having been or become an existentialism were Ferrater Mora, Gaos, Stern, and Rodríguez Alcalá. Ferrater Mora had first recognized him as such in 1936,[4] more than thirty years before Morón Arroyo.

Stubbornly and yielding little, Ortega had persisted till death in denying that his philosophy was existentialism, or at least he *seemed* to do so, just as previously he had denied that it was pragmatism or phenomenology. His Hispanic disciples therefore continued to defend his "vital (or 'living') reason" as something apart and unparalleled, as an Orteguismo sufficient unto itself. Can Ortega, the Orteguistas, and other critics all be right? How did we get such contrary views and definitions?

"TO BE OR NOT TO BE?": "WHAT'S IN A NAME?" (8:265)

In view of all their differences, it was appropriate, argued Ortega, "that not all of us who start from [life] be jumbled together, because *already in starting* we separate from one another and go our own ways" (8:296). So if he was perhaps once an existentialist, did he remain one? He disliked the word even more than some of the substance. Thus he protested the confusion and "frivolity" that resulted by 1949 from attributing to "existentialism" certain ideas about life that Dilthey and he, even Cohen, had enunciated many years before (9:587).

3. See supplemental note 3, chap. 6.

4. José Sánchez Villaseñor, *José Ortega y Gasset, Existentialist*. See Iriarte, *Ortega*, 101, where he first linked him to Heidegger, and idem, "Las lineas fundamentales de la filosofía de Ortega," *Razón y Fe*, no. 138 (May 1949): 416–17, 419. He stressed much more the historicism from Dilthey in Ortega than the existentialism from Heidegger. Ferrater Mora, *Outline* (1956); also see R 20 (1936), for the letter from Ferrater Mora on his article comparing Ortega to Dilthey and Heidegger. These authors and works are cited in the bibliographical essay, but also see the notes below.

The very name "existentialism," seized upon by Sartre in 1946, struck Ortega as unsuitable for his own or for any other genuine philosophy, and he thought that Heidegger had rejected it too (7:495n). The number of times that Ortega put it in quotation marks in later years—"so-called existentialism"—shows his permanent distaste for it. That word was not "radical" enough to describe the "root" reality that was human *life*.

Even "philosophy of existence," as it was called originally in Germany, was—to his judgment, in 1934—"mistaken and arbitrary" (7:45). More than once he explained that "besides existing, it *consists* of something" (6:198–99 and n.). In context, this meant that Ortega preferred the words "life" and "history" to mere "existence" in order to denote basic human reality. For him, terms like "consciousness," "being," and "existence" were pallid compared to "life" (see, for example, 8:277), and human life had for him a "historical consistency" (6:198; 8:656–58). Stern called this ontological aspect in Ortega "essentialist," from his phenomenological stress on "essence."[5]

If he could have had his way, Ortega would have called this new philosophy of life not "existentialism" but a "philosophy of vital reason" (8:47) and of "historical reason." These phrases were more "substantial," ontological, and related to the life "essence" (8:44). Even his earlier term "coexistence" (1:487–88) was preferable to existence, more realistic and comprehensive (8:51, 53), for it covered the life reality of "self *and* circumstance."

The adjective "existential" was no more to his liking, although he had used it from his youth. If he regarded authentic philosophizing as a *rational* response to a crisis situation (6:406; 8:276–77), the meaning of "existential thinking" in Søren Kierkegaard was *too* charged with crisis: it was "born of despair of thinking," was oriented less to thought than to "direct action." For that reason, he very much doubted that any philosophy could adequately be defined as a "philosophy of existence" (8:46). Later (1947), he pointed out that "existential" (as Kierkegaard had rightly used it) signified not philosophy but religion (8:315).

Although he had not been able to give an acceptable popular name to this new philosophy, Ortega evidently decided that, with pride of priority, he had to acknowledge for himself some kind of anticipatory and participatory relationship to "existentialism," but he did so with much misgiving and

5. After Ortega's death, Alfred Stern was one of the first to give his existentialism a cogent analysis—as one with a difference: "¿Ortega, existencialista o esencialista?" *La Torre* 4 (July–December 1956): 383–99, as "essentialism" (description of variable essences)—but not Husserl's *phenomenological* existentialism (392) and not idealist (338). Over Sartre and Heidegger, Stern conceded Ortega's "absolute priority" in "everything essential" (386), even as early as "Adam in Paradise" (388), wherein he proclaimed "the principle of modern existentialism," which "without hyphens" (388) constituted, with historicism, a *dualism* in his philosophy (399). This early analysis remained basic to Stern's later views of Ortega.

peevishness. In 1934 he was prepared to admit to the Germans that "twenty-one years ago (1913) I found myself installed immediately in something resembling what was recently discovered in Germany" as "philosophy of existence" (8:45). Again in the Toynbee lectures (1948–1949), he referred to "so-called 'existentialists'" in France as being "twenty years behind Heidegger and over thirty in regard to us" in launching out into what he now explicitly called "the philosophy of life" (9:85–86, 215–16). At Hamburg in 1949, in regard to life being oriented on the future (9:587), and again at Geneva in 1951 at a conference on man, he claimed that his idea that life involves "worry" (*Sorge*) about the future preceded Heidegger's by "thirteen years" (9:654). Two days later in a private exchange with French existentialists such as Jean Wahl and "structuralist" Merleau-Ponty, he again stressed his own precedence in expressing their common fund of ideas— "being" excepted.[6]

Accordingly, it is clear that, despite all his reservations and objections, Ortega knew that to an appreciable extent and in significant ways he was in fact one of those whom the public had come to know as the "existentialists"— even though he had avoided their negativeness and some of their "errors" and in other respects had gone "beyond" them. The query of Juliet in Shakespeare, "What's in a name?" described his predicament. Like it or not, he was stuck with "existentialism."

To admit of existentialism more openly was simply not Ortega's way—not frankness and candor but qualification and evasion, always leaving a path of escape. Besides, by openly confessing to existentialism, he would have exposed himself to more charges of "atheism" by the Spanish clergy. No word more suitable than "life," he felt, described what he had in mind, but he could not persuade the public, much less Heidegger or Merleau-Ponty, to accept "philosophy of life" instead of "philosophy of existence" to describe their common venture. Like Gabriel Marcel, Ortega was a *reluctant* existentialist, comfortable neither with that word, nor with some positions and doctrines of his fellow existentialists, Heidegger and Sartre.

PROBLEMS OF IDENTIFYING
VITAL REASON AS EXISTENTIALISM

Because Ortega scarcely ever mentioned existentialism explicitly in works published during his lifetime, nor even adverted thus to Heidegger after 1932,[7] neither loyal disciples nor learned critics were able to know very much

6. Ortega, "Troisième entretien privé," 19.
7. For example, on Heidegger, see Ortega 4:57n, 403–4n, 541n; 5:37. Otherwise, Ortega did not refer to "existentialism" except in posthumous works.

about his opinions of it until the posthumous works came out. Hence, errors of identification and interpretation were made about him that were repeated and so became deeply entrenched. Posthumous critical reassessments, some of them scholarly and penetrating on his existentialism, have not been able to expunge erroneous perceptions from the consciousness of public and critics.

If they were attentive to his few footnotes and to passing references, critics before 1955 could have determined only that Ortega agreed with Heidegger on some things and disagreed on others, but that he considered their positions distinct, even if converging. He seemed first to have noticed their similarity early in 1928, when he found both "subtle truths" and "subtle errors" in Heidegger's *Being and Time* (5:54m). Actually, in 1927 he had seen a "parallelism"—"even more with Heidegger" than with Dilthey on "life" as primarily essential "problems" and "solutions" (R 40). In 1929 he hoped Heidegger would agree that Kant's contemporary significance was to lead us "beyond" idealism and realism (4:57). Then, to answer critics among ignorant or malicious students, he added a long footnote to "Goethe from Within" (1932), where he granted some points of similarity with Heidegger but defended his own priority and differences, including the "definition of life" as the basic reality (4:403–4n). In his "Galileo" lectures (*Man and Crisis*) in 1933 he acknowledged that Dilthey had "made us see" it, and Heidegger had "reiterated" that "life is time"—personal and historical time (5:37)—although Ortega himself obviously had held a similar idea long before Heidegger had put it so felicitously as "historicity." Indeed, life and history had always been the two paramount interests in the Spaniard's philosophy, and very explicitly so since he had published it in a more mature form in *Modern Theme* (1923). Thus he sought to combine and to transcend traditional idealism and realism. Coincidence in the key points of life and historicity (if not of transcendence too) showed close affinity between a historical "vital reason" and an existentialism leaning to historicism.

As we have seen, despite Ortega's reserve, clerical and lay critics "nailed" him as both existentialist and historicist in the 1940s and 1950s, though disciples denied it. Copleston saw "obvious affinities with existentialism," pragmatism, and "life-philosophies." However, the posthumous works revealed an unsuspected Ortega, one who was very critical of Heidegger, Sartre, and "existentialism." Then loyal disciples overdid his vindication. Believing that their master was unique, they ignored obvious similarities and exaggerated the undoubted personal and national peculiarities of his thought. Relying on Ortega's idiosyncratic nomenclature, they insisted on calling his philosophy only "perspectivism," "vital reason," or "ratiovitalism," a purely "Spanish philosophy" unrelated to any other European philosophy, including existentialism. Like Marías, who has always resisted assigning any general labels to him, Vela insisted that texts in *Leibniz* and *Man and People* proved that he was actually "freeing us" from existentialism. That was clearly *not* the case, but they inhibited others more disposed to see the existentialist in him. In 1960, K. S. Reid identified the question asked "most frequently of all: 'Is he an existentialist?'"[8] He was indeed, as critics rediscovered.

Assessing the same later works, several scholars from the 1960s definitely situated Ortega as an existentialist, with convincing comparisons and textual demonstration. This happened first in the Americas, where already before 1960 both Stern and Rodríguez Alcalá judged him an existentialist of Heidegger's and Sartre's type but something else besides—for "historical reason." His affinity with the existentialists was also competently assessed in the 1960s in the United States by Janet Winecoff Díaz, who saw in him several main themes paralleling existentialism, and by Stern, who saw in him "historicist existentialism" of an "essentialist" variety akin to Sartre. In Spain, Morón Arroyo identified him in 1968 as a Heideggerian kind of existentialist. Reflecting post–Vatican II openness, Jesuit González Caminero also viewed Ortega positively as an existentialist like Heidegger, sometimes even where he had thought he was different, yet overall as prior and independent, apparently within a "philosophy of life." That was pretty close to how Ortega actually saw himself. More attentive to differences, however, most German and French critics have never put him with existentialism or any current type of philosophy. More recently, Orringer has found "new sources" for Ortega's existentialism but overstates the dependence on Heidegger.[9]

Altogether, therefore, despite denials and anomalous views, a respectable bloc of scholarly opinion in the Hispanic and English-speaking worlds has long since come to view Ortega as an existentialist.[10] There is, however, no general agreement on what characteristic existentialist terms, themes, and interests he manifested first, nor on what type of existentialist he was, nor on what else he was *besides* in his overall philosophy.

Because Ortega's "existentialism" is a very complicated problem, which starts not with Heidegger but with James and Unamuno, and even with Kierkegaard, we must explore first his initial relationship with such pre-existentialists. Only then may we compare him with Heidegger, Sartre, and other secular and Christian existentialists. It is a complex picture that shows Ortega as an existentialist *malgré lui* (against his will). But he was clearly something else besides, or "beyond," the existentialism he knew: by his Jamesian realism, positive affirmation of life, and Diltheyan emphasis on history.

---

8. See supplemental note 8, chap. 6.
9. See supplemental note 9, chap. 6.
10. See supplemental note 10, chap. 6.

PRE-EXISTENTIALIST ROOTS:
JAMES, KIERKEGAARD, UNAMUNO

Before attempting to describe an overall structure of unity and relationships for the extraordinary complexity that Ortega's philosophy presented by the 1970s, one must first demarcate the chronological limits and ideological affinities of his peculiar variety of existentialism, which was his so-called ratiovitalism. As he claimed (4:403n), he had aspired to something new in philosophy from "around 1911" forward (7:41), and he believed that (with his generation) he had begun to achieve this from 1923 onward (3:151–52, 193). Although he had always adverted to "coexistence" of self and world in "life" and occasionally mentioned "existence" and "existential," he was not conscious of anything like "existentialism," until Heidegger and Sartre gave such a name to the new mode of thinking. After 1913, Ortega's phenomenological method (as "perspectivism") had merged logically with a historical "vital reason" in *The Modern Theme* (1923). After pragmatism, by its very nature and content, this "ratiovitalism" then soon became linked to Heidegger's *Being and Time,* and it was also closely akin to Dilthey's "historical reason," "worldview," and "philosophy of life." But Ortega's metaphysics was still rooted in James, so that his existentialism continued, no less than his phenomenology and historicism, with pragmatist roots and flavor. Because of his lifelong reticence, we must combine careful textual analysis with a historical approach to the problem of Ortega's existentialism: how soon, what type, and how far? Thus, we cannot adequately gauge his initial debt to Unamuno from the early texts and letters alone; we must take account of relevant statements from later works too. Moreover, some of his most striking anticipations and some of his most incisive criticisms of Heidegger's existentialism are still in unpublished research and class notes that cannot be dated precisely but could fit anywhere from 1907 to 1917 in the one case and from 1931 into the 1940s in the other.[11]

In fragments of early lectures from perhaps 1907 or 1908 up through 1916–1917, and in the same context of pragmatist or of phenomenological topics (R 76), Ortega adverted at times to "the real, existential being" as the basic problem—"the real or existential." "Existence = being temporal-spatial." "This is Being as Existence—being that is." Indeed, "the fact of the existence of things is the point of departure in every philosophy." Nevertheless, "Being cannot mean existing: mathematical objects do not exist but are." Without the complete texts and precise dates, it might be rash to suppose

---

11. Ortega's notes on Heidegger are listed in the index, *Hispanic Focus,* ed. Everette E. Larson (Washington: Library of Congress, 1982), as in R 39, but R 20, 40, 53, and 57 also have relevant material, and R 3 has some correspondence.

that these isolated phrases manifested proto-"existentialism" in gestation so soon, especially since he later rejected the word. At least they do suggest that his later existentialism was an appropriate outgrowth of his earlier pragmatism and phenomenology. In a variation of his course "What Is Philosophy?" (1930), he meant to start with a series of problems on phenomenology and existentialism, on "being" and "existence." His second lecture was to be on "doing philosophy" beyond realism and idealism (R 78), and in fact culminated with pragmatism and with Kant. Apparently the source for his dual approach was in his own roots and beginnings, not from Heidegger but from James and Unamuno.

The variety of interests expressed by James in *The Will to Believe* had included not only "radical empiricism" and "pluralism" but also a concern with "life," or "existence." In its first two essays, "Is Life Worth Living?" and "The Sentiment of Rationality," James's book may well have been one source (in both time and substance) for Ortega's later existentialism and philosophy of life. In the first essay he turned from "the surface glamour of existence" to "the profounder bass-note of life," considered the problem of suicide in negativism and pessimism, which he regarded as "a religious disease." To this he preferred a "joyous," "daylight view of things." How melancholic, "poisonous," *unheimlich*, was the "death-in-life paradox." James continued this theme in the second essay. "Existence then will be a brute fact to which as a whole the emotion of ontological worlds shall rightly cleave but remain entirely unsatisfied." "The entire man, who feels all needs by turns, will take nothing as equivalent for life but the fullness of living itself"—under conditions of "space and time." Besides "purely theoretic rationality," life involves "the heart," "ultimate irrationality," and "practical interests." He rejected materialism and atheism. "A nameless *unheimlichkeit* comes over us at the thought of there being nothing eternal in our final purposes. . . ." Moreover, "a philosophy which showed only legitimate emotions [of fear, disgust, despair, or doubt, without hope, rapture, admiration, earnestness] . . . , would be sure to leave the mind prey to discontent and craving." All of this, in addition to phrases like "the radical question of life," "the lonely emergencies of life," and "the game of life," distinctly reminds one of Ortega's view of life as "radical reality," as "crisis," and as "sportive."[12]

In James's aversion to possible negative considerations in life philosophy, we can see striking parallels to Ortega's later reaction to Heidegger and Sartre. Moreover, in the first essay James's appeal to "faith" as a "working hypothesis," as a "test of belief" in the "readiness to act in a cause," and as

---

12. James, *The Will to Believe and Other Essays in Popular Philosophy* (Cambridge: Harvard University Press, 1979), 34–42, 61–86.

"a necessary ingredient of a rational philosophy" also struck a sensitive nerve in Ortega. For James, and later for Ortega, that faith was neither the traditional Christian one nor atheism.

A Jamesian spirit and coloration certainly seem to have pervaded both Ortega's existentialism and his reaction to that of Heidegger and Sartre. In *Meaning of Truth,* James preferred the tested, active truth of pragmatism to the "existential truth" of "intellectualists," the latter being contained within the former, which was the larger.[13] In a similar way Ortega claimed to go beyond Heidegger, who was less practical and more idealist.

Was James the first source of Ortega's existentialism? Or was it Unamuno, who also read James but without deriving "joy" and "sport" therefrom? Ortega assures us that he did not get his inspiration from the gloomy romantic, Kierkegaard, whose negative influence he saw in Unamuno, Heidegger, and Sartre.

Historically surveying his inspiration (prior to the German existentialists) for the "Idea of Life" as the truly "radical reality," Ortega granted in 1934 that—had he derived it from a personal source—it could have come from Dilthey, whose "philosophy of life" he did not then know, or from Kierkegaard, whose works and style he had never been able to stomach (8:45–46). In fact, however, by 1909, Ortega had read James and more than "five pages" of Kierkegaard (10:115), whom he had seen as related in a comedic-tragic way to Unamuno's situation in 1914 (10:263). Later he would regard Kierkegaard as an example of "that eternal Christian who bases his Christianity not in something positive, open, generous, and fresh, but precisely in the fact that reason be something limited and tragic." " . . . That Christianity is merely an objection that presumes to be something positive and to live of itself." "That Christianity is constitutively and permanently bankruptcy of reason and despair of man." And that is what "existential thought" was for Kierkegaard: not philosophy but *religious* "despair of thinking" in favor of "arbitrary and irritable resolution, even 'direct action'" (8:46). His "romantic frenzy," "histrionic at root," which the existentialists had rehabilitated as "anxiety" and "extreme situations," did not assist "calm" deliberation in the human sciences (7:24). Not a little of Kierkegaard's decadent romantic and "provincial" personality, with its ridiculous pretensions to martyrdom, to the "extraordinary" and the "original," he suspected, had infected and "poisoned" the existentialists of the following century (8:299–301)—Unamuno, Heidegger, and Sartre.[14]

13. James, *Meaning of Truth* (1975), 110; there (49) James also adverted to "the *dramatic temperament* of nature and life."

14. On Kierkegaard and Ortega, see Ramoon Cenal Lorente, "Kierkegaard, Unamuno y Ortega," *Ya,* December 18, 1963; and Luis Farré, "Hegel, Kierkegaard y los españoles," *La Nación,* July 21, 1963.

Clearly, it was Unamuno to whom Ortega was adverting when he said: "I have known another man very like Kierkegaard, and for that reason I know the latter very well" (8:302). What Ortega disliked in Kierkegaard's contribution to existentialism was, in brief, an infusion of a romantic and religious irrationalism, such as he found in Unamuno.[15] A similar residue of irrationalism he also feared in the secular existentialists, Heidegger and Sartre.

Unamuno was an unmentioned secondary source of inspiration for Ortega's idea of life. Moreover, from Unamuno's explicit distrust of reason, especially "pure reason," he may first have developed—by way of reaction—the initial idea of a "vital reason." Marta López Gil has pointed out that in *The Tragic Sense of Life* (1913)—published a year before Ortega's basic work—Unamuno declared that "everything vital is antirational and everything rational is antivital."[16] Sooner or later, Ortega had "inverted" the meaning of Unamuno's words so as to say that life *is* rational and reason vital, for a beginning of a new rational way of philosophizing. Indeed, *Meditations on Quixote* (1:353–54) laid just such foundations for the idea of a "vital reason," which he made explicit (privately) only in 1916.

Few studies of Unamuno suspect any connection between his "existentialism" and Ortega, but Raúl Roa notes that, despite the age difference and the generational conflict, the two finally made much the same journey of mind, including both existentialism and historical thinking, in different (though adjacent) "saddles."[17] Besides putting reason over unreason in life, Ortega differed from Unamuno (even as he said of Heidegger) by a matter of "tastes," of distinct generations (1898 and 1911) varying in personal and regional cultures—Basque versus "Celtiberian."

No one questions the young Ortega's positive response to Unamuno as

15. Victor Ouimette, *Reason Aflame—Unamuno and the Heroic Will* (New Haven: Yale University Press, 1974), 213, observed that Unamuno's ideas of "the crisis of self" and "tragic sense of life" were the bridge between Kierkegaard and Heidegger, who (with Sartre and Camus) incorporated him directly. Also see José Huertas Jourda, *The Existentialism of Miguel de Unamuno* (Gainesville: University of Florida Press, 1963); and Paul Ilie, *Unamuno: An Existentialist View of Self and Society* (Madison: University of Wisconsin Press, 1967).

16. Unamuno to Ortega, November 21, 1912, in "Epistolario entre Unamuno y Ortega," *Revista de Occidente*, no. 19 (October 1964): 21; M. López Gil, "Ortega y la razón vital," 325–42. The same inverse relation to Unamuno was noted later by Anthony Kerrigan, introduction to *Revolt of the Masses* (1985), xviii: Unamuno's "Reason is not vital" was stood "on its head"; Kerrigan detected not James's pragmatism in their shared idea that man is what he does (xix), but an existentialism and historicism (xxi).

17. Raúl Roa, "Dichos y hechos de Ortega y Gasset," *Cuadernos Americanos* 85 (January–February 1956): 120–31. For other studies of the relationships of Ortega and Unamuno, see supplemental note 2, chap. 27, esp. Alonso Fueyo, Stern, and González Caminero. Also see Nemesio González Caminero, "Unamuno, Ortega y Zubiri vistos en continuidad histórica," *Gregorianum* 50 (1969): 263–90.

preceptor before the latter's open irrationalism, admiration of mysticism, and equivocations on Hispanizing or Europeanizing divided them in 1909. One wonders whether, after the period from 1898 to 1909, Ortega continued to experience personally any of the agonies of disorientation, doubt, despair, and desperation that he later ascribed to life in crisis. Were his "existentialist" insights until the mid-1930s mainly the vicarious experience of an acute observer (*espectador*) of life, making a "diagnosis" of the alienation felt by Unamuno and other contemporaries?

The heartfelt outpourings of Unamuno may well have been sources for Ortega's notions of the tragic content of life and of history as crisis. Unamuno's *Tragic Sense of Life* (1913) and *The Agony of Christianity* (1925 trans.) developed some of the earliest existentialist conceptions and terminology of a crisis type, similar to what emerged at about the same time in Ortega. Thus, in the former work, is a chapter ("In the Depths of the Abyss") on Cartesian doubt and justification of despair, and, in the latter, an emphasis on "agony," contradictions, and antitheses. Doubt engendered existential anxiety, and, in the conflict between reason and life, the latter always won— the history of reason being "inseparable from the history of religion." A character in Unamuno's novels, Alejandro Gómez, typifies the isolated self (the *yo*) reduced to desperation, with life as will and destiny as blind, in a crisis of death and suicide. In *Niebla* (1914), life and destiny are seen as inauthentic and absurd.[18] Such glimpses of life and existence in crisis clearly antedated Heidegger and Sartre, and, before them, Ortega incorporated similar negative conceptions into his own construction of the crisis situation in life and history.

Ortega's idea of *ensimismamiento* approximated Unamuno's *adentamiento* in meaning, and both ideas are instinctive "withdrawal" responses to crisis and ultimately an effective way to begin resolving crisis personally. Nevertheless, since it reflected a crisis situation, Ortega did not accept "the 'tragic sense of life' as the ultimate form of human existing." "Life is not, nor can it be, tragedy." This, he maintained, was not an authentic Christian view of life but was instead the product of a sick "romantic imagination," which had "poisoned" the Christianity of Kierkegaard, who had passed it on first to Unamuno and then to Heidegger (8:299).

On the later and positive side of his relation to Unamuno, Ortega conceded in the 1930s (from James?) that "belief," "faith," or firm conviction of some kind is psychologically necessary to human life and action, and hence is an inevitable ingredient in history. Loss of such faith, he held, was in large

18. Few studies on Unamuno go on to affirm or establish any connection with Ortega that has philosophical consequence. In most of them, however, one can easily detect possible points of contact and influence, such as Huertas Jourda, *Existentialism of Unamuno;* and Ouimette, *Reason Aflame.*

measure the cause of great historical crises and, where the response was not extreme or irrational, also the spur to authentic philosophizing.

ORTEGA AND HEIDEGGER

Almost from the appearance of *Being and Time* in 1927 there have been those who have suspected Ortega of "cribbing" from Heidegger, despite all of his denials, clear evidence, and the distinctions. The most persuasive case that Ortega became a Heideggerian existentialist after 1928 came from Morón Arroyo in the fifth chapter of his *Sistema* (1968). Probably it is true that Ortega did not develop his fullest definition of "being" until after he had absorbed Heidegger, but he developed it *against* him, as we shall see. As the archival materials already cited show, it is not true that (until he encountered Heidegger) he did not use the word *ser* (being) or life "in the sense of existence." Morón granted that any influence—which he claimed was "notorious" after 1928—was not "servile," and that his "applications" to history, sociology, and theory of life remained original. Morón assumed too much influence on the particulars, I think.[19] A continuing tendency to overrate Ortega's dependence on Heidegger is evident in Orringer, despite his intent not to exaggerate. He was following up Morón's view of the "mature" existentialism in *What Is Philosophy?*, in reaction to Marías's persistent denials of *any* influence. In regard to Ortega's becoming aware of "existentialism" as a new system of philosophy now in *general* circulation, I do not doubt or dispute Orringer's contention that Heidegger had provoked him "to put his thought in order and to formulate it in concepts more or less stable and clear." However, his immediate *specific* example is not at all evident, for "the basic doctrines of human life as radical reality" did not come to him from Heidegger. On the contrary, life as basic ("radical") reality was first enunciated by Ortega, as we have seen, in his first philosophical works (1909–1910), and Orringer admitted as much. If Ortega first derived that idea from anyone, it would have been from Nietzsche, Bergson, or James. "Adam in Paradise" is "what we call life"—"The life of a thing is its being" (1:480–81). Of course, his "radical" connotation came in only gradually, via the "radical empiricism" and "philosophical radicalism" of James and Husserl.

Already in 1914–1915, dealing with Rickert and Scheler on value, Ortega stated that in his "theory of life," "radical reality" was always concrete and involved a realism of *things* in contrast to *consciousness* in idealism (R 36). It may be true, however, that till 1930 in "What Is Philosophy?" he did not say

19. Morón Arroyo, *Sistema,* 140–41, 356; for an early example (1931) of "executive self" ("doing") and life as Ortega's response to *being,* which related to Heidegger and Hartmann, but also to James, see Ortega, *¿Qué es conocimiento?* (1984), 14, 16, 120–37, 144, 149–57, where he viewed Hartmann as "superficial" and in error (142).

precisely: "The new fact or radical reality is 'our life,' that of everyone" (7:423), but did it appear so precisely in Hartmann or Heidegger either? If Heidegger evoked this response in Ortega, was it by imitation or by reaction, because the latter did not find it there and wanted to make it the most "radical" distinction separating him from Heidegger? In some particulars (notably, use of such terms as "authenticity," "historicity," "hermeneutics," and maybe "dramatism"), Heidegger apparently did influence him directly, although Orringer noted that the factual equivalent of circular hermeneutic was already in Ortega's usage by 1914 (1:327). The same is also true of historicity. Thus, whereas Heidegger's *Being and Time* made Ortega conscious of his own priority in certain concepts and terms that they had in common, the main influence was first and foremost to reveal to him that he was himself already an "existentialist," like it or not. As Scheler had beaten him to using phenomenology first as a method, in a more or less realist way on the problem of man and life, Heidegger had beaten him in integrating all the essential elements thereof (including even history in principle) into a coherent new *philosophy* called "existentialism," for better or worse. What was left to Ortega as still his own was precisely the radicality of his emphasis on life and history, as well as his applications, where he went far "beyond" Heidegger.[20]

Among those who were intrigued by the relationship with Heidegger by the mid-1930s was Hella Weyl, Ortega's German editor in Zurich and wife of Einstein's colleague Hermann Weyl. In an oddly circumspect reply (undated), he refused to give her a direct answer to the "enigma" but offered her one *"full of strictest silence"* by urging her to read and think about "Silence, Great Brahman [Wisdom]," an undated article of 1925 from volume 7 of *El Espectador.* Otherwise, "it is not possible for me to attempt the clarification of the secret that is my life, since only by going over it as a whole can one *perhaps* clarify it." Those pages, he claimed, revealed *"the radical point of departure of philosophy* compared to every particular science," including history. Just substitute for "'living' or 'life'" the German word *'Dasein'* and once that is done think about Heidegger." Those lines "leave Heidegger radically behind" (R 57). And what were the implications of that article? It was about "life," the object not so much of philosophy but of a new "ordered and systematic" theory, or "new science." This was a most difficult thing to develop and elaborate because most people prudently die without revealing what they have learned, because such wisdom or knowledge is of so personal a kind that it is usually wisely left "silent," unsaid, unwritten, even "censored" or taboo in Freud's manner. However, a scientific knowledge of life, which is so concrete and intimately individual, requires communication and "collaboration," if it is to develop. But, in its

20. See supplemental note 20, chap. 6.

"initial stage," it is necessarily "silent," carefully guarding its "secret treasure" (2:626–32). Alas, his secret remained so.

What did Ortega mean by that cryptic undated advice? He evidently meant that he had developed his philosophy of life long before Heidegger's existentialism but had worked secretly in isolation and had not openly communicated it to others. Also, he implied that *vida* (life) was more radically reality than was "existence," although *Dasein* too implied that life (of self and "of others") was basic in a concrete and individual way. Finally, by making it "systematic," he was taking his "new science" for life well beyond what Heidegger was attempting. His reference to this new "anthropology" (recalling Scheler's efforts at the time) was oriented toward his own "systematic" metahistorical "historiology" of 1928.

Dating Ortega's later critical views of Heidegger also becomes complicated by the problem of distinguishing "first" and "second" main stages in the thinking of both philosophers. González Caminero has attempted this in an extensive exposition, but there is little clear indication that Ortega himself was aware that there was such a "second Heidegger." Did he know that Heidegger had abandoned the initial project of *Being and Time* for another that was equally valid, much as he himself had transformed his intended "Critique of Vital Reason" (4:404n) into a "Critique of Historical Reason"?[21]

In fact, Ortega's general appraisal of Heidegger and of existentialism changed much less in respect to the fundamentals over the years than did his specific reactions, as dictated largely by historic circumstances. From a sympathetic openness to Heidegger from 1928 to 1932, he then became harshly critical of the Nazi "activist" until the late 1940s, but after 1951, if not already from 1949, he resumed his tolerant and partial agreement, despite continuing reservations and distinctions. In other words, there were for Ortega not two Heideggers but three, depending on his view at the time.

Heidegger, First Public View: Sympathy and Anxiety

In his several brief critiques of existentialism that have been published, Ortega was concerned more with Martin Heidegger than with Kierkegaard, Unamuno, Jaspers, Sartre, or Camus, because it was with him, the most powerful and original thinker of the group, that this philosophy had emerged

21. Nemesio González Caminero, "Ortega y el primer Heidegger" and "Ortega y el segundo Heidegger," *Gregorianum* 56 (1975): 89–139, 733–63, subordinates Ortega's existentialism to his "philosophy of life" (91, 128, 136) and the more radical material dimension (734–36). This bifurcated interpretation has more similarity to my study in this chapter than any other works cited herein but used more illustrative texts, lacked the archival materials, and missed some of Ortega's warming to Heidegger in the last few years. On Ortega's limited awareness of a "second Heidegger," see 762.

as something new and distinct in the world.[22] From his first comment a year after the "admirable" *Being and Time* (1927) until the last in 1953, Ortega detected "subtle errors" amid Heidegger's "subtle truths" (4:541n; 9:641–42), in questions relating to life, death, and history (9:710), not to mention being. As it turned out so paradoxically, nothing separated them more than those two most basic ideas of "being" and "time," how to interpret the one and how to use the other.

In "positive" fashion, Ortega at first generally stressed what he and Heidegger had in common by putting the broadest possible interpretation on the idea of "life" in *Sein und Zeit*. For example, his initial reaction even to the emphasis on death as the end of life was that one *could* discover there "an *a priori* difference between the structure of the historical and that of the living individual. History can never die and its movements are not governed by the idea of an end and consummation" (4:541n). He went on to annex Heidegger's and Dilthey's parallel idea that "life is time" to his own concept of generations in the "Galileo" lectures of 1933 (5:37). Neither did he show at first any difficulty in also accepting Heidegger's stress on *Angst*, or his view that "life is care," worry (*Sorge*) (8:436). Similarly, in Heidegger "to live" was interpreted as "living *with*" (*convivir*) one's "world," or "circumstance" (7:416). So far, his approach was a sympathetic interpretation, therefore clearly a hope that Heidegger's philosophy was going to converge with his own in development. In his own eyes, if we disregard "religious" forerunners like Unamuno, that would have made Ortega the prescient "father"—midwife at least—of a European "school" of philosophy, despite his having been unable to give it a generally acceptable name or recognizably coherent structure.

Discovering Heidegger in 1927 had come somewhat as a shock to Ortega, so much did they *seem* to have in common. His generous promoting of Heidegger in Spain, moreover, soon brought him pain and embarrassment, because an uncritical cult of enthusiasts for Heidegger's doctrines quickly sprang up among his students.[23] Blind to the weaknesses he detected there

22. On Heidegger and Ortega, besides studies already cited, see Pedro Cerezo Galán, "El nivel del radicalismo orteguiano: La confrontación Ortega y Heidegger," *Teorema* (Valencia) 13 (1983): 345–84; Priscilla Cohen, "Ortega y Heidegger," *Sur*, no. 353 (July–December 1983) 27–40; Nemesio González Caminero, "Ortega y Heidegger: Postrera valoración mutua," 5–38; A. Guy, "Ortega y Gasset, critique de Heidegger," *Annales . . . Université de Toulouse-La Mirail* 8:3 (1972): 123–41; U. Rukser, "Ortega y Heidegger," *Humboldt* 45 (1971): 60–67; and Juan Vaya Menéndez, "La cuestión de la técnica en una doble meditación de Ortega y Heidegger," *Convivium*, no. 9–12 (1961): 64–98.

23. Ortega introduced Heidegger's *Sein und Zeit* to his students; thus Marías read it around 1934: Marías, "Presence and Absence of Existentialism in Spain," trans. Janet A. Weiss, *Philosophy and Phenomenological Research* 15 (December 1954): 182; González Caminero, "Primer Heidegger," 100–101; Silver, *Ortega as Phenomenologist*, 152; McClintock, *Ortega as Educator*, 123, 423–24.

and scornful of his caution, even Zubiri and Gaos thereafter had listened less to him and much more to Heidegger. Finding Heidegger more *systematic* in philosophy, they inclined to question Ortega's originality and his genuine differences (8:272). These disturbing circumstances produced what one might call a minor identity crisis that he finally felt obliged to address in his own defense.

To establish his own independence and priority, Ortega therefore wrote in 1932: "I could not say what is the proximity between Heidegger's philosophy and that which has always inspired my writings, because Heidegger's work is not finished, nor, on the other hand, are my thoughts adequately developed in *printed* form; but I have to declare that I owe this author scarcely any debt" (4:403n). By page and chapter he went on to point out how many of Heidegger's concepts of 1927 had been expressed in his *Meditations* of 1914 and in subsequent lectures or writings on "perspectivism": "life as disquiet, worry, and insecurity," "culture as security," and "the application of this [previous] thought to the history of thought and culture," "liberation from 'substantialism' in every 'thing' in the idea of being," "life as . . . self and its circumstance" or "world," "structure of life as futurition," "truth as *aletheia*" (or etymological unveiling). And the basic conception of living (or "existing") together (*convivir* or *coexistir*) was even earlier. That claim to priority was confirmed by Stern.[24] For some of his ideas he had been "enormously indebted to German philosophy"—to Cohen, for example, not to Heidegger. "But perhaps I have exaggerated this aspect and have concealed too much my own radical discoveries" (5:410n). Most important here was Ortega's conviction "that philosophy is consubstantial with human life," reaching out for "the world" as the "horizon" of totality above things and distinct from them. Even before 1923 he had named this philosophy "vital reason" (12:392), a dual term (like ratiovitalism) that, he rued, none of his followers—who mistook his style for his thought—had ever bothered to try to think through "together" (4:404n).

By emphasizing the *rationality* of life, Ortega stressed in 1934, his own "philosophy of vital reason" was more like Dilthey's "philosophy of life" than like existentialism (8:46–47). Admiration for Dilthey during these years

24. Stern, "¿Ortega, existencialista?" (1956), 386, affirmed Ortega's "absolute priority" to Heidegger in essentials, such as *convivir* (388). Marías, *Circumstance and Vocation*, 435–37, of course, held to Ortega's priority, as in *aletheia*, and so did Morón Arroyo, *Sistema*, 138–41, 355, 442, who said the influence was "not servile," for Ortega was original in applications, for example, his "synthesis" of Dilthey and Heidegger. Later, in the 1940s, Ortega claimed that "authenticity and inauthenticity of life" was an old and constant theme of his own, as was life (self-circumstance) as "radical reality" (1916), the "radical insecurity" of life (1914), and man as the central problem of philosophy—years before Scheler (or Heidegger). See *Sobre la razón histórica*, 80, 82, 86, 220.

strictly limited Heidegger's influence on him, more than Morón Arroyo has allowed but as Stern and González Caminero have seen.[25]

As with Husserl's later development, so with Heidegger's early development—Ortega discovered that he had been doing first much of what they were doing subsequently. This was the reverse of his relationship with Dilthey, who had already done much that Ortega was driven to repeat unknowingly. In Dilthey's case, Ortega attributed striking parallels not just to coincidence but to the prevailing "spirit of the time," or "worldview," which impelled quite unconnected people to pursue the same problems and to arrive at similar answers (6:166). More obviously than for him and Dilthey, this common experience for him and the other existentialists was the great crisis afflicting Europe.[26] This impersonal atmosphere more than any "personal influence" from common individual sources explained the similarities also between him and Heidegger's "philosophy of existence" (8:43, 45). However, he did not concede that Heidegger had surpassed him yet in anything except systematic exposition, certainly not in either depth ("radicality") or comprehensiveness. His "intuition," or discovery, of life as the "radical reality" had not come to him from Heidegger, nor Dilthey, nor Kierkegaard. He had never been able to endure reading Kierkegaard (8:46), that romantic poseur and extremist, who was acknowledged as the forerunner of Unamuno, Heidegger, and Sartre (7:29; 8:299–303). Nietzsche he ignored because of his irrationalism.

A Second Look at Heidegger: Antagonism and Rejection

If we look only at his published views on Heidegger in 1932, it is easy to see why the clerics later lumped Ortega with him as atheistic existentialists. Unknown to them, however, Ortega had meanwhile severely criticized Heidegger in private and had dissociated himself philosophically from him. For about fifteen years thereafter he was alienated from and sharply antagonistic

25. See Stern, "¿Ortega, existencialista?" 392–93, on the "irrationalism" of Heidegger and Sartre, after Kierkegaard, and on Dilthey limiting Heidegger's influence on Ortega.

26. On the crisis experience as common to the existentialists, see *Dictionary of the History of Ideas* (1973), s.v. "Existentialism," 190–91; as popular in times of crises, see Adrienne Koch, *Philosophy for a Time of Crisis* (New York: Dutton, 1959), 247–49 (on Sartre). Jean Wahl, "Philosophie existentielle," in *Philosophy in the Mid-Century*, ed. R. Klibansky (Florence: Nuova Italia, 1959), 2:73 (on L. Pareyson). Ernest Breisach, *Introduction to Modern Existentialism* (New York: Grove Press, 1970), 3, 11 ("the mood of crisis," the constant "word crisis," for this so-called Age of Crisis). Of the numerous instances of such expression in Ortega, none is more striking than this one from 1913: "Thus philosophy is born in a desperate situation" (12:489). See also, 4:397; 8:280. Partly echoing Ortega, José Ferrater Mora, *Man at the Crossroads*, trans. W. R. Trask (1957; New York: Greenwood, 1968), 10, 63, 72, refers to crises of the few, the many, and of all. Cf. Howard G. Ballard, *Philosophy at the Crossroads* (Baton Rouge: Louisiana State University Press, 1971).

toward Heidegger and his "so-called existentialism," so much so that he looked not for points of agreement but for differences and contradictions. From that part of his works that they came to know as posthumous, Marías and Vela therefore concluded that Ortega was not an existentialist at all. What looked like rejection to them, however, was only a passing antagonism, but it served very well to *distinguish* Ortega's existentialism from that of Heidegger and Sartre. Such sharpening of differences, where not overdone at the expense of similarities, makes Marias's work on Ortega helpful for right understanding. It deters us from premature, incautious "lumping," but this, continued adamantly so long, blocks valid generalization with an indefensible nominalism of the unique. Ortega was not *that* unique.

Following his comments of 1932, Ortega advised that he would again be silent publicly about Heidegger for a "long time" (4:404n). By 1934, however, his private opinion of Heidegger had taken such a turn for the worse that we can easily detect the antagonism in his "Preface for Germans" for *Modern Theme,* which he refused to publish amid the upsurge of Nazi hatred and violence. Significantly, he did not even mention Heidegger by name in the "Preface," nor did he refer to him again in print, until Germany lay in ruins after World War II. The reason for his sudden aversion is not hard to find. A clue is his attack on Kierkegaard as the pernicious, ultra-romantic, irrationalist, and antihumanist (even "anti-Christian") proponent of "direct action" and as the forerunner and inspirer of "existential thought" (8:46–47). In his *Revolt of the Masses* and in his "Galileo" lectures on crisis, this "direct action" characterized those "new barbarians," who were now so evident in Nazi Germany, as well as Communist Russia and Fascist Italy. Apparently he learned of Heidegger's initial cooperation with the Nazis and did not want to be identified with him. Forthwith he sharply dissociated his own "philosophy of vital reason" from "any equivocal 'existential thought.'" Kierkegaard's romantic irrationalism, he believed, had tainted existentialism, if it had not indeed "poisoned" it in regard to "life" and "reason." In 1934 he deliberately described his own vital reason as "a new rationalism of life" (6:196), despite his earlier opposition to rationalism as "intellectualism," utopian and uchronic (3:158–62). Never did he change his mind about the irrationalist, activist danger latent in existentialism as it was oriented by Heidegger first to the totalitarian right, later by Sartre to the totalitarian left, and in between to "nihilism" (9:566).

The outrage that Ortega felt toward Heidegger related in some part to the mistreatment and exclusion of Jewish and liberal professors in Nazi Germany. Strangely, Heidegger wrote to Ortega twice in February 1935 to inquire about positions in Spain for his Jewish docent, Brock, who had lost his chair, and for Karl Löwith of Marburg too (R 3). Among those seeking refuge and academic employment in Spain was Hermann Weyl, who instead went (with

Einstein) to Princeton, where Hella Weyl was later to invite Ortega after civil war had made him flee the country.

Death, Existence, Life

At the Library of Congress are more than a score of pages of Ortega's notes in Reel 39 dealing critically with Heidegger and existentialism. They appear to have been written in the 1930s, begun perhaps as a critical reexamination of *Sein und Zeit* before responding to his students in 1932. "Heidegger's lack of reflection on his method is suspicious. One whole side of his book—the side of Thinking correlative to that of Being—fails! It is a book half paralyzed." But now he objected to "Being" altogether, and he felt that "Time" was inadequately and inconsistently developed, especially in regard to being. This view of *Being and Time* was repeated in his lectures entitled "On Historical Reason" in Buenos Aires in 1940: Heidegger had remained "palsied and almost paralyzed" in thought, although Ortega agreed that man exists before he theorizes and that his "true existence" is in a hostile "world," which he himself had called "circumstance" ever since 1914 (12:192).

Some of Ortega's notes bear such captions as "Against Heidegger," "Existential," "Death and *Dasein*," "Savor of Life," and "Patheticism of the German Theater." The legible parts do not fundamentally change published reservations that Ortega later expressed on Heidegger, but they do considerably illuminate, enrich, and modify them. Here we see an Ortega who had by then become "suspicious" and generally hostile, convinced that the differences between them now outweighed any similarities, that "Life" in his own philosophy was a more radical reality than "Death" in Heidegger's, more radical even than "Being," which he claimed was a "historical invention" that had now become "quite problematical" (R 39). If Heidegger had forced Ortega at last to grapple more seriously with the metaphysical problem of being (Morón Arroyo), it is clear that the Spaniard's "historical sense," or sense of "historicity," even as related to being, was *already* entrenched and stronger than any merely existential criterion of truth and reality. Ultimately Ortega's private critique of Heidegger boiled down to a conflict between life and death—which is paramount for man? As Ortega put it, " . . . it turns out that we have different tastes." "We do not have to seek norms within philosophy [in] imaginary and pathetic false causes. '*Angst*' has every air of this," and so did "*Tod*," or death (R 39). The inconsistencies and excesses he detected in Heidegger's systematic exposition prompted him to observe: "To philosophize is to philosophize with order . . . or, as St. Thomas says: *sapientia est ordinari*."[27]

27. Morón Arroyo, *Sistema*, 355, is an exaggerated view, for Ortega rightly claimed to

In opposition to the word "existential," Ortega offered a history of "existentialism" that implicitly was a restatement of "coexistence," or his principle of "self and circumstance," and it recalls his opposition to Husserl's "consciousness of." "Man, like every entity, is not only existent of—not that everything that exists consists, has *in* existence a consistence, although there is in man here *free* coexistence, although he coexists in not consisting." Here mere consistence, or being, struck him as too one-sided and as attributing to man a "nature" of "soul-body" that in fact was only an "interpretation" of the "function" of "transnatural man." Ortega preferred a different, more open duality in *life* as both "center and periphery," as not only the uniqueness (*Eigentlichkeit*) of self but the dailyness (*cotidianidad*) of circumstance. "Following this by itself differentiates me from Heidegger—if it demonstrates that life at its center *is* in every part. The same duality is pursued in thinking" (R 39).

Reading Heidegger's systematic exposition of Being (*Dasein*) might have prompted Ortega (reluctantly an "ontologist" now) to concentrate more closely on that problem than in 1925, but now he also reacted strongly against "being" as a problematical "historical invention." "It is not certain that man has knowledge of being constitutively—neither of being *qua* being nor of determinate being. . . . But anyway, it does not help to decree it in man by edict nor in any other Entity. . . ." Instead, we have to ask "what is the intelligibility" of being; "of what does it consist and how can man absorb it." It was "nonsense" to justify "being" as metaphysical, any more than "stamp collecting, bull fighting, religion, and science," for "being" is our "invention." "What is there, as Reality, is not an *esse* but a *posse*[—]the *poss est* of Cusa—a something that is making itself constantly"—as man in fact does always (R 39). He is becoming. From his first contact with Heidegger, therefore, Ortega had preferred the historicist "becoming" to the too-metaphysical "being" of existentialism. Life is dynamic and *historical*, not static "being."

Ortega had never been comfortable with the concept of "being"—a "terrible word from metaphysics," full of errors—but he could come up with no alternative except "life," unless it were "becoming." In contrast, before 1930 he came to prefer to "essence" James's word "consistency" (6:28n, 199n).[28]

---

have begun an exploration of being by a new vitalist-historical-phenomenological method in 1925 (8:273), and the archive yields other instances much earlier still (R 36—1916): "'Antecedent attributes' of Being—A proof of Being is only a historical form of a human need, which can be defined abstractly in my theory of life but which always has concrete form—is in the fact that the *Ente* question consists in many antecedent attributes that are in common with other questions prior historically to ontology." As stated earlier, Ortega's notes that are cited and quoted in excerpts over these several pages are from Reel 39, Library of Congress; elsewhere there are rare passing references (R 40 and 57).

28. Ortega, "Investigaciones psycológicas" (1916), *Obras Completas*, 12:431, said that *being* bristled with errors, like "a Medusa's head that we don't know where to grab." It rested on a "Belief," in our "consciousness that something *is*—independently of this

As historical, however, human life was modifiable in its inherited "consistency," was not a "*fixed*, static" one as "being" was traditionally conceived. If not from 1916, at least from 1946 he had worked on a "history of being," wherein he would reject Heidegger's "formula that man *is* a question of being" (9:774), because that question had undergone continual changes of meaning since Parmenides. Although he had a historical view of being long before Heidegger, the latter provoked him to a more careful historical and analytical examination of that concept, to which he always preferred "life"— with its modifiable "consistency."

Ortega disagreed strongly with Heidegger's contention that "the analysis of an interpretation of life," if it is to have "direction," must be a function of being. "But this is to muddy the question already," because "Being is now only an (ancient) interpretation of life and the natural that seems to have no being." Moreover, "that (ancient) 'Being' does not exist, is not, and falls into the void." As an interpretation, being presupposes "a correlative thinking," by which Ortega meant something like his own vital and historical reason. "On discovering a new 'being'—life—(which precisely *is not Being*) and not preparing an ad hoc thinking, he [Heidegger] is left also on that side in Nothingness, and thus all his philosophy is annihilation, in truth, 'destruction of philosophy'" (R 39). In private reflections, Ortega thus turned Heidegger's emotionally charged terminology against him, a destroyer of philosophy instead of a restorer of metaphysics and ontology.

The one problem in Heidegger's existentialism that long privately disturbed Ortega more than any other was that of *death* as related to *life*. On a page entitled "Death and *Dasein*," he argued "against Heidegger": "It is improbable that Life has no '*eigentliche Möglichkeit*' [proper possibility]— because then it would have an essence. The fact that man dies does not mean to say that 'he is there' in order to die—immortality is not impossible—and therefore neither is the non-regressive perpetuation of Life." A lengthy note, "Death in Heidegger," argued that his preoccupation with death was off the mark philosophically, that death was both an "inflated" concept and too narrow to be taken as either the salient characteristic of life or as the neces-

---

consciousness of mine." In 1929, Ortega stated in his "Annex to Kant," without reference to Heidegger: "And it happened that philosophy had been and always will be above all, a question about being. But this question: what is being? contains a radical mistake. On one side it means the inquiry of *who* is being, of what kind of objects primarily meet that predicate. The history of philosophy, almost wholly, from Thales to Kant, consists in a series of replies to such a question" (4:54). This does indeed read like influence from Heidegger. James, *Meaning of Truth*, 58–59. For other references to "consistency," see Ortega, 4:510 (in opposition to the *essence* of phenomenology); 5:136 (inappropriate as "being" for human life), 531 (equivalent to being); 6:656 (applied to man in history, inherited and modifiable).

sary end of life. "From outside," he said, "it costs [too] much effort to believe that the 'most authentic possibility' of life is death." Ortega's four (long) objections viewed life as constituting the "proto-mystery," which did not exclude immortality. "Man *is* neither unquestionably mortal nor impossibly immortal—we do not know"; life itself does not "state" nor "declare" it (R 39). Death, however, he felt, stemmed at least as much from life as life from death, so Heidegger's proposition was too narrow to be the whole truth.

Ortega's conclusion about Heidegger's pessimism is a striking affirmation of life over death and of life as both unity and diversity. As "many-sided" (Dilthey), "Life is never *one* thing, never determination—it would be entirely happy." "Life therefore is not *this*, nor is it 'this *or* that'—but 'this *and* that.' There is no dilemma in deciding—'Kierkegaardian choice'—but instead an imperative to integrate the multiplicity that aspires to, that needs to be appeased in[,] a 'superior unity,' which is hurt not to be *one, unitary, unified*" (R 39). Those words bring to mind James's idea of unity and plurality, as well as Ortega's own central doctrine that life as reality is a "radical unitary duality" (8:43)—also from the 1930s. Those reflections on life and death and immortality, which Heidegger provoked in him, make it very improbable that Ortega had no interest in anything except the here and now of *this* life.[29] This life was simply all he could examine by the light of reason and history, which were all that he had as legitimate tools to investigate life philosophically.

One note, "Savor of Life," pretty well summed up Ortega's relationship to Heidegger as he saw it into the 1940s: agreement on some few points, or "tangents," but overall divergence and disagreement that persisted (R 39). Thus he conceded that the reality of "Life consists above all in a savor, [or] temper," but he optimistically resisted giving in to the "bitter taste" that life in the 1930s and 1940s had for him. More briefly, "it turns out that we have different tastes." (What a Jamesian distinction over "temperaments.") Thus, it seemed to Ortega that Heidegger and he were rather far apart by the 1940s, despite his own much greater pessimism then about life and history. "No one has imposed on worldly reality the obligation of ending well, as is required in American movies," like a "sweet comedy of manners" instead of being "an immense tragedy." Unable to swallow the philosophical optimism of the ancients, of Thomist scholastics, or of Leibniz, however, he could not opt for the current "intellectual pessimism" either. How much more profound than "inveterate optimism" seemed the old Christian view that, in-

29. José Ferrater Mora, "Ortega, filósofo del futuro," *Sur,* no. 352 (January–June 1983): 5–20. I recall such a viewpoint in his response to questions at the Library of Congress, September 30 and October 1, 1982.

deed, this world is "a vale of tears" (9:69)—but not existential *despair.* In its normal "consistency" life has joy.

The most fundamental and extensive of Ortega's reflections on existentialism that were published posthumously were in his *Leibniz,* which summed up two decades of his growing critical awareness by 1947. There, significantly wedged between his references to "historical reason"[30] and to the "historicity" of man (8:268, 286), he emphasized—and not gently—the basic differences between his philosophy and Heidegger's. Instead of "happy visions," Heidegger had sown "general confusion" about philosophy, man, and being through abuse or exaggeration of concepts, in a display of the *furor teutonicus* that so often characterized German thinkers (8:271). His "initial error" was to maintain that philosophy originates in man when he is "alienated" from his world, whereas in fact he is from birth always so alienated, although he philosophizes rarely. Hence, it is not true that "man *is* philosophy," nor that "he has always been asking himself about Being" (8:285), nor, consequently, that "he has an inborn understanding of Being" (8:275–76). All that was an "arbitrary thesis." But historical reason (8:268) showed that no one had thought about being until after 480 B.C. in Greece, and that many philosophers thereafter had not directly concerned themselves with it, including Descartes and Leibniz.

To turn man himself into a "question about Being" was to "inflate" the concept of being into an "omnibus concept" that ran counter to an inclination of the time to restrict it to a more exact meaning. Such inflation is an "automatic tendency" of every merely "*received* concept" that is not "created from its very root." Thus he contrasted his own metaphysical efforts and "historiological" projects for "restating the problem of Being" between 1925 and 1929 with *Being and Time,* which, despite Heidegger's promise to do so, did not actually *restate* it nor define its meaning, but only furnished being with variations of meaning or classifications of type (chiefly *Dasein*) that were comparable to Aristotle's distinctions (8:272–73).

Heidegger did not get down to the "roots"; he was not "radical" enough in his perception of the basic reality with which philosophy should begin. Modern linguistics shows that "being" comes from roots of the verb "to be" that were relatively late in appearing and extremely diverse in origin. The "radical" ('root') reality, Ortega stressed, is not being nor entity—each was "secondary, derived, and not primitive"—but "*life,*" or the "universal event that is our living," which includes "every other reality" (8:274–76). Except for the problem of truth (and there too, not in its "constitutive historicity"), Heidegger, despite his genius, did not penetrate to the *roots* of the great

---

30. Ortega's emphasis on historical reason after the 1930s and in *Leibniz* in fact increasingly separated him from Heidegger.

problems of philosophy, not even of being (8:279–80 n. 2). That was what "profoundly separates" Heidegger's philosophy from his own, according to Ortega.[31] "But I can accept scarcely any of his positions besides those that are common to us where we start from living reality" (8:275). We are reminded here, however briefly, of Ortega's evident pleasure in the early 1930s, when he detected in *Being and Time* a view of life similar to his own prior expression in 1923 and other related concepts that he traced back to the *Meditations on Quixote* of 1914 (4:403–4). In this retrospect on *Sein und Zeit* in 1947, however, Ortega mentioned such a perception of *life* only in Heidegger's equation of *Dasein* and *Existenz* (thereby signifying man's "mode of existing"), although generally being (*Dasein*) is substituted (by a "terminological arbitrariness") for the "simple and natural term 'life.'" Heidegger's distinction between being and *ens* attributed wrongly to the Greeks a merely static sense of being, which arose from conceptualizing it, for Aristotle held it to be active "from within" (8:276–77).

Was Ortega quibbling over words? If Morón Arroyo did not think so, Stern did.[32] Actually, Ortega preferred other terms more technical than "life" to substitute for modern "existence" and for ancient "being," an outmoded scholastic heritage. In treating of Dilthey, he opted for James's term ("consistency") or Husserl's ("essence"). "Traditional philosophy distinguishes in one thing its *essence* and its *existence*. But the term *essence* carries several meanings together that it would be proper to keep separated. . . . Now the primary and least exigent meaning of *essence* is that everything, besides *existing*, *consists* of something." So he opposed "consistency" to "existence" (6:198n), as he opposed "life" to "being."

Like Descartes, who was also insufficiently "radical," Heidegger started from scholasticism, with a distinction between essence and existence as old as Saint Thomas that he translated into the outworn terms "ontological" and "ontic"—distinctions neither clear nor fundamental (8:279 and n.). Ortega concluded that Heidegger had not attained to the "radicalism that our

31. Morón Arroyo, *Sistema*, 357–58; on the matter of history and being, Morón thinks Ortega's position was realized as a "radical historization" of being in terms of time in Heidegger's "later evolution," as in "On the History of Being" (1946). Clearly there was historicism in both of them, although conceptually quite distinct. See Ortega, 9:767–69, on the "history of Being."

32. Morón Arroyo saw that there were "great differences" between them over the concept of life (*Sistema*, 133–38). Stern (*Sartre: His Philosophy and Existential Psychoanalysis*, 2d ed. [New York: Delacorte, 1967], 4) at first regarded Ortega's objection as a valid distinction, since Heidegger warned not to confuse life with existence ("One has one's life but one *is* one's existence"). Later, in *Search for Meaning*, Stern concluded that Ortega's distinction between "life" and "existence" was more apparent than real, if kept on the etymological basis where he had put it (265), yet he also rejected Ortega's insistence on "essence" as truly distinguishing his type of existentialism from Heidegger's.

level of philosophical experience demands" in these times of crisis in "every-thing," even in the principles (or roots) of our very culture and civiliza-tion (8:280–84). In short, existentialism in Heidegger was not sufficient even for a philosophy of crisis, much less for a philosophy of life as a balanced whole.

Pessimism or Optimism

After denying that philosophy is properly a "question about being" (8:306) instead of about "life," Ortega resumed the argument against Heidegger on another (moral) plane. Neither philosophy nor life is properly just a *negative* question of *Angst,* death, or nothingness (8:296). In a chapter entitled "The Dramatic Side of Philosophy," he found Heidegger far too "melodramatic" (compare 7:495)—like Kierkegaard and Nietzsche (8:301–3, 323n). Regarding the pessimistic outlook of existentialism as valid for only one side of life, he balanced it with Dilthey's optimistic view of life as "many-sided," and also with the "sportive" and happier aspects that he himself had always stressed (8:296–97). Reflecting that more positive side of life, philosophy itself (as *theory*) is a "game" and had been so since Parmenides and Heraclitus, in-stead of Heidegger's "bad-tempered and somber" display. To be realistic, one also has to be positive about life.[33]

In his one-sided "liking" for "Death" and "Nothingness," Heidegger was actually an "aficionado of Angst." Since he paradoxically "likes to be miser-able," he makes a sport and theory, or philosophy, of it (8:296, 299). Accord-ingly, Ortega doubted that the pessimism of the existentialists, who enjoyed "wallowing in depression" (9:632), was genuine. Instead, it was more posing and pretense, in Kierkegaard's way. Without retracting his criticism of tradi-tional philosophical optimism in ontology, Ortega reserved his greater con-tempt for Heidegger's only *apparent* radical ontological pessimism—with its "patheticisms, gesticulations, words of terror, heart-wrenching, unleashing of all the 'scare words' in the dictionary: *Angst,* disgust (*Unheimlichkeit*), abyss (*Abgrund*), 'Nothingness.'" These were merely secondary aspects of life, which his French disciples repeated like cackling "jackdaws." "The 'exis-tentialist' sets out resolved that it is not possible to know what man is and, with him, the World. Whatever is not an abyss, an irreducible mystery, a dark cave, unknowable, and nauseous, is not worth investigating . . ." (8:298). Thus had Heidegger infected Sartre.

The existentialist, a "typical 'conceited little master'"—and a "great snob

33. Stern, *Search for Meaning,* 266, thought Ortega right to chastise Kierkegaard's his-torical and negative romanticism, and its carryover into Heidegger and Sartre, but he doubted that it was profitable to argue whether "anxiety or sport," pessimism or optim-ism, was preponderant in life.

before the Most High—will not deal with just anyone, that is, with those who understand and, like Goethe, 'from the obscure—aspire to the clear'" (8:298). "Like the opium addict his drug, he craves darkness, Death, and Nothingness." These existentialists made him "laugh" and recall macabre lines from post-civil-war Madrid: "I like a cemetery with the dead well stuffed. . . ." Were life merely "Nothing," if *Angst* and death were its only end, then the only logical thing to do is to commit suicide—immediately (8:296).

But life is also "infinite sportive happiness," and "death is in the hand of Life. . . ." "Life is precisely the radical and antagonistic unity of those two dimensions: death and constant resurrection or will to exist *malgré tout,* danger and joyful defiance of danger, 'despair' and celebration, in short, 'anxiety' and 'sport.'" No exclusively "tragic sense of life" for Ortega (8:297). For many years he had felt that "the man for whom life has a sportive and festive meaning" was a new man who required a new type of philosophy (3:348)—an audacious idea that he had been almost afraid to develop.[34] "Nietzsche was right! 'That is life? Good, come again!'" (8:229). Heidegger's oversimplification of life on the dark, negative side (8:45) was, Ortega concluded, at best confusion and at worst a "deplorable retrocession," when compared to Husserl's clarity and to Dilthey's calmness and broad view of life as "many-sided" (8:297–98; 9:632).

A Third Look at Heidegger: Rapprochement after 1950

After World War II, gradually and cautiously, Ortega recovered some of his former respect for Heidegger, whom he now acknowledged as "one of the greatest philosophers there has been"—a bouquet with thorns, however. Although he was "profound," he was not really deep (or "radical") nor clear (9:631–32). Ortega had regarded *Being and Time* as a "book of genius" (8:306), but it was still incomplete as a philosophy—insufficient in both epistemological and ontological, or historical, respects. Since he had not developed a "philosophy of life" and history as anticipated, Ortega insisted, Heidegger had not been "radical" enough, had not really gotten to the "roots" of things (of life, being, death, the "nature" of man and of philosophy). His *merely* etymological method did not get to either the vital roots of philosophy or to its historico-social origins and context. Since, like Dilthey, he had not written his second volume, "historicity" (or time) remained for

34. Ortega's optimistic view of life in part reflects *The Gay Science* (1882) of Nietzsche (preface): after suffering and sickness, he hailed hope, spring, and "merrymaking" (trans. Walter Kaufmann [New York: Random House, 1974]). It also may reflect James, who concluded his *Pluralistic Universe* with "cheerfulness of heart, 'Ring out, ring out my mournful rhymes,' but ring the fuller minstrel in" (in *Writings*, 810).

him a principle but did not really become a matter of application (8:279).[35] Finally, his emphases were too gloomy and his style was more suited to somber and affected professorial profundity than to merry, creative exploration in a literary form that could reach and move the public.

In brief, insufficient radicality, historicity, and positivity were Ortega's main objections to Heidegger. Where he had insisted throughout on his own priority and independence, dating even from the *Meditations on Quixote* (1914), from the 1940s he claimed that he had gone "beyond" Heidegger and the existentialists, even as he had gone beyond Husserl and Dilthey. His own vital reason and historical reason, he was convinced, represented a fuller, more realistic, and more authentic philosophy of *life* than could be found in Heidegger, Sartre, or any of the existentialists, in all of whom—except perhaps for Jaspers—he detected also an inclination to irrational activism.

González Caminero has shown that there was a rapprochement between Ortega and Heidegger in 1951, despite their "crossing swords" twice in public debate. Their good will extended to more than tolerant acceptance of each other's peculiar ideas and styles. A mutual respect, even friendliness, now ruled their attitudes and relationship. At one of their conferences, Ortega's gentle exercise of disarming wit saved Heidegger from a very embarrassing attack. He came to refer to the other as "my friend Heidegger."[36]

After the Spaniard died, Heidegger remembered the several encounters of August 1951 in Darmstadt and in the Black Forest. He recalled vividly Ortega debating skillfully or prudently silent, "in his mannerisms, in his gentlemanliness, his solitude, his frankness, his sadness, his many-sided knowledge, and his captivating irony." Yet, he noted, Ortega's apparent frankness was "a thousand miles from candor"; he sensed that Ortega's courtesy and reserve toward his writings masked a "certain uneasiness toward a part of my thought that seemed to threaten his own originality."[37] In contrast, Ortega's private reservations were more in number and were more basic, but he was striving to avoid any rancorous exchanges in public.

They disagreed publicly only on the etymology and meaning of words: "dwelling," or living in, and, with a little more heat and substance, "being." Heidegger was surprised at the apparently spontaneous ease with which Ortega could improvise on the theme "The Spaniard and Death." Discovering him alone late one night, seated on the grass with his big hat and a glass

35. Actually, with the *principle* of historical time relative to life, Heidegger was almost as early as Ortega. See Heidegger, "The Concept of Time in the Science of History" (1916), *Journal for the British Society of Phenomenology* 9 (January 1978): 3–10 (trans. Hans W. Uffelmann and G. S. Taylor); cf. esp. 7–8 with Ortega.

36. See González Caminero, "Segundo Heidegger."

37. Martin Heidegger, "Encuentros con Ortega y Gasset en Alemania," *Clavileño* 7:39 (1956): 1–2.

of wine but clearly very depressed, Heidegger found out that his "great sadness" reflected his sense of despair at the impotence of the thinker before the worldly powers that be, and at his isolation and inability to affect external circumstances.[38]

The German philosopher confessed that he knew "very few" of Ortega's works and "only in translation"—among them, most probably, the *Revolt of the Masses*. Noting that he was "well versed" in "the sciences," he detected in him "a kind of positivism" that he could not define.[39] Did he mean *The Modern Theme*, with its "rigorous positivism," or *History as a System*, where Comte was mentioned several times and where the historical orientation on being and time was also prominent? Compared to those few impressionistic words, Ortega's critique of Heidegger had been much deeper and more extensive, but at last it was again irenic in spirit.

By 1951, then, one can detect another, a third and final change, in Ortega's attitude toward Heidegger, back toward the initial sympathy and interest. Following his disillusioned and rather angry rejection of Heidegger in the period from 1934 to 1947, he once more tended to minimize their differences while still regarding his own philosophy as a more "radical" (vitalistic and historical) philosophy of *life*.

Now that he was an old man—a "survivor," in terms of his generations schema—Ortega seems to have recognized that his reaction to Heidegger some fifteen or so years earlier during his prime had been a bit extreme, at least toward the idea of death as man's basic, radical experience and reality, or toward "end" as "constituting his very essence." "Man is, in effect, from his very birth already dying, as Calderón said: therefore, he begins by ending and he lives from his death" (9:636). This concession was more like his initial inclination to see "acute truths as well as acute errors" in Heidegger. The prospect of an impending end in death, even for those joyfully and tenaciously attached to life, thus saddens and mellows us all. Nietzsche's wistful words, which Ortega had quoted often, finally summed it up, perhaps with more hope than gloom: "'That is life? Good, come again!'"

Stressing similarities again as well as differences, the elderly Ortega remained to the end critical of several errors or "failings" in Heidegger: his claim that "man *is* philosophy" and his effort to "resuscitate" an ontology of "being."[40] In the latter instance he felt that both Heidegger and Sartre were emphasizing mere words over the reality that was life, which should properly be called "life," not "being." He admired Heidegger's literary style and his related etymological method, but he thought they fell short of that fullness

---

38. Ibid.
39. Ibid.; and as reported by González Caminero, "Segundo Heidegger," 758.
40. Ortega, "Medio siglo," 6, 18.

that would have made him more easily understood and helped him avoid mistakes. Ready to grant that Heidegger was "always profound"—too profound, since "at times he itches to wallow in the abysmal" and "suffers a mania for profundities"—Ortega preferred the Cartesian clarity of Husserl to balance such one-sidedness (9:630–32).

Unlike the Germans, he had come to see Heidegger as not "particularly difficult" or occult—no more, that is, than any thinker who glimpses new reality for the first time and must try to describe it in words. Rather than a bad writer who "tortured the German language," Heidegger had "a marvelous style" for the *creative* purposes of philosophical thought, but not for the decorous and rhetorical purposes of literature (9:634–35, 638). Unlike Ortega, Heidegger possessed to a high degree that "denominating talent" of being able effectively to name his discoveries, not by terminological and syntactical inventions but by getting down to the forgotten roots of everyday language (9:635–36). However, Ortega was never to concede that "existential" was a good name for their more or less common philosophy of life, and he disagreed with some of Heidegger's derivations as careless or merely verbal.

Heidegger's etymological method was comparable to what Ortega had used since 1914 and had recently made one of his chief tools of historical reason. This method went *beyond* the "true meaning" that logical (linguistic) positivism had stressed earlier in the century by trying to make the oldest meaning "relive." To Ortega, however, that goal meant going "backward" historically as well as merely etymologically, to discover a word's origin as a "verbal reaction to a *typical* life situation" of the past (9:636–37, 641). In contrast, Heidegger's philosophical style "consists above all in etymologizing" back to hidden roots that were merely verbal. The historical part is what Ortega meant by saying that philosophy should make a "vertical excursion" below, behind, and backward—a "constant retrocession" to a primal reality more basic than daily "principles," secondary commonplaces, or conventional wisdom (9:631, 635, 641).

Heidegger's "voluptuous" and rather "baroque" style, so imitative of Holderin (9:633, compare 638–37), was "very successful" (9:637), but on occasion he was insufficiently careful with his etymology and failed to get to the "authentic," vital roots of words. Thus *bauen* and *wohnen*, Ortega maintained, most basically had meant "I am," or "I live" (9:641)—and previously he had criticized Heidegger's "Being," or *Dasein*, as not really so basic and primary as "life" or "living."

Implicitly Ortega was comparing Heidegger's denser style and sparser verbal method with his own clearer literary style and a method that was more vitally and historically oriented. His own etymological technique of historical reason was less prominent than Heidegger's etymologizing, but he thought it more "radical." Etymology, he insisted, was not a bauble or a philological game to add to philosophical analysis but was a necessary "method of investigation" for a philosophy of life, for uncovering "the essential structure of human life" (9:642). "Now to every pragmatic field [of life—religion, philosophy, art, and business, including history and sociology, of course] there corresponds a linguistic field" of words "that tell us something about the whole, great subject of humanity" (9:643). Heidegger's mistake in treating etymologies was to see them as "isolated" from their proper "region of vital reality."

We have examined two main differences Ortega saw between his own and Heidegger's philosophy: *radicality* ("Life" and history over "Being") and moderate ("merry") *tone* over the pessimistic ("moody") temperament (8:306, 316). Now we can grasp that what "radically" separated them seemed to him to be of such a degree or spirit as to become almost a matter of *kind*. His own philosophy, he believed, was holistic, in its reflecting human life reality on both sides, in its totality—contemporary and historical, and future as well. Ortega felt he had developed a "positive" philosophy that suited Western man in the changeable circumstances of contemporary life—that is, not only for the negative crisis situation but for a creative response based on history, which might rescue him from the Abyss of Nothingness and set him on the path to a stable and balanced existence again in a future epoch of normalcy. In contrast, European existentialism was "negative," an incomplete or half-philosophy that found modern man "in the dumps" (so to speak) and left him sitting there (9:566). He would grant that "Heidegger recognizes . . . , in general, that man is historical; but he does not do this well in his analysis of any particular theme" (8:279, n. 2). Content with philosophical theory, he shunned the praxis side of history—applications to historical interpretation, such as both Jaspers and Ortega used.[41]

JASPERS AND ORTEGA

Although he never mentioned Karl Jaspers in any of his publications, Ortega was well aware of him for works both philosophical and historical. In 1940 he referred to him in lectures as "a psychiatrist who shifted at an unseasonable age to philosophy and made an interpretation with certain insights but an insufficient one for lack of technique" (12:192). Later (1953) he wrote "Fragments on the Origin of Philosophy"—about the pre-Socratics—for a festschrift dedicated to Jaspers (9:347–48, 396).[42]

41. Compare Ortega's critique of abstract historicity in Heidegger with the latter's *Heraklit* (Frankfurt am Main: Klosterman, 1970)—strictly abstract analyses in contrast to Ortega's *Origin of Philosophy*.

42. See supplemental note 42, chap. 6.

Jaspers, likewise, was aware of Ortega. In *The Origin and Goal of History* (trans. 1953), he cited *Revolt of the Masses* on how "the mass" is distinct from "the people" and "the individual." For reflections on history, Ortega was certainly closer to Jaspers in *Man in the Modern Age* (1951) than to anything by Heidegger, who had merely stated a *principle* of historicity. Besides some sociological and historical interests coinciding, however, there was no consciousness on Jaspers's part of the several other ways in which their thought harmonized. On the rationality and historical dimensions of life and philosophy, he was more like Ortega than were other existentialists, but no specific *philosophical* influence has been demonstrated on either side. It is noteworthy perhaps that Ortega's favorites among the "great philosophers" before Hegel were generally also Jaspers's choice: Heraclitus, Anselm, Cusa, Leibniz, and Kant. At one time, both of them regarded philosophy as a "faith" and as something that is possible for "everyman." Surely their relatability needs more study.[43]

FRENCH EXISTENTIALISM: SARTRE, CAMUS, AND MERLEAU-PONTY

Whereas Ortega esteemed Heidegger and was disappointed that he had not continued to develop parallel to himself, he did not bother in 1947–1948 to conceal his contempt for the French existentialists as inauthentic and unoriginal imitators of Heidegger, shallow epigones whose philosophy was a "provincial" sham (9:85; 8:307n). First taking note of this derivative "existentialism" in 1946, as "today so fashionable after a delay of twenty years," he criticized its "flightiness" as a "symptom of immaturity and ignorance" (7:495). For philosophy as distinct from literature and religion, that existentialism was Sartre's and Merleau-Ponty's more than Camus's or Gabriel Marcel's. Ortega's very harsh rejection of it no one would take at face value today, for indeed he and Sartre have been judged to have had much in common, as he himself found that he now shared much with Merleau-Ponty. Sartre he called the enfant terrible of the new philosophy, because he con-

43. Karl Jaspers, *The Origin and Goal of History,* trans. Michael Bullock (1953; New Haven: Yale University Press, 1959), 281, cf. 128; in various places, besides *Revolt of the Masses,* this book resembled Ortega's *History as a System* on simplification (134) and "prognosis" (141–43). Dust, "Extremismo existencialista," 146. According to Skorpen, "From Ortega to Jaspers," Jaspers was like Ortega in *equating existing* with "living." Moreover, Jaspers balanced the existential "loneliness of the self" with the joy of life, and he also had a vision of a "federated legal world order." See *The Philosophy of Karl Jaspers,* ed. P. A. Schilpp (New York: Tudor, 1957), 328–29, 751; Jaspers, *Philosophy Is for Everyman* (New York: Harcourt Brace, 1967); and idem, *Der Philosophische Glaube* (Munich: Piper, 1948).

fused the questions of life or being with "dusty" Hegelian terminology in imitation of Heidegger.[44] When he praised Sartre in 1949 for his "great talent," however, he clearly meant his literary output in plays and novels instead of his philosophy.

He had first adverted explicitly, in a footnote in 1947, to the *French* existentialists as "the young men of Montmartre who today play by ear the guitar of 'existentialism'" (8:275n)—and in 1949 he dismissed them as "jackdaws." They more than Heidegger were on his mind when he spoke of certain "groups of European writers" as an "offshoot of nihilistic inspiration that calls itself 'existentialism'" (9:566). Their Montmartre had shrunk and sunk into the "intellectual ghetto" of the earth. Would that "a new Paris" arise, "minus the *fête foraine* of the perverse Picasso, pederasty, and existentialism" (8:307n). His contempt for French existentialism as philosophy did not deter him from examining some of Sartre's basic ideas, but it was Merleau-Ponty who finally won a measure of respect from him.

Although he thought Sartre more given to histrionics than to "historicity," Ortega did not repeat precisely the same objection against *his* radical "negativity of Being" that he had stated against Heidegger. As *engagé*, Sartre had made a personal "commitment" to "action" (9:216). However, was this notorious commitment, obviously "positive" in comparison to his "desperation" and "nihilism," really a *philosophical* response to crisis? Seeing it akin to the typical irrational activism of mass-man, Ortega maintained that in France too existentialism remained mired in negativity, a philosophy *manqué*, if indeed it were philosophy at all, instead of an atheistic, secularist "religion."

Despite his having appropriated and "exploited" the whole baggage of existentialist catchwords, Sartre was less than a philosopher in Ortega's eyes mainly because of three of his main doctrines: "consciousness," *"engagement"* ("commitment"), and "repetition" (8:314–16). In the first he had repeated Husserl's mistake at the very beginnings of philosophical knowledge, in the primary perception of basic, radical reality. In the second, he was trying in vain, in Kierkegaard's way of commitment, to exit from Heidegger's negativism, which he had pushed to nihilistic extremes. Both errors were failures of philosophy *as philosophy,* one at the beginning, the other at the end. For those reasons apparently, Ortega doubted that Sartre's existentialism was authentically philosophy. "Repetition," which Sartre had taken

44. On Ortega and Sartre, see Stern, *Search for Meaning,* 210, 264, 269–73, and idem, *Sartre,* 66–69; H. Rodríguez Alcalá, "Existencia y destino del hombre," 95–103. Like Stern, he saw many similarities, except for Ortega's historical dimension as related to a more holistic structure (100). Brunjulf Strandberg, "Nyere filosofishe retninger i Europa," *Aalborg Stiftstidende* (Denmark), July 10, 1956 (Sartre and Ortega). Ortega, "Medio siglo," 18.

over from Heidegger's *Wiederholung* and ultimately from Kierkegaard, had lost in French its etymological meaning, "search" and "recovery" of times past (9:85). "Well, history is the recovery of *temps perdu* (9:86)," and, more radically than Heidegger, Sartre lacked the indispensable historical dimension of life and reality.

Having discussed at some length the unacceptability of Husserl's phenomenology as a "philosophy" precisely in regard to "consciousness of" (8:273–75 n. 2), Ortega did not tarry to argue with Sartre over the same point. French existentialists were radically unaware that "human living," not "consciousness," was the basic fact to grasp, "without which there is no exit to the high seas of metaphysics" (8:275n). At its root, he emphasized, life is not yet consciousness; it is an "event," or "happening," in which "things" (as "world" or "circumstance") play as much a part as the self, prior to any transcendence such as consciousness, which is only "secondary" and "derivative" (8:274).

Why was not *engagement* the positive response and development that Ortega could not find in Heidegger? As much as James or anyone else, Ortega believed that one thinks in order to act, indeed *must* do so, which is also the justification for philosophy (8:413). However, he did not grant that action (or praxis) may substitute for thought, which is in part how he perceived Sartre's "commitment." As in Heidegger earlier, so now in Sartre's slogan, Ortega feared a "nihilistic" inducement to mindless "direct action" in the neo-romantic heritage from Kierkegaard through "mass-man" (8:301). There were also, however, objections to commitment as philosophical doctrine, similar to his criticism of Heidegger's notion that "alienation" is the origin of philosophy. It would be "superficial" and "frivolous" to "commit oneself," through a "special and . . . deliberate act . . . at a certain moment," when "simple living" is "of itself always and in itself already being committed . . ." (9:216). Furthermore, in the "game"-"theory" that is philosophy, the same as with mathematics or science, it is not "a question of *s'engager*" or of not doing so, nor of the other brave slogans of "provincial" Parisian "existentialism" (8:306 and n.). It is a matter not of "belief" in truths but of "persuasion" about theories, or hypotheses. Nothing was more contrary to philosophizing than to say melodramatically that by it one is concerned with *engager l'homme* in a doctrine (8:314). That would make sense only if philosophy were a belief instead of a theory that is "born of doubt." One may "commit" oneself to philosophy, to reason, but that does not make philosophy itself commitment. Rather, on philosophizing, "man commits himself not to be committed." Therefore, "*engagement* is the most radical contradiction possible of the very essence of *theory*[,] which is permanent revocability." In philosophizing, man always has "the obligation to be skeptical" (8:315).

Against the dangers he saw in Sartre, Ortega came to his most mature, postexistential view of the nature of philosophy: it is *not* a "faith" (belief), after all.

Considering the logical implications of "commitment," he averred again that "'existential philosophy' is impossible *a limine* and a radical *volte-face*."

> Because in Kierkegaard what is "existential" is not philosophy but religion, and in this he acts completely right. Otherwise the gears are going in reverse, and the idea that the philosopher is *s'engager* in the truth in order to be a philosopher will bring with it—it already has happened—that they come to make the fact of commitment the criterion of truth, and then they are going to give out—they already have—the most errant stupidities and follies, as the tritest of commonplaces, etc. (8:315)

Ortega was of the opinion that Sartre's changing commitments of the moment were hardly worth the trouble: "insipid things, the wormiest topics that now walk the streets" (9:216). There one found a "series of irresponsibilities and nonsense" typical of a "pretentious intellectual" (7:495). One need not even wonder what Ortega's judgment would have been of Sartre's later "commitment" to communism: religion, not philosophy. With *engagement*, said Ortega, existentialism made the mistake of taking up something in "secondary and superficial forms and areas, instead of seeing it in the depth of its constitutive and transcendent value" (9:215–16). Sartre's existentialism, in brief, was not "radical enough," did not get down to the primary, vital "roots," not even in regard to commitment.

Although Sartre never referred to Ortega publicly, it seems likely that he knew of him, whether or not he had read him. On some of the basic problems, and for literary style, they were more alike than Ortega acknowledged, as both Rodríguez Alcalá and Stern emphasized. The former saw them as alike in their "theory of man," in resolving the problem of freedom and determinism by denying any fixed "nature," in affirming choice to make oneself, and in trying to reconcile realism and idealism. But Ortega was much the earlier in all of this.[45]

In Stern's view, both Ortega and Sartre recognized that existence precedes essence, and the former's idea of living a responsible "project" for the future was prior to the latter's similar idea of freedom and commitment. In *Revolt of the Masses*, fourteen years before Sartre's *Being and Nothingness*, "Ortega insisted on the moral necessity of man's 'engagement' in, or commitment to,

---

45. Stern, "¿Ortega, existencialista?" 388–89, claimed that Sartre's *L'Etre et le Neant* (1943) tacitly "adopted in every detail" and "developed" the existential ideas of Ortega's *History as a System* (1941); and in fact, Ortega's "circumstance" (even as "situation") long preceded Sartre's "situation" (Stern, *Sartre,* 69). For studies of Sartre that would support Stern's view that he was (like Heidegger and perhaps even more like Ortega) subsequently oriented to history, see Ronald Aronson, "Sartre's Turning Point: The Abandoned *Critique de la raison dialectique,* Volume Two," *The Philosophy of Jean Paul Sartre,* ed. P. A. Schilpp (La Salle, Ill.: Open Court Press, 1981), 685–707. Also see Walgrave, *Filosofía de Ortega,* 181, on Ortega and Sartre on crisis, doubt, and chaos, with the latter more negative.

a definite project," yet "Sartre never recognized his intellectual debt to the great Spanish thinker." (But is a political "program" a philosophical "commitment"?) In addition, Sartre's notion that a new kind of "dialectical" reason was needed is comparable to Ortega's idea of a new vital and historical reason as a new dialectic. Even Sartre's idea that thereby existential idealism and Marxist materialism could be "blended" is parallel to the Spaniard's effort to surmount the old idealism and the old realism with something new that partook of both. A crucial difference that Stern did not notice is that for Ortega the "commitment" could not apply to a particular philosophical *doctrine,* for that is tantamount to abandoning the philosophical quest for truth in order to adhere to a ready-made ideological or religious dogma by sheer act of will. That, Ortega held, is not staying intellectually open, or honestly *un*committed, which authentic philosophizing demands. A different *spirit* of philosophizing, Stern admitted, did indeed distinguish him from both Sartre and Heidegger. "The most morbose elements of authentic existentialism, such as anxiety, nausea, viscosity, are absolutely absent from Ortega's philosophy."[46] That is not quite so, but they are there in a minor (not major) key, and they were balanced by positive ideas.

Most basically of all, let us add finally, Ortega differed from both Heidegger and Sartre by the added historical dimension of "historical reason" as *applied* to man and to his world-circumstance, which was even more fundamental than his optimism in contrast to their pessimism.

Toward the end at least, Albert Camus seemed closer in spirit to Ortega than did Sartre. In "The Wages of Our Generation" (1957) he rejected the current "commitment" craze, and, weary of spiteful nihilism, he wanted to praise as well as condemn, for life is both "wretched and magnificent." He felt he belonged to an "intellectual Europe" that "foreshadows our political future," which Ortega y Gasset had prophesied in *Revolt of the Masses.* "He is perhaps the greatest of European writers after Nietzsche, and yet it would be hard to be more Spanish." In "Why Spain?" Camus wrote that there is no "salvation" from "the whole political society that nauseates us," until "a complete renewal" is found outside it.[47] Did he know that in *Invertebrate Spain,* Ortega had earlier projected a diagnosis, model, and remedy of political "integration" that anticipated the United Europe of *Revolt of the Masses?* In contrast to Sartre's commitment to the "wormy" ideal of Leninist-Marxist communism, Camus finally chose Ortega's Europe.

Still in a euphoric mood after his encounters with Heidegger, Ortega attended the 1951 conference in Geneva, "The Knowledge of Man in the

---

46. Stern, *Search for Meaning,* 267; idem, *Sartre,* 67–68.

47. Albert Camus, "The Wages of Our Generation" (1957), and "Why Spain?" in *Resistance, Rebellion, and Death,* trans. J. O'Brien (New York: Knopf, 1961), 82–83, 242–43.

Twentieth Century," at which he exchanged views with Merleau-Ponty and Jean Wahl. Where his public presentation, "Past and Future for Contemporary Man," agreed with Heidegger's idea of "worry" about the future, in the private exchange afterward he twice stressed what separated them still. In contrast to Heidegger and to the French existentialists who imitated him by going "outside reason," Ortega advised that he himself had "felt obliged to find another form of reason": a "living reason, or, rather, historical reason," of which he assumed the conference was unaware—although Merleau-Ponty too had spoken of "*une raison vivante*." Certain ideas, such as *Sorge,* or worry, he claimed to have stated "thirteen or fourteen years" earlier than Heidegger (9:654). Unfortunately, using "scholastic terminology," Heidegger had reintroduced the concept of being. "His mistake is in having wanted to produce an ontology." "We have to go beyond the idea of Being, for the word *Being* is not capable of expressing this new reality that is life." Apart from that error, he said, he and Heidegger were "now in agreement." To the notion of "being," he preferred Dilthey's "idea of life," of which every philosophical development since then had been only a "different modulation." Despite his genius and his merit as a historian, however, Dilthey had not "arrived at historical reason."[48]

Although Ortega had not wanted to speak of Sartre, "who is a newcomer and does not sufficiently understand these things," Merleau-Ponty, who was both intrigued and piqued, challenged him. "I have not grasped the relation that M. Ortega established between the notion of life and the notion of history, because *Lebensphilosophie* or Bergson's *philosophie de la vie* is something very different." Could *Leben* cover "historicity"? Ortega was "very hard" on existentialists "who make use of the notions of *Non-être* or *Néant* and *Etre,* and of the dialectic of these two notions. But these ideas are nevertheless infinitely more precise than the notion of *Leben*." When Ortega replied that Dilthey had "discovered life as historicity" and had not—any more than Heraclitus—made use of Parmenides' concept of Being, Merleau-Ponty countered with: "So what?" For him, Being and non-Being expressed historicity better than *Leben*. Ortega thereupon granted that *Leben*—and *Lebensphilosophie*—were inadequate to express precisely the new reality that they had perceived. In the interest of conciliation and amity he seems to have conceded too much at this point, for he had just attributed the name "*philosophie de la vie*" to the whole philosophical movement since Dilthey—including Heidegger and existentialism as particular species of that more general phenomenon. Nevertheless, he had also stated: "We must put an end to that habit of designation by a single word things that are quite different"—like "poetry," or his own and Dilthey's different concepts of "historical reason"

48. Ortega, "Troisième entretien privé," 289.

(and perhaps "life" too). He wondered aloud if "what we are now beginning to do is entirely different from what is concretely called philosophy." "To speak of philosophy, we have to proceed slowly."[49]

Clearly both terms, "life" and "history," were essential to describe Ortega's understanding of the human reality. The moderator properly concluded that the "confrontation" between Merleau-Ponty, "who insists on the idea of history," and Ortega, "who insists on the idea of life," was more apparent than real. The two conceptions were "tied to one another" ever since the beginning of romanticism, which had viewed man as organism and as history, and as embodying a "reciprocity of action" between past and future.[50] That was an apt observation, for Ortega had appealed to both life and history, even to "living reason" as "historical reason." Besides, the very first sentence of his discourse, on man's past and future, had emphasized his "structure" (9:645). Tacitly, he was surely going "beyond" philosophy with a "historiology"—a "structural" theory in historical reason that was more methodical and systematic than any "structuralism" in Merleau-Ponty. The historical "beliefs" to which Ortega appealed here as a means of "generalization," rising from concrete individual to a time-bound culture and society, and thus to his "Theory of Human Life" (9:649–50), were "metahistorical" structures.

CHRISTIAN EXISTENTIALISTS

Perhaps because of the "distortions" in Kierkegaard and Unamuno, Ortega never mentioned "Christian existentialists" such as Gabriel Marcel, whom he knew.[51] Ortega's view of life and of Christian doctrine was less pessimistic, less vitalist.

> Christianity in itself involves not a sentiment, not a vague "sense," but directly and formally a precise *idea*, a quasi-tragic interpretation [of] life, but that is precisely because it does not pause to contemplate the phenomenon of Life itself, but what is immediately a solution to the problem of life,

49. Merleau-Ponty, ibid., 293–95.

50. Jean Wahl, ibid., 335–36.

51. Luis Diéz del Corral, *De Historia y Política* (Madrid: Instituto Estudios Políticos, 1956), 31, told of a lunch Ortega had in Paris with Gabriel Marcel and André Siegfried, "where Ortega's talent shone at a height seldom equaled, producing, despite idiomatic obstacles, admiration in his hearers." Not a Christian existentialist, Ortega has nevertheless been compared (or linked) with them: Takehito Kojima, "Ortega maruseru haidegga" (Ortega, Marcel, Heidegger), *Riso* (Tokyo) 273 (1956): 58–65; Marías, "Love in Marcel y Ortega," in *The Philosophy of Gabriel Marcel*, ed. Paul Schilpp (La Salle, Ill.: Open Court Press, 1984), 553–72; Dust, "Extremismo existencialista," 147–48. Ortega's dualism of "tone" also reminds us of Nietzsche's two sides (Apollonian and Dionysian) of human nature and life, in need of harmony and balance. See John Baker, *The Super-Historians* (New York: Scribner, 1982), 220–24.

> salvation. Therefore, I say, it is a conception only quasi-tragic: in the long run, everything ends well and things fall into order. Christianity sees life immediately in relation to God, . . . as something infinitely far from God, . . . Who is absolutely and fully.

Compared to God, then, human life "appears as quasi-Being, as quasi-Nothing, as almost Nothing, or non-Being" (8:300). Always Ortega had concentrated on the immanent values of this life in contrast to the Christian emphasis on the beatific "other life," to which he compared the modern anti-Christian worship (*beatería*) of culture and intellect above life (3:183–85).

As he grew older and no longer so bravely "merry" about life, Ortega became more tolerant of Unamuno's "tragedy" and "mortality" (R 5) and of Heidegger's obsession with death. Then he also accepted the traditional Christian view that this world's setting for life indeed *is* a "vale of tears" (9:69), a viewpoint in keeping with what he recognized as an "authentic" type of "Christian philosophy" (9:212–13) stemming from Saint Augustine. "This definition of life—by one side, sad and deficient—, although stating the truth is not all the truth. Because, it is evident that if life were only that we would quit it as soon as we came to it." In 1940 he preferred to "turn the defect and the misfortune into an enthusiastic task, that is: into adventure and enterprise."

> In such a way, in my doctrine of life there shows through the indissoluble union—in no wise contradictory—the mutual necessity of bringing to synthesis the two great truths about human life: the *Christian*, for whom "to live" is to *be* [*estar*] in a vale of tears; and the *pagan*, who turns this vale of tears into a *stadion* for the sportive undertaking. (12:218–19)

That was said directly not against Christians but against Heidegger's pessimistic and atheistic appropriation from Kierkegaard: life as *Angst*, anxiety. Ortega's own "synthetic" brand of ratiovitalist existentialism was neither naively optimistic nor blackly pessimistic. That was still his attitude near the end of his life: a blend of historic Christian and modern secular ("pagan") views on life.

There is an intriguing possibility that Ortega heard but did not participate in a lively discussion about Christian existentialism compared to atheistic existentialism at Geneva on September 12, 1951, the same day he gave his address on man's past and future. Catholic theologian Jean Danielou asked Merleau-Ponty if he thought a Christian type of existentialism were possible, if one were to distinguish its phenomenological method from its "system" of relativistic values and of becoming instead of being. Rejecting "system" and systematic explanation in philosophy, Merleau-Ponty responded that Christians did in fact use phenomenological method as an entry into philosophy, but he thought that, from a Christian standpoint, the pope had been right to condemn existentialism. Despite Gabriel Marcel, "one cannot speak absolutely of a theistic existentialism." On the contrary, Danielou replied, by not denying the possibility of the absolute, one could indeed be a Christian existentialist. Protestant theologian Charles Westphal asked whether he acknowledged a humanly unknowable area of reality, but Merleau-Ponty preferred to discuss philosophical problems "without introducing the term 'God.'"[52] Probably Ortega agreed with that reservation, but he was more secular than atheist.

During a later private exchange in Geneva, supporting the idea of "transcendence," existentialist Jean Wahl proposed that God manifests himself in history, not only in the past but in today and tomorrow. Although Ortega was not present then, his attitude toward this proposition can be surmised from his reaction to an earlier discussion at the same conference, when Wahl adverted to Einstein on the question of the reality of God in the universe, a reality surpassing human comprehension. "I don't know," said Ortega. "You are too sure about what concerns God. . . . He is too far away." "We must leave God at a distance. In this sense, one must be a little like that first heretic who put God so far away because he respected Him so much. He was the *etre superantissimus.* He had nothing to do with men."[53] This epistemological agnosticism left Ortega right where he wanted to be: somewhere between orthodox theists and the atheists, at odds with both and thus open for "synthesis" of the Christian and "pagan" positions. Although he did not deny the reality of divine transcendence nor of the absolute, he doubted very much that they were within the reach or capacity of the individual man and his natural reason. They were problems more suited to theology than to philosophy.

REFLECTIONS ON A CLOSE RELATIONSHIP

After examining Ortega's scattered critiques of Heidegger, Sartre, Merleau-Ponty, and other existentialists, one ends with the very strong impression that he too was an existentialist, however much he disliked the name "existentialism." Like them, he put "existence" first—or, to be more precise, as a realist, he put "coexistence" first (7:409)—because man's "essence" was developed in conditions of space and time, or history. True, he was "merry," sportive, "positive," more "rational" and more historical but nevertheless an existentialist of the secular (not atheistic) type. Had Heideg-

52. Danielou, in "Troisième entretien privé," 247–48. See McMurrin's article on Ortega in *A History of Philosophy,* 502–6, and his projection from culturally and ethically relativistic perspectivism to a position approaching "the atheistic existentialist point of view."
53. Ortega, "Troisième entretien privé," 335–38, 281, 287–89.

ger been less pessimistic and more restrained and historical in his approach to *life* instead of to "being," and less tainted by Nazism, Ortega might have openly agreed to be "lumped" with him in the same type or "school" of philosophy—even though it was called "existentialism"—against his will and better judgment. But he *was,* also, a historicist—more than Heidegger, Sartre, or Merleau-Ponty. Because of his much greater emphasis on history and historicity, he was equally a historicist for another half of his mature philosophy.

It was not just Ortega's clerical critics who thought he was an existentialist *and* a historicist in his last years. So did his more independent disciple, José Gaos, though emphasizing historicist more than existentialist; but most critics since 1955 have reversed the preponderance. Not all existentialists who were contemporary with Ortega, however, were able to recognize an existentialist in him, because he was so clearly other things besides. Despite their broad areas of agreement, Heidegger was finally unsure about precisely how to define his philosophy. Merleau-Ponty evidently suspected that his position was that of *Lebensphilosophie,* or *"philosophie de la vie,"* akin to Dilthey or to Bergson. Similarly, German existentialist Otto Böllnow identified him as one of those thinkers grouped under the broad name *Lebensphilosophie.* For French existentialist Jean Wahl, on the other hand, he represented a "historizing existentialism,"[54] which is a definition pretty close to Stern's later choice of "historicist existentialism," or the reverse of Gaos's view.

What most distinguished Ortega's type of existentialism from Heidegger's and Sartre's was his "radical" emphasis on *life and history.* Without ceasing to be an existentialist, he thus sought to go "beyond" them. In historizing "being," he also historized "thing" (9:367–71), and thus he "surpassed" Husserl and James too. By his historicism he exceeded all of them, as surely as by emphasizing life as "radical reality." Both positions, however, were compatible with his own existentialism. He pointed out that both Husserl in phenomenology and Heidegger in existentialism had started from "huge errors"—the one by his description of idealist "consciousness" and the other by his description of the phenomenon Life, which was reduced to static "being" or even to a gloomy "Nothing" that ignored the happy "many-sidedness" (8:296–97) that history revealed.

In sum, we have increasing difficulty following Ortega and defending his "vital reason" as a *unique* philosophy in itself, instead of seeing it as an early and original variety of existentialism, compounded with phenomenology and resting on a pragmatist base. "Vital reason" was "a fuller reason, for

54. Gaos, *Sobre Ortega* (1957); also see my chap. 7. Böllnow, *Lebensphilosophie* (1958). On Böllnow as existentialist, see J. Grooten and G. J. Steinbergen, *New Encyclopedia of Philosophy* (New York: Philosophical Library, 1972), 143. Jean Wahl, "Philosophie existentielle," 74; he also identified Böllnow as an existentialist (71, 79).

which no few objects are rational that to the old *raison,* conceptual reason or pure reason, are in effect irrational" (7:327). On several occasions he would say almost the same of "historical reason" (3:264; 6:43, 49; 9:392). Was he therefore an existentialist, or a historicist, or both—within a covering "philosophy of life" (8:463; 12:192)?

Chapter 7

STAGE II

"Historical Reason" as Historicism
(1924+)

round 1860, Dilthey, the greatest thinker of the second half of the nineteenth century, made the discovery of a new reality: human life" (12:326). So wrote Ortega in 1935 as the opening sentence of "The Dawn of Historical Reason," a short article announcing to North Americans this form of reason as a new worldview, a "new revelation"—a theme he reiterated in 1936 in English in "History as a System" as his "second voyage" (6:29, 45–51). But how were we to take this bold "new" departure—as philosophy of life, philosophy of history, or historicism? Actually, it involved all of these, but as philosophy it was not so new (for him). It was a vitalist historicism he had developed since 1924—on a pragmatist base and by phenomenological method.

For the ongoing study of or revival of interest in pragmatism, historicism, and phenomenology, Ortega thus offers a challenging case study of interpenetration and integration in philosophy in this century. His new historicism was contained within his older philosophy of life but was eventually the equal of existentialism in his "system." Finally it inspired a new *critical* "philosophy of history" that led him "beyond" philosophy itself after 1936.

Historical reason in Ortega always related to a "philosophy of history" such as Raymond Aron saw in Dilthey's philosophy of life, a "historical philosophy" that was "also in a sense a philosophy of history." Such a philosophy of history was not like the speculative systems and sweeping interpretations of world history from Hegel and Marx to Spengler and Toynbee. This kind of philosophy of history was instead "an interpretation of present or past as linked to a philosophical concept of existence," or life, and as tied to its time and "the future it foresees." It is at once an introduction and a conclusion to philosophy.[1] Now Aron's definition fitted Ortega (8:266) as well as it did Dilthey. "One philosophizes from within life" and in time, claimed Ortega, for philosophy is a "historical occupation" in a "historical condition" (8:269). Indeed, "there is no *philosophia perennis.*" Philosophy is born, dies, and is reborn in time or history (8:245, 262).

In 1983, by "authentic analogy," Hans Gadamer also compared Ortega with Dilthey, whom all had assigned to "the historical school" instead of philosophy until Heidegger had placed him as "a thinker on the historical reality of life." Gadamer saw Ortega as combining Nietzsche and Dilthey in vitalism and historicism with his own Latin traditions, but as going "beyond" both of them while remaining faithful to "the primacy of life" and "the historical vision" alike.[2]

In Ortega a philosophy of history was compatible with a philosophy of life, as it was in Dilthey and was earlier still in Friedrich Schlegel: a philosophy of life *and* history. However, his new historicism also involved him in a new kind of "critical" philosophy of history that anticipated "analytical" philosophy of history.[3] Here, however, we are concerned only with history as a part of his philosophy of life, although it led "beyond."

As the second stage, or second branch, of his philosophy of life, historicism was something Ortega had been preparing (in private mainly) from his very beginnings in 1904. For him, history had always been a coordinate of life. In 1924 he had first announced historical reason to the public, but he then developed it as subordinate to vital reason until after 1930. Clearly, historical reason was central to the "second voyage" in his thinking to which he (citing Plato) adverted in the preface to the first edition of his selected works in 1932 (6:356),[4] for it obviously dominated his production thereafter. "History is precisely the second look that manages to find reason in apparent unreason" (7:285). Historical reason was also a "second love" and a second "style,"

1. Raymond Aron, *Introduction to the Philosophy of History,* trans. G. J. Irwin (Boston: Beacon, 1962), 12–13. For another such perspective, see Ilse N. Bulhof, "Structure and Change in Wilhelm Dilthey's Philosophy of History," *History and Theory* 16 (1977): 21–32.

2. Hans Gadamer, "Wilhelm Dilthey y Ortega y Gasset: un capítulo de la historia intelectual de Europa," 78–79, 85, 88.

3. Meyerhoff, ed., *Philosophy of History,* 36, 44, 86, on philosophy of history and historicism, with a pragmatist relation.

4. Often adverted to by critics and expositors, Ortega's idea of "second voyage" was not always transparently and simply history, or historical reason. In an earlier reference (Ortega, 7:315), it seems to be the second look at reality by philosophy (or metaphysics) compared to mere physics, but thus fuller, truer reality; on a later occasion (6:29), it seemed to relate to Kant's "Copernican revolution," *distinguishing* (as well as elsewhere uniting) knowing (conceptual) and being (basic reality), to avoid "intellectualism" (abstract idealism). Here, however, I take the historical view of it, as did McClintock. The term should not be confused with "circumnavigation" (7:315; 8:222), which is roughly equivalent to Ortega's circular "hermeneutic."

because it was "born already carrying on its shoulders the experience of the first" (6:237), that is, of vital reason.

Had Ortega published "Dawn of Historical Reason" and "History as a System" in Spain in 1935–1936, he might have been recognized immediately as a historicist, but he did not reveal his new turn there before 1941. The critics had not yet identified the "first Ortega," when they had to cope with a "second Ortega," as Gaos noted. By then he had obscured his identity philosophically in Buenos Aires in a lecture series (1940) entitled "On Historical Reason," wherein he emphasized history far less than the idea of life, which he now attributed not only to Dilthey and himself but also to the existentialists Heidegger and Jaspers (12:192). For linking life (or being) to history, the others are at times called historicists. Surely Ortega, who did more with history than any of them, must (like Croce) also be directly and explicitly identified with a new historicism. If relatively few have done so—most with hostility—until lately,[5] it is because he failed to publish a "book" called *The Dawn of Historical Reason* that he promised for more than fifteen years after 1940.

Ortega's "second voyage" gave us the "second Ortega," who was like the "second Dilthey," the "second Husserl," and even the "second Heidegger" (as seen herein) by becoming especially oriented on history. None of them brought their "second voyages" to full conclusion before death, but Ortega, as critic of the others (and perhaps because of that) went the furthest, "beyond" all of them—with a "radical," new historicism.[6]

HISTORICAL REASON IN ITSELF—AS HISTORICISM

Just what is "historical reason" specifically—that is, as constituting a type of historicism? Ortega never identified it publicly by that name nor expounded it formally in any extensive way. None of the disciples and very few of the critics, except Walgrave and Ouimette, were able to set out in detail how he saw it or what it was supposed to "do." So, neither philosophers nor historians really know anything about it and may be excused for suspecting that it was just an empty phrase meant to catch attention. Because he wrote no book entitled *The Dawn of Historical Reason*, it is hard to know precisely what that type of reasoning was. Our main source is not *Historical Reason* (1983) but is still "History as a System," where, just after his very notable historicist definition ("*man has no nature, but instead he has . . . history*"), he defended "historicism" for its variable view of reality (6:41)—which was *indirectly* to admit historicism.[7]

5. See supplemental note 5, chap. 7.
6. Morón Arroyo, *Sistema*, 305, 355, on Ortega's "radical" (or "total") historicism.
7. Ouimette, *Ortega* (1982). For an earlier good analysis of the content of historical

The lectures "On Historical Reason" (1940 and 1944, but not published till 1983) greatly disappointed those who have wanted to understand this ill-defined term.[8] Such lack of solid and explicit treatment therein was typical, very comparable to his *Modern Theme,* where "vital reason" itself appeared only twice (3:178, 201), or less often than "historical reason" in "History as a System." Still, that even greater dearth of terminology and definition has not at all deterred studies of his existentialism as it has seemed to discourage investigation of his historicism. Although there are twice the indexed loci to "historical reason" as to "vital reason," ample to support analytical study in depth, there have been so few philosophers who have liked historicism or wanted anything to do with it.

We need not take seriously Ortega's claim that "historical reason" was as simple as "good morning!" (8:265, 315), but we cannot now turn aside to repeat and to analyze at length all the scattered passages on historical reason. Here our concern must be with "history" as part of his total *philosophy,* not with his critique of the historians' methods of historical reasoning. Since historical reason as philosophy, however, is so nebulous and undefined, we have to know in general whence it comes and what it signifies and "does." For this purpose, let Ortega be his own spokesman. In his "Metaphysics of Vital Reason" (1933) he explained that the non-personal half of reality that was his world, or "circumstance," was concerned with the temporal, the spatial, and the social (12:51–52),[9] which directly implied a *historical* reason (added to vital reason) and a sociology.

A few lines from Ortega show the historicist essence of this historical reason. "We can understand nothing historical—and everything human is historical, and man in his substance is nothing else but history—if we do [not] situate it and locate it with full rigor in its place, within that vast chain that is history" (6:236). Historical reason is, "literally, *what has happened to*

---

reason, see Walgrave, *Filosofía de Ortega* (1960). Only a few Ortega specialists have had even the foggiest of ideas of what "historical reason" was in Ortega's thought (or in Dilthey's either) or what it was expected to "do" for history or philosophy. There is nothing on it in either encyclopedias or general histories of philosophy or in texts on historiography and method. That passage on man having a history instead of a "nature" and the reference to "historicism" have been taken as tantamount to Ortega acknowledging historicism for himself: see Meyerhoff, ed., *Philosophy of History,* 61–62; and Stern, *Search for Meaning,* 259, 271.

8. For example, see the review of Ortega's *Historical Reason,* trans. Philip Silver (New York: Norton, 1983), by Hayden V. White in *Times Literary Supplement,* January 31, 1986, pp. 109–10, who saw it as "a pastiche of notes" giving "an existentialist twist" to Dilthey's tradition, as "more of an attitude than a method of reasoning," and "naive and inconsequential" as a whole. Those lectures, also in Ortega, 12:145–330, were never intended to stand alone as a complete treatise but need to be placed within a context of development, within his project "Dawn of Historical Reason."

9. Marías, *Trayectorias,* 209.

man, as constituting its substantive reason, the revelation of a reality transcending man's theories and which is man himself underlying his theories" (6:49). "Historical reason is, then, *ratio, logos,* a rigorous concept." It "accepts nothing as mere fact but makes every fact fluid in the *becoming* from which it proceeds . . ." (6:50).

If the statements above are insufficient for a full grasp of what was historical reason, they are enough to demonstrate that it was in fact a form of historicism.[10] Therein human reality (ontology) is seen in terms of historical life as ever changing and *becoming,* not as static "being" and categories (6:42). To define Ortega's historicism adequately, however, we must not only consult the critics but compare it with other historicisms of his predecessors and contemporaries, chiefly those of Croce and Dilthey and the other existentialists.

CRITICS AND DEFINITIONS OF ORTEGA'S HISTORICISM

Within his "philosophy of life," besides a pragmatist metaphysics, phenomenological method, and existentialism, Ortega then also developed a distinct historicism. Did he share with contemporaries a fund of ideas that constituted for them a common historicism? Was he closer to one kind of historicism than to another? If Dilthey's historicism was "transcendental," Croce's "absolute," and Heidegger's "existentialist," then what was his? The only distinctive name ever given it was by Gaos in 1950: "ratio-historicism." But is that unique name enough, or do we need other qualifiers, just as for "ratiovitalism"?

In Ortega, historicism becomes doubly a problem: what kind was it, and how was it—in his own thinking? Even in his lifetime it became a problem, which is with us still, for it has been investigated critically very little, and therefore it has never been resolved satisfactorily. But his historicism is a problem that will not go away, now that the posthumous works have come to include not only *An Interpretation of Universal History* but his lectures as *Historical Reason.* Was Ortega then finally just an existentialist of "vital reason," or was he also a historicist of "historical reason"—or somehow both things, either successively or simultaneously? And, if this was truly historicism, was it something new by surmounting the skepticism and rela-

10. In Ortega's *Origin of Philosophy* (Ortega, 9:366n) is a good, concise statement of historical reason (as historicism), applied to both history of philosophy and to history in general—in contrast to traditional rationalism from Aristotle to Hegel ("abstract, imprecise, utopian and uchronic"—invariable and eternal reason); "if *there is* reason it will have to be 'concrete reason,'" that is, "the historicity of reason." "I think that it is urgent to invert Hegel's formula and to say that, so far from history being 'rational,' it happens that reason itself, authentic reason, is historical."

tivism previously associated with it? If it was new in kind, then in what ways did it differ by comparison to others?

Owing to "History as a System," by the 1940s the clerical critics Iriarte and Sánchez Villaseñor had identified Ortega with historicism, which they wrongly equated with the "atheistic" and skeptical relativism of old and so damned accordingly. It was the same work that Nicol identified in 1950 as historicist and denounced as a "fraud"—because he assumed that Ortega, like Croce, had simply replaced metaphysics with history, although he noted that Ortega had tried to rise above Dilthey's relativism by means of a "historiology" that was to serve as a new ontology. In contrast, disciple José Gaos liked the idea of a historical reason and that same year gave it an apparently very fitting name: "ratio-historicism," the counterpart of "ratiovitalism." After these few in the 1940s and 1950s, however, little more attention was given to his *historicism* as such, not even in French studies that at least put "historical reason" into the structure of his thought alongside vital reason.[11]

From the standpoint of historicism, little has been written on Ortega's relationship to other historicists. His difference from the romantic historicism of Hegel, who was his "captain" of "historiologists" (4:521), has not been examined. Although Croce and he referred to each other, Italian scholars have shown little interest in the Spaniard's *ragione storica* as similar in some ways to the former's idealist notion of reason in history, so fruitful comparison on historicism still has not developed. Surprisingly, even on his relation to Dilthey's "transcendental" historicism, there has been nothing of length and depth—not even in Germany or in Mexico, where pertinent works of both philosophers have been available since the late 1940s.[12] This is a strange omission, since that is the only close kinship in thinking that Ortega readily and repeatedly acknowledged. One good reason for the neglect of this problem in the United States was that there were until recently few efforts in English to elucidate even Dilthey himself, apart from Ortega's own labored exposition of 1933–1934, of which scholars still take account.

Among the pages, articles, and chapters on Ortega's historicism or on his philosophy of life, few if any even try to reconcile these two philosophical positions in him or him and Dilthey. Reiterating Nicol, Morón Arroyo affirmed a "total" or "radical" historicism as a consequence of his "Heideggerian" existentialism, but he did not further relate the two nor examine the historicism. Among other studies of Ortega and existentialism, only Alfred Stern also explored independently the related problem of *historicism*. More,

11. On Iriarte, Sánchez Villaseñor, Nicol, and Gaos, also see the bibliographical essay herein. For identifying Ortega's historical reason by Gaos's term as "well nuanced" and subordinate to life as basic reality, but without any significant analysis or differentiation of the concept, see Guy, *Ortega ou la raison vitale*, 46.

12. See supplemental note 12, chap. 7.

in fact, have been reluctant to see that historical reason is historicism than have been ready to equate vital reason with existentialism. Ortega himself saw his philosophy as *equally* vitalist and historical, so, after vital reason (existentialism) as first stage, the second stage of "historical reason" was "historicism," which he admitted privately but not openly to the public (R 80).[13]

There are a number of unresolved questions that a *duality* of life and history involves. If he could finally acknowledge Dilthey as "the man to whom we owe most on the idea of life" (9:362)—and, by implication, for a "philosophy of life"—did not that include history as its most prominent component (6:166–68, 175–77, 200n, 205)? Can we then also assign to Dilthey a major influence over Ortega's *development* of historical reason as a contemporary historicism? But was he just a continuator of the so-called transcendental historicism of Dilthey? Did he not also have much in common with the "absolute" historicism of Croce and with the "existentialist" historicism of Heidegger, Sartre, and Jaspers? Was his historicism a "genetic" variation of phenomenology, as Silver saw it? Or, finally, by having been rooted in a pragmatist metaphysics, was it maybe unique as also a *pragmatist* variety of historicism? One's answer depends on how one defines historicism and its sources.

HISTORICISM IN GENERAL AND IN PARTICULAR

The original identifications of historicism—and most of the redefinitions subsequently—have come from philosophers who were denouncing what they deemed *philosophical* "heresy"—apostasy in their ranks that reflected the work, methods, and results (changing, dynamic reality) of historians, especially Ranke and the Prussian historical school. Meinecke's *Historismus* (1936) brought intellectual historians into the controversy too. By their emphasis on the neglected *historical* roots and temporal development of historicism, with variations according to area, individual, and era, they compounded the problem of definition.[14] Although philosophical definitions like those of Popper are too facile, too cut-and-dried as contrasting ideal-types, to fit many concrete cases, the sum of all historical variations does not equal one good generalization about the phenomenon itself. Philosopher Maurice Mandelbaum, however, has given a simple, usable, "analytical" distillation of what is presumed to be common to all varieties: an underlying attitude toward reality as changing in respect to time and place. Still, the historical variations themselves cannot be ignored in the comparisons that are necessary for defining the historicism of any particular person, group, or era.

13. See supplemental note 13, chap. 7.
14. See supplemental note 14, chap. 7.

Hans Meyerhoff's three types in historical succession (romantic, positivist or scientistic, and Diltheyan-existential) is too restrictive for the eighteenth-century origins and for all twentieth-century variations.[15] It is arguable whether there was a historicism (true historical consciousness) already in and of the Enlightenment, but in the twentieth century Dilthey's type was not quite existentialist, Croce's was different still, and Ortega's was unique as a whole, however much it resembled the others at some points.

By accepted definitions, Ortega was undoubtedly some kind of historicist, although many have not recognized the fact and he never confessed it publicly. But what kind and what else was he? Although many philosophers, such as Karl Löwith, Leo Strauss, Leszek Kolokowsky, and Karl Popper, have condemned historicism, it has been sympathetically viewed by Ernst Cassirer and by Alfred Stern, and, since Friedrich Meinecke, by intellectual historians such as H. S. Hughes. Generally, philosophers have opposed and "refuted" historicism, because it seems tantamount to utter relativism, or radical skepticism, as allowing for no permanent, stable, general truth, value, or reality, which they treasure above all else in this world of flux and change. By contrast, historians are instinctively very suspicious of "laws," universal concepts, and metaphysical absolutes that do not move and change in time and space, and they may therefore favor the outlook of historicism precisely because it focuses on the concrete and the variable. Like J. H. Hexter approving of Ortega's account of Dilthey, historians reject abstract Kantian "categories" as absolute, eternal, or necessary, and they see them instead as man-made and changing in response to the basic reality of historical life.[16]

With historical reason Ortega sought to bridge those two polar views of reality, to join the concrete and individual to the abstract and general, so as to give a greater realism to both history and philosophy, as he said in 1930 in *What Is Philosophy?* (7:281, 283–85). His synthesis of the empirical and the conceptual in life and history was by means of a realist metaphysics of "things" and a "supra-historical" metahistory.

---

15. See supplemental note 15, chap. 7.

16. On anti-historicist philosophers (besides Popper)—Löwith, Strauss, Kolokowsky, Gerhard Kruger—see Michael Ermarth, *Wilhelm Dilthey: The Critique of Historical Reason* (Chicago: University of Chicago Press, 1978), 354; in their view "historizing historicism" was "logically specious and morally pernicious," an "all-forgiving relativism," an opposition Ermarth sees as transitory and time-bound. Stern, *Philosophy of History*, chap. 6, on historicism as a form of existentialism; H. S. Hughes, *Consciousness and Society, 1890–1930* (New York: Vintage Books, 1958), 239–48 (on Dilthey, Croce, Troeltsch, Meinecke). J. H. Hexter, review of Ortega's *Concord and Liberty*, in *New York Times Book Review*, September 1, 1946, p. 8. For a consideration of relativism by a historian, see Bert J. Loewenberg, "Some Problems Raised by Historical Relativism" and a response by analytic philosopher Wilson H. Coates, "Relativism and the Use of Hypothesis in History," *Journal of Modern History* 21 (1941): 17–27.

ORTEGA'S HISTORICISM COMPARED TO OTHER TYPES

Whenever Ortega adverted to historicism by name (rarely) in his published works, he was referring critically to the earlier romanticist and positivist kinds. Personally he was much closer to still unnamed contemporary types. In private notes he would define his own idea that "Man is making himself"—or that "man has no nature, but . . . history"—as "naturalism [realism] and historicism" (R 80), even as he implied in "History as a System" when he chided the opponents of historicism (6:41). Also privately, he identified as "historicism" both Dilthey's "perspectivism" (R 40) and the idea of progress as imperfectly a historical outlook in the Enlightenment (R 46; R 80). Obviously he recognized at least four historicisms prior to his own. Hence, he was much more concerned with historicism than we could have guessed from the few published references, and he meant to avoid the errors of earlier kinds.

In 1911, Ortega had seen a romantic historicism in Herder, Schelling, and Hegel as "a way of viewing the world" that sought "to see in history the field of metaphysical experience, the place where the universal spirit gave its revelations . . . [as] the spirit of peoples" (1:166, 168), and he found positivist historicism in Renan, Taine, Treitschke, and Costa. With the exception of Hegel, both types of earlier historicism forgot "the higher unity" of world history and of Europe in order to concentrate on the history of particular nations.

Hegel's error was the "intellectualization" of history, that is, it was known by concepts and these "concepts are its essence," in contrast to his own historiology (R 76). Historical reality was not a "conceptual dialectic" of pure reason (5:135), as in Hegel, who had imposed an abstract, logical reason on history (from outside) instead of finding a reason within history (6:49). But when Hegel had affirmed that history was "rational," his "reason was not historical," no more than Aristotle's. For philosophy and for historicism, more to the point than Hegel's *panlogism* of history (7:326) was Ortega's conception of the "historicity" of reason itself. "I think that it is urgent to invert Hegel's formula and to say that, so far from history being 'rational,' it happens that reason itself, authentic reason, is historical," not "abstract, imprecise, utopian and uchronic" (9:366n). Later he weighed historization of reason against Dilthey too.

Historically the second sort of historicism was positivist. With this type, especially Comte's, Ortega still had more than a little in common. Although it is clear that he rejected its "laws" and any close identification of the epistemology and methods of history and of the social sciences with physics and the natural sciences (6:183–84)—which Popper condemned—he did not reject "prediction" in a loose and general way (3:152–54; 4:127, 175). Echoing

Comte, he mingled a kind of scientism of expected results by "foresight" (6:50) with an a priori perception of reality in his dream of a new "human science" based on life. That scientistic "carryover" from the old positivism gave historian Brinton some misgivings about *History as a System*.[17]

Later, things found in Comte by Ortega confirmed his own historicism. He detected the idea of "historicity" there before Dilthey had enunciated it (R 40). Comte also had conceived, more or less, an idea that man makes himself in history: "the human is substantially social and, finally, historical." "Man, author of himself," is "modifiable" in his destiny (R 45). His famous three stages of the mind were "definitely historical." Ortega felt that Comte's relativism and historicism were not typical positivism but anticipated Dilthey (5:206; 6:337).[18]

In a context where he treated positivistic historicism in regard to Ranke's "Historical School" (4:525n), Ortega also adverted to Ernst Troeltsch's *Der Historismus und seine Probleme* (1923) and Rothacker's *Einleitung in die Geisteswissenschaften* (1920).[19] Both were partly concerned also with Dilthey's historicism, which he later skirted in regard to the putative "Critique of Historical Reason" (6:185, 194) that Ermarth has recently equated with "transcendental historicism." From those sources he was well aware of that later kind too, and, although he did not name it as such in his study of Dilthey in 1933–1934, he would have thought it more "relativitist" than Comte's.

No one has ever attributed "historicism" to William James, but Ortega was able to draw from his books and doctrines some of the basic components of his own historicism, which appeared when he was preparing to emphasize his historicist position in the 1930s. *A Pluralistic Universe* was the most relatable to history of all of James's works. There he had emphasized the "pluralism" that Ortega formally took over into his historical worldview by the 1920s (3:302–4). James also ridiculed the triadic "jargon" of Hegel's dialectic, even while admitting that it was somehow to be found in historical reality and not just in thought, perhaps as a "zig-zag" movement that calls for "endless description" of "circumstances" and activities. Finally, he pointed out that the monist absolute has no history but that pluralist beings do have a history. At the same time, in *Essays in Radical Empiricism,* he adverted to

17. Popper, *Poverty of Historicism,* 143, 147–50, rejects natural science methods and epistemology for history. Crane Brinton, "Toward a Philosophy of History," *Saturday Review of Literature* 23 (April 5, 1941): 5 (essay retitled in 1962).

18. There are no studies of Ortega and Comte, despite Ortega's repeated praise of him (for historical sense and historicity: 4:135, 288; 9:346) and his intention to write a book on him (6:29).

19. Among others, Troeltsch was probably a source of Ortega's idea that historical reason was a new "revelation" (6:49–50), because he regarded history as "the gradual revelation, through time, of an inaccessible God," according to Aron, *Introduction to the Philosophy of History,* 291.

the "change," "event," "happening," and "doing" that take place in the real, historical world, and he saw this world as only "more or less" rational, and as having to be loosely connected by "hypotheses" following daily experience.[20] Broadly speaking, that is all very much like what Ortega saw and practiced in his historiology. One half of this new discipline was structurally from James.

Later, in "Preface for Germans," Ortega repeated (against Husserl and "intellectualist" idealism) several main principles of "Adam in Paradise," his first (Jamesian) work in philosophy: not only life as "given" and "coexistence" of self and world, but reality as "pure event" rooted in "space and time." Next, in "History as a System" (1936), some of the Jamesian concepts and terms again came through, such as "faith" and "revelation" (of a new historicism of historical reason), "intellectualism" rejected, life as Heraclitean "happening," "instrumentalism" of concepts, and pluralism of reality. Unacknowledged, that dependence has been missed by all except John William Miller, whose "Afterword" (1960) pinned the label of "historicism" on that work and loosely linked it with James.[21]

When Ortega remarked in 1908 that he had already been "meditating on the problems of historical phenomenology" (10:60), the context was his first discussion of pragmatism (compare 1:117–19, 439). Despite Husserl's and Scheler's earlier rejection of historicism as relativism, did they later manifest elements of a phenomenological historicism? Although Silver did not link any such historicism to "genetic phenomenology," Carr saw it as possibly a logical implication of Husserl's "Crisis."[22] If Ortega did not regard "Crisis" as logically consistent with Husserl's idealism, possibly his own historical reason (as historicism or in historiology) had a realist phenomenological component that could be compared to a "phenomenology of origins."

In 1925, Ortega made a brief detour into a "philosophical anthropology," where he anticipated Scheler. He dropped it in two years as ahistorical, but some study it in him even today.[23]

If "historical phenomenology" was maybe a "phenomenological historicism" in Ortega, it was surely related to his "existential historicism" from 1923 to 1935. Heidegger, Jaspers, and Sartre also used phenomenology and had a historical perspective too. Did Ortega's examination of Heidegger

20. James, *Pluralistic Universe* (1947), 86–91 (dialectic); idem, *Essays in Radical Empiricism. Pluralistic Universe* (Gloucester, Mass.: Smith, 1967), pt. 2, pp. 47–49, 74, 160–63.

21. Ortega, 8:44, 47–53; idem, *History as a System* (1936; New York: Norton, 1962), 223, 229–30, 195–99, 200–203, 176 (222), 166. John W. Miller, "Afterword" (1960), *History as a System*, 238, 240, 269.

22. Spiegelberg, *Phenomenological Movement*, 1:337–39; David Carr, *Phenomenology and the Problem of History. A Study of Husserl's Transcendental Phenomenology* (Evanston, Ill.: Northwestern University Press, 1974), chap. 10, "Historical Relativity," 156, 160.

23. See supplemental note 23, chap. 7.

between 1927 and 1935 propel him onward into a "total historicism" within existentialism, as Morón Arroyo claimed,[24] or did it make him react to Heidegger as historically insufficient, so that he established historicism as distinct from and independent of (equal to) existentialism by 1936?

The only thing like a "total historicism" in the 1930s was Croce's so-called absolute (or "pure") historicism. Even if Ortega were dependent on Croce, was his historicism also pure or absolute? Was a Crocean character what essentially defined him as different from all the other historicists? Of course, Croce was a Hegelian idealist, where Ortega was a Jamesian *realist* at basis, but in some other respects he learned from Croce.

Since there were historicist implications in James, did his pragmatist metaphysics and outlook finally give Ortega a *unique* historicism? Among philosophers of pragmatist lineage, neither Dewey nor Santayana (his famous dictum notwithstanding) was nearly so developed in historicism as was Ortega. However, Whitehead developed a historical outlook that has been compared to both Croce and Ortega.[25] Unquestionably, Ortega went much further than those other "pragmatists" into genuine historicism, and his historicism definitely evinced pragmatist qualities that distinguished it from all the other kinds. It was first and finally a "pragmatist historicism," but it showed evidence of the other philosophical movements too. Especially, he resembled Dilthey in historicism, even in its "pragmatist" features.

By "relativity" of outlook and orientation to life, despite his professed "antihistorism" (6:180), Dilthey was not so very different from Ortega in historicism except for his idealist basis (6:183n). Yet regarding him as also partly positivist at bottom (6:184; 8:31), Ortega attributed to him a "radical empiricism" as in James (6:190, 202) or a "radical positivism" as in his own metaphysics (6:210) . This fact shows that he minimized his own differences from Dilthey's historicism, which is called "relativistic," "humanistic," or "transcendental" in type. Mainly it is in his archival notes that he stated his awareness of their differences, which make his published works now appear to overemphasize the similarities. Dilthey was not James's alter ego to the

24. Morón Arroyo, *Sistema*, 305.

25. Barzun, *Stroll with James*, 303, 309, found Nietzsche a "pragmatist *sans le savoir*," notably for *Use and Abuse of History* (which influenced Ortega); Burckhardt would have been the historian most congenial to James. Paul Weis, "History and Objective Immortality," *The Relevance of Whitehead*, ed. Ivor Leclerc (London: Allen and Unwin, 1961), 324. Whitehead admitted "a deep debt to James" and had adopted James's pluralism and radical empiricism (Edward Pols, *Whitehead's Metaphysics* [Carbondale: Southern Illinois University Press, 1967], 131). Lewis S. Ford, ed., *Explorations in Whitehead's Philosophy* (New York: Fordham University Press, 1983), 307. Whitehead's view of man as "a 'becoming,'" a "living process," with no "substance" but a "history" emergent to the future is very like Ortega. See William N. Pittenger, *Whitehead* (Richmond: John Knox Press, 1969), 29. Ortega's only references to Whitehead (7:317; 9:663) were not on history.

extent that Bergson was, and James, of course, was not openly or consciously historicist.

Timid in facing relativism, Ortega was afraid to profess historicism boldly, despite its respectable genealogy and contemporary affinities. We can see this plainly in "History as a System" (1936). After affirming the historicity of man and also describing his own idea of historical reason in terms of Dilthey's *Realdialektic* (6:40–41), he remarked:

> It is supremely comical that historicism should be condemned because it produces or corroborates in us the consciousness that the human is changeable in its every direction, that nothing concrete in it is stable. As if stable being—the stone, for example—were preferable to the changeable! "Substantial" mutation is the condition from which an entity as such can be progressive, from which its being may consist in progress. Now it must be said of man, not only that his being is variable, but also that his being grows, and, in this sense, . . . progresses. (6:41)

But did he then directly affirm that his "new" historical reason was a new historicism? No, he simply ignored, evaded the issue. Despite later attacks on his historicist relativism, he remained silent. In 1951 he again asserted publicly that "man has no nature" but history and "variation" instead: no "fixed being" but "pure mobility"—"always under way" (9:646–47). His unusual position was not as radical, pure, or absolute as it sounded, however, for he recognized some fixed traits in human behavior.

When he obliquely acknowledged historicism in "History as a System," he knew that it was already an intellectual movement of the past, or at least in disfavor at the time. In 1928 he had seen that a "crisis of historicism"—over relativism—was said to be occurring (4:525n). Born out of that crisis, and meant to resolve it, Ortega's "historical reason" was a new and more radical (but also more cautious) form of historicism that still is in need of a distinctive name. Neither by meaning nor by their names did the several earlier stages of historicism describe his thinking adequately, for he tried to avoid previous relativism and to go beyond the earlier types—even Dilthey's transcendental kind. In Ortega historicism had a substantial and distinctive content of its own in theory and method, particularly as related to "doing" history "pragmatically"—something that must be more fully demonstrated in a later study.

RELATIVISM, RELATIVITY, AND WORLDVIEW

Philosophers have customarily identified historicism with relativism. Like scholars who have recently reassessed Dilthey's reputed relativism, Ortega saw it (and his own) as new in kind and as more consistent with Einstein's idea of "relativity" (6:196–200), which was opposite to the "old type" of relativism that regarded thought (perception, concepts) as relative but saw reality as absolute (3:233). Here Dilthey, Einstein, and also James represented for Ortega a new "worldview" for this century.

Like Dilthey's historicism, Ortega's newer variety was "relativitist" and humanistic in character. The first function he assigned to his new "historical reason" in 1924 was to recognize the *relativity* of all things as historical, but to rise above that limitation to quasi-"absolute" conceptual forms that inhere in them, forms that might (allowing for changing "variables") be applied holistically, or universally, to interpret and reconstruct history, the temporal and spatial dimension of our human life-reality (3:313). "Historical reason," he said, "advances in two directions." One, a "psychology of evolution," is concerned with the "structure" of different stages of human knowledge, or "categories of the human mind," which seem to parallel Comte's types of mind and Dilthey's worldviews, except that Ortega turned them into *recurring* "constants." Apparently the other direction was "relativity," which for him meant recognizing the "variability" of the "type of man," life, mentality, and culture in the "whole of the human past." Without this, one could not speak of a true "historical sense," which he believed had not existed before romanticism and had been lost again by liberal positivists, Darwinists, and Marxists in the era of scientist naturalism. No more than Dilthey, did he accept the old radical "relativism" that posited the absoluteness of historical reality (3:303, 311–13)—contrary to Iriarte and Nicol.

The problem of relativism in historicism, which so many philosophers have felt compelled to condemn for presumed radical skepticism and nihilism, is one with which Ortega wrestled before he would have been called a historicist. For him as for Dilthey and James, the awkward term "relativitist" (in the sense of relativity) might be more accurate, as he pointed out in *Modern Theme*. It is ironic, therefore, that he, who opposed relativ*ism* as skepticism, was himself later charged with being a relativist and a skeptic.[26]

In 1915, long before he *developed* historicism or was well acquainted with Dilthey's thought, before he quite grasped what the new idea of "relativity" meant in Michelson, Minkowski, and Einstein (12:345–47, 498), Ortega took up the traditional problems of relativism in a psychology course at the Center for Historical Studies in Madrid. Even then, however, he perceived that

26. On Ortega and relativism, see Jorge Biturro, "El relativismo de Ortega," *Estudios*, no. 489 (November–December 1957): 1–34; Copleston, "Ortega and Philosophical Relativism," 172–84; Paulino Garagorri, "Ni relativismo ni absolutismo," *Letras de Deusto* (Bilbao) 13 (May–August 1983): 203–9; Jesús Iturrioz, "Relativismo histórico," *Pensamiento* 2 (1946): 326–32; José M. Millas Valliorosa, "Sobre el relativismo moral de Ortega y Gasset," *Punta Europa*, no. 78 (1962): 57–66; Miguel Oromi, "Cosas Orteguianas—Relatividad y absolutismo," *Revista de la Universidad de Buenos Aires* 8 (January–March 1951): 127–52. Marías (*Trayectorias*, 168–71) denied Ortega's relativism, against such critics as Sánchez Villaseñor; Copleston was tolerant and sympathetic.

Einstein's "Special Theory of Relativity" was a work of philosophy and psychology as well as of physics that had been anticipated in several fields and that had revolutionary implications for traditional notions of space and time. Although he mentioned the history of philosophy and the philosophy of history in regard to relativity (12:348–50), history per se he left out of this problem until *Modern Theme* (1923). In those earlier arguments against relativism, where he acknowledged a debt especially to Husserl, Polzano, and Huber (12:434–35, 439, 444), his own position was already, like James's and Dilthey's, closer to the new relativity than to the old relativism.[27]

Without denying the relative character of our individual and collective knowledge of truth, he sought to exclude the pure relativism about truth itself that is skepticism, which is the theoretical "problem of problems" (12:426). Taking up Pilate's notorious question, "What is truth?," he reduced its meaning to "What do we understand by truth?" (12:429, 437). Absolute skepticism he deemed absurd, as self-contradictory as the squared circle, for one cannot doubt that one doubts (12:428). "Contemporary relativism," which he acknowledged was already yesterday's problem in philosophy but still a very current general outlook (12:441), regarded truth as "something relative to the subject that knows," since what is true or false is not things or reality (absolutes) but what we think, judge, or believe about them. Thus Ortega inverted the relation.

Carefully he developed James's relationship of *belief* to truth, even affirming that "when one believes that truth is something relative, he believes it absolutely"—although this does not affect the character of truth itself (12:430–32). Even "probability" is turned into sureness by belief. Of course, belief can be wrong, and counterevidences can and do undermine and destroy a belief that something is true. Truth, however, does not depend on the "peculiar structure" or location of the subject. "Truth for me" is really not different from "truth in itself"; otherwise, one comes to the logical absurdity that "oranges are not blue but they are blue for me" (12:435).

Selectively he disposed of several objections from the subjective-idealistic point of view (12:438–40), such as the supposition that two plus two may be five on Sirius. On the contrary, truth is given in unique "perspectives." "In effect, where I stand, no one else is, and the world sends me a perspective, takes an aspect that only I can see." But "all aspects and perspectives are truly those of the object," regardless of whether those "pieces" of the world are perceived by races, epochs, or individuals, and no one, except God alone, contains the universe. Objections such as the possible nonexistence of world

27. Theodore Plantinga, *Historical Understanding in the Thought of William Dilthey* (Toronto: University of Toronto Press, 1980), 134–36, said that "relativity," which Dilthey used often, did not mean the same thing for him as it did for other historicists, that is, relativism and skepticism; Ermarth has the same view of Dilthey, in *Critique*, 335–36.

and self he viewed as "serious frivolity"—an effort at "not understanding oneself" (12:439–40).

In summing up a variety of objections, Ortega did not pretend to have eradicated relativism by showing in a schematic way the mistake of conditioning truth by the subject and its situation or constitution "in every formula where they speak of *truth for*"—man, extraterrestrial, or God (12:441). "All that is not to declare that, if truth exists, what is true is absolutely true, and that what is true for me . . . will be so for every other subject whatever be its condition. . . ." That would be absurd, for man's possession of truth has "obvious limits." "In effect, we neither possess all truths nor can we possess them all. In this sense it is clear that truth is relative; but that meaning is ill-stated thusly. It is not truth that is relative to man but the number and kinds of truth that we can possess." In this "trivial" sense (here he echoed James), relativism was right (12:442). Clearly the subject conditions the truth in some sense—by the mere fact that his body, senses, and nervous system intervene between his consciousness and the universe, like a sieve that lets through only a limited amount of reality. Man's eye and the honeybee's eye both see the visible world but in very different ways. Which sees it as it "really" is, that is, *all* that it is?

Reality is open to many ways of seeing and to many perspectives, all proper to the object. "What comes to the subject, therefore, depends immediately on his organic, specific, and individual structure," but especially his *psychic* structure (12:443). For one fascinated by mathematics, physics, and chemistry, the problems and truths of biology, religion, and art may not exist, that is, not draw his attention. Only that part of the world on which "the basic activities of life" operate is common to everyone, and still lesser parts to collective groupings. The individual, finally, "possesses certain corners of truth and reality" uniquely visible and appropriate to him alone, parts of which he cannot even express to others. "Every individual is an organ of perception into something distinct from all others, like a tentacle that reaches out to parts of the universe closed off to others" (12:444). If only psychology could determine the unique "psychic contexture" of a Newton or a Cervantes.

When Ortega took up the problem of relativism again in the *Modern Theme* (1923)—chapter 3, "Relativism and Rationalism"—he still retained the perspectivist and realist approach to it, but now he grasped how Einstein's "*General* Theory of Relativity" fitted into a new and comprehensive worldview with historical implications. It was the latter that he had in mind when he adverted to "the supposition that there exists an intimate affinity between scientific systems and generations or epochs."

Does this mean that science, and especially philosophy, is a complex of convictions that are valid as truth only for a determined time? If we accept

> in this way the transitory character of all truth, we shall remain enrolled in the armies of "relativist" doctrine, which is one of the more typical emanations of the nineteenth century. While we are talking about escaping this epoch, we shall only be slipping back into it. (3:157)

Truth, he granted, had to be "one and invariable" in order to reflect adequately "what things are," but "human life, in its multiform development, that is, in history, has changed constantly in opinion, consecrating as 'truth' whatever it adopted in every case." Faced with this fact, the "'relativist' doctrine" concludes that, if every people and individual always holds its own beliefs as true "for" it, then *the* truth does not exist but only truths "relative" to every subject and situation. "But," he added, "this renunciation of truth, made so genteelly by relativism, is more difficult than it seems at first glance" (3:157–58).

The pretended impartiality of relativism in regard to the mass of vital, historical facts was accomplished at the cost of logic, life, and reason. If "truth does not exist," then we must deny that relativism itself is true. Besides, since "faith in truth is a radical fact of human life," to destroy it is to leave life illusory, absurd, worthless. "Relativism is skepticism, after all, and skepticism, justified as an objection to every theory, is a suicidal theory." He supposed that it was inspired by the noble intent to save the vital from rationalism, but it was a "failed attempt." Modern rationalism, on the contrary, in trying to save truth, had renounced life. "If truth is one, absolute, and invariable, it cannot be attributed to our individual, corruptible, and changing persons," but must instead be assigned to something "abstract," to Descartes's "pure reason" or Kant's "rational entity," which are not subject to time, place, and change. "Rationalism is antihistorical," from Descartes forward. It represented a "complete inversion" of the "natural perspective" on man (3:158–60).

Summing up the effect of the "two antagonistic tendencies" of relativism and rationalism in confronting the problem of truth, Ortega found both were "insufficient," both mutilated life in opposite ways (3:163). "Rationalism sticks with truth and abandons life. Relativism prefers the mobility of existence to quiet and immutable truth." Disavowing both of the old positions, he claimed to belong to his own epoch and to "fight" them equally. "Dualism," a "double face," was evident in both life and thought (3:165), but not such as would support either relativism or rationalism. The "new sensibility" of the time was a "double imperative" to combine its two "dimensions," "the biological and the spiritual," the vital and the cultural (3:169, 174). "*The theme of our time* consists in subjecting reason to vitality, locating it within the biological, . . . to show that culture, reason, art, ethics are to serve life" (3:178). But, lest this be understood (as it was by Nicol and Morón Arroyo) as a merely biological vitalism, he stressed that "both powers, the immanent in the biological and the transcendent in culture" have "equal titles" in the "synthesis" he proposed for going beyond them (3:197–98). If rationalism did not admit that truth (eternal, one, and invariable) could exist in the changes of life and history, relativism denied any transcendent truth and reality.

Applying *perspective* to these two different points of view (3:199), he came up with "vital reason," a reason of place, movement, development, with "vital, historical, perspectivist dimension[s]" (3:201). This "viewpoint" seems very close to what Scheler called "historical perspectivism," which Ortega soon regarded as similar to his own historical reason.[28]

Years later Ortega put his proposition in a much more emphatically historicist sense, but privately. Then the "theme of our time" was a "radical new theory of knowledge," one to disintellectualize the intellect: "intellect chronizes itself" as "historical reason" and "historicism" (R 80). "That reason of the non-identical as such, mobilism, mobile—is historical reason," in opposition to the pure reason of idealism. "I conceive historical reason when, confronting the present, I take account of what happened in succession before now, . . . the prior is intelligible. The dialectic of experiences. . . . History as system." "Every new epoch is a new situation in the universe—therefore a new perspective. Some new things are seen and accustomed things are seen with a new aspect" (R 80). That "theme" of circa 1936 was historicism, but anti-"intellectualism" was also pragmatism, and the "aspect" was still perspectivism.

Appended to *Modern Theme* in 1923 was a section called "The Historical Meaning of Einstein's Theory," which considered the great "historical phenomenon" (3:231).[29] Actually, it was on the philosophical implications of the "General Theory" for the history of the old physics, more than for history in general. First, relativity differed from the old relativism that was implicit in Galileo and Newton; second, as a kind of "perspectivism," it had been anticipated by himself and others in philosophy; and, third, it had broader consequences for history and for a new worldview.

"Einstein's relativism," he held, "is strictly inverse to that of Galileo and Newton" on "absolutes." In the latter, *actual* space, time, and movement were less real than a priori Euclidean *absolutism* of those three coordinates of

28. See Scheler, *Philosophical Perspectives*, trans. O. A. Haac (Boston: Beacon, 1958), 68–69, on "historical perspectivism" as related to "philosophical anthropology"; the work was first published in 1926. Cf. Rabade Romeo, *Ortega filósofo* (1983), in reference to "historicity" and "perspectivism"; also Enrique Lynch, "La perspectiva y la crítica del pensamiento," *Cuadernos Hispanoamericanos*, no. 403–5 (January–March 1984): 81–92.

29. On Einstein and Ortega, see Lysander Z. D. Galtier, "Einstein, Milosz y Ortega y Gasset," *La Nación*, August 9, 1959, sec. 3, p. 2; and James Sharkey, "Ortega, Einstein and Perspectivism," *Romance Notes* 12 (1970): 21–25.

matter in motion, an abstraction in which they believed absolutely. For Einstein, however, reality lay in the individual observer himself moving at a particular place and time—a "relative reality" that was nevertheless "absolute" and for which the old absolutes of time, space, and motion were no longer valid (3:232–33). Since the laws of physics are thus true regardless of the "system of reference," but since space and time vary according to the point of view, then the old proposition about the viewpoint from Sirius is nonsense (3:233–35). The errors of the old physics sprang from the abstract Cartesian mode of deduction, geometric a priori, which Newton himself manifested in the law of inertia, and also from an "excessive estimation of man," who was made in effect "the center of the universe, when he is only a corner." Thanks to that "optical error" and to the old geometry, the physics of Galileo and Newton had now become "provincial"—a system for nearby space but not for the universe (3:234–35). It depended on the "point of view," or perspective, that was taken.

Ortega had already in 1915 identified thinkers and a whole trend of Western thinking as anticipating Einstein. Now he claimed that his first issue (January 1916) of *El Espectador,* preceding the "General Theory of Relativity," had expounded a "doctrine of perspectivism" that was philosophically similar but broader (3:235). Thus, he regarded relativity as a "sign of the times" for a new general "way of thinking," in which many had collaborated unwittingly long before Einstein (3:231–32)—all the way back through Comte (5:387; 6:337) and even to Kant (3:236). By 1923 he claimed that relativity denoted a revolutionary switch in thinking from "utopian" and "uchronic" rationalism and from the Newtonian idea of abstract and absolute space and time to a new world of "finitism," a closed, curved, finite universe (3:237–39, 241)— rather like James's notions. Other changes he detected were "discontinuity" now replacing Darwinian and Comtian continuity, abandonment of the classical theory of causality for a Bergsonian "cinematic" view, and Jamesian "pluralism" instead of nineteenth-century unitary principles (3:241n, 303). With these, relativity was the paramount feature of a new general "worldview" that would become much broader than physical science and philosophy in its implications. "Einstein's theory is a marvelous justification for the harmonious multiplicity of all points of view. Extend this idea to the moral and to the aesthetical [for] a new way of perceiving history and life" (3:237).

FROM RELATIVITY TO "SUPRA-HISTORICAL" IN HISTORICAL REASON

After two decades of strong tendencies toward historicism, in 1924 (in "Atlantises"), Ortega first "extended" relativity to history in the guise of a new "historical reason," a critique of the "extemporaneous relativism" in Frobenius's ethnology and in Spengler's *Decline of the West* (3:300). They erred by making "cultures" (or civilizations) into hermetic organic systems that were the protagonists of history, or the "basic phenomena" of historical reality, for which peoples and individuals were only vehicles. Their cultures were abstract absolutes to which real human beings were merely *relative,* much like Newtonian absolute space and time as related to the observer. As "absolute, metaphysical" entities, such cultures smacked of the "unitary" fixation of Hegel, Marx, and Comte (3:302–3). Ortega preferred the discontinuous and "pluralistic" outlook of quantum physics, Einstein's relativity, and post-Darwinian biology, which he transferred analogously to history (3:309). With their absolute constructs, Frobenius and Spengler had abandoned historical empiricism and thereby the possibility of fruitful comparison and verification befitting historical "reason."

Nevertheless, Ortega saw implied "relativity" in their recognition of independent cultures other than the European, cultures that were not to be judged simply by the Europe-centered "universal history" and criterion of "progress" of the past three centuries (3:305–6). If ethnology represented a historical "long view" (like Einstein's physics in contrast to Newton's), history—unlike physics—does not try to *explain general* material phenomena that lack meaning but seeks to *understand concrete* human facts that of themselves do possess meaning. "Every epoch understands what is true for it. Ours understands the theory of relativity." Now "the problem of historical science" is to grasp the meaning of people, epochs, and events that are *not* contemporary for us. The problem for the "historical optic" is to be far enough away to distinguish something cultural from ourselves but near enough to recognize it as human and meaningful. All cultures and eras, even those of barbarity and savagery, have a "point of reason" (3:310–12).

"Spengler's work," said Ortega, "is strangled by not noticing that to explain the relativity of cultures—of human historical facts—is to do an absolute task. On recognizing the relativity of human forms, history introduces a form free of relativity."[30] These forms, or "norms and modules," have a "supra-historical character," although they are discovered by means of history. Such a form, for example "worldview," may arise in the culture of European man, but that does not prevent it from having an "absolute character." "The discovery of a truth is always an event with precise date and locality. But truth once discovered is ubiquitous and uchronic." So it could be with *history,* which "is historical reason, therefore an effort and an instrument to overcome the variability of historical material," just as physics is

---

30. On Spengler and Ortega, see Ciro T. de Padua, *O Homen e a Tecnica (Ensaio sobre as ideias de Spengler e Ortega y Gasset)* (Curitiba, Brazil, 1942).

"pure reason" in an "effort to dominate matter." "This reflection which liberates us from [our particular] historical limitation is precisely history. . . . Reason, organ of the absolute, is complete only if it becomes whole, by making itself, besides pure reason, clear historical reason" (3:312–14)—and, of course, "vital reason." One of the advantages of historical reason was that institutions and beliefs of other cultures and of earlier ages, which to pure reason always seem "irrational or unintelligible," seem "natural and comprehensible" to the former as "narrative reason" (5:106). Ideally, the ongoing account should be set in a frame of "universal history" (6:236–37).

The use of historical reason in such a way as to obtain transcendent, "supra-historical" forms, such as "generations," was what Ortega had called "metahistory" in 1923 and "historiology" after 1928. Dilthey's "worldview" and James's collective "belief" were two of the more general of these forms, or models, that he adopted. His reflections on relativism and relativity were of the same decade in which he developed "perspectivism," "vital reason" (12:392), and finally "historical reason"—all of which were closely related to that problem.

Whether or not Ortega rightly understood relativity, or correctly distinguished it from relativism, cannot be decided here. It is very clear, however, that he *meant* to reject relativism itself (as skepticism) from 1915 onward, long before "History as a System." The critics who accused his essay of a historicism tantamount to pure relativism and skepticism neither knew of his early lectures nor grasped the "supra-historical" function of historical reason. They disallowed or misconstrued the perspectivist vital reason of *Modern Theme,* but his chapter entitled "Relativism and Rationalism" was viewed by the Dutch scholar Walgrave after 1949 as indeed supporting not relativism but relativity.[31] By intent, he had already disposed of that issue before going on to develop historicism. If everything about man, individually and collectively, is "relative," including his "truths," he held, truth of itself is not relative but absolute. In a practical sense, so are our "beliefs" about truth, but our *perception* of truth is always *limited,* hence "relative" to our own makeup, time, and place. This outlook, similar to James's, was meant to be more akin to the new relativity than to the old relativism, which included the historicisms of the nineteenth century.

When he took up the issue of relativism again in 1930, Ortega denied that history (historiography) implied "radical relativism." History's function was to establish the "meaning and truth" of every epoch, culture, and type of human life in a "rational structure." In this way, history "overcomes radically whatever there be in relativism that is incompatible with belief in a transrelative [*transrelativo*] and eternal destiny in man" (7:285). His own

---

31. See supplemental note 31, chap. 7.

purpose, he explained, was to combine philosophy's liking for "the eternal and invariable" with history's attention to "the fickle and changing." He had done that systematically with "Historiology" in 1928.

In historiology, Ortega used historical reason with the intent to transcend relativism and skepticism. For, if only individual and equivocal perception of truth is possible, even *in* history, then the undisputed sway of the unique and the concrete, or particular, would tend to have consequences of skepticism and pure relativism. Metahistory as historiology was meant to *limit,* to transcend, this condition of the traditional history still in use and to arrive at some valid "supra-historical" concepts to apply to history and to human life in general.[32]

As Nicol noted, Ortega was by 1924 probably using some of Dilthey's *historical* concepts, or he was unconsciously paralleling them, in his idea of "historical reason."[33] This was in fact a variety of historicism, as metahistory was its ontology and historiology was its chief method, or application. But how should we define that historicism—if not uniquely his own, was it beyond Dilthey's type? Will the "ratio-historicism" of Gaos suffice, or shall we need other correlatives to identify it properly, just as "ratiovitalism" requires us to take into account pragmatism, phenomenology, and existentialism? Besides Dilthey's type, two other contemporary forms of historicism seem related to his own: Croce's and Heidegger's with Jaspers's—or transcendental, absolute, and existential. Comparison with these three types should help isolate what is peculiar to his own historicism. Croce's influence apparently preceded Dilthey's.

"ABSOLUTE HISTORICISM": CROCE

Several critics have detected a "pure historicism"—usually meaning "pure relativism"—not only in Croce but in Dilthey and Ortega, although the

32. On historiology, see Graham "Historiology and Interdisciplinarity," 37–46; also see Walgrave, *Filosofía de Ortega,* 99–112, 124–27, and chap. 4, "The Anatomy of Historical Reality" (139–42), for one of the surest grasps of historiology as a kind of science of models. Nicol, *Historicismo y Existencialismo,* 320–21, 330–31, regarded Ortega's historiology as a "science" concerned with ontology, as combining "metaphysics and epistemology," but (hence) "absurd." Among the very few studies (four) specifically on historiology, see especially Walter Garayochea Villar, "La teoría de la historia en Ortega y Gasset: Historiología y perspectivismo," *Hombre y Mundo* (Peru) 2:3 (1967): 59–83; and A. L. Machado Neto, "A ciencia histórica como historiología ou a filosofía de historia de Ortega y Gasset," *Revista Brasileira de Filosofía* 7 (1957): 331–43.

33. Nicol, *Historicismo y Existencialismo,* 317, seemed to suspect that Ortega's avowed parallels with Dilthey were maybe a little less than pure coincidence in the "Atlantises" of 1924. Possibly Ortega had by then obtained the *Einleitung* (1883; new edition, 1923), which he did not regard as actually Dilthey's *philosophy,* which he claimed not to know before 1929.

latter two never admitted publicly to any kind of historicism. Among twentieth-century philosophers the better candidate was certainly Benedetto Croce (1866–1952), who was openly and avowedly for "absolute historicism." In fact, he went so far as to resolve "philosophy into history." For him all true philosophy is "philosophy of the Spirit" (Mind), which "can in the concrete only be, and has in effect always only been, historical thought, or History," reflecting "upon its own method." History "includes in itself Philosophy which lives only in history and as history."[34]

With roots of inspiration in Vico, Goethe, Kant, and finally Dilthey, but especially in "Hegel's historicism," Croce naturally had much in common with Ortega,[35] except that his bold and poetic idealism contrasts sharply to the Spaniard's realist subtleties and reservations. To critics, the former's was a "pure historicism," but, in regard to truth and to a genuine distinction between philosophy and history, the latter's realist historicism was diluted and limited, despite allegations to the contrary. In some respects, however, Ortega's historicism seemed as "pure" and "absolute" as was Croce's. More than a quarter of a century ahead of Ortega in publicly advocating historicist principles, Croce never doubted that historicism was right, for he reiterated it all the rest of his life. In comparison, Ortega equivocated in public and did not openly acknowledge being a historicist, even in "History as a System" (1936). Never did he go so far as to proclaim that history *is* philosophy, or vice versa, however closely he interrelated the two.

Coming so much earlier to explicit historicism—if not by 1902, then by 1916 at the latest, through Vico, Hegel, and aesthetics—Croce certainly influenced Ortega. In his unfinished "Half-Century of Philosophy" (about 1951) he put Croce with the neo-Kantians and neo-Hegelians, as having mixed Kant with Hegel in his *Logic as Science of the Pure Concept* (1902). So this implied that Croce's work was a starting point for him, along with Cohen and Rickert, not just for emphasis on culture but, with Rickert, probably also for historical thinking. Where he came to differ from them was in his basic pragmatic realism: "Reason [is] not from logic but [is] of the 'thing itself'" (R 36). Later he accumulated at least ten of Croce's works in

34. Benedetto Croce, *History: Its Theory and Practice* (1916), trans. D. Ainslie (New York: Russell, 1960), 83, 151, 153n (on "philosophy as history" and "history as philosophy"), and 312 on "Spirit" ("idealism" as basic reality); idem, *Philosophy, Poetry, History,* trans. C. Sprigge (London and New York: Oxford University Press, 1966), "The Logic of History" ("Philosophy as Absolute Historicism," 1939), 13–14.

35. Croce, *Philosophy, Poetry, History,* 45 (on pragmatism), and the essay "What Is Living and What Is Dead in Hegel" (1906), 4–12. G. H. Douglas, "The Pragmatic Element in Croce's Philosophy," *Rivista di Studi Crociana* 10 (January–March 1973): 50–59. Probably Ortega's reference to autobiography as historical reason in "Medio siglo," 5–6, was prompted by Croce's "History as Autobiography and Vice Versa" (1946), in *Philosophy, Poetry, History,* 539–41.

Italian and French editions, including his Hegel, his Vico, and his *Theory and History of Historiography*.[36]

In Croce's work of 1902 there had already appeared the ideas of the "identity of philosophy and history," history as narrative method, individuality of historical judgment, intuition in research, prediction, "variety" in history as surmountable by means of the concept, the subjective versus the objective in history and values, the relation of history to natural science and its practical character, and the cycle as in Vico. There was enough there for Ortega to "chew" on for years to come. In his "What Is Living and What Is Dead in Hegel" (1906), Croce had advanced beyond Hegel, and Ortega professed to have done the same thing with Kant (4:51, 58), yet each was much indebted to both philosophers. For Croce and Ortega, Kant's "Copernican revolution," an "a priori synthesis" of sensate and "intellectualist," real and ideal, intuition and concept, was basic. Thus, in both of them we see efforts to combine the a priori and the a posteriori in a new synthetic method, which for Ortega was "historiology" (4:530). Both followed Hegel in finding historical reality rational, but neither agreed with his imposing an a priori metaphysical reason *on* history. Both linked the "dualism" of inner and outer reality in a "transcendent unity," although they rejected any "unitary" interpretation of history—either Hegelian or Marxist "historical determinism." Finally, despite principles that theoretically sanctioned practice, neither could satisfy the impatience of some of their disciples for "action" *now*, either on the Fascist political right or on the Marxist political left. And, toward the end, both founded "institutes" of history and the humanities in almost the same year (1947–1948).[37] Over all, Ortega shared many things with Croce.

36. Ortega, "Medio siglo," 13 (Croce). On Croce and Ortega, see Franco Meregalli, "Ortega en Italia," *Cuadernos Hispanoamericanos,* no. 403–5 (January–March 1984): 449–50, for a brief general comparison that does not deal with historicism, but he notes that Croce only once adverted to Ortega, in 1943. Similarly, Pellicani, *Introduzione a Ortega,* 13 (citing F. Romero), affirmed Ortega's affinity to Croce in philosophy but failed to develop it in chap. 3 ("The Dialectic of History"), where his historicism is likened instead to Dilthey's; he also affirmed that Ortega's historicism was not the messianic kind that Popper and Löwith criticized in Hegel and Marx (89–90). Armando Savignano, "Utopismo e 'ragione storica' in José Ortega y Gasset," *Filosofia* (Turin) 34 (January 1983): 19–38, with no reference to Croce, confirmed the historicism in Ortega but linked it to existentialism, as both "historicist ratiovitalism" and "vitalist ratio-historicism" (29, 32, 34). Ortega's library contains ten studies by Croce, including *Etudes sur Hegel* (Paris: Colin, 1931); *La filosofia di Giambatista Vico,* 2d ed. rev. (Bari: Gius-Laterza, 1922); *Teoria e storia della storiografia,* 3d ed. (Bari: Gius-Laterza, 1927); and *Problemi di estetica e contributi alla storia dell'estetica italiana* (Bari: Gius-Laterza, 1910).

37. On Croce's historicism, with several references to Ortega, see David D. Roberts, *Benedetto Croce and the Uses of Historicism* (Berkeley and Los Angeles: University of California Press, 1987), 6, 29, 311, 313–14, 322, 115–16. Also see H. Wildon Carr, *The Philosophy of Benedetto Croce: The Problem of Art and History* (1917; New York: Russell, 1969), 20–21,

Despite all the similarities, fundamental differences (other than realism versus idealism) came to separate Ortega's historicism from Croce's. After adolescent crises of belief, both came to new philosophical "faiths" of historicism and stoicism, but the elder came to historicism from historiography, whereas the younger came to it more from philosophy. Croce's ideas were not "thought through" as well as Ortega's, whose basic realism and plain speaking would be more acceptable to practical historians than the confusing echoes of idealism and paradox in Croce. Ortega emphasized "life" more than Croce, and he did not so nearly idolize either history or culture.

Not so opposed to attempts at "universal concepts" and "universal history" as was Croce, Ortega recognized that philosophical thinking and historical thinking are two different kinds and levels of operation—generalizing or universalizing in the one case and concrete and individual in the other. These two levels were to be combined in a new kind of conceptualization, which metahistory or historiology exemplified but which was only an unrealized aspiration in Croce. For Ortega "supra-historical" concepts were a legitimate "transcendence" in history; for Croce, despite his idealism and reifying of spiritual forces, they were apparently not deemed quite legitimate. Where the one reduced philosophy merely to historical *methodology*, the other put an *ontological* emphasis into historiology, in preference to methodology per se (4:539).[38]

Whereas both agreed that the viewpoint and interests of the present impose themselves in all history, Croce strained credibility with his play on words: that "all history is contemporary history" and that all else is "dead history." Paradoxically, Ortega was not the paralyzed captive of the historical past that Croce was recognized to be, but he regarded past, present, and future as a continuum and planned for the future as not *just* the consequence of the past and present but as present free choice informed by the past. He could not accept Croce's view that knowledge of the past is useless for present or future action.[39] "Progress" was still a valid, living "belief" for Croce, regardless of

---

who says that Croce, taking philosophy not as ontology but as methodology, "philosophizes as a historian and he writes history as a philosopher." Ortega likewise came to reject ontology, but he replaced it with a metahistory that (by historiology) served as a new ontology. See Gian N. G. Orsini, *Benedetto Croce, Philosopher of Art and Literary Critic* (Carbondale: Southern Illinois University Press, 1961), 178, for his denunciation (between 1930 and 1933) of contemporary irrationalism, as in fascism, which Ortega denounced a decade earlier; and his religious crisis before taking up philosophy as another faith (294). Ortega was almost certainly indebted to Croce's *Vico* for some ideas in "Historiology" (1928).

38. See Croce, *Theory and History of History*, trans. D. Ainslie (London: Harrap, 1921), on theory and methodology, or *Philosophy, Poetry, History*, 497–624 (ten parts).

39. Croce, "History, Chronicle, Pseudo-History" (1937), *Philosophy, Poetry, History*, 498, 503.

cases of historical "recurrence" (such as classical and renaissance); Ortega was much more skeptical about it all.

Both, of course, were liberal in preference and values, although Ortega was more measured, concrete, and historical in his response to liberalism. More than Croce, his conservative instincts did *not* let him—even briefly—embrace the omnicompetent nation or state as the remedy for impending chaos or anarchy.

Finally, of course, Ortega could never agree with Croce that "philosophy and history coincide and are identical."[40] However close he came to doing so, the nuances and reservations were crucial differences. When he affirmed the "pure historicity of the concept of 'being,'" and "with it the radical historicity of everything human" (R 80), he seemed not far removed from Croce's "absolute historicism." Reason too was historical for Ortega, and so was philosophy. But that was *not identity*.

As Michael Ermarth denied Ernst Troeltsch's claim that Dilthey represented "pure historicism" at its fullest, so must we reject that identification, with its imputation of "pure relativism," for Ortega. By reserving "truth" (as suprahuman), like Scheler, his was not, finally, a "pure" but a *limited* historicism, more like Dilthey's. If he owed much to Croce for details, his historicism should better be called "radical" (as by Morón Arroyo) than "absolute" or "pure."

"TRANSCENDENTAL HISTORICISM": DILTHEY

If Croce's "absolute" historicism was too extreme for Ortega, Dilthey's muted and unconscious historicism was more to his liking. Strangely, although the first linkage between his historicism and Dilthey's was made by Iriarte, Nicol, and Gaos more than a generation ago, there have been since then no careful and impartial investigations, either intensive or extensive, of their common ground and essential differences in this respect. Although some (such as Walgrave, Guy, and Ouimette) expounded Ortega's "historical reason" in meaning or application, they refrained from making obvious connections with both historicism and Dilthey, and others who have asserted such have done so without adequate demonstration. In one of the better earlier analyses of Dilthey, Raymond Aron did not connect him with Ortega in any way, but he knew the latter held similar ideas.[41]

---

40. Croce, "Vico" (1910), *Philosophy, Poetry, History,* claimed that Vico had identified thought with being and (like Ortega) traced it on to Kant (138), but Croce went further in identifying history with philosophy in 1939 (29) and 1945 (10–11).

41. Raymond Aron, *La Philosophie critique de l'histoire,* 2d ed. (Paris: J. Vrin, 1950). An often-cited passage on p. 25 is not what it has been said to be: Aron did not say that Dilthey

Perhaps the lack of international consensus about just what *was* Dilthey's philosophy—and Ortega's too—has discouraged comparison, but some very worthy scholarship (since the 1960s) on Dilthey, as well as the many special studies on Ortega, now make this possible. With both Dilthey and Ortega, the very diversity of their thought has tended to impede generalizations about the nature of their philosophies as a whole and to draw attention to the more specific concepts, methods, and parts, such as hermeneutics, world-views, phenomenology, aesthetics, or politics. Nevertheless, several scholars, such as Tuttle in 1969, Makkreel in 1975, and especially Ermarth in 1978, have refined the looser attributions of historicism made till now in respect to Dilthey. While only Plantinga (1980) gave any thought to comparing Dilthey with Ortega, he has done so by minimizing historicism again in favor of "life philosophy," just the reverse of Ermarth. Those studies, however, lend a solid basis for fruitful comparative examination of their respective historicisms, as has Ilse Bulhof (1980), although her emphasis (like Makkreel's), was less on historical reason as historicism than on hermeneutics as the new interdisciplinary epistemology, which in Ortega's case was more specifically a metahistorical historiology.[42]

Critics of Dilthey's Historicism

Makkreel's case for Dilthey's historicism as a clear *part* of his total philosophy was limited to distinguishing it from other historicisms and to affirming that (perhaps thanks to Husserl's accusations) Dilthey recognized in the historicism he denied a real danger of relativism or skepticism. Moreover, Ranke's merely historical historicism was in itself too purely empirical for Dilthey. In contrast, noted Makkreel, the historicism of "historical idealists," Croce and Collingwood, was later to exemplify the opposite (theoretical) excess coming out of Hegelian historicism. Herder's romantic historicism,

---

did not make "a critique of historical reason but a historical critique of reason" (cf. Rudolph A. Makkreel, *Dilthey, Philosopher of the Human Studies* [Princeton: Princeton University Press, 1975], 244, on Aron's criticism). In his middle years, explained Aron, Dilthey was trying to complete Kant's idea of a critique of the knowledge we derive from the historical world—even as Ortega said of Dilthey (6:195–96). Where Ortega differed was by definitely attempting to do *both* things. Also see some older studies in Calvin G. Rand, "Two Meanings of Historicism in the Writings of Dilthey, Troeltsch, and Meinecke," *Journal of the History of Ideas* 25 (October–December 1964): 503–18; Hajo Holborn, "Dilthey and the Critique of Historical Reason," *Journal of the History of Ideas* 11 (January 1950): 94–110.

42. The newer crop of U.S. studies on Dilthey includes Howard N. Tuttle, *Wilhelm Dilthey's Philosophy of Historical Understanding* (Leiden: E. J. Brill, 1969); Makkreel, *Dilthey;* Ermarth, *Critique;* Hans P. Rickman, *Pioneer of the Human Studies* (London: Elek, 1979); and Ilse N. Bulhof, *Wilhelm Dilthey: A Hermeneutic Approach to the Study of History and Culture* (The Hague: Martinus Nijhoff, 1980).

with its emphasis on the *Zeitgeist* and *Volkgeist* of individual nations, seemed to Dilthey to be in need of the check and contrast of "universal history." Seeking to claim the virtues and to avoid the vices of these several types of historicism, Dilthey replied to Husserl that he did not limit himself to the factual, concrete, and individual emphasis of history but insisted also on the analysis, theory, and universals of philosophy. He recognized, says Makkreel, that historicism ends in relativism, unless a new "epistemological grounding" were provided—meaning, it seems, that hermeneutics replaced the old metaphysics and logic, which his own "worldview philosophy" had shown to be historically relative instead of absolute.[43]

Ermarth goes much further than Makkreel in identifying the new kind of historicism that Dilthey represented, one which was *not,* he emphasizes, the "pure historicism" seen by Troeltsch, nor the historizing but non-historical existentialism or allied structuralism alleged by later critics. Historicism is seen as an inexact and overloaded term, impossible to define briefly, so as to embrace all its variations. Nevertheless, the repeated linking of Dilthey to historicism cannot be rejected as wholly erroneous; the problem is to distinguish types. "If historicism has come to mean an all-encompassing relativism, an interest in the past [solely] for its own sake, or the belief in some overarching meaning or direction in history, then Dilthey cannot be accounted an historicist"—nor if it means a commitment only to the individual and the unique in genetic development. He always "insisted on the importance of generalizing, typifying, and comparative methods," as well as "circulation" among the "human sciences," or "historical science beyond [current] historicism." Unlike the optimistic and quietist historicists of his era, he reacted to the incipient cultural crisis with a commitment to action and resolution, which did not separate understanding from doing. Although he made no explicit comparison with Croce, Ermarth stresses that Dilthey did not "deify" history nor see it as an extension of religion nor as a metaphysics by another means. Neither was his "historicity" that of the existentialists, whose "a-historical *Existenz*" amounted to the "neglect of history."[44]

After distinguishing Dilthey from the other historicists, Ermarth finally calls his mode of thinking a "transcendental historicism," by which he means that history is the "primary perspective" on man and the basis of his "possibilities of self-realization," which point to something further that is *transcendental* or "transhistorical," absolute and eternal in man. This supratemporal aspect was not a metaphysical a priori, nor a phenomenological

43. Makkreel, *Dilthey,* 4–5, 18, 29, 53, 273–79.
44. Ermarth, *Critique,* 15–19, 207, 352–53, 356–57. "The reciprocity of philosophy and history and the 'circulation' of the human sciences as a whole precludes any 'pure' historicism" in Dilthey, who aimed at a "'historical science beyond' historicism" (353). The same can be said of Ortega.

fixed "essence," but a capacity for human creativity—especially through the mind—ever surpassing itself, that is, an "open" nature. (This is the feature of human historicity—"man has no nature, but instead he has . . . a history"— that Plantinga thinks Ortega thus expressed better than Dilthey.) Beyond this element of striving and freedom, which was rooted in historical experience and knowledge, Ermarth did not define Dilthey's "transcendental historicism." But, if that name goes "beyond Dilthey's own terms, his phrase 'history with philosophical intent' amounts to the same thing." So, if "transcendental" here refers not to a Hegelian or Kantian idealism but to man always transcending himself in history, then surely Dilthey's *Idealismus-Realismus* anticipated Ortega's conceptual realism.[45]

In the most historically oriented of the newer studies, Ilse Bulhof's *Dilthey* seemed *almost* to deny Ermarth's equation of historical reason with historicism, but in fact she affirmed it. In 1859–1860—which corresponds to Ortega's idea of the crucial twenty-sixth year—Dilthey's student journal recorded his gradual discovery of his intellectual mission: the combination of philosophy and history to get a "new kind of history" (and of philosophy)— an intent, incidentally, that Ortega echoed in "What Is Philosophy?" (1930). Such a goal would require a new critique of reason, with his life's goal being "to understand the importance of religious life," both traditionally as in history and secularized as at present—not as dogma but as feeling, *believing* life.

Formulated finally as a religious, historical, and philosophical worldview for his time, Dilthey's purpose led him through a diversity of efforts to the end of his life. Of his two most notable works, *Introduction to the Human Sciences* (1883) was aimed against both positivism and the old historicism and promised a second volume later on the "critique of historical reason." Ortega thought that thirty years were not enough to finish the latter because it was so much ahead of its time in regard to concepts and terminology (7:59–61). The latter project proved so difficult that he could finally more or less realize it

---

45. Plantinga, *Historical Understanding in Dilthey*, 14–16, definitely downgraded even "philosophy of history" in him in preference for "philosophy of life" (chap. 4) as Dilthey's intended "point of departure" for philosophy, just as Ortega had discerned it. Such "*Lebensphilosophie*" (in common with Jaspers, Ortega, and others) had "resurfaced" in existentialism, despite Heidegger's dislike of the term as too vague and redundant (70–73). Ermarth, in contrast, disagreed (351), apparently because of the "irrationalist" connotations linked to *Lebensphilosophie*, which (more than Ortega) he strictly limited. Others who utilized Ortega as a basis for understanding Dilthey included Gerhard Masur, "Wilhelm Dilthey and the History of Ideas," *Journal of the History of Ideas* 13 (January 1952): 94–107 (97 on Ortega's parallels); Holborn, "Dilthey and the Critique of Historical Reason," had three references to Ortega's essay (93, 96, 100) and resembled his interpretation in several respects (114–16), as by making his critique subordinate to (within) his philosophy of life. Ermarth, *Critique*, 333, 344, 355, 366; he pointed out that the name "transcendental historicism" was first assigned to Dilthey in 1928 by Ludwig Landgrebe.

only in *The Types of World View* (1911), which Bulhof regarded as his long-promised "meta-philosophy," or a "philosophy of history" that was the fruit of his hermeneutical approach. Thus, hermeneutics as dialogue between interpreter and text (reality) is tantamount to "historical reason" ending in a "structure" of worldviews. Editors have pieced together a volume two on historical reason out of a mass of fragments put into the seventh volume of his works.[46]

Husserl's attack on worldviews in 1911 as "historicism" (relativism in truth and values) and Dilthey's denial and claim to have overcome historicism need some explanation. Bulhof noted that in opposition to the negative effects of the contemporary historicism of historians—as historical relativism or as "idolatry of history"—Dilthey's "hermeneutic philosophy of worldviews [represented] historicism's positive aspect," by which she meant its tolerant and "affirmative attitude toward past and present cultures" and corresponding worldviews. So Dilthey's hermeneutical method and worldview typology were an outgrowth of his lifelong quest for a historical reason to restore reason (mind) to the sovereignty over life and history that it had lost with the defeat of the old metaphysical philosophy by "historical consciousness" during the nineteenth century. Historical reason itself was a new kind of "positive" historicism. Nevertheless, Dilthey refused to recognize the intrinsic or the permanent superiority of any one type of worldview, but he preferred "objective idealism."[47]

Thus, we end with an "anarchy" of worldview systems, as Dilthey twice acknowledged (1905, 1911). Interested in worldviews since 1906 (1:46) and in Dilthey's *Weltanschauung* (12:392) in 1916, as part of his own "system," Ortega later reduced that anarchy to order by definitely historizing the worldviews as *successive* "beliefs," including historical reason itself as a *new* type. In fact he defined historical reason in itself as a kind of "sequential" understanding of things (R 37). And, in contrast to the existentialists' pessimistic view of life in crisis, he saw a "positive" role for historical reason in the resolution of historical crises.

Ortega's Historicism Compared to Dilthey's

Although recent investigations of Dilthey's "Critique of Historical Reason" as historicism are very helpful, the other half of the equation—the

---

46. Bulhof, *Dilthey*, 31–32, stated that the second volume was not written because of conflict with Rickert and Windelband, but it resulted finally (via hermeneutics) in worldview types. See Bernard Groethuysen, preface (1926) to Dilthey's *Gesammelte Schriften*, vol. 7, *Dei Aufbau der Geschichtlichen Welt in den Geisteswissenschaften*, 2d ed. (Stuttgart: Leubner, 1958), vi, where he called this volume "Kritik der historischen Vernunft," being what Dilthey had promised in 1883.

47. Bulhof, *Dilthey*, 30 (cf. 92–95, 195, on historicism), 101 (anarchy of worldviews).

comparison of Ortega and Dilthey—still remains to be done.[48] How close were the two in historical thought? What elements relate to a common historicism? How independent and original was Ortega? Did he go "beyond" Dilthey enough to justify calling his own a distinct kind of historicism? These problems are not easy to answer, although Ortega left us a great deal of analysis and opinion on Dilthey, some of which (his notes) are often critical and show important differences.

When Ortega denied studying Dilthey's *philosophical* works before 1929, he did not mean that he had read nothing of his *historical* works until then. Perhaps he did peruse *Schleimacher* (1870), or *Das Erlebnis und die Dichtung* (1905) while he studied in Germany after 1906 (6:171). If he did not read the *Einleitung* (1883) then, he could have read it in 1923 when it reappeared in his collected works, and he had accepted "worldview" by 1916. Like Nicol and Rabade, I suspect that he had read the *Einleitung* before he began to publish on historical reason in 1924.[49] That expression originated there with Dilthey, whom he regarded as the philosopher with the greatest "historical sensibility" (9:603). Undoubtedly Dilthey influenced his thought on "historical consciousness," "historical reason," and even "historiology" from 1924 to 1928.

History, Historicity, and Historicism

Where Ortega derived the greatest encouragement and help from Dilthey was not for a traditionally "philosophical" thing, even an "ontology of life" as the basic reality. It was for his historical thought, especially for having emphasized the *historicity* of human life as the basic feature of his so-called transcendental historicism. If not necessarily for the actual word,[50] he credited Dilthey with giving us the formal *concept* of "historicity," or "reality as historicity" (6:396–97). "To denote this character of our reality," meaning that the past is active in and beyond the present, "we have no other word than 'historicity'" (6:394). " . . . More radically than his predecessors—Hegel or Comte—he taught us to see historicity as the character constitutive of the human being" (9:396). For Dilthey, "man is relativity, historicity" (6:196). Historicity (*Geschichtlichkeit*) in Dilthey "means simply relativity" (R 40).

Although Ortega had oriented his thought to history for almost three

48. As stated earlier, almost nothing comparing Ortega's historicism with Dilthey's, beyond mere relation or contrast, has been done (see supplemental notes 12 and 13, chap. 7). Hence, what follows in the text will have to stand on its own as a first serious effort. For Ortega's possession of Dilthey's essential works, such as *Introduction to the Human Sciences* (1883), see appropriate notes in the next chapter on contents of his library in Madrid.

49. Ermarth, *Critique*, 351. Rabade Romeo, *Ortega filósofo*, 25: at first Ortega absorbed Dilthey by "osmosis," instead of by direct study. For works on Dilthey in Spanish possibly available to Ortega, see Garagorri, "Ni relativismo ni absolutismo."

50. Dilthey, "The Dream" (1893), in *Philosophy of History*, ed. Meyerhoff, 43: "What man is, only his history tells."

decades, he found Dilthey's idea of historicity most helpful in thinking through various historical problems of human existence. He had not used the term "historicity" before, but now he extended it to everything human, not excepting even man's very existence, "being," or life, in a more radical way than either Dilthey or Heidegger (6:196). At the end, he affirmed "the pure historicity of the concept of 'being' and with it *in nuce* the radical historicity of everything human" (R 80). Thus he applied the test of historicity to the temporal origins of "historical consciousness," where he both praised and criticized Dilthey's view of the eighteenth century's introductory role (6:180; 9:648), for it had come to an "optic of historifying," but it still kept "naturalism" and "antihistorism." He disagreed more pointedly about the origins of philosophy itself, where he found Dilthey myopic (8:221). "Nearly all of history, and almost all men are not philosophical." "The case is he did not historize the fact [of] philosophy, religion, poetry, etc." (R 40). His "capital and ahistorical error" was in failing to make his three types of worldviews definitely successive in history, if not repetitive (8:313; 9:397).[51] He therefore historized Dilthey's worldviews, even as he did with "being," "reason," and philosophy itself (5:404–6; 6:206; 8:286). His notes were definitely more critical of "Dilthey's *un*historicity" in matters of philosophy (R 40).

Ortega later criticized Dilthey too for not having discarded completely the idea of a human "nature" (6:197), so as "to think of human reality as something historical on the run" (8:286). As he said in "History as a System," "man's authentic 'being'" is commensurate with his whole past, with "what has happened to him, [and with] what he has done" (6:41). "In short, *man has no nature, but instead he has . . . history.*" Several times in earlier notes he argued not nature but history. Man *is* not but *lives* (R 76). He is forever "migrating," always moving, in his "being." In a variation of his lectures called "On Historical Reason" (1940), he insisted in chapter 1 that, since man is not being but history, philosophy must drop the use of such terms as "being" and "substance." Later he stressed that "the method for understanding human life, which is the radical reality, is not pure reason but historical reason, the ultra-Eleatic reason" (R 80). Historical reason puts man "anew into tremendous contact with a transcendent reality—that of his destiny" (R 79). "But man does not *have* a being—a fixed and determinate consistency, [for he] . . . is only what happens to him. His essence is precisely his incessant dramatism, forever a peripeteia that for that reason cannot be defined but only told"—by narrative, historical reason, as he had said in "History as a System."

More basically than himself, in Ortega's view, Dilthey as a philosopher was also a *historian*. Emphasizing the predominantly historical side of Dilthey's

---

51. Makkreel, *Dilthey,* 347, sees no "developmental sequence" nor hierarchy of his worldviews.

thought, which he related to the positivistic historicism of the "generation of 1850" (6:183–84, compare 4:525n), was as close as he came to identifying him publicly with historicism, although he did so privately (R 80). Later he claimed that Dilthey had stated his lifelong program as historical already in his *On the Study of the History of the Sciences of Man, Society, and the State* (1875) (7:65). His exposition of Dilthey in 1934, therefore, was presented not as a philosophical investigation but as a study in the "history of ideas" (6:167). "The historical studies of Dilthey are, perhaps, the best ever written in history [but only] . . . for him who possesses the secret of his thought" (6:171).

That "secret," Dilthey's "fundamental idea," was threefold: not just "life" but "historical consciousness," therefore "historicity" of human life, therefore implying a historical "science of the human," or a "basic discipline" as the ultimate concern of philosophy (6:196–97). All of that was not just philosophy of life but philosophy of history—in a new and special sense. Beyond philosophy, historicism (both Dilthey's and Ortega's) concerned history and the other "human sciences."

"Historical reason" applied to the *history* of the human sciences, as in Dilthey's *Einleitung* (1883), interested Ortega much less than his ever-promised "basic discipline," or "fundamental science," relating to all of them. Dilthey had turned from associationist psychology as the "science of fundamentals" for all the sciences to a more intimate self-analysis (*Selbstbesinnung*, or "autognosis") that resembled a "vital" reason but also included history and "historical consciousness" as the "authentic philosophy" of the human whole, or a "philosophy of life" (6:205, 208). The composite vaguely anticipated Ortega's vital and historical reason. For Dilthey, however, his basic discipline finally meant chiefly a hermeneutic, ending in a worldview typology. For Ortega, who was more committed to "system" than was Dilthey (R 80), it was to be a "metahistory," or "historiology," of human "forms" and processes extending from the past into the present and the future. He thought of historiology as historical reason's systematic, vitalistic alternative to the "mechanics" of "physical reason," the "model of knowing" for the old historicism (4:184, 193–94).

Holism and History

"History is a system . . . of human experiences linked in a single, inexorable chain. Hence, nothing can be truly clear in history until everything is clear" (6:43). By this exacting universalist (but plainly impossible) proposition, Ortega meant only that we cannot understand a modern European "rationalist," without first knowing what the medieval Christian and the ancient Stoic were, for example (5:151–52; 6:43). We need to know something about our *whole* historical past in its successive types of man and of world-view, or "belief"—at least of a given spatial-cultural context, or civilization, like Europe.

This broad and general understanding of man's past is the task of historical reason, an "epistemology" that was rooted in man's total nature as "historicity" (6:186, 196). Having studied him long and deeply, Ortega complained that Dilthey, despite all his "historical thinking, never came to adequate possession of historical reason" (8:268), for he excluded philosophy itself from the principle of historicity. More "radical" in historicism, Ortega excluded nothing human from historicity.

Dilthey was a main source for that ideal of "totality" that, in principle at least, has countered during this century the fractious tendency of historical specialization. Such a universalist ideal, which Popper criticized as historicist "holism," Ortega shared with Dilthey (8:32)—and with James—in regard to understanding the part only in relation to the whole, and vice versa. Neither naively believed in the possibility of knowing all facts of history, or truly "universal history." For them, the *relative* "whole" took several forms: (1) the predominant worldview, or social "belief," such as the Enlightenment, positivism, or their own "great Idea of life," as "connecting" and informing all things human at a given time (5:401–3; 6:200–202); (2) the interdisciplinary dream of integrating the "human sciences" through a "basic discipline" (7:11–13); and, finally, (3) general concepts taken as schematic models for systematic use as "constants" in historical interpretation (6:44n). Dilthey's basic discipline became a "meta-philosophy" of worldviews[52] while Ortega's was metahistorical historiology.

On Reason in Life and History and as "Transcendent"

"The idea of *vital reason* represents, in the problem of life, a higher level than the idea of *historical reason,* where Dilthey ended. This book means to demonstrate it minutely" (6:175). Regrettably, Ortega never finished his book on Dilthey, so the comparison is not easy to understand. In his notes, however, with reference to Dilthey's "Critique of Historical Reason," he advised (R 40): "in order to see how limited this idea is compared to vital reason, see the meaning of the former in [Dilthey's] 8: 264."[53] In that context Ortega stressed Dilthey's lack of radicalism, his uncertainty that life is the radical reality, for his "psychologism" placed living or being only in the conscious-

52. Popper, *Poverty of Historicism,* 17–19, seems to reject a historical notion of structure as related to holism. On Dilthey's holism, see Ermarth, *Critique,* 239; and Dilthey, *Selected Writings,* ed. H. P. Rickman (Cambridge: Harvard University Press, 1976), 244, on "the whole" and its parts relative to history. James had a similar idea of a whole of parts (see my chap. 4). Bulhof, *Dilthey,* 80, 89–91 (related to Dilthey's *Gesammelte Schriften,* 8:206).

53. Dilthey, *Weltanschauungslehre,* in *Gesammelte Schriften,* 8:264.

ness. His idealism left living (present or past) only things of the mind, of thought, or consciousness.

Ortega's stress on reason *in* history and on the *rational* character of historical thinking, even as simple narrative, seems to exceed Dilthey's position on these polar principles of the new historicism. Ortega himself was not entirely clear and unequivocal on the difference, however. In unpublished notes (R 40), he first characterized Dilthey's idea of historical reason as counter to the naturalistic reason of mathematics, physics, and biology. But then he saw it as a "Cartesian reason" that was rooted in "intellectualism" and Kantianism—yet it was "pure, 'scientific,' and naturalist" reason at the same time. It is hard to see how he could have it both ways at once, but again he said that Dilthey's "'historical reason' is pure . . . empirical reason." Nevertheless, he finally summed it up this way:

> What Dilthey calls "historical reason" differs radically from what I denote with this expression. For Dilthey deals only with the mode of knowledge that historical science exercises compared to what physical science uses. Hence, historical reason is opposed simply to naturalistic reason and it is only the particular method of a particular science. But whoever thinks like I that radical reality is historical understands by "historical reason" the only, whole and universal reason—of which every other form of reason is only part, derivative, and abstraction. (R 40)

In short, Ortega took "historical reason" not just as that kind employed by historians but as a new general, *philosophical* conception that embraced it and "pure" and scientific reason.

In his view, every type of reason has been historical—as human, as a response to the pressures of life (the radical reality) at a certain time and place. Dilthey's historical reason, though it analyzed reason in the purely "empirical" historians, was, at bottom, also idealist—like Collingwood's. Ortega's historical reason was not only more realist but was intended to be comprehensive too. For him, all human thinking (even the primitive hunter's) was "reason" (not just the Greek's logic nor the modern's mathematized science) and as such was "historical." In addition, he also defended, however, a special mode and method of historical reason for historians and for all who deal with particular "human sciences." And here, too, he went beyond Dilthey, and beyond mere narration and cause-and-effect history, notably with metahistory (concepts) and historiology (working models).

Therefore, the difference between historical reason in Dilthey and in Ortega was not *mainly* one of degree in regard to rationality (for example, "ratio-historicism"). It was a question of comprehensiveness of reason and how it straddled the dichotomy of idealism and realism, or rationality in what and at which level. Actually, Dilthey's *Idealismus-Realismus* was like Ortega's "realism-idealism," in that both were conceived as worldviews combining subjective and objective, ideal and real, which for the former was "objective idealism."[54]

We can more easily distinguish Ortega's historicism from Dilthey's "transcendental" historicism by contrasting the greater realism of the one with the greater idealism of the other. When Ortega adverted to history as a "science," his "supra-historical" models (3:313) had what he called a "transcendent" character but were more realist than Dilthey's "transcendental" forms, if the latter means "idealist."[55] Ortega's metahistorical "forms," "schemas," or "models" that were to give structure, "system," and meaning to the history of events were not—in his notion of historiography as a "science"—extrinsic, ideal, and "absolute" like the concepts of the old rationalism. True, they were derived (abstracted) by the human mind, yet not out of itself as "consciousness" but out of history, out of "things" (facts) that "transcended" the self (3:166). As conceptual constructs, they were *not* of the same order as external, concrete facts and events, although they were rooted in them and were manifested in them and in human life, both present and historical. Since life varied in time and place, they were both "supra-historical," or "constant," and "variable" at once, for they moved and changed, appeared, disappeared, and reappeared with modifications.

When speaking of either vital reason or historical reason, Ortega had shown that (for him) "transcendent" referred to a reality (the world-circumstance) that was partly external to individual man, that thus "transcended" the self (or being).[56] But since he was in constant relation to it and dependent on it, he was nevertheless a *part* of that reality. Particularly through intellectual operations, however, he reached beyond "things" of the encompassing organic world to a "transvital order" of a cultural kind (3:165–66). Conversely, what happened in history was revealed by historical reason to be "a reality transcending man's theories and that is his [past and collective] self underlying his theories" (6:49). There are, therefore, dual (even opposite) meanings of "transcendent" in Ortega: theory transcending the factual world, and real world (with self as a part of it) both preceding and "transcending" any theories. Thus, any implication of conceptual idealism is immediately countered (or balanced) by a "radical" realism. If Ortega's historicism were to be called "transcendental" like Dilthey's, that dual aspect would make the latter's *Idealismus-Realismus* almost equivalent to James's

54. Bulhof, *Dilthey*, 192.

55. On "transcendence" in Ortega, see Arturo García Astrada, "Transcendencia y realidad en el pensar de Ortega y Gasset," *Sur*, no. 353 (July–December 1983): 41–48; Joseph Moreau, "Extériorité et transcendance," *Teoresi* 28 (January–June 1973): 3–23; and Miguel Oltra, "La transcendencia de la vida en la filosofía de la razón vital," *Verdad y Vida*, no. 5 (1947): 337–48.

56. Compare with Plantinga, *Historical Understanding in Dilthey*, 152–53.

"radical empiricism," as Ortega made it (6:190). But James and Dilthey were not exchangeable.[57]

Thus, to relate Ortega's historicism closely with Dilthey's is clearly not to identify it as entirely of that type. Coming later, Ortega thought he had gone "beyond" him, in both theory and practice. Dilthey (like Croce) came to historicism mainly from history (if not so radically), but Ortega approached it more from philosophy. Nevertheless, they *started* from much the same principle and purpose, but they diverged in *development*. By his own judgment, Ortega was more of a realist, more of a rationalist about both life and history, and finally more of a historicist by historizing almost everything: not only man and life but reason and the origins of philosophy and types of worldview too. In 1938, for instance, he remarked: "It would be a residue of 'naturalism' and infidelity to the radical historization of every concept such as my system defends, if we were to regard as until now all have—Dilthey included—considered poetry: as a permanent possibility for man" (compare 5:404; 8:313). He attributed to any flourishing of poetry, as also to related worldviews, a cyclic recurrence and dominance—historized.

"EXISTENTIAL HISTORICISM": HEIDEGGER, JASPERS, SARTRE

To refine the definition of Ortega's historicism further, beyond Dilthey, in relation to yet another kind of historicism that accepted life as basic and as somewhat historical is to link it with existentialism. Meyerhoff and Stern called it an "existential historicism," which has also been suggested for Dilthey.[58] Here "existence" must be taken as equivalent to "life," however— a proposition that Ortega sometimes denied but at other times admitted (for example, 12:192). Even more than in comparison with Dilthey, we shall see that he was a more radical historizer and "rationalist" than Heidegger and Sartre and more adept than they or Jaspers in historical application.

One of the most persuasive analyses of the historicism in Ortega was that by Stern in 1962. Without reference to Dilthey, he placed Ortega with the existentialists, with Heidegger and especially Sartre, whom others too have seen as "existential historicists." In Stern's view, however, the Spaniard was

57. Actually some of the terminology that Ortega had found first in James (as "intellectualism" rejected) he did indeed later discover also in Dilthey. See Ermarth, *Critique,* 350; if Dilthey's *Empirik* (253) was not "radical empiricism" or "radical positivism," he did refer to a "new" critical brand of positivism (329). Also see Dilthey, "Übersicht meines Systems," in *Gesammelte Schriften,* 8:264, "Intellektualismus."

58. Stern, *Search for Meaning,* 271: "Thus, to the extent that he was an historicist, Ortega was also, willy-nilly, an existentialist"; idem, *Philosophy of History,* 174–76. Ermarth, *Critique,* 356–57.

much earlier, more fully, and more consciously a historicist than the other two.[59] Were the differences owing to his closer kinship with Dilthey and maybe also with Scheler, so that he was something more, less, or other than an *existential* historicist? There were still other "variables" in his "ratio"-historicism, of course, including influences from Croce, James, and Husserl.

To both existentialism and historicism, Stern preferred "essentialism," which he detected in Ortega, who had finally preferred James's "consistency" to Husserl's "essence" (4:510; 5:531). Logically such phenomenological concern with something stable should have "limited" the relativism of any alleged "pure historicism." The current form of contemporary historicism was, in Stern's view, existentialist. "Historicism reappears in Existentialism," because "existence" (in contrast to classical "nature" or "essence" of "man in general") deals of necessity with the "here and now" of specific space and time, or "world." "Thus, Historicism appears to be an unavoidable consequence of radical Existentialism"—at least implicitly, even in Sartre.[60]

According to Stern, existential historicism in Ortega, Heidegger, and Sartre had its logical starting point in the historicity (or "mutability") of man, which Heidegger had expressed as "being-in-the-world" and Ortega by the dictum that man has "no nature" but a history instead. Possibly Ortega first encountered Dilthey's term "historicity" in Heidegger and also "concretion" (of time), but (as Gaos noted) one cannot deny that he had stated the ideas of "historical reason" and "historical sense" three years before *Being and Time* was published.[61] The historicity of truth—*veritas filia temporis*—is the second assumption held in common by the three. As a consequence, there are no stable concepts that are fully "supra-historical." For Stern, that relativity was the "core of Historicism," but it was not necessarily the same as *pure* relativism. A third position, which he attributed to Sartre but not to Ortega, was historicity (or relativism) of values. In fact, Ortega did not fully accept the historicity of truth—just its subjective, human perspective.

Those first two principles of existentialist historicism Stern regarded as true and irrefutable *for our times*. But that kind of historicism, he thought, did admit of limits, so that in fact it was not "pure," nor absolute. One of

---

59. Christopher Fynsk, *Heidegger, Thought, Historicity* (Ithaca: Cornell University Press, 1986). Gaos, *Sobre Ortega*, 186, 242, saw Ortega as synthesizing "historicity" from Heidegger's merely theoretical orientation to history with Dilthey's non-ontological type of historicism—largely reflecting Nicol's views, *Historicismo y Existencialismo*, 324–27. Stern, *Philosophy of History*, 174, said Ortega anticipated "some of the positions of Heidegger's Existential Historicism" and also of Sartre's (176), but Ortega's was a "pure Historicism" (175, 177), more radical than Heidegger's but less radical (he thought) than Sartre's.

60. Stern, *Search for Meaning*, 270, 271 ("historicism is also a form of existentialism"); idem, *Philosophy of History*, chap. 6 on historicism; "Historicism reappears in Existentialism" (172) as "an unavoidable consequence of radical Existentialism" (177).

61. Gaos, *Sobre Ortega*, 235; Stern, *Philosophy of History*, 173–74.

these "implicit" limits was the historical human "situation," as Sartre put it, in which all men always and everywhere found themselves existing or living—in love and hate, suffering and death—which were so universal that they could be called transhistorical. Had he looked, Stern could have found this limit also in Ortega's idea of "circumstance," which he had rendered as "situation" in regard to crisis (3:171–72, 193) long before Sartre. However, he found their ideas of liberty similar, as well as Sartre's individual existential "projects" and Ortega's collective "programs" of life as freely realized in the state. But the human freedom to choose, Stern warned, was "always historically, economically, culturally, and socially conditioned" and "limited"—there being no "escape from the prison of history." "We cannot jump out of our time," or "skin."[62]

On the third historicist assumption, the historicity of values, Ortega and Sartre were evidently at odds, the latter accepting an unqualified *moral* relativism, whereas the former agreed with the phenomenologists Scheler and Hartmann that moral values were "absolute, timeless, suprahistorical essences." Although he was himself "essentialist" by conviction, Stern was strangely "diametrically opposed" to Ortega and sided with Sartre on this point. For him, the historical projects of the nation or the state are the very *source* of "codes of values," so that both change in the course of history. But, if that were true for the ancient Hebrews, obviously he would not have granted the legitimacy of such change for Hitler's Germans.

In Stern's rather self-contradictory view, Ortega evinced a "pure historicism"—even though he had said that existential historicism was not "pure," or absolute, and despite obvious inconsistency about values. But Ortega was an existentialist as well, because (like Heidegger and Sartre) he put existence before essence. Since essence for him was not absolute but varied historically, he was an "existentialist historicist." In *History as a System*, Stern claimed, Ortega adopted historicism "freely and consciously," unlike Sartre, who was more radically but only implicitly (unconsciously) historicist. "As a dynamic Heraclitean thinker opposed to Eleaticism, Ortega declares that whoever tries to understand man, this reality *in via*, this eternal pilgrim, must get rid of all stable concepts and learn how to think by virtue of dynamic concepts" that are "a function of historical time."[63] But was that (alone) "pure historicism"?

Stern made it clear that he himself was not trying to refute historicism but only to set *limits* to it,[64] limits that in fact were similar to those adopted by Ortega in 1923 with reference to relativism. To weigh all that he has said about Ortega's historicism against all that he did not say about it is to have to

---

62. Stern, *Search for Meaning*, 258; idem, *Philosophy of History*, 177–81, 185.
63. Stern, *Philosophy of History*, 175–76.
64. Ibid., 178–79, 185.

conclude that Stern was closer to Ortega than he realized, for he himself seemed to be a historicist as well as an "essential" existentialist. Because Stern could not know all of Ortega's works, especially later ones oriented to history, he could not treat of his whole philosophy adequately.

Not only is it true that Ortega accepted the permanence of certain basic experiences within the total life "situation" of men in all times and places and the *ethical* values that would apply to those vital and "transhistorical" experiences, but he also accepted as variable and changing the individual and collective "programs" of *historical* life. In some unpublished reflections, Ortega remarked on "the historical sense as consciousness of the variability of the human type. This supposes some identity. The historical antinomy: the man who is like us is not like us. The understanding of the Other—is a quasi-transmigration" (R 75), comparable to sympathetic "reliving" to a certain extent (9:85). In the 1940s he emphasized that the fact of historicity, or constant change, impermanence, and ending in all things human, "does not mean that there is *nothing* constant in man. Otherwise, we could not speak of man, of human life, of a human being" (9:396).

In his "Metaphysics of Vital Reason" (1933) Ortega had made clear the crucial distinction between changing and perduring elements in man: "We are not concerned here with doing history, with what human life is in one epoch as different from what it is in another. We are dealing, on the contrary, with sketching the permanent structure of human life, with what it always is. In all epochs there functions the system of essential actions in which life consists . . ." (12:88–89). And these acts were not just the homely and humble events of being born and dying, marrying and begetting, sleeping and eating, but others just as structured and occasional but historically more significant. For example, Descartes's life experiences as he recounted them in the *Discourse on Method* struck Ortega as "the essential biography of every intellectual, and, in general, of every man" (12:194). This was true not only in reference to turning points of personal life and thought (like the twenty-sixth or fiftieth to fifty-first year) that Ortega applied to himself, to Dilthey, and to others, but also to the collective experience of and reaction to a situation of historical crisis (12:296–97). These observations were parts of what Ortega called a "General Theory of Life."

Stern closed his eyes to the fact that in *The Revolt of the Masses,* Ortega was dealing not with a "project" and related values of one people or nation-state (where Stern determined to rest his case) but was urging a *supra-national* program (a United States of Europe) for a group of national states that had outlived the viability of their historic national projects and codes. More than Stern, Ortega recognized the *relativity* of *all* collective projects. Where Stern concluded, however, as against the relativism of Max Weber, that we should "recognize that the human project of living is the *a priori* condition of all other projects—and that it is itself transhistorical," which avoids "Historicist nihilism" and skepticism, Ortega would have agreed readily. Likewise, he would have gone along with keeping to the "middle of the road between the extremes of absolutism and the total relativism of an unbridled Historicism."[65] Once again, even in Stern's generally very perceptive analysis of his historicism, the elusive Ortega ended up a straw man of sorts—criticized for a "pure" historicism that he did not hold.

Although Stern slighted Heidegger and ignored Jaspers to concentrate on the *implied* historicism in Sartre, he could have made a better case for either of the earlier existentialists. If Ortega regarded Heidegger as having done very little to *apply* Dilthey's principle of historicity to either philosophy or history, that inconsistency became less true of Heidegger after Ortega's death. Some of Heidegger's belated "historicism" may even have been owing to influence from Ortega's *History as a System* (German, 1943, 1951) or "Origin of Philosophy" (German, 1953). Yet Heidegger's parallel development concluded very differently. It is noteworthy that his later works—one of which was an inverse *Time and Being*—often ended by bringing in history and (or) language, the logical validity of which addenda has been questioned,[66] much as Ortega doubted that Husserl's conversion to history at the end was logical, even if real.

Very like Ortega's, however, was Heidegger's distinction between historiography, as merely "factual" history, and "authentic" (or "actual") history, except that he never came to believe that the latter could be really "discovered" in its true meaning or intent, for example, in regard to "forgotten" *being*. In contrast to Ortega's wide interest in history of all sorts, the only kind or dimension of "history" that ever really exercised Heidegger was the history of philosophy. Even there, where he continued to believe that *Dasein* was historical being, he did not radically historize the concept of being itself in Ortega's fashion. Despite Heidegger's belated interest in historical thinking, as in the Heraclitus Seminar,[67] Ortega was both much earlier and much more authentically historicist.

Existenz in Jaspers intrudes into everything historical as does "life" in Ortega, but one finds there nothing like "historical reason" or "historiology."[68] His whole discussion of history strikes one as much more amateurish

---

65. Ibid., 185–87, 219, 243.

66. Martin Heidegger, *On Time and Being*, trans. Joan Stambaugh (New York: Harper, Row, 1972).

67. Heidegger and Eugen Funk, *Heraklit* Seminar, 1966–1967. It scarcely resembles Ortega's historical approach in any way.

68. Most notable of Karl Jaspers's works in philosophy of history, much later than Ortega's entry into that field, was *The Origin and Goal of History*, first printed in 1949; like Ortega, he stressed the "lack of faith" in traditional values and the rise of ideological

than Ortega's parallel views, both for thought-content and for the opaque, wooden, Germanic style. Jaspers's tortured definition of "historicity" in reference to things historical is a good example of what Ortega called his "lack of technique." At least Jaspers supported "absolute historicity" as "universal" and "supra-rational" as against "irrationality." If at first Ortega savored Curtius's attacks in 1949 on "the confused, abstruse, and diffuse" in Jaspers, he soon protested the belligerence of the critique,[69] for he knew that he had much in common with him in historical thought and orientation.

Since Stern subordinated Ortega's historicism to his existentialism in a later study, where he reversed himself by calling the whole a "historicist existentialism,"[70] we may assume that he finally decided that historicism after all had to modify and to serve life, and not vice versa. The later view is consistent therefore with seeing Ortega's historicism (and existentialism) as subordinate to his general "philosophy of life." Such a conclusion is the end toward which this study has been converging, chapter by chapter.

ORTEGA'S HISTORICISM: REALIST, PRAGMATIST, VITALIST

Was Ortega's later body of thought about "historical reason" sufficiently different and coherent to justify naming it a distinct species of historicism? Did he, for instance, put a greater stress on historical reason? Intentionally he was not only more *historizing* than Dilthey and the existentialists, but as a pragmatist he was more *practical* and *realist* than they or Croce, in all of whom he discerned idealism—and a savor of *ir*rationalism—excepting maybe Jaspers. Besides, he was more *vitalist* with his heavy emphasis on *life* as history. But were these differences finally more of degree than of kind?

"Ratio-historicism" might make more sense by contrast to the age-old antipathy to history by rationalist philosophers. But Ortega was not alone in defending historians' practice as indeed rational in its own way—witness Rickert, Dilthey, Croce, and Collingwood. If he put more emphasis on reason *in* history as events, it was as *in life*. This proviso served to distinguish him from Hegel, and in fact it made of him more *completely* a "rational"

"faiths" offering "salvation." Also see his *The Future of Mankind* (1961). In *Man in the Modern Age,* trans. C. Paul (London: Routledge and Kegan Paul, 1951), Jaspers not only obviously was utilizing Ortega (without acknowledgment) on "Mass Rule" and "mass man" (38–39), but he also mentioned pragmatism as once a hopeful alternative to "traditional idealism" but that proved too crude and optimistic (176). That makes a major difference in their historicisms.

69. Ortega to Curtius, May 31, 1949, on Jaspers, in "Epistolario entre Ortega y Curtius," *Revista de Occidente,* no. 7 (June 1963): 19.

70. Stern, *Search for Meaning,* 271, on Ortega's "historicist existentialism."

historicist than Croce, Dilthey, and existentialists other than Jaspers.[71] Evidently Ortega thought that as idealists they left "reason" in history still external to life. For them, reason covered only a *part* of life—thought and the conscious purpose of the "self" but not all (or most) acts in the world as history. By its degree of difference, therefore, the "ratio-historicism" of Gaos does not define Ortega well. Although it matches "ratiovitalism," it is redundant in meaning.

A distinctive pragmatist cast to Ortega's historicism was evident already in "What Is Philosophy?" (1930), wherein he openly considered pragmatism as well as historicism. Stressing time and place, James had opposed utter relativism, and Ortega too argued against the old positivist historicism: "History's profound assumption is . . . contrary to a radical relativism." We cannot "prescind from both dimensions: the temporal and the eternal. The great philosophical task of the present generation has to be to unite the two [history and philosophy] together, for which I managed to introduce a method . . . with the name of 'perspectivism'" (7:285–86). He combined basic factual realism with a conceptual idealism, as "the theme of our time" (7:388–90, 407–9)—in 1930 even as in 1923, when phenomenology as perspectivism had weighed more with him, for now he reaffirmed his "radical" and "absolute positivism" of 1916 (7:352). That basic pragmatism or "practicism" (7:297, 310) lay within his historicism as the metaphysical basis for a "metahistory."

His "Metaphysics of Vital Reason" (1933) saw philosophy, like life, as basically "what to do" (12:47). Metaphysics, like man himself, is "pure doing" (12:24). In "Leibniz" (1947) his philosophy, vital and historical, implied "always the 'primacy of practical reason'"—clearly not just Kant's—but as the "*science of what to do*" (8:268). His emphasis on *doing* and practicality carried over from his basic pragmatism into his historicism, to make it a uniquely "pragmatist historicism." Even the old "pragmatic history," which he had connected with "historical reason" as "clear example and precursor" (6:431), had a different meaning in Ortega's background than it had for Kant or for Hegel.[72] It implied a *pragmatist* historicism.

71. Angelo de Gennaro, *The Philosophy of Benedetto Croce: An Introduction* (New York: Greenwood, 1968), 47: a "fundamental motif" of Croce's philosophy and conception of history was "the rationality of reality"—in the concrete, but not in the general (as in Dilthey's worldview); see Croce, *Philosophy, Poetry, History,* 1071 (1966), on a "new idea of History" that joins "the real and the rational."

72. Meyerhoff, ed., *Philosophy of History,* 44, might imply existence of a *pragmatic* historicism in Croce, Ortega, Dewey, Becker, Beard, and even Collingwood (also cf. 86— apparently a contradiction). In his *Analytic Philosophy of History* (Cambridge, 1968), chap. 5, Arthur Danto denied that pragmatism could logically apply to history and philosophy of history. Nevertheless, Jacques Barzun held that "Pragmatism did not discard the historical method, far from it . . ." (*Darwin, Marx, and Wagner,* 2d ed. [New York: Doubleday,

It is now possible to summarize the main differences that distinguish Ortega's historicism from his contemporaries and from Dilthey. Where philosopher Karl Popper rejected all kinds of historicism in a lump, both "pronaturalistic" (realist) and "anti-naturalistic" (idealist) types, others have distinguished *historically* several successive kinds: romantic, positivist, relativistic (or humanistic), and existential. The last two types, which cover first Dilthey and Croce and then Heidegger, Jaspers, and Sartre, apparently lay beyond the cognizance of Popper, who identified none of them as historicists—nor Ortega.

The more emphatic vitalism, historicity, realism, and pragmatist practicality for historical usage seen in Ortega's historicism warrant our giving it a distinct, specific name other than "ratio-historicism." These characteristics may not be enough to make it a new species of historicism, but it is at least a very distinct *sub*-species akin to Dilthey's. In Ortega, relativistic historicism would be specified better as "immanent" than as "transcendental." Although he represented a more *radical* historicism finally than did Dilthey or Heidegger, because he was more fully historizing, his type was still not a "pure" or "absolute historicism" of Croce's kind, nor pure "idealist" like Collingwood's. With the phenomenologists, he had reserved some things that were conceptual (notably truth and ethical values) as "absolute," so he imposed *more* limits on relativity in things historically human than other existentialists, notably Sartre. And he balanced conceptual idealism with basic factual realism. Although it is more accurate to call Ortega's "historical reason" at once a pragmatist and realist historicism than simply another existentialist historicism, in fact by its complexity it involved all such aspects.[73] If it is more distinctive, however, to define it by what was muted or lacking in others, then let us call it a *realist, pragmatist, vitalist* historicism. More like Dilthey than the others, he placed his historicism within a covering "philosophy of life"—in a unitary-dualist sense.

1958], 350). Moreover, a pragmatic tradition has continued in historians such as Conkin and Stromberg, *Heritage and Challenge* (1989), both by adscription (88–90) and in the authors themselves (138–41 and 195), who several times cited Ortega (48, 106, 243, 251). On "pragmatic history," which of course is not the same as pragmatist history, see G. W. F. Hegel, *Reason in History: A General Introduction to the Philosophy of History*, trans. R. S. Hartman (Indianapolis: Bobbs-Merrill, 1953), 7–8, who characterized it as reflective, present-minded history.

73. The pragmatism recently detected in Heidegger by Mark Okrent, *Heidegger's Pragmatism* (Ithaca: Cornell University Press, 1988), is not a very prominent or distinguishing feature therein, as compared to Ortega, and, of course, is not historicist. Also see the connection with positivism, via phenomenology, made by P. L. Bourgeois and S. B. Rosenthal, *Mead and Merleau-Ponty* (Albany: SUNY Press, 1991), 1–2.

Chapter 8

UNITY

"General Theory of Life" as Philosophy of Life (1934+)

aving examined in turn the special problems of pragmatism, phenomenology, existentialism, and historicism, for their place in Ortega's thought, we can now venture from analysis of specific parts into *synthetic generalization* about his philosophy as a *whole*. By 1934, Ortega himself was ready to return to a *general* theory of life, which he had abandoned after "Adam in Paradise" (1910) for primarily a personal and national philosophy. For this purpose he now needed a more general name than he had used for his philosophy to date. It also happened that by 1934 he had come to regard his total philosophy as a *philosophy of life,* which, as an aggregate of all of the earlier parts, reduced to a "radical unitary duality" (8:43) that extended from his basic metaphysical principle of life as "radical reality" of self and circumstance on into his two main stages of existentialism and historicism. All of this plurality now seemed to him to have been (or to have become) a "philosophy of life" like Dilthey's (8:46–47), an omnibus name that included not only his first "voyage" of vital reason but also his "second voyage" of historical reason. In his quasi-"autobiographical" study of Dilthey in 1934, he implied that their shared "idea of life" and introspective method amounted to a "philosophy of life" (6:205). Again he implied as much in 1940 and 1944 in his lectures entitled "On Historical Reason" (12:192, 298), where he also referred to a "General Theory of Life" (12:302; compare 9:396, 650). As late as 1951, moreover, he let Merleau-Ponty understand that he still preferred the name "philosophy of life."[1]

Few critics (except Bruno Ibeas in 1935 and Vicente Marrero in 1961) have ever identified Ortega with philosophy of life, although Angel González

---

1. Ortega, in "Troisième entretien privé," 289. Age fifty-one was for synthesis (8:41)

Alvarez in 1956 saw his thought as a "philosophy of life" that attempted to rise above idealism and realism, personalism and relativism. Until 1990, only Otto Böllnow in 1956 and S. I. Levi in 1967 had actually investigated such a philosophy in him, and only Julián Marías, insistent on the sufficiency of vital reason, has ever taken the trouble to deny it—adamantly.[2] For North Americans the gifted Hella Weyl in 1937–1938 affirmed on sound evidence that Ortega's philosophy was then a "philosophy of life," for man *is* "his life," but she then confused the issue by repeating that "Man as man belongs not to nature but to history."[3] Was his position therefore a philosophy of life or a philosophy of history, or somehow both philosophy of life *and* history? That quandary inevitably makes my three final chapters somewhat problematic on the unity and hierarchical structure of Ortega's philosophy.

If Ortega finally acknowledged having a philosophy of life, was it in any way clearly different from his "philosophy of vital reason" (8:46–47)? Is this just another argument over words instead of substance? If there were a "unity of knowing and being," was his philosophy of life about an ontology of life, whereas vital reason was mainly a rational epistemology (or method) for life? If the vital reason of *Modern Theme* were, in a loose sense, a personal philosophy of life for himself in "our time," did Ortega also aim higher, for a *general* philosophy of life, whose conclusions might apply to "each and every one," or to "humanity," anytime in history? Some critics thought so.[4]

2. See supplemental note 2, chap. 8.

3. Helene (Hella) Weyl, "José Ortega y Gasset," *Toronto Quarterly* 6 (1937–1938): 476, 478, 479. Earlier Ortega explained to her his existential position vis-à-vis Heidegger (see chap. 6), so if here she decided that his total position was a philosophy of life, we assume that it was on good authority from Ortega.

4. Clearly there can be no sharp or absolute distinction between philosophy of life as ontology and vital reason as epistemology (or perspectivist method), especially since we have made out vital reason to be also existentialism, in which life (as existence) is obviously involved. As Ortega said in 1930: "Hence, without having a clear understanding of it, every theory of knowledge, against its will, has been an ontology, that is, a doctrine about what is being, for its part, and what is, for its part, thinking (finally a being or particular thing), and thus a comparison between the two" (7:325). Such was his doctrine of "unity of knowing and being." There are, accordingly, no *sharp* lines of division in Ortega's philosophy between its parts and stages (as between vital reason and historical reason), but only aggregate distinctions that apply to vital reason and philosophy of life. Against critics who objected to the historicism in perspectivism, as too personalist, relativist, and limited, Frederick Copleston held that Ortega implied a more "perennial" philosophy, which he was reluctant to call "a metaphilosophy" yet did not call a general philosophy of life either. "If I understand him rightly, Ortega does not deny, for example, that there is a fundamental human situation which recurs in all concrete historic situations, and we can therefore make universal statements, which apply to man and his world in all epochs. In this sense we can get our heads above water. At the same time this fundamental and universal human situation is an abstraction. It never exists as such. We never have man as such, but only primitive man, Greek man, . . . and so on." So, "perspectivism has the last word" ("Ortega and Philosophical Relativism," 182).

As *philosophie de la vie* (or *Lebensphilosophie*), philosophy of life was a turn-of-the-century type in France and Germany that is now largely forgotten or ignored among North American academic philosophers. "Filosofía de la vida" is not even indexed in Ortega's works, although "life" (*vida*) is the most often cited of his many recurring themes, with four columns, compared to three for "history," and two each for "philosophy" and "man." Certainly "life" entered into his philosophy from beginning to end, and into almost everything he wrote. Life was the "root" and center of the multifarious human phenomena that Ortega treated from the beginning: culture, art, technology, reason and truth, ethics and values, history, and world. He began to treat of life "in itself"—ontologically—mainly from the time (about 1929–1930) that he began to read Dilthey for philosophy, for a philosophy of life. However, he found him unsatisfying on what life *is*. Thereafter, perhaps in reaction to Heidegger too,[5] he explicitly affirmed, again and again through twenty-five years of thought, that life (not being) is the "radical reality" and the very basis of philosophy.

Under the broad canopy of *philosophy of life,* as an open "system" or "covering" philosophy, one can bring together in summary fashion the subordinate aspects, themes, parts, levels, and stages of Ortega's thought through over a half-century and thus view it as a comprehensive, developing whole. All of his numerous parallels and sources that have always seemed to be discordant can "fit" under this capacious "cover," which loosely suffices from beginning to end: from Nietzsche, James, Bergson, Unamuno, Husserl, and Scheler, even to Heidegger and Sartre, and to Croce and Dilthey. A "unity in duality" (or plurality), his philosophy of life included his early vitalism, pragmatism, and phenomenology, and it culminated in his mature existentialism and historicism. As with historicism, Dilthey had a great impact on Ortega's mature philosophy of life too, but earlier not only James but Nietzsche, Bergson, and Schlegel were major influences.

Small wonder that no one was able to discern clearly the unitary-dual structure of Ortega's "system" as a philosophy of life comprising existentialism and historicism. Although half a dozen critics before 1955 detected the latter dualism, no one saw the larger unity in a "philosophy of life," except in the narrow, truncated way of Marías or in the idealist sense of Morón Arroyo and Marrero.[6] In works published during Ortega's lifetime, the phrase "phi-

---

5. Citing Orringer (who got it from Morón Arroyo), Armando Savignano attributed to Heidegger's "decisive influence" from 1928 to 1934 Ortega's work on "the ontology of life as biography and history" (historical reason), as related to either existentialism or *Lebensphilosophie* (Savignano, "La Filosofia di J. Ortega y Gasset," *Rivista di filosofia neoscolastica* [Milan] 75 [July–September 1983]: 435).

6. Morón Arroyo, *Sistema,* 216, 218, 238, and chap. 11, for a fuller explanation of Ortega as an "ultra-idealist." Vicente Marrero, *Ortega, filósofo "mondain,"* 248.

losophy of life" appeared only *once,* in 1934 (6:205). Later it seems to have surfaced only twice more in posthumous works till now, as related to Dilthey (again) in 1934 and to Heidegger in 1949 (8:46; 9:86). Also in the "Preface for Germans," however, he presented the idea of *life* as a "radical unitary duality," for the first and only time in *all* of his works (8:43). Did that loose connection of rare and unique expressions have a general function and meaning for Ortega's very complex philosophy?

ORIGINS OF CONCEPTS AND TERMS

By his keen interest in contemporary thought, Ortega was familiar with "philosophy of life" as a general type of philosophy, and his aspiration to unify dualities in life also went back to his beginnings. As he wrote many years later, Dilthey and he had independently "discovered" the "idea of life" in their "26th year"—in 1861 and 1909, respectively (R 40). As we saw, first in "Adam in Paradise" (1910), he had made life basic to his philosophy and tried to unify realism and idealism, although life's duality of "self" and "world" he did not unify as "I and circumstance" until 1914 in *Meditations on Quixote.* By then he had taken note of "Bergsonism" as a "philosophy of life" (or "vitalism") in a lecture in 1912–1913 (R 76), but he was then contemptuous of that equation of "knowing and living" as an *irrational* attempt to "live" problems instead of thinking them. He read a work of 1913 by Scheler (6:330n), wherein he had promised to take up the "philosophy of life," but Ortega judged later that he had not put man or life at the center (12:317).[7]

Although his own philosophy of "vital *reason*" was obviously some kind of philosophy of life, Ortega disliked the irrational aspect in Bergson too much to consider adopting that name for himself in 1910 or 1914. Dilthey, whom he began to read for philosophy in 1929 (6:170), changed his mind. He noted with excitement that Dilthey had given as a title for his long-promised "Critique of Historical Reason" the name "*Philosophie des Lebens*!!!" "Here life is the object of philosophy, where every philosophy is *of* life as subject and agent of it" (R 40).[8]

In "W. Dilthey and the Idea of Life" (1934) Ortega took note (6:173n) of Georg Misch's study of him, *Philosophy of Life and Phenomenology* (1930). Later in the same essay he referred to him as a "philosopher of 'life'" and

7. In 1951, Ortega claimed that Scheler had "not the least idea" that Dilthey was a philosopher, so that his philosophy had no influence on Scheler ("Troisième entretien privé," 289).

8. The reference by Ortega was apparently to Dilthey's *Gesammelte Schriften* vol.5, *Die Gestige Welt: Enleitung in die Philosophie des Lebens,* 2d ed. (Stuttgart: Leubner, 1958). In the introduction by Misch both *Lebensphilosophie* (xxv, xl) and *Philosophie des Lebens* (xxxix) were mentioned.

then identified his "philosophy of awareness," or self-reflection, as parallel to his own "vital reason" and as being "a philosophy of life" (6:200n, 205). With the many "parallels" he detected, more than just the preamble was "autobiographical" (8:175).

Those parallels between Dilthey and Ortega in philosophy of life were immediately reinforced in 1934 in a then-unpublished "Preface for Germans" for a new edition of his *Modern Theme* (1923). There he sought to explain what his "philosophy of vital reason" (8:47) had been in terms of German and European philosophy. He made it clear that "phenomenology was not for us a philosophy" even in 1913 but an "instrument." Despite the similarities, he also rejected "philosophy of existence" as a name (8:42, 46). The only close compatibility he admitted was with Dilthey, whom he praised extravagantly as "the most important philosopher of the second half of the nineteenth century," as having "an authentic philosophy of the highest rank," which he called explicitly a "philosophy of life." And to Dilthey he assigned the "radical tendencies that nourish us today" (8:31–32), meaning himself and his own "generation of 1911."

Was "philosophy of life," therefore, only a more general name for his "philosophy of vital reason," just as he later sought to annex existentialism to philosophy of life (9:85–86)? Or did it stand for a more general, more comprehensive *philosophy*, one that could include history in a more extensive way than did Heidegger: historicism as coequal of existentialism?

Also in the "Preface" he described his own general philosophy as a "radical unitary duality" based in *life* as the "I and its circumstances" (8:43). He saw his system as like a "bi-lobar ginkgo" tree—a tree of life—as a "*one-two*," beginning at its "roots" with a unitary-dual principle of life as reality in self and world. However, he omitted what is now obvious: that by use of phenomenology as method, he had developed his vitalist, dual metaphysical basis of Jamesian "radical empiricism" into two branches, first an existentialism and then a historicism that he then still closely linked as "vital and historical reason" (6:23). All together, they constituted his general philosophy of life. Distinctly "unitary," as compared to either of its two dual parts (even "vital reason"), his philosophy of life as a whole was, for all levels, methods, and stages an umbrella concept that itself may seem to have little specific content.

Despite his intention announced in 1932, Ortega was never ready to publish a synthesis of his general philosophy on life (and history)—not after 1923 as a *Critique of Vital Reason* (4:404n), nor after 1936 as a "systematic" treatise entitled *On Living Reason* on a "*prima philosophia*" (6:38n), nor after 1949, as a collaborative study that he proposed at Aspen, *Experience of Life* (9:574). Possibly he meant his unpublished "Metaphysics of Vital Reason" (1933) to come out under the second title, and the last project could have been a collective *title*, perhaps an anthology of selections from his vitalist works (like *Meditations on Quixote* and *Modern Theme*) and those by others. As it turned out, none of those three putative books on "life" were ever published, and no single extant work can be equated with his "philosophy of life," which itself was a *covering* conception to deal with *overall* purpose, structure, and relationships through a half-century of his philosophizing. However, his "Dilthey and the Idea of Life" (1934), which he meant to make into a "book" both biographical and autobiographical (6:175), was the one most informative study on his own philosophy of life. Notes on which it was to be based are very revealing.

Scattered parts of his works that were intimately related to his "covering" philosophy of life were his theories of life and generations, which linked his philosophizing to turning points, or crises, in the life of "everyone." Thus, as we have seen, the experiences of Ortega's own life were reflected in his philosophy of life, not just by the content of self-analysis (autognosis) that he equated with "philosophy of life" (6:205), but by theoretical connections between the stages, "ages," and "crises" of *personal life* for all, for generations, and for societies. As explanatory, integrating factors, most of those relationships have been neglected. Marías has made a good synthesis of his theory of generations, but only fragments exist of his ever inchoate "General Theory of Life," of which he began to speak from the 1940s (12:302; 9:396, 650).[9] As both individual and social (7:137), it pointed beyond autobiography and biography to history and sociology, but its source was in his philosophy of life. Seeking regularities and pattern, Ortega gave his life to serve "the idea of life."

As a "General Theory of Life," Ortega's philosophy of life included both the more personal and present life of vital reason and the more general historical and social life of historical reason. In fact, most of his later production was given over to the latter, to the social and circumstantial world in its historical dimension, whose scope simply outgrew vital reason.

9. Marías, *El Método histórico de las generaciones* (Madrid: Revista de Occidente, 1949), in English as *Generations: A Historical Method*, trans. Harold Raley (1970). Notable too is Daniel J. Levinson's *Seasons of a Man's Life* (New York: Knopf, 1978), 28–29, 214–15, 323. For other aspects of history of life, also see Manuel García Morente, "Ontología de la vida," *Lecciones preliminares de filosofía* (Buenos Aires: Losada, 1938), 386–403; Juan Roig Gironella, *Filosofía y Vida. Cuatro ensayos sobre actitudes: Nietzsche, Ortega y Gasset, Unamuno y Croce* (Barcelona: Barna, 1946); Sonia Baraldi de Marsal, "Vida, generación e historia en Ortega," *Universidad* (Santa Fe, Argentina), no. 34 (April 1957): 195–209; Borel, *Raison et vie chez Ortega;* Tuttle, "Ortega's Vitalism"; Juan Zaragueta, *Filosofía y vida* (Madrid: Instituto Filosofía de Luis Vives, 1950); Luis Valenciano Gaya, "Configuración de vida humana y psicopatología," *Psicopatología* 2 (April–June 1983): 147–54. Donoso and Raley also list three dissertations on Ortega's idea, theory, or structure of human life, including Ronnie L. Booker, "The Concept of Life in the Philosophy of José Ortega y Gasset" (University of Tennessee, Knoxville, 1979).

STAGES, LEVELS, DIMENSIONS OF
ORTEGA'S PHILOSOPHY OF LIFE

Considering the complexity and subtlety of life, which Dilthey had called a "many-sided" thing (7:553), one could just as well describe Ortega's "philosophy of life" the same way, or perhaps as a "many-layered" thing, a "radical unitary *plurality*." "Philosophical thinking is system, and in a system every concept includes all the others" (6:170). That was true especially of "the great Idea of life." Ortega defined a complex and dynamic idea not just by its first but by its last mature and creative stage, which included compatible positions that were earlier and intermediate in his thinking. In history of philosophy, he maintained, "it is the new ideas, the daughter ideas, that carry their mothers in their wombs."

His philosophy of life included successive but overlapping levels and "stages," chiefly (in order): pragmatic "radical positivism," phenomenological "perspectivism," existentialist "vital reason," and historicist "historical reason." In all of these supposedly distinct phases, however, he was indebted to still earlier sources that predated his first "independent" philosophizing from 1909–1910, his "twenty-sixth year."

Those early sources included mainly Renan and Taine with positivist historicism, Nietzsche with voluntarist historicism and vitalism, Bergson and intuitional vitalism, Hegel and romantic-idealist historicism, and Kant and Cohen's neo-Kantian idealism. But what let him integrate all of them at the very beginning of his philosophizing was James's radical-empirical pragmatism. In their compatible parts, all those earlier influences carried into and through Ortega's mature philosophy after 1923, even after 1934, when vital *and* historical reason became in effect a "philosophy of life" in existentialism and historicism. With a temporal-spatial dimension and historical method, historical reason overlapped with vital reason, which contained phenomenological *method* for description of (or "perspectives" on) "essences" of the basic life-reality. As an "instrument" for "looking" and "seeing," the phenomenological method (perspectivism) in turn rested upon a basic ontology of James's radical empiricism with which he had grasped *life as self and world* already in 1910. Thus, he had built up his total philosophy as an integrated *plurality* from that original basic "radical unitary duality," and that unitary-dual aspect carried through the mature hierarchical structure as a whole.

No doubt an easier way to have presented Ortega's complex philosophy would have been simply to *add* two or three more to the several successive "stages" already alleged by others and to describe them topically. Then let the reader wonder just what were still in effect at the end, how one stage might relate to another, and what one name we might finally give to all these untidy, proliferating units of thought. That kind of evasion would only increase the confusion instead of affording a clearer and simpler view of a *very* complicated subject that seems to have had an overall order, structure, "system," and relationship—at least, as Ortega put it, in his own mind, if not in print.

But were there more than *two* stages, properly speaking, in Ortega's thought? Did each successive, more expansive "phase" simply absorb whole, or swallow up all its predecessors like spiraling circles within circles, Chinese boxes inside boxes, or "mothers within daughters"? There were clearly some dross and discard at each juncture, wherein the whole past, Ortega tells us, is reassessed from a new center of the circle, which had advanced beyond the previous centers. Similarly modern man is (as Ortega saw) his whole accumulated past, from paleolithic man (and woman) forward: Stoic, Christian, rationalist, and positivist. For Ortega, the same progression was true of his personal philosophical past. As he wrote in 1936, as a child he was a Christian, but he was no longer so as a mature man, except that, by *having been one,* an inevitable residue of his earlier ideas, beliefs, and values was still in his makeup. He had "to absorb and to assimilate," "to keep and to discard," and always to convert the vital heritage into "something completely new" as an integral part of himself. He approved of Hegel's mandate: "Dare to make mistakes." For him, the whole philosophical past represented progressive errors as much as progressive truths, but there were some gains as well as continuity evident in recurring ideas, questions, and answers, and so it was in his thinking too, as he had moved beyond his earlier phases.

Obviously, not all of those alleged "stages" in Ortega's thinking are of the same weight and value for assessing what finally was his mature philosophy as a whole. Some are physical, metaphysical, or methodological *levels* rather than stages. Unlike Nicol or Morón Arroyo, I do not regard "biologism" as a *stage* in his thought.[10] For him, life is biological (material, organic) at its primary level, but vital reason had "transcended" that irrational basis (4:341)— tacitly by 1916 (1:400; 12:392) and openly by 1923–1924 (3:271–73). To his mind, moreover, his youthful Nietzscheanism was a pre-philosophical mood quickly outgrown, although he carried over some important *inclinations* toward a philosophy of life, with historicity, elitism, and cyclical outlook. Likewise, his Jamesian radical empiricism was not properly a "stage" at all, since it served as his basic metaphysics from 1910 onward, under a variety of names relating to a self-presenting, dual reality of life. Although Silver held that Ortega's whole philosophy was covered by phenomenology, I think that the latter was instead mainly "perspectivism," a methodological level of the "stage" of vital reason. He kept phenomenology throughout, of course, as *part* of his epistemology and his method of "seeing" and "describing."

10. On "biologism of a material, organic sort," see chap. 2, n. 3.

It is one of the theses of this present study that Ortega's systematic philosophy really had only *two stages* (in the sense of distinct and major developmental phases) and that these were vital reason and historical reason, both comprehended finally within a covering philosophy of life. As he put it in 1934, his philosophy as a whole had always been a "radical unitary duality" that started with life as self and circumstance. Vital reason and historical reason were dual stages of *development* of those unitary-dual origins from life. This means that all other presumed stages, earlier or later, were actually only bases, levels, dimensions, or related themes, aspects, and interests.

From its informal debut in "Adam in Paradise" and from its formal inauguration in the *Meditations on Quixote* and ever after, Ortega's philosophy was primarily about *life* (1:320). From the first, "life" was dual in "self" and "world"—a "unity of life in two worlds," a "unitive" *coexistence* (1:487–88). As he said of Renan in 1909, "this dualism is impossible"; the centaurs have to decide on a "third world," as a compromise between the two (1:451). Beginning thus, his philosophy of life was implicitly a *vital* reason, or *logos* (1:321), and eventually also a historical reason, for "the [historical] past . . . [is] a mode of life" (1:325). As he observed in 1919, "life is duration and change; it is born, flowers, dies and leaves behind it the occasion for other successive and distinct lives" (2:231). But also, "To live is to live with . . ." (3:291), that is, with the world-circumstance and with others (5:251) in material, social, and historical dimensions. In 1930 he wrote that it is the business of history "to grasp what was the life of this or that epoch in its deepest intimacy" (2:736), and from 1932 he defined life in terms of past, present, and future (4:396; 9:652). Although history and life flow together, Ortega at first concentrated on contemporary life ("*nuestro tiempo*") and only subsequently on the historicity of that life (as in 3:293; 9:646–47). Is this combination of life and history to be called pragmatism, phenomenology, existentialism, or historicism, or instead—more properly—philosophy of life, including all of them, the last-born "daughter" holding all?

As Ortega put it in 1923, authentic philosophy requires a "*vital, historical, perspectivist dimension*" (3:201). As we have seen, "perspectivism" was mainly phenomenological "method" mingled with a pragmatist metaphysics. Ultimately, therefore, his philosophy of life reduces to only *two* stages (ontological "dimensions"), vital and historical, that are summed up in the compound names of vital reason and (thereafter) historical reason. Vital reason was not replaced by historical reason; they were coordinates, co-dimensions, of his "philosophy of life," which he described in 1934 as "bi-lobar" like a ginkgo tree, a "radical unitary duality," a "*one-two*" (8:43).

Although those terms of combined unity and duality in association with the metaphorical ginkgo tree occurred only once in Ortega's published works in reference to philosophy, they are in the very self-revealing "Preface for Germans" (1934), near the midpoint of his long philosophical career. Perhaps from James and Schlegel as well as Goethe (8:43), that "tree" metaphor and the one-two terminology should not be ignored, for Ortega reiterated the theme of unitary duality twice again in the same work under a metaphor of the *Dii consentes*,[11] Dioscuri or like-minded gods Castor and Pollux, the Gemini or Twins (8:51). He had first used these latter images and the thesis they represented—"the coexistence of man and world"—in lectures in 1915 and 1916 (8:53; 12:388). Moreover, he repeated these alternate terms in lectures on vital reason and historical reason in the 1940s (12:181). Clearly the "bi-lobar" ginkgo tree was not a momentary whim but a metaphor of permanent significance for describing the character of Ortega's very complex but unitary philosophy.

The immediate or ("radical") reference point for these "one-two" terms was Ortega's perception of the basic life-reality as "self and circumstance." Nevertheless, by logical extension and by development in time, this ontological first principle gradually became manifest in a philosophy articulated on two levels and in two stages: vital reason and historical reason, which together signified two variations on the "unity" of "knowing and being" in *dualities* of epistemology and ontology. This aspect of dualism was preserved, moreover, in "vital reason" and "historical reason" as compound terms. "Philosophy of life" provided the common link and unity.

Several times in 1934, in reference to their common "Idea of life," Ortega inconspicuously identified it in Dilthey as "philosophy of life" (6:200 n. 5, 205; 8:46). Although he seems not to have used that term in print before 1934, it had the advantage of being more general, or generic, and hence more than commensurate with "philosophy of vital reason" (8:47) as the earlier stage of his philosophical development and also broad enough to encompass "historical reason" as the second stage. The lectures of "On Historical Reason" (1940, 1944) make patent that, although it "emerges" from vital reason, historical reason is something distinct and specific, "beyond" vital reason. Only a name like "philosophy of life" can contain both of these stages of Ortega's philosophy, as existentialism *and* historicism. If "philosophy of life" were not in his usage, then, we should need to "invent" it. Moreover, European "philosophy of life" in general was dualistic in content though unitary in name and object—and most explicitly so in Ortega's principle: "radical unitary duality."

---

11. James, *Writings*, 476 ("Some Problems of Philosophy"): a metaphor about philosophy as a tree with branches. There are a score of studies on Ortega's use of metaphors, but for this particular one (Gemini), see Marías, *Circumstance and Vocation*, 279, 335, 400—in relation of "self and circumstance"; for locations in Ortega himself, see 7:417; 12:35, 181, 388; 8:53.

AN ONTOLOGY OF LIFE

Not in "Dilthey and the Idea of Life" (1934), despite its "autobiographical" character, can we find an adequate exposition of Ortega's own idea of life, which was scattered throughout his years and works, but especially in notes after his discovery of Dilthey's *philosophy* around 1929. To describe life's "essence" (or "consistency," as James put it) seemed to be an ontological task, except that he came to the conclusion that life is not "being," so that an "ontology" of this "radical reality" is (strictly speaking) nonsense.[12] Originally he had set out to give "descriptions" of life, but that "phenomenon" had turned out to be not an "essence," or "nature," but an "event" or happening—something "present" that was oriented on the historical past and directed to the future (5:460; 9:391). Since he also felt the need for theory, or generalization, however, he was driven toward an "ontology" of life, even though it was a "historical ontology," or "metahistory."

In his classes and diary for the year 1916, comparing life to "being" and already taking a historical approach to the latter, he became concerned with ontology. The problem of being or the condition of reality involved ontology. Searching for the history of the word "being," he attributed that concept (meaning *stability*) to Parmenides. This abstraction he contrasted with "my theory of life," as related to the idea of becoming (change) from Heraclitus. Clearly, it was *not* Heidegger who first started Ortega thinking on the problem of being and ontology, when he had turned to Scheler (and Rickert) on the problem of values (R 36). After 1927, however, Heidegger caused him to intensify his ongoing inquiry into life as compared with being or "existence." In 1918–1919, when current German philosophy seemed no longer ontological, he was uncertain whether being (or "existence") was prior to knowing, but his "radicalism" about life fitted neither traditional realism nor idealism (R 77). In *Modern Theme* (1923) he declared life historical. "*Life* is particularity, change, development, in a word, *history*" (3:198). By 1928, in an unused prologue to "Historiology," he saw this "new discipline" as providing a new "ontology of historical reality," a "historical ontology," or a "metahistory" (R 68).

Although it became his *desideratum* and goal, Ortega never put together a "General Theory of Human Life," or "biognosis," in a study entitled *Experience of Life*, or in any other work. Here and there, we encounter tantalizing tidbits but never a treatise on the subject. Ironically, two concentrations of such occasional observations appeared in the last two "books" of his lectures that have lately been published: *What Is Knowledge?* (1930) and *Historical Reason* (1940–1944), which both formally dealt with epistemology instead of

12. See supplemental note 12, chap. 8.

ontology. In his view, however, epistemology always involved ontology (and vice versa) in a "unity of knowing and being" (7:325).

In the series "What Is Knowledge?" Ortega promised a "rigorous analysis" of the "gigantic phenomenon of life." With ratiovitalism as equivalent to existentialism, he approached life on three levels, with the titles "Life as Execution"; "On Radical Reality"; and "What Is Life?" First, he defined life in terms of its subject, the "executive self" ("who am I?"), and in terms of "my world," for the self is never isolated and passive, or inactive, as in idealism and phenomenology. Those three levels constitute *life* as "radical reality," in which "everything is absolute"—at least so "I believe" and "act"—in its "consistency," as "unicity" and "uniqueness." The argument became circular: "The unicity of life is, therefore, its absolutivity." "To live is to have to be unique." "To live is to exist absolutely." This active view of life, or existence, was not idealism, not "consciousness," he insisted. Instead, life's *being* is to *do,* or to "make oneself." Later he resumed with "being," to argue that "being" is simply a "supposition and construction that we make in view of another mode of being, of reality"—in short, *life,* which is "executive being." This view goes "radically beyond all idealism." "Existence is living," is being "concerned with the things of the world." "To live is to be projected in the double sense of program and projection of it onto the world. I am, above all, a certain vital program." Here, as Stern saw, he anticipated Sartre. His "trajectory" was "a type of life in this world." But our relation with things of the world is not primarily knowing or thinking, which was the "fundamental—'intellectualist'—error" of Descartes and of modern idealism. "I think because I exist, because life poses rough inexorable problems for me." But this was not a naively optimistic, self-sufficient, self-centered viewpoint, for "human life is by nature defective, needy, fallible." "Life runs; life is rush." Life is "insecurity"—constitutionally—and "perdition," for we do not know the future. The idea of "being" itself was something man has constructed to give him a belief or feeling of security and salvation. "Therefore the being of a thing is not a thing or a super-thing; it is an intellectual schema." We have to live from our beliefs and from such convictions: "Life is absolute conviction." "Life is neither entrance nor exit," for no one assists at his birth or at his death. He concluded: "all the problems of metaphysics . . . have their roots in the study of life, in vital reason."[13]

In the lecture series entitled "On Historical Reason" Ortega linked Heidegger and Jaspers with himself and with Dilthey in having tried to "ground philosophy in the new idea of life." Thus he repeated as a maxim: "One philosophizes because one lives." "*Theory* has its beginning and its essential roots in life." Theory is not life; but, at the same time, one cannot live

13. Ortega, *¿Qué es conocimiento?* 13–18, 94, 120–58.

without "theorizing." Especially, one philosophizes authentically when life has descended into crisis, as for Descartes, for whom all was doubtful. But life never became the *object* of philosophy until Dilthey discovered it as the basic, radical reality. What we call "experience of life" forms an "essential part of life itself." If we can recover "life lived" over the millennia, we only "elevate" it to theory by history, by "historical reason." That was a very "juicy theme," that "experience of life," if only we could turn it into a kind of biographical "biology"—truly a theoretical-historical "study of life" above the "autobiographical" level of the individual "everybody," to an "ontology of the concrete being" that was not traditional abstract "being in general." In the 1940–1944 lectures he would have called the result of such a concrete-general "architecture, anatomy, or structure" by the name "Biognosis," or "General Theory of Human Life." It was unsaid but now obvious that he would have tried to get there by means of history, historical reason, and historiology (as "historical ontology") as surely as by vital reason.[14] In fact, almost his whole approach to philosophy of life had become historical by the 1940s. After existentialism, historicism thus also served his search for a General Theory of Life (9:650), or philosophy of life.

Of course, the foregoing two commentaries did not begin to cover what Ortega said about "life" over a long lifetime. Life was most basic, the "radical reality," but it was so much else at a higher and wider level. As Dilthey had stated, life was "many-sided" (5:191; 7:104) and "multiformed" (8:297). Life was solitary and convivial, individual and social (4:539–41; 5:403; 6:106); it was vulgar and it was noble (6:180–85), easy and difficult (5:337), fake and authentic (4:211–13; 5:73–75), historically falling and rising (7:289–90), determined and free (2:682; 6:34; 7:431); shipwreck and voyage (1:479–81; 4:254; 5:472). If it were best "balanced" (2:74; 5:480) between such opposing dualities, so often it was not; it was "drama" (4:77; 5:31; 9:511), or "worry" (7:436), or "insecurity" (4:168; 5:32–34) and "despair" (5:92–94; 6:405) in times of crisis. Such existential modes, however, were but half of the story for Ortega, for life was also joy, hope, striving, project. Life was not only isolated self but world and others too. If death were life's end, perhaps so was "resurrection" (8:297), or "the will to exist *malgre tout.*" No one, as Ortega pointed out, consciously assists at his own birth or death. Life is what is in between: "Life is what we do and what happens to us" (12:32). Life is such constant change and challenge that Ortega adopted for his motto in middle and later years the phrase *mobile in mobilis* (5:494; 9:255). The old "aficionado of history" (4:158) was also always an "aficionado of living" (8:405). For him, as a philosopher, philosophy is a "form of living" (7:430).

---

14. Ortega, *Sobre la razón histórica,* 67–68, 197–202.

"PHILOSOPHY OF LIFE" AS A NAME

For his public, Ortega well knew that he had not put a *substantive*, generic name (with or without "-ism") on his own philosophy until he had been philosophizing independently for several years. "Only in philosophy can one at first . . . proceed without a suitable terminology," because philosophy is not a "science" (9:710). Probably the difficulty that Ortega encountered in providing "life" with a suitable rationale, *logos* (1:320–21), or "reason" from shifting "perspectives" on merely contemporary scenes or fleeting experiences of existence here-and-now, is what made him in 1924 add "historical reason" to "historical" vital reason. The name "philosophy of life," however, which he had seen assigned to Dilthey in 1933 (6:173n), could cover both life and history. In 1934 he gave that name to a way of thinking (*percatación*) that in fact he shared with Dilthey (6:205), and he clearly preferred that term to either "existentialism" or phenomenology (8:44–46). "Philosophy of life" was able to encompass his "philosophy of vital reason" (even as existentialism) *and* "historical reason" (historicism)—in a "radical unitary duality" (8:43, 46–47). "Idea of life" was more prominent in Ortega's terminology (6:165–67) than "philosophy of life," but in both cases his intent was equivalent to dominant "belief" or "worldview" and seemed comparable to such other general philosophies as "stoicism, rationalism, idealism, positivism" of the past. This new name comprised both life and history, but with "life" on a "higher level" (6:175) and also as more "radical."

Do life and history really "fit" together? In Hegel's idealist "philosophy of history" (2:160–61), Ortega had still sensed a conflict between the vital and the historical as late as 1917. Such a "rational interpretation of life" failed to coincide with the "vital text" of the heart of individual life—palpitating, passionate, desperate, lonely. "And this immediately present life, these emotions of everybody, are for everyone the first things in the world. Like it or not, all else is secondary. . . ." But where does the intimate happiness or bitterness of yesterday's youth go, when we become mature and grow old? ". . . Nothing dies in man so long as the whole man does not die." Yesterday's self "survives in a submerged existence of our spirit." The truly civilized man possesses his whole self "religiously," past as well as present, by "frequent reliving [*revivencia*]" of it all, like a "solicitous spectator" and an "alert investigator," to correct, harmonize, and direct it to worthy ends (2:161–62). Thus he aspired to replace Hegel's idealistic reason *over* history by a new "historical sensitivity" attuned to individual and social life *in* past and present (9:366n)—by "vital reason" and "historical reason" together.

It is clear that by the late 1940s, Ortega knew that he had not managed to assign to his unitary-dual philosophy a generally acceptable name or names. He lacked the lucky originality, or "denominative talent," that he envied in

Husserl and even in Heidegger (9:636), despite his dislike of the "so-called existentialism." This dubious term represented "only the last of four attempts [by Dilthey, Ortega, Jaspers, and Heidegger] to found philosophy in the new idea of life, in the great idea of life that, like it or not, will be that on which philosophy is going to live in the next stage of humanity" (12:192; compare 9:85–86), that is, as a new "realist" worldview beyond Dilthey's triadic typology of materialistic "naturalism," "subjective idealism," and "objective idealism." His own efforts, in "expression or printed formulation," were probably, he granted, "the most inadequate of all." (He meant, apparently, his public names "perspectivism," "vital reason," and "ratiovitalism.")

To existential terminology, Ortega preferred his own—instead of "world," "circumstance"; in place of "existence," "life"; and over "existentialism," "vital reason," from which "emerges" the idea of "historical reason," which starts from "one's life" as the "radical reality" (12:195). "We need, then, a whole new philosophy, a whole new repertory of basic and original concepts" to deal with that "radical reality" that is life, which is "*purely and exclusively* 'happening'" (12:196). However, historical reason, which was only a "particular theme" of "the general architecture of my philosophical doctrine" (12:195), was not an adequate nomenclature for life. Nor was his "vital reason" enough, although he affirmed that "Reason, in its authenticity, is vital reason" (12:193) that is rooted in life. For the general "theme" and "radical thesis" of life, vital reason was only his "initial thesis," as a "practical knowing" that still remained below the level of the *theory* that must deal with the "structure" and "consistency" of life (12:299–300). In the context of the 1940s, however, he avoided using Dilthey's alternative of "philosophy of life" and spoke instead only of a "*general Theory of human life*" (12:302), which he expected to attain by historical reason, beyond the basic vital reason.

What went unsaid above is that, in this case, perhaps the one with the greatest luck at finding appropriate words to name the "new philosophy"— simply as *Philosophie des Lebens,* that is, "philosophy of life"—was Dilthey himself, whom Ortega had pitied previously for his denominative poverty (6:173). If the proper general name for "the theory charged to resolve what is that radical reality" of life is "philosophy," then "philosophy of life" may be as good a name as any other for the new species, although before Dilthey philosophers had always ignored life. A name like biognosis—literally, "knowledge [or theory] of life"—that Ortega coined in 1940 (12:302) was really not better but worse. Dilthey's alternative term *Selbstbesinnung* he had rendered as autognosis ("self-knowledge")—similar to his own "philosophy of awareness"—was "the same," he had conceded, as "a philosophy of life" (6:205, compare 207–8). In 1946 he again lamented that it was a "shame" that "there does not exist in the whole history of philosophy an adequate *terminology* for speaking formally of the phenomenon life" (7:467n). Nor was there an adequate name for it as new general type of philosophy. Perhaps there was still nothing better than the vague and commonplace "philosophy of life." Maybe his ongoing difficulty in finding an appropriate name explains his statement in 1941 that he had "for some years now" called his philosophy "historical reason" (5:534), whereas in fact this was only one *part* of it—as incomplete by itself as was "vital reason." In his "Metaphysics of Vital Reason" (1933), he had made it clear that ultimately he was aiming at "the general structure of our life" above and beyond the "concrete instance" of personal or individual life (12:788; compare 9:649–50) in which the general actually inhered and was verified. This "permanent structure of life" was also distinct from what "human life is in any epoch" of history (12:89). So his general philosophy of life was at a higher level than either vital reason or historical reason. If it was inadequate as a name, philosophy of life was, finally, the integrator, the integral (holistic) form of his philosophy. But Ortega's philosophy of life was significantly *different* from others of that name, including Dilthey's.

SOURCES AND CHARACTERISTICS
OF PHILOSOPHY OF LIFE

What was "philosophy of life," or "Life Philosophy," in terms of its time, adherents, and main characteristics? Dictionaries and encyclopedias of philosophy distinguish between a broadly construed and practical notion dating from the eighteenth century and the more specific and formal mode of thinking by that name that arose in the late nineteenth and early twentieth centuries with Dilthey and Bergson. Forerunners included Friedrich Schlegel (who first used the term *Philosophie des Lebens* in 1827 in relation to a body of speculative thought), Søren Kierkegaard, and Friedrich Nietzsche. Böllnow's study *Lebensphilosophie* (1958) extended the duration of this ill-known philosophy forward from Nietzsche, Bergson, and Dilthey through Simmel and Scheler to include (among others) Ortega himself—and Dewey's pragmatism besides—till the rise and triumph of existentialism, on which it had considerable influence.[15]

Main characteristics that Böllnow detected in philosophy of life were the following: dualism; life as "becoming"; human historicity; emphasis on continuity and form; "perspectivism"; vitalist implications for art, culture, mo-

---

15. Böllnow, *Lebensphilosophie*, I, 131, 142; on Ortega, see 7, 15, 42, 44–45, 54–55, 56, 57, 90, 146; on Dewey's pragmatism as fitting with the category, see 8, 11, 15–16, 59–60, 66, 70–71, 100–101, 123–25, 147. His primary cases were Nietzsche, Dilthey, and Bergson. Also see the following on "philosophy of life": *Historische Wörterbuch der Philosophie* (1980), s.v. "Lebensphilosophie"; Walter Brugger, ed. *Philosophical Dictionary* (Spokane: Gonzaga University Press, 1967), s.v. "Life Philosophy."

rality, and death; "transcendence"; hermeneutic method; and concern with the "human sciences." Although Böllnow examined Ortega on only three or four of those points, all of them (except fascination with death) were prominent enough to justify the view that his thought as a whole was a "philosophy of life." Since the only essays by Ortega that Böllnow cited were *Revolt of the Masses, Man and Crisis,* and *History as a System,* which fall between 1930 and 1936, one suspects that had he also known about parallels with Dilthey in "W. Dilthey and the Idea of Life" and in the "Preface for Germans" he might have identified Ortega with *Lebensphilosophie* more fully and much more confidently.

Such characteristics of philosophy of life as hermeneutics and basic discipline for the human sciences, of which there are both close parallels and major differences in Dilthey and Ortega, are better left for consideration separate from philosophy. The connection of these methods, or "instruments," to their thought on the "human sciences" makes them transitional problems that, in a sense, go "beyond philosophy" to ambitious projects to "unify" the plurality of those human sciences with philosophy.

Ortega's Earlier Philosophical Sources

Although Ortega knew writings by all of the thinkers that Böllnow listed, he had at first learned more about the *idea* of life, if not the so-called philosophy of life, from Nietzsche, Schlegel, James, Bergson, and Simmel (but not necessarily in that order) than from any others, since he could not endure Kierkegaard, knew little of Klages, and did not read Dilthey for his *philosophy* before 1929. Like Kierkegaard, Nietzsche and Bergson were viewed by Ortega as irrationalists who did not contribute to his own idea of vital *reason,* and later he claimed to find even in Dilthey a residue of irrationalism in marked contrast to his own "new rationalism of life" (6:196n). His highly esteemed teacher (6:235), Simmel, had offered him some "acute" ideas on life, probably through his "insufficient" studies of Goethe and Nietzsche (1:92–93; 3:166; 4:398). However, Ortega regarded his "good friend" Scheler as merely a phenomenologist, as not aware of Dilthey's great "idea of life" (4:507–9; 6:173). Ortega saw himself as having been one of several who explored the idea of life philosophically after Dilthey's "discovery" of it around 1860, but his cast of main characters differs from Böllnow's by including, after Dilthey and himself (independently), only Jaspers and Heidegger but not Husserl, Scheler, or Spengler (12:192). Strangely, although Böllnow included Dewey, neither he nor Ortega mentioned James, but Marías did.[16]

16. Despite his numerous references to life, few have identified James with "philosophy

If we judge by kindred thinkers and concepts, this philosophy falls some-where between existentialism and historicism, and on the periphery of prag-matism and Husserlian phenomenology, too. In Ortega himself, then, it included all of these types, but, by comprehending them, by absorbing some features and discarding some, he went "beyond" the others—to excogitate an "authentic" and distinct kind of philosophy of life—at least according to his own estimation.

By the 1930s, Ortega sensed that he was contributing to a new genre of life philosophy. Although he had regarded "life" as the primary object of his philosophy, evidently he did not use for it precisely the name "philosophy of life" until 1934, when he *twice* linked Dilthey and himself. He seems not to have used it again until the period 1949 to 1951, when it was again his own term of choice. It had not been his first choice, however, so he was not quite satisfied with it because it was vague and inexact, but he needed it. By the 1930s he had in appearance a twofold or double philosophy: vital reason *and* historical reason. But how was he to proceed to systematization, if his philos-ophy lacked unity? From his youth (in 1912) he had been aware of "philoso-phy of life" in Bergson (R 76), perhaps finding it again in Friedrich Schlegel before reading it after 1929 in Dilthey (R 40), who answered the problem of unity in diversity: "historical reason" *was* a "philosophy of life." Of course, James had already given him a convenient rationale for a philosophy *from* life that represented a "radical unitary duality." So had Goethe (9:579). While he concentrated on developing a vitalist "historical reason" from 1924 into the 1930s, philosophy of life was never out of his mind. It was the last of the several names that he used, but this one described his philosophy as a whole.

Literary Sources: Goethe and Novelists

In 1949 he pointed out that it was "only in the last seventy years or so that philosophers had begun to take into account that they had turned their backs on this reality [of life] prior to all others, and that if they were philoso-phizing it was because before philosophizing they were already living. First one lives, then one philosophizes" (9:573). With that idea he was paraphras-ing Vico—or Scheler—in noting (6:49) that Descartes's *cogito, ergo sum* should be: "*I think because I exist*," or "live" (12:192, 194). But his own first inspirations toward the idea of life pretty clearly came from literary sources that, apart from Schlegel, are not properly called "*philosophy* of life." "Among us only the poets in verse and the novelists in prose offer us some diffuse

---

of life," except for Royce, *William James;* and Marías, *Circumstance and Vocation,* 79. Another was Theodore Plantinga, *Historical Understanding in the Thought of William Dilthey* (Toronto: University of Toronto Press, 1980), 70–73.

glimmers on what our life is, that is, on our radical reality."[17] Goethe especially, but also Schlegel, Balzac, Flaubert, and Spanish novelists of the "generation of 1898" supplied him vital images. From Goethe came metaphors of the ginkgo as a tree of life, which represented the unity and duality of his philosophy of life, and the "protophenomenon" that anticipated his schema of historiology (7:349; 9:368).

There were, of course, other identifiable literary sources for Ortega's extremely variegated "idea of life." The Spanish novelists, especially Azorín and Pío Baroja, were prime sources, and it is clear that "literary" works of such philosophers as Nietzsche and Unamuno either earlier or later were grist for Ortega's mill, as he sought ever more vicarious "experience of life." Nor were religious sources ignored, for he acknowledged the "wisdom literature" of the Old Testament—Job, for example—and of other cultures and times (9:572). Life is the *radical* reality, he explained, not because it is the only or the highest reality but because it is "the root of all the others," which somehow have to make themselves felt in our own "individual existence." "To be God to us, God has to make Himself burn in the bush or to sail like the frigate birds above Golgothas of three gibbets."[18] On occasion, Ortega himself could wax as eloquent about life as any novelist or poet.

SCHLEGEL'S POETIC PHILOSOPHIES OF LIFE, HISTORY, LANGUAGE

First of all, the German Romantic poet Friedrich Schlegel had introduced the name and concept of a "philosophy of life" as something meant to be philosophical. He also used metaphors that Ortega repeated in his own philosophy: a "tree" of life, growing and symmetrical, and the bold navigator sailing to unknown coasts. After his basic debt to James, knowledge of Schlegel's poetic *Philosophie des Lebens* could well have been a seminal influence on Ortega's philosophy by its view of life as basic (and double) reality. Except for idealist "spirit" and "consciousness," Schlegel's "simple basis," or "foundation of the whole" in the "experience" of life, was like Ortega's notion of life as "basic reality." Schlegel's "architectural structure" with "all its parts in unison" certainly resembles Ortega's "radical unitary duality." The poet-thinker had also opposed the abstractions of "philosophy of the school"—both its "metaphysical castles" and its "politics" of immersion in the world. If his narrow Germanic preoccupation with the "self" (*Ich*) were balanced with "circumstance," which appeared only haphazardly in Schle-

17. By accident I lost and could not rediscover the precise source in Ortega for this and the next note, because the index does not coincide with these passages, but compare with similar statements by him: 1:21, 45, 50; 3:371, 407; 5:31, 229.

18. Cf. Ortega, 7:145; 8:262.

gel, then Ortega's *dualistic* discovery was but a step beyond. Granted the differences of his more formal philosophy, some parallels and resemblances are so striking that I suspect that (besides James) Schlegel was an early source.[19]

Although Ortega did not directly acknowledge Schlegel as a source for "philosophy of life," he quoted him several times on life and on history: notably, life as an "endless dialogue"; and the historian as "a prophet in reverse" (3:153; 5:136). Unlike the notion of life as "drama" that he repeated (4:77; 9:585), the other ideas were not from Schlegel's *Philosophy of Life* (1827), but from his *Philosophy of History* (1828). And his "Philosophy of Language" (1829) also contained coincidences and parallels with Ortega's thinking and manner of expression, including elaborate crisis thinking (such as "crisis of doubt") and references to "historical science." The most striking and extensive parallel is Schlegel's acknowledgment of the dual character on two levels of his *one* philosophy, which started from "life": "the first part, 'The Philosophy of Life,' treats of consciousness, or of the inner man [the I, ego, or self]; the second, this Philosophy of History, . . . considers the outward man, or the [historical] progress of states and nations. . . ." We "think as two," he remarked, and he noted that this was "historical philosophy" as done by a "philosophic historian." In relation to this "truly vital philosophy," one also finds allusions to "the dawn" of a coming age of new "revelation," "regeneration," and stability. Ortega himself could have drawn Schlegel's picture of how he starts from life as the center and "circles" around and around that basic idea, always returning to the central theme, as he branches out into the "whole range of life and thought," yet "always presenting it in some new light and relation."[20] But Schlegel was so poetic, so theological.

Despite all the parallels between Schlegel's philosophy of life and Ortega's, we cannot be sure that it was in fact a source. We simply do not know if or when he read Schlegel's relevant works on philosophy. He quoted the novel *Lucinde* as early as 1909, but he did not mention Schlegel again in print until

19. Friedrich Schlegel, *The Philosophy of Life and Philosophy of Language*, trans. A. J. W. Morrison (London: Bell, 1872). Its object (4–7) was the "inner mental life" and the broader spiritual life of man, including (chap. 8) the history of the world and of states—the "whole man" (187), more than a "mere science of reason and nature" (189). Obviously, however, in both philosophy of life and philosophy of history, Schlegel was very much more religious and theological in orientation than was Ortega, who took a carefully secular approach. Donoso and Raley list no studies of Schlegel's possible influence on Ortega, and the linkage seen by Ibeas and Böllnow was in very general terms.

20. Schlegel, *The Philosophy of History*, trans. J. B. Robertson, 2d ed. (London: Bell, 1893), xii, 66–69, 73, 276, 282, 390, 394. As part of a "general philosophy," subordinate to his philosophy of life, this dealt with origins, middle, and end—drawn from the events and facts of "the whole of history" and aiming at a "science of history," which related his survey (not "too systematically") to "the whole system of human life," which includes periodic "decisive crises," even a "general crisis" in the epochs of world history.

1921. At about that time, however, an anonymous article on him in the *Enciclopedia Universal Ilustrada* mentioned his philosophies of life and of history, which were also named (as pertaining to a *unity* in "triplicity") in the Spanish edition of Vorländer that Ortega published in 1921. Perhaps, then, Ortega pondered Schlegel along with Dilthey over the next several years. Otherwise, all those parallels may be sheer coincidence, as he claimed in the case of Dilthey. If Dilthey also knew Schlegel well (and there is good evidence that he did), then maybe here is a reason other than familiarity with James for Ortega's "parallels" with Dilthey.[21] Possibly Dilthey and he strove separately to "philosophize" ("systematize") Schlegel's poetic "philosophy of life." Careful scrutiny of Ortega's library and archive might yield more certain answers.

In fact, Ortega had several of Schlegel's works in his library, but apparently only one had a philosophical title.[22] Moreover, references in his unpublished notes show that he saw that Dilthey had been influenced by Schlegel in "reducing systems to simple conviction" (R 40). Finally, he cited Schlegel's contribution to the three "great tendencies of the century in *Wissenschafts-lehre*," or theory of knowledge (R 46)—probably meaning his three philosophies of life, history, and language. At root, before he had studied Dilthey's philosophy, Ortega was thus possibly influenced to attempt the same three fields of endeavor, which he, like Dilthey, followed for a lifetime.

DILTHEY'S PHILOSOPHY OF LIFE

A truly kindred spirit, the philosophical mind that had most fully anticipated his own way of thinking by a strange and persistent "parallelism": so Ortega came to regard Wilhelm Dilthey (1833–1911). Claiming not to have read Dilthey for his *philosophy* until about 1929, he wrote an ongoing series in 1933–1934 for *Revista de Occidente*, "Dilthey and the Idea of Life," which for decades was one of the most basic interpretations available, one he had

21. *Enciclopedia Universal Ilustrada* (reprint, 1964), s.v. "Schlegel." Dating from the 1920s, this mentions his "philosophies of life and history" and was possibly by Ortega. See Ortega, R 40, on Dilthey and Schlegel. Also see Rudolph A. Makkreel, *Dilthey, Philosopher of the Human Studies* (Princeton: Princeton University Press, 1975), 152, 261; Michael Ermarth, *Wilhelm Dilthey: The Critique of Historical Reason* (Chicago: University of Chicago Press, 1978), 270.

22. The only philosophical work by Schlegel that was in Ortega's library—*Neue philosophische Schriften*, ed. J. Körner (Frankfurt am Main: G. Schulte-Bulmke, 1935)—did not contain any of the three "philosophies," only "philosophy of philosophy," which Dilthey echoed. Ortega put out (with a prologue by himself) a translation of Karl Vorländer, *Historia de la filosofía*, 6th ed., 2 vols., trans. J. V. Vigueira (Madrid: Beltran, 1921), noting Schlegel's "triplicity" with a "superior unity," in relation to his *Philosophy of Life* and *Philosophy of History*, with "Philosophy of Language" thus implied (2:255). The same information was in the German edition of 1908, which Ortega had probably used first.

meant to develop into a book. Subsequently (1944) he published a translation of Dilthey's final work, *The Types of World View* (1911), and he intended to do the same with the *Einleitung* (1883), for which he started to write a prologue in 1946—regrettably unfinished, perhaps because a Mexican translation had appeared meanwhile. He had acquired Dilthey's collected works in nine volumes, as well as four of the Mexican translations, including the *Introduction*.[23]

From the 1930s, Ortega saw Dilthey as "the most important philosopher of the second half of the nineteenth century" (6:165)—"in and outside of Germany" (8:31)—and his esteem and affection for him continued to rise. Dilthey's "authentic philosophy" was of the "highest rank," the best of the generation of 1830, who (with James, and like Ortega himself) were "men of the flood, born in shipwreck" (crisis), working with "infidels" (8:30; compare 1:311). Their "radical tendencies" were still "the future of philosophy." Concluding from his positivist background that philosophy as such (metaphysics at least) had ended historically, Dilthey recoiled from the thought that he might somehow have created a *new* philosophy, "a magnificent ideological system," a "philosophy of life" (8:31, 46, 293). Around 1860, he had discovered "human life" as an object of philosophizing (6:191). The "great Dilthey," however, was (rather like Ortega) one of those "who think without need of arriving at formulas" (9:290). In many respects, as with the "theme" of "experience of life," Ortega saw him as an "admirable and venerable precursor" (9:26), and as "the most profound and veracious thinker" since Kant. Even the "gentle," "humble Dilthey" (8:293, 308n), nevertheless, had several blind spots and errors (6:212; 9:397, 603).[24]

23. Ortega, 6:175. His "Dilthey" in English was in the anthology *Concord and Liberty* (New York: Norton, 1946), which (after H. A. Hodges's 1944 work) was the "introduction" to Dilthey in the United States; the emphasis on "history of ideas" therein encouraged the growth of intellectual history in the States. He began this "book" as a centennial observance of Dilthey's birth (6:165), and it is interesting that such occasions inspired him to other studies: Kant and Hegel and Goethe. At that time (1946), few reviewers were competent to judge his interpretation of Dilthey, which long remained basic, but it was appreciated by J. H. Hexter in *New York Times Book Review*, September 1, 1946, p. 8. Also see H. Magid in *Journal of Philosophy* 44 (February 1947): 135–37. Plantinga, at least, has reaffirmed Ortega's theses. For the Dilthey works in Ortega's library (nineteen items), my thanks to Señora Soledad Ortega; these included the first edition of the *Gesammelte Schriften* (Leipzig: Teubner, 1914)—in eight volumes, minus the first (*Einleitung*), which he obtained in the second edition of 1923. Also see supplemental note 26, chap. 8. The oldest work of Dilthey that he had was *Das Erlebnis und die Dichtung*, 4th ed. (Leipzig, 1913).

24. It is uncertain just how solid was Ortega's critique of Dilthey. Nicol, for example, claimed that he did not understand Dilthey rightly (*Historicismo y Existencialismo*, 308–9), saying he was too perspectival and, in short, too *historicist*. Also Tuttle (see supplemental note 25, chap. 8) claimed Ortega's criticism of Dilthey's idealism and devotion to con-

Despite his genius and priority, Dilthey had not influenced Ortega in his own most basic philosophical principle (6:168)—the immediate perception of life as dual fundamental reality. (Had it been *one* person, it would have been Nietzsche or James.) Instead, he claimed to have gotten the idea of life from the prevailing "worldview" (6:167–68), from "the very problems that philosophy had then posed" (6:196n; 8:47). In contrast, as an idealist, Dilthey always believed with "the faith of a Carbonaro" that "consciousness" was basic (8:275n)—even more than life.

Whether or not Ortega understood Dilthey correctly does not concern us here; we want to consider, rather, what his exposition of Dilthey reveals of himself. The main problems here are to determine to what degree he was indebted to Dilthey, to examine how they differed and how far he developed various of his earlier themes and concepts "beyond" Dilthey, and finally to decide how else we might qualify their presumably *common* philosophy of life, if in fact they shared enough characteristics and specific ideas to justify seeing it so. Of course, to demonstrate adequately the subtle and complex relationship between Ortega and Dilthey on the ideas of life and history could take a book by itself. It is a problem that has not yet been studied with the care and the detail that it requires.[25]

The most important of Ortega's commentaries on Dilthey is the difficult one contained in "Idea of Life" (1933–1934), which indirectly reveals much about the working of his own mind and the structure and direction of his own thought. With good reason Ortega called his essay "autobiographical" in part (6:175), for he *projected* Dilthey's ideas and "radical tendencies" onto the vital and historical "level" of his own mind, intent, and generation (compare 8:32). The Dilthey we find there—the aspects that are emphasized and the way they are explicated—is very explicitly Dilthey *plus* Ortega (6:182), not just Dilthey through Ortega's eyes. He literally "put himself" into that exposition, because otherwise he found him too incoherent and too underdeveloped, since Dilthey had never been able to see as a whole and to formulate systematically the structure of his own intuitions and "decisive tendencies" (6:172–73, 193 n. 1, 196 n. 1). Expounding Dilthey, he took "the problem to a different level, . . . more advanced and fuller"—to reflect his own thinking and to "complete" him (6:175, 198, 207n).

Later, Ortega's prologue (1946) to the *Introduction to the Human Sciences* (1883) was essentially an attempt—using Dilthey's own notions of "genetic" approach and "worldview"—to explain why he had not been able to develop

---

sciousness was not borne out by the texts as a whole, and Dilthey was not so *emphatic* as he on the reality of the world ("with self") as interdependent parts of life. Hans P. Rickman, *Pioneer of the Human Studies* (London: Elek, 1979), says, "The claim that Dilthey was an empiricist is mistaken" (79).

25. See supplemental note 25, chap. 8.

his ideas with greater coherence, completeness, and system (7:59–61). In his very long life he had "lacked time," in the sense of an appropriate general world-view rather than a greater span of years. Too far ahead of his time mentally, Dilthey had therefore lacked the language and full consciousness to express his profound thoughts adequately. At the end, however, he had neither gone far enough in *developing* his basic ideas, nor had he delved *deeply* enough to get to the very "roots." Accordingly, Ortega felt that he not only had gone "beyond" him in elaboration and application but had also been more "radical" at the beginning (thanks to James)—much the same way that he described his relationship to Husserl and to Heidegger, except that he felt closer to Dilthey (6:173–75).

Not really knowing Dilthey until so late, nor studying his "philosophical" works before the years 1929 to 1933, had cost him, Ortega estimated, "around ten years" of his life (6:170). That observation did not refer to his own basic "idea of life," which he said he had "discovered" (or "intuited") and stated at least "twenty years" earlier. Morón Arroyo may have been right to think that it was Heidegger's reference to Dilthey in *Being and Time* (1927) that turned him to serious study of Dilthey's *philosophy*. However, Ortega went on to form his own complex interpretation of Dilthey in 1933–1934, one that was only belatedly indebted to Heidegger. Gaos too was probably right to suspect that Ortega knew of Dilthey's idea of historical reason and some of his biographical and historical works before 1924. Apparently he read the *Einleitung* before he wrote "Historiology" (1928).[26]

In an uncompleted "autobiographical" account (circa 1951) of the history of philosophy in the twentieth century, he remarked that from 1915 to 1930, Dilthey's doctrines had begun to exercise a decisive influence, but not as *philosophy* before 1920, even in Germany.[27] For the "intellectual development" of the idea of life within a *historical* matrix, which (after 1914) had taken Ortega another ten years or more of preparation, he could have progressed more rapidly had he known Dilthey more intimately (6:174). Had he studied him more intensively early in his career, he could have started at that higher level, thus saving himself much of the hard and tentative thinking of the decade 1913 to 1923. As it was, however, he thought that he had already started at a *deeper* conception of "life as the basic reality," and he had surpassed Dilthey in *applications*—historical and sociological—of that philosophical fundament by the 1930s, in "Historiology" and in *Revolt of the Masses* (6:174).

Initial Parallels: Life and History

Admitting "parallels" between himself and Dilthey in "philosophy of life" and "way of thinking," Ortega nevertheless insisted that they did not in any

26. See supplemental note 26, chap. 8.
27. Ortega, "Medio siglo," 15–16.

strict sense *coincide*. He had started from a position more "radical" than Dilthey's in regard to the idea of life, and he had "come further" (6:174–75, 208) with the dimensions of both vital and historical reason, as well as with the "basic discipline" he called historiology (6:184n). Moreover, the ostensible object of his exposition of Dilthey's thought—"the Idea of life"—was not precisely what it seemed to be at first glance, as related merely to vital reason. What Ortega repeatedly emphasized therein as Dilthey's "fundamental idea," or "axis idea," was not simply "life" but "historicity" in man, in the human (6:182, 195–96, 198). "Life" so described was not quite Ortega's ontological idea that life is the basic, "radical reality." Rather like Husserl but from an "empirical" as well as phenomenological viewpoint (8:299), Dilthey had stuck with "consciousness" (8:275n; compare 6:192), instead of probing the life reality to its vital roots. Going further, Ortega had developed his own version of the "fundamental idea"—life as self and circumstance—in two directions: inward, immediate, or psychological; and outward, historical, and social.

A basic duality that he shared with Dilthey (and with James) was evident from 1923 in *Modern Theme* as a "vital reason" that was "historical" too (3:201). His next formulation of this already obviously dual philosophy as a "ratiovitalism" (1924) had briefly seemed to revert to the vital to the exclusion of the historical (3:271–73), but he had begun to develop an explicit, distinctly "historical reason" (3:264) that was still subordinate to the larger vital whole. Increasingly from 1924 forward, however, he turned more attention to the temporal and social side of the "vital and historical" equation—almost wholly so after 1936.

As a "new great Idea" (similar to Saint-Simon's notion), Dilthey's "Idea of life" (6:166–68, 170, 174) was presented by Ortega in 1934 as mainly a new historical "worldview." But he made "Life" and all types of world-view definitely, explicitly historical and successive, instead of vaguely "permanent possibilities" (8:268, 313; 9:296). Thus he felt that he had treated life as more truly historical than had Dilthey.

Perhaps because he knew that Dilthey had already co-opted the term "historical reason" for his putative "Critique" from 1883 onward, Ortega minimized the importance of that "parallel" concept in 1934, as compared to "vital reason" (6:185)—a phrase that Dilthey had never used. "The idea of *vital reason* represents, in the problem of life, a higher level than the idea of *historical reason* where Dilthey left it" (6:175). "As we shall see, *there is scarcely anything in Dilthey that cannot be formally advanced for the decisive terms of vital reason. . . .*" Later, in a long footnote, Ortega explained how his own ratiovitalism had indicted the old rationalism (as "reason alone and apart") of ending in irrationalism, "but that disappears if one bases that 'pure reason' in the totality of 'vital reason,'" in the "clear and ironic rationalism of 'vital reason'" (6:195–96 n. 1). "That is what Dilthey had *wanted* to say . . . and think . . . ," but it was evident only with the publication of his posthumous papers in 1931 (vol. 8). Hence, "now we see that 'vital reason' means something more decisive than glimpsed by Dilthey," who remained "a prisoner of vital irrationalism" in confronting the "intellectual rationalism," or rationalistic "intellectualism," of his day (compare 6:192n, 206–7). He "did not succeed in finding the new rationalism of life," but to the end, he found "something irrational" in the whole conception of life. "Intellectualism" was a term in Dilthey after James.

Thus, in 1934, Ortega *seemed* to absorb Dilthey's historical reason into his own vital reason, as the lesser into the fuller—much as Marías and other commentators have tended to do with *his own* concept of historical reason: to absorb it as a mere aspect, or dimension, of vital reason. However, Ortega was already drawing the conclusion that history is so much vaster than present personal life alone. Very soon the historical *seemed* to absorb the vital in his thinking. In fact, it did not; vital reason and historical reason remained correlatives, co-dimensions, of his philosophy of life even after 1936.

Throughout "Dilthey and the Idea of Life," a "philosophy of life" having a *dual* orientation and method—inward and present, outward and past— was elaborated on the vital and psychological or historical and social levels. Ultimately that dualism fitted Ortega more than Dilthey; vital reason and historical reason were expressions of such a dualism. If one took philosophy to be the understanding of human life as the basic reality and life as "historicity," then that dualism resolved into a unified but twofold approach, interacting.

It is not difficult to follow in the "Preface for Germans" Ortega's intimations about other parallels between his own and Dilthey's "Idea of life." Once Dilthey's name was introduced, the argument returned repeatedly to the "Idea of Life." Life is the "radical reality" of "coexisting" self and circumstance, both of which terms have to be examined under the dual aspects of "time and space"—"this double fundamental inquiry" that treated everything human under the category of becoming, or historicity, where being is reduced to "pure event" in "mutual" and "reciprocal" movement (8:44, 51). For the purpose of defining his own philosophy, it is clear that he regarded Dilthey's ontology of life as also epistemological in the (Jamesian) sense of "self-posited"—or what he here called simply a "radical" empiricism that was still bearing fruit in his own generation (8:31, 53–54).

In the essay of 1934, Ortega had described Dilthey's basic outlook on life reality as either "radical positivism" or "radical empiricism" (6:210). These were actually his own and James's terms, not Dilthey's, and he used them repeatedly, insistently.[28] For such parallels, it is possible to regard the treatise

28. Ortega, 6:190, 199, and esp. 193n, 202n, and 210. It is not meant to deny that Dilthey

on Dilthey as a critique in the spirit of James. Ortega's "first Dilthey" was a somewhat *pragmatist* Dilthey. This orientation (or flavor) was not wholly unjustifiable, for Dilthey admired James, read some of his writings, and perhaps picked up some ideas and terms from him.

Initial consonance with "essential points" in Dilthey, and development of them, put Ortega into similar *general* categories of philosophy on life and history—more or less as a conscious continuator. However, he claimed he had started from different sources, from a later, more advanced level than had Dilthey, and from a "non-idealist" position (6:173–74, 183n). How, then, should we rank those categories? We have seen that they agreed fairly well in *historicism,* but was "philosophy of life" more basic for both of them? Most expositors over the past decade have seen Dilthey's philosophy as historicism—"transcendental" or otherwise—that covers his *Lebensphilosophie.* As a whole, however, Ortega interpreted Dilthey in 1933–1934 in terms not of historicism but of "philosophy of life," a name—*Philosophie des Lebens*—that Dilthey himself had used. Critic Theodore Plantinga returned to that interpretation in 1980 and subordinated the "Critique of Historical Reason" to that presumably more basic philosophy.[29] Such a relationship of the part to the whole was also true for Ortega's philosophy. His "historical reason" was subordinate to a larger, comprehensive "philosophy of life"—which was not just synonymous with the less extensive *personal* philosophy that he called "vital reason" and which implicated Dilthey too (6:196n).

Second Thoughts on Dilthey's "Idea of Life"

In the copious notes on Dilthey (many pages in R 40) in Ortega's archive are some important reconsiderations that vary considerably from the published views of 1933–1934. It is not clear whether all of those notes and

---

himself referred to positivism and empiricism, more or less as Ortega put it plainly (6:184, 201) but apparently not as explicitly "radical," at least not in any prominent way, although H. A. Hodges, *Wilhelm Dilthey: An Introduction* (New York: Oxford University Press, 1944), stated (88) that Dilthey's inspiration was chiefly Kant and "the Anglo French empiricists," and that he had called for a "radical reassessment of the [philosophical] tradition." Hajo Holborn recorded the meeting of Dilthey and James and their mutual admiration, as in Dilthey's praise especially of *Varieties of Religious Experience:* "In retrospect Dilthey's 'philosophy of life' and American pragmatism seem to have faced the identical problems of the age, and their answers offer many analogies" ("Dilthey and the Critique of Historical Reason," *Journal of the History of Ideas* II [January 1950]: 97). Also see H. S. Hughes, *Consciousness and Society, 1890–1930* (New York: Vintage Books, 1958), 197—evidently Holborn's was his source on James and Dilthey, who was called by one critic "the German William James."

29. Plantinga, *Historical Understanding in Dilthey,* 70–73 (Ortega's parallels with Dilthey), also 83, 91, 151. Makkreel and Ermarth mentioned Ortega but made no independent comparison.

comments preceded the published essays (in which such views were muted or absent) or were in large part a continuation of his efforts to make a "book" that finally was not completed. I favor the latter supposition, for he seems, by persisting at investigating in depth Dilthey's complete works, to have concluded that there were too many fundamental differences separating them to justify his original enthusiastic embrace. Moreover, the repeated effort to transfer James's ideas of "radical empiricism" to Dilthey is missing from these notes, and instead we see a tendency to view Dilthey through Heidegger's categories. Now both Dilthey's commitment to life as the basic reality and the coherence and logic of his philosophy of life were called into question by Ortega. He pointed out by contrast what his own positions were on these problems, reiterating his convictions that life was the radical reality and that all philosophy comes "from life."

"Dilthey fails to take life effectively and resolutely as 'radical reality.' This is the only thing that would have provided him a level of conception and a guide for discovering the structure of life." With it as basic, he could have avoided using traditional concepts in ontology and psychology, and he could have distinguished life from its contents and might have discovered its "basic categorical structure." His indecisive notion of the life reality as "a thing that is not" but that "lives for its own purpose" was not a precise enough definition. On the contrary, life precedes consciousness and thought. Life "fills everything and, if there is thinking, such is owing to life before thinking becomes a preoccupation with itself" (R 40).

Then, on a page captioned "Dilthey and Life," he pointed out that for Dilthey "history begins by being a theory of life and of knowledge of life," comparable to incipient physics as a "rational mechanics." That meant that Dilthey saw life as an "object" similar to "phenomena of nature" in physics, so that he never took it "to be radically the 'fundamental reality'" that simply *has* objects on which it works, like the concepts and themes of metaphysics, or *prima philosophia*. He saw life "floating indecisively in traditional 'ontological space,'" undetermined. For Ortega, in contrast, "life is never an object for itself," and it "does not consist primarily in thinking itself and noticing itself, but in being—itself."

Later he cautioned that life must not be confused (as by the positivists—and by Dilthey) with "the immediately given." "Life is neither object nor given—while it is life." On the contrary, "life . . . puts my thought to seeking the given." "What I do is essentially very different from [Dilthey]. I begin by seeking a radical reality as such, I find life with that specific character of radicality, and I advert that it brings with it and imposes an idea of knowledge, of truth, etc., different from that of traditional reason . . ." (R 40).

Despite differences, Ortega persisted in trying to find a more satisfactory definition of life in Dilthey's works, but without much luck in page after page of extracts. "The element most essential to life," he mused, "is the subject—without this there is nothing because life is *what is* (happens) to anyone." That reflection is important if we want to grasp Dilthey's question on "subjects of the secondary order" and "if there is a subject of history and [if] it is, in effect, life." But he found that Dilthey left "the world out of life as correlation" opposed to world, so that his idea of life as "subjectivity" was, finally, "psychologism" and idealism. Dilthey "believes that living and being is to be in one's consciousness." "It is fantastic, his Kantianism *malgré lui*!"

Formally Dilthey "defines life . . . [only] by the mode of his knowledge"— as "the fundamental fact, the point of departure in philosophy." "Time and again we see that on wanting to define life he gets lost and drops the impulse." "Is it possible that he had nothing more to say on *his* theme, on life? Incredible!" At the end he noted that at least Dilthey had started out with better prospects. In his diary in 1861 he had distinguished "system of law and science" from "system of existence" and meaning, or "worldview." "This last, formalized and including the first, would be vital reason," if not yet "historical reason." He wondered, "How explain that in his 26th year Dilthey's idea [of life] came to him? And mine at the same age?" (R 40).

On the "Idea of life," therefore, Dilthey was only Ortega's "precursor." "He did not come to see it, but it led [in him] a latent existence." As a historian, he saw life first and always "like the historian sees it: the outside of it and as the life of others, as an object that he finds in his own 'living world.'" He saw life not as "living but 'thought,' 'ideal,'" not as "*his own* life, from within" but as "the authentic and radical world-in-which-he-lives." Clearly Ortega found "holes" in Dilthey too.

"Today," observed Ortega, "we are already very far from Dilthey" on the question of life. "But we also need to stress to ourselves the deficiency in which we are still." Life is not "a thing," as it was indifferently *in* all things to ancient and medieval thinkers. Instead, it is "a mode of being, formally dramatic." "To itself life is constantly a question, and, in a radical sense, it is no more than that. This question that is life has no primarily theoretical character but has a real one. It concerns above all whether one is going to exist or not in the next instant, and this is the question par excellence. 'To be or not to be: that is the question'"—"whether to live makes sense or not," but also "whether to exist in one way or in another." Here Ortega's view of life sounds like Heidegger and existentialism. In fact, he pointed out such a "parallelism" with Heidegger: "Life is first of all an aggregate of essential problems to which man always answers with an aggregate of solutions." But he signified his own priority: in his "*Teoría Andalucía*, I; 10 April 1927!"— before *Being and Time* (R 40).

Dilthey's idea of life seemed to Ortega to be based too much on his psychology—in fact to manifest "psychologism," even as Husserl had charged. "With psychology one can only get to the mechanisms with which one lives—but not to the living," which is an "enigma" that must be deciphered. To that end the sciences broke the whole of life into its parts for study. However, argued Ortega, "The 'consistency' of life is not in its morphology nor even in its general phenotype—but in its basic implications" from which they derive. And that was a subject not for descriptive psychology but for philosophy, for what is called "ontology"—to get at the "hidden reality." "Life is not, as Dilthey never ceased to believe, a psychological fact," nor a physical or psychic "thing," but *contains* these things.[30] Life "is an absolute fact within which all else has its place."

ORTEGA'S DISENCHANTMENT
WITH "PHILOSOPHY OF LIFE"?

After 1934, Ortega did not continue publicly to relate his effort to explain life dually and rationally by the covering name "philosophy of life." Apparently his seemingly abrupt deviation was owing to his continuing study of Dilthey (R 40), where he detected weaknesses, one-sidedness, and non sequiturs not only in his "idea of life" but also in his so-called philosophy of life. As he felt his way into this topic gradually, he turned from the initial thrill of discovery to become ever more uncertain of the applicability of the term—to Dilthey at least, if not also to his own thought. Clearly he still equated "philosophy of life" at first with ratiovitalism in his own case—but not his vital reason with German *Lebensphilosophie*, which rejected his "systematization."

His first doubts coincided even with his elation at finding life covering history in Dilthey sometime before 1934. "It is revealing of Dilthey's philosophical limitations that still in the year 1911—when he died—he resolved to title the collection of his main philosophical writings (that represented fragments of volume two of *Einleitung*) *Die Geistige Welt* (!)—*Philosophie des Lebens*!!!" He objected not to his putting the "Critique of Historical Reason" formally within a "philosophy of life," for he too was about to do so in imitation. His "limitations" were in making them and "the world" *idealist* and in not seeing that "every philosophy is *of* life as subject and agent of it." But the term "philosophy of life" itself was vague, indeterminate. "Thus . . . can we use an expression like 'philosophy of life' so incorrectly, irresistibly, and indecisively . . . when life can qualify philosophy congruently only by

---

30. All that is reported in the preceding text is from R 40, as is the following section. It is not possible to designate precisely numbered documents for different views, which are extracted very sparingly for effect, not completeness.

making of it a 'philosophy *from* life,' where the latter reacts on the former definitively and informs its concepts" (R 40).

Ortega was thinking of Vico when he wrote later in *Leibniz* on the "origin of philosophy": "First one lives, then one philosophizes" (8:269). But "one philosophizes from within life. . . ." In 1949 he described his own as "a fundamental philosophy that starts from human life, and whose radical and primary phenomenon, most evident and constitutive," is man in perpetual conflict with the world (9:215). Objecting to the idealist notion of life in Husserl and even in Dilthey, he inverted Descartes' famous formula into his own "Cartesianism of life."[31] For man, "to live, to exist, is not to think." "One has put oneself to think, 'because' one already existed . . . as ship-wrecked in something called the world . . ." (5:468).

As his ongoing investigation left him ever more dissatisfied with Dilthey's idea of life, he felt a similar distrust for his use of the term "philosophy of life." "To be exact, it is not enough to speak of a 'philosophy of life' in Dilthey. Precisely he did not, in his concern with life, come to a philosophy, but, instead, he already has a philosophy—that is 'positivist-idealist' in his time[—]and from it he makes of life itself the point of view from which he thinks, [which is equivalent to] vital reason. . . . When his analysis of life seems to turn into philosophy of life or 'ratiovitalism,' he stops" (R 40).

In taking up the philosophy of Dilthey's "second epoch," he maintained that "his philosophy of life cannot nor should arrive at a doctrine or positive *theory* on any intravital problem—but . . . [reflects] his *need* to believe. But this is skepticism in the last instance," if one has nothing positive to believe. So it seems that Ortega concluded that since Dilthey's idea of life was merely external and historical, so was his philosophy—not a philosophy of life so much as an idealist philosophy of history.

Near the end of his notes on Dilthey he briefly defined "*Lebensphiloso-phie*"—in such as Schopenhauer, Wagner, Nietzsche, Tolstoi, Ruskin, and Maeterlinck—as denying "systematicism" and as being "ultimately unsus-tainable" in its metaphysical positions. It is notable that among them he did not finally include Dilthey, with his so-called *Philosophie des Lebens*. Since he found so much wanting in *Lebensphilosophie*, evidently he distinguished both his own and Dilthey's "philosophy of life" from that older category.

Certainly Ortega did not conclude that Dilthey had attained a unity in his thinking by his philosophy of life. "He is left with two worlds, the natural

---

31. For Ortega's "Cartesianism of life," see 4:58 (*"Cogito quia vivo"*); 6:49; 12:194. The very words were in Nietzsche (see chap. 5, n. 31), and the equivalent was in Unamuno and in Scheler, so it was not a very original formula. For James's reaction to Descartes, see *Writings,* 183. A character in a play by G. B. Shaw had turned Descartes's motto upside down—"I am therefore I think." See Roland N. Stromberg, *An Intellectual History of Modern Europe* (New York: Appleton, 1966), 183.

world and the 'historical world,' whose creation or restoration begets the moral [human] sciences. But it is rather clear that it cannot be a philosophical position. It is not possible to accept that . . . plurality of worlds." Ortega granted that Dilthey had aspired to attain and had shared "the unitarist tendency," but he "accentuates the epistemological instead of ontological way of stating problems." Dilthey counterposes two forms of reality—"reality as nature or cosmos and reality as human life." He did not decide between them but left "*two* forms of reality" coexisting in "deadlock." Therefore, he failed on "the radical ontological problem" (R 40). By contrast, Ortega *decided:* life is a "radical unitary duality." As "*one-two*," epistemology and ontology were for him a "unity of knowing and being." As initially and ultimately united in "life," however, Ortega's dualism actually exceeded Dilthey's.

ORTEGA'S PHILOSOPHY OF LIFE: A "UNITARY DUALITY"

One of the leading ideas that Böllnow associated with the philosophy of life for identifying it as a type was its *dualism*, or "double-sidedness," in regard to life and time, but he did not mention any countervailing concern for *unity*. Certainly Ortega stressed both the unity and the duality of his own philosophy in respect to life as the basic reality (6:205; 8:34, 43, 45–46): "radical unitary duality." As we saw in the preface and the introduction, few have affirmed Ortega's unity (system) but more were aware of its duality, even plurality, or many-sidedness. Many fewer have stressed both its unity and its diversity, and none (it seems) Ortega's own formula of "radical unitary duality" for its comprehensive, complex structure as a philosophy of life.[32] Precisely the characteristic of *duality* is very explicit in his metaphysics and is repeated (8:42) in the "Preface for Germans," but in a way unique to Ortega.

Duality

Ortega's ontology was dual in "self and circumstance"; his epistemology was dual as vital reason and historical reason. His emphasis on unity, how-

32. Böllnow, *Lebensphilosophie*, 12–13, on *Doppelseitigkeit*. Typical examples of contrasting criticisms in the 1950s were Gaos, who affirmed the then-evident duality ("two Ortegas") but also insisted on unity (in one reason), and Marías, who emphasized the unity (in vital [or living] reason) but at the expense of real duality or plurality. For attention to linguistic features of his philosophy, see Guillermo Araya Goubert, *Claves filológicas para la comprensión de Ortega* (Madrid: Gredos, 1971), 61–69, which affirmed the "unity" and "unitary character" of his "corpus" but did not demonstrate it.

ever, was even more distinctive—not only as life encompassing man and world but as "unity of knowing and being" (8:70; 12:223) The *unity and duality* (or even plurality) are characteristics that set his philosophy of life apart from all the others and made it unique, at least as much as his insistence on *rationality* and *generality*. Perhaps no more than perspectivism, historicity, or hermeneutics, did such double-sidedness (although it was more emphatic) distinguish Ortega's "philosophy of life" from Dilthey's.[33] And because of its duality it was identical neither with existentialism (vital reason) nor with historicism (historical reason) alone. By its double character it comprised both yet was itself distinct from either one, for he defined it as a "radical unitary duality." Life provided the unity, but life itself was dual—on several levels at once. From *Meditations on Quixote* (1914) forward, Ortega's whole philosophy of life was double-sided: not only with "radical" reality (life) dual, the "coexistence" of self and circumstance, but with ontology tied closely to epistemology, and (at a higher level) with its dual structure of vital reason and historical reason in existentialism and historicism.

Although the essay entitled "Dilthey and the Idea of Life" (1933–1934) did not stress the double character of Ortega's thinking, he made earlier and later references to the duality in life. In *Modern Theme* (1923) he spoke of a "double imperative" (3:169) in "the phenomenon of human life" that has "two faces—the biological and the spiritual," which are also interacting powers. This image became metaphorical as "the two ironies, or Socrates and Don Juan" (3:174), which meant both that reason becomes "a form and function of life" and that life becomes rational in vital reason. A year later he summed up *Modern Theme* as meaning that every problem has "two horns," for in thought there is the immanently biological and the historically transcendent, transvital, "ultra-biological," or rational (8:373). This dual image he repeated in some polarities (for example, 6:477–78) but he rejected it in others.

Several forms of traditional polar duality, such as body and soul, matter

33. "Dualism" (or "duality") is not even indexed in the *Obras Completas,* neither alone nor under "life," but see 12:83 ("Metaphysics of Vital Reason," 1933): "In this way, by living, man discovers the radical duality of his life, feeling that he is in something other than himself." See also 7:329–30, where Ortega resolved the vital duality of pragmatic utility and philosophic uselessness in a unity of sportiveness. Ernst R. Curtius, "Ortega y Gasset," 264: "the polarity 'life-reason' . . . is one of the principal themes of Ortega's thought." Tuttle, "Idea of Life," said that the element of polarity was "present in Dilthey but less developed and less emphasized" than in Ortega (116–17). Another (older) attempt to unify the dualism in Ortega was by Hernán Larraín Acuña, *La génesis de pensamiento de Ortega: La metafísica* (Buenos Aires: Fabril, 1962). In his conclusion (241–52) he observed that "my life = radical reality"; "life = history"; "life = reason"; or "life-reason-history." "But philosophy, work of reason, necessarily has to be like this: vital and historical." "Hence, philosophy is necessarily, like life, also 'history.'" However, he suggested no unified name for this unified philosophy.

and spirit, even realism and idealism, Ortega abandoned in the strict sense for fusion or unity, but not for any "pantheistic" reasons as alleged by Böllnow.[34] Reacting to Heidegger, he had the duality of death and resurrection meet in the unity of life (8:297). His own moderate realism combined elements of the old realism and idealism. In other ways, however, he stressed duality. In *Man and Crisis* life itself is polarized into two historical forms and two successive epochs of solitude and society (5:60–61) or crisis and stability, so anyone caught between two such worlds or epochs is likely to manifest the symptoms of life in crisis (5:93). Examining the life of "colonial man" in contrast to "metropolitan man," he remarked on the "double character" of every life as "project and situation," that is, "self and circumstance" (2:645), and many years later he confirmed that a "duality and contrast—impotence—omnipotence—accompanies man through the whole of history," taking a different form in each period (7:492). Apparently this fact of duality on so many levels reflected what he later called the "dialectical" movement of thought and history, which was based ultimately on life as self and circumstance (9:374–75, 368). In 1949, in the manner of James and Dilthey, he restated the duality in our knowledge of the life reality. It differs from other kinds of knowing, because what we have learned earlier modifies anything that we learn later, so that our knowing works on two levels: the immediate and the memorative, or historical (9:573). And life itself is "double existence"—the one we live authentically and the one others see imperfectly (9:585). At the highest level of his philosophy, finally, that pervasive duality is reflected in vital reason, which attended especially to the present or contemporary self, and historical reason, which examined its world-circumstance in time and space by history and sociology.

According to Böllnow, the "double-sidedness" of life philosophy was expressed by Dilthey as "here life grasps life"—meaning that the idea of life enters into it in two senses, as both the *subject* and the *object* of philosophizing.[35] Ortega recognized the "dual method" in Dilthey (6:211), but he himself claimed to have come to the "Idea of life as radical reality" by substituting for consciousness "the simple coexistence of 'subject' and 'object,' the [unitary-dual] image of the *Dii consentes*" already by 1916 (8:53). He said almost the same thing in *Modern Theme,* where thought, reflecting life, wears a "double face," subjective and objective at once (3:165). That duality, of course, was evident from the beginning of Ortega's independent philosophizing in life as self and circumstance, which he regarded as a "double discovery" (8:44), but which was first in Schlegel and James—without clear unity of expression. The "radical reality which is life," stated Ortega, consists

34. Böllnow, *Lebensphilosophie,* 12, 101, 142.
35. Ibid., 47, 53, 139 (on Dilthey).

not in "consciousness" but in a "radical unitary duality" (8:43): self and world-circumstance.

Unity

Ortega's public silence about "philosophy of life" after 1934 partly reflected the fact that what he was then striving toward was not so much the personal life of "everyone" any longer as it was a *vital and historical whole* of "human" life. With his selected works, he had promised in 1932 an overall *synthesis,* but his effort, for this "second voyage," turned out to be mainly on the level of "historical reason." "Life" had proved simply too vast and complicated for him to ingest by one phenomenological method or in the experience and reflection of one lifetime—as we might also conclude from a long and complex article entitled "Life" (*Vida*) in *Enciclopedia Universal Ilustrada*.[36]

During the year 1936, therefore, he changed focus from *On Living Reason*—his promised work in "*prima philosophia*" (or metaphysics), which would probably have been his 1933 lectures entitled "Metaphysics of Vital Reason"—to a "book" with a different title: *The Dawn of Historical Reason*. The larger (total) project on human life, however, was never out of his mind, as he revealed when, in his lecture entitled "On Historical Reason" (1940), he identified four philosophical approaches to life: Dilthey's, Heidegger's, Jaspers's, and his own (12:192). What he was propounding then and in his second series (1944) was not explicitly "philosophy of life," however, but "a *general Theory of human life*" in society and history. This purpose was still compatible with Dilthey's, but the name was more reminiscent of James's "Theory of Life" in *Will to Believe*. Again, when speaking at Aspen in 1949 on the theme of "our life, I repeat, the life of each and everyone," he still thought of mankind: he proposed a collective work to be undertaken there, one to be called *Experience of Life*.[37] This phrase from *History as a System* (6:37) was repeated in his metaphysics (12:133) and in his Toynbee lectures on world history—"experience of life" was a "high-flying theme" that no one had really treated before except for some lines in Dilthey (9:26). Of course, in the six years left him, he did not attempt personally such a comprehensive book

36. *Enciclopedia Universal Ilustrada* (1929), s.v. "Vida." This strange, seventy-three-page essay relates life to law, art, literature, biology, and religion, and very possibly was written by him.

37. For Ortega's Aspen lecture on Goethe, see *Goethe and the Modern Age,* ed. Arnold Bergstraesser (Chicago: Regnery, 1950), which is *not* entirely as in *Obras Completas*, 9:551–53, 569–75. For reference to the "life of each and everyone" and *Experience of Life,* see 9:573–74. An amusing and informative account of Ortega at Aspen is by James S. Allen, *The Romance of Commerce and Culture* (Chicago: University of Chicago Press, 1983), 197–293. See *History as a System,* 209 (cf. 221); 6:33 (cf. 43), where "experience of life" or "human experience" is connected with "history as a system."

on his own "philosophy of life." It remained only an aspiration, a project too vast for one life or one generation. He settled instead for two major slices of life, that "many-sided" thing, in the forms of vital reason and historical reason, which constituted a major duality in the vast plurality of that larger, mainly putative unity of "experience of life."

What had happened, then, to the intended full development and integration into "systematic" unity of Ortega's now dual philosophy? In attempting an answer, let us modify somewhat the pelagic metaphors he used as he followed Columbuses (Schlegel, James, and Dilthey) to the new world (or "worldview") of "life," which, in his "twenty-sixth year," our mental mariner had first glimpsed, "distant and confusedly," like the dim shore of an "unknown" land (6:166, 70; 12:182). Crying out, "To sea, to sea!" he and his "generation of 1911" had "launched" their ships toward an "imaginary coast" (8:41–42). After he had reached land and named it "vital reason" in 1916, he saw "one fine day" in 1923 or 1924 that he was beached like a "Robinson Crusoe" (6:347), still viewing life in his isolated "self" on offshore islands. The next decade he spent planning and probing, with the method he called "historical reason," to get into the "new intellectual" continent of social and historical "Life" in the now-tangible distance. To reach it he went to sea again after 1932 on a "second voyage" (6:356). Expecting soon to encompass human life, instead he wore himself out trying to map it with historical reason. At his death he was still sailing, the farther bounds of life still largely beyond his grasp.

Modern Theme had summed up Ortega's first voyage, his *individual* "philosophy of life," as "vital reason"; *The Dawn of Historical Reason* should have summed up the "second voyage" as a "philosophy of history" for the historical and social dimensions of *life in general*. These, however, also pointed to a third venture, a kind of "philosophy of language," or *New Philology* (6:393; 9:751–52), which (had he lived yet another decade in better health) he might have developed as still a newer method for *Experience of Life,* an ultimate, final synthesis, an *integrated, general* "philosophy of life." Thus he would have gone "beyond" Schlegel's original threefold plan. When he died, most of the third project was still only planned, though preliminary parts of it perhaps appeared posthumously in *Man and People* chapter titles: "What People Say"; "Language: Toward a New Linguistics"; "'Public Opinion', Social 'Observances', Public Power."

Since "life" remained his basic quest to the end, then "philosophy of life" suffices to cover the whole project. Vital reason dealt with *personal* and mainly "present" life. The difficult problems of trying to recover an enormous vital "lost past" of humanity and to project from it an uncertain future, however, had become Ortega's paramount concern in the 1930s and later. Hence, historical reason, for which historiology and "philology" (at least as "etymology") became new methods. His "philosophy of life" denotes the largely unattained genus (or general type) of philosophy that Ortega intended, and "vital reason" and "historical reason" signify the "twin" species that he managed to effect, more or less, in a long lifetime of philosophizing. He almost completed the two branches, however, before he had done the inverted trunk of a ginkgo tree of life.

A brief article, "The Dawn of Historical Reason" (June 1935), illustrates Ortega's new tack, abruptly taken as he decided not to continue with "living reason" as promised in *History as a System* (6:38n), presumably as a "philosophy of life." He had already established that our "experience of life" is overwhelmingly historical, even in its present aspect, just as the past and the future really *exist* only in the present (5:460, 534; 6:476), or as the past and the present shape our anticipated future (9:587). When he switched over to "Dawn," however, he began by acknowledging that Dilthey around 1860 had discovered "a new reality: human life" (12:326). Then he defined life in a very Jamesian way: this strange, neglected reality was not a thing, neither physical nor psychic, but was a dramatic "happening." Of itself, life has "structure" that consists in "connections," not just individual and concrete but also general and formal—among the more basic and important of which are the "beliefs," even the doubts, in which we live (9:645–47). The belief in which modern man had lived since Galileo and Descartes was physical, mathematical, and natural reason, no less a "faith" than any other. But now "the situation has changed," because European man (again in a deep historical crisis) no longer lives in that belief but seeks answers to "appropriately human problems" for which the fixed, static, and invariable concepts of "nature" of the traditionally modern kind do not suffice (12:328–29).

Since Dilthey, observed Ortega, we know that "man has no nature," but a history of "variations" instead, for his "being" is *becoming*. "Man, who *is* not, goes on *making* himself in the dialectical series of his experiences." Therefore, because of his historicity, "the only thing we can know of man is what he has been." "The past constrains the future." "For that reason, the science of the past, properly understood, is the only science of the future in the very precise sense in which a science of the future is possible." Hence reason must now be freed from the limitations of physics and mathematics and must become a "historical reason," a "very new and saving reason" that had not existed before, because "until now what we had of reason was not historical and what we had of history was not rational" (12:329). This new reason was "historical reason," which was also a "living reason" that was subject to life.

In Ortega's conception, historical reason is subordinate to life, and the intermediate form of "living reason," in which he expressed it as most clearly subject to life, from 1933 to 1937, was directly out of James's *Pragmatism*. As noted previously, that idea probably had inspired in young Ortega the name "vital reason." It first emerged explicitly in his usage in 1933–1934 in essays in *La Nación* that later entered into *Man and Crisis* (5:135) and *History as a System* (6:38n). His only published references to "living reason" in later years (1949, 1951) were in context with the historicity of man (9:589). Historical reason thus emerged gradually out of vital reason—a progressive consequence finally of his recognizing in 1923 that "*Life* is particularity, change, [and] development; in a word, *history*" (3:198). And "we are life" (7:466), or man is life, and therefore is history (5:178). Hence, Dilthey's "many-sided" life (8:297) is—on two sides—at once "vital and historical reason" (6:23). Having attained the former more or less by the 1920s, Ortega thenceforth strove to possess the other dimension more adequately and in synthetic form. That historical reason was (or became) his "second voyage" to Life.

Since Ortega did not write anything where he formally, explicitly, and unequivocally adopted the name "philosophy of life" for his dual body of thought, is it finally justifiable to apply this concept to him? Aside from his notes on Dilthey, he used the term only a few times (and not very conspicuously), mainly in 1933–1934 to identify Dilthey, whom he described as "parallel" to himself in major ways, and later, from 1949 to 1951, to identify himself with the existentialists. Does that concept therefore encompass his ongoing dual philosophy of vital reason *and* historical reason? That it does go on fitting his efforts is supportable by logic and by evidence, such as his continuing parallels with Schlegel and Dilthey.

The unity of Ortega's philosophy would be lost, if it were simply a developing "*one-two*" sequence of "stages" that are not finally a "unitary duality" of self and circumstance as basic life-reality and also of vital reason and historical reason as a "philosophy of life." The textual context is both consistent with and pregnant with this meaning: "two in one."

Without a thoroughgoing unity-with-duality of structure, Ortega's metaphors and images are pointless and meaningless. Several times repeated after 1916 (in "What Is Philosophy?" in 1930, in the "Preface for Germans" in 1934, and in the lectures entitled "On Historical Reason" in 1940), the image of the *Dii consentes* (the Dioscuri, or Gemini) signifies "unanimous" and "twin" concepts, inseparably linked in *life*—but not confounded in a substantial identity, or oneness, that wipes out their duality. The *one* ginkgo tree with its *two* equal branches supplemented Ortega's metaphors on life as "unitary duality": two aspects of the same basic philosophical reality. Although the duality to which he directly alluded with these metaphors was the "root" (meaning "radical") unity of life comprehending the duality of self and circumstance, it seems logically necessary and aesthetically symmetrical to carry that initial structure of "unitary duality" over into the *development* of his philosophy, into its obvious duality of stages, vital and historical. His philosophy began and ended with life, but was it *philosophy of life* throughout?

Any attempt to substantiate either unity or duality in the names that Ortega actually used over a half-century of his philosophizing encounters certain odd lacunae of usage. He did not mention "historical reason" along with vital reason in 1934 in the German preface to *The Modern Theme* (1923), although he had introduced it a decade earlier in 1924. That absence is not so strange as his omitting "vital reason" from all that he published after 1936. Yet the posthumous *Historical Reason* (his 1940 and 1944 lectures) clearly kept vital reason as a first and always equal "theme" (12:182, 193, 299). So his philosophy remained dual then, but did it remain *one* as "philosophy of life"?

After 1934 he became dissatisfied with "philosophy of life," but his efforts in the 1940s to coin a better name in lectures entitled "On Historical Reason" were not felicitous. His intention was to provide for the "experience of life" (of "our life") under the rubric "practical knowledge," so to describe or define its *general* "structure or consistency," its essential "anatomy" (12:300). The names he proposed, however—"biosophy" as "technique of life" (R 37), "biognosis" as "knowledge of life," or "biology" as literally "study of life" distinct from material "zoology," or finally "general Theory of life" (12:299–302)—were even worse ways to designate a *general* philosophy of life. "Life," he said, is necessarily "my life," the life of "each and everyone," so is it possible to "elaborate a *general Theory of life in the singular*"? Fichte said: "To philosophize is not properly called living; life is not properly called philosophy" (12:303). Then, with his typical insouciance, Ortega dropped the theme. But, coming at the end of his lectures, this showed that he aimed at something higher, more general on life than either earlier vital reason or current historical reason.

In his "hermeneutic" fashion, he returned to the problem of how to get a general philosophy (or theory) of life out of the experience of concrete and individual lives at Aspen in 1949. "[T]he 'experience of life' . . . is, almost entirely, non-transferable," so, "as Dilthey said already, each new generation has to begin its own anew." But something could "be done" by reflecting "scientifically on that enormous and infinitely juicy fact that is life's experience," so as to get a *theory* that would "truly be transferable" (9:573–74). That would make a "splendid theme" for collective work at Aspen. Although nothing was done, he thus showed that his own "system" of thought remained by intention a "philosophy of life" that aspired to incorporate a "general theory of life" with the aid of history and the "human sciences." Both vital reason and historical reason dealt directly with the "individual and concrete," but his philosophy of life aimed also at the "general and formal." Aside from some parts and fragments, such as his historical generations theory, life in historical crisis, and stages (ages) of life theory, he did not develop a *generalizing* content for his philosophy of life—not in a specific and coherent "General Theory of Life" that was published, in synthetic or integrated form, in any work of philosophy, history, or sociology.

As Ortega saw it, history is properly concerned with the concrete and the individual, but it too needs a "general theory of human life." But that theory must start out as "a theory of personal life" (9:75). How do we get from the individual to "the aggregate that we call society or collectivity," except by theory? Outside his philosophy, the closest he ever came to a "General Theory of Life" was in his sociology, in *Man and People,* which he was concluding when he died in 1955. Vitalist and pragmatist, his sociology was concerned with the abstract and "general" in "*theory* of life," which was above and beyond "the concrete [content] of my life" and that of every individual (7:137). Our "vital world" is a "paradise" of the concrete that we have had to generalize. "This life is the life of each one, but its theory is, like every theory, general." Thus, at the end, he was returning to "Adam," to general philosophy.

After the notes and essay on Dilthey and the unpublished "Preface for Germans" (1934), Ortega publicly and explicitly referred to "philosophy of life" only twice more: in lectures on Toynbee in 1949 (9:85–86) and in an oral exchange with Merleau-Ponty in 1951. In each case he tried openly to annex both German and French existentialism to a kind of "philosophy of life" that he claimed had properly begun with himself, and both times he also linked philosophy of life to history or historical reason. By claiming from twenty to thirty years' priority for himself, he was identifying his own philosophy as a philosophy of life from well before 1920—approximately—so he included vital reason, at least where it was generalizing. At Geneva in 1951, after his talk entitled "Past and Present for Contemporary Man," he was distinguishing Kantian "pure reason" from "another form of reason" that the crisis in fundamental principles of Western civilization now made necessary: his own "living reason" or (better) "historical reason," of which they had not heard at Geneva. When someone objected that Dilthey had such a concept, Ortega acknowledged that he was "the greatest thinker who . . . had come to this new way of thinking," but he had not actually "arrived at historical reason. What he called historical reason was the customary reason, pure reason applied to historical reality." Dilthey had indeed come first to "a new idea, the idea of life," to a new philosophy of which no one (including Scheler) had "the least idea." Then, before actually naming that philosophy, Ortega made an astonishing claim: "It is after Dilthey that that philosophy of life began, and it began in that little peninsula situated beyond high mountains"— not Italy but Spain. "And it is for it that Heidegger . . . has repeated things that we have said in Spain, thirteen or fourteen years earlier." However, he still had a problem with Heidegger, who preferred "being" to "life," although "con-

sciousness" and "being" were basic ideas now in crisis. "Being" was an outmoded "scholastic terminology." "His mistake is in having wanted to make an
ontology." But "we have to go beyond the idea of Being," for "the word *Being*
is not capable of expressing this new reality that is Life." Man is not "being."[38]

After an interlude, Merleau-Ponty raised the issue of "life and history"
again. Having already expressed "full agreement" with Ortega's "concept of
history," he now disputed what he assigned to him as "*Lebensphilosophie* or
Bergson's *philosophie de la vie*." How could their outworn ideas help his
"concept of life, of historical thinking"? Was Dilthey's vague, inexact notion
of *Leben* sufficient to express *Geisteswissenschaft* or historicity? Was not Ortega too hard on those who preferred *être* and *néant* (or non-being) for a
historical dialectic? Then Ortega said that Dilthey, who "discovered life as
historicity," had never used "being" or "non-being"—and neither had Heraclitus. "So what?" countered Merleau-Ponty. Not "insisting" on the word
Leben, Ortega granted it was not exact enough for him either. "I never use
the expression *Lebensphilosophie*. There is no philosophy of *Leben*." However,
"being" had meant something very different to the Greeks. "To speak philosophy, to think philosophy, one has to go slowly."[39]

Was Ortega playing a game of words with Merleau-Ponty? Was *vie* or *vida*
somehow better than *Leben*? Clearly he continued to prefer "philosophy of
life" for himself. True, in his notes, he had already rejected *Lebensphilosophie*,
both for Dilthey and for himself. By claiming to have started "philosophy of
life" in Spain, he evidently meant something *new*—a philosophy of life that
was more properly, more genuinely such than in Dilthey.

In Spain it has recently been proposed that indeed Ortega's "Spanish
philosophy" was a "philosophy of life" (*vida*) and that he had developed it
either from native Spanish roots or from a Husserlian phenomenology.[40]

---

38. Ortega, remarks in "Troisième entretien privé": "C'est après Dilthey que l'on a
commencé cette philosophie de la vie . . . dans cette petite peninsule"—that is, in Spain
(289).

39. See supplemental note 39, chap. 8.

40. First see Francisco Sánchez Blanco, "Continuidad y discontinuidad de Ortega y
Gasset respecto al pensamiento español del siglo XIX," *Cuadernos Hispanoamericanos*, no.
403–5 (January–March 1984): 602–14. Also see "Man's Self-Interpretation-in-Existence:
Phenomenology and Philosophy of Life—Introducing the Spanish Perspective," *Analecta
Husserliana* 29 (1990)—title of the whole issue. Therein see esp. A.-T. Tymieniecka, "Phe-
nomenology of Life and the New Critique of Reason: From Husserl's Philosophy to the
Phenomenology of Life and of the Human Condition" (3–18); and (Part 2: Philosophy of
Life in Spanish Philosophical Thought) Harold C. Raley, "Phenomenological 'Life': A
New Look at the Philosophical Enterprise in Ortega y Gasset" (93–106); also the essay on
Unamuno by María Avelina Cecilia. Husserl may well have influenced Ortega consciously
or *un*consciously on the idea of life, other than as the "radical reality," but he very strongly
implied the contrary. Apart from the idea of life as basic, however, an influence of Husserl's method is not doubted, even in Ortega's philosophy of life.

Apart from his basic disposition, our evidence shows stronger foreign sources than Husserl in James and Dilthey, if not also Schlegel, for "life" initially and later. If phenomenology was the chief *method* of his earlier personalist "philosophy of life" as vital reason (6:208n; 8:42) or as existentialism (8:46), it was insufficient for historical reason as historicism or for his later philosophy of life as a "General Theory of Life."

We must either accept Ortega's own definition of philosophy of life as a "radical unitary duality" (8:43) that includes both existentialism and historicism, or we must fall back on one of the earlier, unbalanced unitary explanations of Marías, Gaos, or Stern, or an unsatisfactory variation thereof.[41] But Ortega's philosophy of life was never completed; his "General Theory" still needed the fruits of "historical reason" as a new method in both history and sociology. He could not finish his great project merely as a philosophy of *life*, nor as strictly, exclusively, *philosophy* of any kind. Accordingly, he reached for answers that lay "beyond philosophy."

"Beyond Philosophy"

To Merleau-Ponty, Ortega implied not just the uniqueness of his own philosophy of life but also the inadequacy of any philosophy for effective generalization on life. "It is very probable," he had added, "that what we are beginning to do is quite different from what is concretely called philosophy." If this were not *philosophy*, was it then just a "General Theory of Life" (9:396, 650)—or perhaps a "meta-philosophy" like Scheler's? Privately he had adverted to an "ultra-philosophy" (8:266, 314), literally something "beyond philosophy." As philosophy was born "one fine day" in Greece, "philosophizing, all philosophizing" was maybe henceforth too limited as an "instrument," so that alone it no longer "worked" well as a "way of thinking" but required adding "another way of confronting the universe intellectually" (8:270). "Perhaps we are at the dawn of this other 'fine day.'" Obviously, he meant "historical reason," which he applied also beyond philosophy in the "human sciences" such as history and sociology. "The hour of the historical sciences has begun," he had proclaimed in 1940 (12:195, 237), or the dawning of a new age of "historical reason" in *History as a System* (6:49–50) in 1936.

Alas, just as unfinished as his philosophy of life was his *Dawn of Historical Reason* (9:83). On those two great "themes" too long he had responded: "It will be continued" (4:384), until at last there was no more time, no more life. As a new "way of thinking," Ortega's "Dawn" project will have to be "continued" in another study—an interdisciplinary investigation into history and the "human sciences."

41. See supplemental note 41, chap. 8.

Bibliographical Essay

A BRIEF WORLD HISTORY
OF ORTEGA CRITICISM

riticism of Ortega as a philosopher began in Argentina earlier than it did in Spain. By his diversity Ortega confounded all of the earlier Hispanic critics, however, in their efforts to define or to categorize him as a whole. Rarely do critics review journals and newspapers or articles that appear therein—where almost all his early ideas and production were launched. They naturally concentrate on books, of which he had published only two before 1923: the *Meditations on Quixote* (1914) and *Invertebrate Spain* (1921), neither of which was taken seriously as philosophy at the time. He also put out an anthology called *Personas, Obras, Cosas* (Persons, works, things—1916), which contained youthful essays, especially criticism of art and literature and a theory of social and political education. In the prologue he adverted to his opposition to "subjectivism" (1:419) and implied that "objectivism" (Ferrater Mora)—or *realism*—was now his philosophy. Little more than a hint of pragmatism was evident there in his explicit opposition to the old idealism as "intellectualism" (1:439), although one selection, "Adam in Paradise," was more pragmatism than "philosophy of culture."

Ortega's philosophy was first examined for its species and tendencies by auditors of his lectures in Argentina in 1916 and 1917—as on realism and idealism—before they took up his books from 1922 to 1924, especially the perplexing new "Theme of Our Time."

EARLY HISPANIC CRITICS

In the early 1920s, a decade before any North Americans saw affinities, Ortega eluded and misled Argentine critics who came to suspect him of being a crypto-pragmatist in *Modern Theme*.[1] Actually, he did not deny the charge, which was true for his early metaphysical foundations but not for his philosophy in general, which was then becoming existentialist and historicist. Even in 1936, for both Germans and Spaniards, Bruno Ibeas found Ortega undefinable by any of the accepted general names. "Ortega is Ortega," but he resembled philosophy of life too, as in Nietzsche and Dilthey.[2] Scores of earlier critics (collected in Iriarte) had shown even less understanding, and they were less laudatory and more unfavorable on balance. His early philosophical works were so journalistic and scattered, apart from *Modern Theme*, that critics did not know what to make of him. Circumstances made him hold back such works as *History as a System, Ideas and Beliefs*, and *Man and Crisis* ("Galileo") until after 1940. Until then, critics lacked the essentials for a comprehensive evaluation.

The first well-informed critical estimates of Ortega as a philosopher came only during World War II and after. Then, with the publication of the first six volumes of his complete works in 1946–1947, Spain, Europe, and the Americas were able at last to take a reasonably full measure of Ortega's philosophical tenets and development. Although his pragmatism was then almost wholly forgotten, it was soon generally realized that his *Modern Theme* had been a form of proto-existentialism before Heidegger and that "History as a System" (1936) implied some kind of historicism. Critics had to wait even through the 1960s and longer, however, for some of his most important unfinished works in philosophy and history to appear posthumously. When they finally came, they showed that the initial postwar assessments were not so incorrect, however negative and hostile in spirit. They also showed that Ortega clearly was not *just* an existentialist but also a historicist, and even a phenomenologist—and more.

First into the fray was a Spanish Jesuit and neo-Thomist, Joaquín Iriarte, who knew Ortega and his family personally. He mounted an assault through the 1940s that culminated in 1949–1950 with accusations of existentialism and historicism, as if they were godless heresies. Ortega's "newest vision" was historicism and an extreme relativism deriving from Nietzsche and Dilthey, after an amoral and irreligious existentialism from Scheler and Heidegger. Iriarte's hostility was closely echoed by Spanish Dominicans and by the

1. Guglielmini, "Algo más sobre Ortega"; Irwin Edman, review of *Modern Theme*, in *New York Herald Tribune Books*, February 19, 1933, p. 3. Also see Graham, "Pragmatism and Philosophy of History in Ortega." Since our concern is criticism, *influence* from Ortega in the various Latin American nations will not be covered here, but that topic is well indexed by Donoso and Raley for Argentina and Mexico, where he had greatest impact. See essays especially by Leopoldo Zea, Patrick Romanell, and Patrick Dust on Mexico; Kessel Schwartz, Maximo Etchecopar, and Rosa Martínez de Codes on Argentina.

2. Ibeas, "La filosofía de Ortega."

Mexican Jesuit, José Sánchez Villaseñor, whose attack on Ortega as an existentialist was also published in Chicago by Regnery in 1949. The latter saw him as progressing from Nietzsche through Husserl, Heidegger, and Dilthey to an existentialism and a historicism that were rank skepticism (if not atheism) and immorality. Privately, Ortega despised Villaseñor and Regnery (R 33), but publicly he held to his "long silence" toward all critics. He was following the prudent example of William James, who, despairing of convincing critics that their own timeless absolutes were wrong, awaited the judgment of a later generation. Irritated that they could not provoke Ortega to break silence, clerics turned on an "inferior" disciple, the Marxist Gaos, for his "rude frankness."[3]

It was in Mexico that lay professor Eduardo Nicol lambasted Ortega's Diltheyan historicism (existentialism implied) as bad philosophy. In exile there, José Gaos now upheld his master's "ratio-historicism" against charges of "utter" relativism, but he did not realize how far he had developed in later years. His "two Ortegas" embodied Heideggerian existentialism and "pure" historicism, but he defended the "unity" of his thought as a "cultural philosopher"—perhaps the first time that nondescript, inappropriate name was used. For his part, Nicol anticipated Gaos' analysis of the several stages in Ortega's thought and the hostile reaction to historicism by most later critics.[4]

Picking up the main points of critical assessment, a former admirer, Domingo Marrero, who became disillusioned by Ortega's desertion of the Spanish Republic and by his "unchristian" worldliness, described him in 1949 as a "centaur," a hybrid who was half-philosopher and half-litterateur.[5] He was dual also in his original "existential metaphysics" (from 1910) and in his later "metaphysics of historical reason," or historicism.

Under attack from an "inquisition" of clerical scholastic traditionalists and political rightists or Falangists on one side and by lay philosophical tradi-

---

3. Joaquín Iriarte, "La filosofía de Ortega y Gasset," *Razón y Fe* (Madrid), no. 122 (February–April 1941): 102–15; idem, *La ruta mental de Ortega: crítica de su filosofía* (Madrid: Razón y Fe, 1949), 7, 20, 34–36, 55–56, 62–63; idem, *Ortega,* which contains excerpts from earlier critics (243–92). Sánchez Villaseñor, *Ortega Existentialist,* 57, 224; idem, *La Crisis del Historicismo y otros ensayos* (Mexico City: Editorial Jus, 1945), 11, 133 (on Gaos); William James, *Meaning of Truth,* 159.

4. Gaos, *Sobre Ortega,* 87–90, 97, 99–100; Nicol, *Historicismo y Existencialismo,* chap. 9, 308–31. Nicol, like Gaos, posited two "stages" in Ortega, the first a "vitalism of a biological type" that coincided with Heidegger on life and history (312, 314, 317, 323–24) and the second a historicism that he likewise traced only from 1924 to 1936, from "Atlantises" to "History as a System" (312–14, 327); Nicol was very harshly critical (330–31).

5. Domingo Marrero, *El centauro: Persona y pensamiento de Ortega y Gasset,* 15, 21, 51. He disagreed with both Ortega and his neo-Thomist critics, defended his priority and originality in existentialism vis-à-vis both Heidegger and Jaspers, and his perspectivism in regard to Whitehead (18–19, 26).

tionalists and republican leftists on the other, Ortega kept a stubborn silence about the real nature of his doctrines during his last five years. When he died in 1955, his philosophical identity and reputation were therefore somewhat ill-defined. Many commemoratives in 1955–1956 saluted him but rarely with insight. In fact, he had left things in a terrible muddle that has taken decades to sort out.

After the first seven of his posthumous volumes came out in 1958, with "What Is Philosophy?" (1930), the debate resumed. In 1961 from Puerto Rico, Vicente Marrero attacked. A "worldly" (*mondaine*) philosopher, Ortega was only a "brilliant epigone" with an "idealist-vitalist amalgam" of doctrines he had taken from Nietzsche, Dilthey, Bergson, Heidegger, and Scheler. "His philosophy is [thus] no secret. . . ." Within his secondhand "philosophy of life," he was still an existentialist and a "radical" historicist. Despite his hostile and "superficial analysis,"[6] Marrero's was the most comprehensive identification yet of that complex philosophy, but he had outraged Ortega's own "epigones," his disciples, especially Marías, who rejected all those definitions of their master as an unoriginal imitator.

Marías and Defenders from the "School of Madrid"

Julián Marías and Fernando Vela counterattacked by denying the applicability of Marrero's and all such general categories to their hero. They and other loyal Orteguistas of a so-called School of Madrid from the late 1940s through the 1960s and beyond insisted on the uniqueness of Orteguismo, which was to be defined only by the master's own terminology of "vital reason" (or "perspectivism") simply as a "Spanish philosophy," whatever that was supposed to be.[7] Vela scolded critics as "literary maggots" and

6. Vicente Marrero, *Ortega, filósofo "mondain,"* 135–36, 181–89, 242–48. Ventura Doreste's acid review of this hostile book appeared in *Insules* 17 (May 1962), citing especially Marrero's weak scholarship and inconsistencies (3, 12).

7. Marías, *Circumstance and Vocation.* Almost the only background *influences* on Ortega that Marías would admit were Nietzsche's (as a "presence"—187–88) and Chateaubriand, Barrès, and Renan (183); everything else (notably Bergson and vitalism, James and pragmatism, Husserl and phenomenology, Dilthey and historicism, Unamuno and existentialism, and "philosophy of life," or *Lebensphilosophie*) was all just "part of his vital perspective" (336) or "situation" that he deliberately omitted (95–96). Marías gave no specific (or even identifiable) general influence, but had strange assumptions (see 171). Fernando Vela, *Ortega y los existencialismos* (Madrid: Revista de Occidente, 1961), 39–41. On Marías, see Morón Arroyo, *Sistema,* 26–28. Also see Paul Ilie, "Philosophy as Performance: The Anti-Ortegans," in *José Ortega y Gasset,* ed. Nora Marval McNair (New York: Greenwood, 1987), 51–56, on alienated Ortegans of left and right. Eduardo Nicol, *El Problema de la filosofía española* (Madrid: Editorial Tecnos, 1961), 7–9, 119–39, on "the Orteguist stage" and its "end," which he welcomed because of Ortega's alleged failure in professional, "scientific"

insisted that the posthumous works (the *Leibniz* especially) proved that Ortega had actually delivered them from existentialism. Marías rejected the entire batch of foreign imputations as he endeavored to show that Ortega had gone "beyond" them, one and all, with his unique "ratiovitalism."

Protest or ignore it as they might, the loyal disciples, who then suffered from a siege mentality, could not stem the tide of generalizing interpretation. Obviously, Ortega was more than merely a *Spanish* philosopher of "perspectivism" or "ratiovitalism." If it was too much to impute existentialism to him, despite its growing Western respectability, the "relativist" historicism was still unspeakable for Marías. And philosophy of life, or phenomenology? Not if Marías could help it, so he redoubled his efforts to restrict Ortega to "vital reason," which fully absorbed "historical reason" for him until 1983.

Strangely, while acknowledging his influence on Ortega, Marías had recognized Dilthey's "amalgam" of vitalism and historicism in a "philosophy of life." Of course, he made a good point that Ortega was more "rational" and "realist" than his German idealist sources, but was he so "unique" for that? Still, he was Spain's greatest philosopher, if not—given his terminal place in Marías's *History of Philosophy*—the world's last and greatest philosopher.[8] Was that idolatrous *beatería* toward Ortega?

Gradually, but never completely, Marías seemed to have rather effectively convinced or cowed Hispanic critics. From the 1960s through the 1970s they became noticeably less prone to interpret Ortega in terms of general European philosophy. *Vive la différence.* Marías overdid it, however, as he all but wiped away earlier valid perceptions of similarity and affinity. It is not so much that his analysis of Ortega erred in specific *details*, where he was rich and reliable, but he was wrong about the *whole*. Regrettably, he persisted even in misnaming the parts, or levels and stages, of Ortega's philosophy, so that they were never to be named as existentialism and historicism. Marías made such a fetish of Ortega's originality in almost everything that he could not see that what really mattered was only that he be original as a *whole*, regardless of borrowed parts. And that whole was not just vital reason, but equally historical reason.

---

technique and methods, his writing only "essays" for the dull public and ignoring traditional approved "forms" of philosophy. For Ortega on his "Spanish" philosophy, see 4:33–37 and 7:194; also compare with his earlier views that "Spanish philosophy" meant explanation "in words that are fully meaningful for Spaniards," by participating (1913) in a "renaissance" of *European* philosophy, which had been decadent *in* Spain (1:244, 265n).

8. Marías, "Ortega y su filosofía de la razón vital," *Historia de la filosofía*, 10th ed. (Madrid: Revista de Occidente, 1958), vol. 1; idem, *Circumstance and Vocation*, 68, 72–74, 90–91.

Earlier Hispanic Syntheses

Without benefit of all the later historically oriented but posthumous works, which no one anywhere to date has utilized sufficiently, it was not possible before the 1980s to get a full and accurate grasp of Ortega's development. One sympathetic critic, however, Ferrater Mora, even from 1936, had done better than the others. In his *Outline* (1956) he discerned three "stages" in Ortega's development, but (like Marías) he preferred Ortega's own typology and terminology in order to offset the growing tendency to identify his "Spanish philosophy" too closely with other existentialists. Distrusting the historicism he detected, he (again like Marías) thus halted Ortega's "authentic" development at too early a level: at "vital reason." But this "ratiovitalism" he found not so different from existentialism, nor from "philosophy of life," which (unlike Marías) he half-allowed, as he did later with historicism.[9]

Since it was hard to classify the "unity" and "diversity" in Ortega's "open" type of "system," Ferrater's interpretation remained open too. In "historical reason" he saw "a theme that will grow bigger in Ortega's thought: historicism"—evidently seen as still within his "philosophy of human existence" or "philosophy of human life." Later (1959) he found Ortega's development akin to existentialist "philosophical anthropology" as a "philosophy of man," but not one of "culture." By 1961 he defined Ortega's "radical form of thinking" as historical and systematic, as in his newly published *Leibniz*. In the fifth edition of his *Diccionario de Filosofía* (1965) he clearly regarded Ortega's philosophy as more historicist than was Heidegger's but still not a "pure and simple historicism." He, unlike Marías, saw that Ortega (like Dilthey) put historicism in "a philosophy of life as a total phenomenon" that contained the historical. Altogether Ferrater's developing view of Ortega was the most comprehensive to date, rather like Marrero's but instead *realist* and sympathetic. Moreover, he recognized that Ortega's thought extended "beyond" into an "ultra-philosophy."[10]

In 1986, Ferrater again summed up Ortega's philosophy as an "objectivism" of things and ideas at base but as also becoming a "historicism," or "historicist

---

9. José Ferrater Mora to Ortega, January 10, 1936, with copy of his article on Ortega's "philosophical personality," prepared for the ninth edition of *Dictionary of Philosophy,* ed. Heinrich Schmidt (R 20). Ferrater was perhaps the only critic for whom Ortega broke his "silence" to answer—positively, perhaps because he accorded him priority to Heidegger, affirmed his independence of "biologism," and his "overcoming" of the old realism and idealism (March 7, 1936, in R 32). Also see Ferrater's *Outline* and his *Ortega y Gasset: Etapas de una filosofía* (Barcelona: Barral, 1958).

10. Ferrater Mora, *Outline,* 45–46 (and n.); idem, "Ortega y Gasset," in *Philosophy in the Mid-Century,* ed. R. Klibansky (Florence: Nuova Italia, 1959), 2:214–16; idem, "On a Radical Form of Thinking," *Texas Quarterly* 4 (Spring 1961): 32–38; idem, "Ortega y Gasset," *Diccionario de Filosofía,* 5th ed. (Buenos Aires: Sudamericana, 1965).

realism" at the end, though still bound to life as "radical reality" and "crisis."[11] His rather inchoate concept of objectivism as Ortega's first stage was compatible with what Philip Silver later found in his relation to Husserl and with what I have found in his affinity to James: a basic *realism* in both cases.

After Ferrater Mora's briefer schematic analysis, others then began to dig deeper into Ortega and with more favorable assessments than before. The corpus of his philosophy, which was growing with posthumous tomes (1958–1962), was still too massive to take in as a whole. One of his disciples then in Caracas, Manuel Granell, in 1960 tried to define his "system," despite the "unsystematic" forms of his thought, as existing at least in his *mind*—or maybe in his missing "Dawn of Historical Reason." But he was unable yet to move from basics (life as a radical reality of "things" and "ideas," or realism *and* idealism), to any *general* categories that related vital reason and historical reason to phenomenology, existentialism, or historicism. Then, in 1962, another disciple, Arturo Gaete, attempted in vain to define Ortega's "mature system" more or less on Marías's terms and contrary to Marrero. Ortega's philosophy was "original" and also was compatible with Christianity, and its vital reason and historical reason were united *not* in *Lebensphilosophie* but in a plurality of "life, reason, and history" as interchangeable concepts for radical reality.[12] However, since Ortega did not regard reason as synonymous with life and history, Gaete granted too much to Marías and sought unity at the expense of generality.

Starting from Nicol, Gaos, Marrero, and Ferrater Mora, Ciriaco Morón Arroyo in 1968 took up the problem of "structure" in Ortega's "system," which was still such an enigma that he was little used. Going deeply into complex textual analysis and more openly critical of Marías, Morón put more nuances into Ferrater's three "stages." His "one system" of four stages was, however, in origin almost exclusively German, including Cohen's neo-Kantianism, phenomenology from Scheler, and a nonspecific philosophy of life related to both Heidegger's existentialism and Dilthey's historicism, which together made up a last stage. Thus, he ended with an overall "Heideggerian" existentialism—after an earlier stage of "biologism" that was more hypothetical than real, for he later reduced it to a mere "tone." We may wonder why there was not finally a fifth stage, if historicism was truly "radical" and "total" and represented "a new order of ideas."[13] Instead, like

11. Ferrater Mora, *Diccionario de Grandes Filósofos* (Madrid: Alianza, 1986), 341–47.

12. Granell, *Ortega*, 131–53 ("El Sistema de Ortega"); Gaete, *Sistema maduro de Ortega*, 95, 101–2, 105, 122–23, 261. Gaete opposed the positions taken by both Domingo Marrero and Vicente Marrero, and he defended a unity in his "original" philosophy.

13. Morón Arroyo, *Sistema*, 7, 29–30, 59–63, 81–84, 305, 355–56, 440 (on a "biological" stage). This idea, like "pure historicism," seems first to have surfaced in Nicol and then in Gaos, *Sobre Ortega*, 90, 182, 235, both of whom considered either two stages (as do I) or four (as does Morón Arroyo).

Marías, Morón identified historical reason at the end with vital reason, but he took the whole for idealist. His chapter on Ortega's "doctrine of history" did not fully exploit the historical texts that were then available, but his *Sistema* was a truly formidable work of sound scholarship.

Where Morón Arroyo elevated existentialism over historicism in Ortega, José Luis Abellán had come to an opposite imbalance, more or less like Gaos had done. In a study in 1966 he had seen Ortega as a "philosopher of history." But if his historicist denial of "human nature" was the "downfall of metaphysics," why did not Abellán then stress Ortega's "metahistory"? Even as the rational opposite of the mysticism of Unamuno, a "Renaissance humanism" was no better for defining his "Hispanic philosophy" than was Gaos's "culturalism." Evidently in a later book (1970) on Ortega's "life and philosophy" he finally placed his "total historicism" above his Spanish ratiovitalism. Already in 1961, Arturo García Astrada of Argentina had put even more emphasis on Ortega's historical thought as paramount, and he had produced one of the first studies (1957) of his theory of history and historiology.[14] Still, historical reason as historicism got very little analysis from Hispanic scholars from 1955 into the 1970s.

ORTEGA SCHOLARSHIP IN NON-HISPANIC COUNTRIES

The widespread admiration for Ortega's *Revolt of the Masses* in the 1930s and for selected works translated since then long ensured him of readers and scholars (individuals or small bands) all around the Western world and, since 1945, around much of the westernized world, including eastern European countries (even the former U.S.S.R.) and Japan. Expansion of scholarly participation, however, has been limited by the fact that, except for German, his "Complete Works" have been translated into no other language. Individually, many major works have been translated, and nowhere more than in the United States, where W. W. Norton, which became his publisher of preference during his lifetime, has continued to bring out his posthumous works in English, with *Historical Reason* in 1983.

Ortega in the United States

After the failure of Ortega's hopes that Jaime Benítez of Puerto Rico might interest North Americans in his philosophy, it was mainly thanks to

14. Abellán, *Ortega*, 109, 113, 126, 131, 139, 143, and chap. 6; idem, *Vida y filosofía* (Madrid: Ibérico-Europea, 1970), also on Ortega; Arturo García Astrada, "Historia, ciencia histórica e historiología en Ortega y Gasset," *Humanitas* 3 (1957): 107–15; idem, *Pensamiento de Ortega*.

the studies of Alfred Stern, Ferrater Mora, Marías, and Morón Arroyo that he has been investigated in depth in the United States since 1970. Outside Spain and the Hispanic world, Ortega has come to be better liked and better understood by specialists in the United States than anywhere else in the world. That turn was unexpected, for popular histories of philosophy, like Will Durant's, had modern philosophy march triumphantly through James to Dewey and to the quasi-pragmatist Santayana, but with little concern for European historicism or existentialism. Ortega was interested in all three American philosophers, but they were unaware of it. No one picked up newer but still rare perceptions of his pragmatism, such as Copleston's.[15]

Although by a much diminished circle, the belated scholarly interest in Ortega of the 1970s may have reflected unconscious affinity in the United States with Ortega's mute pragmatism. By 1983, Antón Donoso had counted more than four hundred studies of all kinds there, which included thirty-three Ph.D. dissertations.[16] Although most studies were by Hispanists who taught Spanish literature, a few have been from philosophy, history, and other fields. Some of them were very perceptive, even innovative and synthetic by intent.

Most significant among earlier studies of Ortega in the United States were those by Alfred Stern, an émigré German Jewish philosopher, who studied his philosophy as broadly as was possible in the 1950s and 1960s. He confirmed the now-evident "dualism" in Ortega's philosophy of "perspectivism," but he shifted the emphasis to existentialism (as always historicist) and to what he called "essentialism" (as phenomenological). Yet his solution to the problem of unity—all possible perspectives added together—was not satisfactory. But he established well his existentialism, and its historicist dimension. In a dissertation (1961) that was published in 1970, Janet Winecoff (Díaz) identified "major themes of existentialism" in Ortega.[17] After Stern,

15. Jaime Benítez had done an M.A. thesis, "Political and Philosophical Theories of Ortega y Gasset" (University of Chicago, 1939), and he later corresponded with Ortega. Marías was negotiating in 1955 to publish under Paul Schilpp's aegis a study in English on Ortega's philosophy, but this was dropped when the subject (who had to be still living) died that year. Frederick C. Copleston, "Ortega y Gasset and Modern Spanish Thought," *The Listener*, November 29, 1951, p. 933.

16. Antón Donoso, "Bibliografía estadounidense sobre Ortega," *Quinto centenario* (Madrid) 6 (1983): 177–212. The volume title is "Ortega y América."

17. Alfred Stern, "Ortega y Gasset, Existentialism and Phenomenology," *Search for Meaning*, 263–78, sees Ortega's basis in Leibniz's perspectivism (227) and as contrasted to Unamuno (254–55) and as a forerunner of the existentialism of Sartre and Heidegger (211) but ill-defined here as "perspectivism" (278). Idem, *Philosophy of History*, 87, 170–87, on Ortega's historicism within existentialism or "existential historicism" (174); also 139–61, for a rare view of historicism that was not unsympathetic. Janet Winecoff Díaz, *The Major Themes*, 13–14. Against most of Ortega's disciples and critics, she upheld his existentialism—in concepts, if not in terminology, earlier than in Heidegger.

North Americans have seen Ortega as an existentialist—but as much more besides.

The most massive and comprehensive single volume on Ortega to date was not by Marías but by Robert McClintock, a student of Barzun's, for a Columbia University dissertation that was published in 1971. In *Man and His Circumstances: Ortega as Educator,* he provided a complete inventory of Ortega's philosophical plurality in two parts: Spanish circumstance and "second voyage"—the latter as historical reason, or historicism. He also connected him with phenomenology, existentialism, and philosophy of life, and he even sensed (unindexed) a Deweyite link with pragmatism at the end.[18] All of the main elements of his philosophy were at last detected by one critic—more comprehensive than anyone before, including Ferrater and Morón Arroyo, whom he cited but without deciding for "realism" or "idealism." However, since he mainly emphasized the pedagogue, his *structure* of Ortega's philosophy did not stand out as a *unity* in a coherent relationship of its parts, nor did any basic realism yet appear as pragmatism.

Also attributing to Ortega at least four positions in philosophy in the 1970s, U.S. scholars Harold Raley and O. W. Holmes likewise did not address the problem of unity by providing any integrating "architecture" for so much philosophical diversity. The former related his philosophy to "European unity"; the latter, to the "social world."[19] Obviously the unity of his philosophy is not enhanced by such off-center approaches to it, but no more so than in the majority of generalizing studies worldwide. Ortega's philosophy can thus be entered fruitfully from almost any of his manifold "perspectives" and "themes"—from "crisis," in my case.

Perhaps the most ambitious and ingenious effort yet to unify Ortega's pluralism within brief compass was in Philip Silver's study of his phenomenology (1978). In a "genetic"-"historical" attempt at synthesis Silver reexamined carefully what Ortega himself revealed about his thinking by exploiting his neglected early phenomenological essays. The posthumous works showed him that, contrary to Herbert Spiegelberg in the 1960s, Ortega was more than just a tireless promoter and sharp critic of Husserl's phenomenology. He was intimately involved with it in a *realist,* or "mundane," sense.[20]

18. Boldly reidentifying Ortega as a historicist was McClintock, *Ortega as Educator,* x, 130–31, 405, who did not make historicism central to his "second voyage" (pt. 2, pp. 237–488), although he included "Form of Historical Reason" as a chapter title (chap. 15). He also compared Ortega with Dewey but not actually with James (513, 562–63) on pragmatism and "instrumentalism."

19. Raley, *Philosopher of European Unity;* Holmes, *Human Reality.*

20. Silver, *Ortega as Phenomenologist,* xi, 95, 108, where he attributes to Ortega an early interest in both pragmatism and philosophy of life; idem, introduction, *Phenomenology and Art;* Herbert Spiegelberg, "Spain: Ortega's Part and Its Significance," *Phenomenological Movement,* 2:611–19.

Was he a full-fledged phenomenologist in his total "system" of philosophy, however, or something less (or more) than that? By close analysis Silver covered only Ortega's vitalist "first voyage," so that he did not fully account for the historicist "second voyage." However, neither of these two major stages—nor the metaphysical basis—can be *reduced* so radically to phenomenology. Although Silver overlooks pragmatism at one end and philosophy of life at the other, his study is excellent for an entry into Ortega's phenomenology, never before studied in depth. If in nature, extent, and relationship, phenomenology remains a problem in Ortega after that fine introduction, no one in the United States since has equaled or surpassed Silver for his original insights into that always problematic philosophy.

Ortega in Germany

In Germany, Ortega studies did not prosper after his death. Ernst Curtius had written the earliest definition of Ortega's philosophy—as "perspectivism"—in 1924. A quarter of a century later he tried to summarize his friend's development in the meantime. Although he regarded the Spaniard as "one of the dozen peers of the European intellect," his final overview greatly irritated Ortega. It was not just that Curtius saw no *unity* in his philosophy, but (like Gaos and opposite Marías) he absorbed vital reason into historical reason. Moreover, like Marías, he rejected any suggestion of a philosophy of life.[21] After the historian Curtius failed, no philosopher effectively unified Ortega's complexity, so to promote him attractively there.

Despite Rukser (1962, 1971), few in Germany took Ortega seriously as an existentialist, as a forerunner or competitor of Heidegger and Jaspers. The only notable effort to come to terms with what else his philosophy might be was by existentialist Otto Böllnow (1958), who stressed that his thought was essentially philosophy of life (*Lebensphilosophie*). No one prior to Böllnow—nor since him—has placed Ortega in the category of philosophy of life as a result of detailed comparative study.[22] He might have been more persuasive

21. Ernst R. Curtius, "Spanische Perspektiven," *Die neue Rundschau* 35 (1927): 1229–47; idem, "Ortega." Emilio Garrigues, *Ortega en su circunstancia alemana* (Bonn: Inter Naciones, 1981), judged that Curtius's interpretative essay did Ortega permanent injury in Germany (36–41): they retained a "bad understanding" of him in regard to both Goethe and Heidegger (41–52).

22. Udo Rukser, "Ortega und die Existentialisten," *Neue Zürcher Zeitung*, April 14, 1962; idem, "Ortega y Heidegger," *Humboldt* 45 (1971): 60–67. Böllnow, *Lebensphilosophie*, 44–45, 54–57, on Ortega; he included also Nietzsche, Dilthey, Simmel, Bergson, and Klages. Charles E. Lewalter, "Zu Ortega y Gassets Philosophie des Lebens," *Die Zeit* (Hamburg), no. 46 (January 6, 1951): 4; Tuttle, "Ortega's Vitalism"; Salvador Cabot-Rossello, "Pädagogische Konsequenzen der Lebensphilosophie Ortega y Gassets" (thesis, University of

and more discriminating had he known the posthumous works that were mainly historical in approach to life. How could the historicism wherein Ortega ended be fully contained under a philosophy of life like Dilthey's, any more effectively than under an existentialism like Heidegger's?

Heidegger himself could never decide what Ortega was in general philosophy, apart from sharing in existentialism, where he knew they also differed sharply. Was he some kind of new "positivist"?[23] His emphatic historicism escaped Heidegger.

In 1984, Niedermayer confirmed his own earlier view of 1959: German critics had not admired Ortega as a *philosopher*. Used to heavy tomes, they deemed his essays unsuitable (too superficial) and his total production too wordy—there was so much, it was hard to get a firm grasp on it all. As an elitist, Niedermayer felt, he interested only intellectuals,[24] who admired *Revolt of the Masses* (which Jaspers too cited), but even they regarded him as inferior in philosophy not only to Heidegger but to Sartre.

Ortega in France

It is strange that Ortega has won more praise and better understanding of his philosophy from a few French Hispanists than from all of his many German admirers, but they too had trouble seeing his existentialism, as they concentrated on the historical side. Charles Cascalès, who was interested in his philosophy of history in 1957, defined his general philosophy very loosely, merely as a "Humanisme" that recognized life as radical reality. Although in passing he considered history and historiology, he was unable to see that historical reason was historicism. Soon Jean-Paul Borel in 1959 and Alain Guy in 1969 could place almost equal emphasis on vital reason and historical reason.[25] In fact, however, that structural balance was more apparent than real, for (like Marías) they reduced the latter to the former. Borel recognized in vital reason both phenomenology and existentialism but saw no historicism in historical reason. His approach was broadly speculative instead of demonstrative.

If Alain Guy's view was similar to Borel's, he continued working on Ortega's critiques of Heidegger and of Aristotle. When he summed up his grasp

Vienna, 1966); L. Incisa, "La filosofía de la vitta di Ortega y Gasset," *Minerva,* no. 63 (1953): 420–23. For the most recent studies of Ortega's "philosophy of life" (1990), see *Analecta Husserliana* 29 (1990): pt. 2 (93–216).

23. Martin Heidegger, "Encuentros con Ortega y Gasset en Alemania," *Clavileño* 7:39 (1956): 1–2.

24. Franz Niedermayer, "José Ortega y Gasset desde la perspectiva alemana," *Cuadernos Hispanoamericanos,* no. 304–5 (January–March 1984): 425–40.

25. Cascalès, *L'Humanisme d'Ortega,* vii, 112–16; Borel, *Raison et vie chez Ortega,* 13, 261, and chaps. 2 and 3.

of Ortega in 1984, however, he still had not moved beyond perspectivism and ratiovitalism, which he did not see as phenomenology and existentialism. If he stressed "historicity," he did not really see it as historicism, despite his awareness that Gaos had defined it as "ratio-historicism." He still agreed with Marías that vital reason, as "historical in essence and consistency," included historical reason. Although Ortega engaged in "dialogue" with idealism, phenomenology, and existentialism, he did not (properly speaking) belong to any of them, but he had *used* phenomenological method. His philosophy, decided Guy, was finally a ratiovitalist Orteguisme. But Guy linked Ortega's ideas to recent movements in French philosophy, with the structuralism of Lévi-Strauss and Foucault, with the hermeneutics of Sartre, Gadamer, and Ricoeur, and with Franco-American linguistics. Philosophy aside, he has found Ortega still "an incomparable master of thought for our time."[26]

Among noted professional philosophers in France, Bergson was as contemptuous of Ortega as a philosopher as Ortega was of him: he was only a "journalist of genius." Sartre seemed to have ignored Ortega, despite notable similarities, but Jean Wahl recognized him as a "historizing existentialist."[27] As a literary existentialist, Camus truly admired Ortega for both thought and style, but not for philosophy per se.

Ortega Elsewhere

In Britain and the Netherlands, professional lay critics ignored Ortega for philosophy. Bertrand Russell, to whom he was basically indebted, made no reference to him in his *History of Philosophy* (1946), for he could not have guessed that he related to pragmatism and even to analytical philosophy. Among clerical critics in both countries, however, Ortega was taken more seriously as a philosopher.

In 1951 the Jesuit Frederick Copleston said Ortega's philosophy was characterized by "the idea of life" as "radical reality," with a central theme of man as a "historic being" in a "historical situation." As such, he felt, it had

26. See Guy, *Ortega ou la raison vitale,* chap. 2, on historical reason. He seemed about to arrive at a very "nuanced" historicism but finally ended by subjecting it to vital reason as perspectivism, rather than as existentialism (41, 46, 77, 93). His view of Ortega's philosophy as a unique Orteguisme had not changed from the beginning: idem, *Les Philosophes espagnols d'hier et d'aujourd'hui* (Toulouse, 1956), reviewed by Raymond Bayer, *Revue de Synthese* 77 (1957): 205–6; Guy, "Ortega y Gasset y su puesto en la filosofía contemporanea," *Cuadernos Hispanoamericanos,* no. 403–5 (January–March 1984): 25–42, esp. 30, 33, 37, 40–42.

27. Henri Bergson, quoted by Salvador de Madariaga, "Nota sobre Ortega," *Sur,* no. 241 (July–August 1956): 13; Jean Wahl, "Philosophie existentielle," in *Philosophy in the Mid-Century,* ed. Klibansky, 2:73–74.

affinities with existentialism, life philosophies, and even pragmatism—without being eclectic. A quarter of a century later, Copleston returned to the old problem of relativism (historicism), and again he defended Ortega against his Hispanic detractors, both religious and secular.[28]

A Dutch Dominican, Jan Walgrave, made a detailed analysis of Ortega's philosophy in 1949 (revised in 1960) that was very penetrating for that time. Starting with an article that turned into a book, he still had to settle for less than the whole, as he centered on historical reason, historicity, and historiology. Although he did not make the logical connection with the dreaded historicism, he linked historiology correctly with modeling, and he equated vital reason with existentialism, as also being historical. Like Copleston and the Franciscan Alluntis, he did not regard Ortega's "relativity" as the old relativism. While affirming his "strong and resolute realism," he doubted that Ortega had ever developed a metaphysics because of his "openness" to the outer historical reality. Recognizing that Ortega's "vital philosophy" of "historico-vital reason" had remained unfinished, he regarded it as a "project" that was "radically revolutionary" in character. He took Ortega for "the greatest philosopher-journalist of all time"—"the great modern master of the philosophical essay."[29] Like Cascalès in France, he was inclined to call his philosophy "humanism."

Another Dutch Dominican scholar, John Nota, continued (in the United States) where Walgrave left off. He saw applications of a phenomenological kind for Ortega's historiology in history as a "science."[30] But that is another story, for a later volume.

GENERAL VIEWS FROM THE CENTENNIAL

The centennial years brought several noteworthy studies of a partially generalizing sort, those by Julián Marías, Victor Ouimette (1982), Sergio Rabade Romeo (1983), and Pedro Cerezo Galán (1984). In the United States, Ouimette demonstrated how Ortega regarded his own evolution as culminating in "historical reason," as Marías too finally admitted in 1983 in *Trayectorias* (Trajectories). Still, the old aversion to general categories prevented either of them from actually naming the *historicism* that his final form of "reason" was in fact. Nor did either really explain how he got there from

28. Copleston, "Ortega and Philosophical Relativism," *Philosophers and Philosophies* 172–84; idem, "Ortega and Modern Spanish Thought."

29. Walgrave, *Filosofía de Ortega*, 10–11, 12, 15, 96–114, 124–28, 131, 139, 302, 307, 312–15. Four Dutch editions were published between 1949 and 1967.

30. John H. Nota, *Phenomenology and History*, trans. L. Grooten (Chicago: Loyola University Press, 1967). See also idem, "Le point de départ de la philosophie de l'histoire," *Actes du XI Congrès International de Philosophie* (Madrid, 1952).

vital reason, as through phenomenology and existentialism. Ouimette's exposition of historical reason was much clearer and fuller than was that of Marías, however. To the end, Marías continued to see historical reason as only a "practical" dimension of vital reason.[31]

Reflecting Ortega's most recent work (*Sobre la razón histórica*, 1979), Rabade Romeo produced a sort of running anthology of texts in bits and pieces out of Ortega that were supposed to "speak for themselves." He held that Ortega's "philosophy of man" comprised "vitalism and historicism" coinciding, the latter as merely a "deepening" of the former, finally as (or within) a "philosophy of life." "As vital, reason comes to be historical." He affirmed the "structural and systematic unity" of Ortega's philosophy out of the themes "man, life, history." By ignoring existentialism, he let historical vitalism thus preserve an overall unity, but with extra-vital and metahistorical dimensions.[32]

The most substantial book from the centennial years was *La Voluntad de aventura* by Pedro Cerezo Galán in 1984. Mining the most recently published of Ortega's lecture courses, *¿Qué es conocimiento?* (What is knowledge?) from 1930, Cerezo did not manage to get much beyond "What Is Philosophy?" from that same year, however. Hence, he did not really take in his philosophy as a whole. Nevertheless, by affirming both phenomenology and existentialism within a realist ratiovitalism, he achieved his purpose of putting Ortega in a "European context." He had followed Ferrater Mora's scheme from objectivism through ratiovitalism but went no further. His concept of "practical reason" did not suffice for historical reason, for he did not discern historicism as Ortega's last stage of development after 1936.[33] Regrettably, this recent scholarly study from Spain therefore again presented a truncated version of Ortega's philosophy. By his neglect of the later years Cerezo did not greatly advance our comprehension of the whole as a philosophy of life. And although he detected linguistic "pragmatics" in Ortega, he did not see that "the executive I"—the "doing" self—was related to pragmatism in his basic metaphysics. The early Argentine critique of his pragmatism had been utterly forgotten.

Among the few generalizing studies on Ortega in the 1980s, there was one that may be very significant for future research. Marías's *Trayectorias* (1983), which followed the long-delayed posthumous publication of all of Ortega's historical works, made belated and very grudging admission that historical reason was indeed the final and culminating phase of his philosophy—but as

31. Ouimette, *Ortega;* Marías, *Trayectorias,* 197–202 ("Vital Reason and Historical Reason"); here the latter was still not developed as the "second voyage."

32. Rabade Romeo, *Ortega filósofo,* 17, 22, 23, 82, 125.

33. Cerezo Galán, *Voluntad de aventura,* 11, 15–16 (and n. 1), 119, 191–255, 376–82.

vital reason in the "concrete."[34] That chary, hedged concession to historical reason thus "legitimized" studies of it thereafter, for Marías had long been the main obstacle to placing Ortega within the philosophical movements of the era. Since Morón Arroyo (1968), however, Marías had often been ignored by sympathetic critics who again assigned general Western names to Ortega's philosophy, including historicism. At last Marías too opened up to reassessing Ortega, notably for historical reason.

With Marías's last work, he got back at Nicol and Gaos, but without *directly* admitting existentialism and historicism. Meanwhile, few critics yet have been so bold as Gaos to *defend* historical reason as a "*ratio-historicism*" or even as Stern's "historicist existentialism." Thanks to Marías, critics have become reluctant to call Ortega "historicist." Nevertheless, he was so at the end, although his historicism was still subordinated somehow to his "philosophy of life" but *equal* to phenomenological existentialism, without *being* it. Ultimately, historical reason was *not* vital reason, but something distinct, "beyond" it.

During the 1980s, there was continuing attention to life and to history (even as historicism) as the acme of Ortega's "way of thinking"—as related to the social too. There were several earlier looks at history in his philosophy, such as Walgrave's emphasis in "Life, Man, and History" (1960), Granell's focus also in 1960 on "life and history" as the nucleus of his system, and Gaete's stress in "Life, Reason, and History" (1962). Reaffirming an earlier Italian interest in Ortega's historical thought, Luciano Pellicani in 1978 called him an "authentic philosopher," who (like Croce) concentrated on the "historical character of human life" and who combined existential analysis with "historical sociology." In 1983, Rabade Romeo emphasized historical reason over vital reason in a "philosophy of man, life, and history," and in the next year Federico Ríu made "life and history" the center of Ortega's philosophy. A mainly sociological study of him in 1984 by Ariel del Val had a chapter entitled "History as Philosophy"—a very Crocean concept. Andrew Weigert's study of Ortega's social thought, *Life and Society* (1983), knit these two aspects together, as had Oliver W. Holmes. After his "Philosophy of Man, Society, and History" in 1971, Holmes united philosophy, history, and man as a "new synthesis" for Ortega's social thought in 1985. Since not all of the newer studies affirmed any historicism, Marías clearly still exercised an inhibiting influence. Nevertheless, Teresa Rodríguez de Lecea claimed in 1983 that Ortega's influence in the Hispanic world thenceforth would rest on his historical thought.[35]

---

34. Marías, *Trayectorias,* esp. 210–13 (ever evasive on historical reason).

35. See nn. 12 (on Granell and Gaete) and 29 (on Walgrave). Pellicani, *Introduzione a Ortega,* 13–14, 16; idem, "La teoría epistemológica de Ortega," *Cuadernos Hispanoamer-*

A growth of interest in Ortega's broadly sociohistorical thought, as grounded in his philosophy of life, was evident in the 1980s. In a revival of an earlier occasional concern, there was an unusual concentration on his "philosophical anthropology" among Spanish centennial essays. Then Alberto del Campo, Pedro Gómez Bosque, Carlos Gurméndez, Miguel Montes González, Antonio Pintor-Ramos, and Miguel Diego Sánchez Meca all wrote on that passing theme of 1924–1925, although Ortega's quest for a "metahistory" finally resulted in "historiology" in 1928.[36] Such aspects of his "hermeneutic" will be considered in a following volume, but the sudden surge of interest bespeaks an impatience to get on with Ortega's thought on the particular "human sciences," even before his underlying philosophy has been securely defined.

Since studies of Ortega continued on past the centennial and up to the present, the world has not yet finished with his philosophy, nor with the many other aspects of his thought. If reexamined, his themes and facets can still yield novelty. At the World Congress of Philosophy at the University of Córdoba in Argentina in 1987, a session of six papers on him included mine, entitled "Pragmatism and Philosophy of History"—a connection not previously made, although interest in his parallels with Dewey, if not with James, had been growing in the 1980s. New books on Ortega in 1989 were a biography on his "modernity" by Rockwell Gray and a study of his "politics and philosophy" by Andrew Dobson. Both gave greater emphasis to history and historical reason than has been customary, and Gray asserted (but did not demonstrate) that James's pragmatism too was important in his background. Late in 1989 appeared a volume of essays on the "modernity" theme for *Hispanic Issues*, to which Dust, Morón Arroyo, Donoso, Holmes, Orringer, and Cerezo Galán contributed. Long seen as a modernizer, Ortega is now regarded as anti- or post-modern, too. With Donoso, Raley has also contrib-

---

icanos, no. 403–5 (January–March 1984): 71–79; Rabade Romeo, *Ortega filósofo,* 8, 125; Ríu, *Vida e historia.* Fernando Ariel del Val, *Historia e ilegitimidad . . . Fragmentos de una sociología del poder* (Madrid: Universidad Complutense, 1984), chap. 2, "History as Philosophy," does not actually mention Croce, but see 57–59 for references to Pareto and Mosca compared to Ortega's elite. Andrew J. Weigert, *Life and Society: A Meditation on the Social Thought of José Ortega y Gasset;* Oliver W. Holmes, "La fenomenología y la historia en Ortega," in *Ortega Hoy,* ed. Manuel Durán (Xalapa: Veracruz University Press, 1985), 225–36; Teresa Rodríguez de Lecea, "Ortega: Evolución de un pensador frente a su circunstancia," *Razón y Fe* (Madrid) 207 (May 1983): 487–94. Her reluctance to follow general European-Western nomenclature for Ortega is evident also in a former student of Ortega's, Alvarez González, *Pensamiento de Ortega,* who considered him the "high point" in Spanish thought in this century, but he avoided all general labels, preferred "perspectivism."

36. On Ortega's philosophical anthropology in the 1980s, see Gómez Bosque, *Alma, cuerpo, vocación;* see other authors as listed by Donoso and Raley. Compare with Graham, "Historiology and Interdisciplinarity," on historiology as a new "basic discipline" and a variety of "schematic models" for the human sciences.

uted to a new tome (1990) of the *Analecta Husserliana* on "phenomenology and philosophy of life," wherein his and several other essays are on Ortega's *Spanish* "philosophy of life."[37]

Too late for me to obtain Proceedings or copies to analyze, the *Boletín Orteguiano* gave notice of recent conferences, books, and articles on Ortega in Spain from 1990 to 1993. It appears that concern with his philosophy continues—deeper and more extensive—among Spanish and Argentine philosophers than in the decade before the centennial. Perhaps this development presages a resurgence of interest in Ortega as a philosopher throughout the Hispanic world, which in turn may help kindle or reawaken it elsewhere. An international seminar on Ortega and Leibniz took place in Buenos Aires in 1989, and in Madrid a conference on Ortega and Husserl was sponsored by the Spanish Society of Phenomenology in 1990 and one entitled "Spanish Philosophy Since Ortega" by the University of Madrid (Complutense) in 1992. The second conference examined Ortega's relation with Husserl and phenomenology from many special angles, but only the general views by Professor Javier San Martín, who published them in *Revista de Occidente,* are accessible to me at present.[38]

From historical perspective as well as philosophical analysis of texts, San Martín has come to conclusions very compatible with my own views in chapter 5. He sees both Ortega and Husserl as *developing* their philosophies through several phases, from 1913 (or 1900) into the 1930s, especially from the latter's *Ideas* through his *Crisis of the European Sciences.* Because Ortega innocently misinterpreted the "inharmonious" (if not contradictory) *intent* of Husserl's *Ideas,* he had rejected not only Husserl's notion of "consciousness" of life, things, and world (as reflective and idealist instead of direct and realist), he later rejected the authenticity of Husserl's thought in *Crisis.* Nevertheless, like Silver (whom he cited), San Martín discerns a phenomenology also in Ortega, although he only implies that it was "mundane," or realist—as "objectivist." Ortega's phenomenology, moreover, was directed not to the "theory" (the philosophy per se) but to the "practical," to phenomenology as "method," even as I have maintained. And San Martín also believes that, despite Ortega's "disidentification" with Husserl as idealist (like Kant), he was actually positively related to him—almost against his

---

37. Roberto E. Aras, "Ortega o la distancia," *Universitas* (Buenos Aires) 68 (1983): 9–16. Aras personally alerted me to materials at the Biblioteca Nacional in Buenos Aires, where he had examined previously non-utilized publications by Ortega in Argentinian newspapers. Gray, *Imperative of Modernity;* Andrew Dobson, *An Introduction to the Politics and Philosophy of José Ortega y Gasset;* Antón Donoso, "Ortega's Anti-modernity in Epistemology and Metaphysics," 95–126. See *Analecta Husserliana* 29 (1990): pt. 2 (93–216).

38. Soledad Ortega, ed., *Boletín Orteguiano* (Madrid: Fundación Ortega y Gasset, 1993), 3:5–34; Javier San Martín, "Ortega y Husserl: A vueltas con una relación polémica," *Revista de Occidente,* no. 132 (May 1992): 107–27.

will—in the later turn (by both) to life and world through history and crisis.[39]

Thus do topics old and new continue to be explored with regard to Ortega's astonishing diversity. If we now have a much fuller view of the man Ortega in Gray's "intellectual biography" than previously, we have still lacked an integration of the structure of his philosophy to cover all of its main aspects in terms of general types of Western philosophy. Such *is* possible, and this study attempts it on two levels: criticism and sources.

39. San Martín, "Ortega y Husserl," 107–27.

Supplemental Notes

CHAPTER 2
Background: Life, History, Philosophy (1883–1914+)

23. Ortega twice explicitly rejected "extreme biologism" (as material-organic in a Darwinist sense), as early as 1916–1917 (R 77) in Argentina. On a reputed "biologism," or "biologist stage," see Morón Arroyo, *Sistema*, 80–81, 440; in his view, Spengler's biologism was more related to Ortega's thought than was Darwin's. Also see Victor Ouimette, *José Ortega y Gasset*, 79–80, 116, on a "biologistic" stage in his educational theory. Actually, he had always rejected any *merely* "biological phenomenon" in man's life and history, for life in the human sense related to crisis, not just organic function (6: 350). Marías regarded any "biologism" as "marginal" (*Circumstance and Vocation*, 360–61). Not distinct as a "stage" in itself, Uexküll's new vitalist ("life") and phenomenological approach was contrasted to the old materialistic one (McClintock, *Ortega as Educator*, 24, 298, 301–3, 494, 551–52). Also rejecting biologism as improperly imputed was Oliver W. Holmes, *Human Reality and the Social World: Ortega's Philosophy of History*, 55–56 (but cf. 60). Manuel Benavides, "La retícula biológica en el pensamiento de Ortega," *Cuadernos Hispanoamericanos*, nos. 403–5 (January–March 1984): 119, found *"el cedazo biológico"* in his work on history, sociology, art, and pedagogy, a Leibnizian and neo-Kantian element that Benavides deemed not present in either his first or last period. Francisco Sánchez Blanco, "Continuidad y discontinuidad de Ortega y Gasset respecto al pensamiento español del siglo XX," *Cuadernos Hispanoamericanos*, nos. 403–5 (January–March 1984): 603–4, 606, stated that a biologism dominated all currents of Spanish thought (as materialistic) at the end of the nineteenth century, so Ortega's opposition was new.

25. Ortega (R 48) left some illuminating notes on Maistre and on Bonald from February 1934. Aware that Edmund Burke had exercised considerable influence on Maistre's *Considerations on France,* he was amused at the latter's "huge error on America"; he noted that Maistre was always mistaken about the future—not at all strange, because he always turned his head backward. He found Bonald, however, more absolutist in thought and temperament. Ortega's odd similarity to both Guizot's and Donoso Cortés's ideological position of "moderatism" ("doctrinaire" liberalism in the 1830s) was not then in regard to support for constitutional monarchy, which Manuel Ortega attributed to his father in the 1950s (*Mi padre,* 188–89), but to opposition to extremes of both left and right. Oddly, Ortega and Donoso capitalized "Power" (*Poder*), like Rousseau, but by going to the far right in 1848, Donoso did not please Ortega. Although his early eclecticism might have interested Ortega for its attitude of compromise and comprehension, the later Donoso's

romanticism in "philosophy" (if we can still call it so) was too like Kierkegaard's extremism for Ortega to tolerate it, even as an anticipation of existentialism or philosophy of life.

26. See John Graham, *Juan Donoso Cortés: Utopian Romanticist and Political Realist* (Columbia: University of Missouri Press, 1974), 1 (Ortega), 103–9 (Vico), 130–33 n. 64 (preexistentialism); and Sánchez Blanco, "Continuidad," 609, on Donoso Cortés and on Ortega's notion of a genetic "history of ideas." If (as a lad) Ortega read Donoso's oncefamous *Essay on Catholicism, Liberalism, and Socialism* (1851), which is not improbable, he encountered an opposition to both rationalism and materialism, an emphasis on "faith" (or belief) as basic to human living and knowing, "Adam" as a metaphor for the human "species" (mankind), "coexistence" and "unity and diversity" as metaphysical principles, and rejection of inevitable "progress" for cyclic ideas. The latter historical ideas Ortega could also have found in "Historical Sketches" (1847), which he might have perused around 1930, when (according to what his daughter Soledad told me) he talked with Eugenio D'Ors about Donoso Cortés. In this later period, too, he may have read Donoso's great speeches on dictatorship (1849) and on Europe (1850), with their predictions of a terrible general crisis in Europe that would bring revolutions and demagogic and socialist dictators (he included Russia). Such an interest fitted with Ortega's reading of Maistre and Bonald then. However, we cannot *demonstrate* those influences on Ortega, early or later.

27. "Epistolario entre Unamuno y Ortega," *Revista de Occidente*, no. 19 (October 1964): 3–28 (life as "existential," p. 12). Also see *Epistolario completo Ortega-Unamuno*, ed. L. Robles Carcedo (Madrid: Arquero, 1987), from 1904 into the 1930s. In 1907, to Cejador (R 32), Ortega defined Unamuno's genius as romantic and anti-classical; against his individualism he appealed to humanity and to universal history. José Luis Abellán, *Ortega y Gasset en la filosofía española*, chap. 5 and pp. 91, 142, affirmed "unequivocally" Unamuno's influence as the most philosophical figure of the previous generation, and said that Unamuno and Ortega were the most "authentic" of Spanish philosophers. There is a sizable literature on Ortega and Unamuno, much of it incidental, but some is specific. See Sabino Alonso Fueyo, "Existencialismo espanhol: Ortega y Gasset e Unamuno," *Banderra* 8 (March–June 1960): 10–15; Manuel Fernández de la Cera, "El epistolario Unamuno-Ortega," *Cuadernos de la Cátedra Miguel de Unamuno* (Salamanca) 23 (1972): 103–18; Gonzalo Fernández de la Mora, "Unamuno: Frente a Ortega," in his *Pensamiento español, 1964, de Unamuno a D'Ors* (Madrid: Rialp, 1965), 195–201; Paulino Garagorri, *Unamuno, Ortega, Zubiri en la filosofía española* (Madrid: Alianza, 1968); Nemesio González Caminero, "Unamuno y Ortega," *Unamuno* (Santander: Universidad Pontificia de Comillas, 1948); J. S. Gandique, "Ortega contra Unamuno," *Humanitas* (Monterrey) 11 (1970): 149–62; Alfred Stern, "Unamuno and Ortega: The Renewal of Philosophy in Spain," *Pacific Spectator* 8 (February 1954): 310–24. On *adentamiento* as compared with Ortega's *ensimismamiento*, see José Ferrater Mora, *Unamuno: A Philosophy of Tragedy*, trans. P. Silver (Berkeley and Los Angeles: University of California Press, 1960); Ferrater also comments on Unamuno as Hispanizer and Ortega as Europeanizer (73).

36. On Nietzsche's relatability to pragmatism, see George G. Stack, "Nietzsche's Influence on Pragmatic Humanism," *Journal of the History of Philosophy* 20 (October 1982): 369–406; Max O. Hollman, "Nietzsche and Pragmatism," *Kinesis* 14 (Spring 1985): 63–78; also Barzun, *Stroll with James,* on Nietzsche as "then unknown" to James but very comparable (19, 85, 133). For other relevant Nietzsche studies, see Paul Ilie, "Nietzsche in Spain," *PMLA* 79 (March 1964): 85; Juan Roig Gironella, *Filosofía y Vida. Cuatro ensayos sobre actitudes: Nietzsche, Ortega y Gasset, Unamuno y Croce* (Barcelona: Barna, 1946); Udo Rukser, *Nietzsche in der Hispania* (Bern: Franckes, 1962), 346–47. The fullest study is by Gonzalo Sobrejano, *Nietzsche en España,* which identifies Ortega with about a half-dozen (e.g., Maeztu, Baroja, Azorín) of the "generation of 1898" now recognized as Nietzscheans (10, 25, 93–94, 526–65). He traces Nietzsche's influence on Ortega in regard to vitalism back to "Adam in Paradise" (1910) and in regard to "perspectivism" up through the 1920s

and 1930s, and in regard to elitism ("aristocraticism") on into *Revolt of the Masses*. Gonzalo Sobrejano sees no "plagiarism" in Ortega (559), only creative *influence*, and so does not find (564) Sánchez Villaseñor's "minor Nietzsche." In 1984, Federico Ríu judged that Ortega derived his original vitalism from Nietzsche and Bergson but that their irrationalism, so his "vital reason" was something new (*Vida e historia*, 9), and his emphasis on philosophy as a sportive undertaking resulting from "solitude." Compare the preface to Nietzsche's "The Dawn of Day" (1881) and *The Gay Science* (1882).

40. Very little has been written specifically on Ortega and Britain. Unfortunately "empiricism" is not indexed in Ortega's *Obras Completas,* so it is easy to miss references to it. On the English "dimension" in Ortega's thought, see Joaquín Iriarte, "Ortega y la dimensión anglo-sajona de su pensamiento," *Razón y Fe* (Madrid), no. 140 (July–August 1949): 8–10. See Marías, *Circumstance and Vocation,* 174, on the English romantic influence—on Spain rather than Ortega. Reel 39 contains undated notes on Bentham (1 page), Locke (2 pages from works of 1908 or later in German and English), Hobbes (3 pages from Cassirer's *Der Erkenntnisse* of 1907), and Bacon (at least 15 pages apparently from the *New Organon* mainly, wherein he took note of the idea of "idols"—and later the affirmation of the "Fundamental superiority over Antiquity"—as a "state of mind" that "is the formal basis of 'modernity'." He found Bacon's views on science and religion, philosophy and theology "very interesting." These notes from Bacon could fit either *Man and Crisis* (1933) or the idea of modernization that Ortega set forth in *An Interpretation of Universal History* (1949).

Ortega, "Medio siglo," 12; Carlos Mellizo, "Creencias orteguianas y 'belief' humeana," *Los Ensayistas* 4:6–7 (March 1979): 65–74. In contrast to Dilthey, who disbelieved in a human "nature" as a fixed mode of "being," Hume *seemed* to represent just the opposite view, but Ortega found him "the least 'rationalistic' of his entire century"; "Hume above all requires very careful study" (Ortega, 6:197 n. 3, 180 n. 1).

42. Virtually nothing is indexed for "pragmatism" by Donoso and Raley, *Ortega,* except Guillermo A. Nicolas, *El Hombre, un ser en vías de realización* (Madrid: Gredos, 1974), and (unindexed) Juan David García Bacca, *Nuevos grandes filósofos contemporaneos y sus temas,* 2 vols. (Caracas: Imprenta Nacional, 1947). I have not seen Nicolas, but García Bacca detected no direct *connection.* However, McClintock, in notes to *Ortega as Educator* (562–63), compared Ortega with Dewey's pragmatism, and he found James's works also illuminating for grasping Ortega (570). Also, with reference to McClintock, Antón Donoso's paper "Ortega's Critique of Pragmatism" (1987) explored his links with Dewey and cited several other scholars with that current interest: Luis Recasens Siches, Lorenzo Luzuriaga, José Arsenio Torres, Patrick Dust, and Robert Vichot. Although all our interests in Ortega and pragmatism are complementary, mine arose by 1985 without awareness of other such interests and relates primarily to James. By contrast, I see Ortega's earlier denunciations of pragmatism as having to be taken *cum grano salis,* those *partial* rejections intended to mislead critics.

CHAPTER 3
Beginnings: General, National, and Personal (1904–1916)

18. On Kant's so-called Copernican revolution, see the following, none of whom quite agree with each other on what it was: Henry E. Allison, *Kant's Transcendental Idealism* (New Haven: Yale University Press, 1983), 28–30; Ernst Cassirer, *Kant's Life and Thought,* trans. J. Haden (New Haven: Yale University Press, 1981), 143–52; Graham Bird, *Kant's Theory of Knowledge* (London: Routledge, 1962), 191–93; Lucien Goldmann, *Immanuel Kant* (London: NLB, 1971), 14–15, 105; and T. E. Wilkerson, *Kant's Critique of Pure Reason*

(Oxford: Clarendon Press, 1976), 187. Allison's analysis, lengthier and more persuasive, shows that what Kant meant by the phrase is still a moot question with philosophers.

There are several studies specifically on Ortega and Kant. See H. Herrigel, "Ortega von aussen: Kritische Beimerkungen zu Ortegas Aufsätzen über Kant und Goethe," *Die Sammlung Zeitschrift für Kultur und Erziehung* 10 (1955): 25–31; Julio Enrique Blanco, "Ortega ante Kante y la filosofía pura," *UDEM* 3–4 (Universidad de Medellín, Colombia): 5–6 (July 1959–February 1960): 105–22, 329–45, on *Modern Theme;* Octavio Uña Juárez, "Lecturas sobre la tradición kantiana (Heimsoeth, Buber, Ortega)," *La Ciudad de Dios* 191 (January–March 1978): 93–106; and Maximiliano Fartos Martínez, "Analogía entre Kant y Ortega y sentido de la filosofía," *Arbor* 114 (January 1983): 69–75. Also see Orringer, *Fuentes germánicas,* 56–57; and Marías, *Trayectorias,* 184–96.

35. On Adamism, see Marías, *Circumstance and Vocation,* 5, 61; he defined it as a lack of "historical continuity" or objective "circumstances," like a "first man." This was in contrast to "Robinsonism" ("Robinson Crusoeism"), a condition of "exile" or "shipwreck" in life and beliefs. For other references to Adam (as "type"), see Ortega, 12:83–84, where he is a being (thereafter) obliged to live in a world that resists the self. Thus the two concepts are related—after Adams, we are naturally Robinsons when troubles strike. No one has noticed how often Ortega alluded to Adam (as a type, distinct from the 1910 essay) in his later work: for example, in the "Meditations on Quixote" (1:354–55), where he offered a "psychology of Adams," which he typified by Goya as a "man without age or history," as a perpetual "first man," even while Spanish culture was without past or progress, a "frontier culture" in perpetual struggle with the elemental" (1:354–55); also, metaphysics notwithstanding, all having to *live* like "a first man, to be the eternal Adam" (5:178—1934); or the utopian ("Eleatic" rationalist) view that was applicable to "prehistoric man" (8:406—1939) as opposite to *historical* man (6:43—1936), to man in the world-circumstance (9:210—1949); or a condition where everything resolves into individual perspectives of "compresence" (7:117-19—1949); or (for an opposite sense) "Adam" as naive ancient realism, "philosophical ingenuousness" (7:388-89n); finally, in Andalucía, living Adam's paradisiacal life (6:117-20—1927).

Three times Ortega cited Scheler's *Formalism in Ethics* (1913) in connection with vitalist "values" (Ortega, 6:329n, 330n). Also see Scheler, *Gesammelte Werke* (Bern, 1955), 2:311–41, as cited by David R. Lachterman, introduction to Scheler, *Selected Philosophical Essays* (Evanston, Ill.: Northwestern University Press, 1973), xiii.

42. In *Circumstance and Vocation,* Marías called attention to "a new level" in "Adam" that "Ortega is *seeing* and does not yet know how to name"; nor did Marías, who apparently linked it to Husserl's phenomenology (326–27), but not to James's pragmatism. Marías noted that Ortega appealed to "*concrete positive* reasons" against idealism and for realism and "objectivism" and already expressed it as "those *Dii consentes, I and my circumstance*" and *duality* (329, 343)—several but not all of the metaphysical elements set forth there. More of these basic elements were noted by one influenced by Marías's earlier emphasis on Ortega's exclusively "Spanish philosophy": Rodríguez Huéscar, *Perspectiva y verdad,* saw "Adam in Paradise" as emphasizing mainly "life" and "perspective"—Ortega's later perspectivism (47–59). In origins (sources) "self and circumstance" seems to have been more Germanic-Nordic in the first term and more Mediterranean-Latin in the second. See Ortega, 7:61, on "milieu" (in Taine). For other probable sources of "circumstances," see Marías, *Circumstance and Vocation,* 353–55, 361–62, 364 (Uexküll).

54. James, *The Meaning of Truth* (1909), which was surely not available in time to affect "Adam in Paradise," contains several references to one's "world" as one's "circumstance" (91–93). In *Essays in Radical Empiricism*—also with *A Pluralistic Universe* (1909)—James mentioned separately both "self" and "circumstance" (or "situation"), in one instance used both in one paragraph (165), but not the unified formula as in Ortega, along with "will" to overcome resistance in one's world, and "space and time" as qualities of life

"given us to be known" and for "endless description" (163–67). James had been searching for "the right word," for a "unifying . . . formula," that for him was "radical empiricism"; Ortega called it "self and circumstance" (1914), or "absolute positivism" (1916), or "radical unitary duality" (1934). For this formula in its first *dual* form, see Edmund Husserl, *Ideas: General Introduction to Pure Phenomenology,* trans. W. R. B. Gibson (London: Allen and Unwin, 1931), 101 ("I and my world about me"), 103 (*"my world-about-me"* plus "ego"). However, Husserl "bracketed" that "natural world" and (as Ortega said) made it "disappear" as reality in favor of "consciousness" of his "transcendental" idealism in the *Ideen.* Also see supplemental note 6, chap. 4.

CHAPTER 4
Metaphysics: "Radicalism" as Pragmatism (1909+)

2. Morón Arroyo, *Sistema,* 208–9. The reference from the archive (R 75) applied to a long-term project and did not necessarily relate to Ortega's specific 1933 course, "Principles of Metaphysics According to Vital Reason" (12:13), which first appeared as *Some Lessons in Metaphysics,* trans. M. Adams (New York: Norton, 1969), where, "doing" metaphysics (12:24–26), he identified the "fundamental principle" and "first truth" of his "system" as having to be "radical," a "root truth"; his new "realist thesis" was "Reality is my coexistence with the thing" (12:115, 119). That course was the subject of a study by Manuel Mindan, "El último curso de Ortega en la Universidad de Madrid: Principios de metafísica según la razón vital," *Revista de filosofía* 16 (1957): 141–94. See Luis Recasens Siches, "José Ortega y Gasset: Su metafísica, su sociología y su filosofía social," *La Torre* 4 (1956): 305–35, a good exposition of Ortega's basic concepts (reality is life as self and circumstance) but giving no generic name to it. In 1960, Walgrave, still unaware of that course, held that "Ortega never succeeded in developing a metaphysics" (*Filosofía de Ortega,* 316). Similarly, Osvaldo Lira, *Ortega en su espíritu,* vol. 1, *Metafísica y estética* (Santiago: Universidad Católica de Chile, 1965), regretting his apparent failure to produce a "metaphysics of vital reason," and finding only "germinal intuitions" that were "rudimentary, weak," and contradictory, concluded that in his "irrealism" Ortega was not an "authentic metaphysician" but a "panlogist" (by identifying being with concept), so his metaphysics was without "being" and without efficient or final causality (67–70, 241–42). Also see Hernán Larraín Acuña, *La génesis de pensamiento de Ortega: La metafísica* (Buenos Aires: Fabril, 1962). The later publishing of Ortega's "metaphysics of vital reason" as *Some Lessons in Metaphysics* (1969) and in 1983 in Spanish (12:13–130) has not much enhanced awareness of Ortega's metaphysics, much less of its pragmatist genre. Alfonso López Quintás, "Santayana, Husserl y Ortega: Necesidad de una revisión metodológica," *Arbor* 82 (June–August 1972): 5–16, was concerned not with Ortega but with Santayana and "the theory of compresence" as related to "meta-empirical realities" (12). Similarly failing to connect Ortega's "compresence" with James (but with Husserl) was Jaime de Salas, "A. Rodrígues Huéscar: Recuerdo y presencia de Ortega," *Revista de Occidente,* no. 60 (May 1986), 121, who at least credited Ortega, a "metaphysician" from his "roots," with a "radical reform" in philosophy and metaphysics (131). In "Ortega and Metaphysics," Enrique Tierno Galván related his ideas to Bergson, Brentano, and Natorp, but openly denied any interest in "pragmatism," past or present (*Actas del coloquio celebrado con motivo del centenario . . . de Ortega y Gasset,* ed. H. L. Lope [Frankfurt am Main: Lang, 1986], 55, 58, 61–630. Also see Jorge Acevedo, *Hombre y Mundo: Sobre el punto de partida de la filosofía actual* (Santiago: Editorial Universitaria, 1983), wherein the use of the concept "presence" in regard to life as radical reality and the explicit pragmatist terms of Ortega's *Man and People* then were *not* brought together (33–34, 110–11). On other critics of his metaphysics, see supplemental note 6, chap. 4.

3. For a view that "pragmatism . . . is back," see Mark Migotti, "Recent Work in Pragmatism," *Philosophical Books* 39 (April 1988): 65–66. Richard J. Bernstein, *Philosophical Profiles: Essays in a Pragmatic Mode* (Cambridge, Eng.: Polity Press, 1986): "the pragmatic tradition is neither passé nor dead" but "ahead . . . of time" and now undergoing a "return" (x). Alfred North Whitehead seems to have taken James's radical empiricism for a metaphysics: see n. 25 in my chap. 7. Among the many studies on James or pragmatism there is wide disagreement about whether he had a metaphysics, and, if so, what it was. See Sidney Hook, "The Metaphysics of the Instrument" (method), in *The Metaphysics of Pragmatism* (Chicago: Open Court Press, 1976): 6, 17–18. Paul K. Conkin, *Puritans and Pragmatists,* said, James's "final philosophical goal" was "a new metaphysical system"— never completed," but "his essays on radical empiricism . . . contained the most significant metaphysical innovations since Kant" (322). Thomas R. Martland, Jr., *The Metaphysics of William James and John Dewey* (New York: Philosophical Library, 1963), chap. 3 on James's metaphysics as radical empiricism (76–77) but thus also concerned with "pure experience" and the "flow" of life and thought (79, 83). Wild, *Radical Empiricism,* did not regard radical empiricism as metaphysics but as phenomenology in potentiality. Also see McDermott, *Writings of James,* 134–36 (linkage, arrangement). John E. Smith, *Purpose and Thought: The Meaning of Pragmatism* (New Haven: Yale University Press, 1978), chap. 5 ("Pragmatism and Metaphysics"), granted that there may be *no unified* "metaphysics of pragmatism" among Peirce, James, and Dewey, and he saw a "tension" (if not contradiction) between James's pragmatism and empiricism, between practical results and concepts; some of James's "metaphysical issues" were "the one and the many," or "monism and pluralism" (121, 123). Sandra Rosenthal, "Pragmatism and the Methodology of Metaphysics," *Monist* 57 (April 1973): 252–64, discusses the paradoxical (in Peirce and Lewis); idem, *The Pragmatic A Priori* (St. Louis: W. H. Green, 1976), on "the given" (82) and the concrete (68, 94, 100). James Edie held that James rejected "speculative metaphysics" for a "metaphysics of experience" in radical empiricism, but meant to "replace metaphysics, so to speak, with 'philosophical anthropology'" (*An Invitation to Phenomenology: Studies in the Philosophy of Experience* [Chicago: Quadrangle Books, 1965], 115, 120, 122). Compare that with Ortega's going beyond a metaphysics of radical empiricism to metahistory, philosophical anthropology, and historiology (see Antonio Pintor-Ramos, "Metafísica, historia y antropología: Sobre el pensamiento de la antropología filosófica," *Pensamiento* 41 [1985]:3–36).

5. Guglielmini, "Algo más sobre Ortega"; Alberto Rouges, "El perspectivismo de Ortega y Gasset." A Jamesian pragmatism was almost detected in Ortega in a work by his disciple, Juan David García Bacca, *Nuevos grandes filósofos contemporáneos y sus temas,* vol. 2, *James, Ortega y Gasset, Whitehead* (Caracas: Imprenta Nacional, 1947), 45–186. In a chaotic anthology of texts, with only minimal critical commentary, he claimed (1:5) that he could connect his selected themes through a series of authors, but in fact he mentioned only the "limits of rationality" as in Hartmann, Ortega, and Whitehead and a "realism of truth" (11) in James and in Ortega with regard to things in the world appearing as phenomena, as a "presence" to man, but he failed either to suggest or to demonstrate any connection between those thinkers. Clearly he knew little of James, for he was blind to elements in Ortega's thought that came from James: anti-intellectualism (45), pluralism (153–54), and unity and plurality (154–55), as well as "the given" (155), "beliefs," and "consistency" (176). Marías considered pragmatism as part of Ortega's general "circumstance" but did not see any kind of specific influence on him, in *History of Philosophy* (1948), trans. S. Appelbaum (New York: Dover, 1967), 394–98; *Circumstance and Vocation,* 71, 80–82.

6. "Radical positivism" is not even indexed for Ortega, but philosophical "radicalism" is (8:280–82). See Martin Heidegger, "Encuentros con Ortega y Gasset en Alemania," *Clavileño* 7:39 (1956): 1–2, for Heidegger's reaction to the undefinable "positivism" in Ortega. Crane Brinton, "Toward a Philosophy of History," *Saturday Review of Literature* 23

(April 5, 1941): 5 (essay retitled in 1962). Silver, in *Ortega as Phenomenologist* (153, 157), detected a "super-positivism" as a metaphysical concept dealing with "radical reality," and Marías had noted that term from 1916 (Argentina) and linked it loosely to "philosophy of life" (*Circumstance and Vocation*, 278–79), but neither study stressed it or developed it. Also see Marías, "Metaphysics as a Science of Fundamental Reality," in *Spanish Philosophy: An Anthology*, ed. A. R. Caponigri (Notre Dame: University of Notre Dame Press, 1967), 351–72, comparing Ortega with Heidegger on whether "life" or "man" is basic. Although a number of critics looked but failed to find his metaphysics, most general studies of Ortega's philosophy at least affirm or even briefly consider his basic metaphysics, like Marías in *Circumstance and Vocation*, 418, and (by implication therein) in "The Structure of Reality," 419–23, and in *Trayectorias*, 267–314. See Abellán, *Ortega;* Cascalès, *L'Humanisme d'Ortega;* Arturo García Astrada, *El Pensamiento de Ortega y Gasset;* and Arturo Gaete, *El sistema maduro de Ortega y Gasset—La metafísica*. Specific studies of Ortega's *nameless* "metaphysics" are José Luis Abellán, "Ortega y el fracaso de la metafísica," *Cuadernos Americanos* 140 (May–June 1965): 108–19; John W. Dixon, Jr., "Ortega and the Redefinition of Metaphysics," *Cross Currents* 29 (Fall 1979): 281–99; Arturo García Astrada, "Transcendencia y realidad en el pensar de Ortega y Gasset," *Sur,* no. 353 (July–December 1983): 41–48; Nemesio González Caminero, "Metafísica de la realidad radical y sociología de la cultura en el último de Ortega y Gasset," *Pensamiento* 20 (1964): 174–204; and Rigoberto Juárez Paz, "Ortega y la renovación del problema del ser, o un filósofo malogrado," *Cuadernos Hispanoamericanos* 13 (1960): 273–79. Larraín Acuña, *La génesis del pensamiento de Ortega,* discusses life as radical reality. See also Miguel Montes González, "Papel de lo histórico en la metafísica, antropología y hermenéutica orteguiana," *Lumen* 33 (1984): 328–66; Augusto Andrés Ortega, "La vida y su metafísica (Ortega y Gasset)," *Cuadernos Salamantinos de Filosofía* 10 (1983): 311–23; Pintor-Ramos, "Metafísica, historia y antropología"; and Udo Rukser, "Ortega y Gasset como pensador metafísico," *Humboldt* 8 (1967): 83–84.

15. "Un filósofo de la nueva generación," *Inicial* (1924): 58–63, esp. 59–60; there was at least an attempt to distinguish Ortega from "the points of view of pragmatism" by his added *historical* perspective, and subsequently to compare him with Nietzsche for his "sportive" sense of life and culture. Whoever wrote the review sympathized with Italian fascism.

The length of this study has compelled me to omit a critical appendix on Ortega's very probable writing (at least editing) of some articles on pragmatism for Espasa-Calpe's *Enciclopedia Universal Ilustrada;* they "fit" by tone and internal evidences with what we can determine of his published views. See unsigned articles s.v. "Pragmatismo" (1922) and "Guillermo James" (1926); the latter was a second, revised edition, without a date of first printing. Several letters (with Calpe letterhead) to Ortega in the years 1922 to 1924 implied that he was serving in some general editorial capacity. Helene (Hella) Weyl, "José Ortega y Gasset," *Toronto Quarterly* 6 (1937–1938): 464, stated that he had "played an important role in the foundation of . . . Espasa-Calpe." That encyclopedia carried a commendatory article on Ortega in 1919 and also a long supplement in 1932, which identified a variety of his editorial ventures, some of which were connected with Espasa-Calpe series or collections such as *Los Filósofos, Los grandes pensadores, Estudios sociológicos, Musas lejanas, Historiología,* and *Libros y cuadernos de política*. Miguel Ortega, *Mi padre,* 69, mentions what we would call "hack work"—if for newspapers, maybe also for Espasa's encyclopedia? In response to inquiry, an editor at Espasa-Calpe wrote me in the 1980s that archival records of the publishing firm were virtually all destroyed during the civil war (1936–1939), so that it was impossible to identify any specific contributors, since the articles were always printed as anonymous. A list of contributors, without any assignment of areas of expertise, was given in vol. 70 of the *Enciclopedia* (1930), vi–xvi, but none seem ever to have been associated with publications on pragmatism, so Ortega is the more likely author.

37. For James on "intellectualism," see *Writings*, 519, 561–63; idem, *Essays in Radical Empiricism. Pluralistic Universe* (Gloucester, Mass.: Smith, 1967), pt. 2, pp. 72–74, refers to abstract "absolutes" and extremes of rationality. For some instances of the use of "intellectualism" by Ortega, see 1:439; 4:321; 5:305–6, 382; 6:192, 206–8; 7:93; 6:30, 32, 33n ("History as a System"); 8:32, 44, 47, 52 ("Preface for Germans"). Doubly pragmatist was this statement from the first edition of his selected works in 1932: "I have been *anti-intellectualist*. During my youth there ruled in Europe a cult of the intellect that seemed to me idolatrous and a great humbug [*beatería*]. But today we have to react against the opposite vice, by renewing that faith, not in the intellect, which is only an organic *instrument*, but in its vital utility, in thought" (6:354; emphasis added). Ortega, *¿Que es conocimiento?* 144, 150; James, *Pluralistic Universe* (1977), 50–52; idem, *Writings*, 238–39; idem, *Pluralistic Universe* (1947), on Bergson and intellectualism, 226–28, 237. See Crane Brinton, *The Fate of Man* (New York: Braziller, 1961), 304–8 on "intellectualisms," with James and Bergson as cases of "anti-intellectualism," which he identified (313) as "anti-rationalism," or a "chastened rationalism" that was realist and relativist. Max Weber in *The Sociology of Religion* (1922) also treated of "intellectualism" (chap. 8).

CHAPTER 5
Method: "Perspectivism" as Phenomenology (1912+)

2. Barzun, *Stroll with James*, listed more than twenty-five references to James's "perspectivism" and clearly suggested a link with Ortega (215). Wild, *Radical Empiricism*, concluded that James, in a "broader sense," was "primarily 'a phenomenologist'" and identified radical empiricism as affiliated with the general phenomenological movement in a "very broad sense" that was not Husserl's transcendental phenomenology (414)—the same point to be made about Ortega. The logic in Ortega's movement from pragmatism over to phenomenology is evident from a number of other studies since 1960 on James and Husserl, as recently as James Edie, *James and Phenomenology* (1987) on the "intentionality of consciousness," or his *New Essays in Phenomenology* (Chicago: Quadrangle Books, 1969) for three essays on James; Johannes Linschoten, *On the Way Toward a Phenomenological Analysis: The Psychology of William James;* Bruce Wilshire, *William James and Phenomenology* (Bloomington: Indiana University Press, 1968). Also see Edie, "James and Phenomenology"; Patrick Bourgeois and Sandra Rosenthal, "Pragmatism and Phenomenology: The Common Context of Meaning," *Southern Journal of Philosophy* 18 (1980): 481–87. After citing Gurwitsch on the "strong affinity" between James and Husserl (17), Linschoten found an "implicit phenomenology" in James's psychology (58) and viewed James as a "forerunner" of Husserl's phenomenology (307); Wilshire found James's "protophenomenology" to be "completely understandable" as a keen interest for Husserl, whose "metaphysics" was also an "outgrowth" from Kant (3–8). Edie ("James and Phenomenology," 486) said James often "preceded" the phenomenologists with "phenomenological themes"; and in *Invitation to Phenomenology: Studies in the Philosophy of Experience* (Chicago: Quadrangle Books, 1965), chap. 6 ("Notes on the Philosophical Anthropology of William James," 110–32), he saw James as "an 'empiricist' or 'phenomenologist' who eschewed grand systems" for specific studies (114) and conceded extensive parallels between James and Husserl, even that they were working "in convergent directions" (131–32). Alfred Schutz—himself a phenomenologist, who shared "gray cats" with Ortega and sources such as Husserl, James, Bergson, Simmel, and Scheler—connected him only with Scheler, but he affirmed Husserl's "admiration" for James's *Principles of Psychology,* and he saw "certain essential starting points" and views common to them, without making the one a phenomenologist or the other a pragmatist (*Collected Papers,* ed. A. Brodersen [The Hague: Nijhoff, 1964], 2:ix, 3:1 and 133, 135, 145 [Ortega and Scheler]). Ortega and Husserl

might have been struck by James's first sentence in chapter 1 of *The Principles of Psychology,* 2 vols. (1890; New York: Dover, 1950): "Psychology is the science of mental life, both of its phenomena and their conditions"—by means of "description" (1:vii). Since Husserl first acknowledged James in *Logische Untersuchen* (1901), it is possible Ortega noticed there so early a connection between phenomenology and pragmatism. "Perspective" in James is comparable to "perspectivism" in Ortega: see Edie, "James and Phenomenology," 522. See Martin Farber, *The Aims of Phenomenology. The Motives, Methods and Impact of Husserl's Thought,* 45, on Husserl's early "neutral" (or open) position relative to idealism and "naive" naturalism. Farber saw Husserl's intention as being both method and "universal system" (13), but as less successful with culture, history, and philosophy of history—all areas, incidentally, that Ortega developed much further than Husserl—whether or not by phenomenological method. Morón Arroyo (*Sistema,* 208) saw a "natural affinity for phenomenology" in Ortega's *Meditations on Quixote.*

3. Victoria Ocampo, *Autobiografía* (Buenos Aires, 1952, 1983), 8, 40–41 (Ortega to Chestov and Valerie); Edmund Husserl, *Briefe an Roman Ingarden* (The Hague: Nijhoff, 1968), 90. There were two articles on phenomenology in Ortega's *Revista de Occidente* in 1928–1929 by Arnold Metzger, "La situación presente de la fenomenología" (no. 56, pp. 177–201; no. 58, pp. 178–209), which updated phenomenology relative to Scheler and to Heidegger; Ortega also had three of Husserl's and one of Scheler's works translated. Marías, "Presence and Absence of Existentialism in Spain," *Philosophy and Phenomenological Research* 15 (December 1954): 182.

In *Analecta Husserliana* 29 (1990), see Anna-Teresa Tymieniecka, "Phenomenology of Life and the New Critique of Reason: From Husserl's Philosophy to the Phenomenology of Life and of the Human Condition" (3–18); Harold C. Raley, "Phenomenological 'Life': A New Look at the Philosophical Enterprise in Ortega y Gasset" (93–106); and Nel Rodríguez Rial, "Ortega—Phenomenologist: Man's Self-Interpretation-in-Existence" (107–34). Note that both the first and the third essays appeal to Marías's authority on Ortega's philosophy of life and phenomenology, although (in nothing I have seen) did Marías concede either the presence of the one or the paramountcy of the other in Ortega. Raley raised the question of how Ortega could both deny that phenomenology was his philosophy and yet "abandon" it on "receiving it," and he seems to have answered by distinguishing his phenomenology as only a method, or instrument (93–95)—as do I—and found the "system" not in his philosophy but in "the 'radical' system of phenomenological life that he discovered" (103). However, he views the search for his sources as "sheer problematicity," but not from Germany alone. Strangely, none of the three cite Silver's realist interpretation, but the view of Rodríguez Rial may be an idealist opposite, unless he means by "transcendental" (113, 115, 117, 121–22) only what I define (in chap. 7) as a reciprocally conceptual-ontological sense of "transcendent" in Ortega. Although he remarks that from 1914 Ortega meant to "supersede the idealism" in Husserl, he seems to me to have made the very dubious assumption that what was in Husserl's "later works," first as "existential" and then as "historical" (3:124–27), was *always* in him, even in the *Ideen* (1913)—although first *developed* by Ortega. Hence, he did not look for any other sources of Ortega's phenomenology beyond Husserl himself, and he found an eventual compatibility between them throughout, even on consciousness, the "natural" standpoint, and the historical orientation, which was *not* Ortega's view of their relationship, nor his "intention." Does he therefore think that Ortega did not know what he (or Husserl at least) was doing, or was deceiving his public about it? Raley rejected "piracy" or "plagiarism" (97, 101, 105). Rodríguez Rial offers an insight into Ortega's phenomenological method—a "great epistemological novelty"—as a "new epistemological paradigm" that unites subject and object, consciousness and world (113–15), pretty much what Ortega called "unity of knowing and being," as derived from Kant.

6. See Husserl, *Ideas. General Introduction to Pure Phenomenology* (1913; trans. W. R. B.

Gibson [New York: Collier-Macmillan, 1967]), sec. 2, chap. 1, on "Suspension" of "the world as the natural standpoint: I and my world about me." Ortega rejected such phenomenological reduction (*epoché*) to "pure consciousness" (chaps. 3 and 4). That subtitle on p. 101 was surely the most direct source (after James) of Ortega's "I and my circumstance," but here are also "compresence" and "presence" (101–2) and here too (unlike 1901) "the given" (66–67, 192–93, 378–79), and "viewpoint"—all of which were first in James as realism, in contrast to Husserl's idealism. See Spiegelberg, *Phenomenological Movement,* 1:128, on "givenness" as applying to what "presents itself to us by 'intuition'," as having been in positivism, Bergson, and James (radical empiricism). Before Husserl with his "striking similarity," James had stressed the concrete and individual. Husserl, *Logical Investigations* (1901), trans. F. N. Findley (New York: Humanities Press, 1970), 2:624–26, 639, 351, on "positing" and "presentation," but in reference to Brentano rather than James. For a good example of Ortega's transition, for his blending of pragmatism with phenomenology, see 1:248–51 (1913), on basic "presentative acts" and equating "perception" and "intuition," with reference to Husserl's *Ideen*. Rodríguez Rial detected "pragmatic" aspects to Ortega's phenomenology, and he also unconsciously repeated some of the Jamesian terminology, without realizing that it was from James ("Ortega—Phenomenologist," 116–17, cf. 122, 124, 126). In the "English Preface" (circa 1930?) to the *Ideas,* Husserl explicitly denied that this work constituted a "phenomenological philosophy," although he hoped to come to one eventually (28–29); Ortega may have seen that preface by the 1940s and have drawn from it the idea of "radicalism" in "first philosophy" on "foundations," such as we find in his "Leibniz." In the text of 1913, Husserl made it very clear that this was not a "natural" (realist) approach to "essential Being" but an idealist transcendentalism (44–46). Although he stated in the first chapter that "Our first judgment upon life is that of natural human beings, imaging, judging, feeling, willing, '*from the natural standpoint*'" (101), such was not the effect of his "reduction." Ortega's judgment on Husserl (from that work) thus seems justified by its content. Of course, he could well have chosen then to fasten on the neglected "natural" outlook of man's "life" as more properly basic. Holmes, *Human Reality,* 37: "It is not a system that [Husserl and other early phenomenologists] share," but intuition into structures; he found no "direct evidence" that Husserl's ideas influenced Ortega.

8. Silver, *Ortega as Phenomenologist* (1978), on the *Meditations on Quixote,* defined "Ortega's philosophy as a mundane phenomenology," as part of the European movement of "existential phenomenology" (ix, xi). By contrast, in 1975, Holmes, *Human Reality,* 37–38, citing relevant passages from the "Preface for Germans" and earlier phenomenological essays for his chap. 3, "The Phenomenological Dimension of Man and Social Order," assessed phenomenology's relevance for Ortega's "philosophy of man, society, and history" and concluded that Husserl's phenomenology was not a "system" but was instead a *method* and that Ortega's relationship to it was "ambiguous, ambivalent." He nevertheless chose to "lump" phenomenological and existentialist viewpoints together (92). Morón Arroyo, *Sistema,* 211–18; Robert O'Connor, "Ortega's Reformulation of Husserlian Phenomenology," *Philosophy and Phenomenological Research* 40 (September 1979): 53–63; Rodríguez Rial, "Ortega—Phenomenologist," 107–34. Other more general studies than Silver's that considered phenomenology in reference to Ortega were those by Marías, Salmerón, Guy, Holmes, and Cerezo Galán. Also see Howard N. Tuttle, "Ortega's Vitalism in Relation to Aspects of 'Lebensphilosophie' and Phenomenology"; Lorenzo Merino Barragán, "Fenomenología y metafísica de la acción humana en Santo Tomas y Ortega y Gasset," *Revista de Filosofía* 28 (1969): 171–96; and Alfonso López Quintás, "Santayana, Husserl y Ortega: Necesidad de una revisión metodológica," *Arbor* 82 (June–August 1972): 5–16.

9. Have I misunderstood Silver's intent? In his earlier *Phenomenology and Art* (1975), he had stressed aesthetics and "phenomenological method" (9), although even then he called

Ortega "the first existential phenomenologist of all" (7), "in the main stream" of phenomenology. See *Ortega as Phenomenologist* (ix and xi), but compare his quoting and acknowledging Ortega's claim in 1934 that "phenomenology was never a philosophy for us," because it was "incapable of a systematic form" (49). "Still," said Silver, "in the light of what we know today about phenomenology," Ortega seems inconsistent, for phenomenology was even more "systematic" than neo-Kantianism, and Husserl had already declared phenomenology a "scientific philosophy" (50–57). Since Silver is no clearer on the question of Ortega's "philosophy" and "system" than was Ortega to him, one has to rely on the sense of the "Preface for Germans": his "philosophy" as *system* or *general* philosophy. I would disagree with Silver's contention that phenomenology was "the First Philosophy he had returned to Germany to discover" (55)—his metaphysics was first and chiefly from James's radical empiricism, although phenomenological in form. Hence, I also disagree with both ends of his statement: "By using . . . the new ontological theses [life as basic reality (149)] he extracted from Scheler and the *Ideas* as a first story, he constructed a mundane phenomenology he was pleased to call Vital or Historical Reason" (89). Historical reason was distinct from vital reason and was more than phenomenology. See Spiegelberg, *Phenomenological Movement,* 2:619: "At no time . . . does Husserl present us with a philosophical system. Certainly he never aspired to develop his philosophy into a philosophical system." "His was a philosophy which remained constantly in the making" (1:75)—like Ortega's, we may add. See my Introduction on Ortega's distinction between method (epistemology) and ontology in defining philosophy. Rodríguez Rial, "Ortega—Phenomenologist," 121–23, 124, 126. Also see supplemental notes, chap. 5.

36. Alfred Stern thought Ortega took his perspectivism from Leibniz: *Philosophy of History and the Problem of Values,* 87; H. M. Kallen thought he got it from Nietzsche; and Jacques Barzun, from James—probably from both. For Scheler's "perspectivism," see J. R. Staude, *Max Scheler: An Intellectual Portrait* (New York: Free Press, 1967), 155, 159–61, 221, as important for his entire "system," and with both social and historicist relativistic dimensions. Although Staude claims that Scheler influenced Ortega (60–63, 255), it is not clear whose perspectivism was the earlier. Nevertheless, their meanings (viewpoints) were similar. In Germany, Ortega's early philosophy was called perspectivism by Ernst R. Curtius, "Spanische Perspecktiven," *Die neue Rundschau* 35 (1927): 1229–47. Notably, on pages 1246–47, he referred to *Modern Theme* and *Meditations on Quixote;* this essay was the first thing published on Ortega in Germany. In 1927 the first of his "occasional" essays appeared in Germany—years before his *Modern Theme* was translated, but apparently it was to Curtius that Ortega referred in 1929 when he called "perspectivism" a "method" that the Germans "have baptized for me" by that name (7:286). But he himself had adopted that name in 1923 at the latest (3:200n, 234). Although the footnotes added to vol. 1 of *El Espectador* (1916) are of uncertain date, where he first mentioned "perpectivism" was in the context of a reference to Hans Vaihinger's *Die Philosophie des Als Ob* (1911) as "recent" (2:18–19 n. 1). I assume that he meant the first German edition instead of a later Spanish translation, which would probably establish the date of the term as 1916 too, unlike notes appended to vol. 2 (1917) from 1921 or later (2:131). Hence, it was apparently Ortega himself, not the Germans, who first called his early "method" by the name "perspectivism," even as early as 1913 in courses (3:200n).

38. Most general studies have pages or sections on Ortega's perspectivism, most notably Rodríguez Huéscar, *Perspectiva y verdad.* Moreover, specific studies reveal great variety (and contraries) of definition: Antón Donoso, "Truth as Perspectival and Man as History," American Catholic Philosophical Association *Proceedings* 43 (1969): 139–47; Alfonso Borroso Nieto, "Ortega y Gasset y el perspectivismo," *Verdad y Vida,* no. 4 (1946): 405–36; José D. Camacho, "Verdad, perspectiva y circunstancia," *La Nueva Democracia* 41 (1961): 76–82; A. Cazzanigo, "Sulla concezione prospettivista della venta," *Scientia* 90 (1955): 87–92; José Gaos, "El tema de nuestro tiempo (Filosofía de la perspectiva)," *Revista*

de Occidente no. 3 (October–December 1923): 374; Walter Garaycochea Villar, "La teoría de la historia en Ortega y Gasset: Historiología y perspectivismo," *Hombre y Mundo* 2 (1967): 59–83; Lorenzo Giusso, "Ortega y Gasset," in his *Idealismo e prospettivismo* (Naples: Tipomeccanica, 1939), 167–82; Robert G. Havard, "Guillén, Salinas and Ortega: Circumstances and Perspective," *Bulletin of Hispanic Studies* 60 (October 1983): 305–18; Francisco Larroyo, *La filosofía de los valores: El perspectivismo metafísico* (Mexico City: Porrua, 1936), 131–33; Enrique Lynch, "La perspectiva y la crítica del pensamiento," *Cuadernos Hispano-americanos*, nos. 403–5 (January–March 1984): 81–92; Rodríguez Huéscar, "Concepto central del perspectivismo ortegiano," *Diálogos* 1 (September 1964): 63–79; Patrick Romanell, "Perspectivism and Existentialism in Mexico. Ortega in Mexico," in Romanell, ed., *Making of the Mexican Mind* (Notre Dame: University of Notre Dame Press, 1967), 141–85; Rouges, "El perspectivismo"; Juan Saiz Barberá, "El perspectivismo. Fundamento y orígen de esta teoría orteguiana; su sentido idealista," *Revista de Espiritualidad* (Madrid), no. 9 (1950): 74–87.

48. In his library Ortega possessed thirty distinct works and editions of Scheler's productions (dated from 1913 forward), four from his own press at *Revista de Occidente* and another (*El porvenir del hombre,* 1942) from Espasa-Calpe and for which he wrote a prologue—apparently not reproduced in the *Obras Completas.* (Courtesy of Soledad Ortega.) Also see Orringer, *Nuevas fuentes germánica,* 12–13 and n. Although there are no letters between Ortega and Scheler, the latter's name appears in his letters from and to Curtius (December 10, 1923; March 9, 1925), in "Epistolario entre Ortega y Curtius," *Revista de Occidente,* no. 6–7 (June 1963): 329, 330, 333. It was from Scheler that Curtius had learned about Ortega, who asked: "Is there anyone who represents in history a way of thinking and feeling that coincides with what we ourselves bring into philosophy and literature?" "What is Scheler doing? In his *Sociology of Knowledge,* I have found the most surprising coincidences with my last work, published several months ahead of Scheler's, that is titled *Atlantises.*" He found Scheler's pages "always succulent and ingenious but more than ever hasty."

Just as with Heidegger, Scheler can easily be identified as an influence on Ortega, whereas the latter was actually first with an idea. For example, it would be wrong to suppose that Ortega knew that Scheler had called phenomenology "the most radical empiricism and positivism ever developed"—an expression very close to his own pragmatist "radical positivism"—because it appeared only in 1933 (Spiegelberg, *Phenomenological Movement,* 1:241). If "man" was forever a problem for Scheler, Ortega answered it—more radically than Scheler had done—as "history" (Hans Meyerhoff, "Introduction," Scheler, *Man's Place in Nature* [New York: Noonday Press, 1961]: xi, xxiii–xxiv, cf. Scheler, ibid., 5–7, 88). Ortega never claimed to have contributed anything to Scheler, who in contrast claimed that Ortega had "followed" him in both "value theory" and "sociological thought" (Scheler, *Formalism in Ethics and Non-Formal Ethics of Value,* trans. M. S. Frings and R. L. Funk [Evanston, Ill.: Northwestern University Press, 1973], xxxii–xxxiii)—but he confessed to neglecting history. Moreover, contrary to Orringer (*Nuevas fuentes germánicas,* 38), Ortega did not learn crisis thinking about the sciences from Scheler (or from Husserl) but expressed it in 1915 very clearly (12:343–45). P. Heath, "Introduction," Scheler, *The Nature of Sympathy* (New Haven: Yale University Press, 1954), states that Scheler's basics were from Brentano (xi–xiii) and his doctrine of "the spirit" on the one hand and his frank "biologism" on the other (xxxviii) would have distinguished him from Ortega—as did his intended "Idealismus-Realismus," which apparently was almost the reverse in emphasis of Ortega's earlier attempted synthesis of realism and idealism. This was ultimately the case with their positions on pragmatism, although Scheler too rejected Husserl's consciousness as basic and sought a middle ground between modern idealism and classical realism (Eugene Kelly, *Max Scheler* [Boston: Twayne, 1977], 75–78). Scheler's notion of "idols" (pre-1914 or 1921?) perhaps was too late to inspire Ortega (Scheler, *Philosophical Perspectives,* trans. O. A. Haac [Boston: Beacon, 1958], 1 and 3), and it also seems that for the latter's "Robinsonism" the former's "Robinson Crusoe" (1916) came too late (Nota, *Scheler*, 133, cf. Scheler's "Formalismus in der Ethik," pat. 2, *Jahrbuch für Philosophie und phänomenologische Forschung* 2 (1916): 24–25. See Manfred S. Frings, *Max Scheler* (Pittsburgh: Duquesne University Press, 1965), 139–40; also 37 (on Ortega and Scheler) and 28 (on Scheler's "philosophical anthropology"). Frings later claimed that life was central to Scheler instead of consciousness, that he saw reality as "objective," and that he made phenomenology not an end in itself but a basis for metaphysics (*Max Scheler: Centennial Essays* [The Hague: Nijhoff, 1974], viii–ix). Hence, Scheler and Ortega had much in common, at least in a general sense—as Holmes said in *Human Reality*, 48, where he found "no explicit evidence" that Scheler directly influenced Ortega, despite obvious "affinities in thought." See F. Vela, "Notas—De antropología filosófica," *Revista de Occidente* 87 (September 1930): 393–400, which shows deeply "all the currents of our time," his dualism of life and spirit (reason?) reduced to "existence." "To think, theorize, . . . is a mode of existing," as Ortega had said, or reason is a function of life.

56. Miguel Ortega, *Mi padre*, wrote of going with his father to visit Husserl in 1934: "they were enchanted with my father's books. They had read them all and were talking about them" (*Mi padre*, 122). For Husserl's reference to Ortega, see his *Briefe an Ingarden*, 90 (letter of November 26, 1934): "In the past week we had a very interesting philosopher visitor: Ortega y Gasset, who brought us a great surprise: He is very deeply acquainted with my writings. Daily with me and Fink he held long and serious conversations, his questions pressing into the most difficult depths. He is active not only as a writer and educator of the new Spain, but as professor and leader of a school of phenomenology. Now there comes from him a translation of the *Meditations* and even the selected Works. . . . Over all, a wonderful man." Editor Ingarden erred in thinking that Husserl was referring (at the end) to his own works. As Manuel Ortega reveals, they were Ortega's works—not the *Meditations on Quixote*, which was obviously influenced by Husserl, but instead his *Studies on Love* (*Uber die Liebe: Meditationen*, trans. Helene Weyl [Stuttgart: Deutsche Verlags-Anstalt, 1933]), the only such work then available, as shown in Udo Rukser, *Bibliografía de Ortega* (Madrid: Revista de Occidente, 1971), 20. Silver, *Ortega as Phenomenologist*, 154, saw Ortega's *Modern Theme* as "the rough equivalent of Husserl's *Crisis*," but, in diagnosing crisis as related to life, "they pass each other while going in opposite directions" (154–55).

57. From the point of view of "philosophy of history," the first to raise the question of phenomenology and history in Ortega was John H. Nota, "Le point de départ de la philosophie de l'historie," *Proceedings of the Eleventh International Congress of Philosophy* (Amsterdam, 1953), later expanded into *Phenomenology and History* (1967), cf. 1–10 (through Romein). Holmes, *Human Reality*, says that Ortega used phenomenological analysis in his systematic work on reality, being, and society in the 1930s (37); his "phenomenological perspective" coincided with his existentialist and historicist points of view; for his synthesis of these three perspectives as applied to man, society, and history, see 138–39. In "La fenomenología," 225–36, Holmes saw phenomenology as "a method of analysis, ontological and historical," and he saw vital reason and historical reason as "interchangable terms" (228–33). See Cirilo Flóres Miguel, "La razón histórica y el cambio de paradigma en la historia: De la conciencia a la acción," *Cuadernos Salamantinos de Filosofía* 11 (1984): 279–94; on the basis of *Sobre la razón histórica*, he saw historical reason in Ortega as comparable to "mundane phenomenology" in Merleau-Ponty (cf. Silver) but that he was much more besides (existentialism and historicism), although he called the whole a "philosophy of action" instead of a philosophy of life (280).

58. Olga Monsalve, "La aparición del otro: Comentarios a la posición de Edmund Husserl y su recepción en Ortega y Gasset," *Lecciones y Ensayos* no. 12 (1959): 97–102. Michael Theunissen, *The Other: Studies in the Social Ontology of Husserl, Heidegger, Sartre,*

and Buber, trans. C. Macann (Cambridge: MIT Press, 1984). On Husserl's "shift" from consciousness as static to a Jamesian "time-consciousness" of *life* as "flow" or "developing process," first expressed soon after 1900 but not published until 1928, yet always with *historical* implications, see Ronald Bruzina, *Logos and Eidos: The Concept in Phenomenology* (The Hague: Mouton, 1970), chap. 5: "From the Static to the Genetic," 126–27, 133; also Farber, *Aims of Phenomenology,* 85–86, on "time-consciousness" as *subjective* in Husserl's notion of "stream of consciousness." Edie, *Invitation to Phenomenology,* 118, judged that "the final Husserl is not as far from James" as was his *Ideas* of 1913—that "final" Husserl having allowed for (or returned to?) the "real world" and "the real, existing historical object itself in the world."

CHAPTER 6
Stage I: "Vital Reason" as Existentialism (1914–1923+)

3. Obviously, no reviewers of *Modern Theme* in or around 1923 (nor in the United States in the 1930s) could see existentialism in it yet, but instead (as stated already) they linked it with James and pragmatism or with Nietzsche. A few critics since then have made the existential connection—for "crisis" more than for *life* as "existence" or as "sport" (3:186, 189, 195). See Hayden V. White, *The Ordeal of Liberal Humanism* (New York: McGraw-Hill, 1970), 2:347. Perhaps the connection of that book to phenomenology is clearer, but maybe it owed less to Husserl for life-"phenomenon" and "intuition" (3:169–70) than to Scheler for the more conspicuous "perspectivism," "values," and new historical orientation (3:153, 179, 187, 200). Ortega himself made the connection with *Meditations on Quixote,* as he said, some seventeen years before Heidegger, but scholars have had to dig out the relationships. For critics, the problem of Ortega's existentialism is illustrated in *El Pensamiento de Ortega y Gasset,* by Francisco Alvarez González, who recognized the existential themes but, because of his different ("sportive") spirit, refused to put that label on his philosophy.

8. Frederick C. Copleston, "Ortega y Gasset and Modern Spanish Thought," *The Listener,* November 29, 1951, p. 933. Among the "epigones," Marías was the chief spokesman; in a flood of defensive expository publications, he denied that Ortega was an existentialist, properly understood. In *Ortega y la idea de la razón vital* (Madrid: Antonio Zuñiga, 1948), 80–88, he dissociated Ortega's vital reason from both phenomenology (Scheler, Husserl) and existentialism (Heidegger). In 1954, Marías half admitted that both Unamuno and Ortega represented existentialism in Spain but then denied it, because the one lacked a metaphysics and the other did not match the phenomenological and irrationalist "tendencies" in existentialism. Hence, Marías never really changed his opinion expressed in 1948: Heidegger represented existentialism, and Heidegger after 1927 had become too "closed," irrationalist, even antihistorical to lump with Ortega's "historical and vital reason"— which represented an "overcoming" (*superación*) of both phenomenology and existentialism. Marías did not become aware of Ortega's rapprochement with Heidegger after 1948, only of his antagonism before then. The most negative epigone (unequal to the task) was Fernando Vela, who called the critics "vultures" (*Ortega y los existencialismos* [Madrid: Revista de Occidente, 1961], 39–41); since his master had disliked the word "existentialism," he had "transcended" the philosophy. Also too influenced by Marías was Marta López Gil, who denied that Ortega's theory of vital reason was pragmatism, phenomenology, or existentialism ("Ortega y la razón vital," *Cuadernos de Filosofía* [Buenos Aires] 8 [July–December 1968]: 342). K. S. Reid, "Two Periods in the Philosophical Development of Ortega y Gasset," in *Essays Presented to C. M. Girdleston* (Durham, N.C.: Duke University Press, 1960), 265, concluded that Ortega's second period was Heideggerian existentialism, for which neo-Kantianism and Husserl had prepared him (275).

9. Hugo Rodríguez Alcalá, "Existencia y destino del hombre según José Ortega y Gasset

y Jean Paul Sartre," *Cuadernos Americanos* 110 (May–June 1960): 89–109; Stern, *Search for Meaning*, 269–73, sees Ortega as anticipating Heidegger and Sartre in many ways. Echoing Stern's view (existentialism as essentialist and historical) was Mario Casanas, "Philosophie et histoire de la philosophie chez Ortega y Gasset," *Revue Philosophique de Louvain* 75 (1980): 5–21 (11–12). Janet Winecoff Díaz, *The Major Themes of Existentialism in the Works of José Ortega y Gasset*, on critics pro and con and themes such as "life and its insecurity," "individuality and its loss," liberty and necessity (cf. Ortega, 6:291). Morón Arroyo, *Sistema*, says that existentialism was his fourth, crowning stage, but he reduced historical reason to vital reason, as Marías did (85, 440–41). Alain Guy, *Ortega y Gasset ou la raison vitale et historique;* Udo Rukser, "Ortega und die Existentialisten," *Neue Zurcher Zeitung*, April 14, 1962; Alfonso Cobian y Macchiavello, "Tres temas de la filosofía existencial," *Ariete*, no. 2 (1959): 14–35. Echoing Morón was Nelson R. Orringer, *Nuevas fuentes germánicas de ¿Que es Filosofía? de Ortega* (Madrid: Consejo Superior de Investigaciones Científicas, Instituto de Filosofía Luis Vives, 1984), 8–10, 20–24, 25–27.

10. Apparently convinced by the evidence and arguments of Marías and other disciples, a great many critics since the 1950s have doubted, refrained, or refused to identify Ortega as an existentialist. One of the more recent such was Patrick Dust, "Ortega entre el naufragio y la cultura," *Aporia* 6 (1983–1984): 125–54, who instead defined his philosophy as tending toward a "ratio-historicist phenomenology," with characteristics of life as "desperation" (idem, "El extremismo existencialista a la luz de la razón histórica," *Cuadernos Hispanoamericanos*, nos. 403–5 [January–March 1984]: 142). Ortega, he claimed, viewed existentialism as a "pure extremism" (146), and his philosophy was of neither type (pure "radical" or impure "positive") but went "beyond" them by "overcoming" them (148). Dust forgot that for Ortega "*superación*" meant "keeping" them as part of something bigger.

Also on Ortega as existentialist, see *Dictionary of the History of Ideas* (1973), s.v. "Existentialism" (by Anthony Manser). He notes that the great innovators (among them, Heidegger) did not like the name existentialism, and that there were "as many existentialisms as existentialists," Husserl's phenomenology providing their main methods (like "back to the things themselves"). In those respects, as in Manser's definition of existentialism in terms of "authenticity" and *life* as "project," Ortega certainly fitted, but in regard to both Heidegger's and Sartre's evident negativism, subjective stress on the absurd, exaggeration, and emotionalism, he did not. Otherwise, in some ways he preceded; in others he imitated and followed, but always he was critical of the others. In *Encyclopedia of Philosophy* (1967), s.v. "Spanish Philosophy" (by Neil McInnes), vital reason was connected to pragmatism and biologism on one side and to existentialism on the other; in "Ortega y Gasset," he linked Ortega's perspectivism with existentialism but dissociated it later from vitalism as he projected it forward to history. Sterling M. McMurrin, "Recent Spanish Philosophy— Ortega y Gasset," *A History of Philosophy*, ed. B. A. Fuller, 3d rev. ed. (New York: Henry Holt, 1945), 502–6, projecting Ortega through his culturally and ethically relativistic perspectivism, said his position approached "the atheistic existentialist point of view."

20. Orringer, *Nuevas fuentes germánicas*, 8–9, 20–23, 102. On Ortega's recognition of life as basic, for other instances between 1910 and 1930, see 12:399 (1916), on "absolute positivism"; 1:252, 255–56 (1913), on phenomenology in a "natural mode" for "consciousness of" reality in "the lived as *Erlebnis, vivencia*, or in the life of specific people"; and 3:561 (1926–1927), on "the problem of life, radical point of departure." By 1930 this "radical" mode was long since fixed in Ortega's "usage." See, for example, his Diary, March 24, 1916—"We need a prototype of reality, or radical reality" (R 32). One parallel not mentioned by Orringer or Morón Arroyo was Ortega's (inverse) "Cartesianism of life," I exist [live] and so I think," which was already in Unamuno (as later in Scheler) "fifteen years" before Heidegger expressed it (Stern, "¿Ortega, existencialista?" 385). However, for Ortega's later use of such terms as "inauthentic," see 4:401 (1932); and 7:31–32. Federico Ríu, in *Vida e Historia*, 9–10, puts great emphasis on the impact of Heidegger's *Sein und Zeit* on Ortega's

thought, forcing him to reinterpret his own earlier vitalism, which (he held) had a bad effect by bringing him over to "a transcendental philosophy that situated him outside history" and so undercut his own idea of "historical becoming." (Ríu was wrong; Ortega remained a realist in existentialism, just as he was in phenomenology, and so also in historicism.) Ríu thought it was a "hermeneutical scandal" for Ortega's disciples to continue defending his priority to Heidegger, especially for the idea of life. (Wrong again; as stated above, Ortega owed Heidegger much more for the *general* philosophy than for its *particular* concepts, where he was indeed usually prior.) Both the disciples and their critics have misstated and misfocused the relationship between Ortega and Heidegger. Marías was wrong but so were critics who so overstated Heidegger's influence, reducing Ortega to an imitator who drew even his basic existentialist doctrines from him instead of being prior or independent in most respects. Cf. Martin Heidegger, *Being and Time,* trans. John Macquarrie and E. Robinson (London and New York: Harper, 1962), wherein not only "historicality" or "historicity" is prominent as a principle, but such statements (so like Ortega previously) as *"Dasein* is historical" (Heidegger, *On Time and Being,* trans. Joan Stambaugh [New York: Harper, 1972], 332), "Being-in-the-world" as spatial (299, 335, 351), and "circumspectual." He conceded that "Life in its own right is a kind of Being; but essentially it is accessible only in *Dasein*" (450), and he had objected that "life" (and "man") were terms too partial or "reified" to substitute for *Dasein* (43). The term "historiology"—as a mere translation of *Historie* in Heidegger (332, 398)—should not make us leap to assign it as an influence or borrowing by Ortega, who had used it *before* 1927.

42. On Ortega and Jaspers, see Fernando Uriarte, "La crisis de la creencia en Ortega y Jaspers," *Anales de la Universidad de Chile* 100 (1955): 81–84; Aleksander Rogalski, "Dwaj diagnosci kultury wspolczesnej, Ortega i Jaspers," *Zycie i Myal,* no. 5–6 (1958): 27–50; Erling Skorpen, "From Ortega to Jaspers. Thoughts on Situating Vital Reason," in *José Ortega y Gasset,* ed. Nora Marval-McMair (New York: Greenwood, 1987), 81–90. See R 2 (letters from Curtius of March 8, 1938, referring to a new book by Jaspers on the world crisis). Also see correspondence with Curtius, "Epistolario," *Revista de Occidente* 7 (June 1963): 19–21, for the year 1949, where Ortega indirectly defended Jaspers against Curtius's attacks; Arthur R. Evans, ed., *Of Four Modern Humanists* (Princeton: Princeton University Press, 1970), 144–45 (on Curtius), 131–32 (on his attack on Jaspers), and 136 (on his admiration for Ortega). Reflecting Ortega's earlier interest in and judgment on Jaspers, José Antonio Maravall, "Notas," *Revista de Occidente* 125 (November 1933): 215–20, on the "ambiente espiritual de nuestro tiempo." Reviewing a book on Jaspers by Ramón de la Serna, Maravall thought Jaspers had definitely confirmed "the situation of crisis in our time," as developed previously by Ortega in *Modern Theme* and in the "Galileo" lectures. R 33 contains a letter from Ortega to Xavier de Salas, saying that he had worked like a "horse" to edit his contribution to Jaspers's festschrift; also Ortega to M. C. Ramírez de Arellano, February 24, 1953, in which he said that that book was about to come out in Munich and that his chapter was on "a purely philosophical theme"; by March 5 he had received a copy of the book.

CHAPTER 7
Stage II: "Historical Reason" as Historicism (1924+)

5. Strangely, Ortega's crucial historicist "turn" in "History as a System" was offered first to the British and then to the North Americans (1936–1941), neither of whom then seized upon its historicism—not until a second U.S. edition in 1960 (see n. 21, chap. 7). A reviewer of "Atlantises" for Argentina, Fernando Márquez Miranda, could not fathom Ortega's "changes of orientation" in this "ethnographic-historical" work, apart from his "improvi-

sation" and style, in terms of "philosophical-historical consideration" (*Humanidades* 10 [1925]: 487, 489). The maligned Sánchez Villaseñor was apparently the first publicly to identify historicism in Ortega, as in his disciple: *Gaos en mascarones: La crisis del historicismo y otros ensayos* (Mexico City: Jus, 1945). Gaos, "Los dos Ortegas," *La Torre* 4 (1956): 127–40. For other older critics of Ortega's "historicism," some cited in our Introduction or later in the bibliographical essay, see Iriarte, *La ruta mental de Ortega: Crítica de su filosofía* (Madrid: Razón y Fe, 1949); Eduardo Nicol, "La Crítica de la razón histórica: Ortega y Gasset," *Historicismo y Existencialismo;* Alfonso Castro Pallarés, "Ortega y Gasset, historicista escéptico," *Duc in Altum,* no. 13 (1948): 25–32; Agustín Basave Fernández del Valle, *Miguel de Unamuno y José Ortega y Gasset* (Mexico City: Jus, 1950). A later critic was Francisco Goyenchea, *Ateísmo e historicismo: Ortega y Gasset* (Madrid: Christianidad, 1971). Older defenders were Gaos, "De paso por el 'Historicismo y existencialismo'," *Cuadernos Americanos* 50 (March–April 1950): 122–35; Juan López Morrillas, "Ortega y Gasset: Historicism vs. Classicism," *Yale French Studies* 6 (December 1950): 63–74. Only Gaos stoutly defended Ortega's historicism. In the United States, after López Morrillas found it already in the "metahistory" of *Modern Theme,* a sympathetic acceptance of that historicism was evident in McClintock, *Ortega as Educator* (1971), 130–31, 524. A recognition that historicism was somehow part of his thought appears in Holmes, *Human Reality* (1975), and in Harold C. Raley, *José Ortega y Gasset: Philosopher of European Unity* (1971). No one anywhere has published an analysis of Ortega's historicism in depth, but there was a short dissertation on it: Frank J. Kelly, "The Historicism of José Ortega y Gasset" (University of Oklahoma, 1973). More recently, see Rabade Romeo, *Ortega filósofo,* chap. 7; Ramon Xirau, *José Ortega y Gasset: Razón histórica, razón vital, Velázquez, Goya y otros temas* (Mexico City: Colegio Nacional, 1983); José M. Rubio Ferreres, "Razón histórica y razón utópica en Ortega y Gasset," *Studium* (Madrid) 24 (1984): 347–56. Marta López Gil, "Ortega y la razón vital," *Cuadernos de Filosofía* (Buenos Aires) 8 (July–December 1968): 331–42, accepted Morón Arroyo's and Garagorri's view of his "radical" historicism, but explained it only in terms of historiology, as going beyond the metahistory of vital reason. Armando Savignano, "La Filosofia di J. Ortega y Gasset," *Rivista di filosofia neo-scolastica* (Milan) 75 (July–September 1983): 453.

12. Several of ten studies indexed (by Donoso and Raley) on Hegel and Ortega concern philosophy of history or history of philosophy but are evidently unconcerned with historicism per se: Ramiro Flórez Flórez, "El Hegel de Ortega," *Actas del III Seminario de Historia de la Filosofía Española* (Salamanca, 1983): 253–74; Juan Roig Gironella, "Haeckel, Hegel, Ortega y Gasset: Tres interpretaciones filosóficas de la historia," *Cristiandad* 2 (1945): 314–22. Benedetto Croce, "Estudios sobre el amor," *Nuove Pagini Sparsi* (Milan: Riccardi, 1949), 2:162–64. On Croce and Ortega, see Angelo A. de Gennaro, "Croce e Ortega," *Itálica* (1954): 237–43; and supplemental note 15, chap. 7, for additional studies. On Dilthey and Ortega, see Curtius, "Alemania y el pensamiento español actual (Ortega y Dilthey)," *Cuadernos Hispanoamericanos,* no. 28 (1952): 3–20; and Edward Nicol, "La Crítica de la razón histórica," *Historicismo y Existencialismo,* 276–331 (chaps. 3, 9), or (on Ortega), 308–31. I have been unable to find anything of consequence (like Tuttle's study on "the idea of life") comparing their historicisms—only passing opinions not well supported by documentation, or rather summary views in general studies of Ortega; better among the latter type are those by McClintock and Guy.

13. The most notable failure on Dilthey and Ortega was by Marías, *Circumstance and Vocation,* where he considered Dilthey in regard to both historicism and philosophy of life (82, 90–91) but barely related Ortega to him early in the century (191–92); idem, *Generations,* 10–11, 153–54, and chap. 3. McClintock by contrast affirmed that Ortega was "deeply influenced by historicism, especially by the historicism of Dilthey" (*Ortega as Educator,* 405, 569), and he showed well its "ratio," if not "rationalistic" character (404), but he did not develop that relationship or consider "philosophy of life." Stern, *Philosophy of History*

and the Problem of Values (1962), chap. 6, "Historicism, Natural Rights, and Values" and *Search for Meaning* (1970), 271; Morón Arroyo, *Sistema*, 305, 355, and chap. 9 ("Doctrine of History"). Guy, *Ortega ou la raison vitale,* had chapters (1, 2) on vital and historical reason, and also took up the problems of phenomenology and existentialism, and realism and idealism. Franco Díaz de Cerio, a Jesuit professor of historiology at the Gregorianum, unlike his predecessors Iriarte and Sánchez Villaseñor, viewed Ortega with equanimity as very early both historicist and existentialist, without any inner contradiction: *José Ortega y Gasset y la conquista de la conciencia histórica (Mocedad: 1905–15),* 56–57, 268. One of the few recent critics who has shown a generally correct view, by confirming historicism in Ortega and by relating it also to phenomenology, existentialism, and life (but not philosophy of life), was Cirilo Flórez Miguel, "La razón histórica y el cambio de paradigma en la historia: De la conciencia a la acción," *Cuadernos Salamantinos de Filosofía* 11 (1984): 284–86 and 288–92 (related chiefly to Bergson, Husserl, and Dilthey). Most critics who have treated of Ortega's "historical reason" have left it (a la Marías) subordinated to vital reason, existentialism, or else perspectivism but have not seen it as historicism. But see Rubio Ferreres, "Razón histórica y razón utópica," 347–56, on vital reason "reduced" to historical reason— like Gaos, and just the opposite of Marías. Similarly Miguel Montes González, "Papel de lo histórico en la metafísica, antropología y hermenéutica orteguiana," *Lumen* 33 (1984), accepted historicity in Ortega (346) but rejected historicism because he deemed it relativism (347), which he later seemed to concede (349). It is also possible to see Ortega's historical reason as the equal of (or greater than) vital reason but still not call it historicism— also a legacy from Marías: José L. Abellán, *Ortega en filosofía española* (Madrid: Tecnos, 1966) and Ouimette, *Ortega* (1982). Abellán saw Ortega as chiefly a "philosopher of history," whose thought reached its "maximum radicalization in the theme of history" (109). The notes in R 80 are hard to date, but Ortega's admission of historicism there is patent.

14. For definitions of historicism by historians, especially intellectual historians, see Friedrich Meinecke, *Die Entstehung des Historismus,* 2 vols. (Munich, 1936), translated by H. D. Schmidt as *Historism: The Rise of a New Historical Outlook* (London: Routledge and Kegan Paul, 1972); Dwight E. Lee and R. N. Beck, "The Meaning of Historicism," *American Historical Review* 59 (April 1954): 568–77; Paul K. Conkin and Roland N. Stromberg, *Heritage and Challenge: The History and Theory of History* (Arlington Heights, Ill.: Forum, 1989), 61–69 ("Varieties of Historicism"), 93, 193—a "loaded word" that is "time-qualified" and changing from Enlightened, to Romantic, Positivist, and Crocean (if not Diltheyan) types and perhaps "humanistic" with Ortega (251); George L. Mosse, *The Culture of Western Europe* (Chicago: Rand McNally, 1961), 145–48; Peter H. Reill, *The German Enlightenment and the Rise of Historicism* (Berkeley and Los Angeles: University of California Press, 1975), 213 (citing D. E. Lee and H. V. White on its meaning) and 214, 217, for his own stress on the ideas of development and individuality; Berthold P. Riesterer, *Karl Löwith's View of History: A Critical Appraisal of Historicism* (The Hague: Martinus Nijhoff, 1969). For the recent and ongoing revival of historicism, especially in relation to literature and linguistics, see Roy H. Pearce, *Historicism Once More* (Princeton: Princeton University Press, 1969); Wesley Morris, *Toward a New Historicism* (Princeton: Princeton University Press, 1972); Robert D'Amico, *Historicism and Knowledge* (New York: Routledge, 1988); N. E. Collinge, "The New Historicism and its Battles," *Folia Linguística Histórica* 7 (1986): 3–16; H. V. White, "New Historicism: A Comment," in *The New Historicism,* ed. H. A. Veeser (New York: Routledge, 1989). Also, for a Marxist perspective, see John E. Grimley, *History and Totality: Radical Historicism from Hegel to Foucault* (London: Routledge, 1989).

15. Karl Popper, *The Poverty of Historicism* (London: Routledge, 1957), 159–60: neither of his two types, naturalist and anti-naturalist (pts. 1–2), which are basically romantic and positivist, fit Ortega's historicism but, on characteristics of historicism, he was often in

agreement with Popper in what he allowed or disparaged (for "scientific" method and models in history; against biological or sociological theory and monist-unitary interpretations for history). Stern, *Philosophy of History*, 181, says, "Historicism is the *enfante terrible* of contemporary philosophy" and "a philosophical doctrine and not a historical one." *Encyclopedia of Philosophy* (1967), s.v. "Historicism" (by Maurice Mandelbaum), 4:24; but cf. his *Anatomy of Historical Knowledge* (Baltimore: Johns Hopkins University Press, 1977), as reviewed by Louis O. Mink in *History and Theory* 17:2 (1978): 211–23. There is also a newer historians' historicism ("rhetorical" relativism) in H. V. White and J. H. Hexter. On continuing general opposition of philosophers to historicism, see Bulhof, *Dilthey*, 198. Meyerhoff, ed., *Philosophy of History*, 10–17; on p. 27 he gives a complex definition of historicism in three parts: "(1) the denial of any 'systematic' approach to history; (2) the repudiation of any single, unified interpretation of history; and (3) the positive assertions (a) that the basic concepts of history are change and particularity, (b) that historicism has a special way of explaining things by telling a story, and (c) that history is all pervasive, that historical categories permeate all aspects of human life, including morality and philosophy." Ortega's "History as a System" (which fits all but the first) was included here for historicism supposedly in the tradition of Dilthey, Croce, and Collingwood (36). Of course, Ortega was not "systematic" like Marx or Comte; that is, he had a system not of the whole but one of *concepts*. Meyerhoff seemed to regard Ortega's as *existential* historicism (57). He was very wrong, however, to set him "off sharply" from the "empirical, pragmatic, or analytical approach to history" that supposedly characterized North American historians and philosophers (86).

23. Scheler claimed to be making much progress on his "anthropology" in April 1924, but his "meta-anthropology" did not emerge for several more years (posthumously in 1928). See John H. Nota, *Max Scheler: The Man and His Work*, trans. T. Plantinga (Chicago: Franciscan Herald Press, 1983), 153, 156. Scheler's *Sociology of Knowledge* (1924) was definitely still anti-historical (*Problems of a Sociology of Knowledge*, trans. M. S. Frings [London: Routledge, 1980], 119, 150–51). So it is doubtful that Scheler was Ortega's source. Evidence that Ortega sooner or later knew of Scheler's project in philosophical anthropology is in F. Vela's "Notas—De antropología filosófica," *Revista de Occidente* 87 (September 1930): 393–400, where he speaks of Scheler's work trying to synthesize "reason and life." Apparently thinking that the idea was original with himself, although he was clearly indebted to Ortega's ideas, Marías published *Antropología metafísica* (Madrid: Revista de Occidente, 1970); see Antón Donoso, *Julián Marías*, chap. 3. Before Marías, disciple J. D. García Bacca had included Scheler, Heidegger, and Sartre in *Antropología filosófica contemporanea* (1955; reprint, Barcelona: Antropos Editorial del Hombre, 1982), in which Ortega was put between them and Christian existentialism in Marcel (185) because of his doctrine that man has no "nature" to be thus defined—a program, not a (phenomenological) "essence"—a view that should have excluded also Heidegger and Sartre. After Marías, Zubiri also published on the subject, with only occasional reference to Ortega: *Siete ensayos de antropología filosófica* (Bogotá: Universitas de Santo Tomas, 1982), 11, 13, 196. *Encyclopedia of Philosophy* (1967), s.v. "Philosophical Anthropology" (by H. O. Pappe), 159–65, affirms its affinities with pragmatism, phenomenology, existentialism, *Lebensphilosophie*, and, in its *cultural* form, with "historical morphology," historicism, and sociology. Dilthey and Husserl aspired to go on to "a coordinating discipline," and Ortega went "beyond" it into historiology. Ortega's historical "anthropology" in "History as a System" was grasped in part by Ernst Cassirer, *Antropología filosófica: Introducción a una filosofía de la Cultura* (Mexico City: Fonda de Cultura Economica, 1944, 1963), 252–55. Others who have more recently investigated the theme of "philosophical anthropology" in Ortega himself include: Montes González, "Papel de lo histórico," 325–66; Pedro Gómez Bosque, *Alma, cuerpo, vocación. Reflexiones en torno a la antropología filosófica de Ortega;* Carlos Gurméndez, "Ortega y la antropología," *Teorema* (Valencia) 13 (1983): 407–19; Miguel Diego

Sánchez Meca, "Una hermenéutica del destino humano: El pensamiento antropológico de Ortega," *La Ciudad de Dios* 196 (September–December 1983): 435–78; Pintor-Ramos, "Metafísica, historia y antropología," 3–36, saw a "historical tradition" in anthropology but preferred a post-historicist solution (27, 35).

31. Among the general critics who scored Ortega for relativism and skepticism were Iriarte, Sánchez Villaseñor, and Nicol. A U.S. reviewer of *Modern Theme,* Orlie Pell, utterly mistook Ortega's intent by calling his perspectivism "a radical relativism" (*Journal of Philosophy* 30 [August 1933]: 471). Ortega's Mexican admirer, philosopher Samuel Ramos, denied that perspectivism in *Modern Theme* was relativism in fact, but was an optimistic "new relativism" that promised a "radical reform of philosophy," wherein "metahistory" would replace metaphysics (Patrick Romanell, "Ortega in Mexico: A Tribute to Samuel Ramos," *Journal of the History of Ideas* 21 [October–December 1960]: 601–3). Walgrave, *Filosofía de Ortega* (trans. L. G. Daal, 1949), 57, 264–65, 317, defended Ortega's views as "relativity"; Marías also denied relativism in Ortega, but historicism, too. Díaz de Cerio, *Ortega y la conciencia histórica,* 52, saw Ortega's classicism as a remedy against relativism. In *Philosophy of History,* Stern accepted a *limited* relativism in historicism, including Ortega's (182–90). Denying charges by Spanish critics that Ortega's perspectivism (in *Modern Theme*) was "pure relativism," Copleston argued that he recognized "a transsubjective reality," wherein "all truth is [not] relative" ("Ortega and Philosophical Relativism," 176–79). For a contention that "relativity" has been "widely misinterpreted as relativism," but is indeed opposite in meaning, see Isaiah Berlin, *Personal Impressions* (New York: Viking, 1949, 1980), 145. Despite Ortega's protests, duly acknowledged, F. Alluntis decided finally that his philosophy was relativist (not relativitist) in both ontology and epistemology ("La Razón Vital en Ortega," *Pensamiento* 39 [1983]: 435).

CHAPTER 8
Unity: "General Theory of Life" as Philosophy of Life (1934+)

2. For the latest identification of Ortega's system as a "phenomenological" philosophy of life, see *Analecta Husserliana* 29 (1990), as in chap. 8, n. 40. Perhaps the sharpest of early Spanish critics of Ortega, but still flawed by errors and imbalance, Bruno Ibeas in 1935 was the first to identify him with German "philosophy of life" (*Lebensphilosophie*) from Schlegel through Nietzsche, Dilthey, and Simmel; although claiming to have read his "works" and meditated on them, he concentrated on *Modern Theme* (1923) and possibly made a little use of the essays on Dilthey (1933–1934). However, this very limited assessment of Ortega's "unity and totality" on the German "idealist" side failed to discover James's realism (20) in his "absolute positivism" (7), and Ibeas completely ignored the existentialism, besides historical reason and historicism, while concentrating on philosophy of life ("La filosofía de Ortega," 6–21). A disciple of Ortega who identified him with "philosophy of life" but denied existentialism or historicism in him was García Bacca in 1947 in a very minimal comparison with James's realism (see supplemental note 5, chap. 4). Also see Angel González Alvarez, "Evasion de Modernidad," *Cuadernos Hispanoamericanos* no. 73 (1956): 125. Arthur Hübscher connected Ortega's perspectivism with *Lebensphilosophie* through Nietzsche, Bergson, and Dilthey (*Denker unserer Zeit* [Munich: Piper, 1956], 98). Böllnow, *Lebensphilosophie,* 44–45, 54–55, and passim. On Böllnow as an existentialist, see note 54, chap. 6. Marías, *Circumstance and Vocation,* 79–82, 380–81, called it "entirely alien": "the connection of Ortega's philosophy with *Lebensphilosophie* is minimal; beginning with the fact that what Ortega understands by life has scarcely anything to do with" it, in contrast to Bergson, Klages, Troeltsch, Spengler, and Unamuno. Although Marías cited (279) Ortega's use of the expression "philosophy of life" in 1916 in Argentina, in 1948 he had already distinguished Bergson's *biological* philosophy of life from the "historical or

biographical" idea of vital reason (*History of Philosophy* [1948], trans. S. Appelbaum [New York: Dover, 1967], 389). In a review of Marías in 1960, Eugenio Frutos observed that human life was undoubtedly Ortega's "central fundamental theme," that Marías had shown that it was not "so-called *Lebensphilosophie*," but "to what it corresponds, then, is more difficult to know" ("El 'Ortega' de Julián Marías," *Revista de Filosofía* 19 [1960]: 500). Marías did not see that Ortega could represent a different (personal) *variety* of that general phenomenon, as, for example, it seemed to Sánchez Blanco in 1984, "Continuidad," 606: "Philosophy of life is a cultural current that is developed simultaneously in France, Germany, and Spain, without an interdependence between Bergson, Klages, and Ortega being evident." That is only partly true, for Ortega was very aware of Bergson (and Nietzsche), but not so aware of possible Spanish roots for it (607–10) as the author assumed—Forner, Donoso Cortés, Menéndez y Pelayo, and Giner de los Ríos, for example. A reviewer of *What Is Philosophy?* claimed that Dilthey's "*Lebensphilosophie* has left on him [Ortega] an indelible impression" (Albert W. Levi, *Saturday Review of Literature* 44 [June 24, 1961]: 15–16).

   Not even indexed as such by either Garagorri for the *Obras Completas* nor by Donoso and Raley, "philosophy of life" has thus rarely been proposed in the many studies of Ortega's philosophy. The few exceptions include: Solomon I. Levy, *Mechdv filosofiala na chivola i ekzistencialism* (Between philosophy of life and existentialism) (Sophia, 1967)—its 300 pages are evidently a much more substantial study than Böllnow's but is unavailable to me, since I do not read Bulgarian; Charles E. Lewalter, "Zu Ortega y Gassets Philosophie des Lebens," *Die Zeit* (Hamburg), no. 46 (January 6, 1951): 4; N. Loeser, *Ortega y Gasset en de Philosophie van Het Leven* (The Hague: H. P. Leopold, 1941, 1949); Félix Martí Ibáñez, "Un filósofo de la vida," *El Espectador* (Bogotá) 67 (December 11, 1955): sec. 2, 3, p. 490; L. Incisa, "La filosofia de la vitta di Ortega y Gasset," *Minerva*, no. 63 (1953): 420–23; and Udo Rukser, "Grundzüge von Ortegas Philosophie," *Zeitschrift für philosophische Forschung* 19 (1965): 672—Ortega's diversity was too much for Rukser to sort out properly. Better was Helmut Schoeck, "Ortega y Gasset" *Zeitschrift für philosophische Forschung* 4 (1949): 279–83, who linked Ortega to *Lebensphilosophie* from the older *Historismus*, from Nietzsche to Dilthey, but as different from them.

   12. To follow the mounting problems Ortega had with ontology after 1929 as he confronted the "ontology" of traditional "being" and "nature" with life and history, see *Obras Completas*, 6:27; 7:325, 396; 8:207n, 217, 231, 246, 341–57. Also see *Sobre la razón histórica* (1979), 42, 62, 78–80, 90–93, 95–96, 110–48, 121. Ortega at first objected that ontology had properly "happened" to the ancient "Eleatic" Greeks and could not again happen to anyone later except homologously, such as to medieval scholastics and to modern thinkers since Descartes, to whom "being" signified "thinking" (8:217). Added to that objection was the "inert," passive sense of being among the ancients compared to the "executive" active sense of "life" and "self" and "history" in his own neo-Heraclitean conception of "radical reality" (7:396; 12:236–37). In dealing with Leibniz's ontology of "modality of being," he remarked that "in effect, there is no word in philosophy in our Romance languages fully adequate to denote rigorously what people call 'reality'" (8:344). He was more interested in the modalities of "contingency" and "possibility" (8:350), it seems, because they related closely to "life" as historical and future-oriented. If reality were taken as problematic or questionable, it would require "a radical reform in the very notion of being" and could "turn traditional ontology upside down" (8:350–51). But that is precisely what he proposed to do. By 1951 he wanted simply to discard the word "ontology" (as in Heidegger) as inaccurate and confusing. "Troisième entretien privé," 289.

   25. The ten studies on Ortega and Dilthey listed by Donoso and Raley are all very limited in scope and all are parts of general studies or articles (such as Borel, Curtius, Iriarte, Marías, Morón Arroyo, and Rabade Romeo), but Nicol was omitted. Since Nicol,

the only comparative studies on Ortega and Dilthey seem to be by Howard N. Tuttle of the University of New Mexico. His first effort, "Ortega's Vitalism" (1981), did not actually place Ortega in "the *Lebensphilosophie* movement" but compared and related his "vitalism" to Dilthey and Husserl; he accepted Ortega's claim to realism and to originality, as for orienting life outward from self ("consciousness") to world in contrast to the subjective idealism in both Husserl and Dilthey. " . . . Because of Ortega's additions, modifications, and restrictions to his notion of life, he has made an original contribution to the history of ideas" (92). Tuttle's more recent study is "The Idea of Life in Wilhelm Dilthey and Ortega y Gasset," *Ortega y Gasset Centennial, University of New Mexico* (Madrid: Turanzas, 1985), where he affirmed "philosophy of life" as also in Ortega (112), whom he regarded as the most world-oriented (as in existential phenomenology) of Dilthey's "successors" in the life-philosophy tradition (116–17). Without quoting or citing the relevant text in Ortega, he affirmed (as do I) his "unitary duality of person and object, a fusion of the 'I' and its actual world circumstances" (115–16). He found their "idea of life" as "radical reality" to be central to both and "similar but not identical" (105, 111, 114), but the "alleged idealism" and "pure" consciousness in Dilthey were overstated (114–15).

26. There is an odd disparity in the works of Dilthey that Ortega owned. The *Einleitung* (1883) is the second edition (1923), whereas the rest of the collected works are the first edition (1914). This fact suggests that he obtained the latter eight volumes *after* (not before) the *Einleitung,* because he had already gotten this one volume when he had an opportunity to get the rest of the first edition. That he probably got the *Einleitung* in 1923 rather than later is suggested by his having several other works from the time—the *Leben Schleiermachers* (2d ed., 1922) and the correspondence of Dilthey and York (1923), in which the idea of a "Critique of Historical Reason" had been advanced. However, the fifth volume of the works that Ortega cited with such surprise in his Dilthey notes of the 1930s was from the newer second edition, with an amended title by Misch. This implies either that he obtained the first edition after the *Einleitung* and *Schleiermacher* and correspondence, or that (if he had them) he did not read them till later (some historical works were not included in his purchase of the first edition).

Prior to his receipt of those works, his Spanish edition of Vorländer was not very revealing on Dilthey (2:406–25)—no references to either *Lebensphilosophie* or *Historismus,* but several to his "vitalism."

Ortega may have read the *Schleiermacher* (1810) by 1914 (2:339, 202). The idea of *Erlebnis* (life experience) he assigned to Dilthey in 1913 (1:256n), and he had appropriated *Weltanschauung* (worldview) by 1916 (12:392).

39. Ortega, remarks in "Troisième entretien privé," 287, 293–95: "Il n'y a pas une philosophie du *Leben* . . ." (294). In view of his notes on Dilthey, perhaps he meant to stress "of," since he preferred "from." Compare with Marías's denial of *Lebensphilosophie* in Ortega, in *Circumstance and Vocation,* 380–81; although he seemed to concede a "minimal" connection of Ortega with "philosophy of life," he insisted that *Leben* was a *different reality* from what Ortega understood by "life" (*vida*), because Germans (including the existentialists) lacked Ortega's "method" for getting at it—a very dubious distinction, to define a philosophy only by its method, which Ortega would not have allowed—although Marías' stress on the "irrationalism" and vagueness of the meaning of life was more appropriate (79–80, 360, 465). However, his own "adequate" definition of human life was from Ortega's "Dilthey" (349–52). Later still, in "Medio siglo," 6, Ortega commented on Dilthey's failure in another regard: "Historical reason is prolix by its very nature, is an endless telling of stories, is the 'never-finished account.' Therefore, it is not strange that Dilthey, the first one who looked into historical reason and who could dedicate, minus distractions, the whole of a very long life to its themes, is criticized for giving us only incomplete works, fragments, divisions, projects, first volumes, first chapters, sighs, stammerings." Ironically, we can say much the same of Ortega too—even more so of his "philosophy of life."

41. Marta López Gil seemed to offer a variation on Marías, but maybe it was a tacit compromise between Marías and Gaos instead. She ended up with "living reason" (Ortega's term of 1936 in "History as a System") as an idea covering both vital reason and historical reason ("Ortega y la razón vital," *Cuadernos de Filosofía* [Buenos Aires] 8 [July–December 1968]: 342). She explicitly denied that Ortega's philosophy was idealism or realism, existentialism or pragmatism, but since she did not specifically exclude historicism (331) in regard to historical reason, historiology, and metahistory (334–42), possibly she equated historicism (not as relativism) with the "ontological" interpretation of human life (332). So, can we justifiably exclude "philosophy of life" (to which she never adverted) from the integrating, unifying role in his total philosophy? Still another attempt, one which seemed to reflect Gaos, was by Alluntis, "Vital and Historical Reason of José Ortega y Gasset," *Franciscan Studies* 15:2 (1955): 62–63. His notion was of *one* reason (not two) that was at the same time vital *and* historical. In addition, a disposition or notion similar to Ortega's unitary-dual formula was "integrationism," meaning "a *oneness of duality:* plural oneness," that reputedly characterized the thought of Ferrater Mora, who likewise favored relativism and philosophical *realism* over the *idealist* position, a view of Mario Bunge, "Conceptual Existence," in *Transparencies. Philosophical Essays in Honor of J. Ferrater Mora,* ed. Priscilla Cohn (Atlantic Highlands, N.J.: Humanities Press, 1981), 44, 46, 59, 61. Also close to my conception of Ortega's "radical unitary duality" was Jorge Mañach, "dualidad y síntesis en Ortega," *Papeles de Son Armadans* (Palma de Mallorca) 5:13 (1957): 13–32, who did not know that precise phrase or text but extended the basic "self and circumstance" upward through his vital reason (*Modern Theme*) and historical reason (*History as a System*). Mañach postulated a "radical duality" with unity and system over all (13–15) by preserving *unity* of "rationality" (cf. Gaos and Alluntis) in Ortega's formula "vital *and* historical reason" (*History as a System*), which he subordinated (integrated) in "life" as basic reality in coexisting "self and circumstance." However, he did not advert to a "philosophy of life" but preferred "philosophy of culture" (30), in which some kind of pantheistic "panvitalism" (21–22) was certainly alien to Ortega.

Selected Bibliography

PRIMARY SOURCES

Ortega y Gasset, José. *Cartas de un joven español*. Edited by Soledad Ortega. Madrid: Arquero, 1991.

———. "Medio siglo de filosofía." *Revista de Occidente,* no. 3 (October–December 1980): 5–21.

———. *Obras Completas.* 12 vols. Madrid: Revista de Occidente, 1946–1983.

———. *¿Qué es conocimiento?* Madrid: Alianza, 1984.

———. *Sobre la razón histórica.* Madrid: Alianza, 1979.

———. "Troisième entretien privé." In *La Connaissance de l'homme au XXe siècle.* Neuchâtel: Baconnière, 1952.

BIBLIOGRAPHICAL AIDS

Donoso, Antón, and Harold C. Raley. *José Ortega y Gasset: A Bibliography of Secondary Sources.* Bowling Green, Ohio: Philosophy Documentation Center, Bowling Green State University, 1986.

SECONDARY SOURCES

Abellán, José Luis. *Ortega y Gasset en la filosofía española.* Madrid: Editorial Tecnos, 1966.

Alvarez González, Francisco. *El Pensamiento de Ortega y Gasset.* San José: Costa Rica, 1980.

Barzun, Jacques. *A Stroll with William James.* New York: Harper and Row, 1983.

Böllnow, Otto. *Lebensphilosophie.* Berlin: Springer, 1958.

Borel, Jean-Paul. *Raison et vie chez Ortega y Gasset.* Neuchâtel: Baconnière, 1959.

Cascalès, Charles. *L'Humanisme d'Ortega y Gasset.* Paris: Presses Universitaires, 1957.

Cerezo Galán, Pedro. *La voluntad de aventura: Aproximación al pensamiento de Ortega y Gasset.* Barcelona: Ariel, 1984.

Conkin, Paul K. *Puritans and Pragmatists.* New York: Dodd, Mead, 1968.

Copleston, Frederick C. "Ortega y Gasset and Philosophical Relativism." In *Philosophers and Philosophies,* 172–84. London: Search Press, 1976; New York: Barnes and Noble, 1976.

Curtius, Ernst R. "Ortega y Gasset." *Partisan Review,* no. 3 (March 17, 1950): 259–71.

Díaz de Cerio, Franco. *José Ortega y Gasset y la conquista de la conciencia histórica (Mocedad: 1905–15).* Barcelona: Flors, 1961.

Dobson, Andrew. *An Introduction to the Politics and Philosophy of José Ortega y Gasset.* Cambridge, Eng., and New York: Cambridge University Press, 1989.

Donoso, Antón. *Julián Marías.* Boston: Twayne, 1982.

———. "Ortega's Anti-modernity in Epistemology and Metaphysics." *Hispanic Issues,* no. 5 (1989): 95–126.

Edie, James. *James and Phenomenology.* Bloomington: Indiana University Press, 1987.

———. "William James and Phenomenology." *Review of Metaphysics* 23 (March 1970): 481–526.

Farber, Marvin. *The Aims of Phenomenology. The Motives, Methods and Impact of Husserl's Thought.* New York: Harper, 1966.

Ferrater Mora, José. *Ortega y Gasset: An Outline of His Philosophy.* New Haven: Yale University Press, 1956.

Gadamer, Hans. "Wilhelm Dilthey y Ortega y Gasset: Un capítulo de la historia intelectual de Europa." *Revista de Occidente,* no. 46–50 (May 1985): 78–88.

Gaete, Arturo. *El sistema maduro de Ortega y Gasset—La metafísica.* Buenos Aires: Universidad Católica and General Fabril, 1962.

Galego Morell, Antonio. "Ortega en Marburg." *Cuadernos Hispanoamericanos,* nos. 403–5 (January–March 1984): 441–44.

Gaos, José. *Sobre Ortega y Gasset y otros trabajos.* Mexico City: Imprenta Universitaria, 1957.

García Astrada, Arturo. *El Pensamiento de Ortega y Gasset.* Buenos Aires: Troquel, 1961.

Gómez Bosque, Pedro. *Alma, cuerpo, vocación: Reflexiones en torno a la antropología filosófica de Ortega.* Santander: M. Botín, 1984.

González Caminero, Nemesio. "Ortega y Heidegger: Postrera valoración mutua." *Miscelanea Comillas* (Madrid) 34 (1976): 5–38.

Graham, John T. "Historiology and Interdisciplinarity." In *José Ortega y Gasset,* edited by Nora Marval-McNair, 35–50. New York: Greenwood, 1987.

———. "Pragmatism and Philosophy of History in Ortega y Gasset." *Acta,* Congreso Internacional Extraordinario de Filosofía, Córdoba, Argentina, 3 (1988): 1329–53.

Granell, Manuel. *Ortega y su filosofía.* Madrid: Revista de Occidente, 1960.

Gray, Rockwell. *The Imperative of Modernity: An Intellectual Biography of José Ortega y Gasset.* Berkeley and Los Angeles: University of California Press, 1989.

Guglielmini, Homero M. "Algo más sobre Ortega y Gasset." *Inicial* (Buenos Aires) (1924): 30–34.

Guy, Alain. *Ortega y Gasset ou la raison vitale et historique.* Paris: Seghers, 1969.

Herzberger, David K. "Ortega y Gasset and the 'Critics of Consciousness.'" *Journal of Aesthetics and Art Criticism* 34 (1975): 455–59.

Holmes, Oliver W. *Human Reality and the Social World: Ortega's Philosophy of History.* Amherst: University of Massachusetts Press, 1975.

Ibeas, P. Bruno. "La filosofía de Ortega y Gasset." *Acción Española* 13:74 (1935): 6–21.

Iriarte, Joaquín. *Ortega y Gasset, su persona y su doctrina.* Madrid: Editorial Razón y Fe, 1942.

James, William. *Essays in Philosophy.* Cambridge: Harvard University Press, 1978.

———. *Essays in Radical Empiricism:* 1912. Cambridge: Harvard University Press, 1976.

———. *The Meaning of Truth.* 1909. Cambridge: Harvard University Press, 1975.

———. *The Philosophy of William James.* Ed. Horace M. Kallen. New York: Modern Library, 1925.

———. *A Pluralistic Universe.* 1909. Cambridge: Harvard University Press, 1977.

———. *Pragmatism.* 1907. Cambridge: Harvard University Press, 1975.

———. *The Writings of William James.* Ed. John J. McDermott. New York: Random House, 1967.

Linschoten, Johannes. *On the Way Toward a Phenomenological Analysis: The Psychology of William James.* Pittsburgh: Duquesne University Press, 1968.

McClintock, Robert. *Man and His Circumstances: Ortega as Educator.* New York: Columbia University Press, 1971.

Marías, Julián. *Generations: A Historical Method.* Trans. Harold Raley. University: University of Alabama Press, 1970.

———. *Ortega: Las Trayectorias.* Madrid: Alianza, 1983.

———. *Ortega y Gasset: Circumstance and Vocation.* Trans. F. M. López Morillas. Norman: University of Oklahoma Press, 1970.

Marrero, Domingo. *El centauro: Persona y pensamiento de Ortega y Gasset.* Río Piedras: University of Puerto Rico Press, 1947.

Marrero, Vicente. *Ortega, filósofo "mondain."* Madrid: Rialp, 1961.

Meyerhoff, Hans, ed. *The Philosophy of History in Our Time.* Garden City, N.Y.: Doubleday-Anchor, 1959.

Morón Arroyo, Ciriaco. *El sistema de Ortega y Gasset.* Madrid: Alcalá, 1968.

Nicol, Eduardo. *Historicismo y Existencialismo.* Mexico City: Colegio de Mexico, 1950.

Niedermayer, Franz. *José Ortega y Gasset.* Trans. Peter Tirner. New York: Frederick Ungar, 1973.

Orringer, Nelson R. *Ortega y sus fuentes germánicas.* Madrid: Gredos, 1979.

Ortega, Miguel. *Ortega y Gasset, mi padre.* Barcelona: Planeta, 1983.

Ouimette, Victor. *José Ortega y Gasset.* Boston: Twayne, 1982.

Pellicani, Luciano. *Introduzione a Ortega y Gasset.* Naples: Ligouri, 1978.

Pintor-Ramos, Antonio. "Metafísica, historia y antropología: Sobre el pensamiento de la antropología filosófica." *Pensamiento* 41 (1985): 3–36.

Rabade Romeo, Sergio. *Ortega y Gasset: Filósofo, hombre, conocimiento, razón.* Barcelona: Humanitas, 1983.

Raley, Harold C. *José Ortega y Gasset: Philosopher of European Unity.* University: University of Alabama Press, 1971.

Ríu, Federico. *Vida e historia en Ortega y Gasset: Pensamiento filosófico.* Caracas: Monte Avila, 1985.

Rodríguez Huéscar, Antonio. *Perspectiva y verdad: El problema de la verdad en Ortega*. Madrid: Revista de Occidente, 1966.

Rouges, Alberto. "El perspectivismo de Ortega y Gasset." *Nosotros* (Buenos Aires) 192 (May 1925): 337–51.

Royce, Josiah. *William James and Other Essays on the Philosophy of Life*. New York: Macmillan, 1912.

Salmerón, Fernando. *Las mocedades de Ortega y Gasset*. Mexico City: Colegio de Mexico, 1959.

Sánchez Villaseñor, José. *José Ortega y Gasset, Existentialist*. Chicago: Regnery, 1949.

Silver, Philip W. *Ortega y Gasset as Phenomenologist: The Genesis of Meditations on Quixote*. New York: Columbia University Press, 1978.

———. *Phenomenology and Art*. New York: Norton, 1975.

Spiegelberg, Herbert. *The Phenomenological Movement. An Historical Introduction*. 2 vols. The Hague: Nijhoff, 1960, 2d ed. 1965.

Stern, Alfred. *Philosophy of History and the Problem of Values*. The Hague: Mouton, 1962.

———. *The Search for Meaning: Philosophical Vistas*. Memphis, Tenn.: Memphis State University Press, 1971.

Tuttle, Howard N. "Ortega's Vitalism in Relation to Aspects of 'Lebensphilosophie' and Phenomenology." *Southwest Philosophical Studies* 6 (1981): 88–92.

Tymieniecka, Anna-Teresa, ed. "Man's Self-Interpretation-in-Existence: Phenomenology and Philosophy of Life—Introducing the Spanish Perspective." *Analecta Husserliana* 29 (1990).

Walgrave, Jan H. *La Filosofía de Ortega y Gasset*. Trans. L. G. Daal from the Dutch ed. of 1949. Madrid: Revista de Occidente, 1960.

Weigert, Andrew J. *Life and Society: A Meditation on the Social Thought of José Ortega y Gasset*. New York: Irvington, 1983.

Weintraub, Karl J. *Visions of Culture. Voltaire, Guizot, Burckhardt, Lamprecht, Huizinga, Ortega y Gasset*. Chicago: University of Chicago Press, 1966.

Wild, John B. *The Radical Empiricism of William James*. New York: Doubleday, 1969.

Winecoff Díaz, Janet. *The Major Themes of Existentialism in the Works of José Ortega y Gasset*. Chapel Hill: University of North Carolina Press, 1970.

Index

Action (activism), 120, 121, 237, 239, 261, 293, 309, 389

Adler, Mortimer, 2, 3

Aesthetics, 119, 124, 126–27, 128, 129, 198, 200, 288

America, 377

Anselm, St., 259

Anthropology, 222. *See also* Philosophical anthropology

A priori, 156, 293 (a posteriori), 297

Aquinas, Thomas, 83, 247

Aristotle, 73, 79, 83, 137, 176, 251, 252, 368

Aron, Raymond, 113, 169, 270–71, 279, 295

Art, 125, 140, 200, 285, 286, 329; life as, 65; Spanish, 81; as de-realization, 124, 200. *See also* Aesthetics

Augustine, St., 266

Aulard, Alfonse, 102

Authenticity, 3, 16, 29, 137, 199, 213, 239, 241, 244, 266, 310, 328, 331, 342, 378, 391. *See also* Existentialism

Avenarius, Richard H. L., 113, 116, 146, 157

Azorín (Ruiz, José Martínez), 69, 150, 332, 378

Bacon, Francis, 71, 96, 379

Balmes, Jaime, 82

Balzac, Honoré de, 64, 332

Barbarians, 246, 289

Baroja, Pío, 121, 150, 332

Barrès, Maurice, 70, 71, 72, 86, 363

Barzun, Jacques: on William James, 146, 160. *See also* Ortega y Gasset, critics of

"Basic discipline," 302, 330, 373, 395

Baudelaire, Charles, 92

Beard, Charles, 312

Beatería. See Philosophy in Ortega

Becker, Carl. *See* Ortega y Gasset, critics of

Beliefs (faiths), 35, 39, 70, 87, 148 (James), 151, 156, 161, 165, 168, 189, 226, 236, 265, 280, 286, 290, 294 (Croce), 298 (Dilthey), 299, 303, 325, 327, 336, 350, 378, 379, 380

Bentham, Jeremy, 379

Bergson, Henri, xi, 15, 42, 44, 85, 87–90, 98, 103, 105, 111, 112, 113, 135, 141, 146, 147–51 *passim*, 158, 161, 162, 163, 179, 183, 196, 198, 245, 264, 268, 288, 316, 317, 320, 328, 330, 331, 379, 381, 384, 396

Bible, 332

Bloom, Alan, 3

Bonald, Count Louis, 82, 377

Breisac, Ernst, 245

Brentano, Franz, 40, 112, 113, 120, 124, 189, 191, 199–200, 381, 388

Brinton, Crane. *See* Ortega y Gasset, critics of

Bulhoff, Ilse N., 271, 296, 298, 299, 300, 303, 304, 395

Burckhardt, Jacob, 93

Burke, Edmund, 377

Caponigri, A. R., 208, 383

"Cartesianism of life," 3, 23, 121, 162, 166, 205, 331, 344, 391

Voltaire, 66, 68
Vorländer, Karl, 73, 106, 113, 334, 398

Wahl, Jean, 232, 264, 267, 268, 369
Weber, Max, 29, 200
Weintraub, Karl J. *See* Ortega y Gasset, critics of
Wells, H. G., 150
Weyl, Hermann, 241, 246–47
White, Hayden V., xi, 273, 390, 394
Whitehead, Alfred North, 23, 96, 97, 146–47, 177, 186, 281, 359, 382

Will to life, 326
Worldview, 17, 77, 78, 80, 95, 121, 139, 151, 152, 164, 168, 245, 278, 279, 283, 287, 288, 289, 290, 296, 297 (*Zeitgeist*), 299 (Dilthey), 300–306 *passim*
Worringer, Wilhelm, 129

Ziehen, Theodor, 136, 146, 152, 170
Zubiri, Xavier, 188, 244, 395